The Bed & Breakfast Guide to Great Britain

The Bed & Breakfast Guide to Great Britain

Susan Causin, Elsie Dillard,
and the Editors of Consumer Reports Books

Consumer Reports Books
A Division of Consumers Union
Yonkers, New York

Published by Consumers Union of United States, Inc., Yonkers, New York 10703, by arrangement with K. S. Giniger Co., Inc., New York.

Library of Congress Cataloging-in-Publication Data

Causin, Susan.
The bed & breakfast guide to Great Britain : the best values in B&B accommodations throughout England, Scotland, and Wales / Susan Causin, Elsie Dillard, and the editors of Consumer Reports Books.
p. cm.
Includes index.
ISBN 0-89043-477-8
1. Bed and breakfast accommodations—Great Britain—Guidebooks.
I. Dillard, Elsie. II. Consumer Reports Books. III. Title.
IV. Title: Bed and breakfast guide to Great Britain.
TX907.5.G7C38 1992
647.944103—dc20 92-7712
CIP

Design by Tim Higgins
Cover illustration by Karen Lee Carmack
Text illustrations by Paul Saunders
Maps by Eugene Fleury
Indexes by Paul Nash

First printing, March 1992
Manufactured in the United States of America

The Bed & Breakfast Guide to Great Britain is a Consumer Reports Book published by Consumers Union, the nonprofit organization that publishes *Consumer Reports*, the monthly magazine of test reports, product Ratings, and buying guidance. Established in 1936, Consumers Union is chartered under the Not-for-Profit Corporation Law of the State of New York.

The purposes of Consumers Union, as stated in its charter, are to provide consumers with information and counsel on consumer goods and services, to give information on all matters relating to the expenditure of the family income, and to initiate and to cooperate with individual and group efforts seeking to create and maintain decent living standards.

Consumers Union derives its income solely from the sale of *Consumer Reports* and other publications. In addition, expenses of occasional public service efforts may be met, in part, by nonrestrictive, noncommercial contributions, grants, and fees. Consumers Union accepts no advertising or product samples and is not beholden in any way to any commercial interest. Its Ratings and reports are solely for the use of the readers of its publications. Neither the Ratings, nor the reports, nor any Consumers Union publication, including this book, may be used in advertising or for any commercial purpose. Consumers Union will take all steps open to it to prevent such uses of its material, its name, or the name of *Consumer Reports*.

Contents

Introduction

This totally revised edition of *The Bed & Breakfast Guide to Great Britain* is the ideal touring companion for those who want to stay in clean, comfortable, inexpensive, and perhaps unusual accommodations on their next visit to Britain. The *Guide* describes 1,000 of the best B&Bs in England, Scotland, and Wales, in city, town, and countryside. The authors have personally visited and inspected all of the B&Bs, exploring places as far away as the Scilly Isles, Shetland, Orkney, the Western Isles, the Isle of Man, and even Sark, in the Channel Islands, as well as all areas of the mainland.

The criteria for selection include a warm welcome, cleanliness, a friendly and comfortable atmosphere, and, wherever possible, a building in a particularly attractive setting and of some architectural or historical interest. The descriptions of each B&B are as factual as possible, taken from inspection reports. The basic details, such as price and room information, have been provided by the owners themselves in response to questionnaires.

No free hospitality has been accepted by the authors, and owners are neither charged a fee for being listed in the guide nor allowed to publicize their inclusion in the book. Of course, there is no guarantee that all B&Bs will remain true to their descriptions. A change of ownership, for example, can lead to price fluctuations, new decor, and a complete change in ambience.

This guide offers a wide variety of establishments from which to choose: Georgian and Victorian town houses, coaching inns, old vicarages and rectories, former mills, old forges, windmills, farmhouses, manor houses, castles, lodges, seaside guesthouses, crofters' cottages, old bakeries, even a medieval monks' hostel and a lighthouse.

The Evolving B&B

British B&Bs have adapted over the years to meet new demands. More and more private (*en suite*) bathrooms have been added, televisions and facilities for making tea and coffee are now common, and many other amenities—such as room telephones, hair dryers, and trouser presses—are becoming increasingly familiar.

In fact, a significant number of B&Bs have made a definite move upmarket. This is reflected in substantial price increases, but also in additional comfort—more bathrooms, more four-poster beds, more extras in bedrooms, expensive fabrics and wallpapers. These places are still a good value (perhaps around £25 per person per night), and they fill the gap between the very basic guesthouse and the plush country-house type of hotel.

There are also regional variations. Taking a sample of West Country (Cornwall, Devon, Dorset, Somerset, Wiltshire) entries, prices have risen by about 25 percent on average since early 1990, while the increase in the Southeast area (Kent, Surrey, East and West Sussex) is approximately 15 percent. The best bargains can be found in Scotland and Wales, where good £10-a-night B&Bs still exist.

How to Use This Guide

The Bed & Breakfast Guide to Great Britain divides England into seven regions, with separate sections for Scotland, Wales, and the Channel Islands. Maps and indexes at the back of the book can help you pinpoint particular B&Bs and locations. Many B&Bs are in remote areas and may be difficult for the visitor to find, so it is always best to ask for specific directions when reserving a room.

When owners have supplied a fax number, it has been included. Each entry notes any restrictions that apply to children, pets, and smoking—check, though, when booking your room, as owners may change their policy. The term "car park" has been added to entries that offer some kind of off-street parking facility; if not mentioned, parking could prove difficult. Unfortunately, few B&Bs can adequately accommodate the disabled, but it is mentioned in an entry if suitable rooms are available. The number of rooms with TV and/or telephone is stated, and, if there is no central heating, this is also indicated.

Many B&Bs are good places to dine. Many have special

combination dinner/bed and breakfast rates (some places offer B&B accommodations *only* with dinner). Guests with special dietary requirements should notify the owner when first reserving the room. A growing number of B&Bs provide vegetarian food at dinner, as well as packed lunches if desired. A license to sell alcohol on the premises is indicated in the guide, or, if an establishment is unlicensed, it is stated whether or not you can bring your own wine to dinner.

As a B&B is also someone's home, it is important to know the name of the owner. B&B owners usually stick to the opening times provided, but these can be affected by holidays or illness. Please check beforehand to avoid any surprises. The number and type of rooms in a B&B may also vary; for instance, a twin may also be used as a family room. The number of rooms with private bathroom facilities is listed, as is the number provided with a sink or washbasin.

Prices. Owners were asked to estimate their prices a number of months before publication, so discrepancies may occur. The prices stated are per person per night for visitors sharing a twin or double room, with appropriate variations for four-posters, singles, or single occupancy of a twin/double or family room. Any reductions for children are specified, as are any payment stipulations, such as a deposit or full payment due on arrival. Prices for dinner and/or dinner, bed, and breakfast are also given.

The price ceiling for inclusion in the guide was set at £30 (£35 in London) per person per night in a twin or double room. One or two exceptional places exceed this figure, and a number of B&Bs charge considerably more for single occupancy of a twin or double. In all cases it is advisable to check prices and mention any particular needs and concerns when you are booking your room. Prices and facilities listed in this guide were correct at the time of publication, but changes do occur, and it is important to confirm all details to avoid disappointment.

Most B&Bs do not accept credit cards, although all the major U.S. credit cards—American Express, Diners Club, MasterCard and Visa—have outlets in Britain. It's best to carry only small amounts of cash, and use traveler's checks to replenish your funds as you travel.

Tips and Hints for the American Visitor

- The more remote B&Bs are often open only in the summer months, while B&Bs in small towns and cities are open all year round.
- August is an especially busy month for tourism—try to avoid travel in Britain at that time.
- When reserving a room, specify whether you desire twin beds or a double bed; double beds tend to be smaller than those in the United States. If a B&B does have private baths, specify whether you prefer a tub or shower.
- If you must cancel your reservation, British law allows the proprietor to keep your deposit until the room is rented to someone else for the same dates. If you cancel, do so as early as possible.
- Many of the places listed in this guide are very popular, so try to make your reservations well in advance. Write a letter stating your dates and requirements. If time is short, the convenience of a transatlantic telephone call is well worth the extra expense.
- The standard voltage throughout Britain is 240v; it is 110v in the United States and Canada. Some B&Bs have electric shaver adapters, but they usually do not have adapters for hair dryers or traveling irons. It's a good idea to bring your own.
- If you like to read in bed, buy a 60-watt bulb upon your arrival, as bedside lamps in many B&Bs may have weak illumination.
- Washcloths (or facecloths) are not usually provided in British hotels or B&Bs, so bring your own. It's a good idea to pack some plastic bags for the washcloth and other items.
- Most theaters, especially those in London, begin at 7:30P.M., so plan to dine early before the performance or after the show. Some theaters have buffets, so you can get a drink or a snack between acts. The levels in a British theater are called (from ground level up) the stalls, the circle or dress circle, the upper circle, and the balcony.

The Bed & Breakfast Guide to Great Britain

The South-West

Avon

Cornwall

Devon

Dorset

Isles of Scilly

Somerset

AVETON GIFFORD Devon map 1

Court Barton Farmhouse

Aveton Gifford, Kingsbridge TQ7 4LE
KINGSBRIDGE (0548) 550312

This lovely sixteenth-century stone-built farmhouse is on a 300-acre arable farm, 100 yards from the village of Aveton Gifford, beside the Norman church. John Balkwill is the third generation of the family to live in the house; he and Jill are a very friendly couple with four children. You enter the house through an impressive stone arched porchway with massive front door into a wide flagstone hallway. All bedrooms have recently been made *en suite*, redecorated and newly carpeted. They are of a good size and have been simply furnished and decorated. The comfortable lounge has TV and reading material, and breakfast only is served in the dining-room. Packed lunches can be provided. Guests are welcome to use the swimming-pool and games-room. There is a spiral staircase in the oldest part of the house. Families are always welcome here. No pets in the lounge. Car park.

OWNERS John and Jill Balkwill OPEN All year, exc Christmas
ROOMS 2 family, 2 double, 2 twin, 1 single; all rooms with bath/shower TERMS B&B £18–£25 (reductions for children sharing parents' room); deposit 25%

BATH Avon map 2

Audley House

Park Gardens, Bath BA1 2XP
BATH (0225) 333110 Fax (0225) 482879

Close to lovely Victoria Park and a little way from the centre of Bath, Audley House offers a peaceful, quiet stay. It is a beautifully proportioned Victorian house, built in 1842, and standing in an acre of beautifully kept gardens, with expanses of sweeping lawns and mature trees. It is approached down a quiet, private narrow lane, through gates to a circular driveway, and the entrance to the house is under a covered porch. The interior retains the fine craftsmanship and beautiful features of early Victorian architecture, and has been exquisitely furnished and decorated. Each of the three bedrooms has its own luxurious bathroom, TV and telephone; two of the bedrooms are exceptionally large. Guests have use of a drawing-room and a dining-room, where excellent breakfasts, including kedgeree, kippers and porridge, are served. Dinner, including vegetarian choices, can be served by prior arrangement 7–8pm. There is no alcohol licence, but guests are welcome to bring their own wine. No children under 14. No pets. No smoking. Car park.

OWNERS Mr G. A. and Mrs S. Talbot OPEN All year, exc Christmas ROOMS 3 double/twin (with bath/shower) TERMS B&B £30, (single occupancy of twin/double) £40; dinner £16; Access, Visa

Bathurst

11 Walcot Parade, London Road, Bath BA1 5NF
BATH (0225) 421884

This listed Georgian town house, built in 1768, is on a raised terrace overlooking the busy London Road, convenient for the centre of Bath, beside Hedgemead Park. The front rooms have double glazing, which excludes most of the traffic noise. The house has recently undergone alterations and redecoration. Two bedrooms are now *en suite*, a triple has been reduced to a double and a small double to a single. For those without a bathroom, there is still quite a trek from the top floor to the bathrooms on the first. Bathrobes are provided for the trip. All bedrooms have TV. There is a comfortable lounge, which has a piano, games table, puzzles and books. The Bathurst is a pleasant friendly place and represents good value. Breakfast only is served. Children welcome. No pets. No smoking. Parking for three cars.

OWNER Mrs Elizabeth P. Tovey OPEN All year, exc Christmas and New Year ROOMS 1 four-poster (with bath/shower), 1 double (with wash-basin), 2 twin (1 with bath/shower, 1 with wash-basin), 2 single (with wash-basin) TERMS B&B £15–£17.50 (children under 3 free, 3–13 half-price sharing with both parents); deposit half-night or 1 night charge

Bloomfield House

146 Bloomfield Road, Bath BA2 2AS
BATH (0225) 420105

Bloomfield House was built in the 1820s by one of Bath's principal architects. It is a large building, in a quiet residential area with wonderful views of the whole city. Inside, it is somewhat theatrical, one of the proprietors having once designed opera sets, including some for Joan Sutherland. Photographs of opera sets decorate the stairway, and the circular entrance porch has a mural painted by Mr Pascoe. The guest accommodation is all located on the second floor. The bedrooms, all with TV, are comfortably furnished and have private bathrooms panelled in mahogany, most of which are not *en suite*. There is also a small sitting-room on this level. Additional beds can be provided to make up family rooms. Breakfast only is served in the ground-floor dining-room at one big table. Packed lunches can be provided. There are two self-contained self-catering apartments on the first floor. Children welcome. No pets. No smoking in the dining-room and some bedrooms. Car park.

OWNERS T. Argiris and J. Pascoe OPEN All year ROOMS 1 four-poster, 3 double, 2 twin, 1 single; all rooms with bath/shower TERMS B&B £17.50–£30, (single occupancy of twin/double) from £35, (family room) £56 (reductions for children by arrangement); deposit 20%; Access, Visa

Cheriton House

9 Upper Oldfield Park, Bath BA2 3JX
BATH (0225) 429862

Dating from 1880, this late-Victorian guesthouse is in a quiet street on the southern slopes of Bath with magnificent views over the city. It is set in a very pretty garden, with a pleasant lawned area behind the house, and space for parking. Already attaining a high standard, the Babbages have recently redecorated several of the bedrooms, which are bright, spotlessly clean, restful and simply furnished. All bedrooms have TV. There is a wide, tiled entrance hallway, and a lounge with plenty of books and brochures is available. Breakfast only is served in the dining-room, which overlooks Bath. Packed lunches can be provided. Children by arrangement. No pets. Car park.

OWNERS I. M. and J. M. Babbage OPEN All year, exc Christmas and New Year ROOMS 1 family, 6 double, 3 twin; all rooms with bath/shower TERMS B&B £22.50–£27.50, (single occupancy of twin/double) £32–£38, (family room) £18 third person; deposit; Access, Visa

Cranleigh

159 Newbridge Hill, Bath BA1 3PX
BATH (0225) 310197

Cranleigh is about a mile from the town (buses stop almost at the door), on a gentle rise, and is a beautiful Victorian house renovated by Chris and Arthur Webber. The bedrooms are spacious and tastefully decorated with beautiful matching fabrics; most have their own bathroom and TV. Some of the back rooms have magnificent views of Bath. The Webbers themselves are an added bonus. They are a charming couple, dedicated to their guests' comfort. Breakfast, including fresh fruits, yoghurts, cereals, followed by a cooked course, is excellent and is served in the charming dining-room overlooking the garden. Packed lunches can be provided. There are no evening meals. Street parking is available. There are no facilities for babies, but there are reductions for children, depending on age and time of year. No pets. No smoking.

OWNERS Chris and Arthur Webber OPEN All year ROOMS 2 family (1 with bath/shower, 1 with wash-basin), 1 four-poster (with bath/shower), 2 double (with wash-basin), 2 twin (1 with bath/shower, 1 with wash-basin), 1 single (with wash-basin) TERMS B&B £18–£27.50, (single occupancy of twin/double) £30–£35; Access, Visa

Haydon House

9 Bloomfield Park, Bath BA2 2BY
BATH (0225) 444919/427351

Haydon House is almost impossible to fault. Magdalene Ashman has achieved a high standard, and both she and her husband are most welcoming hosts. It is an Edwardian semi-detached house in a quiet residential street. The house has been furnished and decorated with great taste. There is an elegant drawing-room, which leads out on to an exquisite garden where guests can sit out on warm days, and a tiny sitting-room. Breakfast only is served at one big table in the dining-room. Packed lunches can be provided. The bedrooms are charming and all have private bathroom, TV and telephone. Children by arrangement. No pets. No smoking. On-street parking.

OWNER Mrs Magdalene Ashman OPEN All year ROOMS 3 double, 1 twin; all rooms with bath/shower TERMS B&B £22.50–£27.50, (single occupancy of twin/double) £35–£40; deposit; Access, Visa

Holly Lodge

8 Upper Oldfield Park, Bath BA2 3JZ
BATH (0225) 424042

Immaculate down to the last detail, Holly Lodge is on a quiet hillside street with wonderful views over Bath, and it is only a short distance from the centre. There are six light, airy bedrooms, all individually decorated and furnished, with bathroom, telephone and TV. There is an elegant, beautifully furnished drawing-room, and breakfast only is served in the pretty conservatory/breakfast room, which enjoys lovely views over the city. George Hall can help out on any local information, and he or Carrolle Sellick are always on hand to make sure their guests have everything they want. Holly Lodge continues to provide an extremely high standard of comfort and a warm welcome, with constant redecoration and updating of facilities. Children by arrangement. No pets. No smoking. Car park.

OWNERS Mrs Carrolle Sellick and Mr George Hall OPEN All year ROOMS 3 double, 2 twin, 1 single; all rooms with bath/shower TERMS B&B £27.50–£30, (single) £45, (single occupancy of twin/double) £55 (children sharing with parents £15); deposit for first night; Access, Amex, Diners, Visa

Leighton House

139 Wells Road, Bath BA2 3AL
BATH (0225) 314769

This detached Victorian residence built in the 1870s has fine views over the city and surrounding hills. It stands just off a main road with parking area and garden and is about a 10-minute walk from the centre, or a short mini-bus ride away. The bedrooms, all with TV and telephone, have recently been done up and some are very large. They are comfortably furnished, all *en suite*, and two are on the ground floor. The ground-floor sitting area incorporates a bar, and there is a newly added dining-room where evenings meals can be served 7–7.30pm by arrangement. A dinner may include carrot and coriander soup or whitebait to start, then lamb with mint and redcurrant sauce or chicken with lime and tarragon to follow, and chocolate rum cake or cinnamon apple flan to finish. Vegetarian choices and packed lunches can also be provided by arrangement. Pets by arrangement. No smoking in the dining-room. Car park.

OWNERS David and Kathleen Slape OPEN All year ROOMS 2 family, 4 double, 2 twin; all rooms with bath/shower TERMS B&B £25–£30, (single occupancy of twin/double) £40–£50, (family room) from £70; dinner £16.50; deposit £20 per person; Access, Visa

B&B rates specified in the details for each entry are per person per night; unless the details state otherwise, they are based on two people sharing a double or twin-bedded room.

Somerset House

35 Bathwick Hill, Bath BA2 6LD
BATH (0225) 466451

Malcolm and Jean Seymour bring years of expertise in tourism and catering to their venture in Bath. They developed an interest in traditional English food during their time as restaurateurs in the Lake District. They grow most of the vegetables and fruit used in the kitchen, and, where possible, everything is home-made, including cakes, pâtés, soups, ice-cream, bread and yoghurt. The house is an elegant, listed Regency building, and the mostly spacious rooms are skilfully converted to provide comfortable and bright bedrooms, some with lovely views over the city. All bedrooms have telephone. There is a conservatory off the downstairs sitting-room, and an upstairs drawing-room is also available. Dinner (at 7pm), which bed and breakfast guests are encouraged to take, and breakfast are served in the attractive basement restaurant, which is also open to non-residents in the evening. Dinner may include cream of leek and celeriac soup with home-made bread, poached hake with an egg and lemon sauce, and Danish lemon cake with fresh pineapple. Vegetarians can be catered for and packed lunches can be provided. The wine list has a good choice, is full of detail and includes some English and Swiss choices. Sunday lunch is available from November to May. The house is set in a most attractive large garden, there is ample parking space, and the property is only three-quarters of a mile from all the central Bath attractions. Malcolm and Jean have now been joined by their son Jonathan, daughter Anna-Clare and son-in-law Timothy Pole in running Somerset House. Special interest and activity weekends, such as Roman Bath, Brunel and Jane Austen, are run for most of the year. No children under 10. Small pets only. No smoking. Car park.

OWNERS Jean, Malcolm and Jonathan Seymour OPEN All year
ROOMS 4 double, 5 twin, 1 single (5 doubles/twins can be used as family rooms); all rooms with bath/shower TERMS B&B £29.20, (single occupancy of twin/double) £44.20 (children 10–13 one-third reduction sharing with parents); D, B&B £46.45; dinner £17.25; deposit £20 per person; Access, Amex, Visa

Bath/shower information in the details refers only to a private bathroom or shower; other bathroom facilities at the establishments will be shared. We say if rooms have wash-basins.

BATHAMPTON Avon map 2

The Tasburgh Bath Hotel

Warminster Road, Bathampton, Bath BA2 6SH
BATH (0225) 425096/463842 Fax (0225) 425096

This substantial house was built in 1890 by John Berryman, a Royal photographer, using red brick, which is unusual for the Bath area. It stands in a spectacular position just off the A46 Warminster road out of Bath on the edge of the Avon valley with wonderful views over the canal and river to the hills beyond. The Tasburgh has seven acres of gardens, lawns and orchards, with plenty of space for sitting and admiring the view on fine summer evenings. The present owners have carried out an extensive refurbishment programme resulting in spacious, very comfortable bedrooms, all with TV and telephone, and some with marvellous views. There are two ground-floor bedrooms. A small conservatory leads off the pleasant lounge and breakfast only is served in the dining-room. Packed lunches can be provided. Children welcome. No dogs. No smoking in the sitting-room, conservatory, dining-room and public areas. Car park.

OWNERS Brian and Audrey Archer OPEN All year, exc Christmas ROOMS 4 family (with bath/shower), 1 four-poster (with bath/shower), 3 double (2 with bath/shower, 1 with wash-basin), 4 twin (3 with bath/shower, 1 with wash-basin), 1 single (with wash-basin) TERMS B&B £27–£30, (single occupancy of twin/double) £30–£40, (family room) £80–£84 (children up to half-price); deposit £25; Access, Amex, Diners, Visa

BATHFORD Avon map 2

The Old School House

Church Street, Bathford, Bath BA1 7RR
BATH (0225) 859593

This small Bath-stone building is almost opposite the church and on the edge of the small conservation village of Bathford. Bath, only three miles away, can be reached by public transport or via a towpath walk along the canal. Until 20 years ago, this was the village school; it has been skilfully converted to provide very comfortable accommodation. You enter the house into what was the schoolroom, now a large sitting- and dining-room with wood-burning stove and comfortable armchairs and sofas. This leads through to a small conservatory, which overlooks the small, sitting-room. No children under 14. No pets. No smoking in bedrooms. Car park.

OWNERS Mr and Mrs John Mitchem OPEN Mar–Oct
ROOMS 2 double, 1 twin; all rooms with bath/shower
TERMS B&B £19–£20, (single occupancy of twin/double) £25–£26; dinner £14.50

BICKINGTON Devon map 1

Penpark

Bickington, Newton Abbot TQ12 6LH
BICKINGTON (0626) 821314

Designed by Clough Williams Ellis in 1928, Penpark is a lovely country house in the Dartmoor National Park, set on a hilltop in five and a half acres of beautifully kept mature gardens and woodland with a tennis court and fabulous views to Dartmoor and as far as the sea. The house has well-proportioned rooms, is beautifully furnished with antiques and decorated in soft restful colours. The one twin-bedded room, which can also be a double, is very large with a balcony and sofa, armchairs and TV. It shares a bathroom with the single room, which also has TV. Normally, the Gregsons take one family or group at a time. Breakfast and dinner, by arrangement only at 7.30pm, are served in the family dining-room. Vegetarians can be catered for. There is no alcohol licence, but guests may bring their own wine. Children welcome. No pets. No smoking. Car park.

OWNERS Michael and Madeleine Gregson OPEN All year, exc Christmas ROOMS 1 double/twin, 1 single; both rooms with wash-basin TERMS B&B £20–£22 (children under 2 free, 2–10 £12); D, B&B £30; deposit

BOSCASTLE Cornwall map 1

The Old Coach House

Tintagel Road, Boscastle PL35 0AS
BOSCASTLE (0840) 250398

An attractive stone-built house, originally a coach-house, that is right on the main road, at the entrance to Boscastle. It is a convenient stopping-off point for exploring this part of the north Cornish coast and Tintagel. The house has been extended at the back with pleasant views from this side and glimpses of the sea from the first-floor rooms. The bedrooms are simply furnished and clean, all *en suite* and with TV; two are on the ground floor and suitable for the disabled. There is a guests' lounge and both evening meals (7–8pm) and breakfast are served in the sun lounge. A dinner may include beef in ale, cashew-nut balls in mushroom sauce and lemon meringue pie. There is a short but adequate wine list. Vegetarians can be catered for and packed lunches can be provided. No children under six. No pets. No smoking in the lounge or the dining-room.

OWNERS Allan and Susan Miller OPEN Mar–Nov ROOMS 1 family, 3 double, 1 twin, 1 single; all rooms with bath/shower TERMS B&B £13–£20, (single occupancy of twin/double) £4 supplement (children 60% of adult rate); dinner £11; deposit £10; Access, Amex, Visa

BOTALLACK Cornwall map 1

Manor Farm

Botallack, St Just, nr Penzance TR19 7QG
PENZANCE (0736) 788525

Featured as 'Nampara' in *Poldark* and as 'Roslyn Farm' in *Penmarric*, Manor Farm is an attractive, seventeenth-century house built of local granite, part of a mixed farm on the edge of the hamlet of Botallack and very close to the sea, offering sea views across fields. It is a delightful place, with lots of atmosphere, colour and character, full of all kinds of interesting antique furniture and every inch of wall is hung with pictures and mirrors. There is a comfortable lounge and a wonderful dining-room with beamed ceiling, where a substantial breakfast choice is available. The bedrooms are comfortable and cosy. Manor Farm offers excellent value. Children welcome. No pets. No smoking in bedrooms. Car park.

OWNER Mrs Joyce Cargeeg OPEN All year, exc Christmas
ROOMS 1 four-poster (with bath/shower), 1 double (with wash-basin), 1 twin (with bath/shower) TERMS B&B £14–£17, (single occupancy of twin/double) £5 surcharge (reductions for children according to age); deposit £10

If you are forced to turn up late into the evening, please telephone to warn the proprietor.

When the family-room rate is given in the details it applies to the cost of the whole room, unless a rate per person is specified.

BOURNEMOUTH Dorset map 2

Clifton Court Hotel

30 Clifton Road, Southbourne, Bournemouth BH6 3PA
BOURNEMOUTH (0202) 427753

The house has recently been redecorated on the outside, giving a clean and neat appearance. It is in a quiet road just off the sea-front and dates from the turn of the century. Inside there are new carpets and the halls and stairs have been done up in blue and cream pastel colours. Almost all bedrooms, except for those on the top floor, are *en suite*, and all save three have sea views. The bedrooms are on the small side, with some small beds. The cliff-top area offers amusements for children, and the sandy beach can be reached by lift as well as by a zigzag path. There is a beach hut which can be rented. Home-cooked evening meals (6pm) are available, including vegetarian choices by arrangement. Packed lunches can be provided if ordered the night before. Children welcome. Dogs by arrangement. No smoking in the dining-room. Car park.

OWNERS M. H. F. Ames and S. A. Rook OPEN All year
ROOMS 3 family/double/twin (2 with bath/shower, 1 with wash-basin), 6 double/twin (3 with bath/shower, 3 with wash-basin), 2 single (1 with bath/shower, 1 with wash-basin) TERMS B&B £16–£20, (single occupancy of twin/double) £26–£30 (babies free, children under 10 half-price, 10–12 two-thirds); dinner £5; deposit £15 per person; Access, Amex, Visa

Parklands Hotel

4 Rushton Crescent, Bournemouth BH3 7AF
BOURNEMOUTH (0202) 552529

This small hotel has a warm, friendly atmosphere and is conveniently located for the centre of Bournemouth in a quiet spot just off a main road. It is a real family concern, with parents, two sons and a daughter-in-law all involved in the running of the hotel. The clean, bright bedrooms, all with TV, are mostly *en suite* and located on the ground and first floors. The hotel entrance leads directly into a cosy, warm lounge with TV and a small bar, beyond which is the dining-room. Evening meals, including a vegetarian choice, can be served at 6pm and packed lunches can

If you have to cancel a reservation for a room, please telephone to warn the proprietor.

be provided. No children under six. No pets. No smoking in the dining-room. Car park.

OWNERS Mr Alan Clark and Mrs Sylvia Clark OPEN All year ROOMS 1 family, 6 double, 3 twin; all rooms, exc 1 twin (wash-basin only), with bath/shower TERMS B&B £19–£25, (single occupancy of twin/double) £4 supplement (children 6–13 25–50% reduction); D, B&B £28.50–£34.50; dinner £12.50; deposit £20 per person; Access, Visa

Sandhurst Private Hotel

16 Southern Road, Southbourne, Bournemouth BH6 3SR
BOURNEMOUTH (0202) 423748

A red-and-cream painted, brick and stucco detached house that dates from the early part of the century. It is in a quiet road, comprising mostly hotels, and close to the sea. The bedrooms, all with TV, are clean and comfortable, some small, some good-sized and some *en suite*. There is a comfortable sitting-room with TV. Home-cooked set dinners are served at 6pm and can include vegetarian choices. There is no alcohol licence, but guests may bring their own wine. Children welcome. No pets. No smoking in the dining-room. Car park.

OWNERS Colin and Jean Du Faur OPEN Mar–Oct ROOMS 2 family (1 with bath/shower, 1 with wash-basin), 4 double (1 with bath/shower, 3 with wash-basin), 1 twin (with bath/shower), 2 single (with wash-basin) TERMS B&B £12–£17, (single occupancy of twin/double) £16–£26 (children under 2 free, 2–8 half-price, 9–14 three-quarters); dinner £5.50; deposit £10

San Remo Hotel

7 Durley Road, Bournemouth BH2 5JQ
BOURNEMOUTH (0202) 290558

The entire hotel has recently been redecorated, each room having a different colour scheme with large floral patterned wallpapers. It is a solid Victorian building, close to the cliffs and town centre. Most bedrooms are *en suite* and all have TV. Two of the rooms, one of which is equipped for the disabled, are on the ground floor. Dinner is available at 6pm in the dining-room, which overlooks the small back garden and putting green. There is also a comfortable lounge. Vegetarians can be catered for and guests may bring their own wine (there is no alcohol licence). No children under five. No smoking in the dining-room. Car park.

OWNERS K. R. and B. Humphrey OPEN Easter–Nov
ROOMS 1 family, 7 double, 6 twin, 4 single; all rooms, exc 4 single (wash-basin only), with bath/shower TERMS B&B £16–£24.50 (children 5–10 50% reduction, 10–15 30%); D, B&B £21–£27.50, dinner £5.50; deposit £20; £2 surcharge for single night

BOVEY TRACEY Devon map 1

Front House Lodge

East Street, Bovey Tracey TQ13 9EL
BOVEY TRACEY (0626) 832202

This listed building, on one of the main streets in town, was built in 1540. The theme, however, is more Victorian, the predominant colour being pink, and the décor and furnishings are highly individual. The whole house is stuffed with dolls, china ornaments, plastic and dried flowers and frilly cushions, making it almost a problem finding anywhere to sit or put down a glass. It is, however, surprisingly spacious. The dining-room leads into a large sitting-room, which in turn leads into the bar and out on to the garden. The bedrooms, all with TV, vary in size; some rooms are quite large, and two of the bathrooms have old baths. Evening meals, including vegetarian choices by arrangement, can be served in the licensed restaurant, but there are also several places to eat in town or close by. Packed lunches can be provided. There is a pretty back garden, beyond which are lovely views, and a large car park is available. Children welcome. Guide dogs only. No smoking.

OWNERS Gail and Ian Campbell OPEN All year ROOMS 1 family, 1 four-poster, 4 double, 2 twin; all rooms, exc 1 twin (wash-basin only), with bath/shower TERMS B&B £18–£19, (single occupancy of twin/double) £25, (family room) £45 (reductions for children under 7); Access, Amex, Visa

BRATTON CLOVELLY Devon map 1

Four Chimneys

Bratton Clovelly, nr Okehampton EX20 4JF
BRATTON CLOVELLY (0837) 87409

This charming place is on the edge of a small village, on a quiet country lane, in pretty, unspoilt and peaceful countryside – a marvellous centre for Dartmoor and the north and south Devon coasts. The house stands in a pretty garden and the neighbours have kindly agreed to allow guests to use their tennis court. Four Chimneys is owned by a most hospitable retired couple, who spent the greater part of their lives in Canada. They welcome children, providing all sorts of games and toys as well as babysitting by arrangement. On arrival, guests are offered a tray of tea or coffee. The absolutely charming dining-room and sitting-room with big open fireplace are crammed with ornaments and collections, and the whole house has a friendly, homely atmosphere. The bedrooms are old-fashioned and comfortable and share a bathroom. The double can be let as a private suite, in which case no other guests are taken. This room is in a separate wing and has its own entrance. A cot, high chair and laundry facilities are available and four-course evening meals can be prepared if booked in advance. Vegetarian choices and packed lunches can be provided. There is no alcohol licence, but guests may bring their own wine to dinner. Dogs and cats welcome. No smoking in bedrooms. Parking for three cars.

OWNERS The Ven. C. H. and Mrs Josephine Butler OPEN 1 Mar–7 Nov ROOMS 1 double/family, 1 twin; both rooms with wash-basin TERMS B&B £17 (children under 2 free, 2–4 £4, 4–9 £9.50); dinner £9 (children 2–4 £2.50, 4–9 £5); deposit 10%

BRIDGWATER Somerset map 1

Cokerhurst Farm

87 Wembdon Hill, Bridgwater TA6 7QA
BRIDGWATER (0278) 422330

The approach to Cokerhurst Farm is inauspicious – a built-up suburb, one and a half miles west of Bridgwater. It is a surprise, therefore, to find old farm buildings at the end of the driveway, and a completely rural outlook over the farm's 100 acres of wheat and 'pick your own' soft fruits. The house is a sixteenth-century longhouse and the owners are the third generation of the family to have farmed at Cokerhurst. The three fresh and bright bedrooms, one with TV, are reached by a spiral staircase. The dining-room, which is available just for breakfast, has a TV and sitting area. There is a raised swimming-pool and small lake in the grounds.

Where a single-occupancy rate is not specified in the details, the cost will be the same as that per person in a twin or double room, or will be included in the range of prices given.

Children welcome. Pets by arrangement. Smoking restricted. Car park.

OWNERS Derrick and Diana Chappell OPEN Easter–Oct ROOMS 1 family (with wash-basin), 1 double (with bath/shower), 1 twin (with wash-basin) TERMS B&B £15–£20, (family room) £40 (children under 2 free, 2–10 £10); deposit 25%

BRISTOL Avon map 2

The Lawns Guest House

91 Hampton Road, Redland, Bristol BS6 6JG
BRISTOL (0272) 738459

This is a friendly, cheerful guesthouse offering simple accommodation and good value for money. A detached Victorian residence built in 1846 and in a quiet area, it is close to a good bus service into the centre and an excellent choice of restaurants. Guests are welcome to use the large garden to one side of the property and the sitting-room, which has TV. Breakfast only is available. All rooms have TV. There is car parking to the rear of the property. Children welcome. Guide dogs only. No smoking in the dining-room.

OWNERS John and Nell Moran OPEN All year, exc Christmas and New Year ROOMS 1 double (with wash-basin), 1 twin/family (with bath/shower), 1 twin (with wash-basin), 2 single (with wash-basin) TERMS B&B £17.50–£20, (single) £22, (single occupancy of twin/double) £30 (reductions for children under 10)

BRUSHFORD Somerset map 1

Perry Farm

Brushford, Dulverton TA22 9LN
DULVERTON (0398) 23248

Perry Farm is one and a half miles from Dulverton. It is an old, square, stone-built farmhouse in very pretty countryside in the middle of nowhere with lovely views of farmland, hills and woods. The owners have six horses which are stabled in the old stone farm buildings arranged around a courtyard adjacent to the house. Apart from hunting they also farm sheep. Hunters or riding horses can be booked for guests in advance – not the owners' own horses. Guests wanting to hunt in the spring must book horses before 1 January to be sure of a mount. There are also both salmon and trout fishing available. The bedrooms are large, traditionally furnished rooms which share one bathroom, and there is a small sitting-room with comfortable chairs and a dining-room where evening meals can be served by arrangement in the spring for hunting parties. There is no alcohol licence, but guests may bring their own wine. The house offers simple accommodation and is a great place for those who enjoy the peace and quiet of the countryside and rural pursuits. Children welcome. 'Well-behaved' pets. Car park.

OWNERS Mr and Mrs P. Horton OPEN All year, exc Nov and Dec ROOMS 1 family, 1 double, 1 twin TERMS B&B £14–£15 (children under 12 £10); D, B&B (in the spring) £30; deposit £10

BRYHER Isles of Scilly map 1

Bank Cottage Guesthouse

Bryher, Isles of Scilly TR23 OPR
SCILLONIA (0720) 22612

Bryher is the smallest of the inhabited Isles of Scilly. This 400-year-old beamed cottage bordering the seashore has a spectacular view of the western rocks and the Atlantic. The bedrooms are bright and airy, and simply and comfortably furnished. The dining-room, where evening meals (including vegetarian choices) are served at 7pm, is in the old part, with a low-beamed ceiling, and the lounge is a bright, comfortable room leading out on to the patio and garden filled with colourful flowers. Mr Mace is a diver and collects sea urchins, selling the shells all over the world. Weekly bookings only are taken during the summer months. Packed lunches can be provided. No children under seven. No pets.

OWNERS Mac and Tracy Mace OPEN Mar–Nov ROOMS 1 double (with bath/shower), 3 twin (2 with bath/shower), 1 single (with wash-basin) TERMS B&B £19 (children £2 reduction); dinner £10; deposit 25%

BUCKFASTLEIGH Devon map 1

Dartbridge Manor

Dart Bridge Road, Buckfastleigh TQ11 ODZ
BUCKFASTLEIGH (0364) 43575

In a prominent position at the entrance to Buckfastleigh, and only a minute's drive from the A38, Dartbridge Manor is in a most convenient position for travellers to Cornwall and is within walking distance of Buckfast Abbey and the Dart Valley Railway. The attractive 500-year-old stone building is well maintained and has a large car park, and a patio at the back where guests are welcome to sit. The dining-room, with separate tables, is a low-beamed room, with the owner's sitting area to one side. Guests have use of a separate sitting-room, with partly natural stone walls, beams and an open fireplace. The bedrooms are all *en suite*, comfortable and well decorated. Breakfast only is available, but the house is licensed. Also available are modern seven-berth caravans located in the grounds and overlooking the valley. Dartbridge Manor offers comfort in a welcoming atmosphere. Children welcome. No pets. No smoking in the dining-room.

OWNER Mr C. Jordan OPEN All year ROOMS 1 family, 8 double, 1 twin; all rooms with bath/shower TERMS B&B £15, (single occupancy of twin/double) £20 (children sharing £5)

CAMELFORD Cornwall map 1

Trethin Manor

Advent, Camelford PL32 9QW
CAMELFORD (0840) 213522

This lovely old granite house with massively thick walls is set in glorious countryside in a very peaceful out-of-the-way place, half a mile south-west of Camelford. The house consisted originally of just one room and has been added on to over the years; the guests' sitting-room was built on in 1650 and has the initials of the then owners over the lovely stone fireplace and a framed copy of their will on the wall. Trethin Manor was the birthplace of Captain Samuel Wallace, discoverer of Tahiti, and also belonged to the Siamese royal family in the early part of this century. There are two pretty *en suite* bedrooms, both with TV, and also 10 self-catering units, beautifully converted from old, stone farm buildings set in gardens. Breakfast only is available. Children welcome. No pets. Car park.

OWNERS Donald and Elizabeth Brocklehurst OPEN All year, exc Dec ROOMS 2 double (with bath/shower) TERMS B&B £14–£18, (single occupancy of double) £21–£27 (children under 3 free, 3–13 half-price); deposit 50%

Bath/shower in the details under each entry means that the rooms have private facilities.

CHAGFORD Devon map 1

Bly House

Nattadon Hill, Chagford TQ13 8BW
CHAGFORD (0647) 432404

This substantial stone-built house, once the rectory, stands in five acres of lovely, well-maintained gardens, including a croquet lawn, with glorious views to Dartmoor. An extensive sun terrace runs along one side of the house. It is a quite amazingly furnished country home, including pink porcelain and pictures. The bedrooms, all with TV, are comfortable and some have four-poster or half-tester beds. There are two lounges, one with TV and an open log fire. Breakfast only is served, but there are many places to eat nearby. The village of Chagford is only a four-minute walk down a country lane. There is also a self-catering cottage. No children under 10. Dogs only. No smoking in the breakfast room. Car park.

OWNERS Mr and Mrs G. B. Thompson OPEN Jan–mid-Nov
ROOMS 3 four-poster, 2 double, 2 twin; all rooms with bath/shower
TERMS B&B £23, (single occupancy) £28; deposit £30 per room

Torr House Hotel

Thorn, Chagford TQ13 8DX
CHAGFORD (0647) 432228/433343

Torr House is in very pretty countryside on the edge of Dartmoor and has lovely views. The 200-year-old house, set in two acres of garden with copse and stream has had a chequered career. It has been a private house, hotel, sanatorium, was derelict for a time, and was occupied by the army during the Second World War. It was also one of the first private houses west of London to have electric light installed. The large, comfortable drawing-room has a grand piano, TV, log fire, books and magazines. The bedrooms are comfortable, clean and practically furnished; three are *en suite* and the remaining rooms share a bathroom and ground-floor shower-room. Home-cooked four-course evening meals, including a vegetarian menu, are available by arrangement at 7.30pm and drinking water comes from a Dartmoor spring. Packed lunches can be provided. Located one and a half miles from Chagford within the Dartmoor National Park, the house offers peace and quiet in a lovely setting. Children welcome. Pets by arrangement. No smoking in the dining-room and bedrooms. Car park.

OWNERS John and Hazel Cork OPEN All year ROOMS 1 family (with wash-basin), 2 double (with bath/shower), 1 twin (with bath/shower), 1 single (with wash-basin) TERMS B&B £22.50, (single) £23, (single occupancy of twin/double) £28.50, (family room) £55 (children under 2 free, child sharing room £10); dinner £13; deposit 10% or £10 per room minimum; Access, Amex, Visa

CHARD Somerset map 1

Yew Tree Cottage

Hornsbury Hill, Chard TA20 3DB
CHARD (0460) 64735

Off the A358 Chard–Ilminster road is this modest house in its own garden of an acre, and with pleasant farmland views to all sides. It is about a 20-minute walk from the centre of Chard. Jenny Wright is a very pleasant, friendly lady, and can offer an evening meal, by arrangement at 6.30pm, which is served in the lounge/dining-room. Vegetarians can be catered for and guests may bring their own wine (there is no alcohol licence). The three bedrooms are fresh-looking and cosy, providing simple and clean accommodation. There is also a self-catering annexe. Children welcome. Pets by arrangement. No smoking. Car park.

OWNER J. Wright OPEN All year, exc Christmas and New Year
ROOMS 1 double, 1 twin, 1 single; all rooms with wash-basin
TERMS B&B £12–£15; dinner £8; deposit

CHIDEOCK Dorset map 1

Chimneys Guest House

Main Street, Chideock, nr Bridport DT6 6JH
CHIDEOCK (0297) 89368

This partly thatched, partly tiled guesthouse was converted in 1930 from three, sixteenth-century merchants' cottages. It has a pretty cottage-style front garden and the property extends to half an acre at the back with shrubs and fruit trees. Chimneys stands right on the main road, but double glazing eliminates most of the traffic noise. The interior is surprisingly large and spacious. The sitting-room has comfy chairs and an unusual heavily beamed ceiling. This room leads through to the panelled dining-room/bar, where evening meals, including vegetarian choices, can be served. Packed lunches can be provided. The bedrooms, which are simply decorated and furnished, are fairly small and the bathrooms are very small. One bedroom has TV. No children under four. No pets. No smoking. Car park.

OWNERS Ann and Brian Hardy OPEN All year, exc Christmas and owners' hol ROOMS 2 four-poster, 1 double, 2 double/twin/family; all rooms, exc 1 (wash-basin only), with bath/shower TERMS B&B £17–£22.50 (children up to half-price depending on age); dinner £11.50–£13.50; deposit 1 night charge

CHISELBOROUGH Somerset map 1

Manor Farm

Chiselborough, Stoke sub Hamdon TA14 6TQ
CHISELBOROUGH (0935) 881203

This manor house of mellow Ham stone was built by Lord Ilchester in 1861 as part of the Ilchester estate. It stands in a wonderful position with marvellous views from the house and terrace. Manor Farm is a working farm of about 500 acres, with dairy cattle and sheep, although the farm buildings are further down the driveway, quite separate from the house. Guests are welcome to put on some wellington boots and walk about the farm or even join in the daily chores. The house offers fairly basic accommodation with the four bedrooms and one bathroom arranged around a central landing with a shower-room downstairs. There is a large sitting-room and dining-room where breakfast only is served. Eileen Holloway has compiled a book on local Somerset recipes as cooked by farmhouse owners in the area. Guests may also use the games-room, and fish in the carp pond. Children welcome. No pets. Car park.

OWNERS G. and E. Holloway OPEN Apr–end Oct ROOMS 1 family, 2 double, 1 twin; all rooms with wash-basin TERMS B&B £16–£18 (children up to 1 laundry only, 1–7 one-third reduction, 7–14 two-thirds); deposit 20%

We asked the proprietors to estimate their 1992 prices in the autumn of 1991, so the rates may have changed since publication.

It is always best to book a room in advance, especially in winter. B&Bs with few rooms may close at short notice for periods not specified in the details.

CHIVELSTONE Devon map 1

South Allington House

Chivelstone, Kingsbridge TQ7 2NB
CHIVELSTONE (054 851) 272

A solid country house that is set in pretty countryside, and part of a 150-acre working able farm. It is a quiet, peaceful spot, and guests are welcome to use the grounds, which are equipped for bowls, croquet and coarse fishing. Edward and Barbara Baker have continued to update the accommodation, and have completed more bedrooms, which have been prettily decorated, several with *en suite* bathrooms. For those rooms not *en suite*, there is an excellent ratio of bedrooms to bathrooms. A sitting area in the entrance hall has a wood-burning stove, and there is a large dining-room where breakfast is served. No evening meal is available, although midday snacks and cream teas are provided in high season. A self-catering flat in the east wing of the house is also available. Children welcome. No dogs in the house. No smoking. Car park.

OWNERS Edward and Barbara Baker OPEN All year
ROOMS 2 family (1 with bath/shower, 1 with wash-basin), 4 double (3 with bath/shower, 1 with wash-basin), 3 twin (1 with bath/shower, 2 with wash-basin), 2 single (with wash-basin) TERMS B&B £14.50–£21.75 (children up to two-thirds reduction if sharing with parents); deposit

COMBE MARTIN Devon map 1

Holdstone Farm

Hunters Inn Road, Combe Martin EX34 0PE
COMBE MARTIN (0271) 883423

This immaculately kept small twelfth-century farmhouse is in a very isolated position, high up on the downs, close to the cliffs and two miles from Combe Martin. The farm – beef and sheep, with a few chickens and the odd cow for house use – has been in the family for some time. As you would expect in a building of this age there are plenty of low ceilings. The large, comfortable lounge has TV and a small open fire, and the attractive dining-room has a large stone fireplace. The two bedrooms are of a good size and fresh and bright. Evening meals are available by arrangement 6.30–7.30pm; guests may bring their own wine (no alcohol licence). There is only part central heating. Children welcome. No pets. No smoking in the dining-room. Car park.

OWNER Mrs S. J. Lerwill OPEN All year, exc Dec ROOMS 1 family, 1 double TERMS B&B from £13 (children £10 in family room); dinner £9; deposit

COMPTON ABBAS Dorset map 2

The Old Forge

Fanners Yard, Compton Abbas, Shaftesbury SP7 0NQ
SHAFTESBURY (0747) 811881

The Old Forge lies on the main Blandford to Shaftesbury road, just a couple of miles from Shaftesbury and on the edge of the hamlet of Compton Abbas. Tucked away under the downs, it has a very rural outlook, and is a marvellous place for walking. Tim and Lucy Kerridge, who have been here since 1986, have done a marvellous job of renovating the house and adjoining barn, creating accommodation that has been simply but imaginatively decorated and furnished. The house has lots of old beams and sloping ceilings, three prettily decorated bedrooms and an attractive breakfast/sitting-room. A self-contained flat, also delightfully converted, adjoins the house. Tim restores cars, especially the vintage variety, in a workshop at the back of the house. Children welcome. No pets in bedrooms. No smoking. Parking for three cars.

OWNERS Tim and Lucy Kerridge OPEN All year ROOMS 2 double/family (1 with bath/shower), 1 single; all rooms with wash-basin TERMS B&B £17–£20, (single occupancy of twin/double) £25, (family room) £50 (child in single room £12); deposit £10

COUNTISBURY Devon map 1

Coombe Farm

Countisbury, Lynton EX35 6NF
BRENDON (059 87) 236

The farm lies on its own, in a slight fold in the hills, within the boundary of Exmoor National Park, just a mile from the spectacular coastline and only a couple of miles from Lynmouth and Lynton off the A39. The stone-built house dates back to the early seventeenth century and forms one side of the farmyard. The Piles farm 365 acres of hill and fields and rear Exmoor Horn

Sheep, Devon Cattle and family horses. The farmhouse, presided over by Mrs Pile, offers simple accommodation consisting of five medium-sized bedrooms. Evening meals are available at 7pm in the lovely dining-room, with old beams and an enormous stone fireplace. There is an alcohol licence and vegetarian choices can be provided by arrangement. Packed lunches are also available. Guests have use of a large lounge with TV. Children welcome. No pets in the house. No smoking in the public areas. Car park.

OWNER Mrs Rosemary Pile OPEN Mar–mid-Dec ROOMS 2 family (with wash-basin), 2 double (with bath/shower), 1 twin (with wash-basin) TERMS B&B £15.75–£18.75 (£5 surcharge for single occupancy; reductions for children under 11 sharing parents' room); dinner £12.50; deposit

CRACKINGTON HAVEN Cornwall map 1

Crackington Manor

Crackington Haven EX23 0JG
ST GENNYS (084 03) 397/536

Built 100 years ago, the house is almost at the end of this small village, at the narrow valley's end, 100 yards from the beach, which has good surfing conditions. It is a marvellous place for walking: the South-West Peninsula Path passes the front door and the Heritage Coast Service has a series of leaflets of circular walks, one starting from the village. The house has a comfortable, relaxed atmosphere, and families are welcome. There are family rooms and high teas are provided for younger children. The restaurant specialises in vegetarian food, although traditional cuisine is served as well, with a daily change of menu. Evening meals are served at 8pm and organic and non-organic wine is available from a carefully selected list. Dinner may include such dishes as black-eye bean curry, lentil and coconut soup, rainbow trout in Pernod and chocoholic log. Packed lunches and sandwiches can be provided. All bedrooms have telephone and many have wood panelling. The large, comfortable lounge is also panelled, and there is a pleasant bar and dining-room. Guests also have use of the sauna, solarium, gym facilities, heated outdoor swimming-pool and a games-room with pool table, table tennis

The description for each entry states when pets are not allowed. Where no details are given, you can assume that pets are allowed. It's always best to check first in any case.

and large selection of board games. Children welcome. No smoking. Car park.

OWNERS Nick and Ruth Compton OPEN All year, exc Christmas ROOMS 2 family (with bath/shower), 6 double (with bath/shower), 5 twin (4 with bath/shower, 1 with wash-basin), 1 single (with wash-basin), 1 bunk-bed room (with wash-basin) TERMS B&B £26 (children up to half-price depending on age); dinner £10 residents, £12.50 non-residents; Access, Visa

Trevigue Farm

Trevigue, Crackington Haven EX23 0LQ
ST GENNYS (084 03) 418

In a wild, remote spot, this wonderful old farmhouse stands a mile and a half south of the tiny village of Crackington Haven with its lovely beach. The early sixteenth-century farmhouse is built round a cobbled courtyard, and is only a few hundred yards from spectacular cliffs. The farm itself is a 500-acre family-run dairy and beef farm, with great emphasis placed on conservation and where many species of wild animals and flowers abound. The house has been beautifully and caringly restored by its owners and has three *en suite* bedrooms, an attractive dining-room and a lounge. Janet Crocker enjoys preparing both traditional and more unusual dinners, served at 7.30pm. Dishes may include cream of lemon soup, pasta with Stilton cream sauce, venison in red wine and cranberry sauce, and hazelnut roulade. Vegetarian choices can be offered and the wine list is good. Lunches are served from Easter to September and packed lunches can be provided. No children under 12. No pets. No smoking in the dining-room and bedrooms. Car park.

OWNER Janet Crocker OPEN Mar–Oct ROOMS 2 double, 1 twin; all rooms with bath/shower TERMS B&B £17–£23, (single occupancy of twin/double) £22–£28; dinner £12; deposit £20 per person

CREWKERNE Somerset map 1

Broadview

42 East Street, Crewkerne TA18 7AG
CREWKERNE (0460) 73424

This colonial-style bungalow stands high above the main road on the outskirts of Crewkerne in an acre of very pretty terraced gardens with a feature water garden including koi and other varieties of fish. This is a friendly, homely place and the house is clean and comfortable with rather heavy furnishings and décor; plates, pictures and knick-knacks cover every wall and surface. The three bedrooms all have TV and bathroom, one with a big corner bath. A lounge has been added on to the back of the house. Evening meals can be served by arrangement at 6.30pm and guests may bring their own wine (there is no alcohol licence). Children welcome. Pets by arrangement. No smoking in the sun porch, dining-room and lounge. Car park.

OWNERS Mr and Mrs Swann OPEN All year ROOMS 1 double, 2 twin; all rooms with bath/shower TERMS B&B £16.50, (single occupancy of twin/double) £25; dinner £8.50; deposit 1 night charge

CROYDE Devon map 1

Combas Farm

Croyde, nr Braunton EX33 1PH
CROYDE (0271) 890398

The farm nestles in a secluded position in a fold in the hills and is approached down a very long well-maintained track. A grapevine and wistaria ramble over the idyllic seventeenth-century whitewashed farmhouse, which stands in a very pretty, immaculately kept small cottage-style garden with lots of colour. The Adamses, who tend a 140-acre beef and sheep farm, with their own cow for home-made yoghurt and cream, have lived here for over 30 years. The bedrooms are well equipped for families with children. They are small and simple, but are clean and freshly decorated; one bedroom is on the ground floor. There is an upstairs bathroom and a separate shower-room and toilet up some steep, narrow stairs beyond the kitchen. There are open stone fireplaces, one with a bread oven, in both the dining-room and sitting-room. Dinner is available by arrangement (at 6.30pm approximately) and vegetarians can be catered for. Packed lunches can be provided. The house is only a 15-minute walk from three miles of golden sands. Children welcome. No pets in the house. No smoking in the bedrooms or upstairs. Car park.

OWNERS Mr F. W. J. and Mrs G. M. Adams OPEN Mar–Nov ROOMS 2 family, 2 double, 1 twin, 1 single; all rooms with wash-basin TERMS B&B £14–£16 (children under 1 75% reduction, 1–3 50%, 3–7 35%, 7–12 25%); dinner £6.50; deposit 20%

Use the maps and indexes at the back of the Guide *to plan your trip.*

DARTMOUTH Devon map 1

Ford House

44 Victoria Road, Dartmouth TQ6 9DX
DARTMOUTH (0803) 834047

This attractive, small Regency house is in a very central location, only 500 yards from Dartmouth's historic quay. The house has a friendly, lived-in atmosphere, and is owned by Richard, from Australia, and Henrietta Turner, who used to be a professional cook – meals are something to look forward to at Ford House. Breakfast is served until noon every day, and such items as devilled kidneys, poached smoked haddock and scrambled eggs with smoked salmon are available if ordered in advance. The evening menus (7–10pm) are imaginative and all items are purchased fresh on the day. A spring menu may offer blinis, best end of spring lamb with spiced aubergines, and rhubarb soufflé laced with orange liqueur. Vegetarian choices can be provided and guests may bring their own wine (no corkage; there is no alcohol licence). Lunches are also available. The three bedrooms, all with TV and telephone, are *en suite*; one is on the first floor, two are on the garden level and all are most attractively decorated. The sitting-room is a comfortable room which leads off the dining-room, where guests eat at one big table. There are special dinner party weekends. 'Well-behaved' children and pets. Car park.

OWNER Richard Turner OPEN Mar–end Dec ROOMS 2 double, 1 twin; all rooms with bath/shower TERMS B&B £25, (single occupancy of twin/double) £35 (children £10 sharing parents' room); dinner £18; deposit £20; credit card surcharge; Access, Visa

Townstal Farmhouse

Townstal Road, Dartmouth TQ6 9HY
DARTMOUTH (0803) 832300

This sixteenth-century farmhouse is one of the oldest houses in Dartmouth. It is somewhat of a surprise, situated as it is among modern suburbia on the outskirts of town. Townstal was a working farm until being converted to a guesthouse at the end of the Second World War. Conversion has left the old beams and inglenook fireplaces and the feel of an old building. There are now two ground-floor rooms and a small dining-room extension. A three-course evening meal is available 6.30–8pm and can include vegetarian choices. There is an alcohol licence and packed lunches can be provided. This is a friendly place and a good base for Dartmouth, the centre of which is just half a mile away. Children welcome. Smoking only in the dining-room. Car park.

OWNER Mrs Jean M. Hall OPEN All year, exc Christmas ROOMS 3 family (1 with bath/shower, 2 with wash-basin), 1 double (with bath/shower), 5 twin (4 with bath/shower, 1 with wash-basin), 1 single (with bath/shower) TERMS B&B £15–£22.50, (single occupancy of twin/double) £25 (children £8 in family room); dinner £8.50; deposit

DORCHESTER Dorset map 2

Westwood House Hotel

29 High West Street, Dorchester DT1 1UP
DORCHESTER (0305) 268018

Right on the main street, this listed Georgian house was built as a coaching house for Lord Ilchester. Double glazing cuts down the noise from the road, and the traffic is less busy at night as there is now a bypass avoiding the town centre. The present owners have lived here since 1990 and have done up the whole house, in keeping with its period. The bedrooms have every possible amenity, including refrigerator with mini-bar, telephone, radio, hair-dryer and TV. Most rooms are *en suite*, and two bathrooms have whirlpool baths. There is a small, comfortable sitting-room leading into a Victorian conservatory, which takes up almost the whole back garden, and where breakfast only is served. Westwood House has an alcohol licence and there are many restaurants close by. Packed lunches can be provided. Children welcome. No smoking in the dining-room.

OWNERS Philip and Kate Sevier-Summers OPEN All year (Christmas by arrangement) ROOMS 1 family (with bath/shower), 3 double (with bath/shower), 2 twin (1 with bath/shower, 1 with wash-basin), 1 single (with wash-basin) TERMS B&B £20–£28, (single occupancy of twin/double) £34–£38, (family room) £48 (children under 1 free, 1–7 £8, 7–16 £16); Access, Visa

Any smoking restrictions that we know of are given in each entry.

Reduced rates for children are normally given when they share their parents' bedroom. If no reductions are specified in the details or text, assume you'll have to pay full rates.

DREWSTEIGNTON Devon map 1

Ford House

Drewsteignton EX6 6RD
DREWSTEIGNTON (0647) 21243

Ford House's isolated position, down a series of narrow lanes, necessitates good directions, available from the owners. A substantial country house, formerly the manor house of Drewsteignton, it stands in 15 acres of pasture and woodland right on the northern edge of Dartmoor. The house is spacious and has large bedrooms, all of which are *en suite*, with sizeable bathrooms. The dining-room, where evening meals can be served by arrangement (usually at 7pm), is at the rear of the house and has an old built-in range with tile surround. Lunches, cream teas and vegetarian choices can be provided. Ford House is licensed. The large Victorian conservatory is now in use and there is also a pleasant sitting-room with TV and a games-room. This is a good place for a quiet, peaceful break. No children under 14. No pets. No smoking. Car park.

OWNERS Michael and Jacqueline Page OPEN All year, exc Christmas and New Year ROOMS 2 double, 1 twin, 1 single, all rooms with bath/shower TERMS B&B £22.50; dinner £12.50; deposit 10%

Hunts Tor House

Drewsteignton EX6 6QW
DREWSTEIGNTON (0647) 21228

This small, solid building is right in the middle of the attractive village of Drewsteignton. The emphasis is on the food and many of the clientele come here to eat and stay the night as well. The bedrooms, one with TV, are comfortable, all *en suite* and most with old fireplaces. The décor and tone of the house are subdued and understated, but the style is interesting none the less. The front part of Hunts Tor dates from the nineteenth century; the back part is much older and it is here that the second, subsidiary dining-room is located – a simple room with an old stone fireplace, tiny bar and a big corner table. The main dining-room, with separate tables, is at the front of the house, and there is also a comfortable sitting-room furnished in a more contemporary fashion. Dinner, served at 7.30pm, may offer such dishes as a warm salad of pigeon breast with bacon and pine nuts, red mullet with fennel and butter sauce, and Normandy apple flan. The wine list has a decent, fair-priced choice. Vegetarians can be catered for. No children under 14. No pets in public rooms. No smoking in the dining-room.

OWNERS Sue and Chris Harrison OPEN Mar–Oct ROOMS 4 double (with bath/shower) TERMS B&B £20–£25, (single occupancy of double) £28; D, B&B £36.50–£44.50; dinner £16.50; deposit £10 per night

DUNSTER Somerset map 1

Dollons House

10 Church Street, Dunster TA24 6SH
DUNSTER (0643) 821880

In the heart of the medieval village of Dunster, Dollons is an attractive seventeenth-century house with elm beams and reed ceilings, once the village pharmacy, and noted for producing such delicious marmalade that it was sent for use at the Houses of Parliament. A lot of thought and care has gone into the décor and furnishings, which are most attractive and show great individuality. The rooms are spotlessly clean and bright and the bedrooms, all with TV, are pretty and chintzy, each with its own theme. One is the teddy bear room, with its own bear-design wallpaper in the bathroom. A craft shop takes up the two front rooms, and there is a delightful sitting-room on the first floor at the rear, with doors out on to a small patio and views of woods and hills. The dining-room is immediately below, where breakfast only is served. The owners are friendly, helpful and efficient. No small children. Pets by arrangement. No smoking.

OWNERS Hannah and Humphrey Bradshaw OPEN All year, exc Christmas and sometimes Jan and Feb ROOMS 2 double, 1 twin; all rooms with bath/shower TERMS B&B £20.50–£22.50, (single occupancy of twin/double) £30.50; deposit; Access, Amex, Visa

Spears Cross Hotel

1 West Street, Dunster TA24 6SN
DUNSTER (0643) 821439

The castle entrance is very close to this fifteenth-century whitewashed hotel in the main street of Dunster. At the side of the house is a pretty garden which has model houses from different periods and areas set amongst the plants. The bedrooms are comfortable and traditionally furnished. Two have the old wooden walls and should be avoided by those who sleep lightly, as the insulation is not up to modern standards. There is a small bar through the lounge and a most attractive small dining-room, prettily decorated where both breakfast and evening meals, by arrangement 7–8pm, are served. Spears Cross is licensed and packed lunches can be provided. No children under 12. Small dogs only. No smoking. Car park.

OWNERS Joyce and Ron Ahern OPEN Mar–Dec, exc Christmas
ROOMS 1 family, 1 double, 1 twin, 1 single; all rooms, exc single, with bath/shower TERMS B&B £16.50–£19; dinner from £8; deposit

EXETER Devon map 1

Park View Hotel

8 Howell Road, Exeter EX4 4LG
EXETER (0392) 71772/53047

This clean and comfortable, listed Georgian house is in a quiet road, a 10-minute walk from the city centre. The accommodation is basic and simple, the bedrooms being a bit on the small side, but all with telephone and TV and many with bath or shower. The breakfast room overlooks the secluded garden. Breakfast only is available, although packed lunches can be provided. This is an excellent base for Exeter, and overlooks Bury Meadow Park. Children welcome. No pets. No smoking in the dining-room. Parking for six cars.

OWNERS Mr and Mrs P. Batho OPEN All year, exc Christmas
ROOMS 2 family (with bath/shower), 7 double (3 with bath/shower, 4 with wash-basin), 3 twin (2 with bath/shower, 1 with wash-basin), 3 single (with wash-basin) TERMS B&B £18–£22, (single) £18–£30, (single occupancy of twin/double) £20–£32, (family room) from £50; deposit £5 per person; Access, Visa

FARWAY Devon map 1

Keeper's Cottage

Farway, Colyton EX13 6DL
FARWAY (040 487) 328

Keeper's Cottage belongs to a charming retired couple, who like to make guests feel thoroughly at home. The house, built as a gamekeeper's cottage, is in a very remote and difficult to find place off the B3174. It is quiet and peaceful, has lovely views of hills and woods and stands in a secluded, pretty and well-kept garden. The house is comfortably furnished; one bedroom is *en suite*, while the other two share a bathroom. Guests have use of the sitting-room, and breakfast is served in the attractive dining-room, which looks over the patio and garden. No children under 10. Restrictions on pets and smoking. Car park.

OWNERS Mr and Mrs L. B. H. Ryrie OPEN All year
ROOMS 1 double, 1 twin (with bath/shower), 1 single
TERMS B&B £16–£20; deposit

FOWEY Cornwall map 1

Trevanion Guest House

70 Lostwithiel Street, Fowey PL23 1BQ
FOWEY (0726) 832602

This attractive sixteenth-century house, on the way into the centre of Fowey and next to the garage, is very convenient for the ferry and town. There are five simply furnished bedrooms, all with TV, which share two bathrooms. Breakfast only is available, although packed lunches can be provided. A comfortable and simple guesthouse. Children welcome. Some restrictions on pets. No smoking. Car park.

OWNER Mrs Joy Rowledge OPEN Easter–Nov ROOMS 2 family, 2 twin, 1 single; all rooms with wash-basin TERMS B&B £15–£16 (children up to 5 £5, over 5 £8); deposit

FREMINGTON Devon map 1

Muddlebridge House

Fremington, nr Barnstaple EX31 2NQ
BARNSTAPLE (0271) 76073

This solid country house, with a restored Regency façade, is thought to have derived its name from the nearby picturesque pack-horse bridge. It stands in three acres of grounds just off the Barnstaple–Bideford road. The grounds contain six self-catering cottages, attractive gardens and a heated swimming-pool. Guests are also welcome to use the games-room, which has facilities for snooker, table tennis and darts, and the fully equipped laundry room. The house has three spacious bedrooms, all with TV and bathroom, and a sitting/dining-room, where breakfast only is served. Children welcome. Small dogs only. No smoking in bedrooms. Car park.

OWNERS Mr and Mrs T. Spencer OPEN Mar–Oct ROOMS 1 family, 1 double, 1 twin; all rooms with bath/shower TERMS B&B £17.50–£20 (children under 12 half-price); deposit 25%

GREAT TORRINGTON Devon map 1

Tarka Country Guest House

8 Halsdon Terrace, Great Torrington EX38 8DX
TORRINGTON (0805) 22948

The guesthouse is named after Tarka the Otter, from the story, written by Henry Williamson in the 1920s, which centres on the area around the rivers Taw and Torridge, where Tarka lived and died. The Tarka Trail is fast becoming a popular attraction, covering a nine-mile stretch along the old Torrington–Bideford railway line. Tarka Country Guest House is an early Victorian building in the centre of a small, historic town perched high on a hilltop overlooking the River Torridge. The bedrooms, all with TV, are quite large and bright and simply furnished. Dinner (7pm), including vegetarian choices, and packed lunches can be provided. The house is licensed. The North Devon coastline is only eight miles away, and Great Torrington is a good base from which to explore Dartmoor and Exmoor. Children welcome. No pets. No smoking.

OWNERS Ken and Hillary Bwye OPEN All year ROOMS 2 family (with wash-basin), 3 double (2 with bath/shower, 1 with wash-basin), 2 single (with wash-basin) TERMS B&B £16–£19, (single occupancy of twin/double) £25 (children under 2 free, under 12 £11, over 12 £13); dinner £11.50; deposit; Access, Visa

GREENHAM Somerset map 1

Greenham Hall

Greenham, nr Wellington TA21 0JJ
GREENHAM (0823) 672603

A glimpse at the illustration over the page will show that this is no ordinary B&B. An imposing, rambling Victorian ex-admiral's house complete with mock-Gothic tower, which guests can climb, Greenham Hall stands above the village and enjoys marvellous views in every direction. The large garden of lawns and shrubs

with croquet lawn, is a plant lover's delight. The entrance leads into an enormous hallway, which is the hub of the house. The rooms are vast and economically furnished, with wonderful views. Two bedrooms are *en suite* and there is a dining/sitting-room with TV. No evening meal is served, but good food can be found at local pubs and restaurants. Self-catering accommodation is also available. There is a 10% discount for stays of three nights or more. Children welcome. Pets by arrangement. Car park.

OWNER Caro Ayre OPEN All year, exc Christmas ROOMS 1 family (with wash-basin), 1 double (with bath/shower), 1 twin (with bath/shower) TERMS B&B £17.50, (single occupancy of twin/double) £20 (reductions for children by arrangement)

HALSTOCK Dorset map 2

Halstock Mill

Halstock, nr Yeovil BA22 9SJ
CORSCOMBE (0935) 891278

Dating from the seventeenth century, Halstock Mill has been under new ownership since 1989, and has reverted to its former name (it was, until recently, known as The Old Mill). It is at the end of a private lane, in a peaceful spot, close to the village centre and surrounded by 10 acres of gardens and paddocks. The conversion has created a house of character and charm, each bedroom decorated in an individual style and with its own bathroom and TV. A couple of bedrooms have sitting areas. The owners pride themselves on their food, growing most of their own fruit and vegetables and using fresh local produce. Evening meals, including vegetarian choices by arrangement, are served 7.30–9pm and may include dishes such as carrot and orange soup, pink trout (caught by a neighbour) with a béarnaise sauce and raspberry soufflé. There is a short but adequate wine list. An open fire in the sitting-room keeps guests warm and a well-stocked bar is available. Stabling can be provided for those guests wishing to bring their own horses, and touring bicycles are usually available for hire. No children under five. Pets by arrangement. Car park.

OWNERS Mr and Mrs Peter Spender OPEN Jan–Nov ROOMS 1 four-poster/family, 1 double, 2 twin; all rooms with bath/shower
TERMS B&B £20–£22; dinner £12; deposit £10 per night; Access, Amex, Visa

HARBERTON Devon map 1

Ford Farm Guest House

Harberton, Totnes TQ9 7SJ
TOTNES (0803) 863539

This charming seventeenth-century house in the tucked-away little village of Harberton has its own secluded garden with a stream and is a peaceful place to return to after a day's sightseeing. The bedrooms are comfortable, if a bit on the small side; all have hair-dryers and the comforting little extra of a tin of biscuits. The upstairs sitting-room has TV and tea- and coffee-making facilities. The house has a warm, friendly atmosphere, and although evening meals are not available there is a wide selection of local pubs and restaurants nearby. Packed lunches can be provided. There are also two self-catering flats available. No children under 12. Small dogs by arrangement. No smoking in the dining-room. Car park.

OWNER Sheila Edwards OPEN All year ROOMS 1 double (with bath/shower), 1 twin (with wash-basin), 1 single (with wash-basin)
TERMS B&B £17.50–£20, (single occupancy of twin/double) £25–£35; deposit £15 per person

HARTLAND Devon map 1

West Titchberry Farm

Hartland, nr Bideford EX39 6AU
HARTLAND (0237) 441287

This is a typical Devon longhouse and was built around 1760. It is set on the rugged North Devon coast within easy access of many of Devon's outstanding beauty spots and only half a mile from Hartland Point and lighthouse. The kitchen and dining-room have beamed ceilings, and there is a large open fireplace in the dining-room and a cosy wood-burning stove in the lounge. The upstairs rooms have individual heaters. Packed lunches are available and evening meals of home-cooked fresh produce and meat from the farm are served (usually at 6pm or 6.30pm) by arrangement. Vegetarians can be catered for and guests may bring their own wine to dinner as there is no alcohol licence. Guests are at liberty to wander around the 150-acre farm, which includes sheep, pigs and dairy cows, and are free to use the games-room. A self-catering cottage is also available. Children welcome. No pets in the house. Car park.

OWNERS Mr and Mrs Heard OPEN All year, exc Christmas
ROOMS 1 family (with wash-basin), 1 double (with wash-basin), 1 twin
TERMS B&B £11 (reductions for children under 12); dinner £7; deposit

HEASLEY MILL Devon map 1

Heasley House Hotel

Heasley Mill, South Molton EX36 3LE
NORTH MOLTON (059 84) 213

In the centre of the small hamlet of Heasley Mill is this roomy, listed Georgian house, originally the copper mine captain's house. It is in a quiet, peaceful spot, in a dip in the hills on the very edge of Exmoor, well away from main roads and traffic. The house has a pleasant, friendly and informal atmosphere. The dining-room has beams and a large fireplace, and guests sit at long tables giving them the chance of getting to know each other. Dinner is available at 7pm and can include vegetarian choices; Heasley House is licensed. Packed lunches can be provided. Of the two lounges one has TV, and at the rear of the property is a pretty terraced garden with pleasant views, where guests may relax after a day's outing. The bedrooms are simply furnished and one *en suite* room is on the ground floor. Children welcome. Smoking only in one lounge. Car park.

OWNERS June and Trevor Tate OPEN All year, exc Feb ROOMS 3 double (2 with bath/shower, 1 with wash-basin), 5 twin (3 with bath/shower, 2 with wash-basin) TERMS B&B £17.90 (children under 8 50% reduction, 8–12 33%); D, B&B £29.95; dinner from £10.50; deposit; Access, Visa

HENSTRIDGE Somerset map 2

Quiet Corner Farm

Henstridge, Templecombe BA8 ORA
STALBRIDGE (0963) 63045

This Victorian house, with a collection of older stone farm buildings, has a pretty garden with lovely views across the Blackmore Vale between Sherborne and Shaftesbury. The smallholding extends to about five acres and supports Shetland ponies and a few sheep. Guests have use of a sitting-room with TV and there is also a sitting area in the flagstoned entrance hall. Breakfast only is available and is taken in a sun porch, reached through the kitchen, or, if the weather is fine enough, on the patio. The three bedrooms are simply furnished and one is *en suite*. There are also two well-equipped self-catering units in the grounds. Children welcome. No cats and dogs. No smoking in bedrooms. Car park.

OWNERS Brian and Patricia Thompson OPEN All year, exc Christmas ROOMS 1 family/twin (with wash-basin), 2 double (1 with bath/shower, 1 with wash-basin) TERMS B&B £15–£17.50, (single occupancy of twin/double) £20–£25 (children in cot £6, up to 12 £10–£12); deposit £10

HINTON CHARTERHOUSE Avon map 2

Green Lane House

1 Green Lane, Hinton Charterhouse BA3 6BL
LIMPLEY STOKE (0225) 723631

Only six miles from Bath and 12 from Bristol is this stone-built cottage dating from around 1725, in the middle of the delightful conservation village of Hinton Charterhouse. The house is very comfortable, the bedrooms are of a good size and there is a comfortable lounge with TV and a pretty breakfast room. Children of all ages are welcome, with children's evening meals and babysitting services provided by arrangement. Packed lunches can be provided. The house is just opposite the village pub, and there are a number of eating-places within a few miles. There is a 10% reduction in price for a stay of five nights or more. No dogs. Smoking only in bedrooms and the lounge. Parking for three cars.

OWNERS Lucille and John Baxter OPEN All year, exc Dec and Jan
ROOMS 2 double (1 with bath/shower, 1 with wash-basin), 2 twin (1 with bath/shower, 1 with wash-basin) TERMS B&B £18–£23.50, (single occupancy of twin/double) £24–£35 (children under 3 free, children sharing adults' room half-price); deposit; Access, Amex, Visa

HOLFORD Somerset map 1

Quantock House

Holford TA5 1RY
HOLFORD (027 874) 439

This very pretty seventeenth-century thatched house is in a quiet, picturesque village on the A39, at the foot of the Quantock Hills. It is a superb base for walking, with access to the hills at the end of the lane – the reason why many people stay here. The house is immaculate, and has been beautifully furnished and decorated. The three very pretty bedrooms, all with TV, have private bathrooms, and the lovely sitting/dining-room, with open fireplace, has doors out on to the colourful garden. Evening meals, including vegetarian choices, are available by arrangement at 7pm, and there are also several inns and restaurants nearby providing meals. Packed lunches can be provided and guests may bring their own wine to dinner (there is no alcohol licence). Children welcome. 'Well-behaved' dogs only. Non-smokers preferred. Car park.

OWNER Mrs P. Laidler OPEN All year, exc Christmas
ROOMS 1 family, 1 double, 1 twin; all rooms with bath/shower
TERMS B&B £15–£18 (children half-price sharing adults' room); dinner £9; deposit £10 for new guests

Those B&Bs that we know can offer some kind of off-street car parking, have 'car park' at the end of the entry. If we are aware of particular car parking difficulties, we mention them.

If there are any bedrooms with TV and/or telephone we mention this in the entry.

HONITON Devon map 1

Colestocks House

Colestocks, nr Honiton EX14 0JR
HONITON (0404) 850633

A lovely thatched sixteenth-century house, with later additions, set in two acres of immaculately kept gardens of lawns, shrubs and flowers surrounded by a high cob wall. The tiny village of Colestocks is situated between the villages of Feniton and Payhembury, two miles north of the A30. The house has spacious bedrooms, including one enormous ground-floor four-poster room. There is a comfortable sitting-room with a good selection of brochures and books and french windows that lead out on to the garden, a lounge bar and a dining-room where dinners are served at 8pm. The menu is changed every day and may include cream of watercress soup, roast Gressingham duckling with apples and calvados, and raspberry and redcurrant trifle. Vegetarian dishes and packed lunches can be provided on request. The wine list offers French bottles only, all interesting and well chosen. There is a putting green in the garden. No children under 10. Guide dogs only. Smoking discouraged in the dining-room. Car park.

OWNERS Mrs Jacqueline and Mr Henri Yot OPEN All year
ROOMS 1 four-poster, 5 double, 3 twin; all rooms with bath/shower
TERMS B&B £27–£29, (single occupancy of twin/double) around £33 (children half-price sharing parents' room); dinner around £15.50; deposit £20; Access, Visa

JACOBSTOWE Devon map 1

Higher Cadham Farm

Jacobstowe, Okehampton EX20 3RB
EXBOURNE (083 785) 647

Originally a Devon longhouse, but considerably altered over the years, the house has, as far as is known, only belonged to two families throughout its history. It was acquired by the King family in 1910; the present owners are the third generation to live here. Approached down a long lane, Higher Cadham Farm is a sixteenth-century oak-beamed farmhouse taking up one side of the farmyard. The farm itself extends to 140 acres supporting sheep and beef, and is set in pretty countryside with a stream at the edge of the fields. Children are most welcome here, and there is a good outside play area, as well as a large games-room with lots of games and toys. The farm is also on the Tarka Trail country walk. There is a licensed dining-room with small open fire, and beyond that is a lounge with TV, books and magazines. Four-course dinners are available by arrangement at 7pm and can include vegetarian choices. There is a kitchenette with facilities for preparing drinks and making up picnics. There are also limited facilities for washing clothes. No children under three. No dogs. No smoking in the dining-room. Car park.

OWNERS John and Jenny King OPEN Mar–end Nov
ROOMS 1 family, 1 double, 1 twin, 1 single; all rooms with wash-basin
TERMS B&B £11–£12, (family room) £33 (children under 10 half-price, under 15 three-quarters-price); dinner £7; deposit

KINGSBRIDGE Devon map 1

Aqua-Vista

19 Lower Warren Road, Kingsbridge TQ7 1LF
KINGSBRIDGE (0548) 856366

The house is set in a quiet, residential area of Kingsbridge with panoramic views over the Salcombe Estuary. Aqua-Vista is an immaculate, small modern house, the friendly owner, Sonia Whitaker, providing comfortable, simple accommodation. All bedrooms are on the ground floor and one double is *en suite*; the other two rooms share a bathroom and separate toilet. Breakfast only is available. Aqua-Vista is an excellent base for exploring the Salcombe Estuary, beaches, headlands, moors and the attractive small town of Kingsbridge. Children welcome. Small dogs only. No smoking in public rooms. Parking for four cars.

OWNER S. J. Whitaker OPEN Easter–Oct ROOMS 2 double (1 with bath/shower), 1 twin TERMS B&B £11–£16 (children half-price sharing parents' room); deposit £10

LANGLEY MARSH Somerset map 1

Deepleigh Country Hotel

Langley Marsh, Wiveliscombe TA4 2UU
WIVELISCOMBE (0984) 23379

Once a farmhouse, this listed sixteenth-century building is set in three acres of hilly farmland at the foot of the Brendon Hills. Close by is an old quarry mined by the Romans, an old

Roman road and, for those interested in riding, the Deepleigh Farm Riding Centre, adjacent to the hotel, offers riding for the beginner and the more experienced rider. The present owner, an energetic, friendly lady, has lived here since 1989 and has redecorated the house. The bedrooms, all with TV, are pretty, with cottage style décor, including some stencilling. The lovely, partly panelled sitting-room has beams, comfortable armchairs and sofas and a wood-burning stove in the huge fireplace. The dining-room has been decorated in blue with robust tables and chairs, and there is a small bar and library/games-room with a small snooker table. Home-cooked, four-course candlelit dinners using locally grown produce are available by arrangement at 7.30pm or 8pm. Vegetarian choices and packed lunches can be provided. Deepleigh is licensed. Children welcome. No pets in the house. No smoking in bedrooms. Car park.

OWNER Christine Lymer OPEN All year, exc Christmas
ROOMS 2 family, 2 double, 1 twin; all rooms with bath/shower
TERMS B&B £21–£26 (children under 5 £10, 5–12 half-price); dinner £14.50; deposit £20 per person

LANHYDROCK Cornwall map 1

Treffry Farm

Lanhydrock, Bodmin PL30 5AF
BODMIN (0208) 74405

The farm sits in peaceful, pretty countryside only 300 yards from Lanhydrock, a superb Victorian house and estate now owned by the National Trust, and within easy access of the A38 and Bodmin, which is two miles away. The Georgian farmhouse has a tile-faced front and adjoins the farmyard, which serves the 170-acre dairy farm, once the home farm of the Lanhydrock Estate. It is a comfortable family farmhouse, listed because of its extra-wide staircase and the Victorian panelling in the charming lounge with comfortable furniture and TV. The bedrooms, all with TV, are very pretty; one has a four-poster bed and two are *en suite* and furnished in pine. The farm buildings have been beautifully converted to provide several self-catering units, which have a laundry room for guests' use. There is a large and secluded garden and a play area for children with swings, slides, see-saw and sandpit. Home-cooked dinners, including home-baked rolls, home-made soups and chutneys, are available by arrangement at 7pm. Vegetarians can be catered for and guests may bring their own wine (there is no alcohol licence). Packed lunches can also be provided. No children under six. No pets. Smoking in the lounge only (non-smokers preferred). Car park.

OWNER Pat Smith OPEN Easter–Oct ROOMS 1 four-poster (with shower), 2 twin (with bath/shower) TERMS B&B £17.50, (single occupancy of twin) £25 (children 6–10 half-price); dinner £7.50; deposit

LANTEGLOS Cornwall map 1

Carneggan House

Carneggan, Lanteglos PL23 1NW
POLRUAN (0726) 870327

This eighteenth-century farmhouse is in quiet, peaceful countryside close to the spectacular coastline. A 20-minute walk brings you to two or three unspoilt beaches across National Trust-owned farmland; for those who want a longer walk, both Polperro and Polruan can be reached along the Cornish coastal path. There are three well-furnished bedrooms, all with TV, sea views and private bathrooms or *en suite* facilities. Excellent simple and home-cooked dinners, using organically home-grown produce, including meat, are served in the dining-room, if ordered in advance, at 8pm. A typical dinner menu may include lentil soup with bacon, pot-roast of Carneggan beef and chocolate truffle. Vegetarian choices, snack lunches and packed lunches can all be provided. There is a reasonably priced wine list. Guests have use of a comfortable lounge with open fireplace. The property extends to six acres and includes a grass tennis court. Children welcome. Pets by arrangement. Car park.

OWNER Mrs S. M. Shakerley OPEN All year, exc Christmas ROOMS 3 twin (with bath/shower) TERMS B&B £18–£25, (single occupancy of twin) £23–£30 (infants free, children under 12 half-price, early supper from £2.50); dinner from £15; deposit 50%; Access, Amex, Visa

LAPFORD Devon map 1

Nymet Bridge Country Guest House

Lapford EX17 6QX
LAPFORD (0363) 83334

This 600-year-old small house lies just off the A377 and stands in a pretty garden with orchard and stream. A railway line runs at the end of the garden, but it is only a local line carrying about eight trains a day, usually of only one carriage. The house is immaculately kept, has an informal atmosphere and is owned by a most friendly lady. There is a cosy sitting-room, with wood-burning stove, leading into the dining-room, where evening meals (on request) and breakfast are served. Vegetarians can be catered for; Nymet Bridge is licensed. There are some very low ceilings and lots of beams. Guests may use the croquet lawn in the garden. No children under 12. No pets. No smoking. Car park

OWNER Linda Hindley OPEN Mar–Nov ROOMS 2 twin (with bath/shower) TERMS B&B £15; dinner £7

LERRYN Cornwall map 1

Mixton House

Lerryn, nr Lostwithiel PL22 0QE
BODMIN (0208) 872781

This most unusual and beautiful Georgian country house is in a lovely position, above the small village of Lerryn, overlooking the picturesque wooded Lerryn valley. The tidal waters and National Trust woodland form a natural habitat for herons, cormorants and swans, and it is said that this peaceful valley was the inspiration for Kenneth Grahame's *Wind in the Willows*. Mixton House belongs to a most delightful couple, who have furnished and decorated the house with flair and imagination, achieving a mixture of elegance and informality. The rooms are spacious and well proportioned, and guests have the run of the house. Breakfast can be served in the conservatory, which has a beautiful view, in the dining-room or in the lovely old kitchen at a central refectory table, with beams and hanging dried flowers. The bedrooms are charming; some have pretty, old lace bedspreads and curtains, and are light, bright and refreshing. Two acres of wild, mature gardens stretch behind the house, where there is also a croquet lawn and a grass tennis court. Cream teas are served in the front garden or conservatory. A boat and moorings are also available for guests to use. No children. No pets. Car park.

OWNERS Michael Stevenson and Janie Flockhart OPEN Apr–Oct ROOMS 2 double, 1 twin; all rooms with bath/shower TERMS B&B £25, (single occupancy of twin/double) £30; deposit

It is always best to book a room in advance, especially in winter. Establishments with few rooms may close at short notice for periods not specified in the details.

LIMPLEY STOKE Avon map 2

Avonside

Limpley Stoke, nr Bath BA3 6EX
LIMPLEY STOKE (0225) 722547

Just four miles from Bath, this eighteenth-century, Bath-stone former farmhouse lies on the banks of the River Avon. (Limpley Stoke is just on the Wiltshire/Avon border on the B3108, though its postal address is Avon.) It stands in one and a half acres of lovely gardens and has a hard tennis court which guests are welcome to use. The house is a comfortable family home, attractively decorated and furnished with antiques, and has good-sized bedrooms. A three-course dinner with aperitif and coffee can be served by arrangement at 8pm, and guests are welcome to bring their own wine as there is no alcohol licence. There is also a restaurant within a five-minute walk. Children welcome. No pets in the house. Car park.

OWNERS Major and Mrs Peter Challen OPEN All year, exc Christmas and New Year ROOMS 2 twin (with wash-basin) TERMS B&B £17–£19 (babies free, children under 12 £8); dinner £11

LIZARD Cornwall map 1

Mounts Bay House Hotel

Penmenner Road, Lizard TR12 7NP
LIZARD (0326) 290305/290393

Along the length of the Lizard Point there is hardly a sight of the sea, so the view here comes as something of a surprise as you round a bend in the drive and look out to sea and distant cliffs. The hotel is perfectly placed, at the end of the Point down a dead-end road, for peace and quiet and an away-from-it-all feeling. The house is Victorian and retains some original features, such as the ceilings and stained-glass windows. There is one *en suite* bedroom on the ground floor and some rooms have marvellous sea views. There is a tiny bar and the dining-room with sea views is the venue for good-value home-cooked evening meals at 7.30pm. Vegetarian choices and packed lunches can be provided. Mounts Bay House is licensed. Within each reach are delightful cliff-top

Many B&Bs are in remote places; always ask for clear directions when booking.

walks, sandy beaches, secluded coves and picturesque fishing harbours. Children welcome. Car park.

OWNERS Sam and Grace Crossley OPEN All year, exc Nov ROOMS 1 family (with bath/shower), 4 double (1 with bath/shower, 3 with shower only), 1 twin (with shower), 1 single (with shower) TERMS B&B £16.50–£22, (single occupancy of twin/double) 50% surcharge July and Aug (children under 3 £1.50, 3–12 half-price sharing or three-quarters-price own room); dinner £9.50; deposit 10%; Access, Visa

LODDISWELL Devon map 1

Alleron

Loddiswell, nr Kingsbridge TQ7 4ED
KINGSBRIDGE (0548) 550306

When Lavinia Davies' parents bought Alleron in the 1950s, they were only the second family to have lived in the house since it was built in the sixteenth century. It stands in three acres of garden, which include an interesting circular, thatched walled garden, and 40 acres of pastureland, in a quiet secluded spot – an ideal place from which to explore this attractive part of Devon. For 20 years Lavinia ran a small, successful restaurant at Alleron and guests have the opportunity of sampling her excellent food at dinner, which is served in the elegant family dining-room at 8pm. Vegetarians can be catered for and alcohol is available. All the bread, marmalade and preserves offered at breakfast, which can be served on the patio, weather permitting, are home-made. There is a sitting-room with TV for guests' use. The estate also has streams and ponds, where coarse fishing is available if required, and a swimming-pool. No children at dinner. No dogs in the house. No smoking. Car park.

OWNERS Jeremy and Lavinia Davies OPEN All year, exc Christmas and New Year ROOMS 2 twin (with bath/shower), 1 single (with wash-basin) TERMS B&B £22–£27, (single) £18–£20 (children £10–£12); dinner £18–£20; deposit

Where a single-occupancy rate is not specified in the details, the cost will be the same as that per person in a twin or double room, or will be included in the range of prices given.

Most B&Bs don't accept credit cards, but when they do we list the cards taken.

LOOE Cornwall map 1

Harescombe Lodge

Watergate, nr Looe PL13 2NE
LOOE (0503) 263158

The Lodge, one-time shooting-lodge of the Trelawne estate, is just one of the three houses that make up the tiny hamlet of Watergate off the A387. It overlooks the upper reaches of the West Looe River; a river path offers a pleasant walk (about half an hour) into Looe. The long narrow garden stretches up the floor of the secluded, wooded valley, bounded by a tumbling stream complete with waterfalls. Flowering shrubs behind stone walls surround the square house. The Lodge is cosy and bright; plates, brass and prints decorate the walls; the bedrooms and dining-room tables have vases of flowers, and there is a copious amount of reading material in the small sitting area with fireplace which leads off from the dining-room. Dinner is available by arrangement at 7pm, and guests may bring their own wine (there is no alcohol licence). Vegetarians can be catered for and packed lunches can be provided. This is a quiet, peaceful place, ideal for nature lovers. No children under 12. No pets. Car park.

OWNERS Barry and Jane Wynn OPEN All year ROOMS 2 double, 1 twin; all rooms with bath/shower TERMS B&B £18.50; dinner £10

Marwinthy Guest House

East Cliff, East Looe PL13 1DE
LOOE (0503) 264382

This small, family-run guesthouse is right in the centre of Looe, yet in a peaceful position on the coastal footpath, up a precipitously steep narrow lane with lovely views over the town, harbour and beach. Both dining-room and sitting-room, shared with the owners, have balconies, and there is a telescope for exploring the view. All bedrooms, except one, have marvellous views. Breakfast only is available, although packed lunches can be provided. Not suitable for very young children. No pets. No smoking in the dining-room.

OWNERS Eddie and Geraldine Mawby OPEN All year
ROOMS 4 family/double/twin, 1 double; all rooms with wash-basin
TERMS B&B £14 (children £8.50 sharing with 2 adults); deposit £3 per person per night

LUCCOMBE Somerset map 1

Stables Cottage

Luccombe, nr Minehead TA24 8TE
PORLOCK (0643) 862190

Set on the very edge of Exmoor, Stables Cottage is in the National Trust-owned village of Luccombe, and an excellent location for riders and walkers. There are several stables in the area where horses can be hired, both for experienced riders as well as beginners. Mrs Howard makes a point of ensuring guests have an enormous breakfast, as most are off to do some strenuous exercise. The brick-built house is about 200 years old and was originally the stables to the big house. It stands in one and a half acres of walled gardens and has chickens, ducks and one pet sheep. The two small bedrooms are decorated in a pleasant cottagey style, with the bathroom downstairs. There is a comfortable TV lounge with a small conservatory leading off it, and a tiny pretty dining-room where breakfast only is served. There are good places to eat in Wootton Courtenay and Porlock, both about three miles away. No children. Car park.

OWNERS Mr and Mrs Howard OPEN All year, exc Christmas
ROOMS 1 double, 1 twin/double; both rooms with wash-basin
TERMS B&B £12.50–£13

LUSTLEIGH Devon map 1

Brookside

Lustleigh, nr Bovey Tracey TQ13 9TJ
LUSTLEIGH (064 77) 310

A small, old stone cottage in the centre of the very picturesque village of Lustleigh, just opposite the fifteenth-century thatched pub, which serves competent food in the evening. From the balcony of the small upstairs TV lounge there are views across the small pretty garden, part of which is a disused railway line, to the cricket field and a small stream flowing under what was the railway bridge. The garden also has a croquet lawn. The small, cottagey bedrooms are on the second floor; the bathroom and two toilets are on the floor below. Breakfast only is served in the dining end of the owners' sitting-room. Packed lunches can be

If any bedrooms are suitable for the disabled we mention this in the entry.

provided. Children welcome. 'Well-behaved' dogs only. No smoking. Small car park.

OWNERS Malcolm and Jennifer Bell OPEN All year, exc Christmas and New Year ROOMS 1 double, 2 twin, 1 single; all rooms with wash-basin TERMS B&B £16, (single occupancy of twin/double) £20 (children under 3 free, over 3 half-price on camp bed); deposit

LYME REGIS Dorset map 1

Old Monmouth Hotel

12 Church Street, Lyme Regis DT7 3BS
LYME REGIS (0297) 442456

This whitewashed sixteenth-century building, only a two-minute walk from the centre of Lyme Regis, is ablaze with colour in summer. There are seven attractively decorated bedrooms, furnished in stripped pine and arranged around a small central landing. Two bedrooms can be used as family rooms. Downstairs there is a small, comfortable lounge with TV, and a large, spacious, beamed dining-room with a small bar in the corner. Breakfast only is available. No children under 12. No pets. No smoking.

OWNERS Terry and Jennifer Fuller OPEN All year, exc Christmas and 2 weeks for owners' hol (usually in Feb) ROOMS 7 double (4 with bath/shower, 3 with wash-basin) TERMS B&B £16–£22 (children £10 in family room)

The Red House

Sidmouth Road, Lyme Regis DT7 3ES
LYME REGIS (0297) 442055

Built in the 1920s by a distinguished mariner, the house is set above Lyme Regis in a pleasant garden and enjoys spectacular views of the coast. It is within walking distance of the town centre and harbour. The house has a pleasant, relaxed atmosphere and the feel of a family home. A balcony runs round the front, and has tables and chairs for sitting out on fine days. The three bedrooms are large, attic-type rooms, all with private bathrooms, and are comfortably furnished with armchairs, TV, fridge and writing desk. Mrs Griffin is an exceptionally friendly Australian lady who

Where we know of any particular payment stipulations we mention them in the details. It is always best to check when booking, however.

moved to England with her English husband when he took early retirement. No children under six. Guide dogs only. Car park.

OWNERS Geoffrey and Elizabeth Griffin OPEN Mar–Nov
ROOMS 1 family, 2 twin; all rooms with bath/shower TERMS B&B £18–£23 (children half-price); deposit

LYNTON Devon map 1

Sylvia House Hotel

Lydiate Lane, Lynton EX35 6HE
LYNTON (0598) 52391

You have to like pink and frills to stay here. Diminutive Italian Marianna and her much larger English husband, David, transformed this Georgian hotel into something that is a bit different and has a lot of character. Marianna, who used to be a schoolteacher in Wales, is a walking history of the area, and both she and David want to make sure their guests are comfortable and have everything they want. There are now only eight bedrooms, most of which are *en suite*; several have four-poster beds and all have TV. The rooms, which were very small, are a bit larger now with the extra space. Guests have use of a lounge, library and gardens, and dinners, including vegetarian choices, are served in the dining-room at 6.30pm. The wine list has a particularly extensive selection of Italian bottles. Children welcome. Small pets only. No smoking in the dining-room.

OWNERS David and Marianna Holdsworth OPEN All year
ROOMS 3 four-poster (with bath/shower), 2 double (with bath/shower), 1 twin (with bath/shower), 2 single (with wash-basin) TERMS B&B £13–£18 (discounts for children in single or twin); dinner £11; deposit

MALPAS Cornwall map 1

Woodbury

Malpas, nr Truro TR1 1SQ
TRURO (0872) 71466

The position of this small, comfortable house is superb. It is set just above a quiet road one mile from Truro overlooking the River Fal. The sitting-room leads through to a marvellous, spacious sun porch/conservatory where breakfast is served overlooking the river. Evening meals are available at 6.30pm by arrangement and there is a pub with a good choice of food in the village, just a few minutes' walk away. Vegetarian choices and packed lunches can be provided. Woodbury has no alcohol licence, but guests may bring their own wine to dinner. The three bedrooms are small and simply furnished, but all have river views and the bathroom is large and well equipped. Guests have use of a billiard table and dartboard. Children welcome. No pets. No smoking in bedrooms. Car park.

OWNER Mrs M. Colwill OPEN All year, exc Christmas ROOMS 2 double (1 with wash-basin), 1 single TERMS B&B £12–£14.50 (children half-price); dinner £8.50; deposit 10% for new guests

MARAZION Cornwall map 1

Castle Gayer

Leys Lane, Marazion TR17 0AQ
PENZANCE (0736) 711548

A substantial, whitewashed Victorian sea captain's house, with many original features and in a superb position, Castle Gayer stands right on the edge of a cliff, encompassed by the sea wall and facing St Michael's Mount with sea views on three sides. The National Trust harbour, where boats leave to go over to the Mount lies just below the house, which is approached down a short, narrow lane directly from the centre of the village. Guests have a choice of three beautifully equipped *en suite* bedrooms, each bathroom with bath and separate shower. The lounge has a baby grand piano, log fire and overlooks the Mount; breakfast only is served in the pleasant dining-room. Mr Ivory carries out his chiropodist practice from the house. At the bottom of the garden is a small listed folly, which looks like the top of a lighthouse. No children. No pets. No smoking. Car park.

OWNERS Brian Ivory and John Trewhella OPEN All year, exc Christmas ROOMS 2 double, 1 twin; all rooms with bath/shower TERMS B&B £22.50–£25; deposit £20 per person

MELLS Somerset map 2

Holwell Farm

Mells, nr Frome BA11 3RH
MELLS (0373) 812650

This farmhouse is at the end of a long driveway outside the village of Mells. The farm itself supports mostly sheep on its 130 acres.

The house has been more or less rebuilt to accommodate eight bedrooms with private bathrooms. The rooms are very attractive and a liberal use has been made of pine, in panelling, floors and furniture. Three of the doubles can also be used as family rooms. What was probably the old kitchen, with flagstoned floor, old aga and pretty dresser, is now the dining-room, which is open to both residents and non-residents for coffee, lunch, cream teas and dinners. Holwell Farm is licensed and vegetarians can be catered for. The comfortable sitting-room has beams and large fireplaces; there is also a tiny bar. The house has an informal atmosphere, and is very much a family-run operation, with all four children taking a part. Fishing, riding and clay pigeon shooting can be arranged. Children welcome. No pets. Car park.

OWNER Dawn Coles OPEN All year ROOMS 7 double, 1 twin; all rooms with bath/shower TERMS B&B £26 (children under 4 free, 4–14 half-price); dinner £12 approx.

MEVAGISSEY Cornwall map 1

Southcliffe Guest House

Polkirt Hill, Mevagissey PL26 6UX
MEVAGISSEY (0726) 842505

Southcliffe is situated between the picturesque towns of Mevagissey and Portmellon: Portmellon is a five-minute walk and Mevagissey a 10-minute walk (slightly longer on the way back as it's uphill). It is an intimate, friendly guesthouse on the cliff road. The terraced gardens, with shrubs and flowers, overlook the sea. The bedrooms, all with TV, are on the small side and simply furnished; most have sea views. Evening meals are served at 7pm by arrangement in the very pleasant dining-room, and the large lounge has a wonderful sea panorama. Vegetarians can be catered for and guests may bring their own wine to dinner (there is no alcohol licence). There is also a self-contained flat, adjacent to the house, that is ideal for families. No children under 14. No pets. Car park.

OWNERS Ronald Haskins and David Templeton OPEN All year, exc Christmas ROOMS 3 double, 1 twin; all rooms with wash-basin TERMS B&B £12–£12.50, (single occupancy of twin/double) £15–£15.50; dinner £9; deposit 10%

It is always best to check prices, especially for single occupancy, when booking.

MILTON ABBAS Dorset map 2

Old Bakery

Milton Abbas, nr Blandford Forum DT11 0BW
MILTON ABBAS (0258) 880327

This is a house full of character – beams, inglenooks and antiques. As the name suggests, this was once the bakery, in the centre of the historic village of Milton Abbas, with its thatched houses, old church and pub. It dates from 1780 when the Earl of Dorchester created this 'model village'. Surprisingly it has 10 acres of pasture and woodlands stretching beyond the attractive terraced garden at the back of the house. Stabling and grazing can be provided for guests' horses. The bedrooms are a bit on the small side but have much charm. There is a small front-facing sitting-room and a dining-room leading off from the kitchen, where breakfast only is served. One bedroom has its own entrance and can be let with an attractive, cosy sitting-room that has an open fireplace. This bedroom is built into the rafters with a very low ceiling and, according to the owner, the smallest bathroom in the world. No children under 12. Dogs by arrangement. No smoking in the breakfast room. Parking for six cars.

OWNER Mrs Margaret Penny OPEN All year ROOMS 2 double (with bath/shower), 1 twin, 2 single (1 with wash-basin) TERMS B&B £14–£20; deposit

MINEHEAD Somerset map 1

Tivington Farm

Minehead TA24 8SU
MINEHEAD (0643) 702468

The house belongs to the National Trust and is a lovely fifteenth-century whitewashed thatched farmhouse on a 600-acre working arable and sheep farm with impressive views to Dunkery Hill and Porlock Vale. It is a wonderful old place, with some unusual features, and many exposed beams. The bedrooms, all with TV, are spacious and comfortable, and one of the two bathrooms is enormous, complete with double basin, bidet and a large bath. Breakfast only is served in the dining-room and there is no guests'

If you have to cancel a reservation for a room, please telephone to warn the proprietor.

sitting-room. Packed lunches can be provided; Tivington Farm is unlicensed. Children welcome. No pets. No smoking. Car park.

OWNER Fiona Dyer OPEN Easter–Oct ROOMS 1 family, 1 double, 1 twin TERMS B&B from £14, (single occupancy of twin/double) £15–£20 (reductions for children according to age and time of year); deposit

MOREBATH Devon map 1

Blights Farm

Morebath, nr Bampton EX16 9DD
BAMPTON (0398) 331423

A simple whitewashed seventeenth-century farmhouse that stands in an elevated position in a very rural location on the edge of Exmoor with lovely views over farmland down into a valley. It offers simple accommodation, and the two bedrooms are quite spacious, comfortable and traditionally furnished and decorated in attractive pastel colours. They both have TV and armchairs; there is no guests' lounge. Breakfast only is served in the dining-room. Children welcome. Car park.

OWNERS G. G. and D. M. Martin OPEN Apr–end Oct ROOMS 1 family, 1 twin; both rooms with wash-basin TERMS B&B £13, (single occupancy of twin) £18 (children 12 and under £7.50 sharing parents' room); deposit £5

MORETON Dorset map 2

Vartrees House

Moreton, Crossways, nr Dorchester DT2 8BE
WARMWELL (0305) 852704

Vartrees is approached from a long driveway, through a mature three-acre garden of woodland, azaleas and rhododendrons. It was built by Hermann Lea, a friend of Thomas Hardy, at the turn of the century. Guests have use of the large, comfortable sitting-room, with wood-burning stove, and the outside terrace overlooking the gardens. Breakfast and evening meals, by special arrangement only, are served in the dining-room, and upstairs are the bedrooms, one with TV, and large, traditionally equipped bathroom. One bedroom is very large and both are somewhat sparsely furnished. The nearby tiny parish church at Moreton is renowned for its unique engraved windows by Lawrence Whistler and as the burial place of 'Lawrence of Arabia'. Vartrees is owned by a charming lady and is in a beautiful setting. No pets in the dining-room. No smoking in bedrooms. Car park.

OWNER Mrs D. M. Haggett OPEN All year, exc Christmas
ROOMS 1 double (with wash-basin), 1 double/twin (with shower)
TERMS B&B £16, (single occupancy of twin/double) £20

MORETONHAMPSTEAD Devon map 1

The Old Post House

18 Court Street, Moretonhampstead TQ13 8LG
MORETONHAMPSTEAD (0647) 40900

As you might expect, this small terraced house, right in the centre of the village, is next to the post office. There is a small patio between the house and the street where guests may sit out. All bedrooms are *en suite* and have TV and room to sit. Evening meals, including vegetarian choices, are available 6.30–8pm in the attractive dining-room on the ground floor and guests may bring their own wine (the place is unlicensed). Lunches are also available. Children welcome. No pets. No smoking in bedrooms.

OWNER Mrs Laura W. Thrippleton OPEN All year, exc Christmas
ROOMS 1 family, 2 double, 2 twin, 1 single; all rooms with bath/shower TERMS B&B £17–£20 (children under 8 half-price); dinner £8; deposit 10%

MORWENSTOW Cornwall map 1

The Old Vicarage

Morwenstow, nr Bude EX23 9SR
MORWENSTOW (028 883) 369

Built in the 1830s by the eccentric Rev R. S. Hawker, this is a handsome stone-built house, at the end of a long narrow lane. Morwenstow consists of the vicarage, the church and what is now a tea-shop. A link footpath of the Coastal Path runs through the grounds of the Old Vicarage, bringing you in a matter of minutes to the splendours of the north Cornish coast. The house is surrounded by National Trust or church land, so is completely unspoilt and very peaceful. Along what is now the Coastal Path, the Rev Hawker built a tiny hut out of wood from the many shipwrecks, where he would write poetry. No less than 47 shipwrecks occurred while he lived at the Old Vicarage, and he and his staff would rescue as many of the bodies as possible and give them a Christian burial in the churchyard. The house is renowned for its chimneys, all of which are different; one is a life-size replica of Rev Hawker's mother's coffin. The house offers comfortable bedrooms, all *en suite*, or with private bathrooms, a lounge, a study with lots of books and a dining-room. Evening meals are available at 8pm (drinks at 7.30pm) and can include vegetarian choices if pre-arranged. A pre-dinner drink and wine are included in the price. Packed lunches can be provided with notice. The Old Vicarage has a comfortable and informal atmosphere. Children welcome. No pets. Smoking in the study only. Car park.

OWNERS Richard and Jill Wellby OPEN All year, exc Dec and Jan
ROOMS 1 double, 1 twin, 1 single; all rooms with bath/shower
TERMS B&B £20 (children under 12 half-price); D, B&B £30; deposit £10 per person

MOUSEHOLE Cornwall map 1

Tavis Vor Hotel

Mousehole, nr Penzance TR19 6PR
PENZANCE (0736) 731306

Tavis Vor was built in 1918 along the lines of a ship's compass, to take full advantage of its unique position above Mousehole Beach, which gives every bedroom and public room an inspiring view of the sea. Approached down a driveway through pleasant gardens which run down to the sea, Tavis Vor is an attractive whitewashed house at the entrance to Mousehole, a pretty fishing village with a small harbour. There is a spacious hall, a lounge bar and a licensed dining-room, where evening meals are served from 7pm onwards. Vegetarian choices are available and packed lunches can be provided. All the spotlessly clean bedrooms have sea views and TV; some are quite small. Buses into Penzance, and also to Lands End and other places of interest, leave at regular intervals from the end of the driveway. No children under five. Dogs by arrangement. Car park.

OWNERS Mrs M. Wall and Mrs J. O'Hanlon OPEN All year
ROOMS 1 family (with bath/shower), 4 double (2 with bath/shower, 2 with wash-basin), 1 twin (with wash-basin), 1 single (with wash-basin) TERMS B&B £20–£21.50, (single occupancy of twin/double) £47–£50, (family room) £59–£62 (children sharing family room £12); dinner £9.50–£10.50; deposit £40 per room

Most B&Bs offer tea/coffee-making facilities in the bedrooms.

NETHERBURY Dorset map 1

Heritage

Netherbury, nr Bridport DT6 5LS
NETHERBURY (030 888) 268

The location of this 50-year-old Tudor-style house is quiet and peaceful. It stands on the edge of the pretty little village of Netherbury, and one of the features is the lovely rear garden, enclosed by a yew hedge; many guests enjoy sitting out on the patio. Run by a charming French lady, the house is neat and spotlessly clean. Access to the garden is through the small, comfortable sitting-room with TV, and next door is the dining-room, where evening meals can be served 7.30–9pm. Lunches and vegetarian choices can be provided. There is no alcohol licence, but guests may bring their own wine. The bedrooms are small and pretty, and there is one bathroom shared among the guests. No children under seven (except babies in cots). No pets. No smoking. Car park.

OWNER Mrs M. Seymour OPEN All year ROOMS 1 double, 1 twin, 1 single TERMS B&B £15 (baby in cot free); dinner £8; deposit 20%

NEWLYN EAST Cornwall map 1

Degembris Farmhouse

Newlyn East, nr Newquay TR8 5HY
MITCHELL (0872) 510555

The house is reached down endless narrow lanes off the A3058 and is in an elevated position with lovely views over a beautiful, peaceful wooded valley. Degembris is a listed farmhouse built in the seventeenth century on the site of the old manor. It is a neat, slate-tile-faced building, part of a 165-acre working arable farm, set to one side of the farmyard, with a beautifully kept small front garden. The bedrooms, all with TV, are immaculately clean and freshly decorated, most with lovely views, and they share a bathroom and shower-room. There is a small dining-room where breakfast and four-course evening meals (6pm) are served, by arrangement. Vegetarian choices and packed lunches can be provided. Degembris is unlicensed, but guests may bring their own wine to dinner. The sitting-room has TV, books and games. A country trail can be followed from the farm. There is partial central heating (all bedrooms have heaters). Children welcome. No pets. Car park.

OWNER Kathy Woodley OPEN Easter–Oct ROOMS 2 family, 1 double, 1 twin, 1 single; all rooms with wash-basin TERMS B&B £14 (children under 10 half-price); dinner £7; deposit

Trewerry Mill Guest House

Trerice, Newlyn East, nr Newquay TR8 5HS
MITCHELL (0872) 510345

This converted watermill, dating from 1639, used to be the corn mill for the Elizabethan manor house of Trerice (owned by the National Trust and open to the public) about half a mile away. Five acres of gardens and uncultivated areas of wild flowers and wildlife surround the mill, which is in a quiet valley by a small stream. There is a terrace for sitting out which overlooks the beautifully kept and designed garden. The whole house has become non-smoking and there is now only the one main lounge for guests, which has a huge stone fireplace and a view of the mill wheel. Lunches and evening meals (6.30pm) are available and served at separate tables in the dining-room, and Cornish cream teas are served in the tea garden, which is run in conjunction with the guesthouse. Trewerry Mill is licensed and vegetarians can be catered for. The bedrooms are small and freshly decorated. A local artist has his paintings on view in one of the barns. No children under seven. No pets. No smoking. Car park.

OWNERS Alan and Ethel Grateley OPEN Easter–end Oct ROOMS 1 family, 2 double, 1 twin, 2 single; all rooms with wash-basin TERMS B&B £13.75 (children under 12 half-price); dinner £5.50; deposit £20 per room

NEWQUAY Cornwall map 1

The Michelle Guest House

3 Manewas Way, Lusty Glaze, Newquay TR7 3AH
NEWQUAY (0637) 874521

Guests are given a welcoming cup of tea when they arrive at this modern bungalow in a quiet, pleasant residential area. The Michelle is just 75 yards from Lusty Glaze Beach, only minutes from Tolcarne and Porth beaches and within easy walking distance of the town centre. The *en suite* bedrooms are of a good size and have been prettily decorated. There is a comfortable TV lounge and the dining-room has been extended. Evening meals are available at 6pm and guests may bring their own wine as there is no alcohol licence. Vegetarian choices and packed lunches can be provided. No children under nine. No pets. No smoking. Car park.

OWNERS Jan and George Wheeler OPEN All year ROOMS 3 family/twin, 3 double; all rooms with bath/shower TERMS B&B £16, (single occupancy of twin/double) £21 (children three-quarters-price sharing with parents); dinner £7; deposit £15 per person per week

NORTHLEIGH Devon map 1

The Old Rectory

Northleigh, Colyton EX13 6BS
FARWAY (040 487) 300

Built in the 1820s, the Old Rectory stands above and a little way out of the village of Northleigh, four miles south-east of Honiton. It is a pleasant country house in an unspoilt Devon valley with lovely views. Mrs Wroe's hobby is horses, and she likes to ride when she has the time. Mr Wroe works in publishing and their four children are at school. The three bedrooms, one of which is *en suite*, have been decorated in restful pastel shades, are comfortable and all have TV. Breakfast only is served in a small conservatory, built on to the front of the house. The Old Rectory makes a good base for exploring East Devon and West Dorset and is a good place for walking. No pets in the house. Car park.

OWNERS Mr and Mrs J. B. Wroe OPEN All year, exc Christmas ROOMS 2 double (1 with bath/shower, 1 with wash-basin), 1 twin (with wash-basin) TERMS B&B £17–£20

NORTHLEW Devon map 1

Howards Gorhuish

Northlew, nr Okehampton EX20 3BT
OKEHAMPTON (0837) 53301

This delightful house is a sixteenth-century Devon longhouse standing in seven acres of gardens, orchard and paddocks, in quiet and peaceful countryside with marvellous views to Dartmoor. The Richards have done a wonderful job renovating the house; although simple, it has been stylishly furnished and decorated. Guests have the run of the house, which includes the use of a sitting-room with wood-burning stove and a beautiful kitchen. The bedrooms are spacious, attractive and comfortable. One of the outhouses has been converted to a games-room with table tennis and darts and an enormous play-room upstairs. Dinner is available at 7pm on four nights of the week, allowing guests the opportunity of trying some of the local hostelrics. Vegetarian choices can be provided with prior notice and guests may bring their own wine (there is no alcohol licence). A dinner menu may include such dishes as lobster and prawn soup, beef with peanut sauce, and apple and blackcurrant crumble with Devon cream. There is also an extremely well-equipped self-catering unit. No children under 10. No pets. No smoking. Car park.

OWNERS Paul and Heather Richards OPEN All year, exc Christmas
ROOMS 2 double (with bath/shower), 1 twin (with wash-basin), 1 single (with wash-basin) TERMS B&B £15–£18; dinner £8; deposit £10

OAKFORD Devon map 1

Newhouse Farm

Oakford, Tiverton EX16 9JE
OAKFORD (039 85) 347

Newhouse Farm is a real working farm complete with cows, sheep and a muddy farmyard, set in 40 acres of peaceful valley with a trout stream and glorious countryside. The farmhouse dates from around 1600 and has lots of original features like huge oak beams, inglenook fireplace, bread-oven and low ceilings. Excellent home-cooked food abounds, including home-baked bread, home-reared beef, eggs and vegetables and home-made soups, pâtés, jams and 13 varieties of marmalade. Evening meals are served at 7.30pm and guests may bring their own wine (there is no alcohol licence). Vegetarian choices are available by arrangement. The family, consisting of parents, daughter, son-in-law and grand-daughter, is friendly and hospitable. The bedrooms are comfortable and attractively decorated; two are now *en suite*, and the third has a bathroom through a tiny kitchen, which is handy for making drinks and picnic lunches. A pretty garden follows the valley down to a stream at the bottom and a long track leads to the house across several fields. No children under 10. No dogs. Car park.

OWNER Ann Boldry OPEN All year, exc Christmas
ROOMS 2 double, 1 twin; all rooms with bath/shower
TERMS B&B £16–£18; D, B&B £24.50; deposit

PELYNT Cornwall map 1

Trenderway Farm

Pelynt, nr Polperro PL13 2LY
LANREATH (0503) 72214

This charming farm dates from the sixteenth century and is in a lovely position with hilly farmland views, about halfway between Looe and Polperro. The 450-acre mixed farm is down a quiet country lane, just south of the A387, half a mile before Pelynt. Mrs Tuckett runs an impeccable house, which she has decorated simply, but very prettily. Some bedrooms have lovely views and one has an old-fashioned bath with claw feet and separate shower. All bedrooms have TV. Breakfast only is served in a more recent sun porch addition, which also has splendid views, and is reached through the comfortable sitting-room with its open fire. The old stone farm buildings are set to one side of the house, and an additional room is in one of the old barns, with beams, whitewashed stone walls, pretty fabrics and comfortable chairs. No evening meals are served, but there are several eating-places nearby, including a local sixteenth-century inn. No children. No pets. No smoking in bedrooms. Car park.

OWNERS Mr and Mrs A. Tuckett OPEN Easter–end Oct
ROOMS 1 four-poster, 2 double, 1 twin; all rooms with bath/shower
TERMS B&B £23–£25, (single occupancy of twin/double) £30; deposit

PENRYN Cornwall map 1

Bella's Mouse

8 Shute Lane, Penryn TR10 8EY
FALMOUTH (0326) 373433

This is a charming little thick-walled, whitewashed 400-year-old cottage on a traffic-free steep lane in the centre of Penryn. As the house is built on the side of a hill the rooms are on different levels. They are small but delightful, fresh and decorated and equipped with care and comfort. There are two very pretty bedrooms, which share a large bathroom. Breakfast is served either in the small dining-room or, on warm days, on the colourful little patio. There is also a book-lined study and cosy sitting-room. No

We asked the proprietors to estimate their 1992 prices in the autumn of 1991, so the rates may have changed since publication.

children under 12. No pets. Non-smokers preferred. Parking space is available.

OWNER Mrs Barbara Buchanan Barbour OPEN 1 Apr–30 Sept
ROOMS 2 double (with wash-basin) TERMS B&B £17.50, (single occupancy of double) £21

Prospect House

1 Church Road, Penryn TR10 8DA
FALMOUTH (0326) 373198

Prospect House is set back from the main A39 road into Falmouth. It is a small listed Regency house, built in 1830, with stained-glass windows, mahogany doors, painted cornices and a small, attractive well-kept walled rose garden. The house has been tastefully and restfully decorated and furnished as much as possible in keeping with the period. The dining-room has a flagstoned floor, large table and unusual Dutch mid-nineteenth-century chairs. The hall and the pleasant lounge have the original ceilings. Dinner is available at 7.30pm if arranged in advance and can include a vegetarian choice. Prospect House is unlicensed, but guests may bring their own wine to dinner. Packed lunches can be provided. No children under 12. No smoking in the dining-room. Car park.

OWNERS Cliff Paul and Barry Sheppard OPEN All year
ROOMS 2 double, 1 twin, 1 single; all rooms, exc single (wash-basin only), with bath/shower TERMS B&B £22–£29.50, (single) £18; dinner £15; deposit

PENZANCE Cornwall map 1

Lombard House

16 Regent Terrace, Penzance TR18 4DW
PENZANCE (0736) 64897

Lombard House is set just one street back from the main sea-front road and is very convenient for the town centre. It is a bright pink house, part of a Regency terrace in a quiet road, with no through traffic and a front garden where you can sit out and admire the sea views. More bathrooms have been added, and general decoration has been carried out, particularly to the bar/dining-room/TV lounge, which has doors out to the garden. There are some original cornices and fireplaces on the ground floor and all the bedrooms are freshly decorated, mostly in pink. The front bedrooms have lovely views and are quite large; the back rooms are smaller. Evening meals, including vegetarian choices, can be served at 6.30pm. Packed lunches can also be provided. Lombard House is licensed. Children welcome. House-trained dogs only. No smoking in the dining-room and bedrooms. Car park.

OWNERS Adrian and Lesley Taylor OPEN All year, exc Christmas ROOMS 4 family (3 with bath/shower, 1 with wash-basin), 2 double (1 with bath/shower, 1 with wash-basin), 2 twin (1 with bath/shower, 1 with wash-basin), 1 single (with wash-basin) TERMS B&B £15–£17.50, (single occupancy of twin/double) £25, (family room) £50–£55 (reductions for children sharing with parents); dinner £7.50–£8.50; deposit; Access, Visa

PETER TAVY Devon map 1

Churchtown

Peter Tavy, Tavistock PL19 9NN
MARY TAVY (0822) 810477

A solid granite-built turn-of-the-century house that stands in an attractive garden with wonderful views to the front and of Dartmoor immediately behind – a great place for walking. It is a comfortable, friendly place, particularly suited to those interested in country pursuits and who enjoy horses and dogs. Major and Mrs Lane keep five or six horses, in training for three-day events, in the large stableyard at the back of the house, and have two miniature long-haired dachshunds that are great favourites with guests. The bedrooms are quite spacious and the owners have added a shower. Breakfast only is available, but food can be had at the neighbouring village pub. Pony-trekking is available nearby, and golf and fishing can be arranged for guests. No children under 10. No dogs in the house. Car park.

OWNERS Major Bill and Mrs Noreen Lane OPEN All year, exc Christmas ROOMS 1 family, 1 double, 1 twin TERMS B&B £12; deposit

PETROCKSTOWE Devon map 1

Hartleigh Barton

Petrockstowe, Okehampton EX20 3QJ
BLACK TORRINGTON (040 923) 344

This attractive farmhouse, surrounded by 230 acres of peaceful farmland, dates from pre-Domesday times, and was once possibly a manor house with deer park. Tony Jones is a local man whose grandparents lived in the nearby pretty village of Sheepwash, where they owned the village shop. The three bedrooms are spacious, charming rooms, prettily decorated and furnished. Evening meals are prepared with care and flair and are good value; they are served 7–10pm in an attractive dining-room that has a big open stone fireplace. Lunches and vegetarian choices are also available, and guests may bring their own wine to dinner as there is no alcohol licence. The large sitting-room has a high, beamed ceiling and open fire. Farmhouse teas and children's high teas are also available. Guests may take advantage of the shooting and fishing facilities available. Children welcome. No dogs in the house. Smoking only in the lounge. Car park.

OWNERS Angela and Tony Jones OPEN Feb–Nov ROOMS 2 double (1 with bath/shower), 1 twin TERMS B&B £14–£17, (single occupancy of twin/double) 75% of room rate (children using cot in parents' room £5); dinner £11; deposit 10%

PLYMOUTH Devon map 1

Wiltun Hotel

39 Grand Parade, West Hoe, Plymouth PL1 3DQ
PLYMOUTH (0752) 667072

Dating from 1860, this end-of-terrace house has a patio and lawn stretching to the sea wall. It is on a corner site and has wonderful views of Drake's Island and Plymouth Sound. The bedrooms, all with TV, are on the small side and basically furnished, some with good sea views. The whole basement and ground floor were flooded during a recent winter storm, when the sea wall was breached, so this has all been renovated. The large, pleasant lounge bar leads out on to the patio and evening meals are served in the small, bright basement licensed dining-room at 6pm. Vegetarian choices and packed lunches can be provided. Children welcome. Pets by arrangement. No smoking in the dining-room.

OWNERS Len and Sandra Hirst OPEN All year, exc Christmas
ROOMS 2 family, 3 double, 3 twin, 1 single; all rooms with wash-basin
TERMS B&B £13–£17.50, (family room) £40–£50; dinner £8; deposit 1 night charge; Access, Visa

Many B&Bs will cater for vegetarians. It is always best, however, to check when booking and make it clear what your requirements are, especially if you need a special diet.

PORT ISAAC Cornwall map 1

Archer Farm Hotel

Trewetha, Port Isaac PL29 3RU
BODMIN (0208) 880522

This was once an almost derelict rambling farmhouse, but the owners have added on to the property and converted it to provide comfortable accommodation. Archer Farm has the appearance of a modern house, both from the outside and the inside. There is a pleasant lounge/bar, a large bright dining-room and a small TV lounge. The bedrooms, three with TV and all with telephone, are simply furnished and vary in size; two have large balconies. Drinks can be taken on one of the outside patios while you admire the view. Picnic or snack lunches can be prepared on request as well as three-course, home-cooked evening meals, including vegetarian choices. Just a 15-minute walk from the picturesque fishing village of Port Isaac, Archer Farm is set in peaceful, unspoilt countryside near beaches, coves and lovely cliff walks. Children welcome. No pets in public rooms. No smoking in the dining-room and smoking only by arrangement in bedrooms. Car park.

OWNERS Mr and Mrs D. J. Welton OPEN Apr–Oct (Christmas Day by arrangement) ROOMS 2 family (with bath/shower), 4 double (3 with bath/shower, 1 with wash-basin), 2 twin (1 with bath/shower, 1 with wash-basin) TERMS B&B £25, (family room) £55 (children under 3 nominal charge, 3–10 20% reduction); dinner £15; deposit 10%

PORTLAND BILL Dorset map 2

The Old Higher Lighthouse

Portland Bill DT5 2JT
PORTLAND (0305) 822300

Built in 1750, this intriguing building served as a lighthouse until 1905. There was also a lower lighthouse, at one time owned by Sir Peter Scott, which is now a bird sanctuary. The Old Higher Lighthouse was once the home of Dr Marie Stopes, who entertained such well-known visitors as George Bernard Shaw, Dame Margot Fonteyn, H. G. Wells and Thomas Hardy. After a long period of decay and neglect the house was bought by the present owners about 10 years ago. They completely restored it themselves and can now offer a tiny dining-room in the bottom circular part of the tower and five small, simply furnished

bedrooms, three with TV, all on the ground floor. Guests have the choice of two, compact downstairs sitting-rooms, both with TV. One sitting-room is non-smoking. At the top of the tower, where the light used to be, there is a glassed-in area with binoculars offering spectacular 360-degree views; on a clear day you can see 40 miles in each direction. Outside there is a heated swimming-pool and jacuzzi. There have been many good reports on this place. Children welcome. No pets. Car park.

OWNER Mr L. Nickson OPEN All year ROOMS 1 family, 2 double, 2 twin; all rooms with wash-basin TERMS B&B £17.50, (single occupancy in twin/double) £17.50–£30, (family room) £45–£60; deposit; full payment on arrival

RINGMORE Devon map 1

Ayrmer House

Ringmore, nr Kingsbridge TQ7 4HL
KINGSBRIDGE (0548) 910391

Built in 1964, this at first unprepossessing house is in a wonderful position standing above a picturesque village off the B3392 with views down the valley to the sea. A track leads down to the relatively unspoilt beach. The house is very bright and light and all main rooms have large windows and wonderful views. The bedrooms, all with TV, are of a good size and comfortably furnished; three of them lead out on to a large balcony. There is also a suite with a twin-bedded room, a double room and a bathroom. A pleasant patio can be reached from the large comfortable lounge, with a dining area at one end, where there is plenty of room to sit out on fine days. Home-cooked evening meals are available by arrangement 6.30–7pm. Ayrmer House is unlicensed, but guests may bring their own wine to dinner. Children welcome. No pets. No smoking. Car park.

OWNER Mrs I. Dodds OPEN All year, exc Christmas ROOMS 1 family (with bath/shower), 1 double (with bath/shower), 2 twin (with wash-basin) TERMS B&B £16–£18, (single occupancy of twin/double) £24 (children under 10 half-price sharing family room); dinner £8; deposit 20%

ROADWATER Somerset map 1

Wood Advent Farm

Roadwater, Watchet TA23 0RR
WASHFORD (0984) 40920

Wood Advent Farm is a lovely place, with a peaceful, relaxing atmosphere. The listed house, built in 1804, is part of a 340-acre working farm, in a beautiful position in a fold in the Brendon Hills within the Exmoor National Park. It has fine views and is only two miles from the main coastal road. The house is spacious and the bedrooms are furnished in an old-fashioned, comfortable style. One double and one twin can be used as a family room. There is a large sitting-room and a licensed dining-room with separate tables where evening meals, using mostly home-grown produce, are available 7–7.30pm if ordered in advance. Sunday lunch, packed lunches and vegetarian choices can all be provided. The grounds include a small heated swimming-pool and imperfect grass tennis court. Horse-riding and clay pigeon shooting can be arranged and well-marked footpaths run across the farm. Children welcome. No pets in the house. No smoking in the dining-room and bedrooms. Car park.

OWNERS John and Diana Brewer OPEN All year ROOMS 3 double (2 with bath/shower, 1 with wash-basin), 2 twin (1 with bath/shower, 1 with wash-basin) TERMS B&B £14.50–£19.50 (children in family room half-price approx); D, B&B £27.50–£31.50; dinner £12; deposit £10 for new guests

ST AGNES Isles of Scilly map 1

Coastguards

St Agnes, Isles of Scilly TR22 0PL
SCILLONIA (0720) 22373

St Agnes is a beautiful island inhabited by a close, caring community that welcomes visitors, who come to relax and enjoy the peace and quiet. Coastguards stands on one of the highest points of the island and has good sea views overlooking Bishop Rock Lighthouse. It is a disused coastguard station, the middle one of three cottages that were built back to front (the fault of the architect). This is a friendly, family home, with everything shared, including the bathroom. There are two small bedrooms. Dinner has to be taken, and guests have the choice of a two-course or four-course meal, served at 6.30pm. Vegetarian choices and packed lunches can be provided. There is no alcohol licence, but guests may bring their own wine to dinner. Pets by arrangement. No smoking.

OWNERS Danny and Wendy Hick OPEN All year, exc Christmas
ROOMS 1 double, 1 twin TERMS D, B&B £20–£23; deposit 25%

Covean Cottage Guest House

St Agnes, Isles of Scilly TR22 0PL
SCILLONIA (0720) 22620

This old cottage, a small guesthouse combined with a tea-room, is a few minutes' walk from the quay. The accommodation now consists of two bedrooms with *en suite* bathroom and TV, one other bedroom and a cottage in the grounds which has a bedroom, bathroom and kitchenette. Evening meals, including vegetarian choices, are served at 7pm. There is no alcohol licence, but guests may bring their own wine. Lunches are also available. No children under 10. Very small dogs only. No smoking in the dining-room.

OWNERS Mr and Mrs P. Sewell OPEN Jan–Nov ROOMS 2 double (1 with bath/shower, 1 with wash-basin), 1 twin (with bath/shower) TERMS B&B £15–£16; D, B&B £23–£27; dinner £8.75; deposit

Many B&Bs will cater for vegetarians. It is always best, however, to check when booking and make it clear what your requirements are, especially if you need a special diet.

ST BLAZEY Cornwall map 1

Nanscawen House

Prideaux Road, St Blazey PL24 2SR
PAR (072 681) 4488

This very pretty Georgian house stands in five acres of well-maintained, mature gardens, high up on the side of a valley with lovely southerly views. Wistaria covers the front entrance and clematis surrounds two old plaques on the wall of the house. Janet and Keith Martin are excellent hosts who provide a very warm welcome and put a tremendous amount of energy and enthusiasm into the house. They do all the work, from the gardening to the cleaning and cooking, and provide a first-class service. The house is elegantly furnished and has an enormous drawing-room with doors out to the conservatory. Afternoon tea and elegant dinners (7.15pm) are served in the hall/dining-room. Vegetarian choices can be provided with notice and guests may bring their own wine. Of the three bedrooms, one is vast and all are very well equipped, with every comfort provided including TV and telephone. A large heated swimming-pool and jacuzzi, together with changing rooms, are available for guests' use from May to September, in a secluded part of the garden. No children under 12. No pets. No smoking. Car park.

OWNERS Janet and Keith Martin OPEN All year, exc Christmas and New Year ROOMS 1 four-poster, 1 double, 1 twin; all rooms with bath/shower TERMS B&B £27.50, (single occupancy of twin/double) £35–£45; dinner £17; deposit; Access, Visa

ST IVES Cornwall map 1

Sunrise Guest House

22 The Warren, St Ives TR26 2EA
ST IVES (0736) 795407

Sunrise is a small terraced guesthouse in a tiny narrow street, just above the sea and a very short distance from the harbour, in one of the oldest parts of St Ives. The accommodation is arranged on different levels. On the lower street level is a tiny TV lounge and a very pretty breakfast room, where a considerable breakfast menu choice is available, including pancakes and vegetarian food. Up some steep, narrow stairs there are some small, attractively decorated bedrooms, all with TV. A door at the back of the house leads out on to more stairs, with two little patio areas for sitting out, that lead up to the top rooms. These are all *en suite*, and the two front rooms have lovely views over St Ives and the sea. This top part has access from the street above and is opposite the bus station. Owned by a very helpful lady who has been in the hotel industry for over 50 years, this guesthouse is very central and good value. Children welcome.

OWNER Vicki Mason OPEN Jan–Oct ROOMS 1 family (with bath/shower), 4 double (2 with bath/shower, 2 with wash-basin), 2 twin (1 with shower, 1 with wash-basin) TERMS B&B £12–£20 (children half-price sharing); deposit

ST KEYNE Cornwall map 1

The Old Rectory Country House Hotel

St Keyne, nr Liskeard PL14 4RL
LISKEARD (0579) 42617

Dating from the early 1800s, the Old Rectory is a solid, stone-built house standing in three acres of grounds and lovely gardens in a quiet peaceful spot just outside the small village of St Keyne. The house is extremely comfortable, and the rooms are spacious and decorated in a variety of floral wallpapers. There are two four-poster bedrooms and one ground-floor room, and all bedrooms have TV and bathroom. Home-cooked evening meals are available 7–8pm and can include vegetarian choices on request. There is a decent wine list and packed lunches can be provided. No children under 12. Dogs £1 per night if in a bedroom. No smoking in the dining-room. Car park.

OWNERS R. G. and K. H. Wolfe OPEN All year, exc 20–29 Dec ROOMS 2 four-poster, 3 double, 2 twin, 1 single; all rooms with bath/shower TERMS B&B £25–£32.50; dinner from £11.50; deposit; Access, Visa

ST MARTIN'S Isles of Scilly map 1

Glenmoor Cottage Guest House

St Martin's, Isles of Scilly TR25 0QL
SCILLONIA (0720) 22816

This cottage stands in Higher Town and has wonderful views over a pretty garden to the beach and islands beyond. It is only a few minutes to the beach along a footpath through bulb fields. There are three small bedrooms and a large lounge/dining-room in an extension with lovely views. John and Barbara Clarke also run a gift shop in the adjacent building. Dinner is available at 7pm and can include vegetarian choices. There is no alcohol licence, but guests may bring their own wine. Packed lunches can be provided. No children under three. House-trained dogs only. No smoking in bedrooms.

OWNERS John and Barbara Clarke OPEN All year ROOMS 1 family, 1 double, 1 single; all rooms, exc single, with wash-basin TERMS B&B £15–£18 (children under 12 half-price, 12–16 two-thirds-price in family room); D, B&B £22; dinner £10; deposit

Polreath

Higher Town, St Martin's, Isles of Scilly TR25 0QL
SCILLONIA (0720) 22046

Polreath, an attractive granite Victorian guesthouse, built as the residence of a local farmer, is in the centre of the island and a few minutes from the quay. It has a separate tea-room, offering a variety of home-made food. The house is sparklingly clean, fresh and bright with simple décor. The bedrooms are small, but some have good views. Breakfast, lunch and dinner (6pm) are available. An evening menu may include seafood croissant, grey mullet stuffed with lemon and bay and fudge tart. Vegetarian choices are available and there is a short but adequate wine list. The little-populated island of St Martin's, with its wonderful unspoilt beaches, fine coastal and country walks and pretty farmland, is a haven of peace and tranquillity. Children welcome. Smoking in the lounge only.

OWNERS Geoff and Elaine Watt OPEN All year, exc Christmas ROOMS 1 family, 2 double, 2 twin, 1 single; all rooms with wash-basin TERMS B&B £16.45–£19.75, (family room) £55–£75 (reductions for children 10%–25%); D, B&B £26.75–£29; dinner £14; deposit 20%

ST MARY'S Isles of Scilly map 1

Bay Tree Cottage

Old Town, St Mary's, Isles of Scilly TR21 0NN
SCILLONIA (0720) 22777

Described in the local museum as 'probably two of the last one-up, one-down cottages on the Islands', Bay Tree Cottage is an attractive, old stone-built property. It stands on the main street of

Old Town, about a mile from the centre of Hugh Town. It offers three comfortable and immaculately maintained bedrooms with private bathrooms. There is an attractive dining-room and a very small sitting-room. As in most establishments on the islands, dinner is almost invariably taken (6.15pm) and can include vegetarian choices by arrangement. Bay Tree Cottage is licensed. There is no central heating, but all rooms have some form of heating. No children under 14. No pets. No smoking.

OWNERS Jackie and John Williams OPEN early Mar–end Oct ROOMS 2 double, 1 twin; all rooms with bath/shower TERMS B&B £19.50 (Mar and Oct only); D, B&B £33.25; deposit; occasionally full payment at start of stay

The Boathouse

St Mary's, Isles of Scilly TR21 OLN
SCILLONIA (0720) 22688

Right on the sea-front, in the centre of town, the Boathouse is a small, narrow guesthouse with superb views of the islands and a pleasant atmosphere. The bedrooms, three with sea views, are on the small side and simply furnished. The first-floor small lounge leads out on to a small patio, and home-cooked evening meals using produce from the vegetable garden are served at 6.45pm in the dining-room. Vegetarian choices and packed lunches can be provided. The Boathouse is unlicensed, but guests may bring their own wine to dinner. No children under eight. Pets by arrangement. No smoking in the dining-room or bedrooms.

OWNER Mrs Maureen Stuttaford OPEN mid-Mar–end Oct ROOMS 3 double, 2 twin; all rooms with wash-basin TERMS B&B £18.80 (children ⅓ reduction sharing with adults); D, B&B£27; dinner £11.75; deposit

ST MAWES Cornwall map 1

Braganza

St Mawes TR2 5BJ
ST MAWES (0326) 270281

This classically elegant, eighteenth-century house, surrounded by gardens sloping down towards St Mawes, stands in a fine position, with marvellous views over the picturesque fishing village. Braganza offers the experience of staying in a typical English country house, with its pre-war bathrooms and fittings, and meeting the charming owner, Zosia Moseley, who among other accomplishments has mastered the Cornish language and writes poetry. Following considerable renovation to the house, much of the interior has recently been redecorated. Fresh flowers are put in the bedrooms, beds get turned down every evening, and breakfast coffee is served from a silver coffee-pot. Breakfast only is available. Car park.

OWNER Mrs Z. Moseley OPEN Easter–end Oct ROOMS 5 twin (3 with bath/shower, 2 with wash-basin), 1 single (with wash-basin) TERMS B&B £17–£20, (single occupancy of twin) £7 surcharge; deposit £20

SALCOMBE Devon map 1

Sunningdale Lodge

Main Road, Salcombe TQ8 8JW
SALCOMBE (054 884) 3513

Sunningdale Lodge is a solid 1930s house, set high above the main road into Salcombe with glorious views out to sea, to Bolt Head and the rolling Devon farmland. It has a well-maintained garden, with a patio where table and chairs are set in summer, and faces south-west, catching the sun. The breakfast room, which doubles as a TV lounge in the evenings, has a bay window and faces south-west, as do the two large, bright and comfortably furnished bedrooms all enjoying the same lovely sea view. There is one bathroom with shower and a second separate toilet. The two bedrooms can form a self-contained suite, ideal for a family or party of four. Breakfast only is available. No children under 12. No pets. No smoking. Car park.

OWNERS Clare and Roy Smethurst OPEN Easter–end Sept ROOMS 1 double, 1 twin; both rooms with wash-basin TERMS B&B from £16, (single occupancy of twin/double) from £28; deposit 1 night charge

SANDFORD Devon map 1

Woolsgrove Farm

Sandford, Crediton EX17 4PS
COPPLESTONE (0363) 84246

This is a picturesque 300-year-old whitewashed house on a 150-acre farm set in very peaceful and lovely countryside just off the

A377 Crediton–Copplestone road. It is a comfortable, traditionally furnished house with spacious bedrooms and one shared bathroom. There is a sitting-room, and breakfast and optional four-course evening meals (6.30pm) are served in the dining-room. Vegetarian choices and packed lunches can be provided. Woolsgrove Farm is not licensed, but guests may bring their own wine. Children welcome. Car park.

OWNER Mrs Rachael Pennington OPEN Feb–Nov ROOMS 1 double, 1 twin, 1 single; all rooms with wash-basin TERMS B&B £14–£15 (reductions for children according to age); deposit

SHALDON Devon map 1

Virginia Cottage

Brook Lane, Shaldon TQ14 0HL
SHALDON (0626) 872634

This lovely whitewashed cottage, dating from the early seventeenth century, is on a narrow, quiet lane, a five-minute walk from the River Teign. It stands in a lovely, partly walled cottage garden. The entrance to the house is through a massive, intricately carved front door with decorated porch timbers, which came from South Africa. The house is attractively furnished and

decorated with three pretty bedrooms. There is a small sitting-room and a dining-room where breakfast only is served, although packed lunches can be provided. Pubs and restaurants can be found in the village. At the rear of the property is a small heated swimming-pool. No children under 12. No pets. No smoking. Car park.

OWNERS Jennifer and Michael Britton OPEN All year, exc Christmas ROOMS 1 family, 2 twin; all rooms with bath/shower TERMS B&B £18.50, (single occupancy of twin) £25 (children 12–14 half-price in family room); deposit

SHEEPWASH Devon map 1

Half Moon Inn

Sheepwash, Beaworthy EX21 5NE
BLACK TORRINGTON (040 923) 376

The Half Moon has been the village inn for over 200 years. Whitewashed and built of cob, it is 400 years old and has a large garden. The Inniss family has run the inn since 1958. Benjie's Bar, with flagstone floor and large stone fireplace, is a popular meeting place for locals and visitors alike; bar snacks are available at lunchtime. Dinner – a four-course set meal – is of a high standard and served in the attractive dining-room 8–8.30pm. Vegetarian choices and packed lunches can be provided. Residents have use of a small lounge with TV off the dining-room. The bedrooms are well equipped with TV, radio and telephone, and three are on the ground floor. The Half Moon attracts a number of fishermen, as it has access to salmon fishing, as well as sea trout and brown trout, on the Torridge. A large rod room, excellent drying facilities, a small shop stocking the basic requirements for fishing, tackle for hire, and tuition and advice are all available if required. For non-fishermen, the inn is a relaxing place to stay and is ideal as a base from which to explore Dartmoor, Exmoor and the North Devon and Cornish coastlines. Children welcome. Car park.

OWNERS Benjamin, Robert and Charles Inniss OPEN All year, exc Jan ROOMS 2 family, 4 double, 8 twin, 2 single; all rooms with bath/shower TERMS B&B £25–£30; dinner £15.50; Access, Visa

Reduced rates for children are normally given when they share their parents' bedroom. If no reductions are specified in the details or text, assume you'll have to pay full rates.

SHERBORNE Dorset map 2

Quinns

Marston Road, Sherborne DT9 4BL
SHERBORNE (0935) 815008

Set back a little from a main road into Sherborne is this modern unassuming house only five minutes' walk from the town and yet close to open countryside and good walks. There is a small dining-room with one communal table, where both lunch and dinner (7–8pm) are served if ordered in advance. Vegetarian choices and packed lunches can be provided. Quinns is not licensed, but guests may bring their own wine. The comfortable sitting-room is very large, and there are three bedrooms, all *en suite*, all with TV and furnished and decorated to a high standard in restful colours. Quinns continues to maintain its high standards and is a good base for exploring Dorset, Somerset and Wiltshire. No children under seven. No pets or smoking in public rooms. Car park.

OWNERS Michael and Janet Quinn OPEN All year ROOMS 1 double, 1 twin, 1 single; all rooms with bath/shower TERMS B&B £20–£24, (single occupancy of twin/double) £25–£30 (children half-price if sharing with 2 adults); dinner £13.50; deposit

STOCKLAND Devon map 1

The Kings' Arms Inn

Stockland, nr Honiton EX14 9BS
STOCKLAND (040 488) 361

This attractive thatched pub dates from the early sixteenth century and used to be a main coach stop between Plymouth and London. It is in the centre of a picturesque out-of-the-way village. The owners have added on to the building and rebuilt a couple of the bars, and have replaced one bar floor with flagstones. In spite of its size and the newer parts, the Kings' Arms retains its character and cosy, friendly atmosphere. There are plenty of pub games such as skittles and cribbage for those who want to indulge. The dining-room is in the older part and has stone walls and an enormous fireplace – a cosy place to be on winter evenings. The three bedrooms all have telephone, TV and bathroom, and one has its own patio. Food is available both at lunchtime and in the evening (6.30/7–9.30pm), and the pub attracts a wide clientele. Vegetarian choices and packed lunches can be provided.

This place is not suitable for people expecting a quiet time, or for those who do not want to mix with the locals. 'Well-behaved' children and pets welcome. Car park.

OWNERS Heinz Kiefer and Paul Divani OPEN All year, exc Christmas ROOMS 2 double, 1 twin; all rooms with bath/shower TERMS B&B £15, (single occupancy of twin/double) £20; dinner £10–£15; deposit 1 night charge

STOKE ST GREGORY Somerset map 1

Slough Court

Stoke St Gregory, nr Taunton TA3 6JQ
NORTH CURRY (0823) 490311

This fourteenth-century moated farmhouse has been in Sally Gothard's family for generations. It is a fascinating and unusual property, which has all the attributes for the ideal bed and breakfast. It is very much a working farm, run by Sally's husband. The house is approached from the farmyard through a stone archway and across a lovely patio area with oval-shaped swimming-pool and a lawned garden which has croquet and a grass tennis court for guests' use in the summer. Slough Court is full of character, with oak beams, mullioned windows and open fires. The three bedrooms are comfortable and tastefully furnished and decorated. Guests are welcome to use the large, comfortable sitting-room with open fireplace and the immaculately kept garden. Excellent home-cooked dinners are available by arrangement at 7.15pm and served in the lovely family dining-room. Vegetarians can be catered for and guests may bring their own wine (there is no alcohol licence). No children under 12. No dogs in the house. No smoking in public rooms. Car park.

OWNER Sally Gothard OPEN mid-Jan–mid-Nov ROOMS 2 double, 1 twin; all rooms with bath/shower TERMS B&B £20, (single occupancy of twin/double) £25; dinner £15

TAUNTON Somerset map 1

Forde House

9 Upper High Street, Taunton TA1 3PX
TAUNTON (0823) 279042

The plain exterior of this period house, standing on a main road right in the centre of Taunton, belies the charm within. It is a large, spacious house, with a beautiful drawing-room – a long room with grand piano and french windows leading out into the large rear garden. This most attractive garden has a wistaria-covered patio running round two sides of the house – a delightful place to sit on a warm day. The breakfast room was probably once the old kitchen and has an old slate floor, pine dresser, inglenook fireplace and beams. Breakfast only is available. The bedrooms are comfortable and spacious and all have TV. This is an ideal base for those visiting Taunton itself or, further away, the Quantock and Blackdown Hills. Children over 10 preferred. No dogs. Car park.

OWNERS Peter and Sheila Naylor OPEN All year, exc Christmas
ROOMS 2 double, 2 twin, 1 single; all rooms with bath/shower
TERMS B&B £22–£25

Spy Post House

Staplehay, Taunton TA3 7HE
TAUNTON (0823) 331527

A Georgian-style home that stands in a small garden in the centre of the village of Staplehay, just two miles south of Taunton. The two bedrooms have a bathroom between them and are only let as one booking; there is also an attractive sitting-room. Mrs Hurrell deals in pictures, is trained in catering and loves cooking – evening meals, served by arrangement, are something to look forward to. Vegetarians can be catered for. Spy Post House is not licensed, but guests may bring their own wine to dinner. Mrs Hurrell is also a West Country tour guide, so guests are in the right place for assistance with planning itineraries. Mr Hurrell is an opera singer, so if you are musical you are likely to find yourself with an impromptu evening of music. Children welcome. No pets in the house. No smoking in bedrooms. Car park.

OWNERS Mr and Mrs S. Hurrell OPEN All year, exc Christmas and New Year ROOMS 1 double, 1 twin; both rooms inter-connect with bath/shower TERMS B&B £19–£20 (babies free, up to 12 half-price); dinner from £10

Most B&Bs don't accept credit cards, but when they do we list the cards taken.

Breakfast at B&Bs tends to mean a cooked breakfast of bacon, eggs and so on. If you prefer a different style of breakfast, discuss this when you make the booking.

TAVISTOCK Devon map 1

Hele Farm

Gulworthy, Tavistock PL19 8PA
TAVISTOCK (0822) 833084

This eighteenth-century slate-fronted farmhouse sits in lovely, peaceful countryside, on a 150-acre dairy farm three miles out of Tavistock. Mrs Steer loves to cater for families, and actually prefers families with small children. The house offers unpretentious farmhouse comfort, with three clean, bright and attractive bedrooms. Downstairs there is one large room for guests' use, one half of which used to be the old dairy; it is a bright, comfortable room with a big dining-room table at one end and a sitting area at the other. There is also a wonderful games-room for children. Evening meals, including limited vegetarian choices, are available if required at 6pm using home-grown organic produce. There is no alcohol licence, but guests may bring their own wine. Packed lunches can also be provided. Hele Farm offers the friendliest of welcomes and is excellent value for money. Children welcome. Non-smokers preferred. Car park.

OWNER Mrs Rosemary Steer OPEN Mar–Oct ROOMS 2 double, 1 twin; all rooms with bath/shower TERMS B&B £12.50–£14 (children under 12 £6); dinner £7

THROWLEIGH Devon map 1

The Stables

Throwleigh, nr Okehampton EX20 2HS
WHIDDON DOWN (064 723)

An old stone house, right in the centre of the tiny Dartmoor village of Throwleigh, that was converted from stables. It stands in a pleasant garden with lovely views to Dartmoor. There are two simply furnished, small twin-bedded rooms and a TV lounge shared with the owner. Breakfast only is served in the dining-room, where guests sit on two old church pews. No children under eight. No smoking in bedrooms. Car park.

OWNER Mrs Freda Ford OPEN All year ROOMS 2 twin (1 with wash-basin) TERMS B&B £11–£12; deposit; Access

If you are forced to turn up late into the evening, please telephone to warn the proprietor.

Well Farm

Throwleigh, nr Okehampton EX20 2JQ
WHIDDON DOWN (064 723) 294

A quite amazing place – dogs, cats, muddy boots and a completely chaotic kitchen – that has masses of charm, and is in a wonderful position, right in the middle of nowhere, down endless narrow lanes, on the edge of Dartmoor. Well Farm is a listed medieval longhouse, with sixteenth-century additions, owned by a delightful couple who have lived here since they married almost 40 years ago. The farm runs to 200 acres, supporting cows and pigs, and also a collection of ornamental pheasants, peacocks and free-range poultry. There are three bedrooms in the house and at the back is a ground-floor annexe with two minute bedrooms, a bathroom and a comfortable sitting-room – particularly suited to the disabled. Fresh produce and local farm cider are included in the evening meal at 8pm, which is eaten at one large table; packed lunches and vegetarian choices can also be provided. There is no alcohol licence, but guests may bring their own wine to dinner. Well Farm is most suited to those who enjoy animals and a country life-style. Children welcome. Dogs by arrangement. No smoking in bedrooms. Parking for six cars.

OWNERS Bryan and Sheelagh Knox OPEN All year, exc Christmas ROOMS 2 family, 1 double, 1 twin; all rooms, exc 1 family, with bath/shower TERMS B&B £15–£16 (reductions for children under 12); dinner £8

TORQUAY Devon map 1

The Amberwood

65 Walnut Road, Chelston, Torquay TQ2 6HU
TORQUAY (0803) 605293

Although there has been a change of owners since 1990, this small guesthouse retains its friendly, homely atmosphere. It is close to the centre of Chelston and only a few minutes' walk from the promenade and Torre Abbey gardens. Coach tours pick up and set down outside the house, which is set back from the road, facing south with a small garden and terrace to the front. The new owners have redecorated the house, and although there is a ground-floor room, the two bathrooms are located on the mezzanine level. All bedrooms have TV. There is a comfortable TV lounge and a dining-room where breakfast only is served. Kay and

Graham Darke are very friendly people; Graham spends part of his time abroad working as a golf pro. No children. No pets. No smoking in the dining-room.

OWNERS Kay and Graham Darke OPEN All year ROOMS 4 double, 1 twin, 1 single; all rooms with wash-basin TERMS B&B £14.50–£16; deposit £10–£25 per person

Fairmount House Hotel

Herbert Road, Chelston, Torquay TQ2 6RW
TORQUAY (0803) 605446

This Victorian house stands in a quiet residential area, on a south-facing hillside just a mile from the harbour. It has a very friendly, welcoming atmosphere and is comfortably furnished. To the rear is a small, pretty garden with good views over Chelston to Brixham. Two of the bedrooms, one of which has wheelchair access, open out on to the garden and there has been a recent addition of another single room. All bedrooms have TV. The TV lounge, which has a sunny balcony, has a small library that includes maps and guidebooks, and there is a conservatory bar. Dinner, 6.30–7.30pm, features good home-cooked food and there is a reasonably priced wine list. Lunches are also available, and vegetarian choices can be provided by arrangement. Children welcome. No pets or smoking in the dining-room. Car park.

OWNERS Noel and Maggie Tolkien OPEN Mar–end Oct ROOMS 3 family/double/twin, 3 double, 2 single; all rooms with bath/shower TERMS B&B £23.50–£26.50, (single occupancy of twin/double) £23.50–£45 (children under 5 £4.50, 5–9 £10, 10–13 £13); dinner £10.50; deposit; Access, Amex, Visa

TRURO Cornwall map 1

Polsue Manor Farm

Tresillian, Truro TR2 4BP
TRESILLIAN (087 252) 234

Up a long, well-maintained track, this farmhouse stands above and well out of sight and sound of the main A390 road into Truro from the east, in glorious countryside with fabulous views from every room. It is a spacious, unpretentious farmhouse, part of a 160-acre mixed farm. The oldest, back part of the house dates from the sixteenth century and the front part, added on 150 years ago, has large rooms with high ceilings. There is a spacious lounge and a pleasant dining-room where breakfast and evening meals (6.30pm) are served. Vegetarians can be catered for by prior arrangement and guests may bring their own wine (there is no alcohol licence). The house is not centrally heated, but there are heaters in all rooms. Children welcome. Dogs by arrangement. Car park.

OWNER Mrs Geraldine Holliday OPEN All year, exc Christmas
ROOMS 2 family, 2 double, 1 twin; all rooms with wash-basin
TERMS B&B £14–£17 (children under 12 half-price); dinner £7; deposit 10%

Woodview

12 Highertown, Truro TR1 3PZ
TRURO (0872) 72859

Woodview belongs to the delightful Miss Spurgeon, who lives here with her maid of 52 years' service. It is just a basic little bungalow, set back from and above a busy and noisy main road, with a beautifully kept small front garden and lovely views to distant woods. The two women divide the duties between them, the maid waiting at table complete with apron and cap. Dinner, cooked by both ladies, is served from 6pm and must represent some of the best value in Cornwall. Vegetarians can be catered for, and guests may bring their own wine as there is no alcohol licence. Packed lunches can be provided. The accommodation is nothing special, but it is comfortable, homely, old-fashioned and spotlessly clean. Miss Spurgeon and her maid spoil their guests, many of whom come back for more. Woodview is a 10-minute walk from the station and centre of town, and is close to the bus stop; it makes an excellent centre for those touring Cornwall without a car. No children under 14. No pets. No smoking. Parking for two or three cars.

OWNER Miss D. M. Spurgeon OPEN All year ROOMS 2 twin (with wash-basin) TERMS B&B £13–£13.50; dinner £5; deposit

UPLODERS Dorset map 2

Upton Manor Farmhouse

Uploders, Bridport DT6 4PQ
POWERSTOCK (030 885) 220

This sixteenth-century former farmhouse is in a lovely setting in a peaceful, sheltered valley on the edge of the pretty village of

Uploders. It is approached down a driveway and across a ford in the stream. When the Lords moved here the house was almost derelict, and they have gradually and lovingly restored it. The two bedrooms are clean, fresh and simply decorated and share a bathroom. Guests have use of a large bright room with an open fireplace, which doubles as sitting-room and breakfast room. Breakfast only is available, although packed lunches can be provided. No children under 10. No dogs. No smoking in bedrooms. Car park.

OWNERS Mr and Mrs C. R. Lord OPEN Mar–end Oct
ROOMS 1 double, 1 twin; both rooms with wash-basin TERMS B&B £13.50–£14.50 approx; deposit

WATERROW Somerset map 1

The Manor Mill

Waterrow, nr Taunton TA4 2AY
WIVELISCOMBE (0984) 23317

This is a wonderful place for a peaceful, relaxing, away-from-it-all stay. The Genreys have turned the Manor Mill, a seventeenth-century stone-built water mill and neighbouring barns, into a handsome complex of buildings. Immaculately kept, the house and adjoining long, low buildings border the stream and face a wooded bank, and are set in the depths of hilly, unspoilt farmland. Trout fishing is available and there is a heated indoor swimming-pool. In addition to the B&B accommodation in the house, there are also five self-catering flats and a cottage. The bedrooms are fairly large, simply and comfortably furnished in country style and immaculately clean. Breakfast is taken at one end of the owners' sitting-room, and there is another sitting-room for guests' use. No evening meal is served, but there is a pub just down the road. Children welcome. No pets. No smoking in bedrooms. Car park.

OWNERS Eddie and Elizabeth Genrey OPEN All year, exc Christmas
ROOMS 1 double (with wash-basin), 1 twin/family (with bath/shower), 1 single TERMS B&B from £15, (single) from £17, (single occupancy of twin/double) from £20 (babies £5, children under 12 half-price sharing); deposit

If you intend to spend several days at a B&B, it is worth asking whether there are reduced rates, particularly if the period is midweek or off-season.

WEARE GIFFARD Devon map 1

Burnards

Weare Giffard, nr Bideford EX39 4QR
BIDEFORD (0237) 473809

A small, neat, whitewashed cottage in the picturesque village of Weare Giffard, Burnards has a very pretty, small garden with a patio for sitting out; it is on the edge of the Torridge valley with peaceful views over the river to wooded hills. One end of the cottage is for guests' use, with a small comfortable sitting-room and dining-room, and two simple bedrooms with bathrooms upstairs. The house has a friendly atmosphere and Mrs Carter, who loves cooking, will prepare evening meals by arrangement at 6.30–8pm. Vegetarians can be catered for and guests may bring their own wine to dinner (Burnards is unlicensed). The pub almost opposite has food in the evenings. No children under 12. No pets. No smoking in bedrooms. Car park.

OWNER Mrs J. Carter OPEN 1 Apr–1 Oct ROOMS 1 double, 1 twin; both rooms with wash-basin TERMS B&B £12; dinner £8; deposit 10%

WELLS Somerset map 2

Bekynton House

7 St Thomas Street, Wells BA5 2UU
WELLS (0749) 672222

Bekynton House is only a three-minute walk from the cathedral, and another short walk through the cathedral green brings you to the bishop's palace, market-place and high street. Owned by the cathedral and named after Bishop Bekynton, a benefactor to Wells, the attractive stone-built house is Georgian with Victorian additions. It stands right on the street with parking space and a sunny patio at the back, full of colourful tubs, baskets and window boxes in summer. It is a comfortable house, clean, well-maintained and constantly redecorated. Three bedrooms are *en suite* and the remaining six share three bath/shower-rooms. All bedrooms have TV. There is a pleasant, comfortable lounge and a

Where a single-occupancy rate is not specified in the details, the cost will be the same as that per person in a twin or double room, or will be included in the range of prices given.

dining-room for breakfast only. No children under five. No pets. No smoking in the breakfast room and bedrooms. Car park.

OWNERS Desmond and Rosaleen Gripper OPEN All year, exc Christmas ROOMS 2 family (1 with bath/shower, 1 with wash-basin), 4 double (1 with bath/shower, 3 with wash-basin), 2 twin (1 with bath/shower, 1 with wash-basin), 1 single (with wash-basin) TERMS B&B £18–£21, (single occupancy of twin/double) £25–£30, (family room) £45–£50; deposit £10 per room; Access, Visa

WEST BUCKLAND Devon map 1

Huxtable Farm

West Buckland, Barnstaple EX32 0SR
FILLEIGH (059 86) 254

This family enterprise is in a secluded position surrounded by open fields, woods and a stream. The farm complex consists of a series of stone buildings, most of which have been converted or renovated; the barn, roundhouse and medieval longhouse are all listed buildings. The house itself dates back to 1520 and has many original features, such as oak beams, screen panelling, open fireplaces with bread ovens, low doorways and uneven floors. It has been furnished and decorated with great care and taste, in a simple style. Two bedrooms have TV and the single and twin share a toilet. The family rooms are in large outbuildings. Both breakfast and high teas (served at 5.30pm) are available for children in a room off the kitchen, leaving the adults to enjoy a more sophisticated atmosphere in the lovely dining-room, where they are also offered a complimentary glass of home-made wine at dinner (7.30pm). Vegetarian choices and packed lunches can be provided. Guests have use of a drawing-room, tiny TV room, sauna and games-room with snooker, darts, bar billiards and table tennis. Children welcome. No pets in the farmhouse. No smoking in the dining-room. Car park.

OWNERS Mrs Jackie and Mr Antony Payne OPEN All year, exc Christmas ROOMS 2 family, 2 double, 1 twin, 1 single; all rooms with bath/shower TERMS B&B £16–£22 (children in cot £5, sharing £8); dinner £10.50; deposit 10% Sept–June, 25% July and Aug

The description for each entry states when pets are not allowed or restricted in any way.

If a deposit is required for an advance booking this is stated at the end of an entry.

WEST MONKTON Somerset map 1

Prockters Farm

West Monkton, nr Taunton TA2 8QN
WEST MONKTON (0823) 412269

This seventeenth-century farmhouse was once whitewashed but now the exterior is stripped back to expose the attractive red, local stone from which the house is built. It has a large, pretty front garden and is part of a 300-acre mixed farm. The house has uneven floors, low doorways, exposed beams and log fires. The three bedrooms in the house are simply decorated with old-fashioned furniture, and there are a further two rooms on ground-floor level in buildings adjacent to the house, one with wheelchair access. Dianne Besley greets her guests with a cup of tea and a slice of cake to help them unwind. Breakfast only is available, although packed lunches can be provided. Children welcome. One pet per room. Car park.

OWNER Mrs Dianne Besley OPEN All year ROOMS 1 family (with wash-basin), 2 double (1 with bath/shower, 1 with wash-basin), 2 twin (1 with bath/shower, 1 with wash-basin) TERMS B&B £15–£19 (children £2–£6 in family room); deposit £15 per room; Amex

WEST PORLOCK Somerset map 1

Bales Mead

West Porlock TA24 8NX
PORLOCK (0643) 862565

One mile west of Porlock is this modest country house in a most wonderful position, on the edge of the small hamlet of West Porlock, with magnificent sea views across Porlock Bay to Hurlestone Point and beyond. It is set in a very pretty garden and behind the house are wood-covered hills – a quiet, peaceful spot. The owners moved here from the Waterloo House in Lynton in 1989 and have done another exquisite renovation job. There are just three small bedrooms, all with TV, two with sea views and one overlooking the garden and hills. All are superbly equipped and individually decorated, with every minute comfort considered. Downstairs there is an elegant and comfortable sitting-room and a small dining-room, with pretty, individual tables, where breakfast and superb weekend dinners (7pm) are served. Vegetarian choices can be provided and guests may bring their own wine (there is no alcohol licence). A typical menu may include Stilton pears, suprême of chicken stuffed with asparagus and a choice of desserts. No children under 14. No pets. No smoking. Car park.

OWNERS Stephen Blue and Peter Clover OPEN All year
ROOMS 3 double (with wash-basin) TERMS B&B £18.50, (single occupancy of twin/double) £22.50; dinner £13.50; deposit

WHEDDON CROSS Somerset map 1

Raleigh Manor Hotel

Wheddon Cross, nr Dunster TA24 7BB
TIMBERSCOMBE (0643) 841484

Raleigh Manor is a well-built, elegant, stone and tile-hung late-nineteenth-century country house. It is approached along a half-mile drive through parkland with grazing sheep and stupendous views across Exmoor and stands in one and a half acres of woods and a pretty front garden. All bedrooms have TV, are elegantly decorated with pretty wallpapers and matching fabrics, and are of a good size – one has a half-tester bed. Most bedrooms have marvellous views. There is a small, attractive library with a good selection of books and brochures, a conservatory and a pleasant sitting-room. The licensed dining-room has magnificent views and is the venue for five-course dinners (7–8pm) featuring good English home cooking. Vegetarian choices and packed lunches can be provided. The wine list has a good choice, including a clutch of New World bottles. Children welcome. No pets in public areas. Car park.

OWNERS Caroline and Barry Westin OPEN Mar–Oct
ROOMS 1 family/double, 2 double, 3 twin, 1 single; all rooms with bath/shower TERMS B&B £25.50–£31.50, (half-tester double) £31–£38 (children under 12 free sharing parents' room); D, B&B £35.50–£48; dinner £15; deposit £15 per person; Access, Visa

WHIMPLE Devon map 1

Down House

Whimple EX5 2QR
WHIMPLE (0404) 822860

A substantial Edwardian farmhouse dating from the 1920s, Down House is surrounded by five acres of gardens with lovely rural views. Children are specially welcome here, with cots, a high chair and pushchair available. It is a quiet, peaceful place, simply furnished, with large rooms. All rooms lead off from the hall and landing and there is an interesting art nouveau staircase. The bedrooms, all with TV, are named after cider apples; one is on the ground floor, and there is a good ratio of bedrooms to bathrooms. The owners enjoy cooking, bread making and organic gardening and evening meals are available if required at 6.30pm, except Mondays. Vegetarian choices can be provided and guests may bring their own wine (there is no alcohol licence). Children welcome. No pets in the house. No smoking in public rooms. Car park.

OWNERS Alan and Vicky Jiggins OPEN Apr–Sept ROOMS 2 family (1 with bath/shower, 1 with wash-basin), 1 double (with wash-basin), 2 twin (1 with bath/shower, 1 with wash-basin), 2 single (with wash-basin) TERMS B&B £12.50–£19, (family room) £25–£38 (children £2 in family room); dinner £8.50

WIDEGATES Cornwall map 1

Coombe Farm

Widegates, nr Looe PL13 1QN
WIDEGATES (050 34) 223

Built in 1927 as a small retirement home, the house stands in ten and a half acres of lawns, meadows, woods and ponds and has magnificent views down an unspoilt valley to the sea. Alexander and Sally Low exude enthusiasm, energy and friendliness and their guests' enjoyment of a stay here is endorsed by the ecstatic comments in the visitors' book. An optional four-course evening meal is served (7–7.30pm) in a candlelit, licensed dining-room that has lovely views. Vegetarians can be catered for and packed lunches can be provided. Breakfast is substantial. The TV lounge, dining-room and bar are furnished with an interesting array of antiques with some more modern pieces, and there are plants everywhere. The bedrooms, most with TV, are bright and all enjoy lovely views. A heated outdoor swimming-pool, a croquet lawn and a games-room are available for guests' use. No children under five. No pets in the house. Non-smokers preferred. Car park.

OWNERS Alexander and Sally Low OPEN 1 Mar–31 Oct ROOMS 4 family (1 with bath/shower, 3 with wash-basin), 2 double (with wash-basin), 2 twin (with wash-basin) TERMS B&B £16.80 (children under 14 25% reduction sharing with parents); dinner £10; deposit £15 per person

WILMINGTON Devon map 1

The Old Forge

Wilmington, nr Honiton EX14 9JR
WILMINGTON (040 483) 297

The original forge and wheelwright's barn, with the remains of the old furnace and anvil block, are still visible in stone outbuildings. The Old Forge itself is a seventeenth-century, detached cottage built of cob under a straw-thatched roof. The house stands right on the A35 and there is half an acre of wooded grounds to the rear of the property. Guests have use of a large beamed sitting-room/dining-room with wood-burning stove. One twin-bedded *en suite* room has two windows overlooking the road, but double glazing keeps out most of the noise. All bedrooms have TV. Evening meals, including vegetarian, can be served at 6.30pm. There is no alcohol licence, but guests may bring their own wine. Packed lunches can also be provided. Children welcome. Smoking only in ground-floor rooms. Car park.

OWNERS Penny and Tony Maynard OPEN All year, exc Christmas ROOMS 1 double, 2 twin (1 with bath/shower) TERMS B&B £15 (children £8 sharing parents' room); D, B&B £20; dinner £6

WIMBORNE Dorset map 2

Ashton Lodge

10 Oakley Hill, Wimborne BH21 1QH
WIMBORNE (0202) 883423

This is a detached family home with pleasant rear garden, set back a little from the A349 on the edge of Wimborne. A long hill leads to the town centre and Wimborne Minster. The bedrooms, all with TV, are fresh and bright. Breakfast only is available, but the pub almost next door serves evening meals. Packed lunches can be provided. Children welcome. No pets. No smoking. Parking available.

OWNER Mrs Margaret Gregory OPEN All year ROOMS 1 family (with bath/shower), 1 double (with bath/shower), 1 twin (with wash-basin), 1 single (with wash-basin) TERMS B&B £14.50–£15.50, (single occupancy of twin/double) £27 (children £7.50 in family room)

Thorburn House

2 Oakley Road, Wimborne BH21 1QJ
WIMBORNE (0202) 883958

A solid 1930s home, set back a little from the main road, that has attractive bow-shaped leaded windows. There are three very pretty bedrooms, all with TV and comfortably furnished, and an excellent ratio of bedrooms to bathrooms. There is no lounge and breakfast only is served in the dining-room. The pub almost next door serves evening meals. Children welcome. No pets. No smoking.

OWNER Eveline Stimpson OPEN All year, exc Christmas ROOMS 2 double (1 with bath/shower, 1 with wash-basin), 1 twin (with wash-basin), 1 single (with wash-basin) TERMS B&B £14.50–£15, (single occupancy of twin/double) £19 (reductions for children sharing parents' room); deposit £10 per person

WINSFORD Somerset map 1

Karslake House Hotel

Winsford, nr Minehead TA24 7JE
WINSFORD (064 385) 242

The house, a fifteenth-century brewer's malt house set in the picturesque village of Winsford in the heart of Exmoor, was named after Sir John Karslake, an eminent Victorian lawyer and MP. It still has uneven floors, low ceilings and inglenook fireplaces, and a fifteenth-century wall cupboard and old mounting block. The house is pleasantly relaxing, comfortably furnished and spotlessly clean. The bedrooms, all with TV, are bright and spacious; three of the bathrooms have corner baths. Home-cooked dinners are available 7.30–8pm and can include vegetarian dishes. Packed lunches can be provided and Karslake House is licensed. This is an ideal spot for walking, riding, shooting and hunting. Children welcome. No pets in the dining-room and bedrooms. No smoking. Car park.

OWNERS Mr C. F. Alderton and Mrs J. M. Young OPEN 1 week before Easter–end Oct, exc 2 weeks July ROOMS 1 four-poster, 4 double, 2 twin; all rooms with bath/shower TERMS B&B £19.50–£28.50, (single occupancy of twin/double) £24.50–£35.50; dinner £12.50

If you have to cancel a reservation for a room, please telephone to warn the proprietor.

WOOTTON FITZPAINE Dorset map 1

Rowan House

Wootton Fitzpaine, Charmouth DT6 6NE
CHARMOUTH (0297) 60574

Linda Dedman has created a charming, characterful home out of a small stone-built house which lies on the edge of the village. It is a quiet, peaceful spot and has lovely views, which can be enjoyed from the patio and small garden. Linda has done up the whole house from top to bottom, including a ground-floor room, which also has its own entrance. The bedrooms are small but prettily decorated and furnished. There is an attractive sitting-room with a built-on conservatory, where breakfast and excellent evening meals, including vegetarian choices, are served. There is no alcohol licence, but guests may bring their own wine. Children welcome. No pets. Smoking only in the sitting-room with other guests' permission. Car park.

OWNER Miss Linda Dedman OPEN All year ROOMS 1 family, 3 double, 1 twin, 1 single; all rooms with bath/shower TERMS B&B £17–£18 (children half-price sharing parents' room, three-quarters-price in own room); dinner £8; deposit 20%

ZENNOR Cornwall map 1

Tregeraint House

Zennor, nr St Ives TR26 3DB
PENZANCE (0736) 797061

A wild, lonely place that enjoys views across fields to the sea and is 15 miles from Lands End and six from St Ives. Built of granite, the house stands above the road on the outskirts of the village of Zennor. It is a cosy, warm, simply constructed farmhouse-style building, which has many of the original materials incorporated into the structure. The bedrooms are simply furnished, comfortable whitewashed rooms, with wash-basins built into old wash stands. There is a cosy dining-room with enormous stone fireplace and a lived-in sitting-room, shared with the owners who also run a publishing business from the house. Breakfast only is available. Children welcome. No pets. No smoking. Parking available.

OWNERS John and Sue Wilson OPEN All year, exc Christmas
ROOMS 1 double/family, 2 twin; all rooms with wash-basin
TERMS B&B £13 (children under 7 free, 7–14 half-price); deposit £5

The South and South-East

East Sussex

Hampshire

Isle of Wight

Kent

Surrey

West Sussex

Wiltshire

AMESBURY Wiltshire map 2

Ratfyn Barrow House

Ratfyn Road, Amesbury SP4 7DZ
AMESBURY (0980) 623422

Ratfyn Barrow House lies just off the main road, on the edge of Amesbury. It is a detached brick building dating from 1938 set in a garden dominated by a bronze-age barrow. The letting bedrooms have now been reduced to a total of three: a double with private bathroom and two twins. They are clean and simply furnished and decorated, and all have TV. Breakfast only is served in the attractive dining-room. No children under five. Smoking in bedrooms only. Small pets only are allowed. Car park.

OWNERS Jean and Larry Bax OPEN 1 Apr–31 Oct ROOMS 1 double (with bath/shower), 2 twin (with wash-basin) TERMS B&B £12–£17; deposit £10 per room

ANDOVER Hampshire map 2

Lotties

23 Winchester Road, Andover SP10 2EQ
ANDOVER (0264) 323825

Lotties is a Victorian house, just off a busy main road, on the edge of town. It is a modest, very well maintained and spotlessly clean guesthouse run by a very friendly couple. The bedrooms are small and simply decorated and furnished, and all have TV. Breakfast only is available. Children welcome. Smoking in lounge only. No pets. Car park.

OWNERS Mr R. C. and Mrs M. L. Waite OPEN All year, exc Christmas ROOMS 1 family, 1 double, 1 twin, 2 single; all rooms with wash-basin TERMS B&B £14, (family room) £30–£45 (children 3–12 half-price); deposit

B&B rates specified in the details for each entry are per person per night; unless the details state otherwise, they are based on two people sharing a double or twin-bedded room.

Where we know of any particular payment stipulations we mention them in the details. It is always best to check when booking, however.

ARLINGTON East Sussex map 3

Bates Green

Arlington, Polegate BN26 6SH
POLEGATE (0323) 482039

Bates Green is a brick-built, tile-hung farmhouse down a quiet lane in woods and fields, part of a 175-acre sheep and turkey farm. In the eighteenth century, the house was a gamekeeper's cottage and subsequent additions have been in keeping with the old style. Bates Green is of particular appeal to gardeners, as Mrs McCutchan has green fingers and her lovely garden, which is planned for year-round interest, is regularly open under the National Garden Scheme. There is also a hard tennis court. The accommodation consists of three attractive, medium-sized bedrooms, all *en suite*, and a large sitting-room upstairs, overlooking the garden. Downstairs there is an appealing sitting-room with open fire and a dining-room where breakfast only is served. Packed lunches and light suppers can be provided by arrangement. No children under 12. No pets. No smoking. Car park.

OWNER Mrs C. McCutchan OPEN All year, exc Christmas
ROOMS 1 double, 2 twin; all rooms with bath/shower
TERMS B&B £19–£21, (single occupancy of twin/double) £28

ASHTON KEYNES Wiltshire map 2

Cove House

2 Cove House, Ashton Keynes SN6 6NS
CIRENCESTER (0285) 861221

The house, which predates the English Civil War, is the original part of a historic old Cotswold manor house, divided into two and set in pretty gardens in the centre of an attractive village which is part of the Cotswold Water Park. It belonged to the Richmond family, in which one brother was a royalist, the other a Roundhead. The royalist brother came on a visit to Cove House, and the Roundhead brother, seeing a royalist, shot him. Horrified with what he had done he sailed to America and founded Taunton, Massachusetts. This is now a comfortable family home, where evening meals, using the owners' own fruit and vegetables, are available 7.30–8pm. The Hartlands often join their guests for dinner. Vegetarian choices can be provided. There is no alcohol licence, but guests may bring their own wine. The bedrooms are of a good size and have their own bathrooms. There is a most attractive large, beamed, family drawing-room in the oldest part of the house and a small lounge for guests' use with detailed wall maps and lots of brochures to help guests plan their activities. A walled patio and the garden lead off from this room, where barbecues are sometimes held in summer. No children under 13 at dinner. Pets by arrangement. No smoking at dinner. Partial central heating. Car park.

OWNERS Major and Mrs P. Hartland OPEN All year, exc Christmas
ROOMS 1 family, 1 double, 1 twin; all rooms with bath/shower
TERMS B&B £22–£23, (single occupancy of twin/double) £31–£32, (family room) £56; dinner £15; deposit £20; surcharge of £1 for single night

BETHERSDEN Kent map 3

Little Hodgeham

Bull Lane, Smarden Road, Bethersden TN26 3HE
HIGH HALDEN (0233) 850323

Turn at the Bull pub in Bethersden towards Smarden, continue for two miles and you will find this idyllic Tudor cottage in rose gardens and surrounded by wooded farmland. Every evening at Little Hodgeham is like a small, intimate dinner party, with the maximum of six guests sitting around the elegant dining-room table. Not only dinner (served at 7.30pm), but breakfast too is a gastronomic delight, everything cooked by Erica Wallace, for whom providing dinner, bed and breakfast for her guests is an art. The china she uses is the very best, as is the silver, and table-mats and napkins are immaculate, all starched by hand. Vegetarian choices can be provided if notice is given. There are three charming bedrooms (including one four-poster) with private bathrooms, a TV lounge and garden room, all supremely comfortable and furnished with exquisite taste. The half-acre garden is a delight and full of colour, with a centrepiece of a pond with waterfalls and pet ducks. There is a good-sized swimming-pool with diving board. Thermos flasks with tea, coffee and milk are offered for day excursions, and laundry (although not ironing) is done, all free of charge. Breakfast can be served in bed if guests

Bath/shower information in the details refers only to a private bathroom or shower; other bathroom facilities at the establishments will be shared. We say if rooms have wash-basins.

prefer. Bed and breakfast are not available without dinner. No babies. No pets in public rooms. Car park.

OWNER Erica Wallace OPEN late Mar–31 Aug ROOMS 1 four-poster, 1 twin, 1 family; all rooms with bath/shower TERMS D, B&B £44.50, (single occupancy of twin/double) £50 (reductions for 4 nights or more); deposit

BIDDENDEN Kent map 3

Birchley

Fosten Green Lane, Biddenden TN27 8DZ
BIDDENDEN (0580) 291413

A long driveway (one mile off the A462, just out of Biddenden towards Sissinghurst) leads up through park-like grounds to the oldest part of this traditional timbered house dating from 1632, with lattice windows. The house is divided into three, but from the front there are no signs of this. The Randalls inhabit the oldest part. There are three enormous, well-appointed and bright bedrooms (all have TV) with glorious views. There is a lovely panelled sitting-room with log fire and breakfast is served in the large dining-room, which has a magnificent carved oak inglenook fireplace. In the grounds you will discover one of Mr Randall's hobbies, a miniature railway which runs round the property, and also a large, covered, heated swimming-pool. Packed lunches can be provided, and evening meals are available by prior arrangement (unlicensed, but guests may bring their own wine). No children under 10. No dogs. No smoking. Car park.

OWNERS Jennifer and Drummond Randall OPEN All year, exc Christmas ROOMS 1 double, 2 twin/double; all rooms with bath/shower TERMS B&B £25–£30, (single occupancy of twin/double) £40–£50; dinner £15; deposit £10 per room; Access, Visa

Tudor Cottage

25 High Street, Biddenden TN27 8AL
BIDDENDEN (0580) 291913

This delightful sixteenth-century black and white timbered cottage is situated in the centre of Biddenden. Tudor Cottage is on the main road, but double glazing keeps out the traffic noise. It has a friendly atmosphere and is charmingly decorated, fresh and bright. All rooms have a bathroom and telephone; two have TV. The attractive double sitting-room is on two levels, with lots of beams and an inglenook fireplace where an open fire is lit on cooler evenings. There are books for guests to read and TV. The dining-room overlooks the garden. Evening meals are available (served at 7pm), and vegetarians can be catered for. There is no licence, but guests may bring their own wine. No pets. Car park.

OWNERS Mr and Mrs J. Wadley OPEN All year ROOMS 2 double, 1 twin; all rooms with bath/shower TERMS B&B £15–£16, (single occupancy of twin/double) £17.50 (children under 2 free); dinner £10; deposit

BIRDHAM West Sussex map 2

Jasmine Cottage

Bell Lane, Birdham PO20 7HZ
BIRDHAM (0243) 512358

This whitewashed 200-year-old cottage with thatched roof is just off the B2198 on the edge of the village of Birdham. It is a comfortably furnished house with low beams. The downstairs small double *en suite* room leads off from the dining-room with its big fireplace. Upstairs there is a pretty twin room with its own private loo and wash-basin, but the shower is down the corridor. Breakfast only is served. No children under 10. No pets. No smoking. Car park.

OWNER Mrs Barbara Hepburn OPEN All year ROOMS 1 double (with shower), 1 twin (with wash-basin) TERMS B&B £16, (single occupancy of twin/double) £20; deposit

BOSHAM West Sussex map 2

White Barn

Crede Lane, Bosham, Chichester PO18 8NX
BOSHAM (0243) 573113

White Barn is a single-storey, interestingly modern house set in its own garden on a quiet private road close to the centre of the picturesque old harbour village of Bosham. The 900-year-old church contains the tomb of King Canute's daughter. Good food is served at White Barn. Guests eat dinner (served at 7.15pm) together at one long refectory table in the dining area, which overlooks a small patio and the landscaped garden. A meal may consist of eggs with smoked salmon and caviare, followed by roast English lamb with a gooseberry and mint sauce, then apricot and almond meringue to finish. Vegetarian dishes can be provided. There is no licence, but guests may bring their own wine. Each bedroom is almost a separate entity, and two of them are in buildings in the garden. This is a comfortable house with a friendly atmosphere. No children under 10. No dogs. No smoking in public rooms. Car park.

OWNERS Susan and Antony Trotman OPEN All year
ROOMS 1 double, 2 twin; all rooms with bath/shower TERMS B&B £19–£30, (single occupancy of twin/double) £25–£32; dinner £17–£18; deposit; Access, Visa

BRADFORD-ON-AVON Wiltshire map 2

Bradford Old Windmill

4 Masons Lane, Bradford-on-Avon BA15 1QN
BATH (0225) 866842

This interesting old windmill, high above the town, has recently been rebuilt to accommodate *en suite* bedrooms. The work has been painstakingly done with nothing of the original atmosphere and features lost. The uniqueness of the building, the welcome and friendliness of the owners, and the high standard of accommodation have been commented on by readers. There is a large, comfortable sitting-room shared with the family, and a large bright dining-room, with one big table and french doors leading out on to a small patio and neatly kept garden with tables and chairs, right on the edge of the hill with wonderful views over Bradford. The rooms have been done up with flair and imagination. One has a water bed, one a rounded bed, and bathrooms have been fitted cleverly into odd angles of the round windmill. Vegetarian dinners only are served, by arrangement, at 8pm. There is no alcohol licence, but guests may bring their own wine. No children under six. No pets. No smoking.

OWNER Priscilla Roberts OPEN All year ROOMS 1 family, 1 double, 1 twin, 1 single; all rooms, exc single (wash-basin), with bath/shower TERMS B&B £19.50–£30, (single occupancy of twin/double) £50, (family room) £75–£90 (children half-price sharing family room); deposit 1 night charge; dinner £18

Most establishments have central heating. We say when this is not the case.

Many B&Bs are in remote places; always ask for clear directions when booking.

BRIGHTON East Sussex map 3

Franklins

41 Regency Square, Brighton BN1 2FJ
BRIGHTON (0273) 27016

This is a small, narrow terraced house just off the sea-front and close to the town centre. It has an attractive sitting-room with TV and two comfortable sofas which leads through to the small breakfast room; both rooms have original fireplaces. The bedrooms, all with TV, vary in size, but are comfortably furnished and well appointed with small *en suite* bathrooms. Evening meals, with vegetarian choices available, are served, and packed lunches can be provided. Room service is offered from noon until 11pm. Children welcome. No pets.

OWNERS Sandra Williams and Katrina Cole OPEN All year, exc Christmas and New Year ROOMS 4 double, 1 twin, 1 single; all rooms with bath/shower TERMS B&B £19–£25, (single) £28–£35, (single occupancy of twin/double) £35–£45; dinner £7.50–£20; deposit 1 night charge; Visa

Sea Breeze

12a Upper Rock Gardens, Brighton BN2 1QE
BRIGHTON (0273) 602608 Fax (0273) 607166

This small, narrow terraced house is in a quiet side street just two minutes' walk from the sea and about a 10-minute walk from the centre of town. Each rather small room has been decorated entirely differently in strong colours and all have TV. There is a pretty dining-room on the ground floor where breakfast only is served. Packed lunches can be provided. No children under 10.

OWNER Brian M. Budgen OPEN All year ROOMS 1 family, 1 four-poster, 3 double, 1 twin, 1 single; all rooms with bath/shower TERMS B&B £17.50–£19, (four-poster) £24, (single) £20–£25, (family room) £45; deposit 1 night charge; all major credit cards

If you intend to spend several days at a B&B, it is worth asking whether there are reduced rates, particularly if the period is midweek or off-season.

Where a single-occupancy rate is not specified in the details, the cost will be the same as that per person in a twin or double room, or will be included in the range of prices given.

BROADCHALKE Wiltshire map 2

Stoke Farmhouse

Broadchalke, Salisbury SP5 5EF
SALISBURY (0722) 780209

This Georgian-style Victorian farmhouse is set in 1100 rolling acres of the Wiltshire Downs. The enormous garden with extensive lawns, hedges, walled gardens and tennis court is available for guests' use. The house has large bedrooms, all with TV, which have been comfortably furnished. The drawing-room has TV, books and games and the original bread oven is a feature of the dining-room, where breakfast and dinner (by arrangement, at 7pm) are served. Vegetarians can be catered for. There is no alcohol licence, but guests may bring their own wine. Children welcome. No pets. No smoking upstairs. Car park.

OWNERS Mr and Mrs Hugh Pickford OPEN Mar–end Oct
ROOMS 3 twin/double (2 with bath/shower) TERMS B&B £19 (children under 12 £15, in parents' room £5); dinner £11.50; deposit £10

BROCKENHURST Hampshire map 2

Cater's Cottage

Latchmoor, Brockenhurst SO42 7UP
LYMINGTON (0590) 23225

For a get-away-from-it-all stay this is a perfect location, in the heart of the New Forest. Unless you already knew about Cater's Cottage you would never find it or even know it existed. To reach it, take the B3055 from Brockenhurst towards Bournemouth, go under one railway bridge and 75 yards later fork right on to a gravel track. Cater's is surrounded by lawns and views of undulating moorland and forest. The pleasant whitewashed building has lawned gardens to the side of the house. The bedrooms (one with TV) are simply furnished, and breakfast only is served at a long refectory table in the pretty panelled rectangular room which serves as both dining- and sitting-room. Packed lunches can be provided. Children welcome. Car park.

OWNERS Mr and Mrs I. D. Onslow OPEN All year, exc Christmas
ROOMS 1 double, 1 twin, 1 single; all rooms with wash-basin
TERMS B&B £16, (single occupancy of twin/double) £20; deposit £10

Setley Lodge

Setley, Brockenhurst SO42 7UG
LYMINGTON (0590) 22146

The lodge is a substantial whitewashed building in a quiet location set in three acres of garden, yet just off the main Brockenhurst–Lymington A337 road. The garden backs on to woodland and the New Forest is only a few hundred yards away. Norman and Thea Gillett have done up most of the house themselves and offer a high standard of comfort. Bed and breakfast guests have the choice of a double or twin-bedded room, both *en suite* and with TV – there is no lounge. Breakfast is served in the kitchen. There are also two very well-equipped self-catering flats with their own entrances. Sailing, riding and fishing are all available nearby, and the house is just behind the Filly Inn, an old country pub offering good food. No children. No pets. Non-smokers preferred. Car park.

OWNERS Norman and Thea Gillett OPEN All year
ROOMS 1 double, 1 twin; both rooms with bath/shower
TERMS B&B £15–£17.50; deposit 10%

BURBAGE Wiltshire map 2

The Old Vicarage

Burbage, Marlborough SN8 3AG
MARLBOROUGH (0672) 810495

This substantial Victorian house built of brick and flint and dating from 1853 was formerly the rectory to the adjoining church. It is set in two acres of lawns, mature trees and shrubs, in the oldest part of Burbage with its pretty cottages. Guests have use of the front part of the house, which includes a drawing-room and dining-room with open fires and a wealth of books and magazines. Each of the three beautiful bedrooms has its original Victorian fireplace, bathroom – including one enormous one with a Mediterranean-style mural covering the entire room – and every possible little extra, like soft drinks, biscuits, sponges and soaps. Jane Cornelius loves to cook, her dinners (8pm) being something of an occasion. A menu may include such things as lovage soup, poached salmon steaks with tarragon, English farmhouse cheeses and summer pudding. Vegetarians can be catered for. There is no alcohol licence, but guests may bring their own wine. Lunch is served on Saturday and Sunday, and hampers can be provided.

The whole house has a relaxed country-house feel and is filled with beautiful flower arrangements. No children. Dogs by arrangement. No smoking. Car park.

OWNERS Jane Cornelius and Robert Hector OPEN All year, exc Christmas and Jan ROOMS 1 double, 1 twin, 1 single; all rooms with bath/shower TERMS B&B £30, (single) £35, (single occupancy of twin/double) £40; dinner £25; deposit £10; Access, Visa

CADNAM Hampshire map 2

Walnut Cottage

Old Romsey Road, Cadnam SO4 2NP
SOUTHAMPTON (0703) 812275

This simple, brick-built whitewashed cottage in a quiet lane is well situated for the New Forest, Southampton and motorway exits. Here are all the amenities of a comfortable family home, including a small, elegant dining-room where breakfast is served at one large table, a lovely, bright, light sitting-room with open fireplace and furnished with antiques, and comfortable chairs in the central hall. All three bedrooms have their own bathroom and TV, and the ground-floor room is particularly suitable for disabled guests. There are four old bikes that are lent out free, and a wealth of information is available on what to do and see in the vicinity. Good food can be found at the old thatched-roof pub, just 200 yards down the road. No children under 14. No dogs. No smoking in the dining-room. Car park.

OWNERS Eric and Charlotte Osgood OPEN All year, exc Christmas ROOMS 1 double, 2 twin; all rooms with bath/shower TERMS B&B £16.50–£17.50, (single occupancy of twin/double) £22; deposit £10

CANTERBURY Kent map 3

Magnolia House

36 St Dunstan's Terrace, Canterbury CT2 8AX
CANTERBURY (0227) 765121

This late-Georgian house is on a quiet street, a pleasant 10-minute stroll from the city centre. An extension has recently been added to the back of the house to give all rooms their own bathroom. This back part of the house and the breakfast room overlook the walled back garden, immaculately kept by the Davies, who are keen gardeners. The bedrooms, all with TV, have been prettily decorated, and there is an open marble fireplace in the TV lounge. Breakfast only is served and packed lunches can be provided. During the quieter periods of the year, however, evening meals are offered by prior arrangement (£8.50 for a three-course dinner). There is also a laundry service. Children welcome. No pets. No smoking in the bedrooms or dining-room. Car park.

OWNERS Ann and John Davies OPEN All year ROOMS 3 double, 2 twin, 1 single; all rooms with bath/shower TERMS B&B £22–£25, (single) £28–£36; deposit; Access, Amex, Carte Blanche, Visa

Yorke Lodge

50 London Road, Canterbury CT2 8LF
CANTERBURY (0227) 451243 Fax (0227) 451243

This immaculate Victorian guesthouse is superbly decorated and furnished in keeping with the period. It has been totally refurbished and provides extremely comfortable accommodation; all the bedrooms have private bathroom, TV and telephone. Guests are invited to enjoy a glass of sherry on their arrival in the library, a cosy room, decorated in dark colours, with an array of books and a piano. Guests can help themselves to fruit and biscuits which are left out in the house. The breakfast room is most attractive and beyond it is the garden room, which leads out on to a walled garden and has an extremely comprehensive collection of leaflets and brochures. Breakfast only is served. There is a fax machine which guests may use. There are also mountain bikes at guests' disposal. The owners are welcoming and the atmosphere is informal. Children welcome. Pets by arrangement. Smoking in the library only. Car park.

OWNER Robin Hall OPEN All year ROOMS 3 family/twin/double, 1 twin/double, 1 double, 1 single; all rooms with bath/shower TERMS B&B £17.50–£22.50, (single) £18–£24, (single occupancy of twin/double) £30–£35, (family room) £50–£60; deposit; Access, Amex, Visa

CHALE Isle of Wight map 2

The Clarendon Hotel and Wight Mouse Inn

Chale PO38 2HA
ISLE OF WIGHT (0983) 730431

Children are particularly welcome at this seventeenth-century coaching-inn with an easy-going, lively holiday atmosphere.

There are amenities such as swings, a seesaw and a slide for them in the garden, and there are sandy beaches close by. The house is bright and airy inside, with a large, prettily decorated dining-room and views over the Needles. Most of the bedrooms (all with TV and telephone) are family rooms and have views of the coast. The Wight Mouse Inn (the pub attached to the hotel) has a lot of charm and a choice of 365 whiskies. There are a children's games-room, log fires and real ales. The oak beams in the pub were rescued from a three-masted sailing ship, the *Clarendon* (after which the hotel was named), when she sank in 1836. Lunches and evening meals (7–10pm) are available in the dining-room or in the bar. Vegetarians can be catered for and packed lunches provided. Car park.

OWNERS John and Jean Bradshaw OPEN All year, exc Christmas ROOMS 1 family suite, 8 family, 5 twin/double; all rooms, exc 1 family and 1 twin/double, with bath/shower TERMS B&B £20–£26 (children 2 and under £2, 3–5 £4, 6–12 half-price, 13–16 two-thirds-price); dinner £10–£16; deposit; Access

CHARING Kent map 3

Barnfield

Charing TN27 0BN
CHARING (023 371) 2421

To reach Barnfield, take the A20 from Charing towards Maidstone, then take the first left down Hook Lane and carry on for two and a half miles. It is a lovely fifteenth-century building, set in very peaceful and beautiful countryside and surrounded by buildings that form part of a 500-acre farm. There is a hard tennis court in the grounds. Barnfield has been in the Pym family since 1936 and has all the beams and inglenook fireplaces that you would expect to find in a house of this age. The bedrooms are comfortable, of a good size and pleasantly furnished. There is one small bathroom shared by guests, who also have use of a large room which is part dining-room and part sitting area with comfortable chairs and shelves of books. The more formal dining-room is used when there are a number of guests. Evening meals, with vegetarian choices available, are served at 7pm. There is no alcohol licence, but guests may bring their own wine. Children welcome (reductions if sharing parents' room). No smoking. Car park.

OWNERS Martin and Phillada Pym OPEN All year, exc Christmas ROOMS 1 family, 1 double, 1 twin, 2 single; all rooms, exc 1 single, with wash-basin TERMS B&B £17.50–£19.50; dinner £10.50; deposit

CHICHESTER West Sussex map 2

Chichester Lodge

Oakwood, Chichester PO18 9AL
CHICHESTER (0243) 786560

Dating from 1740, this attractive one-storey building was one of the lodges for the 'big house', which is now a co-educational preparatory school. It is located at the beginning of the driveway (off the B2178, two miles out of Chichester) and is set in a pretty garden. Mr and Mrs Dridge are not connected with the school. A recent addition to the house allows guests almost self-contained accommodation. There are two, very charming small bedrooms, simply furnished with *en suite* bathrooms and both with TV and four-poster beds. Breakfast can be served in several different areas of the house, to catch the most of the sun and views of the garden. There are also a variety of sitting places in the garden where tea is served to those returning in the late afternoon or evening. No children under five. No pets. No smoking. Car park.

OWNERS Mr and Mrs Dridge OPEN All year, exc Christmas ROOMS 2 four-poster; both rooms with bath/shower TERMS B&B £20, (single occupancy) £30; deposit

CHIDDINGFOLD Surrey map 2

Knipp Cottage

Pickhurst Road, Chiddingfold GU8 4TS
HASLEMERE (0428) 682062 Fax (0428) 684086

The cottage is at the end of a long communal driveway, not far from Chiddingfold's village green. It was originally a simple two-up two-down, but has been extended over the years, and is now a very smart house. Part of the original two-down rooms is now a large, comfortable sitting-room with TV for guests' use, and with a door out on to a patio and swimming-pool; beyond is a hard tennis court. There is also a games-room and office facilities are available, including a fax. The house has been decorated throughout in strong colours. The bedrooms are very comfortable and there is a self-contained suite of a double and twin with private bathroom for four or fewer people travelling together.

If there are any bedrooms with TV and/or telephone we mention this in the entry.

Breakfast only is served, but packed lunches can be provided. Children welcome. Dogs discouraged. Car park.

OWNERS Liz and Tony Douglass OPEN All year ROOMS 1 family suite, 2 double, 1 twin; all rooms with bath/shower TERMS B&B £20.56, (family suite) £58.75 (additional children £8.81, babies usually free)

CHIDHAM West Sussex map 2

The Old Rectory

Chidham PO18 8TA
BOSHAM (0243) 572088

The Old Rectory lies down a quiet country lane, opposite the Saxon church of St Mary, and surrounded by its own garden and farmland. Chidham is on a peninsula, surrounded on three sides by Chichester Harbour, and is a wonderful area for bird-watching, sailing and walking. The house is spacious, with large, well-furnished bedrooms all with their own bathrooms and three with TV. There is a formal drawing-room with TV and a dining-room where breakfast is served. Packed lunches can be provided. Guests are welcome to use the swimming-pool in the garden and food is available at the pub 200 yards down the lane. Children are welcome (reductions available). No smoking in bedrooms or the breakfast room. Car park.

OWNERS Mr and Mrs P. J. Blencowe OPEN All year, exc Christmas ROOMS 2 double/twin, 1 twin, 1 single; all rooms with bath/shower TERMS B&B £20–£22, (single) £25, (single occupancy of twin/double) £28

COPTHORNE West Sussex map 3

Linchens

New Domewood, Copthorne RH10 3HF
COPTHORNE (0342) 713085

This comfortable house, off the A264 east of Copthorne, is on a private estate a quarter of an hour from Gatwick Airport and a quarter of a mile from airport parking. It is a 30-year-old, long, low house with green shutters and a dormer window in three and a half acres of land with lovely views over woods. Mrs Duxbury, who is a very friendly, helpful lady, is used to catering for people leaving or arriving at Gatwick. She will undertake transfers for a reasonable rate any time after 5am. The rooms are well decorated and furnished and have TV, juices and biscuits. There is a good ratio of bedrooms to bathrooms. Breakfast only is available. Children welcome. No smoking. Car park.

OWNER Mrs Margaret Duxbury OPEN All year, exc Christmas ROOMS 1 family, 1 double, 2 twin (1 with bath/shower) TERMS B&B £15–£17.50, (single occupancy of twin/double) £18–£22 (children under 5 free, 6–14 £6, 15–18 £10 – all if sharing with parents); deposit £10 per room

CORSHAM Wiltshire map 2

Pickwick Lodge Farm

Corsham SN13 0PS
CORSHAM (0249) 712207

A good half mile off the A4 past Corsham towards Bath, a Tarmac track leads to this farm, across flat farmland. The back part of the stone-built house dates from the seventeenth century, the front was added much later. Pickwick Lodge is set to one side of the farmyard and serves the 300-acre arable and beef farm. One of the two large family/double bedrooms is on the ground floor. There is a lounge, shared with the family, and through it, down some steps, you reach the attractive dining-room, with one large table where breakfast and dinner (6.30pm or by arrangement) are served. There is no alcohol licence, but guests may bring their own wine. Packed lunches can be provided. The old farm buildings have now been converted into housing, the new farm buildings are located a little further from the house. Children welcome. Dogs only. No smoking. Car park.

OWNERS Guy and Gill Stafford OPEN Feb–end Oct ROOMS 2 family/double (1 with bath/shower, 1 with wash-basin), 1 twin TERMS B&B from £15, (single occupancy of twin/double) £17, (family room) £37.50 (children under 12 sharing parents' room half-price); dinner £8

CRANBROOK Kent map 3

Hancocks Farmhouse

Tilsden Lane, Cranbrook TN17 3PH
CRANBROOK (0580) 714645

This is a lovely timber-framed house, first mentioned in a will of 1520 and extended in the latter half of the sixteenth century,

standing in attractive countryside just outside the village of Cranbrook. It is no longer part of a farm. Evening meals are available 7–8pm and are taken in the large lounge/dining-room with a wood-burning stove in an enormous fireplace. A typical menu may include tomato, orange and basil soup, asparagus and prawn tart with a cheese pastry, and walnut sponge with curd cream. Vegetarian choices can be provided. A complimentary glass of sherry or wine is usually served with dinner and guests may bring their own wine. Packed lunches can also be provided. The three bedrooms, one with TV, are large and have antique furniture; one has a four-poster and the one on the ground floor has private bathroom and its own entrance into the garden. Children welcome – reductions available. No smoking. Car park.

OWNERS Bridget and Robin Oaten OPEN All year, exc Christmas ROOMS 1 four-poster, 2 twin (1 with bath/shower) TERMS B&B £16–£18, (single occupancy of twin/double) £20; dinner £12; deposit

CRAWLEY West Sussex map 3

Water Hall Farm

Prestwood Lane, Ifield Wood, Crawley RH11 0LA
CRAWLEY (0293) 520002

There is a cheerful, friendly atmosphere at this old farmhouse at the end of a narrow country lane north-west of Crawley. It is a working beef farm and is very handy for Gatwick Airport. The airport is the main source of business, with many people staying here before and after a trip and leaving their cars at the farm. Transport is arranged to and from the airport at very reasonable rates (£2–£2.50) and breakfast starts at 4am. The oldest part of the building dates from the sixteenth century, and there has recently been complete renovation to provide nine bedrooms all with private bathroom and TV. A large conservatory has also been added to the back of the house, where evening meals can be served by arrangement. The owners can also arrange for guests to pick up hire cars at the farm. The cars are delivered here and all the paperwork taken care of at the time. Children welcome. No pets in bedrooms. Car park.

OWNER Rosalind Tilson   OPEN All year, exc Christmas
ROOMS 2 family, 4 double, 3 twin; all rooms with bath/shower
TERMS B&B £23–£25, (single occupancy of twin/double) £35, (family room) £53–£60 (cots free); deposit £10

CROCKERTON Wiltshire   map 2

Tanhouse Cottage

Crockerton, Warminster BA12 8AU
WARMINSTER (0985) 214816

This pretty whitewashed cottage was originally a farmhouse and dates from the seventeenth century. It backs on to a main road, so is rather noisy, but the surrounding countryside is quiet and peaceful, and there is an attractive, small, cottage-style enclosed garden and area for sitting out, where breakfast is served on warm mornings. Crockerton lies on the edge of the Longleat Estate, Longleat House being only a couple of miles away. Freshly prepared, home-cooked evening meals, if arranged in advance, are served 7–9pm in the pretty dining-room; vegetarians can be catered for. Packed lunches can be provided. The cosy, comfortable oak-beamed sitting-room is shared by guests and hosts. The four bedrooms are small, plainly furnished and share one bathroom, with another available downstairs. Children welcome. No smoking in the dining-room. Car park.

OWNERS Michael and Sheila Dickinson   OPEN All year
ROOMS 1 family, 1 double, 1 twin, 1 single; all rooms with wash-basin
TERMS B&B £15, (family room) £40 (children under 6 £5, 6–12 £10); dinner £10

If you are forced to turn up late into the evening, please telephone to warn the proprietor.

DEAL Kent map 3

Beaconhill

Great Mongeham, Deal CT14 0HW
DEAL (0304) 372809

Originally a row of simple farm cottages, Beaconhill is over 200 years old. The conversion work has left the house with its old features of narrow stairways and low ceilings. It is set in lovely countryside just east of Deal, and part of the two-acre grounds is a managed nature reserve. Angela and Tony Wiggins call Beaconhill a 'field centre' and offer a variety of special-interest holidays to their guests, including walking, painting and music. There is a fully equipped studio in the grounds, which guests are welcome to use for painting or sketching. Home-cooked evening meals are available (7pm or by arrangement) as is Sunday lunch. Vegetarians can be catered for by arrangement and packed lunches can be provided. A complimentary glass of wine is offered at dinner and guests may bring their own wine (there is no alcohol licence). Beaconhill is difficult to find, so it is advisable to get directions. No dogs. No smoking, except in the smoking room. Car park.

OWNERS Angela and Tony Wiggins OPEN All year ROOMS 3 twin; all rooms with wash-basin TERMS B&B from £14.50, (single occupancy of twin) from £16.50; dinner £8.50; deposit

DEVIZES Wiltshire map 2

Long Street Guest House

27 Long Street, Devizes SN10 1NW
DEVIZES (0380) 724245

Close to the centre on one of the main roads into Devizes, Long Street Guest House is an old, listed timber-framed house with a Georgian brick façade and imposing stone porch entrance. The building has been very cleverly renovated using extra rooms and cupboards to create bathrooms without spoiling the size and shape of the rooms, several of which have their original fireplace. The rooms, all with TV, are comfortably furnished and decorated in restful colours. There is a large lounge and an attractive, small panelled dining-room where breakfast only is served. Packed lunches can be provided. There is some car parking to the rear of the property. Children welcome – reductions available. No pets. No smoking.

OWNERS Philip and Ruth Crudge OPEN All year ROOMS 2 double, 3 twin, 2 single; all rooms, exc 1 single, with bath/shower TERMS B&B £20, (single occupancy of twin/double) £25

DOVER Kent map 3

Number One Guest House

1 Castle Street, Dover CT16 1QH
DOVER (0304) 202007

This charming house dates from the early 1800s. The décor is most unusual, including mural wallpapers, collections of prints and porcelain. The bedrooms have TV and private bathroom and pretty tables where breakfast is served. There is an attractive lounge with a comprehensive brochure display, and a pretty walled back garden where guests are welcome to sit. Lock-up garages are available. Number One is just a few minutes from the town centre and docks. Children welcome. No pets.

OWNERS John and Adeline Reidy OPEN All year, exc Christmas ROOMS 2 family, 2 double, 2 twin; all rooms with bath/shower TERMS B&B £14–£18, (family room) £48; deposit £10

Tower Guest House

98 Priory Hill, Dover CT17 0AD
DOVER (0304) 208212

This unusual building stands in a superb position on top of a hill with spectacular views of the castle, docks and surrounding hills. A water tower until 1850, the warm and inviting house offers guests a kitchen where they can help themselves to tea and coffee. The immaculate half-moon and wedge-shaped bedrooms are prettily decorated with chintz curtains and bedspreads and all have TV and hair-dryer. Breakfast only is served and early meals for those catching ferries can be arranged. The house has a pretty garden and ramps for the disabled. It is in a quiet spot, close to the centre. Children welcome. No pets. No smoking in the dining-room. Two lock-up garages.

OWNER Mrs Doreen Wraight OPEN All year, exc Christmas ROOMS 2 family (1 with bath/shower), 1 double (with bath/shower), 2 twin (1 with bath/shower) TERMS B&B £15–£17.50, (single occupancy of twin/double) £20–£27, (family room) £48–£53; deposit

Valjoy Guest House

237 Folkstone Road, Dover CT17 9SL
DOVER (0304) 212160

The Valjoy is a large Victorian house, 15 minutes from the docks and on the A20; most bedrooms, however, are at the back of the house, and the road will be less busy when the bypass is completed. A warm and informal atmosphere pervades the Valjoy. The rooms are spacious, with high ceilings and old fireplaces and they are simply, though comfortably, furnished. Evening meals, including vegetarian choices, can be provided 6–7pm by prior arrangement. Packed lunches are also available. There is no alcohol licence, but guests may bring their own wine to dinner. Full English breakfast is served from 6am and breakfast trays can be arranged for early travellers. This is a simple guesthouse with very friendly owners. Children welcome. No pets in bedrooms. No smoking in the dining-room. Car park.

OWNERS Brian and Valerie Bowes OPEN All year ROOMS 3 family/double/twin, 1 single; all rooms with wash-basin TERMS B&B £12–£15, (single occupancy of twin/double) £24–£28 (children under 3 £4, 4–12 £6–£7 sharing parents' room); dinner £7; deposit 33%

DOWNTON Wiltshire map 2

The Warren

15 High Street, Downton SP5 3PG
DOWNTON (0725) 20263

A listed building of great interest, the front part dating from the fifteenth century, the Warren has many exposed beams and has been carefully furnished with antiques. It lies on the main street of the pretty village of Downton and has a surprisingly large walled garden to the rear, with views of the village church at the end of the garden. The house has a pleasant, spacious feel, with a large entrance hall. Breakfast only is served in the charming dining-room with french windows leading out on to the garden. The small sitting-room with TV has a fifteenth-century fireplace, which was recently uncovered. The bedrooms are large, comfortable and well decorated. The largest, which overlooks the garden, is a beautiful panelled room; the panelling dates from the seventeenth century and was taken from a nearby manor house. One bedroom has a 500-year-old carved half-tester bed and a large private bathroom. No children under five. Pets by arrangement, in bedrooms only. No smoking in bedrooms or bathrooms. Car park.

OWNERS John and Elizabeth Baxter OPEN All year, exc 15 Dec–6 Jan ROOMS 1 family (with wash-basin), 3 double (2 with bath/shower, 1 with wash-basin), 2 twin (with wash-basin) TERMS B&B £17.50–£20, (single occupancy of twin/double) £28–£30 (children 5–11 £12); deposit

EASTBOURNE East Sussex map 3

Beachy Rise Guest House

20 Beachy Head Road, Eastbourne BN20 7QN
EASTBOURNE (0323) 639171

Built in the 1890s, Beachy Rise is an unassuming semi-detached Victorian house just off the road. It is in the conservation area of Meads Village, between Beachy Head and the town centre. Both the South Downs and the sea can be reached in about a 10-minute walk. Mr and Mrs Cooke have put a tremendous amount of work and loving care into both the house and garden. The house is surprisingly large inside, with a comfortable sitting-room and dining-room where evening meals (6.30pm) as well as breakfast are served. A typical dinner menu may be tomato and herb soup, grilled trout with cucumber sauce and bread-and-butter pudding. The wine list is short but reasonably priced. Vegetarians can be catered for and packed lunches provided. The dining-room leads out on to a south-facing patio with tables and chairs and the garden. The bedrooms, all with TV, are prettily decorated and furnished with much pine furniture; most have original fireplaces. Children welcome. No pets. No smoking in the dining-room.

OWNERS Mr R. and Mrs S. Cooke OPEN All year, exc Christmas ROOMS 1 family (with wash-basin), 4 double (3 with bath/shower, 1 with wash-basin), 1 twin (with bath/shower) TERMS B&B £22, (single occupancy of twin/double) £32, (family room) £19 per person (children under 3 free, 4–9 half-price, 10–14 three-quarters-price); dinner £9; deposit £10 per person; Access, Visa

Where we know an establishment accepts credit cards, we list them. There may be a surcharge if you pay by credit card. It is always best to check whether the card you want to use is acceptable when booking.

When the family-room rate is given in the details it applies to the cost of the whole room, unless a rate per person is specified.

EAST COWES Isle of Wight map 2

Crossways House

Crossways Road, East Cowes PO32 6LJ
ISLE OF WIGHT (0983) 293677

Crossways is a large Victorian house, just off the main road, and close to Osborne House. It was formerly part of the royal estate and built as a residence for Queen Victoria's Admiral Master of Arms, later being used as a school for the Osborne Naval Cadets. The owners are building a bungalow in the grounds for themselves and are converting the bedrooms, all with TV, in the main house so that each has *en suite* facilities. Lunches and evening meals (7–8.30pm) are available and vegetarian choices can be provided. The wine list allows a wide choice. Reductions are available for children, depending on age. Car park.

OWNERS A. J. and E. J. Wood OPEN All year ROOMS 1 family (with bath/shower), 2 double, 1 twin (with wash-basin) TERMS B&B about £20, (single occupancy of twin/double) about £30, (family room) £45–£55; dinner from £10; deposit about 25%; Visa

EAST KNOYLE Wiltshire map 2

Milton Farm

East Knoyle SP3 6BG
EAST KNOYLE (0747) 830247

A former farmhouse, this Queen Anne country house has a most attractive garden with heated swimming-pool, and stands in the middle of very pretty, unspoilt farmland. The house is comfortable, elegant, beautifully furnished and decorated, and has a very pleasant, relaxing atmosphere. The bedrooms, all with TV, are large and homely. Breakfast only is served in the lounge/dining-room. Rough shooting can be arranged. East Knoyle, about half a mile away, is famous as the birthplace of Sir Christopher Wren. The house is situated in the middle of the hamlet of Milton, which is signposted from East Knoyle. Children welcome. No dogs. Car park.

OWNERS Mr and Mrs R. G. Hyde OPEN Mar–Nov
ROOMS 1 double, 1 twin; both rooms with bath/shower
TERMS B&B £18–£22 (children under 8 half-price)

Milton House

East Knoyle SP3 6BG
EAST KNOYLE (0747) 830397

Set in very pretty countryside in a quiet position, this is an attractive, part-Queen Anne country house. It is comfortably furnished in keeping with its period and there is one large twin-bedded room with TV and an adjacent bathroom and separate toilet along the corridor. Breakfast only is served in the lovely dining-room that has an interesting carved ceiling. Packed lunches can be provided. Guests are welcome to use the hard tennis court, or the heated swimming-pool in next-door Milton Farm. Children welcome. Pets by arrangement. Car park.

OWNER Mrs T. P. Wootton OPEN All year ROOMS 1 twin (with bath/shower) TERMS B&B £17.50–£22 (reductions for children negotiable); deposit

Swainscombe

The Green, East Knoyle SP3 6BN
EAST KNOYLE (0747) 830224

Swainscombe is in the middle of the tiny hamlet of The Green, about a mile outside East Knoyle. It is a delightful seventeenth-century thatched cottage that has recently been extended in the same style. The house has all the beams and narrow, steep stairs that you would expect in a house of this vintage. Evening meals (7.30pm) are served by candlelight in the beamed dining-room and may include such dishes as Mediterranean fish soup, stuffed pork tenderloin and crème brûlée. Vegetarians can be catered for and guests may bring their own wine (there is no alcohol licence). Packed lunches can also be provided. A group of guests may use an upstairs suite, reached through the dining-room. This consists of two double bedrooms, one considerably larger than the other, a bathroom and a sitting area on the landing. All rooms have TV. The house is surrounded by a pleasant lawned garden and the hamlet enjoys spectacular views (it is 600 feet above sea level), particularly from the nearby village pub, the Fox & Hounds, which serves basic bar food, both at lunchtime and in the evening.

If any bedrooms are suitable for the disabled we mention this in the entry.

Where we know of any particular payment stipulations we mention them in the details. It is always best to check when booking, however.

Swimming and tennis are available by arrangement. Children welcome. No smoking. Car park.

OWNER Joy Orman OPEN Feb–Nov ROOMS 1 family, 1 four-poster, 2 double, 2 single; all rooms with bath/shower TERMS B&B £18–£20 (children under 10 half-price); dinner £12.50; deposit (July–Aug) 10%

EMSWORTH Hampshire map 2

The Chestnuts Guest House

55 Horndean Road, Emsworth PO10 7PU
EMSWORTH (0243) 372233

Dating from 1890, the Chestnuts was once the home of Joe Childs, George V's jockey. It is a comfortable family house, on the B2148, one mile north of Emsworth and its harbour, and an excellent location for golf (the favourite pastime of the proprietors), sailing and other water-related activities. The accommodation is clean and comfortable; there is a pleasant lounge with open fire and a small sun/sitting-room off the dining-room with views of the garden and small swimming-pool. Breakfast only is available, although packed lunches can be provided. Children welcome. No smoking in the dining-room. Car park.

OWNERS Mr and Mrs G. V. Hobbs OPEN All year ROOMS 1 family, 1 double, 1 twin; all rooms with wash-basin TERMS B&B £15, (single occupancy of twin/double) £20, (family room) £40; deposit

ERLESTOKE Wiltshire map 2

Longwater

Lower Road, Erlestoke, nr Devizes SN10 5UE
DEVIZES (0380) 830095

This modern farmhouse is a long, low building on the edge of a pretty, unspoilt village, in an attractive valley, and named after one of the lakes the house overlooks. The farm is organically managed, and consists of acreage of grass for the beef herd, woodland and two small lakes, the larger stocked for coarse fishing and the smaller a waterfowl conservation area. There is also a small herd of longhorn cattle. All bedrooms have their own bathroom and TV; two are on the ground floor and there is now a unit in one of the outbuildings providing a large family room with private bathroom and a smaller room also with its own bathroom – ideal for families, or a party of friends. There is a spacious, comfortable lounge – a light room with lots of windows and an open fire on cooler evenings – leading into the large, long conservatory which has lovely views over the lakes and leads out on to the patio. The large kitchen/dining-room is decorated with dressers full of blue and white china and displays of Pam Hampton's thimble collection. Longwater is a member of the 'Wiltshire Larder' and evening meals are available (7pm) using home-grown or home-made organic produce. Vegetarians can be catered for and packed lunches provided. Wines from a local vineyard are a speciality. Children welcome. No smoking in the dining-room or the conservatory. Car park.

OWNER Pam Hampton OPEN All year, exc Christmas
ROOMS 1 family, 1 double, 2 twin; all rooms with bath/shower
TERMS B&B £18, (single occupancy of twin/double) £22 (children half-price); dinner £11; deposit

FARNINGHAM Kent map 3

The Bakery

High Street, Farningham DA4 0DH
FARNINGHAM (0322) 864210

A pretty, whitewashed seventeenth-century cottage faced with Kentish weatherboard and opposite the church in the centre of Farningham, the Bakery is close to the A20, M25 junction 3 and the railway station. Mrs Lovering, who is an artist and has her studio in the grounds, was born in Portugal and speaks Portuguese, Spanish, French and Greek, as well as English. The house has the original flagstone floors, and the three bedrooms are clean and comfortable. Breakfast only is served. Children welcome. No pets. No smoking.

OWNERS Mr and Mrs Lovering OPEN All year ROOMS 1 double, 1 twin, 1 single; all rooms, exc single, with wash-basin TERMS B&B £15–£16, (single) £20–£22 (children under 12 sharing room half-price)

Bath/shower information in the details refers only to a private bathroom or shower; other bathroom facilities at the establishments will be shared.

The description for each entry states when pets are not allowed. Where no details are given, you can assume that pets are allowed. It's always best to check first in any case.

FINDON West Sussex map 3

Findon Tower

Cross Lane, Findon, nr Worthing BN14 0UG
FINDON (0903) 873870

This is a substantial Edwardian country house, surrounded by a small garden, and just off the A24. The pretty village centre is about a quarter of a mile away with one or two good places to eat. The house is spacious and offers three good-sized bedrooms, all with *en suite* bathrooms. Guests have use of a drawing-room, a sun lounge, a large snooker room and a family dining-room with one table where breakfast only is served. Packed lunches can be provided. Children welcome. Dogs by arrangement. No smoking in bedrooms. Car park.

OWNERS Thurza and Tony Smith OPEN All year, exc Christmas ROOMS 1 family/double, 1 twin, 1 single; all rooms, exc single, with bath/shower TERMS B&B £17.50–£20, (single) £15–£20, (single occupancy of twin/double) £20–£25 (children £5 in family room); deposit

FLEET Hampshire map 2

8 Chinnock Close

8 Chinnock Close, Fleet GU13 9SN
FLEET (0252) 613646

This family home, in a 20-year-old housing development, stands in a quiet, peaceful spot, with lots of trees and gardens, and not far from the centre of Fleet. The Nixes have their own, separate part of the house and work from home, making figures for dolls' houses, several of which decorate the house. Guests have a restful TV lounge with doors out on to a patio and small back garden. Breakfast only is served, but there is a large selection of eating-places close by. The immaculately clean and comfortable bedrooms (one with TV and telephone) are pleasantly furnished. This is a popular place for business people and those attending the Farnborough Air Show. Not suitable for small children. No dogs. No smoking in one bedroom. Car park.

OWNERS Mrs and Mrs R. Nix OPEN All year ROOMS 1 double, 1 twin, 2 single TERMS B&B £14

FRANT East Sussex map 3

Henley Farm

Frant TN3 9EP
FRANT (089 275) 242

Originally an oast house, the building dates from the early 1800s and stands close to the main road, but in a rural setting. You drive under an arch of the weatherboarded house to park at the back. There is a large attractive garden to the rear with a patio for sitting out and a tennis court. Two bedrooms have TV. Breakfast only is available, and Henley Farm represents excellent value for money. It is located on the B2099 between Frant and Wadhurst. Children welcome. No pets. No smoking in bedrooms. Car park.

OWNER Mrs Ann Fleming OPEN All year ROOMS 1 double, 1 twin, 2 single; 3 rooms with wash-basin TERMS B&B £14 (babies free, children under 5 half-price approx)

The Old Parsonage

Church Lane, Frant TN3 9DX
FRANT (0892) 750773

This substantial Georgian house off a quiet lane in the pretty village of Frant was the rectory until 1989. It was built by the Marquess of Abergavenny for his son who was the parish rector between 1820 and 1845. The present owners have done a lot of work to the house. The big, comfortable bedrooms, all with TV, have their own bathrooms, with raised baths, one of which has a Venus-like lady decorating the tiles. There is a large, pleasant, well-furnished drawing-room and breakfast only is served in the dining-room. Tea and biscuits are offered to guests on arrival in the large conservatory, which has access out on to the enormous terrace. Guests may have a bash at croquet in the walled garden. In the past, two Canadian prime ministers have stayed here while visiting the grave of Colonel By, the founder of Ottawa, who is buried in the churchyard. There is a restaurant just opposite the house and a couple of nearby pubs serving food. Children welcome. No smoking in bedrooms. Car park.

OWNERS Tony and Mary Dakin OPEN All year ROOMS 1 four-poster, 1 double, 2 twin; all rooms with bath/shower TERMS B&B £22.50–£24, (single occupancy of twin/double) £36 (children under 2 free, 3–6 one-third-price, 7–12 half-price)

FRESHWATER Isle of Wight map 2

Brookside Forge Hotel

Brookside Road, Freshwater PO40 9ER
ISLE OF WIGHT (0983) 754644

This very friendly, well-run, small guesthouse is a modest brick-built house, originally the village forge, with a large, pretty rear garden, in a quiet road close to the centre of Freshwater. All except three bedrooms have *en suite* shower/bathrooms; the others have showers, but no toilets. Doors from the small bar lead out on to the patio and back garden, with tables and chairs for sitting out. There is a small, comfortable lounge and dinner is available at 6.30pm or 7pm, depending on the time of the year. Packed lunches can be provided. Brookside Forge also has access to special ferry fares at certain times. Children welcome. Dogs by arrangement. No smoking in the dining-room. Car park.

OWNERS Margaret and Douglas Pollard OPEN All year
ROOMS 2 family (with bath/shower), 4 double (3 with bath/shower, 1 with shower only), 4 twin (3 with bath/shower, 1 with shower only), 1 single (with shower) TERMS B&B £18.50–£22, (single occupancy of twin/double) £22.50–£26, (family room) £55.50–£66 (children under 3 free, 3–12 half-price, 13–15 three-quarters-price); dinner from £9; deposit £20 per person; Access, Visa

Yarlands Country House Hotel

Victoria Road, Freshwater PO40 9PP
ISLE OF WIGHT (0983) 752574

Formerly the rectory, this seventeenth-century country house is set back from the road, with a wide gravel sweep at the front. It stands in two and a half acres of gardens, which stretch down to the River Yar. The house has been furnished throughout in restful pastel colours, including carpets and curtains. The very large, comfortable bedrooms, all with TV, are furnished with simple pine furniture and the private bathrooms have also been finished in pine. There is a large lounge bar, off which is a conservatory leading on to the garden. Dinner, served at 7pm, includes fresh vegetables and fruit from the garden. Dishes may include celery and Stilton soup, poached hake with lemon garlic butter and treacle sponge. Vegetarians are catered for and packed lunches can be provided. The house is very well maintained and is popular with business people. No children under three. No pets. No smoking in the dining-room or lounge. Car park.

OWNERS Mr and Mrs J. L. Fairman OPEN All year ROOMS 2 family, 2 double, 2 twin; all rooms with bath/shower TERMS B&B £22, (single occupancy of twin/double) £27 (children under 14 sharing parents' room half-price); dinner £10; deposit; Visa

GLYNDE East Sussex map 3

Glyndebourne Farm

Glynde, nr Lewes BN8 6SH
LEWES (0273) 812391

From the road you see the not very attractive seventeenth-century addition to the farm, and it is not until you turn into the driveway that the pretty fifteenth-century part comes into view. This family home is owned by a friendly couple who are happy for guests to come and go as they please. The bedrooms are large and have magnificent views of the South Downs. Breakfast only is served. Glyndebourne Farm is one mile off the A27 almost opposite Glyndebourne Opera House. Children by arrangement. No pets. No smoking in bedrooms. Car park.

OWNERS Mr R. and Mrs E. M. Brickell OPEN All year, exc Christmas ROOMS 1 double (with bath/shower), 2 twin TERMS B&B £17.50, (single occupancy of double) £25

GREAT CHART Kent map 3

Worten House

Great Chart, nr Ashford TN23 3BU
ASHFORD (0233) 622944

Great Chart is two miles west of Ashford on the A28. This brick and stone building, probably dating from the eighteenth century, is in a quiet and peaceful spot with a lovely walled garden and pleasant views over farmland. Although it is in a peaceful country area, access to trains is very good. A family home, it is comfortable and pleasantly decorated and furnished and the two bedrooms are light, bright and of a good size. Guests have use of a sitting-room with TV and there is a large, secluded garden. Evening meals are available at 8pm and guests may bring their own wine (there is no alcohol licence). Children welcome. Car park.

OWNERS Denise and Charles Wilkinson OPEN All year, exc Christmas ROOMS 2 twin (with wash-basin) TERMS B&B £16, (single occupancy of twin) £25 (children 10% reduction); dinner £10

GRITTLETON Wiltshire map 2

Church House

Grittleton, nr Chippenham SN14 6AP
CASTLE COMBE (0249) 782562 Fax (0249) 782562

Church House, between the church and the pub, was formerly the rectory in the pretty village of Grittleton. It is an unpretentious, yet elegant and spacious Georgian building that has been in the Moore family for the last 25 years. Church House is very popular with small groups of friends or families who return again and again, partly to experience Anna Moore's cooking. Dinner (8pm) is served in a party atmosphere at the large dining-room table seating 12. Vegetarian choices can be provided with notice and guests may bring their own wine (there is no alcohol licence). Packed lunches are also available. The bedrooms, all with TV, radio/clock-alarm and hair-dryer, are mostly located on the second floor and are good-sized, simply furnished and decorated and all have their own bath or shower and toilet, which are not in a separate room, but screened off in a corner. There is a fax service for guests. The heated and covered swimming-pool, which is floodlit at night, incorporates the walls of the house and walled garden. There are 11 acres of garden and pasture in all, including a croquet lawn in summer. Church House offers an informal, friendly, house-party atmosphere, and is only a short distance from Badminton. No children 2–12. No dogs. No smoking in the dining-room or drawing-room. Car park.

OWNER Mrs Anna Moore OPEN All year ROOMS 1 double, 3 twin; all rooms with bath/shower TERMS B&B £22.50, (single occupancy of twin/double) £27.50 (babies under 2 free, children 12–15 half-price sharing with parents); dinner £13; deposit

Those B&Bs that we know can offer some kind of off-street car parking, have 'car park' at the end of the entry. If we are aware of particular car parking difficulties, we mention them.

It is always best to check prices, especially for single occupancy, when booking.

GURNARD Isle of Wight map 2

Hillbrow Private Hotel

Tuttons Hill, Gurnard, Cowes PO31 8JA
ISLE OF WIGHT (0983) 297240

The centre of Cowes is only a 15-minute walk away from this 1930s house with a small garden and views over farmland to the Solent. Although it does not have a great deal of character, it is very clean and neat, and simply furnished. All bedrooms have TV. Evening meals are available on request at 6.30pm and snacks can be provided at any time. The premises are licensed. Vegetarians can be catered for and packed lunches provided. Horse-riding and golf can be arranged. Children welcome. No pets. No smoking in the dining-room. Car park.

OWNER Paul Mortlock OPEN All year ROOMS 1 family (with bath/shower), 1 double (with wash-basin), 2 twin (1 with wash-basin), 1 single (with wash-basin) TERMS B&B £16, (single occupancy of twin/double) £21 (children sharing parents' room under 2 free, under 5 25%, under 10 50%, under 14 75% of adult rate); dinner £6; deposit

HARTFIELD East Sussex map 3

Bolebroke Watermill

Perry Hill, Edenbridge Road, Hartfield TN7 4JP
HARTFIELD (0892) 770425

Romantically set in six and a half acres of secluded, tranquil woodland, this ancient watermill was first recorded in the Domesday book, and continued as a working corn-mill until 1946. The machinery and olde worlde charm remain, but the mill has been adapted to form delightful, unusual guest accommodation with exceptional character. The Mill and the Miller's Barn each have two bedrooms and can also be converted to take groups of six people. All rooms have TV and bathroom. There are several steep stairways, so the accommodation is not suitable for small children or the disabled. The mill stream runs through the garden. Breakfast only is available, but packed lunches can be provided. No children under seven. No pets. No smoking. Car park.

OWNERS Christine and David Cooper OPEN Mar–mid-Dec
ROOMS 1 four-poster, 2 double, 1 twin; all rooms with bath/shower
TERMS B&B £22.50, (four-poster) £27.50, (single occupancy of twin/double) £40, (family room) from £85; deposit; Amex, Visa

HASLEMERE Surrey map 2

Deerfell

Blackdown Park, nr Haslemere GU27 3LB
HASLEMERE (0428) 653409

Deerfell was once the coach-house to Blackdown Park, which is still a privately owned house. It is an attractive stone building with glorious views towards the South Downs. To reach it, you take the A286 Midhurst road from Haslemere and after crossing the border into West Sussex you turn left into Fernden Lane. After two and a half miles the road bends sharply to the left and you carry straight on through two large stone gates; the last part is down a pot-holed driveway. Guests can have breakfast either in the dining-room or the conservatory. They have use of a sitting-room and there are two attractive bedrooms with their own bathroom and TV. Evening meals are available by arrangement and guests may bring their own wine (there is no alcohol licence). Packed lunches can also be provided. No smoking. Car park.

OWNER Elizabeth Carmichael OPEN Mar–Oct ROOMS 2 twin (with bath/shower) TERMS B&B £16–£18 (children sharing with parents £10); dinner £7.50–£10; deposit for 3 days or more

Houndless Water

Bell Vale Lane, Haslemere GU27 3DJ
HASLEMERE (0428) 642591

About a mile out of Haslemere off the A286 Midhurst road, you will find Houndless Water, down a quiet country lane, and approached by a gravel drive. It is a substantial brick-built house dating back to Tudor times, and a comfortable family home, traditionally built with tile-hung walls and inglenook fireplaces. Originally a farmhouse, it still has the bell tower used for summoning the workers to their meals. There are five acres of grounds, which are especially colourful in May when the azaleas and rhododendrons are in bloom. Evening meals (7pm) and vegetarian choices can be arranged in advance; guests may bring their own wine (there is no alcohol licence). Packed lunches can also be provided. No children under three. No cats. No smoking in bedrooms. Car park.

OWNERS Mr and Mrs A. Mansley OPEN All year, exc Christmas ROOMS 1 double, 2 twin; 2 rooms with wash-basin TERMS B&B £16–£22 (children 3–11 25% reduction); dinner £9–£12; deposit 50%

HAWKHURST Kent map 3

Conghurst Farm

Hawkhurst TN18 4RW
HAWKHURST (0580) 753331

This is a 500-acre working sheep and arable farm, set in beautiful, unspoilt countryside, down a quiet lane a couple of miles out of Hawkhurst. The views from the house are superb. Conghurst has been in the Piper family for hundreds of years and family records in the local church date back to 900, which is when the house was first built. At that time it was surrounded by a moat at the bottom of the hill, on the edge of tidal water. Flooding drove the family up the hill to the house's present site. The oldest part has a stone coat of arms in what was the outside wall, dated 1599; this is now the family's sitting-room. The house has been extended over the years, the front façade being Georgian. There is a large garden and an outdoor swimming-pool. The bedrooms are very spacious and most attractively furnished and decorated and guests can use the lovely drawing-room with log fires and a smaller room for TV and listening to music. Evening meals are available by arrangement at 7.30pm and can include vegetarian choices. There is no alcohol licence, but guests may bring their own wine. Packed lunches can be provided. There are a number of National Trust properties, such as Sissinghurst and Bodiam Castle, in the area, which is also good walking country. Children under seven by arrangement. Pets by arrangement. No smoking. Car park.

OWNER Rosemary Piper OPEN Mar–Nov ROOMS 1 double, 2 twin; all rooms with bath/shower TERMS B&B £16–£19 (children 7–12 half-price); dinner £10

HAYLING ISLAND Hampshire map 2

Cockle Warren Cottage Hotel

36 Seafront, Hayling Island PO11 9HL
HAYLING ISLAND (0705) 464961

The Skeltons built this small brick house in 1979 and have been doing B&B ever since. Cockle Warren is their hobby, and not a year goes by without them making some kind of improvement to the property. The house faces the sea, set back from the main road across a car park, with a heated swimming-pool to the rear. The bedrooms are small, prettily decorated and furnished with all kinds of little touches such as mineral water, a sewing kit and magazines, and are now all *en suite* and have TV and direct-dial telephone. There is one room in an annexe and one room has a four-poster bed. The small lounge with open fire is separated from the dining area by a plant-covered trellis. Food is a very important part of the Cockle Warren operation, and excellent home-cooked set dinners (7.30 for 8pm) are served in an elegant setting in the recently added conservatory. Vegetarians are catered for. No children over eight months and under 12 years old. No pets in bedrooms or public areas. Smoking in the lounge only. Car park.

OWNERS David and Diane Skelton OPEN All year ROOMS 2 four-poster, 3 double; all rooms with bath/shower TERMS B&B £24, (four-poster) £34, (single occupancy of double) £35–£45; dinner £23.50; deposit; Access, Visa

HENFIELD West Sussex map 3

Frylands

Wineham, Henfield BN5 9BP
PARTRIDGE GREEN (0403) 710214

Built in about 1570, this Tudor farmhouse is at the end of a quiet country lane in peaceful farmland, three miles north-east of Henfield. Constructed of brick and timber with a stone roof, it has been in the family, apart from two short breaks, since 1622. The house retains many of its original features, such as the leaded windows, oak beams, flagstone floors and thick stone walls. Bedrooms have wash-basin, TV and radio-alarm. There is over an acre of landscaped gardens surrounded by 250 acres of farmland, which is no longer farmed by the family but let out. Mr Fowler is a swimming-pool consultant, and guests are welcome to try the heated swimming-pool in the garden. Coarse fishing is also available, and there is a self-catering cottage. Breakfast only is served, but packed lunches can be provided. Children welcome. No pets. Car park.

OWNER Mrs Sylvia Fowler OPEN All year, exc Christmas
ROOMS 1 family, 1 double, 1 twin; all rooms with wash-basin
TERMS B&B about £15 (children half-price sharing family room)

Where we know of any particular payment stipulations we mention them in the details. It is always best to check when booking, however.

We asked the proprietors to estimate their 1992 prices in the autumn of 1991, so the rates may have changed since publication.

HORLEY Surrey map 3

Chalet Guest House

77 Massetts Road, Horley RH6 7EB
HORLEY (0293) 821666 Fax (0293) 821619

A neat, small, modern guesthouse on a busy road that is only five minutes from Gatwick Airport. It used to be the Shortlands' family home, but they converted it recently and now live in the bungalow behind. The rooms are a bit on the small side, and all except two of the singles have *en suite*, mostly very small bathrooms. Continental breakfast only is served in the tidy, clean breakfast room. English breakfast can be provided for an extra charge. Children welcome. No dogs. No smoking in public areas. Car park.

OWNER Mrs Daphne Shortland OPEN All year ROOMS 1 double, 2 twin, 4 single; all rooms, exc 2 single (wash-basin only), with bath/shower TERMS B&B £20–£24, (single) £25–£30, (single occupancy of twin/double) £35 (£10 for child's bed in room); deposit £10 per room; Access, Visa

Gainsborough Lodge

39 Massetts Road, Horley RH6 7DT
HORLEY (0293) 783982

The road can be noisy, but this Edwardian house is only about a mile and a half from Gatwick Airport. The dining-room overlooks the pleasant, secluded grounds with lots of shrubs and flowers and a manicured lawn. Guests have the use of a lounge. Breakfast (English, not Continental) only is served. All bedrooms have TV. This is a convenient place to stay at before or after a trip from Gatwick Airport, although no transport service is provided. No smoking in the dining-room. Car park.

OWNER Mrs J. E. Oxenham OPEN All year, exc Christmas ROOMS 2 family, 2 double, 5 twin, 3 single; all rooms with bath/shower TERMS B&B £16–£22, (single) £25.50–£35.50, (single occupancy of twin/double) £37.50, (family room) £45–£59.50; deposit 50% or full payment if flying in late; Access, Visa

Where a single-occupancy rate is not specified in the details, the cost will be the same as that per person in a twin or double room, or will be included in the range of prices given.

The Lawn Guest House

30 Massetts Road, Horley RH6 7DE
HORLEY (0293) 775751

This pleasant Victorian house is on the same noisy road as our other Horley entries, but it is extremely handy for Gatwick Airport, and only a two-minute walk from the town centre. Janet and Ken Stocks are a very friendly, helpful couple. The house is cheerful, bright and comfortably furnished. The bedrooms are spacious and have armchairs and TV; there is a twin room with private bathroom on the ground floor. A light breakfast only is served, but packed lunches can be provided. Children welcome. No smoking in the breakfast room and public areas. Car park.

OWNERS Janet and Ken Stocks OPEN All year, exc Christmas ROOMS 2 double (1 with bath/shower, 1 with wash-basin), 6 twin (3 with bath/shower, 3 with wash-basin) TERMS B&B £17.50–£21, (single occupancy of twin/double) £24–£31; deposit 50%; Access, Visa

HUNTON Kent map 3

The Woolhouse

Grove Lane, Hunton ME15 0SE
HUNTON (062 72) 778

This appealing seventeenth-century building, on a quiet lane in pleasant farmland in the heart of hop country near the River Beult, was originally a barn. It is now a sizeable house, cleverly and tastefully converted and full of beams. The house has clematis around the porch and honeysuckle covering the fences. There is a tennis court in the garden. The bedrooms are simply decorated and furnished. Breakfast only is served in the attractive dining-room. The owners also have a picture-framing business, with their workroom in the house. To find the Woolhouse, you aim for Yalding from Hunton church and after half a mile Grove Lane is on the right. No children. Car park.

OWNERS Mr and Mrs Wetton OPEN All year ROOMS 1 double, 1 twin, 1 single; all rooms with bath/shower TERMS B&B £15–£17.50

Many B&Bs will cater for vegetarians. It is always best, however, to check when booking and make it clear what your requirements are, especially if you need a special diet.

ICKLESHAM East Sussex map 3

The Old Farmhouse

Broad Street, Icklesham, nr Rye TN36 4AU
HASTINGS (0424) 814711

Reached down a country lane and long driveway, this old, Grade II listed house stands in lovely unspoilt countryside only four miles from Rye. It is a large building, which has been extensively modernised, but retains its old beams and an enormous fireplace in the family sitting-room. This is no longer a farm, but the owner keeps a few sheep and angora goats on the seven acres. Breakfast includes home-made muesli and preserves and is taken in the very large family kitchen. All bedrooms have TV. One bedroom is a family room under the high-peaked eaves with skylights and lovely views over the surrounding countryside. Children welcome. Small dogs only. No smoking in bedrooms. Car park.

OWNERS Mr John and Mrs Dianna Epton OPEN 1 Mar–20 Dec ROOMS 1 family, 2 double, 1 twin TERMS B&B £15.50, (single occupancy of twin/double) £20.50 (children under 5 free, over 5 £9 in family room); deposit

ISFIELD East Sussex map 3

Birches Farm

Isfield, nr Uckfield TN22 5TY
ISFIELD (082 575) 304

The oldest part of this attractive brick and part tile-hung, part timber-framed old farmhouse is 300 years old; the newer part dates from the 1920s. No longer a farm, it is located down a quiet country road. The house has many beams and there is an attractive dining-room, where breakfast only is served, and a comfortable sitting-room with views of the garden. The twin-bedded room is delightful and has an open-plan bathroom and good views. Dinner can be served on request and can include vegetarian choices. There is no alcohol licence, but guests may bring their own wine. No children under 12. No pets in the house. No smoking in bedrooms. Car park.

OWNER Mrs Lesley Robertshaw OPEN All year ROOMS 2 double, 1 twin; all rooms with bath/shower TERMS B&B £17.50, (single occupancy of twin/double) £25

KINGSWOOD Surrey map 3

Field House

Babylon Lane, Lower Kingswood KT20 6XE
REIGATE (0737) 221745

Built only eight years ago, this is a fine brick house overlooking fields, down a quiet country lane, yet very close to the M25 and not far from Gatwick. To find Lower Kingswood and Field House, you leave the M25 at junction 8 and take the A217 towards Sutton. At the first roundabout you turn right into Babylon Lane. A large, surprisingly spacious house, it has been beautifully decorated and furnished. The bedrooms, all with TV, are of a good size and very comfortable. The dining-room is enormous, with one table where breakfast only is served. There are gardens and even a gym for guests to enjoy. No pets. No smoking in bedrooms. Car park.

OWNER Mrs B. Pritchard OPEN All year, exc Christmas and hols
ROOMS 1 double (with bath/shower), 1 twin (with wash-basin), 1 single TERMS B&B £21–£25 (children under 3 free, over 3 reductions negotiable)

LEWES East Sussex map 3

Millers

134 High Street, Lewes BN7 1XS
LEWES (0273) 475631

Millers is a sixteenth-century timber-framed house in a conservation area in the centre of Lewes. Its name comes from its tenancy during most of the last century by a succession of millers who sold their produce from the front parlour. A millstone may still be seen in the walled garden. This is a charming house with lots of panelling and natural wood. The delightful front entrance room has a cosy sitting area around the fire and a table for breakfast. The bedrooms, all with TV, are large and quite charming. One has a rose-painted four-poster bed, and another has a shower-room built into what is reputed to have been a priest hole. Breakfast only is served. Reductions are available for stays of more than one night. No small children, but older children can

We state at the end of an entry when children are welcome. If we know of any restrictions, we give them.

be accommodated if they share a separate room. No pets. No smoking.

OWNERS Teré and Tony Tammar OPEN All year, exc Christmas and New Year ROOMS 1 four-poster, 2 double; all rooms with bath/ shower TERMS B&B £18–£21, (single occupancy of double) £31–£37

LINTON Kent map 3

The White Lodge

Linton, nr Maidstone ME17 4AG
MAIDSTONE (0622) 743129

'A happy alternative to hotels' is how Merrilyn Boorman bills her B&B, four miles south of Maidstone and off the B2163 just north of Linton village. This substantial, perfectly kept, classical-looking house is in a beautiful and quiet setting. It seems strange, but this impressive house was once the laundry to Linton Park, former home of Lord Cornwallis. It is thought that it was built on the site of a monastery and has been considerably renovated and altered over the years. It is interestingly decorated with matching wallpapers and curtains. The house has a very informal atmosphere and breakfast only is taken in the kitchen. All bedrooms have TV. Facilities are available for small private conferences. Car park.

OWNER Merrilyn Boorman OPEN All year ROOMS 1 double, 2 twin, 1 single; all rooms with wash-basin TERMS B&B £16 (children under 5 half-price); deposit

LYMINGTON Hampshire map 2

Albany House

Highfield, Lymington SO41 9GB
LYMINGTON (0590) 671900

Built in 1840, Albany House is half of a substantial, elegant town house, in an excellent location, right at the top of the high street in this old port and market town. Wendy Gallagher loves to cook, so is more than happy to prepare evening meals (7pm). When available, local shellfish, Lymington-landed fish and New Forest game will be provided. Vegetarians can be catered for and guests may bring their own wine (there is no alcohol licence). Packed lunches can also be provided. The rooms, most with TV, are very large with high ceilings; private bathrooms have now been added to all but one of the rooms. There is a very pleasant, spacious sitting-room with TV and open fireplace and lots of books, and the dining-room is also a big, well-proportioned room. Reductions for children by arrangement. Children must be well behaved and controlled. Pets by arrangement. No smoking in the dining-room and some bedrooms. Car park.

OWNER Wendy Gallagher OPEN All year, exc winter hol
ROOMS 1 family (with bath/shower), 1 double (with bath/shower), 2 twin (with bath/shower), 1 single (with wash-basin) TERMS B&B £18.50–£24, (single occupancy of twin/double) £24–£38; dinner £9.50–£12.50; deposit

Wheatsheaf House

25 Gosport Street, Lymington SO41 9BG
LYMINGTON (0590) 679208

Wheatsheaf House is a Grade I listed building, originally an inn, built in about 1640. It is in the centre of Lymington, ideal for exploring this delightful old market town and for the Isle of Wight ferries. You enter the house from the street directly into the very unusual and lovely front room with a fireplace to each side, beams, brick pillars and a wooden floor. The house is warm and cosy and furnished very much as a family home, with ornaments and antique furniture. Upstairs there are four good-sized bedrooms, two of which overlook the front, which is on a fairly noisy street. Although the Cutmores have no objection to children staying, the house is really not suitable for small children. There is space for two cars in the courtyard. Pets by arrangement. No smoking.

OWNERS Jennifer and Peter Cutmore OPEN All year
ROOMS 2 double (1 with bath/shower, 1 with wash-basin), 2 twin (1 with bath/shower, 1 with wash-basin) TERMS B&B £18–£28, (family room) £16–£20 per person (children under 12 £2–£5)

LYMINSTER West Sussex map 2

Arundel Vineyard

Church Lane, Lyminster, nr Arundel BN17 7QF
ARUNDEL (0903) 883393

Arundel Vineyard is in the tiny hamlet of Lyminster, one and a quarter miles south of Arundel Castle. Nearby is the legendary Knuckerhole (a bottomless pool where folklore tells of a fearsome dragon being slain by St George). The accommodation is in a rather untidy-looking bungalow. However, the bedrooms are attractive and well equipped, each with its own shower and TV. The large entrance-cum-passageway has comfortable chairs and is where breakfast is served. Mrs Rankin is a good cook and lectures on cookery and farm tourism, but does not provide evening meals, although packed lunches can be provided. The winery is housed in Parkgate Barn – a local fifteenth-century Sussex barn that the present owners were able to save from demolition, carefully transport to its present position and rebuild. Conducted tours and tastings can be arranged for small parties. No children under four. Small pets only. No smoking in public areas. Car park.

OWNERS John and Valerie Rankin OPEN All year, exc Christmas ROOMS 1 family/twin, 1 twin; both rooms with bath/shower TERMS B&B £16–£18, (single occupancy of twin) £21–£24 (children under 10 £10); deposit £10

MAIDSTONE Kent map 3

Court Lodge Farm

The Street, Teston, Maidstone ME18 5AQ
MAIDSTONE (0622) 812570 Fax (0622) 814200

This sixteenth-century farmhouse stands in an elevated position at one end of the small village of Teston (four miles west of Maidstone off the A26), next to the church, with lovely views over the Medway Valley and fruit and hop fields. It is a particularly attractive place at apple-blossom time. Court Lodge Farm was once a meeting place for those campaigning for the abolition of slavery. Breakfast only is available, but there are many eating-places to be found nearby. There is a lovely garden in front of the house. No children under 10. No pets. Non-smokers preferred. Car park.

OWNER Mrs Rosemarie Bannock OPEN All year, exc Christmas and New Year ROOMS 1 double, 2 twin; all rooms with bath/shower TERMS B&B £14–£22.50, (single occupancy of twin/double) £22–£30; deposit

The description for each entry states when pets are not allowed or restricted in any way.

If a deposit is required for an advance booking this is stated at the end of an entry.

MARLBOROUGH Wiltshire map 2

Rosegarth

West Grafton, nr Marlborough SN8 4BY
MARLBOROUGH (0672) 810288

West Grafton is a tiny hamlet just off the A338 Hungerford–Salisbury road, about seven miles south-east of Marlborough. This thatched whitewashed cottage dating from 1580, with bright yellow trim, stands in three acres of garden with pleasant farmland views. Originally, the building was a terrace of four Crown servants' cottages, and was converted into one house about 40 years ago. The guests' accommodation is at one end of the house and consists of a large sitting-room with TV and breakfast area and, up a narrow, steep staircase, two bedrooms. There is a bathroom to go with each bedroom, but access is down the stairs through the sitting-room. Breakfast only is available, but packed lunches can be provided on request. The owners provide a taxi service to and from local pubs or restaurants for guests who have had enough driving for the day. Rosegarth is convenient for Marlborough, Stonehenge, Avebury, Wilton Windmill, Crofton Beam Engines, the Kennet and Avon canal, Savernake Forest and Lacock Abbey. Children welcome. No dogs. No smoking in bedrooms. Car park.

OWNERS Anne and Rick Ruddock-Brown OPEN All year, exc Christmas ROOMS 1 family, 1 twin; both rooms with bath/shower TERMS B&B £15.50, (single occupancy of twin) £22.50, (family room) £13.50 per person; deposit £10 per room

MAYFIELD East Sussex map 3

April Cottage Guesthouse and Tearoom

West Street, Mayfield TN20 6BA
MAYFIELD (0435) 872160

This charming sixteenth-century cottage in the picturesque village of Mayfield has oak beams taken from wrecked Armada ships, low-beamed ceilings and latticed windows. The ground floor is a charming tea-room with an open fire, and this is where breakfast is served. Snacks, including home-made cakes and fresh sandwiches, are available all day, and afternoon teas are available 3–5.30pm. There are two pubs close by that serve evening meals. The bedrooms are simply and very basically furnished; one is *en suite* and the other two share a bathroom and are normally let to family parties or friends only. Parking is in the nearby village car park. Children welcome. No smoking in the dining-room. Storage heaters in bedrooms. The house is locked up at 11.15pm.

OWNER Barbara Powner OPEN All year ROOMS 1 double (with shower), 1 twin, 1 single (with toilet and wash-basin) TERMS B&B £16

MELKSHAM Wiltshire map 2

Shurnhold House

Shurnhold, Melksham SN12 8DG
MELKSHAM (0225) 790555

This most attractive, listed, wistaria-covered Jacobean manor house stands in one and a half acres of pretty gardens. The house has been decorated and furnished imaginatively, in restful colours. In the course of conversion, whole rooms were converted into bathrooms, so both bedrooms and bathrooms are very large. All bedrooms have bathroom, telephone and TV and a couple have recently been converted on the top floor – smaller in size, but full of charm. What started out as the dining-room is now the bar: a small, cosy room, with flagstone floor. The attractive dining-room has individual tables, where breakfast only is served. Continental breakfast is included in the rate, and there is an extra charge for English breakfast. There is also a more formal sitting-room. The house is on the A365, only a mile from Melksham town centre, and still offers excellent value. Children welcome. Dogs by arrangement. Smoking only in lounge bar.
Car park.

OWNERS Sue and Chris Mead OPEN All year ROOMS 1 family, 2 four-poster, 3 double, 2 twin; all rooms with bath/shower
TERMS B&B £30–£34, (single occupancy of twin/double) £45–£48, (family room) £78–£80; deposit; Access, Visa

MERSHAM Kent map 3

The Corner House

Church Road, Mersham, nr Ashford TN25 6NS
ASHFORD (0233) 636117

The Corner House, built around 1920, is situated by the fourteenth-century church, on the edge of the village. It enjoys lovely views and has a very attractive front garden. The house is bright and light and is pleasantly furnished and decorated. The entrance to the house leads into a dining-room-cum-sitting-room with TV and views over the garden. The bedrooms are comfortable and are all on the ground floor. Dinner can be served by arrangement (7–7.30pm) and guests may bring their own wine as there is no alcohol licence. Vegetarians can be catered for and packed lunches provided. Children welcome. Dogs by arrangement. No smoking in bedrooms. Parking for two cars.

OWNER Mrs E. Hayes OPEN All year, exc Christmas
ROOMS 1 double, 1 twin/family, 1 single TERMS B&B £13–£15, (single occupancy of twin/double) by negotiation (babies free, children under 10 half-price); dinner £8; deposit

NETHER WALLOP Hampshire map 2

Broadgate Farm

Nether Wallop, Stockbridge SO20 8HA
ANDOVER (0264) 781439

This eighteenth-century farmhouse is thought to be built on the site of an earlier family home. The family name can be traced back through the village records to the sixteenth century and the farm continues to be a family enterprise, with the Osmonds' son looking after the sheep. It is a 300-acre dairy, arable and sheep farm, and the old farm buildings have been converted into housing with the dairy now situated about a mile away. There is a large walled garden to the rear of the house with a curious little brick-built summer-house at the bottom, complete with fireplace, built by the grandfather as his smoking-room. Breakfast only is served in the traditionally furnished family dining-room, and the comfortable sitting-room is decorated with oil paintings, dating from the last century, of the farm's prize pigs. There are three large, comfortable, attractively furnished bedrooms. The shared bathroom has had a good-pressure shower added above the bath. The house is immediately next to the village pub, and various food options can be found in Stockbridge, four miles away. Packed lunches can be provided. Children welcome. No dogs. Smoking only in the sitting-room. Car park.

OWNERS Richard and Susan Osmond OPEN All year
ROOMS 1 double, 2 twin; all rooms with wash-basin TERMS B&B £15–£17, (single occupancy of twin/double) £18–£20 (reductions for children under 8)

Most B&Bs offer tea/coffee-making facilities in the bedrooms.

NETTON Wiltshire map 2

The Old School House

Netton, nr Salisbury SP4 6AW
MIDDLE WOODFORD (072 273) 491

This 150-year-old house was the schoolhouse until 1977. It is a comfortable family home, with a small prettily decorated dining-room and three fresh, bright and clean bedrooms. It stands in a lovely valley, with a small garden to the rear which guests are welcome to enjoy, and this leads out on to fields with sheep. Breakfast only is available, but there are two country pubs within walking distance. Packed lunches can be provided. Fishing can be arranged and there is a golf course half a mile away. Children welcome. Car park.

OWNER Mrs K. L. Crossley OPEN All year, exc Christmas
ROOMS 1 double, 1 twin, 1 single (with wash-basin) TERMS B&B £16, (single occupancy of twin/double) £20 (children under 8 half-price)

NEWPORT Isle of Wight map 2

Salween House

7 Watergate Road, Newport PO30 1XN
ISLE OF WIGHT (0983) 523456

In a quiet part of Newport, yet only a 10-minute walk into town, stands this spacious Victorian house, with a most attractive back garden and, from the upstairs rooms, views to hills beyond the town. Guests have use of three attractively decorated and comfortable, large bedrooms, all with TV. The shared bathroom has a corner bath and separate shower. Downstairs there is a comfortable sitting-room; breakfast only is served in the beautifully decorated dining-room, which overlooks the garden. Mrs Corke has executed all the décor herself, and as a hobby makes lovely quilts. No children under 10. No pets. No smoking. Car park.

OWNER Mrs Carol Corke OPEN All year, exc Christmas
ROOMS 1 family, 2 twin; all rooms with wash-basin TERMS B&B £14–£16 (children 10–14 £12 sharing with parents); deposit £10

Most B&Bs don't accept credit cards, but when they do we list the cards taken.

NITON Isle of Wight map 2

Springvale Christian Guest House

St Catherine's Road, Niton PO38 2NE
ISLE OF WIGHT (0983) 730388

Springvale is a solidly built guesthouse on the clifftop, with pleasant sea views and half an acre of terraced gardens. Although advertised as being 'Christian', the Christian aspect is not overstressed. The Coopers, with three children of their own, are very pleased to welcome families, and many facilities for children are provided: toys and books inside and garden games, paddling pool and so on outside. The guesthouse provides fairly basic accommodation. The front rooms have sea views and are quite large. All bedrooms have TV. Good-value home-cooked evening meals are available at 7pm, including vegetarian choices, and children's meals can be served at 5pm if required. Springvale is unlicensed, but guests may bring their own wine to dinner. Drying and ironing facilities can also be provided. During July and August no bookings are taken for less than four nights. Children welcome. Dogs by arrangement. No smoking.

OWNERS Phil and Tina Cooper OPEN Easter–Oct ROOMS 2 family (with bath/shower), 2 double (with bath/shower), 2 single (with wash-basin) TERMS B&B £14–£16 (children under 5 free, 5–8 50% adult rate, 9–15 75% adult rate); D, B&B £20; deposit 10%

OTTERDEN Kent map 3

Frith Farm House

Otterden, nr Faversham ME13 0DD
EASTLING (079 589) 701 (from some time 1992: (0795) 890701)

A very attractive late-Georgian farmhouse that sits high on the North Downs in an area of outstanding beauty and is set in six acres of formal gardens and cherry orchard. The owners are an extremely pleasant couple who love music and singing. Markham's collection of china makes an incredible display in the dining-room, which, together with the drawing-room, is decorated in unusual dark colours with dark print curtains. The bedrooms, all with TV, are comfortable and well furnished and there is a conservatory/breakfast room. Susan enjoys cooking and prepares excellent home-cooked dinners by arrangement at

7.30pm, including vegetarian choices if necessary. There is no alcohol licence, but guests may bring their own wine. Packed lunches can be provided. Horse-riding and country drives by landau are available at the adjacent stables. Otterden is a tiny place between the A2 and A20 – make sure you ask for directions. No children under 12. No pets. No smoking in bedrooms. Car park.

OWNERS Markham and Susan Chesterfield OPEN All year
ROOMS 1 four-poster, 1 double, 1 twin; all rooms with bath/shower
TERMS B&B from £19.50, (four-poster) £24.50, (single occupancy of twin/double) from £25; dinner £15; deposit

PENSHURST Kent map 3

Swale Cottage

Old Swaylands Lane, off Poundsbridge Lane,
Penshurst TN11 8AH
PENSHURST (0892) 870738

Handy for Penshurst Place – the home of the Sidney family since 1552 – this listed eighteenth-century Kentish barn is in a peaceful location with wonderful views overlooking the beautiful Weald of Kent countryside. Well converted, with all modern comforts, it remains a house of great character, with oak beams, inglenook fireplace and latticed windows. The atmosphere here is one of peace and tranquillity. Cynthia Dakin is an artist and there is an interesting display of her paintings throughout the house. There are three attractive bedrooms, each with *en suite* bathroom and TV. One has a four-poster, another a pretty Victorian bed and the third has canopied beds. There is also an elegant sitting-room with TV. Breakfast only is served, but there are lots of tea-shops and local inns close by. Swale Cottage is a little tricky to find, so be sure to ask for a brochure with driving directions when booking. No children under 10. No pets. No smoking. Car park.

OWNER Mrs Cynthia Dakin OPEN All year, exc Christmas
ROOMS 1 four-poster, 1 double, 1 twin; all rooms with bath/shower
TERMS B&B £20–£22.50, (single occupancy) £26–£28; deposit

Breakfast at B&Bs tends to mean a cooked breakfast of bacon, eggs and so on. If you prefer a different style of breakfast, discuss this when you make the booking.

Bath/shower in the details under each entry means that the rooms have private facilities.

PETHAM Kent map 3

Upper Ansdore

Upper Ansdore, Petham, nr Canterbury CT4 5QB
PETHAM (0227) 700672

The farmhouse dates from the fourteenth century and once belonged to Sir William Cockaine, Lord Mayor of London in 1619. It sits high up a hillside with spectacular views and is in remote, peaceful countryside just six miles south of Canterbury. There are beamed ceilings, Tudor fireplaces and thick stone walls. An extension has recently been added to the house, so there are now four bedrooms with tiny bathrooms and a separate entrance for guests. One room can be used as a family room. Breakfast only is provided in the farmhouse dining-room/sitting-room, which has a magnificent fireplace. There are three local pubs within two and a half miles offering traditional meals. Children welcome. No pets. No smoking in some areas. Car park.

OWNERS Roger and Susan Lynch OPEN Feb–Nov ROOMS 3 double, 1 twin; all rooms with bath/shower TERMS B&B £16–£18, (single occupancy of twin/double) £24–£28 (children under 5 half-price); deposit

PORTSMOUTH Hampshire map 2

Fortitude Cottage

51 Broad Street, Old Portsmouth PO1 2JD
PORTSMOUTH (0705) 823748

This is a delightful place, in terms of both the friendliness of the welcome and the location, which is right at the very end of Old Portsmouth – much further and you would be in the sea. The house is almost surrounded by water, with views over the harbour to the Isle of Wight and of the ferries coming and going between the mainland and the island. It is also opposite the waterbus for HMS *Victory* and the *Mary Rose*. Mrs Harbeck has lived in the cottage almost all her life. Her parents bought the land and a house at the back at the end of the Second World War. They built the cottage, a tiny narrow brick-built house with bow windows, in keeping with the surrounding architecture. The rooms, all with TV, have recently been redecorated. They are tiny, but very prettily decorated and are warm and cosy. Breakfast only is served at one end of the owner's sitting-room. For other meals there are any number of eating-places nearby. Mrs Harbeck's mother, who lives in the house at the back of the cottage, which can be reached through a pretty courtyard, also does B&B. She has two double rooms, each with wonderful sea views. Mrs Harbeck ensures that her high standards are maintained, with constant updating and redecoration. Children welcome. No pets. No smoking in the breakfast room.

OWNER Mrs Carol A. Harbeck OPEN All year, exc 25 and 26 Dec ROOMS 1 double (with wash-basin), 2 twin (1 with bath/shower, 1 with wash-basin) TERMS B&B £15–£17, (single occupancy of twin/double) £27–£29

REDLYNCH Wiltshire map 2

Templeman's Old Farmhouse

Redlynch, nr Salisbury SP5 2JS
DOWNTON (0725) 20331

This seventeenth-century farmhouse with spacious Victorian additions was part of the Trafalgar Estate, which was presented to Lord Nelson's family by a grateful nation. It stands in a secluded hilltop position with panoramic views over the New Forest. There are 10 acres of gardens, paddocks with a flock of sheep, and a hard tennis court that guests can use. Guests have use also of the elegant drawing-room with TV and the dining-room, where breakfast only is served. The three bedrooms are very large, even the single room, and the twin has lovely New Forest views. The house has a most pleasant family-home atmosphere. Ask for a brochure, as this gives a map of how to find the house. No dogs. No smoking in the dining-room or bedrooms. Car park.

OWNERS June and Peter Dabell OPEN Apr–Oct ROOMS 1 double, 1 twin, 1 single; all rooms with wash-basin TERMS B&B £16–£20 (children under 12 £10); deposit

RINGWOOD Hampshire map 2

Moortown Lodge Hotel and Restaurant

244 Christchurch Road, Ringwood BH24 3AS
RINGWOOD (0425) 471404

This Georgian house lies just off the B3347 about a mile and a half from the town centre and on the edge of the New Forest. Formerly a fishing-lodge, it is part of the Moortownhouse estate, once owned by William Gladstone. The emphasis here is on the food, and it is preferred that guests take dinner (7–8.30pm) if they stay the night. Mrs Burrows-Jones is responsible for the high standard of cooking and presentation of meals using fresh local produce. Dishes may include tomato and mozzarella salad, deep-fried chicken and Gruyère pancake, pork in a plum sauce and salmon with watercress. A vegetarian choice is available on request and packed lunches can be provided. The bedrooms, all with TV and telephone, are small but prettily decorated, and all have bathrooms *en suite*, except for the single, which has sole use of a shower and toilet next door. Residents have the use of a lounge and a licensed bar. There is fishing available on the River Avon, and the area offers good walks, golf and horse-riding. Wednesday is market day. Children welcome. No pets. No smoking in the dining-room. Car park.

OWNERS Mr and Mrs Burrows-Jones OPEN All year, exc 24 Dec–14 Jan ROOMS 1 family, 2 double, 2 twin, 1 single; all rooms, exc single, with bath/shower TERMS B&B £26–£30, (single) £29, (single occupancy of twin/double) £40 (children £5–£15 sharing with 2 adults); dinner £12.50; deposit; Access, Visa

ROCKBOURNE Hampshire map 2

Shearings

Rockbourne, nr Fordingbridge SP6 3NA
ROCKBOURNE (072 53) 256

This delightful sixteenth-century listed thatched cottage facing a stream is in the pretty village of Rockbourne, which has a Roman villa, picturesque old pub and twelfth-century church. It is set in a lovely, well-maintained garden of lawns and shrubs with a sunny patio and summer-house, and has been featured many times on the front of magazines and calendars. There is also a croquet lawn. The house is full of olde worlde charm: uneven floors, oak beams and inglenook fireplaces. Guests are treated as friends and a house-party atmosphere prevails. Dinner is available by arrangement (8–8.15pm with aperitifs at 7.30pm) and guests are usually joined by Brigadier and Mrs Watts. Guests are welcome to bring their own wine, but a half-bottle of wine per person is included in the £18 price. A typical menu may include iced cucumber soup, chicken in a honey and curry sauce and summer pudding with cream. Vegetarian choices can be provided by arrangement as can packed lunches. There is a small sitting-

Most B&Bs offer tea/coffee-making facilities in the bedrooms.

room with TV for guests to use, with books and brochures. No children under 12. No pets. No smoking in bedrooms. Car park.

OWNERS Brigadier and Mrs A. C. D. Watts OPEN mid-Feb–mid-Dec
ROOMS 1 double, 1 twin, 1 single; all rooms with bath/shower
TERMS B&B £20–£24, (single occupancy of twin/double) £27; dinner £12.50–£18

ROGATE West Sussex map 2

Cumbers House

Rogate, nr Petersfield GU31 5EJ
ROGATE (0730) 821401

This brick-built 1930s home is situated down a quiet driveway off the main A272 road, with pleasant views over open countryside and surrounded by three and a half acres of woodland garden. The house is furnished with antiques and there are open fires in both the drawing-room and dining-room. The latter has recently been done up with dark green walls and curtains with a pretty floral design. There is a friendly, relaxed atmosphere and, on the culinary side, Mrs Aslett offers home-baked bread and home-produced vegetables, eggs and honey. Breakfast only is available. The postal address puts Cumbers House in Hampshire, but it is actually just in West Sussex. No children. No pets. Non-smokers preferred. Car park.

OWNERS Major and Mrs Jon Aslett OPEN All year, exc Christmas and Jan ROOMS 2 twin (1 with bath/shower, 1 with wash-basin)
TERMS B&B £17–£22

Mizzards Farm

Rogate, nr Petersfield GU31 5HS
ROGATE (0730) 821656

Mizzards Farm is in peaceful countryside on the edge of the delightful village of Rogate. It is a lovely seventeenth-century farmhouse, a mellow brick and stone building of character in 13 acres of pleasant gardens and fields, with the River Rother flowing through it all. There is also an outdoor swimming-pool. A previous owner was a pop star, and one of the surprises of the house is the main bedroom – a huge room with an impressive bed raised on a hexagonal platform. Leading off it is an ornate marble bathroom full of mirrors. One of the most magnificent rooms is the dining-room at the centre of the house with large stone fireplace, lovely old furniture and interesting pictures. The house has ancient flagstone floors and a beautiful wooden staircase leading to a galleried landing. The drawing-room has been completely redecorated and is a large, elegant room furnished with antiques. All bedrooms have TV. Breakfast only is available, including home-made jams and honey. Guests may have a Continental breakfast in their rooms if they prefer. Mrs Francis continues her extremely high standard of hospitality and comfort, continuously updating and adding little touches here and there. No children under six. No pets in the house. No smoking. Car park.

OWNERS Mr and Mrs J. C. Francis OPEN All year, exc Christmas
ROOMS 1 four-poster, 2 twin; all rooms with bath/shower
TERMS B&B £19–£23, (single occupancy of twin) £26–£32

RYARSH Kent map 3

Heavers Farm

Ryarsh, West Malling ME19 5JU
WEST MALLING (0732) 842074

Heavers stands at the top of the hill on a narrow country lane which leads up from the tiny village of Ryarsh. The seventeenth-century house is typical of a smallholding of the area, with small rooms and low ceilings, and is compact and comfortable. The smallholding supports sheep, geese, chickens and bees. Home-cooked evening meals using home-grown produce can be served by arrangement at 7.30–8.30pm and can include vegetarian choices. There is no alcohol licence, but guests may bring their own wine. Packed lunches can be provided. Guests are treated as members of the family and may enjoy all the facilities of the house. Jean will collect guests from the station at West Malling with advance notice, and there are some who arrive on foot, for the house is just off the North Downs Way. Children welcome. No pets in bedrooms. No smoking. Car park.

OWNERS Jean and James Edwards OPEN All year, exc Christmas
ROOMS 1 double, 1 twin, 1 twin/family; all rooms with wash-basin
TERMS B&B £15–£17, (single occupancy of twin/double) £20 (reductions for children under 10 sharing parents' room); dinner £7–£13; deposit £10 per person

The description for each entry states when pets are not allowed. Where no details are given, you can assume that pets are allowed. It's always best to check first in any case.

RYE East Sussex map 3

Cliff Farm

Iden Lock, nr Rye TN31 7QD
IDEN (0797) 280331

This typical Sussex tiled farmhouse, about 150 years old, has extensive views over Romney Marsh and the River Rother, which flows in front of the house. It is built against a cliff, up to which the sea used to come. Now sheep graze on the cliff above the house. Guests have use of the patio in the front garden, which enjoys the lovely views. There is a small sitting-room with TV and a dining-room where breakfast only is served. Packed lunches can be provided. The bedrooms are small and neat. Iden Lock is two miles east of Rye. Children welcome. Car park.

OWNER Mrs Pat Sullivan OPEN Mar–Oct ROOMS 1 family, 1 double, 1 twin; all rooms with wash-basin TERMS B&B £12.50–£13.50 (children half-price sharing)

Half House

Military Road, Rye TN31 7NY
RYE (0797) 223404

This turn-of-the-century house is just off one of the main roads into Rye, and a 10-minute walk from the centre. The bedrooms are not large, but are bright and prettily decorated, and all have TV. Home-cooked breakfasts are served in the breakfast room. There are no evening meals. Bikes are available for guests' use. Children welcome. No pets. Easy parking.

OWNERS Norman and Agnes Bennett OPEN All year, exc Christmas ROOMS 1 double (with wash-basin), 2 twin/double (1 with bath/shower, 1 with wash-basin) TERMS B&B £15–£17, (single occupancy of twin/double) £15–£34; deposit; Access, Visa

Jeake's House

Mermaid Street, Rye TN31 7ET
RYE (0797) 222828 Fax (0797) 222623

This listed building on one of Britain's most loved streets was originally built in 1689 as a storehouse by a Samuel Jeake; it was later used as a Baptist school. In 1924 the house became the home of the American author Conrad Aiken whose visitors included

writers and artists such as T. S. Eliot, E. F. Benson, Edward Burra, Paul Nash and Radclyffe Hall. It abounds with period features, oak beams, wood panelling and antique furnishings. Jenny Hadfield is an extremely friendly and professional lady, and runs a superb establishment. She has done all the decorating herself with great taste, resulting in a charming house of great character. The beautifully appointed bedrooms, all with TV and telephone, look over the rooftops of the town or across the marsh to the sea. Breakfast only is served in the eighteenth-century dining-room, which was once used as a Quaker meeting-place. All the food is freshly made using local produce, and includes home-made preserves. There is car parking at the bottom of the street. As the approach to Jeake's House is up a steep street, with steep stairs in the house, it is not suitable for the disabled or infirm. Children welcome. No pets or smoking in the dining-room.

OWNERS F. and J. Hadfield OPEN All year ROOMS 3 family, 2 four-poster, 5 double, 1 twin, 1 single; all rooms, exc 1 double and single (wash-basin only), with bath/shower TERMS B&B £18–£25, (single occupation of twin/double) £32–£44, (family room) £63 (children half-price sharing with 2 adults); deposit £20 per room; Access, Amex, Visa

The Old Vicarage Guest House

66 Church Square, Rye TN31 7HF
RYE (0797) 222119

This pink, mainly Georgian, residence is in a delightful setting by the ancient church of St Mary's, overlooking quiet Church Square. It has exposed beams and small, prettily decorated and well-appointed bedrooms, all with TV. These rooms have views mostly over the medieval roofs of Rye and across the churchyard to the sea. The small sitting-room and large dining-room overlook the pretty walled garden. Breakfast includes freshly ground coffee, specially selected teas and freshly baked scones. Rye has a wealth of restaurants and pubs for other meals. The prices include complimentary newspapers and sherry. There is a discount of 15 per cent for stays of three nights or more from November to March. No children under 10. No pets. No smoking in the dining-room or bedrooms.

OWNERS Julia and Paul Masters OPEN All year, exc Christmas ROOMS 2 four-poster (with bath/shower), 3 double (coronet with bath/shower, 2 with wash-basin), 1 twin (with bath/shower) TERMS B&B £17.50–£25, (single occupancy of twin/double) £26–£45; deposit £25

Playden Cottage Guesthouse

Military Road, Rye TN31 7NY
RYE (0797) 222234

An attractive whitewashed house arranged around a lovely garden, built into the side of the cliff and overlooking the River Rother and Romney Marsh. The area of Playden is on the edge of Rye and is a Domesday village. The bedrooms are spacious, all with private bathroom/shower, fresh fruit and lovely views and are individually named 'Hornbeam', 'Wysteria' and 'Badger'. The long sitting-room has books, games, writing paper and TV for guests to use and the writing-room leads out on to a small patio in a secluded part of the garden. Playden Cottage is said to be the origin of the house Grebe in E. F. Benson's Mapp and Lucia novels. Breakfast only is available although supper trays and packed lunches can be provided by arrangement. This is a

B&B rates specified in the details for each entry are per person per night; unless the details state otherwise, they are based on two people sharing a double or twin-bedded room.

relaxing, friendly house in a peaceful spot away from the crowds of Rye. No children under 12. No pets. Car park.

OWNER Mrs Sheelagh Fox OPEN All year ROOMS 1 double, 2 twin; all rooms with bath/shower TERMS B&B £20–£25, (single occupancy of twin/double) £30–£50 (children half-price by arrangement); supper £7.50; deposit £20, single night surcharge £3; Access, Visa

SALISBURY Wiltshire map 2

Hayburn Wyke Guest House

72 Castle Road, Salisbury SP1 3RL
SALISBURY (0722) 412627

The name was given to the house by its builder, who honeymooned in Hayburn Wyke, Scotland. Conveniently located for the centre of Salisbury, this turn-of-the-century guesthouse lies just off the main road to Amesbury. It offers simple, very clean accommodation. The bedrooms, all with TV, are a bit on the small side, but are bright and freshly decorated. Two rooms are up a narrow staircase on the second floor and the two *en suite* rooms have a very small bathroom/shower-room. Breakfast only is served in the dining-room, which also has TV. Children welcome. Guide dogs only. No smoking in the dining-room. Car park.

OWNERS Alan and Dawn Curnow OPEN All year ROOMS 2 family (1 with bath/shower, 1 with wash-basin), 3 double (1 with bath/shower, 2 with wash-basin), 1 twin (with wash-basin) TERMS B&B £15–£18.50, (single occupancy of twin/double) £20–£22 (children 2–5 £7, 5–11 £10 sharing parents' room)

Little Langford Farmhouse

Little Langford, nr Salisbury SP3 4NR
SALISBURY (0722) 790205

The farm is set in a quiet, peaceful valley (except for a main-line railway which runs close by and disturbs the peace for a few seconds every now and again). Just eight miles from Salisbury, it enjoys lovely views of the Wiltshire Downs. It is a most unusual house, part of the Earl of Pembroke's estate, built in 1858 in the Gothic style, complete with tower. Mr Helyer's family have been tenant farmers for more than 50 years, farming 650 acres of arable and dairy land. Families are welcome here and guests are free to walk around the farm and watch cows being milked or calves fed. There are three large, attractive bedrooms, comfortably furnished, and although only one has a wash-basin there are two bathrooms for guests' use. The double room has a Victorian brass bed and can form a family room with an adjoining small room with bunk beds. There is a large, pleasant lounge and a dining-room with one big table, where breakfast only is served. Guests also have use of a games-room with billiard table. Children welcome. Well-behaved dogs only. Smoking in the lounge only. Car park. Little Langford is two miles from the A36 Salisbury–Bath road, on a parallel country road, between Great Wishford and Hanging Langford.

OWNER Mrs Patricia Helyer OPEN All year, exc Christmas ROOMS 1 double/family, 2 twin (1 with wash-basin) TERMS B&B £16–£17.50, (single occupancy of twin/double) £20–£22, (family room) from £48 (children under 12 half-price); deposit

The Old Bakery

35 Bedwin Street, Salisbury SP1 3UT
SALISBURY (0722) 320100

This charming B&B is right in the centre of Salisbury on a busy street, but with double glazing the noise is minimal. A bakery until 1971, it is a sixteenth-century listed building with a double bow-windowed front. There is reputedly a ghost: a Victorian boy who perished when his brother mistakenly lit the oven while he was inside cleaning it. Guests have use of a large, homely TV lounge-cum-breakfast room and there are three small and quite simple bedrooms, all with TV, up narrow staircases and under low beams. Breakfast only is available. No children under 10. No pets. No smoking in the breakfast room.

OWNERS Peter and Evelyn Bunce OPEN All year (room only at Christmas) ROOMS 1 double (with bath/shower), 1 twin (with bath/shower), 1 single (with wash-basin) TERMS B&B £15–£20, (single occupancy of twin/double) £20–£24; deposit 10%

SCAYNES HILL West Sussex map 3

Old Cudwell's Barn

Lewes Road, Scaynes Hill, nr Haywards Heath RH17 7NA
SCAYNES HILL (0444) 831406

This is part of a seventeenth-century house divided into four and set around an attractive courtyard. When the Pontifexes moved here they lived in what was a small cottage, and over the years they have gradually done up the barn. Mr Pontifex, who is a self-employed environmental consultant, has done most of the work himself. Guests have use of one end of the house, which includes a small sitting-room/dining-room with views over the sizeable garden. Upstairs there is a comfortable large double with garden views and a pleasant twin, with a bathroom between them. The accommodation is let to only one party at a time. Mrs Pontifex enjoys cooking and will prepare light evening meals or more elaborate dinners with prior notice. Vegetarians can be catered for, and although there is no alcohol licence, wine is included in the dinner price. Packed lunches can be provided. The owners do not like people turning up on spec. Children welcome. No pets. No smoking in bedrooms. Car park.

OWNERS Roy and Carol Pontifex OPEN All year ROOMS 1 double, 1 twin; both rooms with wash-basin TERMS B&B £19, (single occupancy of twin/double) £22–£26 (young child in parents' room £10); dinner £17.50 (light supper from £6.95); deposit

SHALFLEET Isle of Wight map 2

Shalfleet House

Shalfleet, Newport PO30 4NS
ISLE OF WIGHT (0983) 78280

A substantial Victorian house, built as the vicarage, Shalfleet House stands in extensive gardens, including a hard tennis court, a little outside the village and secluded from the road by trees. It is a comfortable family home with charming owners who have been doing B&B for some years. The bedrooms are large and well furnished. The dining-room has recently been redecorated, including the addition of an attractive Victorian fireplace. This is where breakfast only is served, at one large table. Packed lunches can be provided. Stairs lead from the ground-floor bedroom with its separate entrance to a sitting-room/kitchen. This can also be let separately as a self-catering unit. The house overlooks the Newtown Estuary Nature Reserve and Bird Sanctuary. Children welcome. Dogs only in the ground-floor room. Partial central heating. Car park.

OWNERS Lt. Col. and Mrs J. R. E. Laird OPEN All year, exc Christmas, New Year and Easter ROOMS 1 double, 2 twin (1 with bath/shower, 1 with wash-basin) TERMS B&B £15–£17, (single occupancy of twin/double) £20–£25 (children under 3 free, 3–10 £7, over 10 by arrangement); deposit by arrangement

SHANKLIN Isle of Wight map 2

Cavendish House

8 Eastmount Road, Shanklin PO37 6DN
ISLE OF WIGHT (0983) 862460

This is a substantial Victorian house in a quiet road, close to the centre, cliff path and beach. Guests have a choice of three large and most attractive bedrooms, all with private bathroom, TV, telephone and dining area. English breakfast is ordered in advance and served in the rooms 8.30–10am. Although there is no sitting-room for guests, a small conservatory is available, as is a large back garden with lawns and shrubs. Cavendish House represents excellent value. No children under 12. Pets by arrangement. Car park.

OWNERS Mr and Mrs Cavaciuti OPEN All year, exc Christmas and 2 weeks Feb ROOMS 3 double (with bath/shower) TERMS B&B £15–£18, (single occupancy of double) £17.50–£22; deposit £10; Access, Visa

SHEERNESS Kent map 3

Kingsferry Guest House

247 Queenborough Road, Halfway, Sheerness ME12 3EW
SHEERNESS (0795) 663606

Kingsferry is a family-owned guesthouse, offering very basic, simple accommodation. It is a detached 1950s house overlooking Sheppey Marshes and school playing fields on the A249, close to the sea and convenient for the ferry and railway. The rooms are comfortable and all have TV. Breakfast only is served, and there are pubs and restaurants nearby for other meals. Children welcome. No pets. No smoking in eating areas. Car park.

OWNERS Tina and Rob Smith OPEN All year ROOMS 2 family, 3 twin, 2 single TERMS B&B £15, (family room) £35 (children 5 and under £5); deposit £5

It is always best to book a room in advance, especially in winter. B&Bs with few rooms may close at short notice for periods not specified in the details.

We state at the end of an entry when children are welcome. If we know of any restrictions, we give them.

SHIPTON BELLINGER Hampshire map 2

Parsonage Farm

Shipton Bellinger, Tidworth SP9 7UF
STONEHENGE (0980) 42404

You will find this brick and flint building opposite the church, in the centre of a quiet village on the edge of Salisbury Plain. The oldest part dates from the sixteenth century and is now the dining-room, a lovely room with a beamed ceiling and an enormous dining table. Parsonage Farm is very much a family home; guests are treated like friends and have use of a large sitting-room and the lovely walled garden, where there are tables and chairs for sitting out on warm days. Picnic lunches and evening meals with the family are available by arrangement and there is also food to be had in the village pubs. Guests may bring their own wine to dinner as there is no alcohol licence. Packed lunches can be provided. This is a wonderful area for walking and riding (the owners keep horses), with access right on to Salisbury Plain. Not suitable for infants or young children. No pets. No smoking. Car park.

OWNERS Col. and Mrs J. B. R. Peecock OPEN All year, exc Christmas and New Year ROOMS 1 family (with bath/shower), 2 twin (with wash-basin) TERMS B&B £12, (single occupancy of twin) £15, (family room) from £35; dinner from £5; deposit £10 per room per night

SMARDEN Kent map 3

Munk's Farm

Smarden TN27 8PN
SMARDEN (023 377) 265

Two miles east of Headcorn, on the Headcorn–Smarden road, you will find this listed seventeenth-century oak-beamed and weatherboarded farmhouse, bordering the road and with an extensive garden to the rear and side of the house and a swimming-pool. The old village gaol, which has an interesting history and is also listed, stands in the grounds. The house is full of character and olde worlde charm, including inglenook fireplaces. The rooms are attractively decorated and are of a good size; all have private bathroom. There is a pleasant and comfortable lounge and evening meals (7.30pm) can be arranged in advance for Friday and Saturday evenings only. There is no alcohol licence, but guests may bring their own wine. Vegetarians can be catered for. Children welcome. No pets. Smoking in the lounge only. Car park.

OWNERS Ian and Josephine Scott OPEN All year, exc Christmas ROOMS 2 twin (with bath/shower) TERMS B&B £16–£18, (single occupancy of twin) £19–£21 (children under 2 free); dinner £12; deposit

SOUTHBOROUGH Kent map 3

10 Modest Corner

10 Modest Corner, Southborough, Tunbridge Wells TN4 OLS
TUNBRIDGE WELLS (0892) 22450

Only half a mile from the main road, this small, brick-built terraced house seems miles from anywhere. It is in a quiet cul-de-sac with lovely wooded views to front and rear. It is alleged that Queen Victoria's servants stayed out here while she visited Tunbridge Wells. There are two simply furnished twin-bedded rooms, with TV, on the ground floor and the shared bathroom has a powerful shower. There are small patios at the front and back of the house with tables and chairs for sitting out, and on fine days breakfast can be served on the back patio. Otherwise, breakfast is taken at the kitchen table. Evening meals are available on request at 8pm and vegetarians can be catered for. There is no alcohol licence, but guests may bring their own wine. Packed lunches can be provided. Anneke Reinders is a friendly and helpful Dutch lady, who also has a picture-framing studio on the ground floor. Children welcome. Pets only in bedrooms. Parking for two cars.

OWNER Anneke C. Reinders OPEN All year ROOMS 1 family (with bath/shower), 2 twin TERMS B&B £16–£19, (family room) £45–£57 (reductions for children under 10)

SOUTHSEA Hampshire map 2

The Ashburton Hotel

25 Ashburton Road, Southsea, Portsmouth PO5 3JS
PORTSMOUTH (0705) 871187 Fax (0705) 871177

A small hotel that is located on a quiet road in central Southsea a few minutes' walk from the sea. New owners took over the property in June 1990 and have carried out a total renovation, creating a superb small hotel. The bedrooms are of quite a good size and are decorated in restful greys and pastels. Each room has a bathroom, fruit basket, direct-dial telephone, trouser press and

TV. The dining-room, where a buffet-style breakfast is served, is clean and crisp and there is a sitting-room in the basement. Lunches and evening meals (from 7pm) are available and can include vegetarian choices. An alcohol licence has been applied for, but in the meantime guests may bring their own wine. A fax machine is also available for guests. Children welcome. No pets. No smoking in the restaurant and some bedrooms. Car park.

OWNERS John R. and Margaret E. Basham OPEN All year ROOMS 3 family/twin, 2 double, 2 single; all rooms with bath/shower TERMS B&B £17.50–£19.50, (single) £24–£29, (single occupancy of twin/double) £35–£39, (family room) £38–£60 (children free sharing adults' room); dinner £7; Access, Visa

STONE-IN-OXNEY Kent map 3

The Old Post House

Stone-in-Oxney, Tenterden TN30 7JN
APPLEDORE (023 383) 258

The Old Post House, built in 1772, overlooks the historic expanse of Romney Marsh and the Military Canal built to help keep out Napoleon. What was once the post office is now a most attractive large lounge/dining-room, lined with bookshelves. The bedrooms, all with TV, are small, but bright, light and cheerful, with a good ratio of bathrooms to bedrooms. Breakfast only is served, but there are a couple of pubs offering food in the village, and the market towns of Rye and Tenterden are just a 10-minute drive away. Packed lunches can be provided. No children under eight. No pets in the house. Car park.

OWNER Mrs M. R. O'Connor OPEN All year ROOMS 2 double (1 with bath/shower, 1 with wash-basin), 1 twin (with wash-basin) TERMS B&B £16–£19

TROTTON West Sussex map 2

Trotton Farm

Trotton, Rogate, nr Petersfield GU31 5EN
MIDHURST (0730) 813618

The farmhouse stands in pleasant countryside in the tiny hamlet of Trotton just off the A272 west of Midhurst. Guests stay in an old converted barn which adjoins the house. There are two small, comfortable bedrooms with exposed beams and private bathrooms. On the ground floor is a large games-room/lounge with table tennis table, TV and french windows which lead out on to a patio with lovely views of fields and farmland. Breakfast only is available and is taken in the dining-room of the farmhouse. There are plenty of pubs nearby for evening meals. Children welcome. Guide dogs only. No smoking. Car park.

OWNER Mrs G. W. Baigent OPEN All year ROOMS 2 twin (with bath/shower) TERMS B&B £17.50, (single occupancy of twin) from £25; deposit

TUNBRIDGE WELLS Kent map 3

Town House

64 Dudley Road, Tunbridge Wells TN1 1LF
TUNBRIDGE WELLS (0892) 35130/35100

The Town House is on a quiet street right in the centre of town and within walking distance of all the main attractions of Tunbridge Wells. It dates from 1820 and has a most appealing black and white Elizabethan-style façade. It is a friendly and relaxed house, furnished with antiques. The bedroom, with TV, is clean, fresh and attractively decorated. The house is approached through the small, walled, colourful and well-kept front garden. Street parking is available at night; in the daytime cars have to be left in the public car park, five minutes from the house. Breakfast only is available. Children and pets restricted.

OWNER Mrs R. Wotton OPEN All year, exc Christmas and New Year ROOMS 1 double (with bath/shower) TERMS B&B £19, (single occupancy of double) £33; deposit £10 per night

WEALD Kent map 3

Pond Cottage

Eggpie Lane, Weald, nr Sevenoaks TN14 6NP
SEVENOAKS (0732) 463773

Pond Cottage was built in 1580 and has seventeenth- and early twentieth-century additions. It is surrounded by three and a half acres of land, including a large pond full of fish. There is also a tennis court which guests are welcome to use. There are oak beams, old quarry-tiled floors and a huge inglenook fireplace. The dining-room has a sitting area beside the fireplace, and the sitting-room with TV leads out on to a sunken garden. Afternoon tea is served to guests on arrival and breakfast only is available. Packed lunches can be provided. There are several good pubs and restaurants nearby. Children welcome. Pets by arrangement. No smoking. Car park.

OWNER Amanda Webb OPEN All year, exc Christmas
ROOMS 1 family (with bath/shower), 1 single TERMS B&B £22 (first night)/£20 (subsequent nights), (single) £28 (fight night)/£27 (subsequent nights) (children under 12 half-price); deposit

WEST CHILTINGTON West Sussex map 3

New House Farm

Broadford Bridge Road, West Chiltington,
nr Pulborough RH20 2LA
WEST CHILTINGTON (0798) 812215

This is a delightful fifteenth-century farmhouse, right in the centre of the village of West Chiltington. Mr Steele is now retired from farming, although they still keep 50 acres with a few sheep. The house is immaculately kept, decorated in white with black woodwork inside, and has a most pleasant atmosphere. There is an attractive dining-room/sitting area with open fire, where breakfast is served, and a separate sitting-room that guests may use in summer. The bedrooms, all with TV and bathroom, are comfortably furnished; there is one exceptionally large room, and the tiny double room in the garden annexe is particularly popular with those who cannot cope with stairs. No children under 10. No pets. No smoking in bedrooms. Car park.

OWNER Mrs A. M. Steele OPEN Jan–Nov ROOMS 1 double, 2 double/twin; all rooms with bath/shower TERMS B&B about £18–£22, (single occupancy of twin/double) £25–£35 (children over 10 half-price sharing with parents); deposit

WESTERHAM Kent map 3

Corner Cottage

Toys Hill, Westerham TN16 1PY
IDE HILL (073 275) 362

Toys Hill is a village two miles south-east of Westerham and this delightful, picturesque fifteenth-century cottage is at the top of the hill with magnificent views over the Weald of Kent. It is a long, low building with terraces and lawns facing the views. Full of beams and antiques, including an old green mangle in the entrance hall, Corner Cottage offers one spacious bedroom, with a brass bed and TV; the room is situated on top of the garage block, giving complete privacy. Mrs Olszowska is a charming lady, and with just one guest room is able to offer individual attention to her guests. She is not able to accommodate single guests. Breakfast only is available. Children welcome. No dogs or cats. No smoking in bedrooms. Car park.

OWNER Mrs K. Olszowska OPEN All year ROOMS 1 family (with bath/shower) TERMS B&B £17.50 (children under 12 £8.50); deposit £10

WESTGATE-ON-SEA Kent map 3

White Lodge Guest House

12 Domneva Road, Westgate-on-Sea CT8 8PE
THANET (0843) 31828

This turn-of-the-century gabled house, in a quiet road just 500 yards from Westgate Bay, where the lovely golden sands stretch for miles, is a pleasant stroll from the town and railway station. There is a large TV lounge and an attractive dining-room with small bar and sitting area, and french windows leading out on to the garden. All bedrooms have TV and sea views. Lunches and evening meals are available 6–7pm and vegetarians can be catered for. Packed lunches can also be provided. Children welcome. Smoking in the bar and lounge only. Parking for three cars.

OWNERS Tony and Eve Cutler OPEN All year ROOMS 2 family (with bath/shower), 3 double (with bath/shower), 1 twin (with wash-basin), 1 single (with wash-basin) TERMS B&B £16.50–£22, (family room) £48–£55 (baby in cot free, second child under 5 in family room free); dinner £7; deposit £20 per room

WEST MALLING Kent map 3

Scott House

High Street, West Malling ME19 6QH
WEST MALLING (0732) 841380/870025

West Malling is a small, historically interesting town, with an eleventh-century abbey and Georgian high street, on which this handsome, listed town house is located. The Smiths run an antique business, and the entrance to the house is through the shop. Scott House is beautifully furnished and has been decorated with simplicity and great taste. There is a very comfortable, enormous drawing-room with TV and five very well-appointed bedrooms are available, all with private bathroom, TV and clock/radio-alarms. Breakfast only is served and includes a newspaper. There is a good selection of restaurants and inns to choose from in the town. No children. No pets. No smoking.

OWNERS Margaret and Ernest Smith OPEN All year, exc Christmas ROOMS 2 double, 2 twin; all rooms with bath/shower TERMS B&B £25, (single occupancy of twin/double) £39; deposit 20%; Access, Carte Blanche, Visa

WINCHELSEA East Sussex map 3

The Strand House

Winchelsea TN36 4JT
RYE (0797) 226276

At the foot of the cliff of Winchelsea, this old house enjoys lovely views towards Rye. It is just off the main A259 road and a steep climb brings you to the most attractive town of Winchelsea, a Cinque Port, but far less visited than neighbouring Rye. The house dates from the fourteenth century and is one of the oldest in the area. Almost every bedroom has low ceilings, so those who are six feet or over would have a hard time standing up straight. The bedrooms, all with TV and bathroom, are comfortably furnished. The house still has many of the traditional features including inglenook fireplaces and beams. There is a large breakfast room and a pleasant lounge leading out on to the garden. At the back of the house some fifteenth-century cottages have been converted to provide more bedrooms. No children under seven. Pets by arrangement. Car park.

OWNERS Jeremy and Sally Lee OPEN All year ROOMS 1 family, 1 four-poster, 7 double, 1 twin; all rooms with bath/shower TERMS B&B £14–£21, (single occupancy of twin/double) £20–£32, (family room) £48

Breakfast at B&Bs tends to mean a cooked breakfast of bacon, eggs and so on. If you prefer a different style of breakfast, discuss this when you make the booking.

Use the maps and indexes at the back of the Guide *to plan your trip.*

WINCHESTER Hampshire map 2

Dellbrook

Hubert Road, St Cross, Winchester SO23 9RG
WINCHESTER (0962) 865093

Very much a family home, this attractive Edwardian house is just outside the centre of Winchester. The terrace has views over the attractive garden to the eleventh-century church and ancient St Cross Hospital, and beyond to the Hampshire countryside. A delightful walk through watermeadows takes you to Winchester Cathedral, only a mile away. Christine Leonard is a most welcoming and enthusiastic hostess and the house has a warm friendly atmosphere. The bedrooms are large and bright, and simply decorated and furnished. Dinner, which must be ordered in advance, is served at 7pm in the dining annexe of the large kitchen, the hub of the house. Vegetarians can be catered for and guests may bring their own wine (there is no alcohol licence). Packed lunches can be provided. Tea, offered on arrival, can be taken on the terrace. Children welcome. Pets by arrangement. Parking for four cars.

OWNER Mrs Christine Leonard OPEN Jan–Nov, sometimes Dec ROOMS 2 family (1 with bath/shower, 1 with wash-basin), 1 double/twin (with wash-basin) TERMS B&B £16, (single occupancy of twin/double) £24 (children 3 and under free, 4–9 £4 reduction)

Florum House Hotel

47 St Cross Road, Winchester SO23 9PS
WINCHESTER (0962) 840427

Florum Hotel is a small, brick-built Victorian property just off the main St Cross road, between the centre of Winchester and St Cross Hospital. All the small bedrooms have TV and are *en suite*, with a few in a new extension. Home-cooked, simple evening meals (including a vegetarian choice) are served 6–8.30pm in the pretty dining-room and there is a pleasant sitting-room that leads out on to the patio and garden at the rear. A small bar is also available. Children welcome. No smoking in the dining-room. Car park.

OWNER F. Hollick OPEN All year ROOMS 2 family, 2 double, 4 twin, 2 single; all rooms with bath/shower TERMS B&B £22–£25, (single) £30, (single occupancy of twin/double) £38, (family room) £54–£62; dinner £10–£14; Access, Visa

WINSLEY Wiltshire map 2

Burghope Manor

Winsley, Bradford-on-Avon BA15 2LA
BATH (0225) 723557

Burghope Manor lies on the edge of the village of Winsley, just a couple of miles from Bradford-on-Avon and a little further from Bath. Dating from the thirteenth century, it is an excellent example of a medieval manor house, and has strong links with Henry VIII. Primarily a family home, the Manor has been lovingly preserved and offers guests every possible modern comfort while still retaining a wealth of historical features. These include an enormous fireplace, in the Cranmer Room, which takes up almost one side of the room and is engraved with Elizabethan writing. The bedrooms, all with TV, have been furnished and decorated with taste and elegance. Elaborate dinner parties are held, by arrangement, on a fairly regular basis, which guests are welcome to join. Burghope Manor is not licensed, but guests may bring their own wine. There are a number of excellent country pubs and restaurants nearby. The grounds include a tennis court. No children under 10. No pets. No smoking in bedrooms. Car park.

OWNERS Elizabeth and John Denning OPEN All year
ROOMS 2 double, 4 twin; all rooms with bath/shower TERMS B&B £30–£32.50, (single occupancy of twin/double) £45–£50, (family room) £70–£75; Access, Amex, Visa

WOKING Surrey map 3

Knap Hill Manor

Carthouse Lane, Woking GU21 4XT
CHOBHAM (0276) 857962

Dating from 1780, Knap Hill Manor is a brick-built rambling house which has been added on to over the years. It stands in pleasant countryside and in its own six acres of land, about one mile from Chobham and three miles from Woking. There is a croquet lawn, a hard tennis court, a 1920s swimming-pool converted to a water-lily pond with fountain and a terrace and garden with chairs for sitting out. The bedrooms all have private bathroom and TV and are comfortable and traditionally decorated and furnished. Breakfast and dinner (by arrangement) are served in the pleasant family dining-room that has views out over the garden and fields and woods beyond. There is no alcohol licence, but guests may bring their own wine to dinner. Vegetarians can be catered for. The large, comfortable drawing-room has a wood-burning stove. No children under eight. No pets. Car park.

OWNERS Teresa and Kevin Leeper OPEN All year, exc Christmas ROOMS 2 double, 2 twin; all rooms with bath/shower TERMS B&B £25, (single occupancy of twin/double) £30 (children up to 50% reduction); dinner £18

WOODMANCOTE West Sussex map 3

Eaton Thorne House

Woodmancote, nr Henfield BN5 9BH
HENFIELD (0273) 492591

Eaton Thorne House is midway between the A23 and A281 on the B2116, next to the Wheatsheaf pub. It is a beautiful fifteenth-century cottage set in lovely gardens and paddocks near the South Downs. The Langhornes are a very friendly couple and are great animal lovers, with a particular interest in horses. The bedrooms, all with TV, are attractively decorated and breakfast only is served in the elegant dining-room. Transport from Gatwick Airport and local car hire can be arranged and sightseeing information

If you intend to spend several days at a B&B, it is worth asking whether there are reduced rates, particularly if the period is midweek or off-season.

provided. The pub next door serves evening meals. Children welcome. No pets. Non-smokers preferred. Car park.

OWNERS Mr and Mrs Langhorne OPEN All year, exc Christmas ROOMS 1 family, 2 twin; 2 rooms with wash/basin TERMS B&B £15 (babies free in cot, children under 5 £10)

The Tithe Barn

Woodmancote, nr Henfield BN5 9ST
HENFIELD (0273) 492267

This old barn was originally converted in the 1920s, and a number of alterations have been made since then, in keeping with the style of the building. The large sitting-room-cum-dining-room with wood-burning stove is a most pleasant, comfortable room used by the family and guests. The two bedrooms, both with TV, are attractively decorated and have splendid views across the garden to the South Downs. The house lies just off the A281 in Woodmancote. Breakfast only is available and is served in the large conservatory. Children welcome (but not suitable for very young children). No pets in the house. No smoking. Car park.

OWNERS Michael and Mary Chick OPEN All year, exc Christmas and New Year ROOMS 1 double, 1 twin, 1 single; all rooms with wash-basin TERMS B&B £15–£16 (children under 10 £10 in single, £12 in twin); deposit

WOOTTON BRIDGE Isle of Wight map 2

Bridge House

Kite Hill, Wootton Bridge PO33 4LA
ISLE OF WIGHT (0983) 884163

This listed Georgian house is right next to the bridge on the main road into Ryde, and has a pretty front garden which leads down to the river, where there is a public slipway for sailors. The position is fairly noisy, but inside most of the traffic sound is eliminated by double glazing. The rooms are clean and bright, simply furnished and of a good size. The bathroom has an old claw-foot bath and porcelain loo. There is one table in the dining-room where breakfast only is served and the entrance hall has a small sitting area. Packed lunches can be provided. The owners

If there are any bedrooms with TV and/or telephone we mention this in the entry.

are happy to pick up clients from the ferry. Children welcome. Pets by arrangement. No smoking. Parking for four cars.

OWNERS Derek and Dee Blackman OPEN All year ROOMS 2 double (with wash-basin), 1 twin (with shower) TERMS B&B £15–£17 (children half-price sharing parents' room out of season); deposit; surcharge for single night and single person in high season

WORMSHILL Kent map 3

Saywell Farm House

Bedmonton, Wormshill, nr Sittingbourne ME9 0EH
WORMSHILL (062 784) 444

This old farmhouse is a low, square building, newly whitewashed with black trim, standing in pretty farmland at the end of a quiet lane off the B2163 between Hollingbourne and Bredgar. The oldest part dates from the thirteenth century, and inscribed on the massive carved beam which crosses the large open fireplace in the dining-room is the date 1611. The Carters have lived here since Mr Carter retired in 1986, and they have done a tremendous amount of work to the house. It has been cleverly updated and renovated with great taste, with all the old features retained, and it has comfortable, attractive bedrooms. The farm no longer belongs to the house, and what was the rose garden outside has been turned into a patio. Evening meals can be served by arrangement from 6.30pm and can include vegetarian choices. A meal may include avocado and kiwi fruit with sour cream dressing, beef bourguignonne and pavlova. There is no licence, but guests may bring their own wine. Packed lunches can be provided. No children under 12. No pets. No smoking in bedrooms. Car park.

OWNER Mrs Yvonne Carter OPEN All year, exc Christmas ROOMS 1 double, 2 twin; all rooms with bath/shower TERMS B&B £17.50, (single occupancy of twin/double) £35; dinner from £13.50; deposit £10

YARMOUTH Isle of Wight map 2

Jireh House

St James Square, Yarmouth PO41 0NP
ISLE OF WIGHT (0983) 760513

Jireh House is a seventeenth-century stone-built house, part of a terrace right in the centre of the pretty little town of Yarmouth, within easy reach of the ferry terminal. The guesthouse is combined with a charming tea-room, where breakfast is served, that is open to non-residents for meals most of the day – everything is home-made. Evening meals are available in July, August and September. The bedrooms (five with TV) have all been done up in pretty wallpaper with matching bedcovers, and only four people have to share the bathroom and separate shower-room. An attractive conservatory, which leads off from the dining-room, has recently been added. Children welcome. Non-smokers preferred.

OWNERS Miss Janis Norton and Mr C. R. Jones OPEN Mar–Dec ROOMS 1 family, 1 double (with bath/shower), 2 twin (1 with bath/shower, 1 with wash-basin), 2 single (with wash-basin) TERMS B&B £16.50–£20 (reductions for children under 12 negotiable); deposit

ZEALS Wiltshire map 2

Stag Cottage

Fantley Lane, Zeals BA12 6NX
BOURTON (0747) 840458

A pretty seventeenth-century thatched house, originally three cottages, Stag Cottage is full of charm, with beamed ceilings and inglenook fireplace, and decorated in light colours with cottage-style furnishings. The bedrooms, including one four-poster, are very small and charmingly decorated. They have night storage heaters. Afternoon cream teas are served downstairs and on the lawn opposite the house on fine summer afternoons. Scones and cakes are all home-made. Breakfast only is available and evening meals can be booked for guests at the village inn. Packed lunches can be provided. The cottage stands next to the post office in the centre of the village and is within walking distance of Stourhead Gardens. Children welcome. Small dogs by arrangement. No smoking. Car park.

OWNERS Marie and Peter Boxall OPEN All year ROOMS 1 four-poster, 1 double, 1 twin, 1 single; all rooms with wash-basin TERMS B&B from £12, (single) from £12.50, (single occupancy of twin/double) from £16 (children under 3 free, under 12 half-price); deposit £5

The Heart of England

Bedfordshire

Berkshire

Buckinghamshire

Gloucestershire

Hereford & Worcester

Hertfordshire

Oxfordshire

Warwickshire

ABINGDON Oxfordshire map 4

22 East St Helen Street

22 East St Helen Street, Abingdon OX14 5EB
ABINGDON (0235) 533278

This elegant house dating from about 1730 is in an attractive old street, close to the Thames and right in the centre of town. It has a well-lived-in feel to it. The bedrooms are large and comfortable, and there are antique furnishings throughout the house; an interesting staircase leads to the bedrooms. The house has panelled rooms, old beams and open fireplaces. Breakfast only is served. There is limited on-street parking and a public car park is close by. Children welcome. No pets. No smoking.

OWNER Mrs S. A. M. Howard OPEN All year, exc Christmas ROOMS 1 double, 1 twin; both rooms with wash-basin TERMS B&B £12–£15, (single occupancy of twin/double) £14–£17 (reductions for children depending on age); deposit

ADMINGTON Warwickshire map 4

Corner Cottage

Admington, nr Shipston on Stour CV37 4JN
STRATFORD-UPON-AVON (0789) 450739

Situated in the hamlet of Admington, which lies between Stratford-upon-Avon and Broadway, Corner Cottage is an idyllic sixteenth-century thatched property set in a pretty garden full of flowers and shrubs. It is full of olde worlde charm: low beams, an inglenook fireplace, and an exposed wattle and daub wall in the lounge. Most of the original woodwork has been preserved. Breakfast here will probably see you through the day, with kippers and hash browns on the menu. Packed lunches can be provided on request. Guests must be prepared to accept farmyard noises. Not suitable for children. No pets. No smoking in bedrooms. Parking for five cars.

OWNER Mrs June Ions OPEN Easter–Sept ROOMS 2 double (with bath/shower) TERMS B&B £20; deposit

B&B rates specified in the details for each entry are per person per night; unless the details state otherwise, they are based on two people sharing a double or twin-bedded room.

Corner Cottage, Admington

BAMPTON Oxfordshire map 4

Morar

Weald Street, Bampton OX8 2HL
BAMPTON CASTLE (0993) 850162 Fax (0993) 851738

This small, modern farmhouse is on a 450-acre farm on the edge of the village. It is a great place for animal lovers; there are goats, cats, dogs, guinea-pigs and a tame ram. The small garden is well kept and the three small bedrooms have pleasant views. The lounge has new carpets and offers TV, video and lots of books to browse through. Evening meals, using mostly home-grown produce, are served at 6.30pm from 1 October to April in the licensed dining-room. Packed lunches and vegetarian meals can be provided by arrangement. There is a large guest lounge where Janet Rouse keeps her spinning-wheel; she is willing, time permitting, to demonstrate her skills. The house has a warm and homely atmosphere. No children under six. No pets. No smoking. Car park.

OWNER Janet Rouse OPEN All year, exc Christmas ROOMS 1 double, 2 twin; all rooms with bath/shower TERMS B&B £16–£17, (single occupancy of twin/double) £6 supplement in high season (children 6–11 £2 off adult price); dinner £12.50; deposit one-third; Access, Visa

BANBURY Oxfordshire map 4

Prospect Guest House

70 Oxford Road, Banbury OX16 9AN
BANBURY (0295) 268749/270580

Prospect Guest House is a handsome red-brick property standing in its own grounds one-third of a mile from the town centre. The good-sized bedrooms all have *en suite* bathrooms or shower-rooms and TV. The gardens are lovely, full of flowers and hanging baskets, and were the recipient of Best Floral Display award for Banbury in 1990. Although situated on the A41 Oxford road, the house suffers little from traffic noise thanks to its triple glazing. There is a small bar/lounge and reasonably priced evening meals are available at 7.15pm on request. Vegetarian choices and packed lunches can be provided. Prospect House is licensed. There are two guest lounges with TV, a payphone and a car park. Children welcome. No pets. No smoking in the dining-room.

OWNERS Tony and Stella Amos OPEN All year ROOMS 1 family, 5 double, 2 twin, 1 single; all rooms with bath/shower TERMS B&B £22.50, (single) £35, (family room) £50–£60 (reductions for children); dinner from £7.50; deposit; Access, Amex, Visa

BOURTON ON DUNSMORE Warwickshire map 4

The School House Guest House

Bourton on Dunsmore, nr Rugby CV23 9QY
MARTON (0926) 632959

This pretty Victorian guesthouse with Gothic-style windows and woodboard floors was, as the name suggests, once the village school. The village itself is picturesque and has some thatched houses. There are three spacious and comfortable bedrooms, all with TV, radio and telephone. Breakfast is served in the cheerful dining-room and the choice includes fish and croissants, as well as traditional cooked fare. Dinners are served, if pre-arranged, at 7pm and feature simple home-style cooking with fresh vegetables and local fish and meats. Vegetarians can be catered for and lunches are also available. The School House is unlicensed, but guests may bring their own wine. The lovely landscaped gardens have furniture for guests' use. Draycote Water, a popular fishing spot, is nearby. Children and pets by arrangement. Smoking is discouraged. Car park.

OWNERS Les and Sylvia Buckley OPEN All year ROOMS 1 double (with bath/shower), 1 twin, 1 single (with wash-basin) TERMS B&B £16–£18, (single) £20, (single occupancy of twin/double) £22 (children under 4 free, over 4 half-price); dinner £7.50–£12.50; deposit 20%

BOURTON-ON-THE-WATER Gloucestershire map 4

Camalan House

Station Road, Bourton-on-the-Water GL54 2ER
COTSWOLD (0451) 21302

The house was built by Mr Campbell from Cotswold stone, and is very comfortable, with a homely, relaxed atmosphere. It is in a charming village and has sparklingly clean rooms. There is a separate dining-room where a large fresh-cooked breakfast is served and a sitting-room with TV. No children under five. No pets. No smoking. Car park.

OWNERS Mr and Mrs J. Campbell OPEN Mar–Nov
ROOMS 1 family/double, 2 twin; all rooms with wash-basin
TERMS B&B £14–£15 (children half-price in family room); deposit £10

Lansdowne House

Lansdowne, Bourton-on-the-Water GL54 2AT
COTSWOLD (0451) 20812

This eighteenth-century detached Cotswold stone house, on the edge of the picturesque village, has mullion windows and sits in a pleasant lawned garden. There are blue and white floors, and the house has a mixture of old-fashioned and antique furnishings. Two bedrooms have TV and there is a TV lounge. Breakfast only is served, but there are several eating-places in the village. Packed

Reduced rates for children are normally given when they share their parents' bedroom. If no reductions are specified in the details or text, assume you'll have to pay full rates.

lunches are available by prior arrangement. Children welcome (no cot available). No pets. Smoking in lounge only. Car park.

OWNER Mrs L. P. Garwood OPEN All year, exc Christmas and New Year ROOMS 2 double, 1 twin; all rooms with bath/shower TERMS B&B £14–£17, (single occupancy of twin/double) £20 approx (children £8.50 sharing adults' room on camp bed); deposit £15 per room

BREDENBURY Hereford & Worcester map 4

Grendon Manor

Bredenbury, nr Bromyard HR7 4TH
BROMYARD (0885) 482226

Grendon Manor is a most interesting sixteenth-century farmhouse, part of a 498-acre farm that has corn, cattle, sheep and horses. There are thick stone walls, slanting floors and an inglenook fireplace which is lit every day in winter. There is also a stone fireplace which has carved panelling depicting Adam and Eve and the serpent, and the sacrifice of Isaac. The bedrooms are spacious and decorated with pretty floral wallpapers. Huge breakfasts are cooked on the Aga stove and served with home-made marmalades and preserves; you might ask Mrs Piggott to show you the original bread oven in the kitchen. There is just one huge bathroom, but there are so many redeeming features that this matters little. Also of interest is the church on the property and the original horse-powered cider press. Children welcome. Car park.

OWNERS Mr and Mrs George Piggott OPEN Mar–Nov ROOMS 1 family, 1 double, 1 twin TERMS B&B £12.50 (children under 16 £8)

BREDWARDINE Hereford & Worcester map 6

Bredwardine Hall

Bredwardine, nr Hereford HR3 6DB
MOCCAS (098 17) 596

The village of Bredwardine is in a beautiful and tranquil area and boasts the remains of an ancient castle and a church of Norman origin. It is famous for its connection with Francis Kilvert, the Victorian diarist, who was the Vicar of Bredwardine (1877–9). In fact, Bredwardine Hall was used by the BBC during the filming of 'The Kilvert Diaries'. It is an impressive stone-built mid-nineteenth-century manor house, peacefully situated in extensive wooded grounds. The rooms are spacious and there is a magnificent reception hall and staircase. The Hall's elegant drawing-room, with three floor-to-ceiling windows, has superb views over the garden. The bedrooms are now all *en suite* and have TV. Dinner is available at 7.30pm and packed lunches can be provided on request. There is a cocktail bar in the dining-room and a wine list is provided. Mr Jancey runs the village post office adjacent to the house. This is ideal walking country, close to the Welsh border. No children under 10. No pets in the house. No smoking in the dining-room. Car park.

OWNERS Mr and Mrs W. A. Jancey OPEN Mar–Oct
ROOMS 2 double, 2 twin; all rooms with bath/shower
TERMS B&B from £21, (single occupancy of twin/double) from £27; dinner £10.50; deposit

BRILL Buckinghamshire map 4

Poletrees Farm

Ludgershall Road, Brill, nr Aylesbury HP18 9TZ
BRILL (0844) 238276

This small, listed fifteenth-century farmhouse of brick and stone stands in a compact garden just off the old coaching road between Buckingham and Oxford. Guests may walk around the 165-acre working farm. Many original features of the farmhouse remain, including beamed ceilings, an inglenook fireplace and a fifteenth-century window. The bedrooms are large and comfortable with an old-fashioned atmosphere. Four-course evening meals are served at 6.30pm and consist of farm-style cooking with substantial portions. Vegetarian choices and packed lunches can be provided. There is no alcohol licence, but guests may bring their own wine. All water at the farm is spring water. No children under 10. No pets. No smoking. Car park.

OWNER Anita Cooper OPEN All year ROOMS 1 family, 1 double, 1 twin; all rooms with wash-basin TERMS B&B from £15, (single occupancy of twin/double) £20; deposit £10

Where we know an establishment accepts credit cards, we list them. There may be a surcharge if you pay by credit card. It is always best to check whether the card you want to use is acceptable when booking.

Most establishments have central heating. We say when this is not the case.

BRIMPTON Berkshire map 2

Manor Farm

Brimpton, nr Reading RG7 4SQ
WOOLHAMPTON (0734) 713166

This lovely old farmhouse stands in a pleasant garden separated a little from the farm buildings, which serve a 500-acre arable and dairy farm, on the edge of the small village of Brimpton. It is a very interesting house: Georgian at the front, Tudor at the back, and all sorts of periods inbetween. There are window shutters, a priest's hiding hole and a Norman arch in what is now the kitchen. In the garden is a Norman chapel, now used by the geese. The atmosphere is informal and guests sit around a big table for breakfast in the dining-room, which has a large open fireplace and a well-filled bookcase. There are two small sitting-rooms, one of which has facilities for making picnic-type meals. Jean Bowden is interested in walking and is happy to take guests on local walks, time permitting. Children welcome. No dogs. Smoking in the sitting-room only. Car park.

OWNER Mrs Jean R. Bowden OPEN All year ROOMS 1 double/family, 1 twin TERMS B&B £16–£20 (children under 2 free, 2–9 half-price, 10–15 75% of adult price); deposit

BROADWAY Hereford & Worcester map 4

Cowley House

Church Street, Broadway WR12 7AE
BROADWAY (0386) 853262

Just off the village green, this lovely seventeenth-century Cotswold-stone house was converted from a farmhouse and grain store. It is superbly furnished. The hall has a magnificent polished flagstone floor, exposed beams and a lovely grandfather clock. One of the bedrooms has an Elizabethan four-poster bed. Three bedrooms have TV and there is a sitting-room with TV; tea and coffee are usually offered on arrival. The ground-flour family room is very spacious. Breakfast only is served in the cosy

Bath/shower information in the details refers only to a private bathroom or shower; other bathroom facilities at the establishments will be shared. We say if rooms have wash-basins.

dining-room, which has exposed stone walls. No children under three. No smoking. Car park.

OWNERS Mary and Robert Kemp OPEN All year, exc Christmas
ROOMS 1 family, 1 four-poster (with shower), 2 double (1 with bath/shower), 1 twin (with bath/shower), 1 single (with wash-basin)
TERMS B&B £17.50–£25, (family room) £45; deposit

Leasow House

Laverton Meadows, Broadway WR12 7NA
STANTON (038 673) 526 Fax (038 673) 596

Take the B4632 Cheltenham road from Broadway, turn right towards Wormington and Dumbleton and Leasow House is the first house on the right. It is a traditional seventeenth-century Cotswold farmhouse, situated in open countryside, with the Broadway Tower visible in the distance. The spacious, beautifully appointed bedrooms have elegant furnishings and one has a whirlpool bath. Two of the bedrooms are in a restored bull pen and all have TV and telephone. A ground-floor room is suitable for the disabled and designed to accommodate a wheelchair. The drawing-room/library has new furniture and a magnificent bookcase. A sumptuous breakfast, beautifully presented, is served in the attractive, recently extended dining-room, which looks over the garden and out to open countryside. Packed lunches are available by arrangement. This is a civilised house with a pleasant, informal atmosphere, an idyllic spot in which to relax. Children welcome. No smoking in the dining-room. Car park.

OWNERS Barbara and Gordon Meekings OPEN All year
ROOMS 2 family, 4 double, 3 twin; all rooms with bath/shower
TERMS B&B £21–£26, (single occupancy of twin/double) £38–£46 (babies £3, children under 5 £6, 6–12 £9, 13–16 £11); deposit £30; Access, Amex, Visa

Whiteacres Guest House

Station Road, Broadway WR12 7DE
BROADWAY (0386) 852320

Whiteacres is a turn-of-the-century house on the edge of the village. There are six bedrooms (all with TV), one is on the ground floor with a lace-canopied four-poster and its own bathroom and sitting-room, the rest are all on the first floor, two of which have four-posters. A four-course breakfast is served in the dining-room, which has a pretty plate collection and french doors leading out into the garden. There is also a well-furnished guest lounge. No children under 12. No pets. No smoking in the dining-room and bedrooms. Car park.

OWNERS Alan and Helen Richardson OPEN 1 mar–1 Nov
ROOMS 3 four-poster, 2 double, 1 twin; all rooms with bath/shower
TERMS B&B £18–£20, (single occupancy of twin/double) £25

BROMYARD Hereford & Worcester map 4

The Granary

Church House Farm, Collington, Bromyard HR7 4NA
KYRE (0885) 410345

The Granary, a wonderful away-from-it-all place in which to relax, is situated in the beautiful Kyre Valley three miles from Bromyard on the Tenbury Wells road. For those who enjoy walking, the country lanes are a delight. Riding and fishing facilities are also available nearby. The luxurious ground-floor bedrooms, all with TV, are in a converted barn decorated with delicate fabrics, and have exposed beams and pine furnishings. All bedrooms are suitable for the disabled. Breakfast and dinner (served 6–9.30pm, feature home-cooked fresh food and are served in the cool green dining-room with views out to open countryside. Lunches are available and vegetarians can be catered for. The wine list is short but adequate. There is also a guest lounge with a small, well-stocked bar. Children welcome. Car park.

OWNERS Paul and Margaret Maiden OPEN All year
ROOMS 1 double, 4 twin; all rooms with bath/shower
TERMS B&B from £19; dinner from £10; deposit

BROOKTHORPE Gloucestershire map 4

Gilbert's

Gilbert's Lane, Brookthorpe, nr Gloucester GL4 0UH
PAINSWICK (0452) 812364

This beautiful 400-year-old Cotswold Tudor farmhouse is built from local Cotswold stone and wood from the Severn Valley. There are five acres of grounds supporting sheep and chickens, and an organic vegetable garden including hives, providing fresh, wholesome ingredients for the superb breakfasts cooked on a 50-year-old Aga in the farmhouse kitchen. There are exposed beams and interesting antique pieces, including a very lovely grandfather clock in the hallway. The bedrooms, all with TV and telephone, are very spacious. Guests are welcome to stroll through the farm, which is bounded by a small stream, and are provided with a wealth of local information. Children welcome. No pets in the house. Car park.

OWNER Jenny Beer OPEN All year (Christmas opening varies)
ROOMS 2 double, 1 twin, 1 single; all rooms with bath/shower
TERMS B&B £19–£22.50, (single occupancy of twin/double) £25 (some reductions for children)

BUCKINGHAM Buckinghamshire map 4

Western House

Addington, nr Buckingham MK18 2JS
WINSLOW (029 671) 2540

Advance bookings only are available at this charming cottage conversion set in private parkland, a mile from Winslow and six miles from Buckingham (directions are provided). A sixteenth-century barn and the remains of the village stocks have been preserved. In the nineteenth century the surrounding estate was owned by the first Lord Addington, governor of the Bank of England. The house is very comfortable and elegantly furnished. French doors lead out from the drawing-room to the lovely garden and a conservatory has been added. No pets. Car park.

OWNER Mrs Charmian Bolton OPEN All year ROOMS 1 twin, 1 single; both rooms with bath/shower TERMS B&B £20–£24; dinner £13.50

BURFORD Oxfordshire map 4

Chevrons

Swan Lane, Burford OX8 4SH
BURFORD (099 382) 3416

Chevrons is an early sixteenth-century stone-built house with a small walled garden planted with roses and apple trees. Situated on a quiet side-street, it overlooks the picturesque high street. There are medieval paintings in the form of chevrons on the beams. Both bedrooms have TV. There is a sitting-room with TV. Breakfast only is served, although packed lunches can be provided. Numerous restaurants and pubs are within walking distance. Children welcome. Pets by arrangement. No smoking in bedrooms.

OWNERS Sheila and John Roberts OPEN All year ROOMS 2 twin (with wash-basin) TERMS B&B £14–£15, (single occupancy of twin) £22 (additional child in room £10.50)

CANON PYON Hereford & Worcester map 6

The Hermitage Manor

Canon Pyon HR4 8NR
HEREFORD (0432) 760317

The Manor is a winning combination of country house elegance and a warm and homely atmosphere. It stands at the end of a half-mile-long private drive, and is set in 11 acres of private grounds, much of it deer park, with beautiful views. The spacious oak-panelled lounge with its intricate carving has a Tudor Rose ceiling and cornices, wood-stripped floors and a crystal chandelier. There is also a lovely oak stairway and baronial-style hall. The well-appointed bedrooms are delightfully furnished and have every comfort; two have TV. There are several sitting areas, including a drawing-room, a 'blue' room and a small TV room. Breakfast only is served. The water at the Manor comes from a natural spring and is gravity-fed to the house. This is an ideal spot for walking and bird-watching and a good base for exploring the Wye Valley, Welsh border country and the Malvern Hills. No children under 10. No pets. No smoking in the dining-room and one lounge. Car park.

OWNER Mrs S. E. Hickling OPEN Easter–end Oct ROOMS 4 double, 1 twin; all rooms with bath/shower TERMS B&B from £18, (single occupancy of twin/double) £25; deposit £15

CHELTENHAM Gloucestershire map 4

Hannaford's

20 Evesham Road, Cheltenham GL52 2AB
CHELTENHAM (0242) 515181

Hannaford's is a lovely Regency house, built in 1833 as part of Joseph Pitt's estate, which includes Pitville Park. It has retained much of its original character, including ornate ceilings and marble fireplaces. All bedrooms have TV, telephone and hair-dryer. There is a small lounge bar and a sitting-room with TV.

Evening meals are available Monday to Friday by arrangement at 6.30pm and there is an alcohol licence. Children welcome. No pets. No smoking in the dining-room.

OWNER Dorothy Crowley OPEN All year, exc Christmas ROOMS 1 family, 2 double, 4 twin, 2 single; all rooms, exc 1 single (wash-basin only), with bath/shower TERMS B&B £24–£26, (single occupancy of twin/double) £31–£35, (family room) £58–£65; dinner £12.50; deposit; Access, Visa

Parkview

4 Pittville Crescent, Cheltenham GL52 2QZ
CHELTENHAM (0242) 575567

This Georgian residence, built in 1826, is on a quiet tree-lined crescent just a five-minute walk from the town centre. It has a pretty front garden. The two spacious bedrooms are well appointed, and the bathroom has a whirlpool bath, ideal for weary travellers. Electric blankets are also provided. Most of the furnishings came from a Cotswold cottage and they blend in very well with the rest of the house with its pine and period furniture. Breakfast only is served in the dining-room with its original gold-leaf cornice. The TV lounge also has original features and contains antique furniture. Children welcome. Smoking in bedrooms is discouraged.

OWNERS Mr and Mrs J. F. Sparrey OPEN All year ROOMS 1 family (with wash-basin), 1 twin (with bath/shower), 1 single (with wash-basin) TERMS B&B £14–£15, (single occupancy of twin) £18–£20 (infants free, children under 7 half-price); deposit

COOKHAM DEAN Berkshire map 2

Primrose Hill

Bradcutts Lane, Cookham Dean SL6 9TL
BOURNE END (0628) 528179

This solid whitewashed country house on the top of a hill has an attractive garden and a pleasant rural outlook. The house is divided into two, the owner living in one half, and has a family-home atmosphere with guests sharing the TV lounge with the owner. There is a separate lounge and a dining-room where breakfast only is served. The bedrooms are immaculate, clean and comfortable and have black and white TV. Children welcome (no cot for babies). Pets by arrangement. No smoking in the dining-room and bedrooms. Car park.

OWNER Mrs D. Benson OPEN All year, exc Christmas
ROOMS 1 family (with wash-basin), 1 single TERMS B&B £15–£17.50 (children 2–14 £5–£10); deposit £5

CUSOP Hereford & Worcester map 6

Lansdowne

Cusop, Hay-on-Wye HR3 5RF
HAY-ON-WYE (0497) 820125

This most attractive and immaculate 100-year-old house is in a peaceful setting within walking distance, over the fields, of Hay-on-Wye – known as the second-hand book capital of the world. There are two well-appointed bedrooms, both *en suite* and with TV, plus extra little touches such as fresh flowers. Margaret Flack was formerly a teacher before going into the B&B business and is a charming and dedicated host. Rob Flack has a traditional letter-printing press and can easily be persuaded to demonstrate it for interested guests. Breakfast is a banquet and features fresh fruits, yoghurts, a wide choice of cereal followed by a traditional cooked breakfast. Packed lunches can also be provided. Lansdowne is impeccably maintained and offers extremely good-value accommodation. Very early reservations are suggested for the May/June Literary Festival and August Jazz Festival. There are no facilities for small children. No pets. No smoking. Car park.

OWNERS Rob and Margaret Flack OPEN All year, exc Christmas
ROOMS 1 double, 1 twin; both rooms with bath/shower TERMS B&B £13–£15, (single occupancy of twin/double) £18–£20; deposit

DINTON Buckinghamshire map 4

Wallace Farm

Dinton, nr Aylesbury HP17 8UF
AYLESBURY (0296) 748660 Fax (0296) 748851

In a quiet, peaceful spot, just outside the pretty village of Dinton, is this lovely stone-built sixteenth-century farmhouse, part of a 200-acre mixed-livestock farm supporting sheep, beef cattle and cows. There are pedigree flocks of Suffolk and Jacob sheep as well as a commercial flock. Ducks and geese live on the ponds and free-range chickens provide eggs for breakfast. You enter the house through a stone hallway, which leads into the large family kitchen, one half of which is a dining area with an enormous open fireplace, original bread ovens and wood-burning stove. This is where breakfast is served, at one long table. The sitting-room doubles as a library with several bookcases and has french windows that open out on to a terrace with garden seats. There are three large, comfortably furnished bedrooms, one with an exposed area of wattle and daub. Two of the bedrooms have *en suite* bathrooms, while the third has its own private bathroom. A self-catering cottage is also available. Children welcome. No pets. No smoking in bedrooms. Parking for six cars.

OWNERS Geoffrey and Jackie Cook OPEN All year, exc Christmas ROOMS 1 double, 2 twin; all rooms with bath/shower TERMS B&B from £17, (single occupancy of twin/double) £28 (children under 12 £8 sharing parents' room); deposit 25%; Access, Visa

EVESHAM Hereford & Worcester map 4

Church House

Greenhill Park Road, Evesham WR11 4NL
EVESHAM (0386) 40498

A detached Victorian house, with a pretty front garden, that overlooks the historic town of Evesham. Mr and Mrs Shaw share the work, although Veronica does most of the cooking and takes care of the garden. Guests are offered a glass of home-made wine upon arrival. The well-appointed, colour-co-ordinated bedrooms all have TV and private bathroom with modern fixtures. Excellent breakfasts include home-baked bread and brioche. Packed lunches can also be provided. Children welcome. Parking for three cars.

OWNERS Michael and Veronica Shaw OPEN All year, exc Christmas and New Year ROOMS 1 family, 1 double, 1 twin; all rooms with bath/shower TERMS B&B £15–£19, (single occupancy of twin/double) £25–£30 (children under 12 half-price); deposit

FARINGDON Oxfordshire map 4

Bowling Green Farm

Stanford Road, Faringdon SN7 8EZ
FARINGDON (0367) 240229 Fax (0367) 242568

An attractive brick-built eighteenth-century farmhouse that stands on the site of a bowling-green, used by the Duke of

Buckingham in the fifteenth century. The owners breed horses and Charollais cows on the 30-acre farm. Guests are accommodated in a more recent addition. There are two large bedrooms, one on the ground floor with french doors leading out on to the garden. Both have bathroom, armchair and TV. Breakfast, including fresh free-range eggs, is served in the bedroom. Packed lunches can be provided. Guests also have use of a lounge with TV. Children welcome. No pets in the house. No smoking. Car park.

OWNERS Mr and Mrs D. Barnard OPEN All year ROOMS 2 family (with bath/shower) TERMS B&B £18–£22 (reductions for children according to age); deposit

FIFIELD Oxfordshire map 4

South View

Fifield OX7 6HP
SHIPTON-UNDER-WYCHWOOD (0993) 830723

On the edge of the village, South View is a small stone-built bungalow with lovely views and a very pretty, small back garden. Fifield is a good base from which to tour the Cotswolds, being four miles north of Burford and about 15 miles from Oxford. There are two small, bright bedrooms, simply furnished and both with TV. Guests have exclusive use of two bathrooms. Delicious breakfasts are served on Royal Albert china, often on antique lace tablecloths (collecting these is a hobby of Mrs Rose). No pets. Smoking is not encouraged. Car park.

OWNERS Jean and Tony Rose OPEN All year, exc Christmas ROOMS 1 double, 1 twin TERMS B&B £12–£20

FULBROOK Oxfordshire map 4

Elm Farm House

Meadow Lane, Fulbrook, Burford OX18 4BW
BURFORD (0993) 823611

Set in an attractive walled garden, the house, with its stonesfield slate roof, gables and mullion windows, is a fine example of a Cotswold manor-style farmhouse. It was built at the turn of the century of solid, mellow stone and lies down a quiet lane, one mile from Burford. The spacious hall leads to comfortable bedrooms, all with TV and telephone, decorated in mostly floral wallpapers. Four bedrooms are now *en suite* and the shared bathroom has been completely refurbished. Breakfast and dinner (7.30pm) are served in the elegant licensed dining-room, which has french windows opening out on to a terrace, gardens and a croquet lawn. Vegetarian meals are served on request. There is also a small bar and a sitting-room. No children under 10. No dogs. No smoking in bedrooms. Car park.

OWNERS Mr and Mrs David Catlin OPEN Feb–14 Dec
ROOMS 3 double (with bath/shower), 2 twin (1 with bath/shower), 2 single (with wash-basin) TERMS B&B £20.50–£29.50, (single occupancy of twin/double) £31–£34.50; dinner £15; deposit £20; Access, Amex, Visa

Pytts House

Church Lane, Fulbrook OX18 4BA
BURFORD (0993) 823193

A sixteenth-century Cotswold-stone house, Pytts House is situated in a quiet lane between the owners' working Fulbrook Forge and the twelfth-century church, just half a mile from Burford. The house is reached through a medieval arch and cobbled outer hall. There are beautiful landscaped gardens and a terrace where guests can sit and enjoy a drink on fine days. Tricia Murfitt is a superb hostess, well known for her sumptuous breakfast, with everything prepared fresh each morning. There are several local places that serve food in the evening. Peter Murfitt is happy to show guests around the working forge. The bedrooms, all with TV, are large and pleasantly furnished. Children welcome. Dogs by arrangement. No smoking. Car park.

OWNERS Tricia and Peter Murfitt OPEN All year ROOMS 1 family (with wash-basin), 2 double (with bath/shower) TERMS B&B £13–£17, (single occupancy of double) £20–£28 (children usually half-price); deposit

GAYHURST Buckinghamshire map 4

Mill Farm

Gayhurst, nr Newport Pagnell MK16 8LT
NEWPORT PAGNELL (0908) 611489

This attractive, listed brick-built seventeenth-century farmhouse is set in half an acre of gardens in the middle of a 500-acre working farm, overlooking the Ouse valley. The house sits to one side of the numerous farm buildings, which are neatly maintained.

It is a family home, with large, pleasant and comfortably furnished rooms. All bedrooms have TV. Breakfast only is available. Guests have use of the hard tennis court, and fishing and riding can be arranged. Mill Farm is three miles out of Newport Pagnell, one-quarter of a mile off the B526. Children welcome. Car park.

OWNER Mrs Kaye Adams OPEN All year ROOMS 1 family (with wash-basin), 1 twin (with bath/shower), 1 single (with wash-basin) TERMS B&B £15–£20; deposit

GLOUCESTER Gloucestershire map 4

Lulworth Guest House

12 Midland Road, Gloucester GL1 4UF
GLOUCESTER (0452) 21881

This town guesthouse offers good-value accommodation. It is pleasantly situated close to the park, and is a five-minute walk from the town centre. The bedrooms, all with TV, are of a good size. Breakfast only is served. There is also a guest lounge with TV. Children welcome. Pets by arrangement. No smoking in the dining-room. Car park.

OWNER Mrs J. M. Wiltshire OPEN All year, exc Christmas and last week July ROOMS 2 family (with bath/shower), 3 double (with wash-basin), 2 twin (with wash-basin), 1 single (with wash-basin) TERMS B&B £14–£16, (family room) £40; deposit £10

Notley Guest House

93 Hucclecote Road, Hucclecote, Gloucester GL3 3TR
GLOUCESTER (0452) 611584

A cosy, cleverly converted whitewashed cottage-style house that stands in its own grounds, three miles from the town centre. The immaculate bedrooms are of a good size and all have radio-alarm and TV. Evening meals are served 6–8.30pm and can include vegetarian choices. Notley is unlicensed, but guests may bring their own wine. Packed lunches can be provided. Children can use the play equipment, such as slide and playhouse, in the garden. The Coach House, a self-catering unit, is also available. Children

If you intend to spend several days at a B&B, it is worth asking whether there are reduced rates, particularly if the period is midweek or off-season.

are welcome, and cots and high chairs are provided. No smoking. Car park.

OWNERS Jaki George and Alyn George OPEN All year, exc some days Christmas ROOMS 2 family, 1 four-poster, 1 double, 2 twin, 1 single; all rooms with bath/shower TERMS B&B £16–£23 (babies free, children using bed £7); dinner £9; deposit

GREAT WOLFORD Warwickshire map 4

Lower Farm Barn

Great Wolford, nr Shipston on Stour CV36 5NQ
BARTON-ON-THE-HEATH (060 874) 435

This lovely 100-year-old converted barn stands in its own grounds with a three-quarter-acre garden full of shrubs, flowers and a large collection of flowering tubs. The entrance is very attractive, with a galleried landing, and there is a small conservatory area leading out to the garden, which guests are encouraged to enjoy, including use of the swimming-pool. Several original features remain, such as the exposed beams and stonework. There are three spacious bedrooms and a comfortable sitting-room with a wood-burning stove and TV. Breakfast only is available, but there are several pubs and restaurants in the village. Children welcome. No dogs in the house. Smoking in the sitting-room and dining-room only. Car park.

OWNERS Fred and Rebecca Mawle OPEN All year ROOMS 1 double (with bath/shower), 2 twin (1 with wash-basin) TERMS B&B £13.50–£14.50, (single occupancy of twin/double) £25 (children under 8 half-price); deposit

HAZLETON Gloucestershire map 4

Windrush House

Hazleton, nr Cheltenham GL54 4EB
COTSWOLD (0451) 860364

The house, in the unspoilt village of Hazleton with its medieval church and one mile from the A40, is Cotswold-stone modern and furnished in a comfortable style, with rooms that are immaculate and tastefully decorated. The dining-room is large, and there is a quiet lounge and a small music room with a piano. The garden is full of roses, shrubs and other plants. Guests are offered a glass of sherry or a cup of tea or coffee when they arrive, but it is

Mrs Harrison's cooking that guests regularly return for: home-made bread, soups, traditional local dishes, fresh vegetables prepared to order and mouth-watering puddings. Dinner is served at 7.30pm and can include vegetarian choices with notice. Packed lunches can also be provided. Windrush House is licensed. Riding weekends can be arranged in winter. No children under 12. No pets. No smoking in bedrooms. Car park.

OWNER Sydney Harrison OPEN All year, exc 16 Dec–mid-Jan ROOMS 2 double (1 with bath/shower, 1 with wash-basin), 2 twin (1 with bath/shower, 1 with wash-basin) TERMS B&B £18.75–£20; dinner £15; deposit £10

HENLEY-ON-THAMES Oxfordshire map 2

Aarhus

25 Queen Street, Henley-on-Thames RG9 1AR
HENLEY-ON-THAMES (0491) 576767

This semi-detached, red-brick Edwardian house is in a quiet road, only three minutes from the town centre and the River Thames, where there are beautiful riverside walks, boat trips and boats for hire. This is an unpretentious little guesthouse, offering very clean accommodation with simply furnished bedrooms, the top-floor rooms being the most attractive, with sloping ceilings and pretty wallpapers. There is a small TV lounge-cum-dining-room with a small balcony where breakfast only is served. During the summer the front of the house has lots of pretty hanging baskets and flowerpots. Children welcome. No pets. Car park.

OWNERS Mr and Mrs A. G. and J. G. Collins OPEN Easter–1 Jan ROOMS 1 family, 2 double (with bath/shower), 2 twin, 4 single; 7 rooms with wash-basin TERMS B&B £14, (single) £16.50, (single occupancy of twin/double) £21–£25.50 (children up to 2 free, 2–10 half-price)

HEREFORD Hereford & Worcester map 4

The Old Rectory

Byford, nr Hereford HR4 7LD
BRIDGE SOLLARS (098 122) 218

Georgian in style and used as a rectory until 1960, this house is situated in the unspoilt hamlet of Byford, eight miles west of Hereford on the A438 and a 10-minute walk from the River Wye. There are lovely gardens, with herbaceous borders and a magnificent old cedar tree, and the house also overlooks one hundred acres of parkland. The spacious bedrooms, all with TV, have inlaid mahogany furnishings, in keeping with the character of the house. Breakfast only is served, but there are several eating-places close by and the owners are always happy to recommend local restaurants and pubs. Fishing can be arranged. A real family atmosphere pervades the Old Rectory. Children welcome. No pets in the house. No smoking. Car park.

OWNERS Charles and Audrey Mayson OPEN Mar–end Nov
ROOMS 1 family (with wash-basin), 1 double (with wash-basin), 1 twin (with bath/shower) TERMS B&B £14–£17, (single occupancy of twin/double) £20–£25 (children half-price approx sharing); deposit

The Old Tudor Guest House

33 Breinton Road, Hereford HR4 0JU
HEREFORD (0432) 272765

Built in 1926, this handsome mock-tudor house is situated within striking distance of the cathedral, city centre and riverside walks. The spacious bedrooms, all with TV, are comfortable, have modern furnishings and are named after famous Tudor characters, including Henry VIII and his wives. A sumptuous breakfast includes fresh fruits, yoghurts and filtered coffee; evening meals, featuring traditional roasts, lots of fresh vegetables and also light snacks, are served at 7pm in the dining-room overlooking the garden. Vegetarians can be catered for and packed lunches provided. There is no alcohol licence, but guests may bring their own wine. A quiet lounge and an additional sitting area on the first floor are also available. No children. No smoking. Parking for nine cars.

OWNERS Graham and Chris Brinton OPEN All year
ROOMS 1 double (with bath/shower), 2 twin (1 with bath/shower, 1 with wash-basin), 2 single (with wash-basin)
TERMS B&B £18–£25; dinner £9.50; deposit

The Upper House

Didley, nr Hereford HR2 9DA
WORMBRIDGE (098 121) 212

The Upper House stands in a half-acre garden on a 400-acre working arable farm, six miles south-west of Hereford off the A465. The house is tastefully furnished, combining period furniture with original features such as inglenook fireplaces and exposed oak beams. The two spacious bedrooms are *en suite* and feature elegant Edwardian-style fixtures and extras such as fresh fruit, flowers and toiletries. Breakfast and dinner (7pm in winter, 8pm in summer) are served in the well-furnished dining-room, with its inglenook fireplace, on a large mahogany table and include fresh produce from the garden in season. Vegetarians and special diets can be catered for with advance notice. The Upper House has no alcohol licence, but guests may bring their own wine to dinner. There is a restful lounge with lots of books and local information provided. A visit to the local church at Kilpeck, renowned for its gargoyles and its exquisitely carved Norman arch depicting the tree of life, is highly recommended. Children by arrangement. No dogs in the house. Non-smokers preferred. Car park.

OWNER Mrs Jane Manning OPEN All year, exc Christmas
ROOMS 1 double, 1 twin; both rooms with bath/shower TERMS B&B £22.50, (single occupancy of twin/double) from £29.50; dinner £14.50; deposit

HERTFORD Hertfordshire map 5

Bengeo Hall

New Road, Hertford SG14 3JN
HERTFORD (0992) 582033

This listed seventeenth-century house is in a tranquil setting of three acres, including a 500-year-old oak tree, inhabited by sheep and doves. The bedrooms are large and some overlook the gardens; there are plans to install a four-poster bed, more *en suite* facilities and to continue to improve this lovely old house. One of the bedrooms is *en suite*, another has a shower and basin only. There is a separate sitting-room with TV and a dining-room where breakfast and light refreshments are served. A cup of coffee or tea is offered to guests on arrival. No children under 10. No cats. No smoking. Car park.

OWNER Rachel Savory OPEN spring–autumn (sometimes longer)
ROOMS 1 double (with bath/shower), 2 twin (1 with shower, 1 with wash-basin) TERMS B&B £20–£30

Many B&Bs are in remote places; always ask for clear directions when booking.

If you are forced to turn up late into the evening, please telephone to warn the proprietor.

HOARWITHY Hereford & Worcester map 4

The Old Mill

Hoarwithy, nr Hereford HR2 6QH
CAREY (0432) 840602

The Old Mill in the unspoilt village of Hoarwithy dates from the eighteenth century and is full of character, with oak beams, fireplaces and exposed stone walls. Breakfast and dinner are served in the dining-room, which leads out on to the garden. Modest-priced evening meals (7pm) include home-grown vegetables in season, roasts and casseroles and home-made puddings. Vegetarian choices and packed lunches can be provided. There is no alcohol licence, but guests may bring their own wine. The bedrooms are large and decorated to a high standard. There is a guest lounge with TV and a stone fireplace which has log fires on cool days. Carol Probert is a congenial host who enjoys cooking and riding and also runs the village post office, which is in the Old Mill. Tea and coffee are offered to guests on arrival and at other times on request. Children welcome. Pets by arrangement. No smoking in the dining-room. Car park.

OWNER Carol Probert OPEN All year ROOMS 4 double (3 with bath/shower, 1 with wash-basin), 1 twin (with wash-basin), 1 single
TERMS B&B £14 (children under 2 free, 2–10 half-price); dinner £7

HUNGERFORD Berkshire map 2

Marshgate Cottage

Marsh Lane, Hungerford RG17 0QX
HUNGERFORD (0488) 682307 Fax (0488) 685475

Marshgate Cottage dates from 1637 and was, at one time, used by the people of Hungerford as a recuperation home and later as a pub called the Barge Inn. It stands on the outskirts of Hungerford beside Freeman's Marsh, which is commonland that has been kept in a natural state, attracting birds and unusual flora. It is also next to the canal and a five-to-ten minute walk along the waterway will bring you to the centre of the medieval town. Elsebeth Walker is of Danish descent, and the Scandinavian influence is much in evidence in the décor and furnishings – whitewashed walls, wooden floors, pine furniture, wooden shelves and dried flowers. There is a sitting-room, a dining area, a bar and a library, as well as a courtyard for sitting out on fine days. Evening meals, including a vegetarian choice, are available by arrangement from 7.30pm. Packed lunches can also be provided by arrangement. Snacks are always available. Bike hire and canoeing can be arranged. A popular place with business people. No children under five. Guide dogs only. No smoking in some bedrooms. Car park.

OWNERS Elsebeth and Mike Walker OPEN All year, exc Christmas
ROOMS 2 family, 1 four-poster, 2 double, 3 twin, 1 single; all rooms, exc 1 double and 1 single (wash-basin only), with bath/shower
TERMS B&B £19.75–£24.25, (single) £25.50–£35.50, (family room) £56–£66; dinner from £14.50; deposit £10 per room per night; Access, Amex, Visa

KENILWORTH Warwickshire map 4

Victoria Lodge Hotel

180 Warwick Road, Kenilworth CV8 1HU
KENILWORTH (0926) 512020

The welcome is warm at this Victorian house situated in the town centre, opposite the parish church of St John the Evangelist. The building was divided into flats until 1990 when Malcolm and Joyce Chilvers purchased it and turned it into a small hotel. The bedrooms are decorated in soft pastel colours and all have telephone and TV; three bedrooms have a balcony. The house is immaculate, and high standards prevail. Evening meals, including vegetarian choices, are served (last orders 8.30pm) and lunches can be provided. The wine list is reasonably priced. Children welcome. No pets. No smoking in bedrooms and the dining-room. Car park.

OWNERS Malcolm and Joyce Chilvers OPEN All year
ROOMS 2 double, 2 twin, 1 single; all rooms with bath/shower
TERMS B&B £21–£23, (single) £27–£28, (single occupancy of twin/double) £31–£32; dinner £9 approx; Access, Visa

KINETON Warwickshire map 4

Willowbrook House

Lighthorne Road, Kineton CV35 0JL
KINETON (0926) 640475 Fax (0926) 641747

This welcoming house is in a quiet location, on a four-acre smallholding inhabited by goats, sheep and chickens, which supply the fresh eggs for breakfast. There are several antique pieces and other items about, including a glass bottle collection. The three well-appointed bedrooms range in size from average to large, the most spacious being the 'green' room. Two bedrooms have TV. Breakfast only is served in a long dining-room with a pretty window seat, which leads on to a comfortable lounge with TV. A pleasant garden, a small orchard with plums and apples, and a patio are all available for guests' use. Children welcome. Pets by arrangement. Smoking only in the sitting-room. Parking for seven cars.

OWNERS Carolyn and John Howard OPEN All year, exc Christmas ROOMS 2 double (1 with bath/shower, 1 with wash-basin), 1 twin/family (with wash-basin) TERMS B&B £13–£16, (single occupancy of twin/double) £20 (children under 10 £2.50–£6.50, over 10 £7.50–£10.50 sharing parents' room)

KINGSEY Buckinghamshire map 4

Foxhill

Kingsey, nr Aylesbury HP17 8LZ
HADDENHAM (0844) 291650

This listed seventeenth-century building was formerly a farmhouse, the old timbers of which, clearly visible in one of the bedrooms, may have come from a ship. The house has lots of character with creaky, uneven floors and sloping ceilings. The driveway passes a duck pond, there is a big yard with stables used for lambing and the garden at the back of the house has wonderful rural views and a heated swimming-pool at the far end. There is a huge breakfast room, and upstairs are the three bedrooms, two of which have a private shower. All bedrooms have TV. The house, which belongs to a charming couple who have lived here over 20 years, has a pleasant, relaxed atmosphere and is comfortably furnished. Breakfast only is served, but a portfolio of local restaurants has been assembled for guests. There are also lots of interesting books to choose from. No children under five. No pets. No smoking. Car park.

OWNERS Mary-Joyce and Nicholas Hooper OPEN Feb–end Nov ROOMS 1 double (with shower), 2 twin (1 with shower, 1 with wash-basin) TERMS B&B £16–£19

Those B&Bs that we know can offer some kind of off-street car parking, have 'car park' at the end of the entry. If we are aware of particular car parking difficulties, we mention them.

KINGSTON BAGPUIZE Oxfordshire map 4

Tall Trees

11 Rimes Close, Kingston Bagpuize OX13 5AL
LONGWORTH (0865) 820034

A modern and spacious brick house, six miles west of Abingdon, that stands in one-third of an acre of gardens. This is very much a family home, and there is a large family room with TV and a piano which guests are welcome to play. Breakfast only is served in the dining-room, which leads out to a patio. The immaculate bedrooms, one with TV, are a little small, apart from the twin/family *en suite* room, but are tastefully furnished and comfortable. Children welcome. No smoking in the dining-room. Car park.

OWNER Mrs Margaret Conway OPEN All year, exc Christmas
ROOMS 2 double (with wash-basin), 1 twin/family (with bath/shower)
TERMS B&B £12–£15 (children half-price); deposit

LEDBURY Hereford & Worcester map 4

Wall Hills Country Guest House

Hereford Road, Ledbury HR8 2PR
LEDBURY (0531) 2833

This is an elegant, family-run Georgian guesthouse approached through an orchard and past sheep grazing in the field. The house overlooks Ledbury and enjoys lovely views, including that of a Victorian railway viaduct, from most rooms. The lounge leads out on to the garden where guests can enjoy a drink overlooking the Malvern Hills. A fifteenth-century cruck barn is part of the property and an Iron Age hill fort behind the house may be visited by arrangement. Children are made welcome and they are free to explore the extensive grounds and help feed the chickens. It is, however, the owners' special brand of hospitality and excellent food that guests return for again and again. Local salmon, quail, wild duck and venison are featured on the dinner menu, available 7.30–8.45pm. Vegetarian food is available and the wine list has a good choice. Children welcome. No pets. Smoking in lounge only. Car park.

OWNERS David and Jennifer Slaughter OPEN All year, exc Christmas ROOMS 1 family/double, 1 double, 1 twin; all rooms with bath/shower TERMS B&B £17.50–£19.50, (single occupancy of twin/double) £25–£29 (children £2–£9); dinner £12.50; Access, Visa

LEIGHTON BUZZARD Bedfordshire map 4

Grovebury Farm

Grovebury Road, Leighton Buzzard LU7 8TF
LEIGHTON BUZZARD (0525) 373363

Approaching the farm down a long, unattractive road through an industrial estate, it is hard to imagine there can be anything interesting at the end. Grovebury Farm, which is part of a 450-acre arable and beef farm, is a solid, well-built, whitewashed brick house, standing in very pretty, well-kept gardens, with lovely views over farmland. There is a pleasant dining-room/lounge leading out to the garden and three comfortably furnished, clean and bright bedrooms, all with TV, are available. There are now two bathrooms to share between the bedrooms. The house is full of interesting items including a corner unit displaying dolls' house furniture. No pets in the house. No smoking. Car park.

OWNER Mrs Kinsey OPEN All year ROOMS 1 double, 2 twin
TERMS B&B £13.50, (single occupancy of twin/double) £17–£18

LITTLE MARLOW Buckinghamshire map 2

Monkton Farmhouse

Little Marlow SL7 3RF
HIGH WYCOMBE (0494) 521082 Fax (0494) 443905

The farm lies close to High Wycombe and off the dual-carriageway to Marlow, although only a slight murmur of traffic indicates the proximity of the main road. It consists of 150 acres and includes Ayrshire dairy cows. The fourteenth-century brick-built farmhouse is in lovely countryside with wonderful views from the small garden. The house has lots of beams, crooked walls, uneven floors and the attic-type bedrooms, all with TV, are bright, clean and fresh. Breakfast only is served. There is a large, pleasant lounge/dining-room for guests, but breakfast is eaten at one table to one side of the kitchen. No children under five. No pets. No smoking. Car park.

OWNERS Jane and Warren Kimber OPEN All year ROOMS 1 family, 1 twin, 1 single TERMS B&B from £17.50, (single occupancy of twin) from £20, (family room) from £45 (reductions for children)

Any smoking restrictions that we know of are given in each entry.

LITTLE RISSINGTON Gloucestershire map 4

Badgers Bank

Pound Lane, Little Rissington GL54 2NB
COTSWOLD (0451) 21124

Just one and a half miles from Bourton-on-the-Water and six miles south of Stow-on-the-Wold is this charming house built in 1970 from Cotswold stone. It is in a peaceful spot, amid beautiful landscaped gardens. There are three attractively decorated rooms, tastefully furnished and with everything maintained to a very high standard. There is an elegant sitting-room with TV and hot-drinks facilities which guests may help themselves to at any time. Mrs Harris is very interested in flower arranging, as evidenced by the many attractive displays throughout the house. The twelfth-century church in the village is well worth a visit. Breakfast only is available, although packed lunches can be provided by arrangement. Children welcome. No pets. Smoking in the lounge only. Car park.

OWNERS Mr and Mrs V. W. Harris OPEN All year, exc Christmas and New Year ROOMS 2 double (1 with bath/shower, 1 with wash-basin), 1 twin (with wash-basin) TERMS B&B £14–£16 (children under 10 £5–£8); deposit

LITTLE WITLEY Hereford & Worcester map 4

Ribston House

Little Witley WR6 6LS
WICHENFORD (0886) 888750

Ribston House dates from the sixteenth century and stands in a quiet rural setting with views over the surrounding hills and woods and the imposing ruins of Witley Court. It has been beautifully modernised, sympathetically combining the old with the new. Meeting trains and coaches is all part of the service, and Richard Wells, a patient and knowledgeable guide, is also able to take you to places of interest. Sarah Wells welcomes you on your return with a cup of tea. Several llamas are kept in the field for fleece and breeding, from whose wool Sarah knits designer sweaters. Bookings for bed and breakfast and dinner are preferred. Dinner, which includes wine, is served at 7pm and everything is home-cooked and prepared fresh. Vegetarian choices and packed lunches can be provided. Children welcome. No pets. Smoking restricted. Parking for two cars.

OWNERS Sarah and Richard Wells OPEN All year, exc Christmas and New Year ROOMS 2 double, 1 single; all rooms with bath/shower TERMS B&B £23–£25 (children under 12 half-price); D, B&B £30–£32; deposit £50

LONGDON Hereford & Worcester map 4

The Moat House

Longdon, nr Tewkesbury GL20 6AT
BIRTSMORTON (068 481) 313

A beautiful, black and white Elizabethan building, the Moat House is approached through the stable yard, and across a little bridge over the moat. It has uneven floors, thick stone walls, oak panelling, a wealth of exposed beams and antique furniture. The delightful bedrooms, all with TV, are full of olde worlde charm; two have half-tester beds and the other a brass bed, and all are now *en suite*. There is an abundance of flower baskets, and a wonderful welcoming atmosphere. Dinners are no longer served but there are several eating-places in the area. Sue Virr also runs a veterinary hospital and recuperation centre for racehorses in the

grounds, as well as keeping ducks, guinea-fowl and rare breeds of sheep. Children welcome. No pets. No smoking. Car park.

OWNER Mrs Sue Virr OPEN All year, exc Dec and Jan ROOMS 1 family, 2 double; all rooms with bath/shower TERMS B&B £25, (single occupancy of double) £35 (children under 10 free sharing parents' room – nominal charge for breakfast); deposit; Access, Visa

LONG HANBOROUGH Oxfordshire map 4

The Old Farmhouse

Station Hill, Long Hanborough OX8 8JZ
FREELAND (0993) 882097

Originally a farmhouse, this listed, small stone-built house has lovely views. A small front garden separates it from a rather busy road, but the house is in an elevated position and is set back. The property is very comfortable and tastefully decorated, the bedrooms, one with TV, are large and attractively furnished. The dining-room has one large table and a big pine dresser with pretty china. China pieces also decorate the wall above the big open fireplace in the comfortable sitting-room. Breakfast only is served and on fine days guests can eat in the walled garden overlooking rolling countryside and the distant spires of Oxford. Packed lunches can be provided. No children under 12. No pets. No smoking. Car park.

OWNERS Robert and Vanessa Maundrell OPEN All year, exc Christmas ROOMS 2 double (1 with bath/shower, 1 with wash-basin) TERMS B&B £15–£18, (single occupancy of double) £18–£25

LOXLEY Warwickshire map 4

Loxley Farm

Stratford Road, Loxley CV35 9JN
STRATFORD-UPON-AVON (0789) 840265

In the small village of Loxley, picturesque, thatched Loxley Farm is only three and a half miles from Stratford. The black and white, late-thirteenth-century building is of cruck-frame construction, using wood that is naturally curved to form an arch supporting the end walls. The interior sets off the lovely antique furniture, the Victorian equestrian drawings, the polished wooden floors and gleaming silver. There is a large, comfortable sitting-room, and breakfast is served at the refectory table in the traditional dining-room. There are no evening meals. A family suite is now available, consisting of a double and a single room. There are two *en suite* bedrooms in the barn conversion, as well as a sitting-room, and two rooms have TV. The property extends to six acres, with a pleasant garden, shetland ponies and chickens. Mrs Horton may collect guests from Stratford and even take them there in the morning. Bicycle hire can also be arranged. Children welcome. Car park.

OWNERS Mr and Mrs R. P. K. Horton OPEN All year, exc Christmas ROOMS 1 family, 2 double; all rooms with bath/shower TERMS B&B £18–£19, (single occupancy of double) £25–£26 (children up to 12 half-price); deposit

LUTON Bedfordshire map 5

Belzayne Guest House

70 Lalleford Road, Luton LU2 9JH
LUTON (0582) 36591

This house is very handy for the airport, which is less than a mile away. In a road of recent, brick-built semi-detached houses, Belzayne is on a corner site and has a very neat front garden. There are three small bedrooms and a breakfast room that doubles as lounge and bar. Breakfast only is served. The accommodation is basic, spotlessly clean and modestly priced. A taxi service and breakfast trays for early travellers can be arranged. No children under six. No pets. Smoking in lounge only. Car park.

OWNERS Andy and Elsie Bell OPEN All year, exc Christmas and 2-week hol ROOMS 1 double, 2 twin TERMS B&B £11 (single occupancy of twin/double) £18; deposit £5

LYONSHALL Hereford & Worcester map 6

Church House

Lyonshall, nr Kington HR5 3HR
LYONSHALL (054 48) 350

This small Georgian house stands in four and a half acres of gardens and paddocks with lovely views. The house is furnished in Edwardian style: pretty hats on the hallstand, ribboned cushions, old framed photographs and a pretty plate collection. The bedrooms are fairly large and subtly decorated. There is a pleasant, comfortably furnished guest lounge with TV. Three-course dinners are available at 7.30pm, if pre-arranged; special diets, including vegetarian, can be catered for and guests may bring their own wine (there is no alcohol licence). A self-catering cottage in the grounds is available. Children welcome. No pets. No smoking. Car park.

OWNERS Ted and Eileen Dilley OPEN All year, exc Christmas ROOMS 1 four-poster (with bath/shower), 1 double (with wash-basin), 1 twin (with wash-basin) TERMS B&B £15–£17, (single occupancy of twin/double) £20 (children ⅓–⅔ reduction sharing adult room); dinner £8; deposit 20%

MALVERN WELLS Hereford & Worcester map 4

Mellbreak

177 Wells Road, Malvern Wells WR14 4HE
MALVERN (0684) 561287

A Grade II listed building dating from the 1830s, Mellbreak is a detached, late-Regency three-storey house in a third of an acre of terraced gardens with views over the Severn and Avon valleys. It was formerly a gentleman's residence and at one time the headmaster's house to the Wells House preparatory school. The house is situated on the main road just beyond the Three Counties Showground and is furnished with a mixture of antiques and traditional and twentieth-century craftsman-made furniture. The bedrooms are tastefully decorated with pretty, soft-coloured wallpapers and all have TV, hair-dryer and clock-radio. Mrs Cheeseman is noted for her cooking, based on traditional English recipes. Evening meals, including vegetarian choices, are served 6.30–9pm and may offer such dishes as cream of artichoke soup, roast pheasant and apple and blackcurrant pie. There is a well-stocked wine cellar. Breakfast is hearty, with guests helping themselves buffet-style. Packed lunches can also be provided. 'Well-behaved' children only. Small dogs by arrangement. Car park.

OWNER Mrs R. A. Cheeseman OPEN All year ROOMS 1 family, 1 double, 1 twin, 1 single; all rooms, exc single (wash-basin only), with bath/shower TERMS B&B £16 (children under 8 half-price); dinner £9; deposit 50%

Many B&Bs will cater for vegetarians. It is always best, however, to check when booking and make it clear what your requirements are, especially if you need a special diet.

MAXSTOKE Warwickshire map 4

Maxstoke Priory

Maxstoke, Coleshill B46 2QW
COLESHILL (0675) 462117

Maxstoke Priory is a timber-gabled property set in 300 acres and surrounded by open countryside, eight miles from Birmingham and Coventry. It has been in the same family for over 100 years and is full of character. Entrance to the house is through a sandstone arch and iron-studded doors. The 700-year-old priory gate is still in working order. There is an outdoor, unheated swimming-pool. The house has been beautifully furnished. All rooms have TV. Breakfast only is served in the oak-panelled dining-room, which has a hand-painted ceiling. There is also a comfortably furnished lounge. Children welcome. Car park.

OWNER Mrs P. Tyacke OPEN All year ROOMS 2 twin (with bath/shower) TERMS B&B £18–£19, (single occupancy of twin) £24–£26 (children under 10 half-price)

MORDIFORD Hereford & Worcester map 4

Orchard Farm

Mordiford, nr Hereford HR1 4EJ
HOLME LACY (0432) 870253

Orchard Farm is a stone-built seventeenth-century farmhouse, furnished in keeping with the building's character: oak beams, flagstone floors and an inglenook fireplace. The farm covers 57 acres, inhabited by wild deer, badgers, rabbits, kestrels and owls. There are three comfortable bedrooms, a lounge with TV and a quiet lounge where smoking is permitted. Apart from the idyllic setting and Mrs Barrell's special brand of hospitality, guests return also for the delicious home-made food, complemented by wine from local vineyards and cider and perry made from Herefordshire apples and pears. Mouth-watering scones with home-made preserves are a speciality of the house. Vegetarians can be catered for. The River Lugg runs through the property and one mile of coarse fishing is available. Watch out as you approach the private lane to the house – it is not difficult to end up in the ditch. Orchard Farm is four miles east of Hereford on the B4224.

If any bedrooms are suitable for the disabled we mention this in the entry.

No children under 10. Pets by arrangement. Smoking in one sitting-room only. Car park.

OWNER Mrs Marjorie Barrell OPEN All year, exc Christmas ROOMS 2 double, 1 twin; all rooms with wash-basin TERMS B&B £14, (single occupancy of twin/double) from £16 (reductions for children sharing parents' room); dinner from £10; deposit; Amex

MURSLEY Buckinghamshire map 4

Richmond Lodge

Mursley, nr Milton Keynes MK17 0LE
MURSLEY (0296) 720275

Close to Milton Keynes, this house, built just before the First World War as a shooting lodge, stands in its own grounds of three acres with glorious gardens and paddocks. There are lovely views over the Vale of Aylesbury to Waddesdon. The bedrooms, both with TV, are bright, freshly decorated with lots of extra touches, and colour-co-ordinated with matching fabrics. Breakfast, including home-made jams, and evening meals (7pm by arrangement) are served on the patio weather permitting. Vegetarian choices and packed lunches can be provided. There is no alcohol licence, but guests may bring their own wine to dinner. A beautiful lounge is also available for guests' use. Its proximity to Milton Keynes makes Richmond Lodge a popular choice for business people. No children under seven. Babies welcome. No dogs in the house. No smoking. Car park.

OWNERS Christine and Peter Abbey OPEN All year, exc Christmas ROOMS 2 twin (1 with bath/shower, 1 with wash-basin) TERMS B&B from £18, (single occupancy of twin) from £25 *en suite* (babies £5); deposit

NEWENT Gloucestershire map 4

Orchard House

Aston Ingham Road, Kilcot, nr Newent GL18 1NP
GORSLEY (0989) 82417

This beautifully appointed home, surrounded by five acres of extensive grounds including lawns, paddocks and wooded paths, is in a peaceful setting close to the Wye Valley and Forest of Dean. Anne Thompson, a charming lady, opened her bed and breakfast in May 1991. There are three bedrooms, one *en suite* and two that share a large, luxurious bathroom. There is a TV lounge and a quiet snug area with a good view. Both the lounge and dining-room have wood-burning stoves. Evening meals are served at 8pm in a dinner-party atmosphere, and Anne Thompson, who dines with her guests, is already gaining a reputation for her excellent, imaginative cooking. Lunches and vegetarian choices can be provided and there is an alcohol licence. There are several areas outside for sitting, including a conservatory overlooking the water fountain and terraced courtyard. This is a good base from which to explore the Forest of Dean, Wye Valley and Brecon Beacons. Orchard House is two miles west of Newent on the B4222. 'Well-behaved' children only. No pets in the house. No smoking. Parking for 10 cars.

OWNERS Basil and Anne Thompson OPEN All year
ROOMS 2 double (1 with bath/shower), 1 twin TERMS B&B £17.50–£27.50 (children ½–⅔ reduction depending on age); dinner £12.50; deposit £10 per person; Access, Visa

NEWGATE STREET VILLAGE Hertfordshire map 5

Home Farm

Newgate Street Village, nr Hertford SG13 8RD
CUFFLEY (0707) 872685

Home Farm comes as something of a surprise in this suburban sprawl, although Newgate Street Village itself is quiet and peaceful with a couple of decent pubs. Down a quiet lane, bordered with modern housing, it is a pleasant whitewashed building, standing in its own garden and enjoying wonderful views over woodland. The house offers clean and comfortable accommodation. There are no bedrooms with private facilities, but there are now two shower-rooms plus a bathroom exclusively for guests' use. All bedrooms have TV. Breakfast only is available and is taken at two tables in the dining-room. Mrs Milton Brooks is a friendly, outgoing lady who makes guests feel very much at home. No babies. No pets. Car park.

OWNER R. Milton Brooks OPEN All year, exc Christmas
ROOMS 1 family, 2 double, 1 twin, 2 single; all rooms, exc double, with wash-basin TERMS B&B £17.50 (reductions for children under 10)

Where a single-occupancy rate is not specified in the details, the cost will be the same as that per person in a twin or double room, or will be included in the range of prices given.

NEWNHAM Gloucestershire map 4

Broughtons

Flaxley Road, nr Newnham GL14 1JW
GLOUCESTER (0452) 760328

A warm welcome is guaranteed at Broughtons, the comfortable, elegant home of Captain and Mrs Bill Swinley. Built 200 years ago, it is set in four acres of lovely grounds, on the edge of the Forest of Dean, with glorious views across the River Severn. As a naval family, the Swinleys have lived abroad for many years, and as a special welcome to guests from overseas they fly the appropriate national flag throughout a visit. There are two guest suites, one comprising bedroom, sitting-room and bathroom, the other a large bed-sitting-room and adjacent bathroom; both have TV and panoramic views. There is a tennis court and croquet lawn for guests' use. Arrangements may be made to pick up guests without cars at any point (including airports), and Mrs Swinley is always happy to drive visitors on a tour in her car by prior arrangement. Guests are welcome to use the fully equipped laundry, and there are bicycles for hire. Breakfast only is available and may be served on the terrace on fine days. Sample menus from local pubs and restaurants are provided, and guests are invited to stay here for at least two nights, if possible. Broughton is on the Flaxley road, off the A48 between Newnham and Westbury-on-Severn. No children under seven. No pets. No smoking in bedrooms. Car park.

OWNERS Captain and Mrs Bill Swinley OPEN All year, exc Christmas ROOMS 2 twin (with bath/shower) TERMS B&B £16–£18

NORTHLEACH Gloucestershire map 4

Market House

The Square, Northleach GL54 3EJ
COTSWOLD (0451) 60557
(from mid-summer 1992: (0451) 860557)

Built in 1580 as a covered sheep-fleece market, Market House was converted in 1750 into two residential cottages. In 1950 it was once again converted, into a single dwelling. Several original features remain: inglenook fireplace, flagstone floors and exposed beams. There is a lovely sitting-room with log fires and TV and a complete portfolio on what to see and do in the area. There are three charming bedrooms, one with private bath, exposed stone walls and original fireplaces. Early morning tea or coffee is served at no extra charge and tasty, freshly prepared breakfasts are served. Packed lunches can also be provided. There is a secluded, stone-walled garden full of climbing evergreens, mature trees and shrubs. No children under 10. No pets. No smoking in bedrooms. Car park.

OWNERS Theresa and Mike Eastman OPEN All year
ROOMS 2 double (1 with bath/shower, 1 with wash-basin), 1 twin (with wash-basin) TERMS B&B £14–£15; deposit 1 night charge

Prospect Cottage

West End, Northleach GL54 3HG
COTSWOLD (0451) 60875

This is a delightful cottage made from Cotswold stone and located at the edge of this pretty unspoilt village. One of the best things about the cottage is Mrs Hobley herself, for whom nothing is too much trouble. Breakfast is served at times to suit guests and there are no petty rules. The house has been refurbished but retains many of the original features, including exposed beams and stone walls. The beamed bedrooms, both with TV, gleam and have pretty curtains and fabrics. There is a large, well-furnished dining-room/lounge exclusively for guests. In Northleach, the fascinating Mechanical Music Museum, famous ancient church and the Cotswold Countryside Collection are all well worth a visit. Children and pets by arrangement.

OWNER Mrs Ann Hobley OPEN All year ROOMS 1 double, 1 twin; both rooms with bath/shower TERMS B&B £25; Access, Amex, Visa

OXFORD Oxfordshire map 4

Cotswold House

363 Banbury Road, Oxford OX2 7PL
OXFORD (0865) 310558

Cotswold House has been totally refurbished. It is a neat, fairly modern, small stone-built house on the main Banbury Road into Oxford, about two miles from the centre. It is furnished to a very high standard, with modern furniture, and the pleasant entrance hall with oriental rugs sets the tone. Immaculately clean, the bedrooms are of a good size, all with bathroom, TV, video and fridge. A ground-floor bathroom is now available. Jim and Anne

O'Kane are extremely knowledgeable about the area and are happy to take the time to help guests to plan daily activities. There is a small dining-room where traditional and vegetarian breakfasts only are served. No children under five. No pets. No smoking. Car park.

OWNERS Jim and Anne O'Kane OPEN All year, exc Christmas week ROOMS 2 family, 1 double, 1 twin, 2 single; all rooms with bath/shower TERMS B&B £24, (single) £32, (single occupancy of twin/double) £40, (family room) £58

The Dial House

25 London Road, Headington, Oxford OX3 7RE
OXFORD (0865) 69944

This well-built 1930s house, on the main London Road in Headington, is well placed for bus routes into the centre of Oxford, about a mile and a half away. Spotlessly clean, the bedrooms, all with bathroom, TV, hair-dryer and easy chairs, are of a good size, bright and airy and comfortably furnished; many overlook the pretty garden. There is a small smoking lounge, with doors leading out to the garden, and a bright dining-room where breakfast only is served. The house is well maintained and has been freshly redecorated. No children under six. 'Well-behaved' dogs in bedrooms only. Smoking in guest lounge only. Car park.

OWNERS A. J. and J. M. Lamb OPEN All year, exc Christmas and New Year ROOMS 2 family, 4 double, 2 twin; all rooms with bath/shower TERMS B&B £21–£25, (single occupancy of twin/double) £40–£45, (family room) £57 (children 6–12 half-price); deposit £20 per room

Earlmont Guest House

322/324 Cowley Road, Oxford OX4 2AF
OXFORD (0865) 240236

The Earlmont Guest House is a good base for exploring Oxford. It is a mile from the centre, five to 10 minutes away by bus. The bedrooms, all with TV, are small and simply furnished. There is a compact TV lounge and a dining-room, and on the other side of the road is an annexe with seven bedrooms. Breakfast only is available, although packed lunches can be provided. The owners are happy to help with tour planning and forward booking of

If a deposit is required for an advance booking this is stated at the end of an entry.

other accommodation. No children under five. No pets. Non-smoking rooms available. Parking for nine cars.

OWNERS Mr and Mrs P. B. Facer OPEN All year, exc Christmas and New Year ROOMS 2 family, 4 double (2 with bath/shower), 4 twin, 3 single; 11 rooms with wash-basin TERMS B&B £17–£25, (single) £20–£35 (children under 11 half-price); deposit 1 night charge; Access, Amex, Visa

The Gables

6 Cumnor Hill, Oxford OX2 9HA
OXFORD (0865) 862153

Occupying a corner site on one of the main roads into Oxford and a couple of miles from the centre, the Gables is a pink-washed building providing very clean and simple accommodation. Dianne White took over the business from her mother in June 1990 and has been redecorating and making improvements. The bedrooms, all with TV, are small. Breakfast only is available. There is a tiny lounge off the dining-room. Children welcome. Dogs only. Car park.

OWNER Dianne White OPEN All year, exc Christmas
ROOMS 1 family, 1 double, 2 twin, 1 single; all rooms with bath/shower TERMS B&B £18–£20, (single occupancy of twin/double) £25 (reductions for children); deposit

Norham Guest House

16 Norham Road, Oxford OX2 6SF
OXFORD (0865) 515352

This late-Victorian house is in a conservation area, near the lovely university parks and a 15-minute stroll from the town centre. The Welhams have totally redecorated the house, which is bright and attractive. Breakfast only is available and is served in the sunny dining-room overlooking the pretty front garden with lots of flower-filled window boxes. No children under four. No pets. No smoking in the dining-room and non-smokers preferred. Car park.

OWNERS Rosemary and Peter Welham OPEN All year
ROOMS 2 family, 1 double, 3 twin, 2 single; all rooms with wash-basin
TERMS B&B £19.50–£20, (single occupancy of twin/double) £27–£35, (family room) £60; deposit 50%

Most establishments have central heating. We say when this is not the case.

St Michael's Guest House

26 St Michael's Street, Oxford OX1 2EB
OXFORD (0865) 242101

A modest guesthouse that is within minutes of the city centre, train station and bus station. It is ideal for guests arriving by local transport as parking is just about impossible. Parts of the house date back over 300 years, and sections of the original wall run through the house in the cellar. The bedrooms, all with TV, are a little small, but clean and functional. Children welcome.

OWNERS Paul Wright and Margaret Hoskins OPEN All year
ROOMS 2 family, 1 double, 1 twin, 2 single; all rooms with wash-basin
TERMS B&B £18, (single occupancy of twin/double) £35, (family room) £45 (children £10); deposit £10

OXHILL Warwickshire map 4

Nolands Farm

Oxhill CV35 0RJ
KINETON (0926) 640309

Nolands Farm dates from 1840 and offers guests an opportunity to sample a slice of genuine farm life. The old barns have been carefully converted to provide interesting accommodation. All the bedrooms now have *en suite* facilities and there are six ground-floor rooms, overlooking the old stableyards, fields, a lake with fly and coarse fishing, a large garden and woods full of wildlife and interesting walks. There are two romantic Tudor-style four-poster beds and all bedrooms have TV. There is a drawing-room with log fires, and a separate dining-room, which has a varied breakfast menu. The licensed restaurant, no longer open to non-residents and closed on Sunday, serves excellent evening meals (7pm, reservations recommended), including vegetarian choices by arrangement. Packed lunches are also available. Special weekend breaks are offered, including flower arranging, cookery and painting. Clay pigeon shooting and bicycle hire can be organised.

B&B rates specified in the details for each entry are per person per night; unless the details state otherwise, they are based on two people sharing a double or twin-bedded room.

When the family-room rate is given in the details it applies to the cost of the whole room, unless a rate per person is specified.

A self-catering unit is also available. Children welcome. Guide dogs only. Car park.

OWNER Sue Hutsby OPEN All year, exc Dec ROOMS 1 family, 2 four-poster, 4 double, 1 twin, 1 single; all rooms with bath/shower TERMS B&B from £15, (four poster) from £18, (single) £20–£25, (single occupancy of twin/double) £25, (family room) from £52 (children under 12 from £11); dinner from £13.50; deposit; Access, Visa; surcharge on credit cards

PAINSWICK Gloucestershire map 4

Lower Green House

Green House Lane, Painswick, nr Stroud GL6 6SE
PAINSWICK (0452) 812304

Situated on the Cotswold Way, Lower Green House is ideal for walkers. It is an attractive 300-year-old Cotswold-stone woodworkers' house set in rolling hills overlooking Painswick, a quarter of a mile away. Simon and Libby Graesser bought the property in 1984; it had not been modernised since 1866, so updating it to its current high standard of comfort without detracting from the old charm presented quite a challenge. It is an interesting building with inglenook fireplaces, a bread oven, an internal well, stone-flagged floors and antique furniture. The bedrooms are cosy, with patchwork quilts on the beds, and there is a Victorian bathroom. Full English breakfast, including black pudding, is served. There is also a self-catering apartment which is suitable for the disabled. Dogs must sleep in guests' car. Car park.

OWNERS Simon and Libby Graesser OPEN All year ROOMS 1 double, 1 twin TERMS B&B £18, (single occupancy of twin/double) £24 (children £12 sharing parents' room)

PANGBOURNE Berkshire map 2

Weir View Guest House

9 Shooters Hill, Pangbourne RG8 7DZ
READING (0734) 842120

This family house overlooks the river and weir, right in the centre of Pangbourne, and is set above the main road in terraced gardens. The railway line runs just above the house, and the station is only a two-minute walk away, making Weir View very accessible from London and other major centres. The bedrooms, all with TV, are functional and of a good size. Breakfast only is available. The front rooms have lovely weir views and guests can accompany Mr King to the river on his daily pilgrimage to feed the swans. The Swan pub on the edge of the river serves food. No children under seven. No pets. No smoking. Car park.

OWNERS R. A. and E. King OPEN All year, exc Christmas ROOMS 2 double, (1 with bath/shower, 1 with wash-basin), 1 twin (with wash-basin) TERMS B&B £17.50–£22.50, (single occupancy of twin/double) £28; deposit £10 per room; Access, Visa

READING Berkshire map 2

Abadair House

46 Redlands Road, Reading RG1 5HE
READING (0734) 863792

The house is a spacious, brick-built Edwardian property in a fairly busy road, very conveniently located for the Royal Berkshire Hospital and the university, and a 15-minute walk from the centre of town. It attracts many professional people connected to the university or hospital. Most of the rooms are now *en suite* or have private showers; all of them have TV, are bright and furnished with armchairs. There is a small dining-room where breakfast only is served. Packed lunches can be provided. Children welcome. No pets. No smoking in public areas. Car park.

OWNERS Mr and Mrs Clifford OPEN All year ROOMS 1 double (with shower), 3 twin (with bath/shower), 5 single (3 with bath/shower, 2 with shower) TERMS B&B £15–£19, (single) £23–£27.50 (children under 12 £5–£10)

Ye Olde Coach House

127 South View Avenue, Caversham, Reading RG4 0BB
READING (0734) 476627

This little guesthouse, one of two former coach-houses, is a most surprising find, in a very unobtrusive road in Lower Caversham. It is a modest-looking brick house with a very large, neatly kept rear garden, with lawns, flower-beds, goldfish pond, patio and, at the far end, a gravel parking area. There are six small but neat bedrooms, two of which are on the ground floor. All have TV and are fresh and very clean. Breakfast only is available and is served

If we know a B&Bs has an alcohol licence, we say so.

in the cosy dining-room overlooking the garden. Children welcome. No pets. Car park.

OWNERS Mr David and Mrs Hazel Hinton OPEN All year, exc Christmas ROOMS 1 double (with bath/shower), 1 twin (with bath/shower), 4 single (2 with bath/shower, 2 with wash-basin)
TERMS B&B £20, (single) £23–£25, (single occupancy of twin/double) £30 (reductions for children)

ROSS-ON-WYE Hereford & Worcester map 4

Edde Cross House

Edde Cross Street, Ross-on-Wye HR9 7BZ
ROSS-ON-WYE (0989) 65088

From 1907 to 1913 Sybil, the Dame of Sark, lived here. Edde Cross House is an elegant listed Georgian town house in a charming walled garden on a bluff overlooking a horseshoe bend on the River Wye, yet only minutes from the centre of Ross-on-Wye. The standards here continue to be impeccable. The house is beautifully furnished in old pine and tastefully decorated; the comfortable lounge has books, magazines and various games for guests' use. Breakfast only is available, but a folder with menus from numerous local restaurants, most within a few minutes' walk, is given to guests who want to eat out. All bedrooms have TV. The house is warm and comfortable and retains the welcoming atmosphere of a private home. Drying and ironing facilities are available. Cheap autumn and spring breaks are offered. No children under 10. No pets. No smoking.

OWNER Renate Van Gelderen OPEN Feb–Nov ROOMS 3 double, (2 with bath/shower, 1 with wash-basin), 1 twin (with wash-basin), 1 single (with wash-basin) TERMS B&B £16–£21.50, (single occupancy of twin/double) £24–£35; deposit

Linden House

14 Church Street, Ross-on-Wye HR9 5HN
ROSS-ON-WYE (0989) 65373

Linden House is a town house built around 1680, covered in summer with window boxes and hanging baskets. It is in a quiet street overlooking St Mary's Church and only a couple of minutes from the centre of town. The three-course dinner menu, served at 6.30pm, with everything home-cooked, includes a vegetarian choice, and packed lunches can be prepared on request. A menu may include carrot, apple and cashew-nut soup, Herefordshire chicken and home-made ice-cream. Linden House is licensed. The bedrooms, although a little small, are comfortable, with old pine furniture and brass beds; all have TV. Meals are served in the dining-room, which has a fireplace and a Victorian dresser. Mr and Mrs O'Reilly are happy to collect guests from Hereford and Gloucester, and can lay on dinner parties for small groups. They are also concerned for the environment, using only bio-degradable cleaning products and loo rolls made from recycled paper. No children under eight. No pets. No smoking.

OWNERS Patrick and Clare O'Reilly OPEN All year
ROOMS 3 double (1 with bath/shower), 1 twin, 4 single; 7 rooms with wash-basin TERMS B&B £16.50 approx, (single) £18.50 approx, (single occupancy of twin/double) £26 approx (children 8–13 £9.50 in z-bed); dinner £12 approx; deposit

ROYAL LEAMINGTON SPA Warwickshire map 4

Charnwood Guest House

47 Avenue Road, Royal Leamington Spa CV31 3PF
LEAMINGTON SPA (0926) 831074

This is an attractive semi-detached Victorian house, five minutes' walk from the town centre. The spotless bedrooms, all with TV, vary in size and are traditionally furnished; one has a pine bed and *en suite* corner bath. The owners provide comfortable accommodation in an informal and homely atmosphere. Breakfast is served in a bright dining-room and evening meals are served by prior arrangement weekdays only. Vegetarian choices and packed lunches can be provided. Children welcome. Pets by arrangement. No smoking in the dining-room. Car park.

OWNERS Mr A. Grasby, Mrs A. Phillips and Mr S. Phillips OPEN All year, exc Christmas ROOMS 1 family (with bath/shower), 2 double (1 with bath/shower, 1 with wash-basin), 2 twin (with wash-basin), 1 single (with wash-basin) TERMS B&B £14–£18, (single occupancy of double/twin) £19–£28; dinner £6.50; deposit; Access, Visa

The description for each entry states when pets are not allowed. Where no details are given, you can assume that pets are allowed. It's always best to check first in any case.

Reduced rates for children are normally given when they share their parents' bedroom. If no reductions are specified in the details or text, assume you'll have to pay full rates.

ST ALBANS Hertfordshire map 5

Care Inns

29 Alma Road, St Albans AL1 3AT
ST ALBANS (0727) 867310

A semi-detached Victorian house that is three minutes from the station and seven minutes from the town centre. Karin Arscott, who is a friendly, well-travelled Anglicised German, enjoys people and languages, speaking French, Spanish, Italian and German. All the bedrooms are now *en suite*, and all have TV. Breakfast only is available, but there is a good selection of restaurants and pubs within a two-minute walk. Children welcome. Car park.

OWNER Mrs Karen Arscott OPEN All year ROOMS 1 family/double, 1 twin, 1 single; all rooms with bath/shower TERMS B&B £18–£20, (single occupancy of twin/double) £25 (children under 12 half-price)

ST BRIAVELS Gloucestershire map 4

Cinderhill House

St Briavels GL15 6RH
DEAN (0594) 530393

Cinderhill House is in a superb position just below the Norman castle at St Briavels, overlooking the River Wye, with panoramic views over magnificent countryside to the Sugar Loaf mountain and Brecon Beacons beyond. It is full of character, parts dating from the fourteenth-century, with exposed beams, inglenook fireplaces, flagstone floors and an old bread oven. Gillie Peacock makes her guests feel relaxed and comfortable, and takes pride in ensuring that her meals are well balanced, tasty and interesting, with all diets catered for. In the winter, tea and scones are served around a log fire in the guests' beamed sitting-room or on the sun-facing terrace in the summer. Dinner is served in the licensed dining-room at 7.30pm and packed lunches can be provided. There is a separate guest lounge with TV. All the bedrooms are well appointed and tastefully decorated; one room has TV. There are some lovely walks close by, although the terrain is somewhat hilly. Special-interest weekends, including food, wine, bird-watching and painting, can be arranged throughout the year. There is also a cottage with a four-poster bed, offering the same

Use the maps and indexes at the back of the Guide *to plan your trip.*

high standards as are found in the house. Children welcome. No dogs in the house. Smoking only in the sitting-room. Car park.

OWNER Mrs Gillie Peacock OPEN All year ROOMS 1 four-poster, 3 double, 2 twin; all rooms with bath/shower TERMS B&B from £21, (four-poster) £29.50, (single occupancy of twin/double) from £30 (reductions for children depending on age); dinner £15.50; deposit

ST OWEN'S CROSS Hereford & Worcester map 4

Aberhall Farm

St Owen's Cross, nr Hereford HR2 8LL
HAREWOOD END (098 987) 256

Dating from 1636, and in those days called Aberhall Manor, Aberhall Farm is a working farm, with beef cattle and arable crops. The farm is situated on the B4521, 200 yards off the road, only five miles from the small market town of Ross-on-Wye, and a short distance from Monmouth. The bedrooms have superb views, overlooking the garden and rolling border countryside, and are furnished in keeping with the character of the house. There is a pleasant lounge, separate dining-room, and a games-room in the cellar. A farm-fresh breakfast is served; evening meals are no longer available but there are four pubs within a half a mile. Visitors are welcome to walk around the farm. There is a hard tennis court and a peaceful and tranquil spot in the garden where guests can enjoy a cool drink on fine days. No children under 10. No pets. No smoking. Parking for three cars.

OWNER Freda Davies OPEN Mar–Nov ROOMS 2 double (1 with bath/shower, 1 with wash-basin), 1 twin (with wash-basin) TERMS B&B £13.50–£15.50, (single occupancy of twin/double) £18.50; deposit

SHEFFORD WOODLANDS Berkshire map 2

Fishers Farm

Shefford Woodlands, nr Newbury RG16 7AB
GREAT SHEFFORD (048 839) 466
(from summer 1992: (0488) 648466)

Only a stone's throw from the M4 junction 14 and off the B4000, this charming brick-built farmhouse with roses climbing up the front is in the middle of a 600-acre farm in peaceful countryside. It is a spacious house, furnished as a comfortable family home, with a lovely indoor swimming-pool. The bedrooms are all large and bright, and there is a pleasant sitting-room. Breakfast is served at a table at one end of the kitchen. Evening meals (7.30–9.30pm) and lunches can be provided if arranged in advance. Fishers Farm is unlicensed, but guests may bring their own wine. Mary Wilson speaks German and Spanish. The house is a TV-free zone. No children under 10 for 'long' stays. No pets in the house. Smoking only in the drawing-room. Car park.

OWNER Mary Wilson OPEN All year ROOMS 1 family, 1 double, 1 twin; all rooms with bath/shower TERMS B&B £20, (single occupancy) £30 (children under 10 £10 in parents' room); dinner £15; deposit

SHENINGTON Oxfordshire map 4

Sugarswell Farm

Shenington, nr Banbury OX15 6HW
TYSOE (029 588) 512

A large, well-built modern stone farmhouse standing in lovely open countryside, this house has been furnished to a high standard, with exceptionally large bedrooms and bathrooms. Rosemary Nunneley is a cordon bleu cook and is happy to provide evening meals at 6.30pm if required. There is no alcohol licence, but guests may bring their own wine to dinner. Both dinner and breakfast are served at one big table in the dining-room, which is separated from the hallway by an unusual glass case with a fine display of porcelain. Guests also have use of the large drawing-room, where log fires glow on chilly days. No children under 12. No pets. No smoking. Car park.

OWNER Rosemary Nunneley OPEN All year ROOMS 1 double, 2 twin; all rooms with bath/shower TERMS B&B £18–£20, (single occupancy of twin/double) £25–£28; dinner £15; deposit £10 per person

SHERBOURNE Warwickshire map 4

Fulbrook Edge

Sherbourne Hill, nr Warwick CV35 8AG
BARFORD (0926) 624242

This is a welcoming place in a peaceful location set in two and a half acres of gardens, overlooking the valley of the River Avon and the Cotswold Hills. It is quite easy to locate, midway between

Stratford-upon-Avon and Warwick on the A46. The three very large bedrooms are beautifully appointed, tastefully furnished and decorated, and all have sitting areas and TV; two overlook beautiful countryside. Horses and pheasants can often be found in the five-acre paddock, and a croquet lawn is available for guests. Mr and Mrs Lillywhite are extremely knowledgeable about the area and are always happy to assist guests with itineraries. Tasty, substantial breakfasts are served. Horse-riding and hot-air-balloon flights are available locally. There are also several golf courses close by. Not suitable for small children. No pets. No smoking in bedrooms. Car park.

OWNERS Mr and Mrs R. B. Lillywhite OPEN All year, exc Christmas and New Year ROOMS 1 double, 2 twin; all rooms with wash-basin TERMS B&B £16–£17.50, (single occupancy of twin/double) £25; deposit £10 per room

SLAD Gloucestershire map 4

Chessed

Slad, nr Stroud GL6 7QD
GLOUCESTER (0452) 812253

Chessed is Arabic for warm welcome and guests are assured of just that in this large, unpretentious house, situated on the edge of an unspoilt village. The house is a blaze of colour in summer with lots of beautiful hanging baskets. The bedrooms, both with fireplaces, are furnished with antiques, and one has an antique brass bed. There are several areas for sitting, including a lounge, a conservatory and a terraced garden. Mrs Wood is a charming hostess who prepares excellent evening meals (7–8pm) on request, and there are several eating establishments in the village. Chessed is not licensed, but guests may bring their own wine to dinner. Packed lunches can also be provided. The house is in an elevated, peaceful position, and may not be suitable for the infirm or disabled as there are lots of steps up to the front of the house. The house was built in 1903 and retains many original features including the beautiful stained-glass windows in the hallway. There is also a swimming-pool for guests' use. Children welcome. 'Well-trained' dogs only. Car park.

OWNERS Mr and Mrs Wood OPEN All year ROOMS 1 double/family, 1 twin; both rooms with bath/shower TERMS B&B £18.50, (single occupancy of twin/double) £20–£25 (children £10–£15); dinner £8.50; deposit

STOULTON Hereford & Worcester map 4

Caldewell

Pershore Road, Stoulton WR7 4RL
WORCESTER (0905) 840894

Caldewell is a listed Georgian building, originally a country squire's house, in grounds of 25 acres. There is a small lake for coarse fishing, a slightly bumpy tennis court, croquet, a guests' garden, a 16-acre wood, an old cider mill and stables, plus a miniature steam railway; there are also friendly farm animals such as goats and poultry. The bedrooms are large, well furnished and comfortable. There is now an additional double room which has *en suite* facilities. Breakfast and freshly prepared home-style evening meals (6.30–7pm) are served at a refectory table in the large, flagstone-floored dining-room. Packed lunches and vegetarian meals can be provided. Caldewell is unlicensed, but guests may bring their own wine. Children welcome. Car park.

OWNERS Mrs S. M. Booth and Mrs A. B. Leslie OPEN Mar–Dec, exc Christmas and New Year ROOMS 1 family (with wash-basin), 2 double (1 with bath/shower, 1 with wash-basin), 1 twin (with wash-basin) TERMS B&B £14.50–£19.50 approx (children under 2 free, 2–12 half-price); dinner £7

STOW-ON-THE-WOLD Gloucestershire map 4

Cotstone House

Union Street, Stow-on-the-Wold GL54 1BU
COTSWOLD (0451) 32210 (from 1 April 1992: (0451) 832210)

This attractive three-storey house, built in 1908 of Cotswold stone, is situated in a quiet side-street in this picturesque village. The delightful bedrooms have wrought-iron and brass flower-pattern-design fittings, with stripped-pine and cane furnishings. There is a huge teddy bear on the stairs, and a lovely plate collection in the hallway. Two of the bedrooms are on the first floor; the third bedroom on the top floor is adjacent to the bathroom. Cotstone House is run by Jan Wegerdt who creates a warm and welcoming atmosphere. There is a small guest lounge with TV. Breakfast consists of a wide choice of cereals, fresh fruit and home-baked croissants, followed by a traditional cooked

Most establishments have central heating. We say when this is not the case.

breakfast. There are eating-places within walking distance. No children, pets or smoking. Car park.

OWNER Jan Wegerdt OPEN According to demand ROOMS 2 double/ twin; both rooms with wash-basin TERMS B&B £15, (single occupancy) £20; deposit £10

Wyck Hill Lodge

Wyck Hill, Stow-on-the-Wold GL54 1HT
COTSWOLD (0451) 30141 (from 1 April 1992: (0451) 830141)

This is a listed Victorian lodge in country surroundings with views over the Vale of Bourton. Mrs Alderton took over this already well-established B&B in September 1990. The three bedrooms are all *en suite*. Two are on the ground floor, one having a brass bed, while another leads out directly on to the lovely gardens. All bedrooms have TV. Mrs Alderton prepares excellent breakfasts, and dinners are also served daily (7.15–7.30pm) except Tuesday and Friday. Vegetarian choices and packed lunches can be provided. There is no alcohol licence, but guests may bring their own wine. Mr Alderton is a keen golfer and is happy to advise guests on local courses. No children under 10. No pets. No smoking in bedrooms. Car park.

OWNER Mrs Jacqueline Alderton OPEN All year, exc Christmas ROOMS 2 double, 1 twin; all rooms with bath/shower TERMS B&B £18–£21, (single occupancy of twin/double) £26–£30; dinner £12–£13; deposit

STRATFORD-UPON-AVON Warwickshire map 4

Brook Lodge

192 Alcester Road, Stratford-upon-Avon CV37 9DR
STRATFORD-UPON-AVON (0789) 295988

If you want to see Anne Hathaway's cottage, Brook Lodge is just around the corner, one mile from the city centre, on the edge of open countryside. The immaculate bedrooms are tastefully decorated with pretty wallpapers, and all have TV, radio and hair-dryer. High standards continue to be upheld at this comfortable guesthouse. Breakfast only is served in the pretty

Where a single-occupancy rate is not specified in the details, the cost will be the same as that per person in a twin or double room, or will be included in the range of prices given.

dining-room. Children welcome. No smoking in the dining-room. Parking for 10 cars.

OWNERS Anne and Michael Black OPEN All year, exc Christmas and New Year ROOMS 2 family (1 with bath/shower, 1 with wash-basin), 3 double (with bath/shower), 2 twin (1 with bath/shower, 1 with wash-basin) TERMS B&B £16–£19, (single occupancy of twin/double) £25–£30, (family room) £40–£57 (children 3 and under free, 4–16 half-price sharing parents' room); deposit; Access, Amex, Carte Blanche, Visa

Melita Private Hotel

37 Shipston Road, Stratford-upon-Avon CV37 7LN
STRATFORD-UPON-AVON (0789) 292432

Built around the turn of the century, Melita has preserved much of its original character. There is a pretty award-winning garden, which guests may enjoy. Breakfast only is available and is served in the attractive dining-room. Guests also have use of a comfortable guest lounge with a small bar, plus a bright conservatory which leads out to the garden. All the bedrooms have TV and telephone, and all are *en suite*; three rooms are on the ground floor. The Melita is well located for the theatre, canal and other amenities. Children welcome. No pets in the dining-room. No smoking in the dining-room and eight bedrooms. Car park.

OWNERS Patricia and Russell Andrews OPEN All year, exc Christmas ROOMS 3 family, 4 double, 2 twin, 3 single; all rooms with bath/shower TERMS B&B £26–£28, (single) £30–£40, (single occupancy of twin/double) £40–£47, (family room) £64–£84 (children about half-price); deposit; Access, Amex, Visa

Moonraker House

40 Alcester Road, Stratford-upon-Avon CV37 9DB
STRATFORD-UPON-AVON (0789) 267115/299346

This pretty, flower-bedecked guesthouse on the north side of Stratford-upon-Avon is a pleasant five-minute stroll from the centre. There is also Moonraker II close by. The bedrooms in both guesthouses are decorated to a high standard, some with four-poster beds. All of the rooms have hair-dryer, TV and easy chairs. One room, ideal for a small family or group of friends, has its own sitting-room, bathroom and private entrance. For special occasions, champagne and flowers can be arranged for a modest charge. Breakfast only is available. Taking guests to the station and helping them obtain theatre tickets is all part of the owners' service. Children welcome. Pets by arrangement. No smoking in four bedrooms, including four-posters. Car park.

OWNERS Michael and Maureen Spencer OPEN All year, exc Christmas ROOMS 1 family, 2 four-poster, 4 double, 2 twin; all rooms with bath/shower TERMS B&B £18.50–£19.50, (four-poster) £26–£28, (single occupancy of twin/double) £28–£32 (children £10 in family room); deposit £20; Access, Visa

Victoria Spa Lodge

Bishopton Lane, Stratford-upon-Avon CV37 9QY
STRATFORD-UPON-AVON (0789) 267985 Fax (0789) 204728

Queen Victoria gave her name to this hotel, and her coat of arms is built into the gables. The Lodge is in a peaceful spot overlooking the canal, set in one and a half acres of lovely gardens, one and a half miles from Stratford-upon-Avon. It is an attractive building, built in 1837 as a spa; the hotel and pump rooms were divided into three separate residences. There are seven well-appointed bedrooms, all with TV and comfortable chairs, and some with the original cornices and fireplaces. The attic rooms are ideally suited for families or friends travelling together. Cooked, Continental and vegetarian breakfasts can be served in the elegant dining-room. Dinner is available by arrangement and packed lunches can be provided. Guests are welcome to bring their own wine as there is no alcohol licence. Children welcome. No pets. No smoking in the dining-room. Car park.

OWNERS Paul and Dreen Tozer OPEN All year ROOMS 2 family (1 with bath/shower, 1 with wash-basin), 3 double (with bath/shower), 2 twin (1 with bath/shower, 1 with wash-basin) TERMS B&B £19.50–£22.50, (single occupancy of twin/double) £30–£38; dinner £15; deposit; Access, Visa

STROUD Gloucestershire map 4

Cairngall Guest House

65 Bisley Old Road, Stroud GL5 1NF
STROUD (0453) 764595

Built in 1852, Cairngall is a listed building situated in an elevated position on the edge of town; at the front there are 12 colonnades. The spacious rooms are comfortable and well furnished. The guest lounge is full of interesting items, including an antique carved piano, lovely wood panelling and a mantle. There are lovely gardens, which guests are free to enjoy. Mrs Thacker is a kindly lady who especially enjoys her cats – there are several, all of them friendly. Breakfast only is available, although packed lunches can be provided. Children welcome. Car park.

OWNER Mrs Shelagh Thacker OPEN Mar–end Dec
ROOMS 1 family, 1 double, 1 single; 2 rooms with wash-basin
TERMS B&B £12–£14 (children under 5 half-price)

Woodside

Burleigh, nr Stroud GL5 2PA
BRIMSCOMBE (0453) 884350 Fax (0453) 731129

This seventeenth-century wool merchant's house, two miles east of Stroud on the A419, stands in three acres of grounds overlooking the Golden Valley, one of the most beautiful and unspoilt areas of the Cotswolds. The three spacious, characterful bedrooms all have woodboard floors, a sitting area and TV. There are roaring log fires in the lounge, and lots of books and games for guests' use. The day begins with a sumptuous breakfast consisting of fresh fruits, juices, porridge or local yoghurt, with a choice of a traditional breakfast, kippers or haddock, with home-made preserves and Cotswold honey. Lunches and dinners are available, imaginatively prepared using local produce and vegetables and fruit from the garden. Vegetarian and special diets can be catered for. Woodside is unlicensed, but guests may bring their own wine. A self-catering unit is also available. Children welcome. Pets restricted. Car park.

OWNERS Shirley and Derek Hewson OPEN All year, exc Christmas
ROOMS 2 double, 1 twin/family; all rooms with bath/shower
TERMS B&B from £18, (single occupancy of twin/double) from £23 (reductions for children); dinner from £12.50; deposit £10

SUNNINGDALE Berkshire map 2

Skitten

16 Woodby Drive, Sunningdale SL5 9RD
ASCOT (0344) 25876

This large American/colonial-style home built in 1975 on a quiet cul-de-sac housing development is half a mile from Sunningdale and off the A30. It is comfortably furnished and decorated in bright colours. The dining-room leads out to the patio and to the sizeable, well-kept rear garden with bee hives at the end. Mrs Nel is a qualified guide and can arrange special sightseeing tours. Breakfast only is served and on warm days can be enjoyed on the patio. Skitten is just a five-minute walk from the station and a 20-minute drive from Heathrow. Windsor and many famous golf courses are within striking distance. A £2 supplement is charged for English breakfast. There is also a self-catering flat available with a small balcony leading down to the garden. No children under four. No pets. No smoking.

OWNER A. C. Nel OPEN All year, exc bank hols ROOMS 1 double (with bath/shower), 1 twin (with wash-basin) TERMS B&B £20 approx, (single occupancy of twin/double) £25 approx; deposit

TAYNTON Oxfordshire map 4

Manor Farm Barn

Taynton, nr Burford OX8 4UH
BURFORD (099 382) 2069

As the Guide went to press this establishment stopped offering B & B

TENBURY WELLS Hereford & Worcester map 4

Court Farm

Hanley Childe, nr Tenbury Wells WR15 8QY
KYRE (0885) 410265

Court Farm is a sixteenth-century renovated farmhouse on 200 acres of mixed farming in a fairly remote area ideal for walkers. To find it, take the B4204 from Tenbury Wells for six miles and turn right by the Tally Ho pub for Hanley Childe. Full of character, the house has log beams, a huge stone fireplace, a cast-iron fireplace with ovens, and original hop pockets, doors and latches. There is a guest lounge, which is reached through the kitchen. Mr Yarnold was born at the farm and he is very knowledgeable about the area. Evening meals are not served, but light snacks such as soup and sandwiches are available at a modest cost. Packed lunches can be provided. Guests are welcome to use the large garden. Golf, horse-riding and quiet, country woodland walks are all on offer nearby. Children welcome. No pets. Smoking restricted. Car park.

OWNERS Edward and Margaret Yarnold OPEN Apr–Oct ROOMS 1 family, 1 twin TERMS B&B £15, (single occupancy of twin) £20, (family room) £40 (children under 5 £6, 5–10 £10)

Hunthouse Farm

Frith Common, Tenbury Wells WR15 8JY
CLOWS TOP (0299) 832277

Guests are greeted with tea and home-made cakes on arrival at this beautiful period farmhouse on a 180-acre arable and stock farm. There are breathtaking views, and this is an ideal base for walking and exploring the area. The house is beamed and has an inglenook fireplace. The bedrooms have been redecorated and have new carpets. There is a separate sitting-room and dining-room where scrumptuous breakfasts are served – enough to keep you going for the day. Dinner is not available, but there is a pub that serves food about two miles away. Hunthouse Farm is warm and welcoming and guests are assured of good service from congenial owner Jane Keel. The farm is six miles east of Tenbury Wells between the A456 and the A443. No children under eight (except for tiny babies). No pets in the house. No smoking in bedrooms. Car park.

OWNERS Chris and Jane Keel OPEN Feb–Nov ROOMS 1 family, 1 double, 1 twin; all rooms with bath/shower TERMS B&B £15–£18 (children about £7.50 in family room); deposit

It is always best to book a room in advance, especially in winter. B&Bs with few rooms may close at short notice for periods not specified in the details.

Breakfast at B&Bs tends to mean a cooked breakfast of bacon, eggs and so on. If you prefer a different style of breakfast, discuss this when you make the booking.

TETBURY Gloucestershire map 4

Tavern House

Willesley, nr Tetbury GL8 8QU
WESTONBIRT (0666) 880444

Formerly a sixteenth-century coaching-house, Tavern House is approximately one mile from Westonbirt Arboretum on the A433 Bath–Cirencester road and a few miles south-west of Tetbury. It sits in a half acre of mature gardens where breakfast may be served on warm days. The bedrooms are in excellent decorative order, with antique pine furnishings and sloping beams; all have TV, telephone and hair-dryer. An unusual feature is that each bedroom is reached by a separate staircase. There is a flagstone entry leading to the quiet, elegant lounge overlooking the garden. Breakfast only is available, although packed lunches can be provided. No children under 10. No pets. Smoking in the lounge only. Car park.

OWNERS Janet and Tim Tremellen OPEN All year ROOMS 3 double, 1 twin; all rooms with bath/shower TERMS B&B £22.50–£29.50, (single occupancy of twin/double) from £32 (reductions for children); deposit; Access, Visa

TOWERSEY Oxfordshire map 4

Upper Green Farm

Manor Road, Towersey OX9 3QR
THAME (084 421) 2496

Upper Green Farm is a whitewashed house dating from the fifteenth century on the edge of the small village of Towersey. It has been beautifully thatched and stands in seven acres. Euan and Marjorie Aitken have recently converted an old barn, which now provides an additional six *en suite* rooms, all with TV and video. Guests take breakfast in what was the old kitchen, with Victorian range and bread oven. The house has been decorated with great charm and taste. The old beams and shape of the house dictate much of the décor, and it is simply furnished, partly with antiques and partly with pine furniture. There is also a large pond with

Reduced rates for children are normally given when they share their parents' bedroom. If no reductions are specified in the details or text, assume you'll have to pay full rates.

rowing boat and the house is surrounded by orchard and gardens. No children. No pets. No smoking. Car park.

OWNERS Euan and Marjorie Aitken OPEN All year ROOMS 5 double (4 with bath/shower), 2 twin (with bath/shower), 2 single (1 with bath/shower, 1 with wash-basin) TERMS B&B £15–£27, (single occupancy of twin/double) £22–£37

WARGRAVE Berkshire map 2

Inverloddon Cottage

Ferry Lane, Wargrave RG10 8ET
WARGRAVE (0734) 402230

Fronting the Thames, with lawns running down to the water's edge, Inverloddon has an idyllic setting and is an ideal base during Henley Royal Regatta. On summer afternoons and evenings, afternoon tea and cocktails are served in the summer-house. The building, originally two small flint and timber houses, is about 200 years old, and was at one time a beer-house, frequented by river customers and the ferryman and his passengers. The slightly run-down feel of the house is more than compensated for by the friendly owners and the wonderful position. The rooms have a lived-in feel but they are comfortable, if a little untidy, and the downstairs reception rooms are elegantly furnished and proportioned. The house is full of books and memorabilia. A punt is available for guests' use, and boat trips can be arranged. Breakfast only is available, although packed lunches can be provided. Children welcome. Non-smokers preferred. Car park.

OWNERS Mr and Mrs P. J. Hermon OPEN All year ROOMS 1 family/double (with bath/shower), 1 single (with wash-basin) TERMS B&B £17.50–£20 (children under 5 £10); deposit 10%

WARWICK Warwickshire map 4

The Garden Suite

44 High Street, Warwick CV34 4AX
WARWICK (0926) 401512

This was the first house to be burned in the great fire in the late 1600s. The front of the house was replaced with a Georgian façade in 1720. It is in an excellent location, right in the town centre, a seven-minute walk downhill to the castle, a little longer on the return as it's uphill. The two guest suites, with their own garden entrance, have a small sitting-room and bathroom, fridge, telephone and TV. Both suites have been totally refurbished and are very comfortable. One is on the ground floor and is suitable for the disabled. A freshly cooked breakfast is served in your room or in the garden room. Dinner is available by arrangement. Vegetarian dishes and packed lunches can be provided. There is no alcohol licence, but guests may bring their own wine to dinner. Guests have exclusive use of the garden. Children welcome. No pets. No smoking. Car park.

OWNER Mrs Elizabeth Draisey OPEN All year ROOMS 2 twin/suite (with bath/shower) TERMS B&B £18–£22.50, (single occupancy of twin) £25–£35 (babies free, children 2–10 £5–£10); dinner £8; deposit £10

Pageant Lodge

2 Castle Lane, Warwick CV34 4BU
WARWICK (0926) 491244

Ideally situated, next to both the castle entrance and the Dolls Museum at Oken's House, Pageant Lodge is a listed building first recorded in the castle archives as a humble cottage. The bedrooms, all with TV, are a little small, but are comfortable, clean and delicately decorated with Laura Ashley bedspreads and curtains. A single bed can be added to one of the rooms to make a family room or twin. Breakfast only is available. A morning newspaper of your choice is part of the service. Parking charges are taken care of by the owners. Children welcome. Dogs in bedroom only.

OWNERS Christopher and Linda King OPEN All year
ROOMS 3 double (1 with bath/shower, 2 with wash-basin)
TERMS B&B £15–£20 (children under 6 free, 6–10 half-price)

Warwick Lodge

82 Emscote Road, Warwick CV34 5QJ
WARWICK (0926) 492927

Bernard and Grace Smith continue to improve the standards at Warwick Lodge, and they work hard to ensure guests receive good-value accommodation. The well-appointed bedrooms, all with TV, are bright and airy, with comfortable beds. The downstairs dining-room, where an excellent breakfast is served, is a charming room with Spanish décor. There is also a guest sitting-room with TV. There are no evening meals. Warwick Lodge is just a few minutes' walk from Warwick Castle, 20 minutes' drive from the National Exhibition Centre and only five miles from the National Agricultural Centre. Children welcome. No pets. Car park.

OWNERS Bernard and Grace Smith OPEN All year, exc Christmas
ROOMS 1 family, 2 double, 2 twin, 2 single; all rooms with wash-basin
TERMS B&B £13.50–£15, (single occupancy of twin/double) £16–£18, (family room) £34 (children under 5 free); Access, Visa

WELLINGTON HEATH Hereford & Worcester map 4

Callow Croft

Wellington Heath, nr Ledbury HR8 1NB
LEDBURY (0531) 3758

Callow Croft is a beautiful seventeenth-century black and white timbered house in a secluded rural location set in three acres of garden, with lovely views of farmland and the hills of Wales. It is a fascinating house with a wealth of beams; the dining-room features a stone fireplace and the lounge a wood-burning stove. There are five bedrooms, with lovely lace bedspreads. Hilary Beggs is a warm and friendly lady from Northern Ireland who is adept at making guests feel very much at home, offering tea and cakes on arrival. Breakfast only is served, but there is a pub within walking distance that serves evening meals. Picturesque Ledbury

is just a mile away. Callow Croft is a little tricky to find, so ask for directions. Children welcome. No smoking. Car park.

OWNER Hilary Beggs OPEN All year, exc Christmas and New Year ROOMS 2 family, 2 double (1 with shower), 1 twin TERMS B&B £16.50–£20 (children under 12 half-price)

WIGMORE Hereford & Worcester map 6

Queen's House

Wigmore HR6 9UN
WIGMORE (056 886) 451

Queen's House started life about 500 years ago as two Elizabethan cottages. These have been carefully extended and altered to make a comfortable, rambling house. There are flagstone floors, oak beams, thick stone walls, inglenook fireplaces and lots of brass and copper. The house is in the centre of the sleepy village of Wigmore, and the rear rooms overlook the area from the Mortimer Forest to Leintwardine and across the moors to the River Teme. Home-cooked evening meals are served in the licensed restaurant, which is open to non-residents three days a week. Light meals can be served at any time and packed lunches are available. Vegetarians can be catered for. Children welcome. Car park.

OWNERS Jack and Anne Webb OPEN All year ROOMS 1 family, 1 double, 1 twin, 1 single; all rooms, exc single, with wash-basin TERMS B&B £12–£15 (children under 12 £7); dinner £10; deposit 25%

WINCHCOMBE Gloucestershire map 4

The Homestead

Broadway Road, Footbridge, Winchcombe GL54 5JG
CHELTENHAM (0242) 602536

This most attractive eighteenth-century cottage, built of local stone, is situated on the B4632 on the edge of the unspoilt village of Winchcombe. It is ideal for walkers and country lovers – the Cotswold Walk passes by the front of the house. Maureen Brooker is always happy to assist and provide guests with local information. The house has lots of olde worlde charm, including exposed beams and stone walls. The bedrooms are tastefully decorated with matching fabrics and wallpapers. There are no TVs at all, but many magazines to read. Tea and coffee are available on request. Breakfast only is available, although packed lunches can be provided. A visit to the Winchcombe Railway Museum is suggested. Children welcome. House-trained pets only. No smoking in bedrooms. Car park.

OWNER Maureen Brooker OPEN All year, exc Christmas ROOMS 2 double, 1 twin; all rooms with bath/shower TERMS B&B £14–£20 (children £10 sharing parents' room); deposit £10 per room

WINDSOR Berkshire map 2

Alma House

56 Alma Road, Windsor SL4 3HA
WINDSOR (0753) 862983

Alma House is a simple guesthouse made up of two terraced Victorian houses in a pleasant residential district, not far from the centre, with a driveway to one side which provides limited parking. The accommodation is fairly spacious, clean and bright. The bedrooms all have TV and there is a cheerful little breakfast room. Breakfast only is available but there are numerous restaurants and pubs in the area for evening meals. Children welcome. Car park.

OWNER Mr Shipp OPEN All year ROOMS 1 family (with wash-basin), 2 double/twin (with bath/shower), 1 single (with wash-basin) TERMS B&B £16–£17.50, (single) £20, (single occupancy of twin/double) £30–£33 (children under 2 free if sharing parents' bed or in own cot); deposit

Langton House

46 Alma Road, Windsor SL4 3HA
WINDSOR (0753) 858299

This substantial double-fronted Victorian house is just a few minutes' walk from the town centre. The bedrooms are large, in good decorative order and both have TV and easy chairs. Marjorie and Roy Fogg are a charming, well-travelled couple, and Roy enjoys assisting guests with itinerary planning. A cup of tea or coffee is offered to guests on arrival at no extra charge. The house has a comfortable, lived-in atmosphere. There are price reductions at weekends. Children welcome. No smoking.

OWNER Mrs M. Fogg OPEN All year ROOMS 1 family, 1 double; both rooms with wash-basin TERMS B&B £17, (family room) £48 (children under 10 half-price)

WOODSTOCK Oxfordshire map 4

Pine Trees

44 Green Lane, Woodstock OX7 1JZ
WOODSTOCK (0993) 813333/811587

Pine Trees is an attractive house in a countrified road a few minutes' walk from Woodstock. It is in an elevated position in glorious landscaped gardens, with a fish pond adjacent to the house stocked with goldfish and Koi carp. There are several areas for sitting out in the garden, including a terrace, and several antique farm implements lie in the grounds. The three bedrooms are large, and all have TV. There is also a guest lounge with a log fire. This house may be unsuitable for the infirm as there are several steps up to the entrance. Children welcome. No pets. No smoking in bedrooms. Car park.

OWNERS M. Snell and M. J. Marshall OPEN Jan–Dec
ROOMS 2 family (1 with bath/shower), 1 twin TERMS B&B £16–£18, (single occupancy) £20 (children up to 5 free, 5–12 half-price); deposit

WORCESTER Hereford & Worcester map 4

Burgage House

4 College Precincts, Worcester WR1 2LG
WORCESTER (0905) 25396

Burgage House is only a few minutes' walk from the Commandery, Tudor House Museum, the Royal Worcester Porcelain Works and other places of interest. It is a listed Georgian building in the conservation area adjacent to Worcester Cathedral, with fine views of the cathedral grounds. There is a most unusual, original stone curved staircase leading to the large, comfortable, colour-co-ordinated bedrooms, one of which has a Victorian reproduction of a Jacobean bed. The rooms are located on three floors and the stairs are very steep – not suitable for the elderly and disabled. There is a dining-room, a lounge and an additional sitting area with flagstone floors and inglenook fireplace. Breakfast only is available. Burgage House is a little tricky to find so be sure to get directions when making a reservation. Car parking is available in the cul-de-sac outside the

It is always best to book in advance. Some B&Bs may close temporarily if they have received no bookings.

house, or in Castle Place nearby. Children welcome. No pets. No smoking in bedrooms.

OWNER Mrs Janette Ratcliffe OPEN All year, exc Christmas
ROOMS 1 family, 1 double (with wash-basin), 1 twin, 1 single
TERMS B&B £15–£17, (single) £18–£23 (babies free, children under 10 half-price sharing family room); deposit

Highfield

68 London Road, Worcester WR5 2DY
WORCESTER (0905) 352009

A listed Georgian terraced house that is only five minutes' walk from the centre. Look for the house with a fuschia-coloured front door and a brass knocker. All the bedrooms are large and comfortable, and the attic room, with a beamed ceiling, is particularly charming; all the rooms have TV. The house is spotless and the proprietors are very hospitable. There is also a comfortable guest lounge. Breakfast only is served. Children welcome. No pets. No smoking in the dining-room and bedrooms. Car park.

OWNERS Mr and Mrs B. Humphries OPEN All year
ROOMS 1 family, 2 double, 1 single; all rooms with wash-basin
TERMS B&B £14–£16 (reductions for children)

East Anglia

Cambridgeshire

Essex

Norfolk

Suffolk

ARDLEIGH Essex map 5

Bovills Hall

Ardleigh, Colchester CO7 7RT
COLCHESTER (0206) 230217

Situated on the edge of Dedham Vale, Bovills Hall is an imposing manor house, recorded in the Domesday Book. It is well placed for exploring both Essex and Suffolk. The atmosphere reflects the elegance of this tranquil and historic house, which has oak beams, period and antique furniture, and, on chilly evenings, open fires. Breakfasts are substantial and include home-made marmalade and preserves. The bedrooms are of a good size and all have TV. Guests have a lovely drawing-room which leads out on to the beautiful 14 acres of garden and may use the garden furniture. Children under one and over eight accepted. No pets. Car park.

OWNER Mrs A. F. Bredin OPEN All year, exc Nov–Feb
ROOMS 2 double (with wash-basin), 1 twin (with bath/shower)
TERMS B&B £17–£19, (single occupancy of twin/double) £22–£26, (reductions for children by arrangement); deposit; Visa

BIRCHANGER Essex map 5

The Cottage Guest House

71 Birchanger Lane, Birchanger, nr Bishops Stortford CM23 5QA
BISHOPS STORTFORD (0279) 812349

This seventeenth-century Grade II listed property is set in two acres of beautifully landscaped gardens, including a private woodland walk. There are two lounges, both with inglenook fireplaces and one with Gothic-style windows. Some bedrooms are in the main house with additional *en suite* rooms in a separate wing. All rooms have TV. Breakfast and evening meals, served at 7pm and featuring fresh vegetables from the garden, are taken in the conservatory. Vegetarian choices and packed lunches can be provided. The Cottage is licensed and offers a selection of wines. There are areas for sitting in the garden, including a terrace. Children welcome. No pets in the house. No smoking. Car park.

OWNERS Peter and Rosemary Jones OPEN All year, exc Christmas
ROOMS 1 family, 3 double, 4 twin, 2 single; all rooms, exc 2 single (wash-basin only), with bath/shower TERMS B&B £22.50, (single) £27, (single occupancy of twin/double) £32, (family room) £45, (reductions for children negotiable); dinner £10.50; Access, Visa

BLOFIELD Norfolk map 5

The Lindens

Yarmouth Road, Blofield, nr Norwich NR13 4LG
NORWICH (0603) 713183

A pleasant turn-of-the-century house that is set back from the road in a large garden. The bedrooms are all of a good size and three have TV. There is a large family room with an adjacent single; two bedrooms are in an annexe, which was converted from the original stable block, two are on the ground floor and one can accommodate a wheelchair. The house has solid, old-fashioned furnishings and there is an antique marble washstand. Breakfast only is served in the dining-room/lounge. There are several pubs and restaurants close by. Guests may use the grass tennis court. Reductions for children by arrangement. Children welcome. No dogs. Car park.

OWNER V. L. Baker OPEN All year, exc Christmas ROOMS 2 family, 2 twin, 1 double; 4 rooms with wash-basin TERMS B&B £13–£18, (single occupancy of twin/double) £15–£20, (family room) £40–£48; deposit

BURY ST EDMUNDS Suffolk map 5

The Leys

113 Forham Road, Bury St Edmunds IP2 6AT
BURY ST EDMUNDS (0284) 760225

This attractive Victorian house is set in half an acre of grounds on the edge of town. Although it is situated on the B1106, the house is quiet and peaceful. Built in 1894, it retains many original features, fireplaces and pine stripped doors. The spacious rooms are comfortable and well furnished and all have TV. There is a separate sitting-room where excellent breakfasts that include home-baked bread and home-made preserves are served. A comfortable lounge is available for guests. Children welcome. No smoking in two rooms. No pets. Car park.

OWNERS Mr and Mrs Roger Lee OPEN All year, exc Christmas ROOMS 1 family (with bath/shower), 1 double (with wash-basin), 1 twin (with wash-basin) TERMS B&B £15, (single occupancy of twin/double) £20–£25, (family room) £34 (reductions for children); deposit

If we know a B&Bs has an alcohol licence, we say so.

CAMBRIDGE Cambridgeshire map 5

Regency Guest House

7 Regent Terrace, Cambridge CB2 1AA
CAMBRIDGE (0223) 62655

A modest guesthouse in a Victorian building that overlooks Parker's Piece. This is a new venture for Mr and Mrs Payne who recently returned from South Africa. They are a most congenial couple and offer good-value accommodation in a central location. All the bedrooms have TV. There is partial central heating and each guest room has an electric heater. Breakfasts only are served in the basement dining-room; hot vegetarian choices might include mushrooms or tomato and potato waffles. Children welcome. No smoking in the breakfast room. No pets. Parking is a problem and guests should park at the car park across the green.

OWNERS Jean and Barry Payne OPEN All year ROOMS 1 family, 4 double, 2 single; all rooms with wash-basin TERMS B&B £20–£22, (single) £27–£30, (single occupancy of twin/double) £30–£32, (family room) £45 (children under 10 free if sharing parents' room)

CASTLE HEDINGHAM Essex map 5

The Old School House

St James Street, Castle Hedingham CO9 3EW
HEDINGHAM (0787) 61370 Fax (0787) 61605

This superb Georgian house is situated in a lovely medieval village. The Norman castle, which gives the village its name, is just a few minutes' walk away. The lounge, where guests are often joined by the charming owners, leads on to a beautiful garden with a colourful display of shrubs and flowers; the gardens are open to the public and have been featured in gardening magazines. The house is elegantly furnished and full of interesting items. Of particular interest is the carved chest on the landing. The beamed drawing-room has open log fires in winter. The bedrooms are decorated with matching fabrics, wallpapers and many extra touches such as lavender pouches in the beds. Evening meals (7.30–8pm), including vegetarian dishes, are available by arrangement; a sample three-course dinner may include Stilton mousse, followed by rack of lamb with port and rowanberry sauce, finishing with meringue roulade. A selection of wines is available. There is also a converted two-bedroomed coach-house suitable for those who value privacy; one room has a private sitting-room with TV. A good breakfast is served in the main house. No children under 12. No pets. No smoking. Car park.

OWNER Mrs P. Crawshaw OPEN All year ROOMS 3 twin (with bath/shower) TERMS B&B £18.50–£23.50, (single occupancy of twin) £25–£30; dinner £14; deposit

CLACTON-ON-SEA Essex map 5

Hamelin Hotel

20 Penfold Road, Clacton-on-Sea CO15 1JN
CLACTON (0255) 474456

This Victorian house is on a quiet road, five minutes from the town centre and 200 yards from the sea-front. The décor is black and white mock-Tudor style; the rooms are of a good size and all have TV. The lounge has a small bar where guests can enjoy a drink and converse with George, the colourful parrot. Joy Franklin took over the business in July 1991, and it is very much a family-run affair. Evening meals are available at 6.30pm in the licensed dining-room; vegetarian choices are offered by arrangement. Packed lunches can also be provided. Children welcome. Pets by arrangement. Limited parking only.

OWNERS Joy and Terry Franklin OPEN All year ROOMS 3 family (2 with bath/shower, 1 with wash-basin), 2 double (1 with bath/shower, 1 with wash-basin), 2 twin (with wash-basin), 1 single (with wash-basin) TERMS B&B £16–£20 (children under 10 half-price if sharing parents' room); D, B&B £22–£26; dinner £6; deposit or full payment on arrival

CLARE Suffolk map 5

Bells

37 Bridewell Street, Clare CO10 8QD
CLARE (0787) 277538

This Grade II listed house started life as three cottages, one of which belonged to the local butcher. There are lots of books throughout the house for guests to browse through, and Gillian Bell is happy to chat to guests and advise them on local sight-seeing. The rooms, both with TV, have antique furnishings, and there is a comfortable family atmosphere. Breakfasts are substantial (with good fresh coffee) and are taken in the wood-floored dining-room. Evening meals are served at 7pm, by arrangement; vegetarians can be catered for. There is no alcohol licence, but guests may bring their own wine to dinner. An antique grandfather clock stands in the lounge. Three cats and one docile dog share the house. Children under 10 discouraged. No pets. No smoking.

OWNERS Tim and Gillian Bell OPEN All year, exc Christmas ROOMS 1 double, 1 twin TERMS B&B £15; dinner £10; deposit £10 per room

Cobwebs

26 Nethergate Street, Clare CO10 8NP
CLARE (0787) 277539

An interesting listed house, full of character, parts of which date back to the fifteenth-century. It is situated within easy walking distance of the town centre. The wealth of oak beams and stone walls combine with the antique furnishings to create a feel of antiquity. The bedrooms, all with TV, are of a very high standard, and there is a well-furnished, quiet lounge. Breakfast only is served, and can be taken in the walled garden on warm days. For those who value privacy there is ground-floor accommodation in a cottage in the garden; it has been converted from the stables, and has twin beds and *en suite* facilities. No children under six. No pets. No smoking in bedrooms.

OWNER Mrs Jean Tuffill OPEN All year ROOMS 2 twin (1 with bath/shower, 1 with wash-basin), 1 single (with wash-basin) TERMS B&B £15, (single occupancy of twin) £18; minimum deposit £10

CLINT GREEN Norfolk map 5

Clinton House

Well Hill, Clint Green, Yaxham NR19 1RX
DEREHAM (0362) 692079

A lovely 200-year-old house situated in an acre of gardens, with lawns, mature trees and shrubs. There are three beautifully decorated bedrooms, colour-co-ordinated in pastel floral wallpapers, with comfortable beds. The beamed guest lounge, with TV, has an inglenook fireplace. Breakfast is served in the Victorian-style conservatory. A grass tennis court is being constructed for guests' use. A self-catering unit is available.

Children welcome. No pets. No smoking in public rooms; smoking in bedrooms discouraged. Car park.

OWNER Margaret Searle OPEN All year ROOMS 1 family, 1 double, 1 twin, 1 single; all rooms with wash-basin TERMS B&B £13–£17 (20% reduction for children)

COLCHESTER Essex map 5

Four Sevens Guest House

28 Inglis Road, Colchester CO3 3HU
COLCHESTER (0206) 46093

This Victorian house is set in a beautiful garden, a few minutes' walk from the town centre. From the Colchester Police Station take the B1022 Maldon road, then the second road on the right. Guests are treated as visiting family and there is a relaxed atmosphere. The bedrooms are of a good size and all have satellite TV. Video recorders and tapes are supplied on request. Shower waterflow in the bathrooms is extremely forceful. Huge breakfasts are taken 'family-style' in the dining-room. Evening meals are served, 6–8pm, and vegetarian choices are available. There is no alcohol licence, but guests may bring their own wine. Bicycles are provided for guests' use. There is a private drive with limited parking. Children welcome. No pets. No smoking.

OWNERS Mr and Mrs Demetri OPEN All year ROOMS 3 double/family (1 with bath/shower, 2 with wash-basin), 3 twin/family (1 with bath/shower, 2 with wash-basin) TERMS B&B £15–£18, (single occupancy of twin/double) £20–£30, (family room) from £45 (reductions for children under 10); D, B&B £22–£35; dinner £7

14 Roman Road

14 Roman Road, Colchester CO1 1UR
COLCHESTER (0206) 577905

A Victorian residence on this quiet town-centre square, the house enjoys views of the Norman castle and a Roman wall at the end of the garden. The rooms are of a good size, well furnished and all with their own TV, books and information packs on the area; home-made biscuits are a welcome accompaniment to the tea-making facilities. Ample, well-presented breakfasts include vegetarian choices and are served in the bright dining-room.

Use the maps and indexes at the back of the Guide *to plan your trip.*

Packed lunches are available by arrangement. Children welcome. No pets. No smoking. Parking for one car beside the house.

OWNER Gill Nicholson OPEN All year, exc Christmas
ROOMS 1 double, 2 twin (1 with bath/shower) TERMS B&B £15–£17, (single occupancy of twin/double) £20–£24 (babies free, children under 8 half-price)

The Old Manse

15 Roman Road, Colchester CO1 1UR
COLCHESTER (0206) 45154

In a quiet Victorian square near the centre of this Roman town (there is a Roman wall at the bottom of the garden) is this civilised home. Wendy Anderson is happy to help guests plan their itineraries. The bedrooms are all of a good size with antique furnishings, and all have TV and an information file covering places to visit in Colchester and the surrounding area. One bedroom is on the ground floor. Breakfasts only are served on a large antique wooden table. Packed lunches can be provided on request. Children welcome. Pets by arrangement. No smoking. Car park.

OWNER Wendy Anderson OPEN All year, exc Christmas
ROOMS 1 double (with bath/shower), 1 twin TERMS B&B £15–£18, (single occupancy of twin/double) from £20 (children under 8 half-price)

DOWNHAM MARKET Norfolk map 5

The Dial House

12 Railway Road, Downham Market PE38 9EB
DOWNHAM MARKET (0366) 388358

This listed Jacobean and Georgian building is made from stone quarried locally. Dial House is on the main road through Downham Market, but the rooms are fairly quiet. One of the rooms is very spacious, with the original shutters; another has leaded Jacobean windows; all have TV and comfortable old-fashioned furnishings. Guests are offered a free cup of tea or coffee on arrival, and as often as they want throughout the day and evening. Evening meals are available 6–9pm by prior arrangement, and vegetarian choices can be provided. There is no alcohol licence, but guests may bring their own wine to dinner. Breakfast includes home-made preserves and marmalades. Packed lunches can also be provided, on request. The Dial House is well situated for exploring West Norfolk and Cambridgeshire. No central heating. Children welcome. No pets. No smoking in bedrooms and during meals. Car park.

OWNERS Ann and David Murray OPEN All year ROOMS 1 family, 1 double (with bath/shower), 2 twin (1 with bath/shower, 1 with wash-basin) TERMS B&B £16.25 (children under 2 free, under 12 half-price sharing parents' room); dinner £8.50; deposit 25%

DRY DRAYTON Cambridgeshire map 5

The Coach House

Dry Drayton, nr Cambridge CB3 8BS
CRAFTS HILL (0954) 782439

This beautiful nineteenth-century converted coach-house stands in two acres of delightful grounds overlooking a manicured lawn and a lily pond. The house is very well appointed; the immaculate bedrooms, one with a brass bed, are tastefully furnished and decorated. Catherine Child's house is a haven for those seeking peace and tranquility. Delicious breakfasts, that include home-made preserves, are served in the bright dining-room overlooking the garden. There is a small sitting-room with TV. Electric blankets and sewing kits are provided. No children. No pets. No smoking. Car park.

OWNER Catherine Child OPEN mid-Mar–mid-Dec ROOMS 1 four-poster (with bath/shower), 1 double (with bath/shower), 1 twin (with bath/shower), 1 single (with bath/shower) TERMS B&B £20–£21, (single) £29, (single occupancy of twin/double) £31

ELY Cambridgeshire map 5

The Black Hostelry

The College, The Cathedral Close, Firmary Lane, Ely CB7 4DL
ELY (0353) 662612

One of the finest domestic medieval buildings still in use, standing in the shadow of the imposing and beautiful Ely Cathedral, the house was once the infirmary of the Benedictine monastery, becoming a canon's residence in the sixteenth century. With its eleventh-century Norman arches, old fireplaces and proximity to the cathedral – it is a actually within the walls – the house has a very peaceful atmosphere. The accommodation consists of an apartment with a sitting-room, bedroom and bathroom, a double bedroom and a single; all rooms have TV. The rooms are large and comfortable, and each of the two bedrooms can be converted to accommodate up to four people. The rooms overlook a meadow and gardens. A substantial breakfast is served, including kippers and wholemeal home-made bread. Children welcome. Car park.

OWNER Mrs S. Green OPEN All year, exc Christmas ROOMS 2 twin/family, 1 single; all rooms with bath/shower TERMS B&B £20, (single) £20, (single occupancy of twin) £40, (family room) £40 plus £10 for extra person (babies £2, children 5–10 £5, over 10 £10); deposit

31 Egremont Street

31 Egremont Street, Ely CB6 1AE
ELY (0353) 663118

This spacious seventeenth-century house with Victorian additions is set in a walled garden, with views of the cathedral. It is just a few minutes' walk from the cathedral and town centre. There are two well-appointed bedrooms, both with TV; the twin-bedded room is located in the Victorian addition. Antique furnishings include a chaise-longue and grandfather clock. Breakfast only is served in the cosy dining-room. This is a peaceful location, and guests are welcome to use the lovely gardens, which are open to the public one day a year, as well as the grass tennis court. Car park. Children over 12 preferred. No pets. No smoking.

OWNERS Mr and Mrs Jeremy Friend-Smith OPEN All year, exc Christmas ROOMS 1 double (with wash-basin), 1 twin (with bath/shower) TERMS B&B £17–£18, (single occupancy of twin/double) £23–£25 (£4 reduction for child sharing parents' room); deposit £5

FELIXSTOWE Suffolk map 5

Dorincourt Guest House

16 Garfield Road, Felixstowe IP11 7PU
FELIXSTOWE (0394) 270447

Built in 1902, Dorincourt is an attractive house on a quiet residential street, just minutes from the beach and all amenities. There are steps directly down to the sea 200 yards from the house. The immaculate bedrooms are of a good size, tastefully decorated and all with TV; some have sea views. All the beds are firm and there is one orthopaedic bed. There is also a guests' sitting-room, with TV and lots of games. Breakfast only is served, but there is a very wide choice of places to eat in the town. Packed lunches can be provided. Children welcome (a cot can be provided if necessary). No pets. No smoking. Limited private parking.

OWNER Mrs K. Malapeau OPEN All year, exc Christmas
ROOMS 1 family, 1 double, 1 twin; all rooms with wash-basin
TERMS B&B £13, (single occupancy of twin/double) £15, (family room) £33–£40 (children £7 sharing parents' room); deposit

FELTHORPE Norfolk map 8

Flitcham Cottage

Fir Covert Road, Felthorpe NR10 4DT
NORWICH (0603) 867493

This characterful red-brick and pantile cottage, situated in its own grounds amidst typical Norfolk farmland, just seven miles north of Norwich, offers comfortable accommodation at a very reasonable price. Breakfasts are substantial, and early morning tea and biscuits are available at no extra charge. Packed lunches can be provided, if required. There is a comfortable TV lounge and a conservatory that makes a pleasant spot in which to relax. One of the bedrooms is not very convenient for the bathroom. Children are welcome and baby-sitting can be arranged. No pets. No smoking. Ample parking.

OWNERS Mr and Mrs G. H. Smith OPEN All year, exc Christmas
ROOMS 1 family (with wash-basin), 1 double (with wash-basin), 1 twin (with wash-basin), 1 single TERMS B&B £13.50 (reductions for children under 12); deposit

FORDHAM Essex map 5

Kings Vineyard

Fossetts Lane, Fordham CO6 3NY
COLCHESTER (0206) 240377

Until recently this modern house and three and a half acres of land were part of a working farm. Now the land forms a large, sunny garden and supports a flock of rare black St Kilda sheep. There are beautiful views in all directions of the surrounding farmland. Two of the rooms have TV, and the pretty bedspreads were made by Mrs Tweed. There is also a comfortable lounge where fires burn on chilly days. Breakfast is served in a conservatory that has lovely south-facing views overlooking farmland. Vegetarians can be catered for and packed lunches can be provided. Mrs Tweed is extremely knowledgeable about the local area and speaks Dutch and German. Children welcome (a cot is available). Guide dogs only. No smoking. Ample parking.

OWNER Mrs Inge Tweed OPEN All year ROOMS 1 family, 1 double, 1 twin; all rooms with bath/shower TERMS B&B from £15, (single occupancy of twin/double) from £18, (family room) from £34 (babies £3, children under 10 half-price); deposit

FOXLEY Norfolk map 8

Pol-Na-Chess

Mill Road, Foxley, Dereham NR20 4QX
BAWDESWELL (036 288) 330

This modern bungalow in unspoilt countryside is named after a favourite spot of the owners in Scotland. Mr and Mrs Parfitt have lived here since the late 1960s, and are happy to share their knowledge of what to see and do in the area with their guests. Breakfast only is served in the pleasant dining-room on a refectory table, with patio doors leading out into the garden. The guests' lounge has TV and a large open fireplace faced with local stone. There is a hot-drinks trolley and guests may help themselves at any time. All the bedrooms are on the ground floor. The house is well maintained and spotlessly clean. There is a horse-riding school in the village. Children welcome. Car park.

OWNERS Joan and Richard Parfitt OPEN Mar–31 Oct
ROOMS 1 double, 2 twin; all rooms with wash-basin
TERMS B&B £15 (children under 12 £10)

FRAMINGHAM EARL Norfolk map 5

Oakfield

Yelverton Road, Framingham Earl, nr Norwich NR14 7SD
FRAMINGHAM EARL (050 86) 2605

Framingham Earl is four miles south-east of the historic city of Norwich. Take the A146 Lowestoft road from Norwich, turn right opposite the Gull public house, keep left and turn left at the top of the lane. Oakfield is an attractive modern bungalow set in half an acre of gardens, with four acres of meadowland. The immaculate bedrooms, all on the ground floor, are of a good size and have pastel peach and cream bedspreads. The excellent breakfast, with home-baked bread, is just one of the reasons why guests return. Vegetarians can be catered for. The guest lounge has a TV. No children under 12. No pets. No smoking. Car park.

OWNERS Mr and Mrs N. Thompson OPEN all year, exc Christmas ROOMS 1 double (with bath/shower), 1 twin (with wash-basin), 1 single (with wash-basin) TERMS B&B £13–£15

FULMODESTONE Norfolk map 8

Manor Farm House

Stibbard Road, Fulmodestone, nr Fakenham NR21 0LX
GREAT RYBURGH (032 878) 353

Your arrival at Manor House farm is heralded by a brass bell, which is one of the many original features. This traditional Norfolk farmhouse is in a secluded location in 500 acres of arable farmland, formerly part of the Earl of Leicester's estate. The bedrooms are of a good size, all with easy chairs and TV. There is an interesting doll collection on the landing, and the hand-made stuffed animals and gloves are for sale. Guests may sit out in the acre of formal gardens and there is a croquet lawn set out in summer. Evening meals are available 7–7.30pm by prior arrangement and vegetarian choices can be offered. Mrs Savage is a health-conscious cook who tries to prepare foods that are additive-free. There is no alcohol licence, but guests may bring their own wine to dinner. Guests are encouraged to treat the farmhouse as their own home, and there is a pleasant informal atmosphere. Children welcome. No pets. No smoking.

OWNER Mrs A. Savage OPEN All year ROOMS 1 family, 1 double, 1 twin; all rooms with wash-basin TERMS B&B £17, (family room) £38 (reduction for children sharing parents' room); dinner £9; deposit; Visa

GISSING Norfolk map 5

The Old Rectory

Gissing, nr Diss IP22 3XB
TIVETSHALL (037 977) 575

This lovely Victorian rectory is set in three acres of grounds, in a rural hamlet. Jill and Ian Gillam have restored the house to its original splendour. The three spacious bedrooms are beautifully furnished and colour-co-ordinated; all have TV and hair-dryer. There are lots of extra touches, such as toiletries, notepaper and fresh flowers. Delicious breakfasts and candle-lit dinners, at 7.45pm (if pre-arranged), are served in the elegant dining-room or on the terrace in warm weather. A typical four-course menu might include iced lettuce soup, cod and prawns in white wine with grapes and almonds, and apple and apricot gâteau. Vegetarian and low-fat dishes can be provided. There is no alcohol licence, but guests may bring their own wine to dinner. The drawing-room has a lovely marble fireplace, TV, books and magazines. Guests may play croquet on the lawn, relax on the terrace or swim in the indoor pool. There are also bicycles for hire. Children welcome (but not allowed in the pool under 18). No pets. Smoking only in the drawing-room. Car park.

OWNERS Jill and Ian Gillam OPEN All year ROOMS 1 double, 2 twin; all rooms with bath/shower TERMS B&B £22–£24, (single occupancy of twin/double) £32–£36 (children under 2 free, 2–5 £8, 5–9 £12); D, B&B £38–£40; dinner £16–£18; deposit

GREAT MAPLESTEAD Essex map 5

Monks Lodge Farm House

Gestingthorpe Road, Great Maplestead, Halstead CO9 2RN
HEDINGHAM (0787) 60280

Surrounded by pretty countryside and the Constable country of the Essex/Suffolk border, the farmhouse was transported from Canada in 1881 and rebuilt. It is very much a private home, with few rules and a pleasant informal atmosphere. One bedroom has TV. Breakfast only is served and times are flexible. There are several pubs and restaurants in the village serving bar snacks and meals. Mrs Hook is a friendly lady with a good sense of humour. There is a small private swimming-pool that guests may use in the summer. Car park.

OWNER Mrs Jean Hook OPEN All year, exc Christmas and New Year ROOMS 2 twin TERMS B&B £12 (reductions for children under 10)

If you intend to spend several days at a B&B, it is worth asking whether there are reduced rates, particularly if the period is midweek or off-season.

Any smoking restrictions that we know of are given in each entry.

HARWICH Essex map 5

Reids of Harwich

3 West Street, Harwich CO12 3DA
HARWICH (0255) 506796

A basic property with modest furnishings, handy for the ferries, that is only a few minutes' walk from the town centre. The accommodation is above a studio/gallery run by the proprietor, a local artist, and his wife. There is a fine collection of Mr Reid's watercolours, sketches and hand-painted thimbles on display. There is a very comfortable lounge, with original marble fireplace, where breakfast only is served. Packed lunches can be provided on request. The bedrooms are on the second floor and all have TV. The owners are extremely helpful and provide irons, hair-dryers and sewing kits on request. Children by arrangement. No pets. There is no parking at the property, but a free car park is close by.

OWNERS Gordon and Lorna Reid OPEN All year ROOMS 1 double, 1 twin, 1 single; all rooms with wash-basin TERMS B&B £15, (single occupancy of twin/double) £20 (children under 3 free); deposit; Access, Visa

HEMSBY Norfolk map 8

Old Station House

North Road, Hemsby, nr Great Yarmouth NR29 4EZ
GREAT YARMOUTH (0493) 732022

This turn-of-the-century house was built for the station master and is set in a three-quarter-acre garden in a secluded and peaceful setting six miles from Great Yarmouth, close to the Norfolk Broads. The dining-room and kitchen were converted to a large comfortable lounge, which overlooks the pretty landscaped garden. Mrs Lake is a delightful lady and the house has a warm and relaxed atmosphere. Breakfast only is served, but there are some excellent restaurants and pubs close by. Children welcome. No pets. No smoking. Car park.

OWNERS Mr and Mrs A. Lake OPEN All year, exc Christmas ROOMS 2 family, 1 twin; all rooms with wash-basin TERMS B&B £13, (single occupancy of twin) £18 (reductions for children according to age); deposit

If any bedrooms are suitable for the disabled we mention this in the entry.

HITCHAM Suffolk map 5

Hill Farmhouse

Bury Road, Hitcham IP7 7PT
BILDESTON (0449) 740651

Set in three acres of grounds at the heart of Suffolk's gently rolling farmland, this comfortable farmhouse dates from medieval times, with Georgian/Victorian additions. Furnished mostly with Victorian pieces, the older part of the house has beams and inglenooks and there is a sitting-room with TV for guests. The bedrooms are well furnished and all have their own bathrooms; one room is on the ground floor. There is also a fifteenth-century timbered cottage, ideal for families, with light cooking facilities, although breakfast and evening meals, 6.30–8pm, are available in the main house. Vegetarians can be catered for. Hill Farm is unlicensed, but guests may bring their own wine. Children are welcome, but parents should be warned the property has two ponds. No smoking in one bedroom. Parking available.

OWNERS Andrew and Philippa McLardy OPEN Easter–end Oct
ROOMS 1 double, 2 twin; all rooms with bath/shower TERMS B&B £15 (children under 12 £8.50 in own room); dinner £9.50; deposit

HORNING Norfolk map 8

Oak Tree Cottage

2 Oak Tree Cottage, Norwich Road, Horning, Norwich NR12 8LW
HORNING (0692) 630102

Well situated for the Norfolk Broads, the cottage has three freshly decorated rooms, which are clean, basic and modestly furnished. There are no fancy frills here – the accommodation is down-to-earth and good value. Guests are welcome to use the family lounge. Breakfast only is available, but packed lunches can be provided on request. Car park.

OWNERS Brenda and Colin Bullock OPEN All year, exc Christmas
ROOMS 1 family, 1 double, 1 twin TERMS B&B £11, (single occupancy of twin/double) £12.50, (family room) £30–£40 (children £8) deposit

Most B&Bs offer tea/coffee-making facilities in the bedrooms.

HOWLETT END Essex map 5

The Bungalow

Howlett End, Wimbish, Saffron Walden CB10 2XW
SAFFRON WALDEN (0799) 599616

The Bungalow was built in the 1930s and is situated off the road in a peaceful location. The immaculate bedrooms are tastefully furnished in pine. The one *en suite* bedroom has sloping ceilings and 'duck your head' door. A TV lounge is the first floor, as well as a separate dining-room where breakfasts only are served. A cup of tea or coffee is offered to guests on arrival and on fine days this is served on the patio in the pretty garden. This is an ideal area for bicycling and for visiting Cambridge or Colchester. Transport to and from Stanstead Airport can be arranged. Children welcome. Pets by arrangement. No smoking. Car park.

OWNERS Doreen and John Kennet OPEN All year ROOMS 1 family, 1 double (with bath/shower), 1 twin; all rooms with wash-basin TERMS B&B £15–£17 (reductions for children)

HUNTINGDON Cambridgeshire map 5

Braywood House

27 St Peters Road, Huntingdon PE18 7AA
HUNTINGDON (0480) 459782

Close to Huntingdon town centre, this listed Georgian house stands in its own grounds in a tree-lined area. The house has been decorated to a high standard, and all bedrooms have TV. This was once a judge's house, reflected in the Governor's Bedchamber, Jailer's Room, Solitary Room and Awaiting Trial Room. Two of the bedrooms have four-poster beds and there is one ground-floor bedroom. Substantial breakfasts are served in the bright dining-room, and dinners are available at 6.30pm Monday to Thursday. Vegetarians can be catered for. There is no licence, but guests may bring their own wine. There is a snooker table in the lounge, and also a sauna and sunbed for guests' use. Children welcome. No smoking in the dining-room. Car park.

OWNERS Lynne and Brian Knapp OPEN All year, exc Christmas ROOMS 2 family, 2 double, 2 twin, 2 single; all rooms, exc 1 single (wash-basin only), with bath/shower TERMS B&B £16–£20, (family room) from £37.50 (babies free, children under 10 £7.50); dinner £6; Access, Visa

Braywood House, Huntingdon

IPSWICH Suffolk map 5

Burlington Lodge Guest House

30 Burlington Road, Ipswich IP1 2HS
IPSWICH (0473) 251868

You will find this attractive Victorian property on the corner of a quiet street, just a five-minute walk from the city centre. The bedrooms are large, all with TV and modern, comfortable furnishings; one room is on the ground floor. Burlington Lodge is popular with business people as well as tourists. Breakfast only is served. Children welcome. Pets must be house-trained and their own beds must be provided. No smoking in the dining-room. Car park.

OWNERS David and Jean Wickens OPEN All year, exc Christmas
ROOMS 5 twin; all rooms with bath/shower TERMS B&B £16, (single occupancy of twin) £20

It is always best to check prices, especially for single occupancy, when booking.

KERSEY Suffolk map 5

Red House Farm

Kersey, Ipswich IP7 6EY
BOXFORD (0787) 210245

Situated between the delightful old villages of Kersey and Boxford, this attractive farmhouse, dating from 1850, is surrounded by open countryside. There is a lovely weeping willow fronting the house and a large garden with an abundance of flowers and shrubs. The rooms, all with TV, are large and comfortably furnished. The cosy dining-room has french doors leading out to the garden. Evening meals, served 6–9pm, are available; an extensive menu of traditional dishes is presented to guests upon arrival. Vegetarian choices can be provided. All the vegetables are organically grown, and the eggs are free-range. There is no alcohol licence, but guests may bring their own wine to dinner. Guests may use the large heated swimming-pool in the garden. Children welcome. Car park.

OWNER Mary Alleston OPEN All year ROOMS 1 twin (with bath/shower), 1 single TERMS B&B £15–£16, (single) £18; dinner £8

KING'S LYNN Norfolk map 8

Fairlight Lodge

79 Goodwins Road, King's Lynn PE30 5PE
KING'S LYNN (0553) 762234

This grey-stone Victorian house standing in its own grounds is within walking distance of the town centre and bus and railway stations. The house is tastefully decorated throughout, and the well-appointed bedrooms have TV and hair-dryer. Dinner is served at 7pm (by prior arrangement) and vegetarian dishes can be arranged. Guests may bring their own wine to dinner as there is no alcohol licence. Four of the rooms are on the ground floor in a well-appointed annexe. Children welcome. No smoking in the dining-room. Private parking.

OWNERS Tim and Penny Rowe OPEN All year, exc Christmas ROOMS 2 double (1 with bath/shower, 1 with wash-basin), 3 twin (2 with bath/shower, 1 with wash-basin), 2 single (1 with bath/shower, 1 with wash-basin) TERMS B&B £13–£16, (single) £13–£18, (single occupancy of twin/double) £16–£20, (family room) £38 (children half-price sharing parents' room); dinner £7.50; deposit

Russet House Hotel

53 Goodwins Road, King's Lynn PE30 5PE
KING'S LYNN (0553) 773098

The owners and staff work hard to maintain the high standards set at this lovely Victorian house, where the atmosphere is relaxed. Excellent breakfasts and dinners (7–7.45pm) are served and vegetarian choices can be provided. A small bar/lounge, with a fire, overlooks the garden. There are two additional small lounges for guests to relax in. All bedrooms have TV and telephone and two are on the ground floor. Children are welcome but are not allowed in the bar. No pets in the public rooms. No smoking in the dining-room or four-poster room. Car park.

OWNERS Rae and Barry Muddle OPEN All year, exc Christmas and New Year ROOMS 1 four-poster, 4 double, 4 twin, 3 single; all rooms with bath/shower TERMS B&B £22.50, (four-poster) £30, (single) from £34, (single occupancy of twin/double) £37.50–£39; dinner from £11; Access, Amex, Diners, Visa

LAVENHAM Suffolk map 5

48 Water Street

48 Water Street, Lavenham CO10 9RN
LAVENHAM (0787) 248422

This cosy Victorian cottage on the edge of the village was once the local butcher's shop. There are just two bedrooms, without wash-basins, but there is a bathroom exclusively for guests' use. The lounge is shared with Mrs Morley, a most pleasant hostess who is always happy to assist her guests. The lounge has french doors leading out into a pretty, small walled garden. Evening meals are available on request and vegetarian choices can be provided. There is no alcohol licence, but guests may bring their own wine to dinner. Children welcome. Pets by arrangement.

OWNER Margaret Morley OPEN All year ROOMS 1 double, 1 single TERMS B&B £13.50–£14 (children under 10 half-price); dinner £6

Most B&Bs don't accept credit cards, but when they do we list the cards taken.

Many B&Bs are in remote places; always ask for clear directions when booking.

Weaners Farm

Bears Lane, Lavenham CO10 9RX
LAVENHAM (0787) 247310

This modern farmhouse in 20 acres of land is just one mile from Lavenham. It is on a working farm that supports pigs and a few sheep. The two pretty bedrooms are spacious and there is a very comfortable TV lounge overlooking the garden. Breakfast only is served, featuring home-made sausages and free-range eggs from the farm. It is a peaceful spot and there are some lovely walks close by. No children under 12. No pets. Smoking downstairs only. Car park.

OWNER Hazel Rhodes OPEN All year, exc Christmas
ROOMS 1 double, 2 twin TERMS B&B £15.50, (single occupancy of twin/double) £17; deposit

LETHERINGSETT Norfolk map 8

Glavenside Guest House

Letheringsett, Holt NR25 7AR
HOLT (0263) 713181

This country house dates back to 1654, and was originally known as the Mill House. The working watermill was repaired in 1983, and its own stone-ground flour is on sale. Glavenside is set in idyllic surroundings of four acres of varied garden, and there are croquet and deck tennis on the lawn and paddling in the river and streams. The house has a flagstone entry and all the bedrooms have TV and views of the countryside. The atmosphere is one of peace and tranquillity. Breakfast only is served, and there is a kitchen for guests' use. Bar meals are served in the King's Head pub a few minutes' walk away. Children welcome. Pets by arrangement. No smoking in bedrooms and the dining-room. Car park.

OWNERS Angela and Jonathan Cozens-Hardy OPEN All year
ROOMS 2 family, 3 double (with bath/shower), 2 twin, 1 single
TERMS B&B £10–£16; deposit

It is always best to check prices, especially for single occupancy, when booking.

Bath/shower in the details under each entry means that the rooms have private facilities.

LONG MELFORD Suffolk map 5

1 Westropps

1 Westropps, Long Melford CO10 9HW
SUDBURY (0787) 73660

Mrs Fisher makes guests feel at home in her immaculate, modern house, furnished in traditional style. The rooms, all with TV, are of a good size, bright and decorated in pastel colours. There is a comfortable sitting-room. Breakfast only is served, although packed lunches can be provided. The dining-room leads on to a small conservatory overlooking the pretty garden, which is full of shrubs and flowers. There is also a fish pond with Koi carp which guests can feed. Children welcome. Non-smokers preferred. Car park.

OWNER Mrs A. Fisher OPEN All year ROOMS 1 family (with bath/shower), 1 twin (with wash-basin), 1 single (with wash-basin) TERMS B&B £16 (children under 10 half-price)

LOWESTOFT Suffolk map 5

Coventry Guest House

8 Kirkley Cliff, Lowestoft NR33 0BY
LOWESTOFT (0502) 573865

A three-storey Victorian guesthouse that faces the sea. All the bedrooms (one is at ground-floor level) are immaculate and have alarm clocks and TV. One room has the original marble fireplace. There are pretty flowers and shrubs in the front garden. This is a very popular place, both in winter and summer, with business people as well as tourists. Evening meals, including vegetarian dishes (on request), are served at 6pm; unlicensed, but guests may bring their own wine. Packed lunches can be provided. Weekend breaks out of season. Children welcome. Small dogs only. Car park.

OWNERS Chris and Gill Alden OPEN All year, exc Christmas ROOMS 2 family (with bath/shower), 2 double (with bath/shower), 3 twin (with bath/shower), 2 single (with wash-basin) TERMS B&B £13, (single) £15, (single occupancy of twin/double) £20, (family room) £32.50–£39 (children half-price sharing); dinner £5; deposit

We state at the end of an entry when children are welcome. If we know of any restrictions, we give them.

Longshore Guest House

7 Wellington Esplanade, Lowestoft NR33 0QQ
LOWESTOFT (0502) 565037

The lovely promenade gardens are opposite this Victorian house that faces the sea. All rooms have TV and sitting areas, and most have uninterrupted sea views. Mr and Mrs Nolan took over in October 1990 and they are maintaining the high standards set by the previous owners. The bedrooms are in soft pastel colours with matching fabrics, and all have radio-alarms. Breakfasts only are served. Children welcome. No smoking in the dining-room. Pets by arrangement. Car park.

OWNERS Mr and Mrs F. D. Nolan OPEN All year, exc Christmas
ROOMS 3 family, 1 twin, 1 single; all rooms with wash-basin
TERMS B&B £16–£18, (single occupancy of twin/double) £22, (family room) £32 (children under 7 £5–£7); deposit

MENDLESHAM GREEN Suffolk map 5

Cherry Tree Farm

Mendlesham Green, Stowmarket IP14 5RQ
STOWMARKET (0449) 766376

The owners have lovingly restored this late-fifteenth-century timber-framed Suffolk farmhouse in an unspoilt hamlet. It is surrounded by a large garden with an orchard and duck-pond, and is an ideal base from which to visit the Museum of East Anglian Life at Stowmarket. The charming property is prettily decorated and dotted with antiques. One bedroom overlooks the garden and pond and has a beamed sloping roof and new pine furnishings. Dinners, served at 7pm, are a feature here, offering traditional and imaginative menus using home-grown produce when available, and can include vegetarian dishes if ordered in advance. There is an interesting choice of local wines. The spacious lounge has an inglenook fireplace where logs blaze on cool evenings. No children under eight. No pets. Smoking only in the lounge. Car park.

OWNERS Martin and Diana Ridsdale OPEN All year, exc Dec and Jan ROOMS 2 double (1 with bath/shower, 1 with wash-basin), 1 twin (with wash-basin) TERMS B&B £16.50–£20, (single occupancy of twin/double) £25; dinner £11.50; deposit

Most B&Bs offer tea/coffee-making facilities in the bedrooms.

NEATISHEAD Norfolk map 8

Regency Guest House

Neatishead NR12 8AD
HORNING (0692) 630233

Neatishead is in the heart of the Norfolk Broads and only a few miles from the sandy beaches of the coast. This seventeenth-century house with beamed ceilings is in the centre of this unspoilt pretty village. The rooms are decorated with Laura Ashley fabrics; some have delightful views of the garden. All have TV. The proprietors are well known for their large, well-prepared breakfasts; wholesome packed lunches are also available and vegetarians can be catered for. There are several eating places nearby for evening meals. Children and pets are welcome. No smoking in the breakfast room. Car park.

OWNERS Alan and Sue Wrigley OPEN All year
ROOMS 2 double/1 family, 3 twin/1 family; 3 rooms have bath/shower, all have wash-basin TERMS B&B £16.50, (single occupancy of twin/double) £19, (family room) £40; deposit

NEWMARKET Suffolk map 5

Falmouth House

Falmouth Avenue, Newmarket CB8 ONB
NEWMARKET (0638) 660409

This is an attractive modern house in a quiet cul-de-sac overlooking Fitzroy Paddocks, a few minutes' walk from the town centre and racecourse. Rooms are of a good size, well furnished and in good decorative order. There is an interesting collection of Danish china plates. Evening meals, including vegetarian dishes, are available, by arrangement, 6–7pm. There is no alcohol licence, but guests may bring their own wine. Packed lunches can be provided. There is a sitting-room with TV and a swimming-pool is available. No pets. Car park.

OWNERS Vernon and Evelyn Shaw OPEN All year, exc Christmas
ROOMS 1 double, 2 twin; all rooms with wash-basin TERMS B&B from £15–£16, (single occupancy of twin/double) £20–£30; dinner £7.50; deposit; sometimes full payment in advance

The description for each entry states when pets are not allowed or restricted in any way.

NORTH WALSHAM Norfolk map 8

Toll Barn

Norwich Road, North Walsham NR28 0JB
NORTH WALSHAM (0692) 403063

Toll Barn is in five acres of grounds surrounded by open country. The basic structure of the house is eighteenth-century and it has been tastefully modernised. Several original features remain, such as the oak beams and a beautiful brick arch under which the galleried stairway leads to the bedrooms. The beautifully furnished bedrooms all have TV. There are three ground-floor rooms, one of which is suitable for a wheelchair. Three large rooms in the adjacent annexe form a courtyard around the garden and central fountain. Freshly prepared breakfasts are served in the elegant dining-room. Packed lunches can be provided. There is a comfortable sitting-room with an open fire and TV. The stately homes of Blickling, Felbrigg and Beeston are all close by. No children under five. Pets by arrangement. No smoking. Car park.

OWNERS Annette and Peter Tofts OPEN All year ROOMS 2 family (with bath/shower), 2 double (with wash-basin), 1 twin (with wash-basin) TERMS B&B £16–£21 (children £8 if sharing parents' room); deposit

NORWICH Norfolk map 5

Aspland Hotel

5 Aspland Road, Norwich NR1 1SH
NORWICH (0603) 628999

A Victorian residence that is located in a quiet cul-de-sac, a 10-minute walk from the city centre. Although company-owned, this hotel is one in a chain of only two establishments and is, in effect, family-run. Bedrooms are decorated with Laura Ashley wallpapers and all have TV, hair-dryer and tea and coffee maker. Some of the original features remain, including ceiling cornices, a ceiling rose and marble fireplace in the dining-room. Parking permits are provided for guests. Children welcome.

OWNERS Skeet Hotels OPEN All year, exc Christmas
ROOMS 1 family (with bath/shower), 1 double (with bath/shower), 4 twin (2 with bath/shower, 2 with wash-basin), 1 single (with wash-basin) TERMS B&B £15–£25 (children under 10 free); deposit; Access, Visa

OTLEY Suffolk map 5

Otley House

Helmingham Road, Otley, nr Ipswich IP6 9NR
HELMINGHAM (0473) 890253

This elegant house dating from the seventeenth-century has been tastefully modernised over the years, retaining many original features, including a Grade I listed Queen Anne staircase. The house stands in its own spacious grounds, surrounded by trees; there is also a small lake inhabited by ducks and moorhens. The croquet lawn is available for guests. The house is furnished with fine antiques and other treasures, plus an interesting plate collection. One of the bedrooms has a four-poster bed, three have TV. There is a suite (bedroom/bathroom/drawing-room) on the ground floor. An atmosphere of elegance and luxury pervades Otley House and the service is impeccable. For example, guests can have tea brought to them at any time of the day, anywhere in the house or grounds. Guests also have use of a billiard and TV room. Breakfast and evening meals (7.30pm) are available; Friday and Saturday bookings are accepted on a dinner, bed and breakfast basis only. Dinner is not served on Sunday. Vegetarian dishes can be provided by prior arrangement. The premises are licensed. No children under 12. No pets. Smoking in the billiard room only. Car park.

OWNERS Lise and Michael Hilton OPEN 1 Mar–1 Nov
ROOMS 1 four-poster, 1 double, 2 twin; all rooms with bath/shower
TERMS B&B £21–£24, (single occupancy of twin/double) £34–£38; dinner £15.50; deposit

PETERBOROUGH Cambridgeshire map 5

Willow End Guest House

313 Eastfield Road, Peterborough PE1 4RA
PETERBOROUGH (0733) 62907

Standards are extremely high at this attractive Edwardian house within easy reach of the town centre; everything gleams and sparkles. Owner Mrs Rowell is very creative and the attractive décor reflects her special flair. The bedrooms are large and well furnished, with modern furniture in the TV lounge and dining-room. The gardens are lovely, with flowering shrubs, plants and a fish pond. Breakfast only is served and packed lunches can be provided. This is a comfortable place to stay, with a pleasant, relaxed atmosphere. No children under five. No pets. Car park.

OWNER Mrs L. Rowell OPEN All year, exc Christmas ROOMS 1 family (with wash-basin), 1 double (with wash-basin), 2 twin (1 with bath/shower, 1 with wash-basin) TERMS B&B £14–£20 (children under 12 half-price sharing with parents); deposit

REEPHAM Norfolk map 8

Rookery Farm

Church Street, Reepham, Norwich NR10 4JW
NORWICH (0603) 871847

Close to the attractive market town of Reepham, this old listed farmhouse dates from the seventeenth century; the façade was added in 1810. It is close to the church and main square yet overlooks unspoilt countryside. There is a patio in front of the house with a small garden – a pleasant place to sip drinks on warm evenings – and a children's play area. The Goffs bought the house around 1986 and they continue to upgrade the property. The bedrooms are fresh, brightly painted in pastel colours, with flowered duvets and comfortable furniture. Breakfast includes free-range eggs and home-baked bread and is served in the very spacious guests' dining-room/sitting-room. Light evening snacks can be arranged, including vegetarian dishes. Guests may bring their own wine. No pets in the public rooms, and guests must bring a bed for any pet. No smoking in bedrooms. Car park.

OWNERS Gill and Bob Goff OPEN All year, exc Christmas and New Year ROOMS 1 family, 1 double, 1 twin; all rooms with bath/shower TERMS B&B £16, (single occupancy of twin/double) £21, (family room) £48 (children under 2 free, 3–12 £10); evening snacks £4

SHERINGHAM Norfolk map 8

Fairlawns

26 Hooks Hill Road, Sheringham NR26 8NL
SHERINGHAM (0263) 824717

A large, secluded Victorian house set in a beautiful landscaped garden, a few minutes from the town centre. The bedrooms are spacious and individually decorated; all have TV and a bathroom with both bath and shower. The large dining-room/lounge, with TV, overlooks the gardens. Substantial breakfasts, traditional or Continental, are served. Mrs McGill, who is from Edinburgh, enjoys cooking, and imaginative dinners (if pre-arranged) are available; vegetarians can be catered for. There is a brief wine list. This is an ideal base for those interested in visiting National Trust properties and the north Norfolk coast. Children welcome. Guide dogs only. Car park.

OWNERS Elizabeth and Fred McGill OPEN Easter–Oct
ROOMS 2 double, 2 twin; all rooms with bath/shower TERMS B&B from £18, (single occupancy of twin/double) £22; D, B&B Fri–Sat £55; dinner £11; deposit

SHIPDHAM Norfolk map 5

Ivy Cottage

Blackmoor Road, Shipdham, Thetford IP25 7PU
DEREHAM (0362) 820665

These two sixteenth-century Norfolk cottages have been sympathetically restored and modernised. Original features such as the oak beams, inglenook fireplaces and pantiled roofs have been retained. The cottages are set in an acre of gardens, situated on a quiet lane and surrounded by farmland. The atmosphere is warm and friendly, and Margaret Kirk enjoys chatting to her guests in the small, cosy TV lounge. There are geese, two dogs, three cats and chickens, which provide the fresh eggs for breakfast. One of the cottages is self-catering. Children welcome, but may need supervision near the fish pond.

OWNER Margaret Kirk OPEN All year, exc Christmas
ROOMS 1 family (with wash-basin), 1 double, 1 twin TERMS B&B £15 (children under 12 half-price sharing); deposit

SIBLE HEDINGHAM Essex map 5

Comfrey Cottage

29–31 Queen Street, Sible Hedingham CO9 3RH
HEDINGHAM (0787) 60271

Guests are welcome to use the two acres of pretty gardens that surround the house. The two Victorian cottages converted into one are in a quiet position, set back from the main road. The rooms are cosy, modestly furnished, and there is one *en suite* bedroom; all overlook the pond. There is a comfortable guest lounge with TV. Breakfast only is available. Children welcome. No pets. No smoking in bedrooms. Car park.

OWNER Mrs B. M. Rowney OPEN All year ROOMS 1 family (with bath/shower), 1 twin (with wash-basin), 2 single (1 with wash-basin) TERMS B&B about £12, (family room) £15 per person (reductions for children); deposit

SOUTHEND-ON-SEA Essex map 3

Pebbles Guest House

190 Eastern Esplanade, Thorpe Bay,
Southend-on-Sea SS1 3AA
SOUTHEND-ON-SEA (0702) 582329

This is a comfortable guesthouse, with an attractive whitewashed exterior, and flower baskets and window boxes. The five bedrooms are freshly decorated, with new carpets, and all have TV. Some of the rooms have estuary views and small balconies. Breakfasts and evening meals, 6–7pm, are served in the dining-room, which overlooks the sea. Traditional as well as vegetarian meals are served. There is no alcohol licence, but guests may bring their own wine to dinner. Packed lunches are available upon request. Children welcome. No pets. Smoking allowed only in bedrooms. Street parking, but a free car park is 100 yards away.

OWNERS Edna and Colin Christian OPEN All year ROOMS 1 family, 1 double, 2 twin, 1 single; all rooms with bath/shower TERMS B&B £16, (single) £20 (children under 6 £8); dinner £7.50; deposit

SPIXWORTH Norfolk map 8

Spixworth Motel

145 Crostwick Lane, Spixworth, Norwich NR10 3NG
NORWICH (0603) 898288

This popular chalet-type accommodation is quietly situated at the rear of the main house. There is also a patio and garden with a fish pond. The rooms follow a standard format, all with private bath. Each room has a writing desk and TV, and most of the rooms are on the ground floor. Colin Ward is a cartographic publisher, producing tourist maps, and is always happy to assist guests with itineraries. Although motel-like in appearance, Spixworth Motel still has a friendly feel. À la carte evening meals are served in the small licensed restaurant (6.30–8.30pm); there is also a residential licence. Children welcome. Pets allowed only in ground-floor rooms at a modest cost. No smoking in the dining-room. Car park.

OWNERS Colin and Claude Ward OPEN All year, exc Christmas ROOMS 3 family, 12 double, 4 twin, 4 single; all rooms with bath/shower TERMS B&B £19.25, (single) £24.50–£26.50, (single occupancy of twin/double) £29; deposit; Access, Amex, Diners, Visa

SPORLE Norfolk map 8

Corfield House

Sporle, nr Swaffham PE32 2EA
SWAFFHAM (0760) 23636

This lovely brick farmhouse, built in 1852 with later additions from the 1950s, is situated off the road in a very peaceful position. The guest rooms are in the original part of the house, decorated to a high standard with colour-co-ordinated Laura Ashley designs and wicker and pine furnishings. All have TV and hair-dryer. One bedroom is on the ground floor. Guests have full use of the lovely garden with a footpath bordered by lavender and rose bushes. Linda Hickey works as a volunteer for the local tourist office and is happy to assist with itineraries. Excellent breakfasts and dinners (7.30pm) are available, and vegetarians can be catered for. There is a wine list. Children welcome. Pets by arrangement. No smoking. Car park.

OWNERS Linda and Martin Hickey OPEN Easter–mid-Dec ROOMS 2 double, 2 twin, 2 single; all rooms with bath/shower TERMS B&B £17.50–£19.50, (single) £19.50, (single occupancy of twin/double) £30 (babies free, reductions for children); D, B&B £27–£29; dinner £10.50; deposit; Access, Visa

STOKE BY CLARE Suffolk map 5

Dovecote

Romford Green Lane, Stoke by Clare, Sudbury CO10 8HJ
CLARE (0787) 277331

Set in half an acre of pretty gardens, this is a welcoming place in a quiet location about a quarter of a mile from the village. The original dovecote is now in the dining-room, which has a most attractive wooden ceiling rose. The bedrooms are located in a new addition, and are sparkling clean, of an average size and modestly furnished. Mrs Farrow welcomes guests in the family lounge, and offers a hot drink on arrival. Breakfast only is available, but it is substantial. Reductions for children. No smoking. Car park.

OWNERS Mr and Mrs J. Farrow OPEN All year ROOMS 1 double, 1 twin TERMS B&B £10

STRATFORD ST MARY Suffolk map 5

Teazles

Stratford St Mary, nr Colchester CO7 6LU
COLCHESTER (0206) 323148

A delightful listed timber-framed house built in 1500 by a merchant weaver. The house was completely refurbished in 1971, cleverly combining modern comforts with olde worlde charm. Many original features remain, including the sloping floors, oak beams and a Tudor fireplace. Breakfast only is served in the Suffolk-stone-floored dining-room. The bedrooms are of a good size, and tastefully and individually decorated with antique furnishings. The TV lounge is shared with the family. This is a warm and friendly house, in a peaceful situation ideally situated for touring this lovely region, three quarters of a mile from Stratford St Mary and Dedham and close to Colchester. From Stratford Church, which is well worth a visit, take the B1029 to Dedham; the house is the first on the right after the 'S' bend. Children welcome. No pets in bedrooms. No smoking in bedrooms. Car park.

OWNER Mrs A. Clover OPEN All year ROOMS 1 double, 1 twin (with wash-basin), 1 single TERMS B&B £15–£17.50, (family room) £30–£35 (children under 3 free, £5 under 5, £8 under 10, £10–£12 under 12); deposit

SUDBOURNE Suffolk map 5

Long Meadows

Gorse Lane, Sudbourne, nr Woodbridge IP12 2BD
ORFORD (0394) 450269

A homely, cottage-style bungalow set in half an acre of landscaped gardens, in a semi-rural location situated midway between Snape Maltings and Minsmere Bird Sanctuary. Mr Wood is a keen gardener, and the gardens are open to the public under the National Garden Scheme. The three bedrooms, with period furniture, overlook the gardens; one is *en suite*, and a single and twin share a bathroom. There is a sitting-room with TV and open fire which is lit at the first sign of a chill in the air. There are some lovely walks close by. Laundry facilities are available at no extra charge. No children under 12. Pets by arrangement. Smoking in sitting-room only. Car park.

OWNERS Ann and Stewart Wood OPEN All year, exc Christmas ROOMS 1 double (with bath/shower), 1 twin (with wash-basin), 1 single (with wash-basin) TERMS B&B £11.50–£13.50, (single occupancy of twin/double) £16.50–£18.50; deposit

SUDBURY Suffolk map 5

35 Gainsborough Street

35 Gainsborough Street, Sudbury CO10 6HP
SUDBURY (0787) 881766 Fax (0787) 312039

The deeds to this house date back 500 years. It is situated on the street named after the artist Gainsborough, whose house is open to the public at certain times during the week. The house is very central, just a three-minute walk from the town centre. The beamed bedrooms are well furnished and comfortable. The dining-room, where breakfast and dinner (until 9pm by prior arrangement) are served, leads on to a pretty walled garden which guests may use. There is no licence, but guests may bring their own wine to dinner. Packed lunches can also be arranged. Children welcome. No pets. No smoking in bedrooms. Car park.

OWNERS Mr and Mrs P. Phelan OPEN All year ROOMS 1 double (with bath/shower), 1 twin, 1 single TERMS B&B £13, (single) £15, (single occupancy of twin/double) £18; dinner £7.50; deposit

TERRINGTON ST CLEMENT Norfolk map 8

Homelands

79 Sutton Road, Terrington St Clement, King's Lynn PE34 4PJ
KING'S LYNN (0553) 828401

The gardens at this pleasant detached house are open to the public on alternate years during the Terrington St Clement church festival. Terrington St Clement church is so large that it is known as the 'Cathedral of the Marshland'. The bedrooms (one is on the ground floor) are decorated to a high standard and are well furnished; one has TV. Breakfast only is available. Afternoon tea is served in the sun room or on the garden patio and a cup of tea or coffee is offered to guests on arrival. There is a lounge with TV. Children welcome. No pets. No smoking.

OWNERS Joan and Doug Smith OPEN Mar–Nov ROOMS 2 double (1 with bath/shower), 1 twin (with bath/shower) TERMS B&B £14–£17, (single occupancy of twin/double) £21; deposit

THELNETHAM Suffolk map 5

The Lodge Farm

Weston Road, Thelnetham, Diss IP22 1JL
DISS (0379) 898203

Lodge Farm is a listed, thatched, timber-framed house on a 200-acre arable farm with shire horses and a three-acre vineyard; guests are welcome to put on some wellies and explore the farm. The house is spacious and rambling with exposed beams, a quarry-tiled floor and original fireplaces. There are three well-appointed bedrooms with Laura Ashley designs and old-fashioned furnishings. All have private facilities, one with a whirlpool bath. There is a sitting-room, with log fires and TV, overlooking the walled garden. Evening meals are available (at 7pm if pre-arranged). Dishes are 'farm-style' and all desserts home-baked. There is a table licence and guests may purchase wine from the farm vineyard. Packed lunches can be provided. The well-known Bressingham Gardens and Steam Museum are close by. No children under 10. No pets. No smoking in the dining-room or bedrooms.

OWNERS Michael and Christine Palmer OPEN All year, exc Christmas ROOMS 1 double, 2 twin; all rooms with bath/shower TERMS B&B £16, (single occupancy of twin/double) £20; dinner £10; deposit

THETFORD Norfolk map 5

The Wilderness

Earls Street, Thetford IP24 2AF
THETFORD (0842) 764646

The remains of an old priory are visible in the garden of this mock-Tudor-style house. The town centre is only a two-minute walk. The bedrooms, all with TV, are of a very high standard. The comfortable lounge is furnished with antiques and overlooks the beautiful landscaped garden and the tower of St Stephen's church. Mrs Pomorski welcomes guests with a cup of tea or coffee on arrival. Breakfast only is available. Children welcome. No pets. One bedroom is reserved for smokers; no smoking in the rest of the house. Car park.

OWNERS Mr and Mrs Pomorski OPEN All year ROOMS 2 double, 1 twin; all rooms with bath/shower TERMS B&B £15–£16; deposit

THOMPSON Norfolk map 5

The Thatched House

Pockthorpe Corner, Thompson, nr Thetford IP24 1PJ
CASTON (095 383) 577

All of the bedrooms in this sixteenth-century whitewashed cottage are beamed and full of character; one has the original stable door leading out to the garden; the 'garden room' has french doors leading out on to a patio overlooking the garden. Two rooms are on the ground floor, and two have TV. The upstairs bedrooms, with sloping ceilings, are reached by a narrow, steep staircase. Guests are welcome to join the owner in the family lounge, and facilities are available for making hot drinks at any time. There are two friendly labradors. Breakfasts are excellent and include home-made marmalade. Packed lunches can be provided. No children under seven. Dogs welcome. No smoking. Car park.

OWNER Mrs Brenda Mills OPEN All year, exc Christmas
ROOMS 3 twin (2 with bath/shower), 1 single TERMS B&B £15

UGLEY GREEN Essex map 5

Thatched Cottage

Snakes Lane, Ugley Green, nr Bishops Stortford CM22 6HW
BISHOPS STORTFORD (0279) 812341

This charming Elizabethen black and white timbered thatched cottage is just three miles from Stanstead Airport, and set in nine acres of land with lovely gardens, featuring the original village water pump. Croquet may be played by guests. The house has recently been re-thatched and the interior redecorated. The beamed bedrooms have matching bedspreads and curtains. There is a cosy lounge with TV and lots of books to browse through. Excellent breakfasts are served in the cosy kitchen and are cooked

on the Aga. There are no strict rules here, and the atmosphere is relaxed and informal. Children welcome. Car park.

OWNERS Mr and Mrs D. A. Hilton OPEN All year, exc Christmas ROOMS 3 twin (1 with wash-basin) TERMS B&B £15, (single occupancy of twin) £17.50–£20

WATERDEN Norfolk map 8

The Old Rectory

Waterden, Walsingham NR22 6AT
SOUTH CREAKE (0328) 823298

This charming Victorian rectory is surrounded by views of unspoiled countryside, only six miles from the Norfolk coast. It is part of the Holkham Estate and close to Holkham Park Gardens. There is a flagstone entry, and the house is full of antiques. The rooms are large, and can be a little chilly in winter for those turning up on the off-chance. One room on the ground floor has access either through a small conservatory or direct from the outside. There is a guest lounge with TV and a quiet lounge with a log fire. Hot drinks are offered to guests on arrival. Breakfast only is available. Children welcome. Pets by arrangement. Smoking in the twin room only. Car park.

OWNER R. D. Pile OPEN All year ROOMS 2 double, 1 twin; all rooms with bath/shower TERMS B&B £17.50, (single occupancy of twin/double) £25 (children under 12 £10); deposit

WELLS-NEXT-THE-SEA Norfolk map 8

The Cobblers Guest House

Standard Road, Wells-next-the-Sea NR23 1JU
FAKENHAM (0328) 710155

The house, built in 1924, stands in its own grounds, just two minutes' walk to the harbour. The bedrooms range in size from average to large; they are well furnished and have TV. Two bedrooms have recently been added, a single and double, both *en suite*. The single rooms are on the ground floor. The guest lounge opens out on to a pretty conservatory overlooking the gardens. Evening meals, including vegetarian dishes, are served in the licensed dining-room at 6.30pm; packed lunches can be provided. No children under three. No pets. Smoking allowed only in the lounge. Car park.

OWNERS Andrew and Sylvia Strong OPEN All year, exc Christmas ROOMS 1 family, 4 double (1 with bath/shower), 1 twin, 2 single (1 with bath/shower) TERMS B&B from £14, (single occupancy of twin/double) £17.50 (children over 3 £8.50 in family room); dinner £8.50; deposit

WEST WALTON HIGHWAY Norfolk map 8

Strattons Farm

West Drove North, West Walton Highway PE14 7DP
WISBECH (0945) 880162

This is a modern ranch-style bungalow on 22 acres of beef/dairy farm, with a herd of pedigree Dairy Shorthorns. The bedrooms are very large indeed, with comfortable furniture, a sitting area with easy chairs, radio-alarm and TV. Mrs King is an occupational therapist and one of the bedrooms is specifically designed for guests with wheelchairs. All rooms are at ground level. Breakfast consists of home-cured bacon and sausage, fresh eggs, home-produced milk and preserves. Packed lunches can be provided. Children are encouraged to explore the farm and pet the animals, under supervision. Guests may use the heated swimming-pool in summer. The lake is available for coarse fishing. Home-made

B&B rates specified in the details for each entry are per person per night; unless the details state otherwise, they are based on two people sharing a double or twin-bedded room.

chutneys and marmalades are for sale. No children under five. Guide dogs only. No smoking. Car park.

OWNERS Mr and Mrs Derek King OPEN All year ROOMS 2 double (1 with bath/shower), 2 twin (1 with bath/shower) TERMS B&B £18–£20 (children under 11 half-price); deposit

WITCHFORD Cambridgeshire map 5

Clare Farm House

86/88 Main Street, Witchford CB6 2HQ
ELY (0353) 664135

This modern farmhouse offers excellent accommodation. All the bedrooms have sitting areas, TV and views over open farmland. The bathrooms are modern and attractive. The family room is particularly spacious. There is a large garden where guests can sit or children play. A full English breakfast is served in the family dining-room. Packed lunches are available if ordered the night before. Children welcome. No pets. Car park.

OWNERS Peter and Rita Seymour OPEN All year ROOMS 1 family (with bath/shower), 1 double (with bath/shower) TERMS B&B £13.20–£14.20 (reductions for children); deposit

WIVETON Norfolk map 8

Flintstones Guest House

Wiveton, Holt NR25 7TL
CLEY (0263) 740337

An attractive modern bungalow, with a lovely garden, set in picturesque countryside close to the village green, one mile from Blakeney and Cley-next-the-Sea. Five of the bedrooms are on the ground floor. All have TV and are decorated with delicate floral wallpapers and matching bedspreads. Breakfasts and dinners, 7pm, are served in the licensed dining-room. Packed lunches can be arranged. The guest lounge is well furnished and has a TV and lots of books on bird-watching. Cheap breaks. Pets must have their own beds. Children must share with parents. No smoking. Car park.

OWNERS Mr and Mrs Ormerod OPEN All year, exc Christmas ROOMS 3 family, 1 double, 1 twin, 1 single; all rooms with bath/shower TERMS B&B £14.50, (single occupancy of twin/double) £18.50 (children under 10 £8, over 10 £11); dinner £8.25; deposit

WIX Essex map 5

New Farm House

Spinnell's Lane, Wix, Manningtree CO11 2UJ
CLACTON (0255) 870365

New Farm House is a pleasant modern farmhouse surrounded by a 50-acre working arable farm. Friendliness and hospitality with good farmhouse cooking prevail. The bedrooms, all with TV, are large and tastefully decorated with matching bedspreads and curtains. There are six ground-floor bedrooms and two of them are suitable for the partially disabled, with room for a wheelchair and bathrooms fitted with rails. Children are welcome and the play-area has been extended. The gardens are most attractive and garden furniture has been provided for guests' use. A small kitchenette with microwave oven and facilities for making drinks and snacks is available in the comfortable guest lounge. Evening meals, including vegetarian choices, are available at 6.30pm (winter) or 7pm (summer) as well as packed lunches; menus are in seven European languages. New Farm House is unlicensed, but guests may bring their own wine. Smoking allowed only in two bedrooms and the TV lounge. Laundry facilities are available for a modest charge and irons also provided.

OWNERS Mr G. K. and Mrs H. P. Mitchell OPEN All year
ROOMS 5 family (3 with bath/shower, 2 with wash-basin), 1 double (with bath/shower), 3 twin (2 with bath/shower, 1 with wash-basin), 3 single (1 with bath/shower, 2 with wash-basin) TERMS B&B £16.50–£20 (children under 2 free, 2–4 one-quarter-price, 5–11 half-price, 12–16 three-quarters-price); dinner £8.50; deposit 10%; Access, Visa

WOODBRIDGE Suffolk map 5

Grove Guest House

39 Grove Road, Woodbridge IP12 4LG
WOODBRIDGE (0394) 382202

Built in 1935, with an extension added in 1968, the house lies back from the main road, within minutes of the town centre. Leslie and Jean Kelly run a pleasant, comfortable guesthouse. The bedrooms, all with TV, are of a good size, bright and well decorated. Two additional ground-floor rooms have been added, with *en suite* bathrooms. There is a small lounge with a bar where guests congregate in the evenings. Dinner is available 6.30–7.30pm, and vegetarian choices can be provided by prior arrangement. Packed lunches can also be provided. The Grove is licensed. Woodbridge itself is a small, thriving town with lots of old pubs, a theatre and quaint antique shops. Children welcome. There is a £2 per night charge for pets. No smoking in the dining-room. Car park.

OWNERS Leslie and Jean Kelly OPEN All year ROOMS 1 family (with bath/shower), 1 four-poster (with bath/shower), 1 double (with bath/shower), 4 twin (2 with bath/shower, 2 with wash-basin), 2 single (with wash-basin) TERMS B&B £17–£22.50, (family room) about £40 (children up to 3 free, 3–10 half-price); dinner from £7.70; deposit; Visa

YOXFORD Suffolk map 5

Sans Souci

Main Road, Yoxford IP17 3EX
YOXFORD (072 877) 268

A Georgian residence that is exceptionally well maintained and stands in one and a half acres of walled garden on the outskirts of the village. There are three comfortable bedrooms; one has a brass bed, and all have a sitting area. This is a very popular house with bird-watchers, and it backs on to Rookery Park. A cup of tea or coffee is offered to guests upon arrival. Breakfast only is available and packed lunches can be arranged. Children welcome. Pets by prior arrangement. No smoking in bedrooms. Car park.

OWNERS Stuart and Mary Andrews OPEN All year
ROOMS 2 double, 1 twin; all rooms with wash-basin
TERMS B&B £15–£22 (children under 12 free)

The Midlands

Cheshire

Derbyshire

Leicestershire

Lincolnshire

Northamptonshire

Nottinghamshire

Shropshire

Staffordshire

West Midlands

ASHBOURNE Derbyshire map 7

Stanshope Hall

Stanshope, nr Ashbourne DE6 2AD
ALSTONEFIELD (033 527) 278

Stanshope Hall is a rambling listed country house dating from the sixteenth century in the dairy village of Stanshope, set in the middle of the beautiful surroundings of the Manifold Valley and Dovedale. This is an unusual place to stay for a short break, atmosphere and interest making up for the occasional threadbare armchair. The previous owner was a scene painter and decorated the sitting-room like a moorland scene, with a clear blue sky and white clouds, giving one the impression of sitting out in the open. All bedrooms have TV. The owners, Naomi Chambers and Nicholas Lourie, prepare good, imaginative evening meals, which might include carrot and ginger soup, lamb in red wine and honey and home-made rhubarb ice-cream. Dinner is served at 7pm and vegetarians can be catered for. Sunday lunch is also served and packed lunches can be provided on weekdays. Children welcome. No smoking in the dining-room. Car park.

OWNERS Naomi Chambers and Nicholas Lourie OPEN All year, exc Christmas ROOMS 2 double (1 with bath/shower), 1 twin
TERMS B&B £19.50–£26 (children under 12 two-thirds of adult price); dinner £16.50; deposit

BAKEWELL Derbyshire map 7

Cliffe House

Monsal Head, nr Bakewell DE4 1NL
BAKEWELL (0629) 640376

This attractive 100-year-old stone house is situated at the top of Monsal, overlooking glorious countryside in the heart of the Peak District. There are 10 comfortable bedrooms, all with *en suite* facilities, one of which is ideal for families as there is a double *en suite* bedroom with a triple room adjacent. There is a separate licensed dining-room where breakfast and freshly prepared dinners (from 7.30pm) are served. Packed lunch is also available but needs to be ordered by 10am. There are two lounges, one on the ground floor which is spacious and has a TV, and a small reading-room on the first floor. Monsal Head is just three miles from Bakewell on the B6465, which you turn on to from the A6. Children welcome. No pets. Car park.

OWNERS Mr C. and Mrs S. Harman OPEN All year, exc Christmas
ROOMS 3 family, 6 double, 1 twin; all rooms with bath/shower
TERMS B&B £19–£20, (single occupancy of twin/double) £30, (family room) £46–£62 (half -price reduction for children if sharing with 2 adults); dinner £9; deposit; Access, Visa

Holly Cottage

Rowland, nr Bakewell DE4 1NR
GREAT LONGSTONE (0629) 640624

Holly Cottage is three miles from Bakewell and situated within the Peak District National Park at the end of a most attractive hamlet on a dead-end road leading directly to the hills, where you can just leave the car and walk. The stone-built cottage dates from the eighteenth century and is set among beautifully kept lawned gardens lined with shrubs and flower-beds. An old stone patio runs the length of the front of the house, where guests can sit on warm summer evenings. It has a restful atmosphere and is clean, fresh and bright with comfortable, well-furnished rooms. Guests have the use of the panelled hall, with open fire, an attractive dining-room, where breakfast only is served, and a large comfortable lounge with TV. Mrs Everard, ex-English Ladies Golf Champion, is a charming and friendly hostess. Evening meals are no longer available but Mrs Everard is happy to recommend eating establishments in the area. Chatsworth House, Haddon Hall and Hardwick Hall – as well as several golf courses – are nearby. Children welcome. No smoking. No pets in the house. Car park.

OWNER Mrs Mary Everard OPEN Jan–Oct ROOMS 2 twin
TERMS B&B £16, (single occupancy of twin) £19 (children under 2 free, 3–6 £6, 7–12 £8); deposit

BELPER Derbyshire map 7

Dannah Farm Country Guest House

Bowmans Lane, Shottle, nr Belper DE5 2DR
COWERS LANE (0773) 550630/550273 Fax (0773) 550590

This charming farmhouse, built around 1792, on a farm of 128 acres, is set in beautiful countryside, nestling just below Alport Heights with its panoramic views. The house has been tastefully refurbished, and the bedrooms, all with TV, are well-appointed with matching fabrics and Victorian-style wallpapers. Six of the seven bedrooms now have *en suite* facilities and the seventh has its own private bathroom. Three of the bedrooms are on the ground floor. Meals are a special feature here with the emphasis on wholesome foods. Breakfast is a banquet, with yoghurt, home-made muesli, fresh-baked wholemeal breads, fresh eggs, home-cured meats, juices, crumpets and toast. Evening meals are served 6.30–8.30pm and Dannah Farm is licensed. Vegetarians and special diets can be catered for. Packed lunches can be provided. Children welcome. Guide dogs only. No smoking in bedrooms and the dining-room. Car park.

OWNERS Joan and Martin Slack OPEN All year, exc Christmas Day ROOMS 1 family, 1 four-poster, 2 double, 2 twin, 1 single; all rooms, exc 1 twin (sole use of separate bathroom), with bath/shower TERMS B&B £20–£25 (children half-price in parents' room); dinner £7.95–£22.50; deposit £20 per room; Access, Visa

Shottle Hall Farm Guest House

Shottle, nr Belper DE5 2EB
COWERS LANE (077 389) 276

Set in three acres of colourful gardens and well-kept lawns, Shottle Hall Farm is a secluded, nineteenth-century country house surrounded by farmland. There are two dining-rooms, one usually used for breakfast, the other for dinner, which is served at 7.30pm. Vegetarian meals can be arranged and packed lunches can be provided. There is a lounge with a small bar, and a TV/games-room with a snooker table. The bedrooms are spacious and there is now an additional ground-floor suite with wheelchair access that has two bedrooms, a lounge and its own bathroom. Shottle Hall Farm makes a good base for visiting the Peak District and the Trent Valley. No smoking in bedrooms. No pets in public rooms. Car park.

OWNERS Philip and Phyllis Matthews OPEN All year, exc Christmas ROOMS 3 family (with wash-basin), 6 double (2 with bath/shower), 2 twin (1 with wash-basin), 1 single (with wash-basin) TERMS B&B from £19.50, (single) £23 (reductions for children £1 per year of age); dinner £10.50; deposit £10

Bath/shower information in the details refers only to a private bathroom or shower; other bathroom facilities at the establishments will be shared. We say if rooms have wash-basins.

BIRMINGHAM West Midlands map 4

Heath Lodge Hotel

117 Coleshill Road, Marston Green, Birmingham B37 7HT
021-779 2218

Heath Lodge Hotel is family-run and quietly situated one and a half miles from the National Exhibition Centre and Birmingham Airport. The bedrooms are well appointed and all have telephone and TV; half now have *en suite* facilities. A courtesy car is available to and from the airport, and long-term parking can be arranged. There is a guest lounge with TV as well as a bar. Simple, home-cooked meals are served in the cosy restaurant from 6.30pm. Vegetarian choices are available on request. Packed lunches can also be provided. Children welcome. No smoking. Car park.

OWNER Simeon Collins OPEN All year, exc Christmas
ROOMS 3 double (2 with bath/shower, 1 with wash-basin), 6 twin (3 with bath/shower, 3 with wash-basin), 10 single (5 with bath/shower, 5 with wash-basin) TERMS B&B from £19, (single) from £28.50; deposit; Access, Visa

BOMERE HEATH Shropshire map 6

Fitz Manor

Bomere Heath, nr Shrewsbury SY4 3AS
SHREWSBURY (0743) 850295

Set in spacious grounds overlooking the wide valley of the River Severn, with views of the Shropshire countryside, Fitz Manor is a traditional black and white timbered house dating from the fifteenth century. The garden was laid out in Elizabethan times with rose bushes, herbaceous borders and an extensive fruit and vegetable area from which produce is gathered daily for the evening meals. The house features a huge dining-room, large beds, old-fashioned wash-basins and an oak-panelled sitting-room, all with antique furnishings. Candle-lit dinners are available if pre-arranged, and vegetarians can be catered for. There is no alcohol licence, but guests may bring their own wine. Packed lunches are also available. Guests are welcome to use the solar-heated swimming-pool. There is also a croquet lawn and a play-room with toys. Riding and fishing can also be arranged. Car park.

OWNERS Neil and Dawn Baly OPEN All year, exc Christmas
ROOMS 2 twin, 1 single TERMS B&B £15–£20; dinner £10; deposit

BONSALL Derbyshire map 7

Sycamore House

76 High Street, Town Head, Bonsall, nr Matlock DE4 2AR
MATLOCK (0629) 823903

Sycamore House is an eighteenth-century listed building in an elevated position with views right down the main street of the village and to the hills beyond. The bedrooms are on the small side and simply furnished but some are now *en suite*; all have TV and hair-dryer. Guests have use of the TV lounge, bar and dining-room, where breakfast and evening meals (6.30pm) are served (lunches too, on request). On chilly days a fire is lit enabling guests to enjoy dinner in a warm and cosy atmosphere. Bonsall village is a few minutes from the Historic Canal Terminus at Cromford and the start of the High Peak Trail, which makes Sycamore House a good base for the many places of interest around the area. Children over 11 only. Smoking in lounge only. No pets. Car park.

OWNERS Ray and Pauline Sanders OPEN All year ROOMS 4 double (3 with bath/shower, 1 with wash-basin), 2 twin (1 with bath/shower, 1 with wash-basin), 1 single (with wash-basin) TERMS B&B £16.50–£21; dinner £9; deposit

BOSTON Lincolnshire map 8

Fairfield Guest House

101 London Road, Boston PE21 7EN
BOSTON (0205) 362869

Fairfield Guest House is an impressive turn-of-the-century house standing in its own grounds approximately one mile from the town centre. The gardens are extremely pretty with a colourful display of shrubs and flowers. Many of the original features still remain, such as the oak staircase, fireplace, leaded bay windows and the oak panelling in the entrance. The bedrooms are of a good size and in excellent decorative order, with most rooms having pretty wallpapers and matching furnishings. There is also a TV lounge. Breakfast only is served and packed lunches can be provided on request. Children welcome. Guide dogs only. Car park.

OWNERS Peter James Page and Jean Page OPEN All year, exc Christmas ROOMS 2 family, 4 double, 1 twin, 3 single; all rooms with wash-basin TERMS B&B £14, (single occupancy of twin/double) £20 (children under 5 free, 5–14 half-price if sharing with parents); deposit

BOURNE Lincolnshire map 8

Bourne Eau House

30 South Street, Bourne PE10 9LY
BOURNE (0778) 423621

An air of friendly elegance pervades this beautiful and very interesting house in the little-known market town of Bourne, which still has a twice-weekly street market. The house is furnished with antiques and is comfortable and immaculate. Breakfast and dinner are served in the beautiful Jacobean dining-room, which has an enormous fireplace complete with old bread ovens. A pretty English garden surrounds the house and is bordered on one side by a stream (the Bourne Eau) with swans and geese; beyond the stream is a twelfth-century abbey. The oldest part of the house was built on the site of an old monastery; the more recent additions were made in the Elizabethan and Georgian periods. The sitting-room with TV is in the oldest part of the house. The breakfast room is Elizabethan, the music room Jacobean and the elegant drawing-room Georgian. The lovely bedrooms have *en suite* facilities and TV. Garages and courtyard parking are available. Children welcome. No smoking in bedrooms. No pets.

OWNERS Dr and Mrs G. D. Bishop OPEN All year, exc Christmas, New Year and Easter ROOMS 2 double, 1 twin; all rooms with bath/ shower TERMS B&B £28–£30, (single occupancy of twin/double) £40–£45

BRAMSHALL Staffordshire map 7

West Lodge

Bramshall, Uttoxeter ST14 5BG
UTTOXETER (0889) 566000

This is a modern brick house standing in two acres of beautiful landscaped gardens. The bedrooms are of a good size and comfortably furnished. All have TV. Breakfast only is served in the sunny dining-room, which has an interesting small silver collection on display. In the garden there is a summer-house for guests' use. West Lodge is handy for Alton Towers and the Derbyshire Dales. Children welcome. Reductions for children if

Where we know of any particular payment stipulations we mention them in the details. It is always best to check, however, when booking.

sharing with parents and according to age. No pets. No smoking. Car park.

OWNERS John and Wendy Udall OPEN All year, exc Christmas ROOMS 1 family, 1 double, 1 twin; all rooms with wash-basin TERMS B&B £12.50–£14, (single occupancy of twin/double) £15–£17.50, (family room) £38–£45; deposit

BRAUNSTON Leicestershire map 4

Rutland Cottages

5 Cedar Street, Braunston, nr Oakham LE15 8QS
OAKHAM (0572) 722049

This seventeenth-century stone-built house is in the picturesque conservation village of Braunston and was until 1947 the village bakehouse, where villagers would come to get their Sunday lunches. The bulk of the accommodation is in another house owned by John and Connie Beadman, about a hundred yards away. The bedrooms are somewhat basic but are clean and adequate, and all have TV. Breakfast only is taken in the large dining-room of the main house. Children welcome and babies/small children in their own travelling cots stay free. No pets. No smoking in bedrooms. Car park.

OWNERS John and Connie Beadman OPEN All year, exc Christmas ROOMS 1 double (with bath/shower), 1 twin (with wash-basin), 2 single (with wash-basin) TERMS B&B £15–£18; deposit £10

BUILDWAS Shropshire map 4

Bridge House Guest House

Buildwas, nr Telford TF8 7BN
IRONBRIDGE (0952) 432105

Bridge House is a very interesting, listed seventeenth-century half-timbered house with views over the River Severn, and is one and a half miles from Ironbridge. Many of the timbers used in the construction are reputed to come from the abbey just over the bridge. The house was at one time an inn and in 1925 it was converted into two houses. The panelled lounge has an open fire and the bedrooms have beams and antique furnishings. There is a 'special' bedroom that has a brass bed, Victorian bath and a unique display of antique swords, bayonets and knives. A trolley with tea and biscuits is available for guests' use. There are lots of interesting artefacts and antiques around the house, such as stone hot-water bottles, paintings, statuettes and, in the garden, a display of old farming implements. Breakfast only is available and includes a full English breakfast. Packed lunches can be provided on request. Children welcome. No dogs. Car park.

OWNER Mrs Janet Hedges OPEN All year, exc Christmas ROOMS 1 family (with bath/shower), 2 double (1 with bath/shower, 1 with wash-basin), 2 twin (with wash-basin), 1 single (with wash-basin) TERMS B&B £18–£25, (single) £16–£20, (family room) £52–£58 (children under 4 free, 4–13 half-price); deposit

Hill View Farm

Buildwas, nr Telford TF8 7BP
IRONBRIDGE (0952) 432228

This is a working farm in a rural setting with views of woods and fields. There is over an acre of gardens with a mill-pond stocked with trout and attracting various birds such as kingfishers, heron and mallard. The atmosphere is friendly and the bedrooms are immaculate. Breakfasts are varied and may include kippers and fresh fish. Packed lunches are available by arrangement. The farm is two miles from Ironbridge and close to many places of interest, including the Ironbridge Gorge Museum. No children under 13. Small dogs only by prior arrangement. No smoking. Car park.

OWNERS Mr and Mrs J. Hawkins OPEN All year, exc Christmas and New Year ROOMS 1 family, 1 double; both rooms with wash-basin TERMS B&B £12–£14; (family room) £38–£40; deposit £10

BURLAND Cheshire map 7

Burland Farm

Rexham Road, Burland, nr Nantwich CW5 8ND
NANTWICH (0270) 74210

Burland Farm is a listed red-brick and timber-gabled farmhouse dating from 1865, and standing in a pretty front garden. This country house, with its informal and relaxed atmosphere, has four spacious bedrooms, all individually furnished. One is Victorian in style, another Edwardian, which has an original stencilled wardrobe. All have TV and *en suite* facilities. There is a separate guest lounge with a real fire and a sitting-room/library which has a wood-burning stove. Facilities also include croquet and table tennis. Imaginative evening meals are served by arrangement from

7pm, and all the vegetables and dairy products used for the menu are from the farm. Vegetarians can be catered for and packed lunches can be provided. Guests may bring their own wine to dinner as there is no alcohol licence. No children under 10. 'Well-behaved' dogs only. No smoking. Car park.

OWNERS Michael and Sandra Alwood OPEN All year, exc Christmas and New Year ROOMS 2 double, 2 twin; all rooms with bath/shower TERMS B&B £20–£22.50, (single occupancy of twin/double) £20–£25; dinner £12.50; deposit £10 per person

BUXTON Derbyshire map 7

Hartington Hotel

18 Broad Walk, Buxton SK17 6JR
BUXTON (0298) 22638

Hartington Hotel is a small hotel in a superb position overlooking a park with a lake and ducks and with views beyond to hilly countryside. It is only a short walk to the centre of town and to the famous Opera House. It was established as a hotel in 1958 and has been in the family ever since. The first-floor lounge is large and comfortable. The bedrooms are of good size, light and fresh, and have been individually colour-co-ordinated. All have TV, radio and smoke detector. Two bedrooms on the ground floor are equipped for the disabled and have *en suite* facilities. Dinner is served at 7pm (6.30pm on Sundays) and there is usually a vegetarian dish on the menu. (Dinner is not always available November to Easter.) There is also a cocktail bar. Packed lunches are available on request. Children welcome. Reductions for children when sharing with parents. Guide dogs only. No smoking in the dining-room. Car park.

OWNERS Mr and Mrs M. Whibberley OPEN All year, exc Christmas, New Year and mid-July ROOMS 2 family (1 with bath/shower, 1 with wash-basin), 7 double (4 with bath/shower, 3 with wash-basin), 7 twin (2 with bath/shower, 5 with wash-basin), 1 single (with wash-basin) TERMS B&B £18–£21, (single) £20–£25, (single occupancy of twin/double) £25–£33, (family room) £48–£58; dinner £9.50; deposit; Access, Visa

We asked the proprietors to estimate their 1992 prices in the autumn of 1991, so the rates may have changed since publication.

If a deposit is required for an advance booking this is stated at the end of an entry.

Hawthorn Farm Guest House

Fairfield Road, Buxton SK17 7ED
BUXTON (0298) 23230

This guesthouse has been in the same family for 10 generations and is located on the edge of Buxton, 10 minutes' walk from the centre and with a good bus service passing the door. It is an attractive, whitewashed listed building dating from around 1600 and set in its own grounds. There are leaded windows, thick stone walls and although the ceilings are quite high there are some very low doorways – a potential problem for taller guests. Old farm buildings at the back of the house have been converted into seven bedrooms. These, together with the house, give a courtyard effect. Four of the 11 bedrooms now have *en suite* facilities. A full English breakfast is served and vegetarians can be catered for. Children welcome. Car park.

OWNER David J. S. Smith OPEN Apr–Oct ROOMS 4 family (3 with bath/shower, 1 with wash-basin), 2 double (with wash-basin), 2 twin (1 with bath/shower, 1 with wash-basin), 3 single (with wash-basin) TERMS B&B from £15.50 (children under 16 half-price); deposit

Westbourne Guest House

43 Manchester Road, Buxton SK17 6SR
BUXTON (0298) 71647

Set in half an acre of terraced gardens on the outskirts of Buxton, with lovely views over Buxton to Solomon's Temple, Axe Edge and beyond to the Peak District National Park, Westbourne Guest House is a comfortable and informal Victorian house with a great feeling of light and space. The bedrooms, two of which have glorious south-facing views, are large with built-in furniture, including vanity units. Two bathrooms, one with a Jacuzzi, serve the bedrooms and there is a sauna on the top floor. All bedrooms have TV. There is a private entrance to Cavendish Golf Course, which adjoins the garden, and arrangements can be made for guests to play on this course. Freshly prepared croissants are an option at breakfast. Packed lunches are available on request. Vegetarians and those on special diets can be catered for by prior

B&B rates specified in the details for each entry are per person per night; unless the details state otherwise, they are based on two people sharing a double or twin-bedded room.

arrangement. Children welcome. Non-smokers preferred. Car park.

OWNERS Pat and Gordon Liversidge OPEN All year, exc Christmas
ROOMS 1 family, 1 double, 1 twin; all rooms with wash-basin
TERMS B&B from £15, (single occupancy of twin/double) from £20, (family room) £15 per adult and £10 per child (children under 2 free, 3–15 £10); deposit

CASTLE ASHBY Northamptonshire map 4

Old Rectory Cottage

66 Chadstone, Castle Ashby NN7 1LH
YARDLEY HASTINGS (060 129) 716

Situated in the peaceful hamlet of Chadstone, Old Rectory Cottage is an eighteenth-century stone-built listed building which was originally the coach-house to the large rectory and is in beautiful landscaped gardens. The entrance still has the original flagstone floors and there is lots of olde worlde charm. The two bedrooms are reached by a narrow, steep stairway and are spacious, well appointed and tastefully decorated. There is an office area with a typewriter, desk and telephone – ideal for business people who need these facilities but enjoy staying in a private home. Early morning tea or coffee is served in your room at no extra charge. Evening meals are available, if pre-arranged, and guests have a choice from five menus. Everything is freshly prepared and vegetables and fruit come from the garden. Guests share the family lounge where there is a TV. This is an ideal area for walking, and coarse fishing is available on Castle Ashby lakes, with Castle Ashby itself nearby. Electric blankets are provided. No children under 12. Pets by arrangement. No smoking in the bedrooms. Car park.

OWNERS Mary and Peter Chubb OPEN All year, exc Christmas
ROOMS 1 double, 1 twin; both rooms with wash-basin TERMS B&B £16.50, (single occupancy of twin/double) £19; deposit £10

CASTLETON Derbyshire map 7

Cryer House

Castleton, nr Sheffield S30 2WG
HOPE VALLEY (0433) 620244

In a quiet road next to the pub and in the centre of the pretty, though rather touristy, village of Castleton this listed seventeenth-century cottage also doubles as a tea-room. The walled front garden set with tables and chairs for summer seating is a delight, and indoors there is an attractive conservatory, where breakfast is served on sunny days. The two large double bedrooms are comfortably furnished and freshly decorated; a free bath-towel is provided for stays of three nights or more, otherwise there is a small charge. Breakfast only is served in the tea-shop and packed lunches are available on request. Cryer House is surrounded by wonderful countryside, in the heart of the Peak District, and makes a good base for exploring this beautiful area. Children welcome. Dogs accepted (with own bedding) by arrangement. No smoking in the tea-shop.

OWNERS Mr and Mrs T. Skelton OPEN All year, exc Christmas ROOMS 1 family, 2 double; all rooms with wash-basin TERMS B&B £13.50 approx (children under 12 half-price); deposit

CHEADLE Staffordshire map 7

Ley Fields Farm

Leek Road, Cheadle ST10 2EF
CHEADLE (0538) 752875

Ley Fields is a listed Georgian house and a working dairy farm of 45 acres situated in beautiful countryside. All of the comfortable bedrooms are now *en suite* with TV and an ideal family suite is available in the annexe, which has its own lounge. There is a separate guests' sitting-room with TV and a dining-room where fresh breakfasts are served, with fresh cream and milk from the farm's own cows. Dinner is available, if pre-arranged, from 6pm. Vegetarian meals are also available. There is no alcohol licence, but guests may bring their own wine. Children welcome. Reductions for children if sharing with parents. No pets. No smoking preferred. Car park.

OWNER Kathryn Clowes OPEN Easter–Nov ROOMS 2 family, 2 double; all rooms with bath/shower TERMS B&B £14–£16, (single occupancy of double) £15–£16, (family room) £44–£48; dinner £8; deposit

Where we know an establishment accepts credit cards, we list them. There may be a surcharge if you pay by credit card. It is always best to check whether the card you want to use is acceptable when booking.

Many B&Bs are in remote places; always ask for clear directions when booking.

CHEDDLETON Staffordshire map 7

Choir Cottage and Choir House

Ostlers Lane, Cheddleton, nr Leek ST13 7HS
CHURNET SIDE (0538) 360561

A most surprising find in a quiet rural area, Choir Cottage is a small, stone-built cottage over 300 years old and standing on what was originally a herb garden. There are three bedrooms: the Green Room in the Choir House has countryside views through patio doors and a small private sun lounge with wicker furniture; the Rose Room and the Pine Room (which has a new cast-iron bathtub) in the cottage have magnificent, draped four-poster beds. The rooms are beamed and have delicate wallpaper, elegant furnishings and their own private entrances. There are two ground-floor bedrooms, also with private patio area. There is a comfortable chintzy-style lounge and an interesting mug and cup collection on display. Freshly cooked breakfasts are served in the dining-room; Continental breakfast is served in your room if preferred. Dinner, including vegetarian choices, is available at 6pm, only if pre-arranged. Packed lunches are also available. There is no licence, but guests may bring their own wine. No children under five. No pets. No smoking except in separate sun lounge for smokers. Car park for up to six cars.

OWNERS William and Elaine Sutcliffe OPEN All year, exc Christmas
ROOMS 2 four-poster, 1 twin; all rooms with bath/shower
TERMS B&B £19–£24, (single occupancy of twin/double) £24–£30, (family room) £47–£61 (children half-to-three-quarters of adult rate); dinner £19; deposit

CHESTER Cheshire map 7

Egerton Lodge Hotel

57 Hoole Road, Hoole, Chester CH2 3NJ
CHESTER (0244) 320712

This terraced Victorian town house is a cheerful and bright small hotel, run by a friendly, welcoming couple. It is in good decorative order, with white fitted-furniture. The immaculate bedrooms all have TV and some have hair-dryers. Breakfasts are substantial and guests have a choice of either a cooked breakfast or just fresh fruit, cereal and toast. Egerton Lodge Hotel is close to the centre and the railway station; the bus stop for the town centre is in front of the house. No children under three. No pets. Car park.

OWNERS William and Stephanie Barrow OPEN All year, exc Christmas and New Year ROOMS 3 double/family (with bath/shower), 1 single (with wash-basin) TERMS B&B £16–£19.50, (family room) £40–£48 (children under 16 half-price); deposit; Access, Amex, Diners, Visa

Holly House Guest House

1 Stone Place, Hoole, Chester CH2 3NR
CHESTER (0244) 328967

Holly House is a whitewashed Georgian-style house with a small rose garden in a quiet cul-de-sac. The house is in excellent decorative order, is well maintained and has a cosy atmosphere. The bedrooms are bright and fresh with pretty pastel furnishings. All have TV. There is a window seat on the landing, a pleasant spot for guests to sit and read the books and leaflets provided on what to see and do in Chester and the surrounding area. Children welcome. No pets. Car park.

OWNER Mrs Marilyn Rudham OPEN All year, exc Christmas ROOMS 1 family, 1 double, 1 twin, 1 single; all rooms with wash-basin TERMS B&B £13.50, (single occupancy of twin/double) £16, (family room) £33 (children under 5 free)

CHESTERFIELD Derbyshire map 7

Abigail's Guest House

62/64 Brockwell Lane, Chesterfield S40 4EE
CHESTERFIELD (0246) 279391

Abigail's Guest House is an immaculate turn-of-the-century red-brick building one mile from the town centre. The bedrooms are *en suite* with two single rooms on the ground floor, all tastefully decorated with pretty furnishings. All have TV, and hair-dryer and trouser-press are available on request. There is a quiet lounge and a separate dining-room where a buffet breakfast is served; home-cooked evening meals are available at 6.30pm. Vegetarian choices and packed lunches can be provided. There is no alcohol licence, but guests may bring their own wine. Guests are welcome to use the garden and conservatory, which looks towards the peaks in the distance. There is private car parking and guests would be

If any bedrooms are suitable for the disabled we mention this in the entry.

well advised to take the bus into town, which stops in front of the house. Children welcome.

OWNERS Gail and Michael Onza OPEN All year, exc Christmas
ROOMS 2 double, 2 twin, 2 single; all rooms with bath/shower
TERMS B&B £16, (single occupancy of twin/double) £18.50, (single) £16.50–£18.50 (children under 2 free, 2–12 half-price); dinner £6.50

The Gables Hotel

85–87 Newbold Road, Chesterfield S41 7PU
CHESTERFIELD (0246) 278695

Adjoining a chapel and not far from the centre of Chesterfield, the Gables Hotel offers basic accommodation. Almost all the bedrooms have *en suite* facilities and all have new furniture and TV. The single rooms are quite small. There is a guest lounge with TV, as well as the recent addition of a cosy bar/lounge with a Victorian fireplace. Home-cooked evening meals (5.30–7.30pm), light snacks and packed lunches are available at modest prices. Vegetarians can be catered for. Children are welcome, and high chairs and cots are available on request. The Gables is family-run and the owners, who live on the premises, offer good-value accommodation at reasonable prices. Children welcome. No dogs. Car park.

OWNERS Mrs J. S. Fields and Mr A. Fields OPEN All year
ROOMS 2 family (1 with bath/shower, 1 with wash-basin), 4 double (3 with bath/shower, 1 with wash-basin), 2 twin (1 with bath/shower, 1 with wash-basin), 9 single (2 with bath/shower, 7 with wash-basin)
TERMS B&B £19, (single) £22, (family room) £44 (children under 4 free, 4–14 £9.50); dinner from £6.50; deposit

Sheeplea Cottage Farm

Baslow Road, Eastmoor, nr Chesterfield S42 7DD
CHESTERFIELD (0246) 566785

Sheeplea Cottage is a stone-built farmhouse and provides basic accommodation in a very convenient location (on the A619) for the Peak District, Chatsworth House and Chesterfield. The house is in the middle of farmland and is part of a smallholding supporting sheep and horses. The cottage opens directly into the small, cosy lounge, which also serves as the breakfast room. The house is warm with a homely atmosphere, and knick-knacks adorn every surface and wall area. There are three comfortable and simply furnished bedrooms and all have radio. Breakfast only is served and includes free-range eggs and home-grown produce. Flasks can be filled and packed lunches provided on request. No children under 10. Pets by arrangement. No smoking. Car park.

OWNER Mrs Veronica Worrall OPEN All year, exc Christmas
ROOMS 2 double (with wash-basin and toilet), 1 twin TERMS B&B £14, (single occupancy of twin/double) £18; deposit

COVENHAM Lincolnshire map 8

The Grange

Grange Lane, Covenham, Louth LN11 0PD
FULSTOW (0507) 363678

The Grange is at the end of a country lane, alongside a reservoir which has a bird sanctuary and sailing. The house is an excellent base for those seeking good, simple accommodation in rural surroundings. The comfortable bedrooms are of a good size but very basic and the double rooms can be adapted to accommodate families. Breakfast only is available. There is a large lounge and a separate dining-room with a collection of toby jugs on display. Children welcome. No pets. No smoking in bedrooms. Car park.

OWNERS Phyl and Jim Shaw OPEN All year, exc Christmas
ROOMS 3 double, 2 single TERMS B&B £12.50–£13.50, (single) £12.50

COVENTRY West Midlands map 4

The Crest Guest House

39 Friars Road, Coventry CV1 2LJ
COVENTRY (0203) 227822

Located in the centre of Coventry, just off the ring road in a quiet cul-de-sac, this turn-of-the-century house has very spacious and comfortable bedrooms, all with TV. There are two *en suite* twin bedrooms, and two singles that share a bathroom. Guests enjoy the relaxed atmosphere and the excellent freshly cooked breakfasts. Packed lunches are also available. There is also a well-furnished guest lounge with TV. Children welcome. No pets. Car park.

OWNERS Peggy and Alan Harvey OPEN All year, exc Christmas
ROOMS 2 twin (with bath/shower), 2 single (with wash-basin)
TERMS B&B £20, (single occupancy of twin) £28; deposit

DENSTONE Staffordshire map 7

Stone House

College Road, Denstone, nr Uttoxeter ST14 5HR
ROCESTER (0889) 590526

As the Guide went to press
this establishment stopped
offering B & B

DETHICK Derbyshire map 7

The Manor Farmhouse

Dethick, nr Matlock DE4 5GG
MATLOCK (0629) 534246

This listed 300-year-old farmhouse was built out of the ruins of the thirteenth-century manor house and is set in a delightful, peaceful, unspoilt hamlet at the gateway to the Peak District. Mrs Groom is a most friendly lady and an excellent cook. She will prepare evening meals by arrangement at 7.30pm, using fresh farm produce. The house is furnished comfortably and traditionally and the bedrooms have lovely views. All bedrooms have TV. No children under eight. No pets. No smoking. Parking for six cars.

OWNER Mrs R. A. Groom OPEN All year, exc Christmas
ROOMS 1 double (with bath/shower), 2 twin (with bath/shower), 1 single (with wash-basin) TERMS B&B £16, (single occupancy of twin/double) £25; dinner from £9; deposit

DIDDLEBURY Shropshire map 4

Glebe Farm

Diddlebury, Craven Arms SY7 9DH
MUNSLOW (058 476) 221

This beautiful 400-year-old half-timbered, half-sandstone Elizabethan farmhouse stands in a peaceful setting, with a stream running through the garden. The house is roomy and comfortable, with panelled rooms, inglenook fireplaces and antique furniture. One small wattle-and-daub area has been exposed, enabling guests to view the original construction. There is a bar with TV and a residents' lounge. All the bedrooms have TV and there is also a separate self-catering cottage available. Continental and full English breakfasts are offered. Reductions for children by arrangement. No children under eight. No dogs in the house. No smoking in the bedrooms. Car park.

OWNERS Michael and Eileen Wilkes OPEN Easter–Nov
ROOMS 1 double, 2 twin, 1 single; all rooms with bath/shower
TERMS B&B £24–£26, (single occupancy of twin/double) £5 extra; deposit

EVERTON Nottinghamshire map 7

Gable Cottage Guest House

High Street, Everton, nr Bawtry, Doncaster DN10 5AR
RETFORD (0777) 817601

This is a charming 200-year-old cottage with bow windows, in a conservation village and located in the centre of the Pilgrim Fathers' trail. The immaculate bedrooms are beautifully carpeted and furnished, all individually decorated in soft, restful colours. Double bedrooms can be converted to family rooms if required. Mr Attenborough is a local historian who enjoys sharing his knowledge with guests and will help to arrange daily itineraries and transport to and from the local station. Breakfast only is available and is elegantly presented with fine china and crystal. There is an attractive galleried landing/reading-room for guests'

If there are any bedrooms with TV and/or telephone we mention this in the entry.

Where we know of any particular payment stipulations we mention them in the details. It is always best to check when booking, however.

use. Children welcome (reductions if sharing with parents). No pets. No smoking in the dining-room. Car park.

OWNERS Mr and Mrs C. Attenborough OPEN All year
ROOMS 2 double, 1 twin; all rooms with bath/shower TERMS B&B £16.50–£17.50, (single occupancy of twin/double) £22.50–£25, (family room) £40–£45; deposit

GLENTHAM Lincolnshire map 8

Mill House

Glentham, nr Lincoln LN2 3AW
NORMANBY-BY-SPITAL (067 37) 217

The Mill is an attractive 200-year-old residence situated in an acre of grounds. Although it has been modernised, it still retains its oak beams, brick floors and leaded windows. The beautiful grounds have a fish pond and the original mill grinders, as well as the old barn which was once the steam mill. The comfortable lounge with open fire still has the original bread ovens intact. The two bedrooms both have TV. The tasteful restoration work was all done by the owners and they have succeeded in creating a delightful house in a peaceful atmosphere. Breakfast only is served and includes home-made jams and marmalades. Packed lunches are available on request. Not suitable for children. No pets. No smoking in bedrooms.

OWNER J. Richardson OPEN All year, exc Christmas
ROOMS 1 double, 1 twin TERMS B&B £13; deposit

GRINDON Staffordshire map 7

The White House

Grindon, nr Leek ST13 7TP
ONECOTE (0538) 304250

Built around 1640 as the village inn, the White House retains its character with original stone mullions and oak beams. It stands with its back to the road and faces south over a lovely garden and enjoys uninterrupted views of the Manifold and Hamps valleys. Grindon is a delightful and unspoilt village in the Peak National Park. There are three elegant bedrooms; the blue bedroom has a half-tester bed and pine furnishings. All bedrooms have TV. The beamed guest lounge is a comfortable blend of old and modern, with local information guides and books, and a log fire in the winter. On show are a framed, hand-made quilt that has been in the family for over 150 years, an old grandfather clock and an interesting plate collection. A varied breakfast menu is offered, including home-made bread and preserves. Vegetarians can be catered for. Evening meals are not available but there is a portfolio of the many restaurants in the area. There is also an adjoining self-catering unit for two. No children under 12. No pets in the house. No smoking. Car park.

OWNERS Philomena and Jack Bunce OPEN All year, exc Christmas and New Year ROOMS 2 double, 1 twin; all rooms with bath/shower TERMS B&B £18–£21, (single occupancy of twin/double) £29.50; deposit

GRINGLEY ON THE HILL Nottinghamshire map 7

The Old Vicarage

Gringley on the Hill, nr Doncaster DN10 4RF
RETFORD (0777) 817248

This beautiful old vicarage is in an unspoilt village next to an ancient church. The lovely three-acre gardens include a rock garden and an orchard. The house is beautifully appointed, furnished with antiques, and has four luxurious bedrooms. Mrs Jackson is an experienced cook and keen gardener, growing all her own vegetables. Imaginative home-cooked evening meals are served 7.30–8pm. Vegetarians can be catered for. There is no licence, but guests may bring their own wine. Packed lunches can be provided. Children welcome. Non-smokers preferred. Car park.

OWNER Mrs Helena Jackson OPEN All year ROOMS 1 double/ family, 1 twin, 1 single; all rooms with bath/shower TERMS B&B £25, (single occupancy of twin/double) £30, (family room) £35 (children under 2 free, under 12 half-price); dinner £15

HAMPTON IN ARDEN West Midlands map 4

The Hollies

Kenilworth Road, Hampton in Arden, Solihull B92 0LW
HAMPTON IN ARDEN (0675) 442941

The Hollies is a well-maintained guesthouse set back from the road, off the A452 dual-carriageway on a service road. During the summer there is a lovely display of flowers in the many hanging baskets and tubs. The bedrooms are fairly small but are spotlessly clean and bright, and all have TV. There is an attractive dining-room-cum-lounge with dusty pink décor where breakfast only is served. Packed lunches can be provided. Mr and Mrs Fitzpatrick live in an extension to the main house and they are a friendly, helpful couple who will organise transfers to and from the airport if pre-arranged. This is an ideal location for the NEC, which is three miles away. Children welcome (reductions depending on age). Car park.

OWNERS James and Christine Fitzpatrick OPEN All year
ROOMS 2 double (with bath/shower), 5 twin (3 with bath/shower, 2 with wash-basin), 1 single (with wash-basin) TERMS B&B £18–£20, (single occupancy of twin/double) £28; deposit

HARTINGTON Derbyshire map 7

Raikes Farm

Hulme End, nr Hartington SK17 0HJ
HARTINGTON (0298) 84344

This charming, listed sixteenth-century farmhouse stands in 12 acres, surrounded by woods and just 200 yards from the River Dove. The house has thick stone walls, uneven floors and exposed oak beams. There are several antique furnishings including a 300-year-old fruitwood settle and a pine dresser. Tasty breakfasts are served in the cosy dining-room and evening meals are available by prior arrangement. Vegetarians can be catered for. The lounge is shared with the family, and there are help-yourself tea- and coffee-making facilities. The house overlooks Beresford Dale and there are some lovely walks nearby. Children welcome. No smoking in bedrooms. Car park.

OWNERS Mr A. and Mrs V. Shipley OPEN Mar–Dec
ROOMS 1 family, 2 double; all rooms with wash-basin TERMS B&B £14–£16 (£10 reduction for children); dinner £7; deposit 20%

HATHERSAGE Derbyshire map 7

Highlow Hall

Hathersage, nr Sheffield S30 1AZ
HOPE VALLEY (0433) 650393

Highlow Hall is a listed stone-built sixteenth-century manor house in the heart of the Peak District. It was built by the Eyre family and owned by them until the 1800s, when it was purchased by the Duke of Devonshire. The house retains many of its original features; the banqueting hall is Tudor and there are five large, comfortable bedrooms with electric heaters and electric blankets. Guests may use the lounge where there is a TV. Children welcome. Pets by arrangement. No smoking in the dining-room. Car park.

OWNERS Mr and Mrs T. C. Wain OPEN Mar–Dec ROOMS 2 family, 3 twin, 1 single; all rooms with wash-basin TERMS B&B £20; dinner from £10; deposit

HAYFIELD Derbyshire map 7

The Old Bank House

Hayfield SK12 5EP
NEW MILLS (0663) 747354

This listed Georgian house stands in the centre of the picturesque village of Hayfield. There are three spacious bedrooms: one has a four-poster bed made by the owner, one an antique brass bed and one a lovely pine bed. They all have either a settee or armchair, and TV. There are lots of antique furnishings and a comfortable guest lounge with a Victorian fireplace is available. Breakfasts are served in the dining-room overlooking the pretty walled garden, with a choice of kippers, haddock, Derbyshire oat cakes as well as a traditional cooked breakfast. Evening meals and packed lunches can also be provided on request. There is no alcohol licence, but guests may bring their own wine. John Collier-Johnson has a Mountain Leadership Certificate and can arrange guided walks. Children welcome. Pets by arrangement. No smoking in bedrooms or bathrooms. Car park for four cars.

OWNERS Sheila and John Collier-Johnson OPEN All year, exc Christmas ROOMS 1 family, 2 double, 1 twin; all rooms with wash-basin TERMS B&B £16–£18, (single occupancy of twin/double) £18–£20, (family room) £39–£43 (children under 12 £7.50); dinner £7.50

HOLBEACH Lincolnshire map 8

Pipwell Manor

Washway Road, Saracen's Head, Holbeach PE12 8AL
HOLBEACH (0406) 23119

The owners took over Pipwell Manor in December of 1990 and since then have been busy redecorating and refurbishing this charming Georgian farmhouse. Although the accommodation is basic, the spacious bedrooms have been exquisitely decorated with matching fabrics, chintz curtains (made by Lesley Honnor) and antique furnishings. Some of the bedrooms still have their original fireplaces. The guest sitting-room has an open fire, TV and lots of books to browse through. Breakfast only is served in the farmhouse kitchen, which still has the original butcher's block. Fresh eggs from the owners' own hens are served; jams and marmalades are home-made. No children under 12. No pets. No smoking. Car park.

OWNER Mrs Lesley Honnor OPEN All year, exc Christmas and New Year ROOMS 2 double (1 with bath/shower), 1 twin (with wash-basin), 1 single (with wash-basin) TERMS B&B £16, (single occupancy of twin/double) £22

HOLMESFIELD Derbyshire map 7

Horsleygate Hall

Horsleygate Lane, Holmesfield S18 5WD
SHEFFIELD (0742) 890333

This is a superb country house, built in 1783, standing in two acres of beautiful gardens in a secluded and tranquil setting. There are several areas for sitting out on fine days, including a peaceful terrace, and stabling is available on request. Mr and Mrs Ford purchased the property in 1987 in a fairly run-down condition and they have since tastefully incorporated modern comforts

while retaining the charm and atmosphere of the bygone era. The bedrooms are spacious and furnished in keeping with the character of the house. There is a guest lounge with TV. Delicious breakfasts are cooked on the Aga stove in the huge country kitchen, with choices of Derbyshire oat cakes and fresh fruit from the garden, followed by a traditional cooked breakfast, with home-made breads and preserves. Vegetarians and special diets can be catered for. Margaret Ford is a local lady happy to give advice on what to see and do in the area. No children under five. No pets in the house. No smoking. Car park.

OWNERS Robert and Margaret Ford OPEN All year, exc Christmas ROOMS 1 family (with wash-basin), 1 double (with bath/shower), 1 twin (with wash-basin) TERMS B&B £16–£19.50, (family room) £40 (children half-price); deposit 10%

HOPTON CASTLE Shropshire map 6

Upper House Farm

Hopton Castle, Craven Arms SY7 0QF
BUCKNELL (054 74) 319

Upper House Farm is a handsome Georgian house situated in the beautiful Clun Valley among wooded hills with uninterrupted views. This is a farm of 500 acres producing cereals and seed potatoes, and supporting beef cattle and a flock of Clun forest sheep. The spacious bedrooms, all with fresh flowers, are tastefully decorated and colour-co-ordinated. All have TV. Breakfast is served in a cosy dining-room with an open fire. There are some antique furnishings, including an intricately carved oak settle in the hallway. There is a games-room with a pool-table and a separate guest lounge. Five-course dinners, served at 7pm, may include pheasant casserole cooked in red wine, roast sirloin of beef, fresh vegetables and delicious home-made desserts. Vegetarians can be catered for on request. Guests may enjoy wine with their meal as there is a table licence. Children welcome. No pets in the house. Car park.

OWNER Sue Williams OPEN Feb–Nov ROOMS 1 family, 1 double (with bath/shower), 1 twin TERMS B&B £15.50–£16.50 (children under 12 half-price); dinner £9.50; deposit

Those B&Bs that we know can offer some kind of off-street car parking, have 'car park' at the end of the entry. If we are aware of particular car parking difficulties, we mention them.

ISLEY WALTON Leicestershire map 7

High Barn Farm

Isley Walton, Castle Donington DE7 2RL
DERBY (0332) 810360

This is a working farm of cattle and corn situated up a private farm road, and just one and a half miles from East Midlands Airport. Part of the accommodation is in a cottage adjacent to the farmhouse. Seven of the bedrooms are on the ground floor. The comfortably furnished, well-equipped cottage is ideal for two couples or a family looking for a stay in peaceful, rural surroundings. Five more rooms are available in a barn conversion, one of which is suitable for the disabled. The barn has its own dining-room and a sitting-room with TV. Undercover parking is provided for guests while they are away and transport to and from the airport can be arranged, for a modest fee. Breakfast only is served. Guests staying in the main house share the family lounge. Children welcome. Pets by arrangement but not in the house. Smoking allowed in some of the rooms.

OWNERS Mr J. and Mrs A. Bottomley OPEN All year
ROOMS 1 family (with bath/shower), 2 double (with bath/shower), 5 twin (1 with bath/shower, 4 with wash-basin), 2 single (with wash-basin) TERMS B&B £15–£20, (family room) £45–£50; deposit

Park Farmhouse Hotel

Melbourne Road, Isley Walton, Castle Donington DE7 2RN
DERBY (0332) 862409

Close to Castle Donington racetrack and three miles from East Midlands Airport, this eighteenth-century farmhouse stands in beautiful, unspoilt countryside with a view of Breedon church in the distance. The bedrooms, two of which are on the ground floor, are spacious and upholstered in country farmhouse style. All have TV and telephone. John and Linda Shields continue to make improvements and *en suite* facilities have been added to some of the bedrooms. Most have hair-dryer, trouser press and a small sitting area. The licensed dining-room has the original panelling, a large log fireplace and a beautiful French walnut piano. A barn conversion is available for private hire. Evening meals are available 6–8pm, and packed lunches can be provided. There is a lounge bar and a sitting-room for guests. Children welcome. No pets in public rooms. No smoking in the dining-room. Car park.

OWNERS John and Linda Shields OPEN All year, exc Christmas ROOMS 2 family, 3 double, 3 twin (1 with wash-basin); 7 rooms with bath/shower TERMS B&B £22.50–£26.50, (single occupancy of twin/double) £33–£43; dinner from £8.25 (children's meals from £1.50); deposit £10; Access, Amex, Diners, Visa

KNUTSFORD Cheshire map 7

Tatton Dale Farm

Tatton Park, Ashley Road, Knutsford WA16 6QJ
KNUTSFORD (0565) 654692

Tatton Dale Farm is a Victorian red-brick building in a peaceful location, formerly the estate manager's house for Tatton Park. The spacious bedrooms, all with TV, are individually furnished, have comfortable beds and often fresh flowers. Scrumptious breakfasts are served in the huge family kitchen – Susan Reeves' omelettes are particularly delicious. Packed lunches are available with notice. There is no guest lounge. Children welcome. No pets. No smoking. Car park.

OWNERS Susan and Richard Reeves OPEN All year ROOMS 1 family (with bath/shower), 1 double, 1 twin TERMS B&B £15, (single occupancy of twin/double) £20, (family room) £38 (children £8–£12)

LANGWITH Nottinghamshire map 7

Blue Barn Farm

Langwith, Mansfield NG20 9JD
MANSFIELD (0623) 742248

This 450-acre working mixed arable farm on the Welbeck Estate is set in the middle of rolling fields with lovely rural views. As it is very much a working farm, you may need a pair of boots to get to the 1930s farmhouse. The house is homely, but comfortably furnished and a good spot for a simple holiday. All rooms have had a wash-basin fitted. Breakfast only is available, although packed lunches can be provided on request. Mrs Ibbotson, a Tourist Board Blue Badge Guide, can offer guided tours. There is also a self-catering cottage. Children welcome. No pets in bedrooms and dogs by arrangement. Car park.

OWNER June Ibbotson OPEN All year, exc Christmas
ROOMS 1 double, 1 twin, 1 family; all rooms with wash-basin
TERMS B&B from £13.50 (babies free, children up to 15 £6–£8); deposit £5

LEINTWARDINE Shropshire map 6

Church House

High Street, Leintwardine, Craven Arms SY7 0LB
LEINTWARDINE (054 73) 655

Church House is a seventeenth-century half-timbered cottage within the boundary of the site of a former Roman camp. The accommodation is in a separate wing of the house and guests have their own entrance. The oak-beamed rooms are attractively furnished and there is a sitting-room/dining-room which has a TV. This is ideal for three friends or a small family. Mrs Campbell extends a warm welcome to her guests and will serve hot drinks on arrival. Breakfast and dinner usually include home-grown fruit and vegetables in season. Dinner (6.30pm) is served Monday, Wednesday and Friday and there is a choice of meat or vegetarian dishes. Special diets can be catered for. The home-made ice-cream is a real treat. Church House is not licensed, but guests may bring their own wine. Laundry facilities are available. Guests may choose to go self-catering instead, and plates and cutlery will be provided. Reductions for children under 10. Small dogs only. Car park.

OWNERS Mary Campbell and Paddy Campbell OPEN All year, exc Christmas ROOMS 1 twin, 1 single TERMS B&B £15–£20 (reductions for children under 10); dinner £10.50; deposit 10%; £2 surcharge Nov–Feb for heating

Upper Buckton

Upper Buckton, Leintwardine, Craven Arms SY7 0JU
LEINTWARDINE (054 73) 634

This late-Georgian farmhouse is set in 300 acres and overlooks the River Teme near the Welsh border. The house stands on a slight rise surrounded by tree-clad hills and has a large garden which slopes down to a mill stream. The approach to the farm is three-quarters of a mile off the A4113. Children can help with the animals, enjoy garden games such as croquet, and play table tennis and snooker. There are some lovely walks, where guests may have an opportunity to see some of the abundant wildlife. The house is spacious and the elegant bedrooms are furnished with antiques. Mrs Lloyd is a dedicated cook who offers both traditional and cordon bleu dishes, served on tables set with fine china and crystal. Dinner is at 7pm and special diets can be catered for. Upper Buckton is unlicensed, but guests may bring their own wine. Packed lunches can also be provided on request. Guests can relax on the verandah, enjoy the lovely views and watch the rabbits at play. Children welcome. No pets in the house. No smoking. Car park.

OWNERS Hayden and Yvonne Lloyd OPEN All year
ROOMS 2 double, 2 twin; all rooms with wash-basin TERMS B&B £20 (reductions for children under 12); dinner £12; deposit

LICHFIELD Staffordshire map 4

Old Rectory Cottage

21 Gaia Lane, Lichfield WS13 7LW
LICHFIELD (0543) 254941

This picture-postcard 250-year-old cottage is in an idyllic setting directly behind the cathedral. Formerly two vergers' cottages, it now provides cosy, comfortable accommodation. The two bedrooms, both with TV, are tastefully decorated with pine furnishings and beautiful carpets. There is a varied menu for breakfast, which is cooked to order, with vegetarian and special diets catered for. Packed lunches can be provided if required. No children under five. Pets by arrangement. Non-smokers preferred. Car park.

OWNERS Brian and Patricia Zavou OPEN All year, exc Christmas and New Year ROOMS 1 double/family, 1 twin; both rooms with wash-basin TERMS B&B £15, (single occupancy of twin/double) £19, (family room) £39 (children £9 sharing); deposit

B&B rates specified in the details for each entry are per person per night; unless the details state otherwise, they are based on two people sharing a double or twin-bedded room.

Bath/shower information in the details refers only to a private bathroom or shower; other bathroom facilities at the establishments will be shared.

LINCOLN Lincolnshire map 8

ABC Guest House

126 Yarborough Road, Lincoln LN1 1HP
LINCOLN (0522) 543560

This small guesthouse is convenient for the town centre, situated on the edge of common land with lovely views overlooking the Trent Valley. The bedrooms, all with TV, are comfortable, simply furnished and of a good size. Some have *en suite* facilities and a balcony. An *en suite* ground-floor bedroom has just been added. Breakfast only is served in the dining-room/lounge. No children under 10. Pets by arrangement. No smoking. Car park.

OWNERS Terry and Wendy Cain OPEN All year, exc Christmas ROOMS 1 family (with wash-basin), 5 double (3 with bath/shower, 2 with wash-basin), 2 twin (1 with bath/shower, 1 with wash-basin), 2 single (with wash-basin) TERMS B&B £14, (single occupancy of twin/double) £18, (family room) £45; deposit £10

Carline Guest House

1/3 Carline Road, Lincoln LN1 1HN
LINCOLN (0522) 530422

Carline Guest House, only a five-minute walk from the cathedral, makes an ideal base from which to explore this historic city. Gillian and John Pritchard are local people, very knowledgeable about the area and always pleased to assist guests with what is worth visiting. The bedrooms are prettily decorated, with stripped pine doors. All have radio-alarm, hair-dryer and TV. The dining-room has been enlarged and overlooks a patio where guests can relax on warm days. A quiet lounge is also available. Ten of the 12 rooms have *en suite* bathrooms and three are on the ground floor; some are non-smoking. An excellent breakfast is served using free-range eggs from chickens kept in the big back garden. Limited under-cover and off-street parking is available. There are no facilities for babies. Dogs only allowed if ground-floor rooms are not occupied. No smoking in the dining-room.

OWNERS Gillian and John Pritchard OPEN All year, exc Christmas ROOMS 2 family (with bath/shower), 6 double (5 with bath/shower), 2 twin (with bath/shower), 2 single (with wash-basin) TERMS B&B £16.50, (single) £14–£26, (family room) £42–£50 (reductions for children sharing with parents); deposit

LLANYBLODWEL Shropshire map 6

Fishers Cottage

Llanyblodwel, nr Oswestry SY10 8NF
LLANSANTFFRAID (0691) 828382

This picturesque seventeenth-century white cottage is in an idyllic setting on the banks of the River Tanat at the foot of the Berwyn mountains. It is surrounded by a pretty garden full of rambling roses, clematis, fruit trees and hanging baskets. Fishing can be arranged for guests wishing to try to catch a fresh trout for dinner. There are two comfortable bedrooms with window seats, new carpets and curtains, and private bathrooms. There is only partial central heating so electric over-blankets are provided. There are no TVs in the house – Audrey and Clive Holder prefer getting to know their guests. Delicious four-course dinners are served in the charming dining-room at 7.30pm (unlicensed, but guests may bring their own wine). Packed lunches can be provided. The Snowdonia National Park, Shrewsbury and many National Trust properties are all within easy reach. No children under 12. No pets. Non-smokers preferred. Car park.

OWNERS Audrey and Clive Holder OPEN Mar–end Oct
ROOMS 1 double, 1 twin; both rooms with bath/shower
TERMS B&B £15; dinner £8.50; deposit

LLANYMYNECH Shropshire map 6

Hospitality

Llanymynech SY22 6LG
LLANYMYNECH (0691) 830247

This is a comfortable eighteenth-century house on the edge of the Welsh border, with pleasant outlooks over Shropshire farmland. It has been recently renovated, and there are four immaculate bedrooms, two of which are singles; all have TV. Although there are no *en suite* rooms there are plenty of bathrooms exclusively for guests' use. Owner Carol Fahey, who trained as a caterer at a local college and also lectures on catering, provides excellent home-cooked evening meals (7–7.30pm) at modest prices. Guests are welcome to bring their own wine as there is no alcohol licence. Vegetarians and special diets can be catered for by prior arrangement. Fly fishing and one-day short courses on cookery, embroidery, art and wood-turning can be arranged. Offa's Dyke is half a mile away. Children welcome. Smoking only in the sitting-room. Car park.

OWNER Mrs Carol Fahey OPEN All year, exc Christmas
ROOMS 1 double, 1 twin, 2 single; all rooms with wash-basin
TERMS B&B £12.50 (children under 12 half-price); dinner £6.50

LOUGHBOROUGH Leicestershire map 7

De Montfort Hotel

88 Leicester Road, Loughborough LE11 2AQ
LOUGHBOROUGH (0509) 216061

This is a well-maintained Victorian house on the A6, one mile from the city centre. Mr and Mrs Guise are a most accommodating couple, both local people, who are able to help their guests with what to see and do in the area. The bedrooms, all with TV, are spacious, sparkling and have sitting and writing areas. There is now a bath/shower-room on the top floor and each floor has a bathroom. There is a small lounge bar. Evening meals, including vegetarian if requested, are available at 6pm. Free car parking is available opposite the hotel. Children welcome. Large dogs discouraged. No smoking in the dining-room.

OWNERS Harold and June Guise OPEN All year, exc Christmas
ROOMS 1 family, 1 double, 6 twin, 1 single; all rooms with wash-basin
TERMS B&B £19, (family room) £44 (baby cot £2, children up to 5 half-price); dinner £7; Access, Visa

Garendon Lodge Guest House

136 Leicester Road, Loughborough LE11 2AQ
LOUGHBOROUGH (0509) 211120

This immaculate turn-of-the-century house is just one mile from the town centre. The bedrooms have been decorated to a high standard. All have TV and radio-alarm. There is a small conservatory with wicker furniture and bright, floral-patterned cushions. Breakfast and evening meals, if pre-arranged, are served in the pretty dining-room 6.30–7pm. Guests have the choice of up to three courses, and vegetarian options are available. Garendon Lodge is unlicensed, but guests may bring their own

If you are forced to turn up late into the evening, please telephone to warn the proprietor.

wine. Packed lunches are also available on request. Children welcome. Dogs by arrangement. Car park.

OWNERS Lynda and John Savage OPEN All year, exc Christmas
ROOMS 1 family, 1 double, 2 single; all rooms with bath/shower
TERMS B&B £17.50–£20, (single) £20–£25, (family room) from £35 (children under 5 free); dinner from £4; deposit

LUDLOW Shropshire map 4

Number Eleven

Dinham, Ludlow SY8 1EJ
LUDLOW (0584) 878584

Number Eleven is a beautifully restored Georgian town house built in 1770 overlooking Ludlow Castle, and designed by the architect responsible for St Martin-in-the-Fields in London and the Radcliffe Library in Oxford. The bedrooms are decorated to a very high standard, beautifully appointed and furnished with antiques. There is a four-poster bed, and a brass and cast-iron bed with a lace canopy. The top-floor room is particularly charming with its sloping roof and has a huge private bathroom. Most rooms have castle views. There is an elegant lounge with TV and a 'quiet' lounge for relaxing in and reading. Evening meals are available, if pre-arranged, at 7.30pm and there is an extensive wine list. Packed lunches are provided on request. Special weekend breaks are available over Christmas. Plenty of street parking is available in front of the house. No children under 12. No pets. Smoking in the drawing-room only.

OWNERS Guy Crawley and Michael Martin OPEN All year
ROOMS 1 four-poster, 4 twin; all rooms with bath/shower
TERMS B&B £20–£25; dinner £10.50; Access, Visa

Sunnymede Guest House

Burway Lane, Ludlow SY8 1DT
LUDLOW (0584) 827609

Sunnymede Guest House nestles on a gentle rise half a mile from the town centre and is set in one and a half acres of gardens, with a view of Ludlow Castle and the surrounding countryside. Built in 1929, the house still retains the original tiled fireplaces, leaded-light windows and wood-strip floors. It is a comfortable place, and the rooms are spacious. Extra beds can be provided on request for a family. There is a lounge with a small licensed bar.

Dinner is served at 6.30pm, by arrangement only, at very reasonable prices, and consists of simple home-style cooking. Vegetarian meals are available on request. Children welcome. No pets in the dining-room. Car park.

OWNERS J. E. and N. Robinson OPEN All year ROOMS 2 double, (1 with bath/shower), 1 twin (with bath/shower) TERMS B&B £18, (single occupancy of twin/double) £20 (children under 12 half-price); dinner £8; deposit £10

MACCLESFIELD Cheshire map 7

Chadwick House Hotel

55 Beech Lane, Macclesfield SK10 2DS
MACCLESFIELD (0625) 615558

This attractive Victorian building, originally two private houses, is close to the town centre on the A523. The rooms are superbly furnished with antique pine furnishings, and have been attractively colour-co-ordinated. Eight of the 12 bedrooms have *en suite* facilities and all have satellite TV. There is one luxury suite with a four-poster bed with a white lace canopy, ideal for honeymooners. The cellar has been converted to an exercise area with a sauna and solarium. There is a comfortable lounge with TV, as well as a bar lounge. William and Karen Danson are a friendly couple who used to play in a pop group and still appear locally in cabaret. Dinner is served at 7pm Monday to Friday only and there is an alcohol licence. Packed lunches and vegetarian meals are all provided if required. There is a five per cent surcharge on credit cards. Children welcome. No pets. Smoking allowed in the lounge only. Car park.

OWNERS William and Karen Danson OPEN All year ROOMS 1 four-poster (with bath/shower), 3 double (1 with bath/shower, 2 with wash-basin), 3 twin (2 with bath/shower, 1 with wash-basin), 5 single (4 with bath/shower, 1 with wash-basin) TERMS B&B £27.50–£32.50, (single) £23–£40; dinner £7.95; deposit; Access, Diners, Visa

Goose Green Farm

Oak Road, Mottram St Andrew, nr Macclesfield SK10 4RA
PRESTBURY (0625) 828814

Goose Green Farm is a turn-of-the-century red-brick farmhouse just off the A538 between Prestbury and Wilmslow and has an informal, friendly atmosphere. This is an arable farm but there are horses and cows, and a Belgian Blue Bull. The small fishing lake is stocked with carp. The well-appointed bedrooms, all with TV, are on the small side but have been attractively decorated and have comfortable beds. Guests have use of a lounge, which has a log fire in winter, and a games-room. Breakfast only is cooked to order and served in the pretty dining-room overlooking the garden bordered by mature shrubs and flowers. There are no evening meals but sandwiches can be provided. Dyllis Hatch goes out of her way to ensure her guests are comfortable and the house is impeccably maintained. Manchester Airport is only five miles away and guests may leave their cars at the farm and be taken to the airport. Children welcome. No pets. No smoking in bedrooms and the dining-room. Car park.

OWNER Dyllis Hatch OPEN All year, exc Christmas
ROOMS 1 double (with bath/shower), 1 twin (with wash-basin), 2 single (with wash-basin) TERMS B&B £16–£18; deposit £5

MARKET HARBOROUGH Leicestershire map 4

Millstones Guest House

138 Northampton Road, Market Harborough LE16 9HF
MARKET HARBOROUGH (0858) 465441

This attractive mock-Tudor corner house is one mile from the city centre. Many of the stones for the house came from Rockingham Castle and there are stone-mullioned and stained-glass windows. There is a very pleasant TV lounge with soft blue furnishings and the original marble fireplace. Five of the bedrooms are in the new extension at the rear of the house and furnished to a high standard. Evening meals are available Monday to Friday at 6pm. Millstones is unlicensed, but guests may bring their own wine. Vegetarian choices and packed lunches can be provided. Children welcome. No smoking and no dogs in the dining-room. Car park.

OWNER Mrs J. Blackburn OPEN All year, exc Christmas and 2 weeks
ROOMS 1 family, 3 double, 2 twin, 1 single; all rooms with wash-basin) TERMS B&B £14 (children under 5 £5, 6–10 £7.50, 11–14 £9); dinner £6

Most establishments have central heating. We say when this is not the case.

We state at the end of an entry when children are welcome. If we know of any restrictions, we give them.

MATLOCK BATH Derbyshire map 7

Glena

182 Dale Road, Matlock Bath DE4 3PS
MATLOCK (0629) 583629

Glena is a family-run guesthouse right in the heart of Derbyshire, one mile from the town centre and just a few minutes from the cable-cars to the Heights of Abraham. The immaculate bedrooms are modestly furnished and comfortable. All have TV. An excellent breakfast is served in the bright, cosy breakfast room, which overlooks High Tor. Mrs Gibbs has been doing B&B for well over 30 years and takes excellent care of her guests. There is a pretty terraced garden, with furniture, for guests to use in summer. Partial central heating. Children welcome. No smoking and no pets in the dining-room. Car park.

OWNER Ines May Gibbs OPEN All year, exc Christmas ROOMS 2 family, 1 double, 1 single; all rooms, exc single, with wash-basin TERMS B&B £14, (family room) £35 (reductions for children sharing with parents); deposit

MELTON MOWBRAY Leicestershire map 7

Coniston Guest House

199 Thorpe Road, Melton Mowbray LE13 1SH
MELTON MOWBRAY (0664) 67758

This terraced corner house is situated on the main Grantham Road, in this ancient town famed for Stilton cheese and pork pies. The bedrooms, all with TV, are comfortably furnished and have new wash-basins. The very spacious family room has its own entrance to the house. The exterior of the property has been painted white and has had new leaded-light windows and double glazing installed. There is a lounge/dining-room with TV and video. Breakfast only is available and vegetarians can be catered for. There is plenty of on-street parking. Children welcome. Pets by arrangement. No smoking in bedrooms.

OWNERS Mr and Mrs A. R. Toon OPEN All year ROOMS 1 family (with bath/shower), 2 twin (with wash-basin) TERMS B&B £15 (children under 14 £10); dinner £5

If we know a B&Bs has an alcohol licence, we say so.

MOBBERLY Cheshire map 7

Laburnum Cottage Guest House

Knutsford Road, Mobberly WA16 7PM
MOBBERLY (0565) 872464

This lovely country house, built around 1930, sits in beautifully landscaped gardens which guests have full use of, including the barbecue. The house is luxuriously furnished, and the bedrooms all have colour-co-ordinated matching fabrics. The elegant lounge is very comfortable and has a log-burning fire in winter. The owners can meet guests at the railway station or airport and arrange car hire. Local sightseeing trips can also be organised, with Malcolm Collinge as your guide, and a picnic lunch can be provided at a modest charge. Excellent and plentiful breakfasts are served – enough to take care of you for the day. Light suppers are also available, by arrangement. Early morning tea can be provided. All bedrooms have TV. Mobberly is one and a half miles from Knutsford and three miles from the M6, junction 19. Facilities for very small children are limited – reductions by arrangement. No pets in the house. No smoking. Car park.

OWNERS Shirley Foxwell and Malcolm Collinge OPEN All year, exc Christmas and New Year ROOMS 1 double, 2 twin, 2 single; all rooms with bath/shower TERMS B&B £19–£22.50, (single) £22–£30, (single occupancy of twin/double) £25–£35; deposit £10 per person

NANTWICH Cheshire map 7

Stoke Grange Farm

Chester Road, Nantwich CW5 6BT
NANTWICH (0270) 625525

Stoke Grange Farm is a working dairy farm with chickens and geese and dates from 1828. The bedrooms are spacious and well appointed. The twin bedrooms have *en suite* facilities, and all bedrooms have TV. Guests may use a comfortable lounge with TV, a solarium, a games-room and riding ponies, or simply relax on the verandah and watch the canal boats as they pass by the farmhouse. Breakfast only is available, although packed lunches can be provided. Stoke Grange is two and a half miles from Nantwich off the A51, half a mile before Barbridge. There

Bath/shower in the details under each entry means that the rooms have private facilities.

are two self-catering units available. Children welcome. No pets. No smoking in public rooms. Car park.

OWNER Mrs Georgina West OPEN All year ROOMS 1 double (with wash-basin), 2 twin (with shower) TERMS B&B £15–£17.50 (children 2–5 half-price, 5–14 £10); deposit

NORTHAMPTON Northamptonshire map 4

St Georges Private Hotel

128 St Georges Avenue, Northampton NN2 6JF
NORTHAMPTON (0604) 792755

This is a substantial Victorian house opposite a park, which was formerly a racecourse. The house was in a derelict condition when purchased by the owner, Thomas Goodwin, and refurbishment took three years. The result is a pleasant, tastefully decorated and well-furnished property. There are attractive matching fabrics and curtains in the spacious bedrooms, three of which have an original fireplace. All have TV, and some have clock-radio. There is a large lounge with an original brass and wrought-iron surround fireplace. Guests are encouraged to treat the house as they would their own home and evenings can be quite festive, with cheesecake and coffee served in the lounge. The entrance still retains its stained glass and original mosaic tiles. Breakfast only is served and packed lunches can be provided on request. Children welcome. Pets by arrangement. Car park.

OWNER Mr T. Goodwin OPEN All year, exc Christmas
ROOMS 1 family (with bath/shower), 4 double (2 with bath/shower), 2 twin (1 with bath/shower), 2 single (1 with bath/shower, 1 with wash-basin) TERMS B&B £17.50–£20, (single occupancy of twin/double) £25, (family room) £45 (1 child £10 if sharing with parents, 2 children £5 per child); Access, Visa

NOTTINGHAM Nottinghamshire map 7

Firs Guest House

96 Radcliffe Road, West Bridgford, Nottingham NG2 5HH
NOTTINGHAM (0602) 810199

Firs Guest House is a Victorian corner house only one mile from the city and with a good bus service to the centre. The bedrooms, all with TV, are basic, clean and functional. The dining-room/ lounge has pine furniture and is next to a small aviary. Trent

Bridge cricket ground is just half a mile away. Mrs Beacham is a very amiable lady and is always happy to assist guests with any special requirements. Children welcome. Parking for two cars.

OWNER Margaret Beacham OPEN All year, exc Christmas
ROOMS 3 family, 3 twin, 1 single; all rooms with wash-basin
TERMS B&B £12, (single) £20, (family room) £30 (children half-price)

Gallery Hotel

8–10 Radcliffe Road, West Bridgford, Nottingham NG2 5FW
NOTTINGHAM (0602) 813651

This is a beautifully maintained Victorian house still with its original moulded cornices. The bedrooms are immaculate, well-furnished and comfortable. Some have *en suite* facilities. There is a lounge, dining-room, small bar and gym with pool-table and darts. Breakfast and reasonably priced home-cooked evening meals (6.30pm) are served, and vegetarians can be catered for by arrangement. The owners, Don and Brenda Masson, are a charming couple who are happy to assist guests with itineraries and offer advice on what to do in the area. Don was once a professional footballer and is an American football coach. This hotel is situated one and half miles from the city centre next to Trent Bridge cricket ground. Children welcome. No pets. No smoking. Car park.

OWNERS Don and Brenda Masson OPEN All year ROOMS 4 family (1 with bath/shower, 3 with wash-basin), 4 double (1 with bath/shower, 3 with wash-basin), 5 twin (1 with bath/shower, 4 with wash-basin), 3 single (2 with bath/shower, 1 with wash-basin) TERMS B&B £17, (single) £21–£26, (family room) £13 per person (children under 5 free, 5–12 £10); dinner £7.50

OLD Northamptonshire map 4

Wold Farm

Old, nr Northampton NN6 9RJ
NORTHAMPTON (0604) 781258

This attractive old farmhouse is very much a working farm (300 acres with sheep and beef cattle) and some parts of the building date from the fifteenth century. The house is elegant, tidy and immaculately clean. Guests have use of the large dining-room where evening meals, using home-produced vegetables and meat (vegetarian choices on request), are served at 7pm. There is no

alcohol licence, but guests may bring their own wine. The breakfast room, which is in the oldest part of the house, has a wood-burning stove in the enormous fireplace, oak beams and a dresser. The bedrooms are of a good size, very comfortable and tastefully furnished. Some old farm buildings on the property have recently been converted and now provide three *en suite* bedrooms (one on the ground floor). The rooms overlook the garden and are reached through the rose arbour. The conversion has its own lounge, but guests are welcome to use the large family lounge in the main house. Children welcome. Dogs by arrangement. No smoking in the bedrooms. Car park.

OWNER Anne Engler OPEN All year, exc Christmas and New Year ROOMS 1 family, 2 double, 1 twin, 2 single; all rooms with bath/shower TERMS B&B £18–£20 (children under 14 half-price); dinner £10; deposit

POLEBROOK Northamptonshire map 5

Hall Barn

Main Street, Polebrook, nr Oundle PE8 5LN
OUNDLE (0832) 273195

This 200-year-old completely refurbished barn made of local stone stands in an acre of gardens in the centre of the village, just two miles from Oundle. The spacious bedrooms, all with TV, are well appointed and decorated to a high standard with matching Sanderson fabrics. A sumptuous breakfast is served in the Baronial Hall, an impressive galleried room furnished in keeping with the baronial style. There is also a separate sitting area. Children welcome. No dogs. Car park.

OWNERS Martin and Christine Cooke OPEN All year ROOMS 1 double, 1 twin; both rooms with bath/shower TERMS B&B £20, (single occupancy of twin/double) £28 (children sharing with parents £8)

SHEARSBY Leicestershire map 4

Knaptoft House Farm and The Greenway

Bruntingthorpe Road, Shearsby, nr Lutterworth LE17 6PR
LEICESTER (0533) 478388

Knaptoft House Farm is a traditional mixed farm set in 145 acres of peaceful rolling countryside. There are medieval fish ponds which have been restored and re-stocked, largely with carp, but also with some tench and roach. Guests may fish by arrangement. There have been several recent improvements to both Knaptoft House Farm and the Greenway, including additional shower-rooms and a conservatory. There is a sun lounge, which has superb views, as well a TV lounge with a wood-burning stove. The Greenway is a luxurious bungalow/farmhouse set in the old orchard of Knaptoft House Farm and offering similar facilities, including three ground-floor bedrooms and a sitting-room. Guests are welcome to use the garden and barbecue. Breakfast only is available, although packed lunches can be provided. A fridge and ironing facilities are available. No children under three. No pets in the house. Car park.

OWNERS A. T. Hutchinson and A. M. Knight OPEN All year, exc Christmas ROOMS 1 family, 2 double, 3 twin (1 with wash-basin); 5 rooms with shower TERMS B&B £15, (single occupancy of twin/double) £16–£20, (family room) £38; deposit

Wheathill Farm

Church Lane, Shearsby, nr Lutterworth LE17 6PG
LEICESTER (0533) 478663

This listed building is partly medieval and is on a working dairy farm. It has beamed rooms, inglenook fireplaces with log fires, and even a ghost. Wash-basins have been cleverly built into dressers, and one bedroom has a shower in the chimney stack. Most rooms have views of the countryside. The family room is on the ground floor and comes complete with an old brass bed. The lounge has been newly furnished and carpeted, and leads out through french doors into the garden and down to a small lake. Children are welcome to feed the fish (under supervision). Breakfast only is served and includes free-range eggs from the farm. A conservatory has been added, which is an ideal spot for guests to sit in and chat, or read. Sue Timms is friendly and guests can be assured of genuine old-fashioned hospitality. 'House-trained' children welcome. No pets. No smoking. Off-road parking.

OWNER Sue Timms OPEN All year, exc Christmas ROOMS 1 family (with bath/shower), 1 double (with wash-basin), 1 twin (with shower), 1 single (with wash-basin) TERMS B&B from £15, (single occupancy of twin/double) from £18, (family room) £37 (babies in cot free, children up to 10 half-price); deposit £10

SHREWSBURY Shropshire map 7

Fieldside

38 London Road, Shrewsbury SY2 6NX
SHREWSBURY (0743) 353143

One and a half miles from the town centre, on the A5112, is this elegant Victorian house with attractive gardens. A large statue of Lord Hill and lions makes locating the hotel easy. The tasteful bedrooms, all with TV, are beautifully decorated and have every possible comfort. There is a varied choice at breakfast, which is served in a charming dining-room that overlooks the garden and has some lovely copper pieces and the original iron grate. Breakfast only is served, but there is a wide variety of eating establishments in and around the town centre. The hotel is still an excellent choice at reasonable prices and within each reach of Ironbridge, Chester and the Welsh border. No children under 10. No pets. No smoking. Car park.

OWNERS Pat and Ian Fraser OPEN All year, exc 18 Dec–8 Jan ROOMS 5 double (with bath/shower), 2 twin (1 with bath/shower), 2 single TERMS B&B £20, (single) £18, (single occupancy of twin/double) £28; Access, Amex, Visa

If we know a B&Bs has an alcohol licence, we say so.

The Old House

Ryton, Dorrington, nr Shrewsbury SY5 7LY
DORRINGTON (0743) 73585

About six miles south of Shrewsbury, off the A49, this white-washed seventeenth-century beamed manor house is set in two acres of beautiful gardens and looks out upon the rolling hills of south Shropshire. Susan Paget-Brown arranges dried flowers professionally and teaches flower arranging, and her skill is very evident throughout the house. The attractive bedrooms all have *en suite* facilities and are furnished with antiques. There is a pleasant guest lounge with TV. Tours of the area can be arranged with the owners for a modest charge. Breakfast only is served and packed lunches can be provided on request. There is an extensive garden with croquet lawn and a sitting area. This makes a good base for visiting the border counties and North Wales. Children welcome. No pets in bedrooms or living rooms, but they may stay overnight in the utility room. No smoking. Car park.

OWNERS James and Susan Paget-Brown OPEN All year, exc Christmas ROOMS 1 double, 2 twin; all rooms with bath/shower TERMS B&B £17.50, (single occupancy of twin/double) £26.25; deposit

SLEAFORD Lincolnshire map 8

The Mallards

6 Eastgate, Sleaford NG34 7DJ
SLEAFORD (0529) 303062

Just 100 yards from the market square is this Grade II listed Georgian building with some parts that date back to the sixteenth century. Mr and Mrs Lewin took the place over in April 1990. The small bedrooms are well maintained, and all have TV, radio-alarm and telephone. Three rooms are on the ground floor. Lunches and evening meals (7–9pm) are available in the restaurant at the rear. Vegetarians are catered for. The lounge has a display of Wedgwood china and there is a small bar, cleverly converted from a passage. Children welcome. Pets by arrangement. Car park.

OWNERS Mr and Mrs A. Lewin OPEN All year, exc Christmas ROOMS 1 family, 5 double, 2 twin, 2 single; all rooms with bath/shower TERMS B&B £24.50, (single) £39 (children under 14 free accommodation and half-price meals); dinner; deposit; Access, Amex, Visa

SPALDING Lincolnshire map 8

Belvoir Guest House

13 London Road, Spalding PE11 2TA
SPALDING (0775) 723901

This four-storey listed Georgian house faces the River Welland and is just a two-minute walk from the town centre. The spacious bedrooms, all of which have been freshly decorated, some with new carpets and ceilings, have sitting areas and TV. Evening meals are served 6.30–7.30pm in the licensed dining-room, which faces the river. There is also a small bar. Children welcome (no cot provided). No smoking in the dining-room.

OWNERS Ronald and Helen Cox OPEN All year, exc Christmas ROOMS 1 family, 1 double, 2 twin, 2 single; all rooms with wash-basin TERMS B&B £15, (single occupancy of twin/double) £20 (children under 2 free, 2–10 half-price); dinner £6–£7.50; deposit

STOKE-ON-TRENT Staffordshire map 7

The Corrie Guest House

13 Newton Street, Basford, Stoke-on-Trent ST4 6JN
STOKE-ON-TRENT (0782) 614838

The Corrie Guest House is a pleasant Victorian house off the A53 in a quiet location not far from the centre of town. The bedrooms are a little small, but they are clean, prettily decorated and comfortable; three rooms have TV. A cup of tea or coffee is offered to guests on their arrival and facilities for tea-making are available in the lounge. Modestly priced home-cooked evening meals, served 6–7pm if ordered in advance, are available, and vegetarians can be catered for. The Corrie is not licensed, but guests may bring their own wine. Three bedrooms have TV. The owners live in the adjacent house but are always available should guests have questions. Pottery tours can be arranged. The car park has been enlarged and guests are well advised to leave the car here and take the bus into the town centre. Children welcome (no cot or high chair provided). No pets. No smoking in the dining-room and bedrooms.

OWNERS Rob and Averill Burton OPEN All year ROOMS 1 family, 2 double (1 with bath/shower), 1 twin, 3 single; 6 rooms with wash-basin TERMS B&B £16–£18, (family room) £45 (children under 4 free, 4–12 half-price); dinner £8; deposit £5

Peacock Hay Guest House

Peacock Hay Road, Talke, Stoke-on-Trent ST7 1UN
STOKE-ON-TRENT (0782) 773511

Talke is just off the A34 about five miles north-west of Stoke-on-Trent centre. Peacock Hay is a 200-year-old beamed house in an elevated position and has a warm and relaxing atmosphere. Guests are treated like friends and encouraged to treat the house as their own. There is a dining-room-cum-lounge converted from the cowshed, which has coal fires on chilly evenings. The bedrooms are bright and clean, and simply furnished with comfortable beds; two bedrooms are on the ground floor. Breakfast only is served; guests help themselves to juice and cereals followed by a fresh-cooked traditional breakfast. Children welcome. Pets must be house-trained. Car park.

OWNER Barbara Johnson OPEN All year, exc Christmas ROOMS 3 double (1 with bath/shower, 2 with wash-basin), 4 twin (1 with bath/shower, 3 with wash-basin), 3 single (1 with bath/shower, 2 with wash-basin) TERMS B&B £16–£19, (single occupancy of twin/double) £25 (children free sharing room with 2 adults); deposit 25%; Access, Visa

Westfield House

312 Princes Road, Penkhull, Stoke-on-Trent ST4 7JP
STOKE-ON-TRENT (0782) 44582

This is a well-maintained and modest Victorian house in a residential area about a 10-minute walk from the town centre. The accommodation is simple and clean and there is a TV lounge for guests' use. A substantial breakfast is served; evening meals are not available, but Mrs White is happy to offer advice on where to eat. There are no fancy frills here, you get good-value accommodation in a friendly atmosphere. Children welcome. Dogs only. No smoking in bedrooms.

OWNER Mrs Norma White OPEN All year ROOMS 1 double, 1 twin TERMS B&B £12.50–£15 (children 30% reduction)

It is always best to check prices, especially for single occupancy, when booking.

Any smoking restrictions that we know of are given in each entry.

STURTON BY STOW Lincolnshire map 8

The Village Farm

Sturton by Stow, nr Lincoln LN1 2AE
GAINSBOROUGH (0427) 788309

This nineteenth-century farmhouse is set back from the road, in a big, well-cultivated garden, in the middle of the village. The house is owned by a friendly couple who farm 350 acres supporting Limousin cattle and sheep. Mrs Bradshaw offers evening meals on request, served at 7pm, using home baking, and beef and lamb from the farm. Vegetarian meals can be arranged with prior notice. There is a beautiful guest lounge, rich red carpeting on the stairs and in the hallway, and a display of interesting pictures. The Village Farm is about nine miles from both Gainsborough and Lincoln. No children under 11. No pets. No smoking in bedrooms. Car park.

OWNER Mrs Sheila Bradshaw OPEN Apr–end Oct ROOMS 1 double (with bath/shower), 1 twin (with wash-basin), 1 single (with wash-basin) TERMS B&B £14–£18, (single occupancy of twin/double) £21–£27; dinner £9; deposit

SWINHOPE Lincolnshire map 8

Hoe Hill

Swinhope, nr Binbrook LN3 6HX
BINBROOK (0472) 398206

Hoe Hill is a large, white farmhouse on the B1203, one mile north of Binbrook village. It dates from around 1750 and is in a fairly isolated position on the top of a hill, with lovely views. The house has been freshly decorated and the bedrooms, furnished with pine, are comfortable. There is a large sitting-room, which has TV and french doors leading out on to the patio and lovely gardens, including a croquet lawn. Packed lunches can be provided and evening meals served at 7.30pm by arrangement; vegetarians can be catered for on request. There is no alcohol licence, but guests may bring their own wine. No children under five. No dogs. No smoking in bedrooms. Car park.

OWNERS Ian and Erica Curd OPEN All year, exc Christmas and Jan ROOMS 1 double, 2 twin, 1 single; all rooms with wash-basin TERMS B&B £11–£15 (children 6–12 £10); dinner £10; deposit if staying 3 or more nights

TANSLEY Derbyshire map 7

Packhorse Farm

Tansley, Matlock DE4 5LT
MATLOCK (0629) 582781

Just two miles from Matlock, Packhorse Farm is a 200-year-old farmhouse and former coaching-inn, with more recent additions, on a working farm set in a large garden in Derbyshire's beautiful countryside with views of hills and moors. The bedrooms are clean and light and decorated in soothing colours. The large, sunny dining-room has doors leading out on to a terrace and there is a putting-green and a small nature reserve for guests to explore. There is also a beamed sitting-room overlooking a lovely walled garden. Breakfast only is served, although packed lunches can be provided. No children under three. No pets in the house. Car park.

OWNER Mrs Margaret Haynes OPEN All year, exc Christmas and New Year ROOMS 3 family, 1 double, 1 twin; all rooms with wash-basin TERMS B&B £14–£17; deposit

TETFORD Lincolnshire map 8

Tetford House

East Road, Tetford LN9 6QQ
TETFORD (0507) 533639

Close to the Viking Way is this spacious Victorian house on the edge of the village in two acres of gardens and paddocks. Tetford is mentioned in the Domesday Book, and the next village, Somerby, is the birthplace of Alfred, Lord Tennyson. There are just two simply furnished bedrooms, both with sitting area, *en suite* bathroom and TV. Substantial breakfasts are served in the bedrooms, overlooking the garden. This is good walking country. Children welcome. Pets by arrangement. Car park.

OWNERS Mr and Mrs B. Glendinning OPEN All year, exc Christmas ROOMS 2 double (with bath/shower) TERMS B&B £17–£20 (babies and very young children free sharing room with adults)

Many B&Bs will cater for vegetarians. It is always best, however, to check when booking and make it clear what your requirements are, especially if you need a special diet.

TILSTON Cheshire map 7

Tilston Lodge

Tilston, nr Malpas SY14 7DR
TILSTON (0829) 250223

In a secluded and tranquil setting surrounded by beautiful grounds, Tilston Lodge is a nineteenth-century country house set in 12 acres of land, with a collection of rare-breed poultry, sheep and cattle. Guests are welcome to walk around the landscaped gardens. The rooms are spacious and furnished in keeping with the character of the house. One of the bedrooms has a king-size four-poster bed, two rooms have TV and all but one single are *en suite*. Several original features of the house remain, such as a galleried landing, the stairwell and fireplaces. Evening meals, if pre-arranged, are served in the attractive dining-room/lounge, everything home-made using produce from the garden. Vegetarian choices and packed lunches can be provided. Tilston Lodge is unlicensed, but guests may bring their own wine. Children welcome. No dogs. No smoking in the dining-room and bedroom. Car park.

OWNERS Kathie and Neil Ritchie OPEN All year, exc Christmas ROOMS 1 four-poster/family, 1 twin, 1 single; all rooms, exc single (wash-basin only), with bath/shower TERMS B&B £15–£20 (children up to 12 half-price); dinner £8.50

UPPER ELKSTONE Staffordshire map 7

Mount Pleasant Farmhouse

Elkstone, nr Longnor, Buxton SK17 0LU
BLACKSHAW (053 834) 380

This late-nineteenth-century farmhouse is approached from a private lane off a quiet country road, with lovely views across the Elkstone Valley towards Ecton Hill and the Manifold Valley. There are two acres of land with two pet donkeys which children are welcome to ride. The bedrooms are large, simply furnished and spotlessly clean. There is also a separate lounge with TV, a dining-room, table tennis room, and lots of information leaflets, maps and guides on what to see and do in the area. Excellent evening meals using fresh local produce and meats are available five nights a week at 6.30pm, prepared by Mrs Faulkner, who used to demonstrate cookery. The menu may include local lamb roasted with garlic and rosemary, a fish dish and home-made desserts such as queen of puddings. Vegetarians can be catered for by arrangement. Mount Pleasant is unlicensed, but guests may bring their own wine. No children under six. Dogs by arrangement. No smoking in public rooms. Car park.

OWNER Mrs E. B. Faulkner OPEN Mar–Nov ROOMS 1 double, 2 twin; all rooms with wash-basin TERMS B&B £14–£16 (children £10–£12); dinner £7.50; deposit £30 per room

UPPINGHAM Leicestershire map 4

Rutland House

61 High Street East, Uppingham LE15 9PY
UPPINGHAM (0572) 822497

Uppingham is a historic market town and Rutland House is in a good position in the centre. The owners provide good value, and offer all the facilities of a large hotel, including laundry services, but at a reasonable price. The bedrooms all have TV and easy chairs, and there is a twin room on the ground floor suitable for a wheelchair-user. Breakfast only is available, but packed lunches can be provided. There are nine restaurants or pubs serving food within a few minutes' walk. This is a good base for visiting Rutland Water, Rockingham Castle, Burghley House and Belvoir Castle. Children welcome. No pets in public rooms. Car park.

OWNER Mrs J. Hitchen OPEN All year ROOMS 1 family/double, 1 double, 1 twin, 1 single; all rooms with bath/shower TERMS B&B £18.50, (single) £27, (family room) £45 (children £8 sharing room); deposit

WHISSENDINE Leicestershire map 7

Old Bakehouse

11 Main Street, Whissendine, nr Oakham LE15 7ES
WHISSENDINE (066 479) 691

The Old Bakehouse, dating from 1725 with later additions, was the last bakery in the village. The house is a blaze of colour in summer with many beautiful hanging baskets and tubs full of flowers. The bedrooms are immaculate and beautifully furnished in pine. Breakfasts only are served in the pleasant dining-room and include home-baked bread. There is also a pine and antique furniture shop, which is part of the guesthouse. No children under eight. No pets. No smoking. Car park.

OWNER Mrs W. J. Stevenson OPEN Easter–end Oct
ROOMS 1 family (with wash-basin), 1 double (with bath/shower), 1 twin (with wash-basin) TERMS B&B £11–£14, (family room) £33–£36 (children £7–£8 if sharing); deposit 20%

WINSTER Derbyshire map 7

The Dower House

Main Street, Winster DE4 2DH
WINSTER (0629) 650213

This beautifully restored Grade II listed Elizabethan country house, with a walled garden, is adjacent to the village church. Winster is a delightful village, and in the first week of July you can witness the well-known Winster morris dancers on the Dower House lawn. The large bedrooms are decorated to a high standard, and all have easy chairs and TV. There is also an elegant beamed drawing-room with an open log fire. Superb, freshly prepared breakfasts, including home-made jams and marmalades, are served in the dining-room. Packed lunches can also be provided. No children under 10. No dogs or smoking in the dining-room. Car park.

OWNERS Mrs H. A. Bastin and Mr G. J. Dalton OPEN Mar–Oct
ROOMS 1 double, 2 twin; all rooms with wash-basin TERMS B&B £16, (single occupancy of twin/double) June–Sept £32; deposit £20

WOLVERHAMPTON West Midlands map 4

Wheaton House

285 Stafford Road, Oxley, Wolverhampton WV10 6DQ
WOLVERHAMPTON (0902) 28841

Wheaton House is an attractive turn-of-the-century red-brick and white house standing in its own grounds one and a half miles from the town centre on the A449. It is surrounded by rose bushes, hanging baskets and flower tubs. There are stained-glass windows in the front door, and there is a galleried landing. The bedrooms,

It is always best to book a room in advance, especially in winter. B&Bs with few rooms may close at short notice for periods not specified in the details.

all with TV, are of a good size, have modern furniture and are tastefully decorated with matching fabrics. Breakfasts only are served. There is plenty of parking and the bus to town stops in front of the house. Children welcome. Pets by arrangement. No smoking in the dining-room.

OWNER Mrs Pauline Ward OPEN All year ROOMS 1 family, 3 double; all rooms with bath/shower TERMS B&B £10–£17.50 (children under 4 free, 4–13 half-price); deposit

The North

Cleveland

Cumbria

Co Durham

Greater Manchester

Humberside

Isle of Man

Lancashire

Merseyside

Northumberland

North Yorkshire

South Yorkshire

Tyne & Wear

West Yorkshire

ALNMOUTH Northumberland map 10

The Grange

Northumberland Street, Alnmouth NE66 2RJ
ALNMOUTH (0665) 830401

The Grange is a large, attractive stone-built house dating from 1899, in a peaceful setting overlooking the River Aln and only two minutes' walk to beautiful unspoilt beaches. The bedrooms are spacious and tastefully furnished; two have four-poster beds with pretty lace canopies and are *en suite*. All have TV. The elegant, quiet lounge overlooks the river. Breakfast only is available and vegetarians can be catered for. Children over five welcome. No pets. No smoking. Car park.

OWNERS Mr and Mrs C. R. Homer OPEN All year, exc Christmas and New Year ROOMS 2 four-poster (with bath/shower), 1 double, 1 twin, 1 single; all rooms with wash-basin TERMS B&B £17–£20; deposit

ALNWICK Northumberland map 10

Aydon House Hotel

South Road, Alnwick NE66 2NT
ALNWICK (0665) 602218

An attractive, large, stone-built house that dates from 1899. The immaculate rooms are extremely spacious, modestly furnished, and all with TV. There is a bright and comfortable licensed guest lounge with a wide choice of reading material, and guests may help themselves to tea and coffee. Breakfast only is served, but there are several pubs and restaurants close by. Mr Carroll is very interested in golf and is happy to advise guests on the best local courses. Alnwick Castle is only 10 minutes away. Children welcome. Car park.

OWNERS Jane and Arthur Carroll OPEN All year, exc Christmas ROOMS 2 family (1 with bath/shower, 1 with wash-basin), 3 double (2 with bath/shower, 1 with wash-basin), 3 twin (1 with bath/shower, 2 with wash-basin), 2 single (with wash-basin) TERMS B&B £14–£18, (family room) from £40

Bath/shower information in the details refers only to a private bathroom or shower; other bathroom facilities at the establishments will be shared. We say if rooms have wash-basins.

ALTRINCHAM Greater Manchester map 7

Marron Guest House

15 Manchester Road, Altrincham WA14 4RG
061-941 5603

Marron Guest House is a Victorian house situated on a main road, and just eight miles from Manchester and the airport. It has been redecorated to a very high standard and the bedrooms are large, all with TV and easy chairs; some still have their original fireplaces. Breakfast only is served in the dining-room. Children welcome. No pets. Car park.

OWNER Mr R. W. Bartle OPEN All year ROOMS 3 double/family, 1 twin; all rooms with wash-basin TERMS B&B £20–£25, (family room) £60–£75

AMBLESIDE Cumbria map 9

Brantfell Guest House

Rothay Road, Ambleside LA22 0EE
AMBLESIDE (053 94) 32239

Elaine and John have been in the B&B business since 1989 and have recently improved the house. *En suite* facilities have been added to two of the bedrooms and all have TV. Brantfell offers homely accommodation, close to the centre of Ambleside. Parking is available for one car only. The house is near the park, where guests may play tennis (racquets are available). There is also a residents' lounge with TV. Breakfast and dinner (6.30pm) are served in the attractive licensed dining-room. Children welcome. No pets. No smoking in the dining-room.

OWNERS Elaine and John Morrisroe OPEN All year, exc Christmas ROOMS 1 family (with wash-basin), 2 double (with wash-basin), 2 twin (with bath/shower), 1 single (with wash-basin) TERMS B&B £11.50–£17, (single) £11.50–£13.50, (single occupancy of twin/double) £20–£25, (family room) £32–£44 (children under 2 free, 3–8 £5, 8–12 £7.50, 13 full price); dinner £8; deposit

Where a single-occupancy rate is not specified in the details, the cost will be the same as that per person in a twin or double room, or will be included in the range of prices given.

Most B&Bs don't accept credit cards, but when they do we list the cards taken.

Fern Cottage

6 Waterhead Terrace, Waterhead, Ambleside LA22 0HA
AMBLESIDE (053 94) 33007

On the main road to Windermere, Fern Cottage is in an excellent position, a two-minute walk from the head of the lake and steamer piers. It is a small, immaculate guesthouse, excellent value and a good base from which to tour the Lake District. The bedrooms are small but comfortable; there is only one bathroom for the four guest rooms, and guests are requested not to take showers early in the morning. Home-cooked evening meals are served at 6.30pm, and packed lunches can be provided by prior arrangement. There is no alcohol licence. Vegetarians can be catered for. Car parking is available at the nearby steamer car park. No children under eight. No dogs. No smoking in the dining-room.

OWNER Mrs M. Brown OPEN All year, exc Christmas
ROOMS 2 double, 1 twin; all rooms with wash-basin TERMS B&B £14–£16, (single occupancy of twin/double) from £19; D, B&B £22–£24; deposit £10

Meadowbank

Rydal Road, Ambleside LA22 9BA
AMBLESIDE (053 94) 32710

This spacious Victorian house stands in extensive gardens, five minutes' walk from Ambleside. Ray and Barbara Woollett have created a charming and comfortable house in a peaceful setting. The bedrooms are of a good size, two are non-smoking. There are some interesting Gothic-style carvings throughout the house, stripped Canadian pine doors and a large marble fireplace in the lounge. Most of the rooms overlook the garden and Loughrigg Fell. Breakfast only is served. Children welcome. No pets. Car park.

OWNERS Ray and Barbara Woollett OPEN All year, exc Christmas
ROOMS 2 family/twin (1 with bath/shower), 4 double/twin (3 with bath/shower), 1 single; 4 rooms with wash-basin TERMS B&B £16–£18, (children under 3 free, 3–14 half-price); deposit £10

The description for each entry states when pets are not allowed. Where no details are given, you can assume that pets are allowed. It's always best to check first in any case.

Riverside Lodge Country House

nr Rothay Bridge, Ambleside LA22 0EH
AMBLESIDE (053 94) 34208

This early Georgian house, situated in a unique position right on the river bank overlooking Rothay Bridge, is just a pleasant walk away from Ambleside. There are extensive grounds through which the River Rothay flows and guests are invited to fish. An inscription records that Bonnie Prince Charlie rested here in 1745. The Lodge, with some beamed ceilings, has been refurbished to a very high standard and exudes character and charm. The dining-room overlooks the river and there is a cosy lounge with a log fire

and a small bar. Evening meals are no longer available, but there are plenty of places to eat in Ambleside. The bedrooms all have private bathroom, telephone, hair-dryer, TV and easy chairs. There is one ground-floor bedroom. Self-catering cottages sleeping two to four persons are available. Children welcome. No pets. No smoking in public rooms. Car park.

OWNERS Alan and Gillian Rhone OPEN All year ROOMS 1 family, 3 double, 1 single TERMS B&B £20–£27.50, (single occupancy of double) £30–£40 (children half-price sharing family room); deposit £20; Access, Visa

APPLEBY-IN-WESTMORLAND Cumbria map 10

The Friary

Battlebarrow, Appleby-in-Westmorland CA16 6XT
APPLEBY (076 83) 52702

This is an informal, comfortable house, just a half mile from the historic town of Appleby and the castle. The Friary is a Grade II listed building on the site of a twelfth-century friary, set in an acre of beautiful mature gardens. The rooms are large and tastefully decorated. Guests may relax in the TV lounge or quiet lounge, and log fires are lit on chilly days. Mr Huntington is a former sea captain, and holds a diploma in vegetarian cuisine. A four-course set vegetarian menu, with dishes such as raised pecan, walnut and mushroom pie and aubergine soufflé, is available, as well as a traditional menu. Dinner is served at 7.30pm and there is an alcohol licence. Packed lunches can also be provided. Children welcome. No dogs. No smoking. Car park.

OWNER Mrs Phyliss Huntington OPEN All year, exc Christmas ROOMS 1 family (with wash-basin), 2 double (with bath/shower), 1 twin (with bath/shower) TERMS B&B £20–£24, (family room) £18 per person (children under 8 free, £9 over 8); D, B&B £28–£30; dinner £10; deposit £20

BAMBURGH Northumberland map 10

Greengates

34 Front Street, Bamburgh NE69 7BJ
BAMBURGH (066 84) 535

Greengates is a late-Victorian house situated at the foot of the picturesque village, 100 yards from the castle and 300 yards from the beaches. The house had been empty for 11 years when Mr and Mrs Walton took over the property. They have completely refurbished the spacious rooms, which are attractive and immaculate. The lounge has an open fire and there are books and games for guests' use. Breakfast only is available, but there are plenty of eating establishments in the village. Mr Walton has a small Aviation Museum that can be viewed on request. Children welcome. Smoking in the lounge only. Car park.

OWNER Mrs E. F. Walton OPEN All year, exc Christmas and 3 weeks Nov ROOMS 1 double, 2 twin/family; all rooms with wash-basin TERMS B&B £15 (children under 14 half-price sharing with parents); deposit £10; Access, Visa

BARNARD CASTLE Co Durham map 10

The Homelands

85 Galgate, Barnard Castle DL12 8ES
BARNARD CASTLE (0833) 38757

The Homelands is a large terraced house dating from 1860 in the centre of Barnard Castle. Raby Castle and Bowes Museum are fairly close by. The spacious bedrooms are elegantly furnished, attractively decorated, and all have TV. There is a very comfortable, quiet guest lounge. Mrs Chesman enjoys cooking, gardening and interior decorating, as well as sharing her knowledge of local history with her guests. Home-cooked meals using fresh local produce are served 6.30–8pm in the licensed dining-room. Vegetarian choices can be provided on request. Packed lunches are available with prior notice. Children welcome. No pets.

OWNER Mrs Kath Chesman OPEN All year, exc Christmas
ROOMS 1 double (with wash-basin), 2 twin (with bath/shower)
TERMS B&B £16, (single occupancy of twin/double) £21; dinner £9

BASSENTHWAITE LAKE Cumbria map 9

Link House

Bassenthwaite Lake, Cockermouth CA13 9YD
BASSENTHWAITE LAKE (076 87) 76291

Link House is a Victorian country house in half an acre of garden close to Bassenthwaite Lake, and is a haven of peace and tranquillity. Guests continue to return here for the friendly atmosphere, good food and superb views of the forest and Skiddaw. The comfortable bedrooms (one of which is on the ground floor) are furnished with antiques and period pieces; all have TV. There is also a delightful conservatory. A five-course dinner is served at 7pm in the licensed dining-room. There is always a choice of dishes; the favourite speciality of the house is still the home-made ice-cream. Light lunches are served and packed lunches can be provided. No children under seven. No pets. No smoking in the dining-room. Car park.

OWNERS Brian and May Smith OPEN Feb–Nov ROOMS 3 double, 3 twin, 2 single; all rooms with bath/shower TERMS B&B £19.50–£23.50, (single) £19.50–£23.50; D, B&B £31.50–£35; deposit

BEDALE North Yorkshire map 10

Hyperion House

88 South End, Bedale DL8 2DS
BEDALE (0677) 422334

This attractive, ivy-clad residence was named after a racehorse by a local resident who was lucky enough to have collected a substantial win, and is located just one-and-three-quarter miles from the A1. All the large, comfortable rooms have been freshly decorated and have new curtains. There is a TV lounge and a garden for guests' use. Children welcome. No pets. No smoking. Car park.

OWNERS Sheila and Ron Dean OPEN All year, exc Christmas
ROOMS 2 double, 1 twin, 1 single; all rooms with wash-basin
TERMS B&B £14.50–£17, (single occupancy of twin/double) £20; dinner £8; deposit £15

BELLERBY North Yorkshire map 10

The Old Hall Guest House

Bellerby, nr Leyburn DLA 5QP
WENSLEYDALE (0969) 23028

The Old Hall is a listed sixteenth-century house, in the centre of the village, with a stream in front of the property. An underground tunnel is thought to lead to the manor house. Cromwell's men burnt down the east wing in the belief that royalists were in the house. The beamed bedrooms are large and simply furnished; one of them was the priest's hole. There is a guest lounge with TV and an inglenook fireplace. Evening meals are available (6.30–7pm), all home-cooked. Vegetarians can be catered for. There is no alcohol licence, but guests may bring their own wine to dinner. Packed lunches can also be provided. Guests are offered a hot drink upon arrival. Children welcome. No pets. No smoking in bedrooms. Car park.

OWNERS Mr and Mrs Richard Travell OPEN All year, exc Christmas
ROOMS 1 family, 1 double (with bath/shower), 1 twin (with bath/shower) TERMS B&B from £13.50, (single occupancy of twin/double) from £18 (children under 12 half-price sharing parents' room); dinner £7.50; deposit

BELLINGHAM Northumberland map 10

Ivy Cottage

Lanehead, Bellingham, nr Hexham NE48 1NT
BELLINGHAM (0434) 240337

This attractive cottage, dating from 1797, overlooks the tree-lined Tarset Burn and North Tyne Valley. The spacious bedrooms have pretty wallpapers, matching fabrics and Victorian pitchers and bowls; one room has a canopied bed. All the rooms have TV. One bedroom now has its own shower and another an *en suite* bathroom. Breakfast and dinner (6.30–7pm) are available. Dinner is a special feature at Ivy Cottage; dishes are traditional English, cordon bleu, vegetarian or vegan. The premises are not licensed, but guests may bring their own wine. There is a conservatory lounge with TV, and a separate lounge for smokers. The proprietors hope to offer a number of activities for guests to try, including painting, spinning and photography. Children welcome. Pets by arrangement. No smoking. Car park.

OWNERS Jeanette and Barry Imeson OPEN All year, exc Christmas
ROOMS 1 double (with bath/shower), 2 twin (with wash-basin)
TERMS B&B £14–£17; dinner £8.50; deposit £10

Westfield House

Bellingham, nr Hexham NE48 2DP
BELLINGHAM (0434) 220340

Many of the original Victorian features are preserved at this large, comfortable, detached house; there are some interesting fireplaces and a wood-burning stove in the lounge. The bedrooms (one of which is on the ground floor) are spacious and individually decorated; one has a brass bed. The pretty, decorative drapes are made by June Minchin herself. The pleasant sitting-room overlooks the large garden, which guests are welcome to use. There are drying facilities and hairdressing may also be arranged. Dinner is usually served at 7.30pm. Guests are seated around two large dining tables. Vegetarian meals and packed lunches are available on request. The premises are not licensed, but guests are welcome to bring their own wine to dinner. Walkers are well

Breakfast at B&Bs tends to mean a cooked breakfast of bacon, eggs and so on. If you prefer a different style of breakfast, discuss this when you make the booking.

catered for; the Pennine Way passes nearby. Children welcome. Dogs by arrangement. No smoking.

OWNERS David and June Minchin OPEN All year, exc Dec–Jan ROOMS 1 family (with wash-basin), 2 double (1 with bath/shower, 1 with wash-basin), 2 twin (1 with bath/shower, 1 with wash-basin) TERMS B&B £17–£24, (single occupancy of twin/double) £25–£35 (reduction for children sharing parents' room); dinner £14; deposit £10

BERWICK-UPON-TWEED Northumberland map 10

14 Quay Walls

14 Quay Walls, Berwick-upon-Tweed TD15 1HB
BERWICK-UPON-TWEED (0289) 330796

This eighteenth-century house is located on the quay overlooking the River Tweed. Dinners are available (7pm) if pre-arranged, and guests are joined by the owners. There is no alcohol licence, but guests may bring their own wine to dinner. Vegetarian choices can be provided. The TV lounge is shared. Mr and Mrs McNair-Allen enjoy outlining day-trips for their guests; there is a fine golf course nearby, overlooking the beach. No children. No smoking in bedrooms. A public car park is close by.

OWNERS Robert and Pamela McNair-Allen OPEN All year ROOMS 1 double, 1 twin (with bath/shower) TERMS B&B £15; dinner £5

Middle Ord Farm

Middle Ord, Berwick-upon-Tweed TD15 2XQ
BERWICK-UPON-TWEED (0289) 306323

This elegant Georgian manor house, built in 1783, has been completely redecorated in period style with a chandelier in the dining-room and Adam-style fireplaces. The house is surrounded by a peaceful secluded garden and guests can enjoy all-day access. There are three comfortable bedrooms, and one has TV. Mrs Gray greets visitors with a cup of tea and home-made cakes, and guests are welcome to participate in the farm activities. There are two lounges, one with TV, for non-smokers. Breakfast only is served in the elegant dining-room and includes farm eggs and home-made marmalades and jams. No children. No pets. Car park.

OWNER Mrs J. Gray OPEN Apr–Oct ROOMS 1 four-poster (with bath/shower), 1 double (with wash-basin), 1 twin (with wash-basin) TERMS B&B £15.50, (four-poster) £20.50; deposit £10

Myecroft, Letham Shank Farm

Berwick-upon-Tweed TD15 1UX
BERWICK-UPON-TWEED (0289) 307564

This working arable and sheep farm is set in rolling countryside just outside Berwick. From the town take the A6105 for approximately one mile, then turn left on the B6461 for half a mile. Accommodation is in the spacious 200-year-old country cottage. The two bedrooms are beautifully furnished, mostly with pine, and are very comfortable. There is a delightful conservatory, which overlooks an attractive garden and open countryside down to the sea, and a charming balcony area with lots of plants. Breakfasts are ample, with home-baked bread, home-made marmalades and fresh eggs. Trout fishing and riding are available in the area, and there are two golf courses nearby. No children. No pets. No smoking in bedrooms.

OWNER Mrs P. Cranston OPEN All year, exc Christmas
ROOMS 1 double, 1 twin TERMS B&B from £15.50

Riverview

11 Quay Walls, Berwick-upon-Tweed TD15 1HB
BERWICK-UPON-TWEED (0289) 306295

Due to the location of this Georgian terraced house, cars must approach the property from the rear. It is situated on the thirteenth-century quay walls, overlooking the River Tweed and the three bridges. Mr and Mrs Chappell are local people and very knowledgeable about the surrounding area. The comfortable bedrooms all have TV. Breakfast is served upstairs in the dining-room, which overlooks the river. There is a guest lounge. Lunch and packed lunches can be provided. Dinner is served (6–7.30pm) and vegetarian choices are available. There is a courtesy car service to and from local public transport. Children welcome. No pets. Car park.

OWNER Mrs Margaret Chapell OPEN All year ROOMS 1 double (with bath/shower), 1 twin (with bath/shower), 1 single (with wash-basin) TERMS B&B £18, (single occupancy of twin/double) £30; dinner £8; small deposit; Visa

Bath/shower information in the details refers only to a private bathroom or shower; other bathroom facilities at the establishments will be shared.

BEVERLEY Humberside map 8

Pinewood

45 North Bar Without, Beverley HU17 7AG
HULL (0482) 861366

Pinewood is an elegant, listed, mock-Tudor house situated close to the town centre in a spacious Georgian road, close to St Mary's Church. Veronica Livingston-Raper took over the residence in November 1990; she is an enthusiastic lady, dedicated to ensuring guests' comfort. On chilly mornings fires are lit in the dining-room and lounge. The bedrooms are spacious with comfortable new beds; all rooms have the original fireplaces. The lovely oak stairwell carvings are by the craftsman Elwell, who also executed carvings in Beverley Minster. Dinner can be arranged (with prior notice) and guests may bring their own wine. Packed lunches can be provided. Children welcome. No pets. No smoking. Car park.

OWNER Mrs Veronica Livingston-Raper OPEN All year
ROOMS 1 double (with wash-basin), 2 twin (1 with bath/shower, 1 with wash-basin) TERMS B&B £20, (single occupancy of twin/double) £23 (babies free, reductions for children)

BLACKPOOL Lancashire map 7

Grosvenor View Hotel

7–9 King Edward Avenue, North Shore, Blackpool FY2 9TD
BLACKPOOL (0253) 52851

Helen Kelly and Margaret Spencer are mother and daughter, who have pooled their catering expertise to provide a first-class establishment. Originally two houses, Grosvenor View has been totally refurbished and all rooms have been decorated to a high standard. The bedrooms are bright and airy; there is one ground-floor *en suite* room. Good home-cooked evening meals are served at 5pm; vegetarians can be catered for. Lunch and packed lunches can be arranged. There are two comfortable lounges. The hotel is situated in a quiet area, yet is still close to amenities. Children

We asked the proprietors to estimate their 1992 prices in the autumn of 1991, so the rates may have changed since publication.

Bath/shower in the details under each entry means that the rooms have private facilities.

welcome (cots and high chairs are available). Pets by prior arrangement. Smoking in the lounges only. Car park.

OWNERS Mr and Mrs Kelly, Mr and Mrs Spencer OPEN All year ROOMS 10 double (2 with bath/shower), 9 twin (2 with bath/shower), 2 single; all rooms with wash-basin TERMS B&B £15.50 (reductions for children); D, B&B £18; dinner £4.50–£5; deposit £10 per person; Access, Visa

The Justholme

14 King George Avenue, Blackpool FY2 9SN
BLACKPOOL (0253) 53226

The Justholme continues to be an excellent choice for visitors to Blackpool. An attractive house built in the 1930s, it is five minutes from all of Blackpool's amenities. The lounge, with comfortable furnishings, has a fine display of crystal, china and plants. A small conservatory has been added and is a popular spot for guests to enjoy an after-dinner drink. Evening meals, including vegetarian, are served at 5pm. Lunch and packed lunches can be arranged. No children under five. Car park.

OWNERS Maurice and Derek Green OPEN All year ROOMS 8 double (4 with bath/shower, 4 with wash-basin), 2 twin (with wash-basin) TERMS B&B £15; dinner £4

Lyndene Private Hotel

106 Coronation Street, Blackpool FY1 4QQ
BLACKPOOL (0253) 23222

The hotel's exterior is decorated with colourful hanging baskets. The house has been totally redecorated to a high standard, and the bedrooms, although small, are furnished with pretty wallpapers and attractive curtains. There is a dining-room/lounge and small bar. Cooked breakfasts and a three-course dinner are served (5pm), as well as light snacks during the day; packed lunches can be provided. This hotel caters largely for older guests and offers cheap breaks for senior citizens. No children under seven. No pets. No smoking in the corridors.

OWNERS G. Wright and J. Brown OPEN All year ROOMS 2 family, 6 double, 1 twin, 2 single; all rooms with wash-basin TERMS B&B from £13 (children 7–12 ⅓ reduction); D, B&B £15; deposit £10 per person

Sunray Private Hotel

42 Knowle Avenue, Blackpool FY2 9TQ
BLACKPOOL (0253) 51937

This attractive guesthouse is of the highest standard. New carpets and furnishings have been installed and the house has been freshly decorated. All of the bedrooms have telephone, radio, hair-dryer and TV. Dinners, served at 5pm, feature home-style cooking and fresh produce. Vegetarians can be catered for by prior arrangement. The proprietors Jean and John Dodgson will keep an eye on the children if their parents wish to eat out in the evening. Children welcome. Pets by arrangement. Car park.

OWNERS Jean and John Dodgson OPEN All year, exc Christmas and New Year ROOMS 2 family, 2 double, 2 twin, 3 single; all rooms with bath/shower TERMS B&B £22–£28 (children half-price sharing with parents); D, B&B £31–£39; dinner £10; deposit; Access, Visa

BOWNESS-ON-WINDERMERE Cumbria map 9

Fairfield Country House Hotel

Brantfell Road, Bowness-on-Windermere LA23 3AE
WINDERMERE (053 94) 46565

Fairfield is a small country-house hotel with half an acre of secluded gardens full of rhododendrons and azaleas. Guests may sit out at the tables and chairs in the garden. Breakfast only is served and includes the famous spicy Cumberland sausage. Vegetarians can also be catered for. Log fires blaze on chilly nights, and guests can enjoy a drink from the bar in a cosy atmosphere. There are three ground-floor rooms; all rooms have TV and private bathroom. Self-catering units are also available. Children welcome. Pets by arrangement.

OWNERS Beryl Bush and Lynne Bush OPEN All year, exc Christmas ROOMS 3 family, 4 double, 1 twin; all rooms with bath/shower TERMS B&B £24–£27, (single occupancy of twin/double) £34–£37 (children half-price sharing parents' room); deposit £30 per room; Access, Visa

The description for each entry states when pets are not allowed or restricted in any way.

If a deposit is required for an advance booking this is stated at the end of an entry.

Storrs Gate House

Longtail Hill, Bowness-on-Windermere LA23 3JD
WINDERMERE (053 94) 43272

Built of local stone over 100 years ago, Storrs Gate House is an elegant country residence standing in two acres of secluded gardens. It is 200 yards from the marina and lake. The rooms have been tastefully modernised and are prettily decorated with soft, restful colours and traditional furnishings. Breakfast and dinner (7pm) are served in the dining-room. Vegetarians can be catered for if prior notice is given. There is an alcohol licence. Packed lunches can be arranged. Coffee may be enjoyed in the sitting-room, which has an open coal fire, TV and video. Saturday night only bookings are not accepted. Children welcome. No pets.

OWNERS Les and Margaret Finch OPEN All year ROOMS 2 family (1 with bath/shower, 1 with wash-basin), 2 twin (with bath/shower), 1 single (with wash-basin) TERMS B&B £18–£24, (single occupancy of twin) £30 (children half-price); D, B&B £27–£30; dinner £10; deposit

BRACEWELL Lancashire map 7

New House Farm

Bracewell, nr Skipton BD23 3JU
BARNOLDSWICK (0282) 813026

New House Farm is situated two miles from Gisburn on the B6251. The stone-built farmhouse dates from the 1600s and has beamed rooms and an inglenook fireplace. The rooms are spacious and tastefully decorated, with comfortable beds. Guests are welcome to explore the 222-acre farm with its dairy and beef herds and flocks of sheep. The small village of Bracewell is midway between Skipton and Clitheroe. It is a peaceful base from which to tour the Dales and Brontë country. Breakfast and packed lunches are available and vegetarians can be catered for. Children welcome. No pets.

OWNER Mrs Sheila Mattinson OPEN All year, exc Christmas ROOMS 2 double, 1 twin; all rooms with wash-basin TERMS B&B £12.50 (babies free, children up to 8 £5, 8–13 £7)

If there are any bedrooms with TV and/or telephone we mention this in the entry.

Where we know of any particular payment stipulations we mention them in the details. It is always best to check, however, when booking.

BURNESIDE Cumbria map 9

Garnett House Farm

Burneside, near Kendal LA9 5SF
KENDAL (0539) 724542

Guests continue to enjoy visiting Garnett House Farm, an attractive fifteenth-century farmhouse on a 270-acre mixed farm. Although it appears deceptively small from the outside, inside it is quite spacious, with oak panelling, beams, and four-feet-thick walls. Full breakfasts are served in the dining-room, as are the evening meals (6.30pm) of farmhouse fare. Guests may bring their own wine to dinner. Children are free (under supervision) to enjoy the farm activities. Reductions for children. No pets. Car park.

OWNER Mrs S. Beaty OPEN All year, exc Christmas and New Year ROOMS 2 family, 2 double; all rooms with wash-basin TERMS B&B £12–£13, (family room) £38–£42; dinner £6; deposit

CARLISLE Cumbria map 9

Howard House

27 Howard Place, Carlisle CA1 1HR
CARLISLE (0228) 29159

Situated in a quiet residential area, Howard House is a 120-year-old property. The bedrooms are well appointed, one retaining its original fireplace; all have TV. One of the bedrooms has a four-poster bed, and two bedrooms now have *en suite* facilities. Dinner is served at 6.30pm and vegetarians can be catered for. There is no alcohol licence, but guests may bring their own wine to dinner. Packed lunches can be arranged. Mr Fisher is a former president of a local genealogical society and is happy to share his knowledge and assist guests with their own research, time permitting, and also help guests plan sightseeing itineraries. There is a very comfortable lounge with TV. Children welcome. Pets by arrangement. No smoking in the dining-room.

OWNERS Lawrence and Sandra Fisher OPEN All year, exc Christmas and New Year ROOMS 2 family (with wash-basin), 1 four-poster (with bath/shower), 1 twin (with bath/shower), 1 single (with wash-basin) TERMS B&B £12–£16, (family room) £36, (single) £13, (single occupancy of twin/double) £18–£20; dinner £6

Most B&Bs offer tea/coffee-making facilities in the bedrooms.

Ivy House

101 Warwick Road, Carlisle CA1 1EA
CARLISLE (0228) 30432

This beautiful, ivy-clad late-Georgian house is just a five-minute walk from the town centre. The spacious rooms are well appointed and tastefully furnished; one has a brass bed and all have TV. Substantial breakfasts are served 'family-style' in the attractive dining-room. Mr and Mrs Shaw are friendly, and happy to give advice and to recommend places for evening meals. No children under five. No dogs.

OWNERS Mr and Mrs P. G. Shaw OPEN All year, exc Christmas
ROOMS 2 double (1 with bath/shower, 1 with wash-basin), 1 twin (with wash-basin) TERMS B&B £14–£16; deposit £5

CARNFORTH Lancashire map 7

Thwaite End Farm

Carnforth, Bolton-le-Sands LA5 9TN
CARNFORTH (0524) 732551

Thwaite End Farm is a beamed, seventeenth-century farmhouse with a warm and comfortable atmosphere, on a small beef and sheep farm. The dining-room has Queen Anne-style furnishings, window seats and an original sandstone fireplace. Guests have use of a sitting-room, television lounge and furnished patio. Displayed on the landing is a beautiful, carved antique settle. All bedrooms have TV. Breakfast only is served. There are several pubs for evening meals close by. No children. No pets. No smoking in bedrooms and the dining-room.

OWNERS G. and A. Ireland OPEN All year, exc Christmas
ROOMS 2 double (1 with bath/shower, 1 with wash-basin), 1 twin (with bath/shower), 1 single (with wash-basin) TERMS B&B £16–£20

CHESWICK Northumberland map 10

Ladythorne House

Cheswick, nr Berwick-upon-Tweed TD15 2RW
BERWICK-UPON-TWEED (0289) 87382

Built in 1721, Ladythorne House is a listed building, approached from a tree-lined drive and set in beautiful countryside. The house was virtually derelict when purchased in 1981 and restoration was completed in 1986. It retains the original beams in the dining-room, an inglenook fireplace, stairwell and ceiling rose. The bedrooms are spacious and individually heated. There are two lounges, one is non-smoking, one has a TV. There is an informal, friendly atmosphere and the house is ideally located, being midway between Berwick and Lindisfarne: a good base for walkers or bird-watchers. Children welcome. Smoking allowed in the smoking room only. Car park.

OWNER Mrs V. Parker OPEN All year ROOMS 2 family, 1 double, 2 twin, 1 single; 4 rooms with wash-basin TERMS B&B £12 (children under 2 free, under 5 £2, under 10 £6); deposit £10

CHIPPING Lancashire map 7

Carrside Farm

Chipping PR3 2TS
CHIPPING (0995) 61590

Carrside Farm is a family-run dairy farm, two miles from the charming village of Chipping. The house is attractively decorated; there is a beamed guest lounge with open fire, TV and video. A substantial breakfast is served in the dining-room, which overlooks the countryside. Two of the bedrooms have *en suite* shower facilities; one has TV. The house has a peaceful atmosphere. The farm is a little tricky to find, so telephone for directions. Children welcome. Pets by arrangement. No smoking in bedrooms.

OWNER Janet Cowgill OPEN All year ROOMS 2 double (with shower), 1 twin TERMS B&B £13–£15, (family room) £32 (children under 7 £7, under 12 £10); deposit £5 per person

CLITHEROE Lancashire map 7

Brooklyn Guest House

32 Pimlico Road, Clitheroe BB7 2AH
CLITHEROE (0200) 28268

Flower-filled baskets and window boxes decorate this welcoming detached Victorian town house. All the bedrooms are bright and spotlessly clean and have TV. There are several antique pieces in the house, including an original hall stand. This is a comfortable house with an informal atmosphere. There are four beautifully decorated annexe rooms, one of which is on the ground floor. Guests in the annexe have their own lounge, although meals are taken in the main house. Evening meals are served 6.30–7.30pm, and vegetarians can be catered for. There is a table licence. Packed lunches can be provided. The nearby 800-year-old Norman castle and keep are well worth a visit. Children welcome. No pets. No smoking in the dining-room.

OWNERS Colin and Elizabeth Underwood OPEN All year, exc Christmas ROOMS 5 twin (4 with bath/shower, 1 with wash-basin), 3 single (2 with bath/shower, 1 with wash-basin) TERMS B&B £17–£19, (single occupancy of twin) £20–£21; dinner £9.50; deposit; Access, Visa

CONISTON Cumbria map 9

Beech Tree

Yewdale Road, Coniston LA21 8DB
CONISTON (053 94) 41717

This comfortable, characterful property, formerly the vicarage, stands in its own grounds at the foot of the Old Man of Coniston. The house dates back to 1720, the east wing was added in 1842. There are several antique pieces, including a grandfather clock in the dining-room and marble wash-stand in the hallway. The rooms are comfortably furnished and are fresh and bright. Guests often join Jean and John Watts in their family lounge for a game of scrabble. This is a vegetarian establishment; both breakfast and dinner (6.30–7.30pm) comprise exclusively vegetarian choices. Evening meals include dishes such as spinach soufflé, red bean moussaka and mushroom croustade. A minimum stay of two nights is required. Children up to six months and six years and over welcome. Pets by arrangement. No smoking. Car park.

OWNERS Jean and John Watts OPEN All year ROOMS 1 family (with wash-basin), 3 double (1 with bath/shower), 2 twin (1 with bath/shower) TERMS B&B £14–£18, (single occupancy of twin/double) £22–£30 (children under 8 £10 sharing parents' room); dinner £8.50; deposit

Townson Ground

East of Coniston Water, Coniston LA21 8AA
CONISTON (053 94) 41272

Townson Ground is a 400-year-old country house on the eastern side of Coniston Water. From Coniston village take the

Hawkshead road to the head of the lake, turn right on to the road marked 'Brantwood, East of Lake' and the house is the first residence on the left. Tastefully refurbished, the rooms are decorated in soft, pastel shades, and all but the singles have *en suite* facilities. Breakfast and dinner (6.30pm) must be taken; vegetarians can be catered for with prior notice. There is a brief wine list. A wood-burning stove heats the comfortable guest lounge. Home-made scones and tea are served at no extra charge. Laundry facilities are available. There are several charming self-catering units available. Children over three years welcome. Pets by arrangement. No smoking in the dining-room. Car park.

OWNERS Mr and Mrs Nelson OPEN mid-Jan–mid-Nov ROOMS 2 family, 1 double, 1 twin, 2 single; all rooms, exc singles (wash-basin only), with bath/shower TERMS B&B £18–£20 (children under 11 half-price, 11–15 two-thirds-price sharing parents' room); dinner £9.50; deposit £30–£50 per room

CORBRIDGE Northumberland map 10

Clive House

Appletree Lane, Corbridge NE45 5DN
HEXHAM (0434) 632617

This lovely stone house was built in 1840 for the headmaster of Corbridge Church of England School and stands in a large garden with a terrace. It is in a quiet position, down a lane (no thoroughfare), in the centre of the village. All the bedrooms are named after butterflies: Tortoiseshell, Swallowtail and Holly Blue. One of the rooms has a four-poster with a lace canopy. All of the rooms are *en suite* and have TV, telephone and radio. Breakfast is served in a beamed, galleried room with a log fire. There are antique furnishings, plenty of fresh flowers and even sweets provided for guests. Packed lunches can be provided. There are several eating-places within a five-minute walk. No children under 12. No pets. No smoking in bedrooms. Car park.

OWNER Mrs Edith Clarke OPEN All year ROOMS 1 four-poster, 1 double, 1 twin; all rooms with bath/shower TERMS B&B £18–£20, (single occupancy of twin/double) £28–£30; Access, Visa

If you are forced to turn up late into the evening, please telephone to warn the proprietor.

If you intend to spend several days at a B&B, it is worth asking whether there are reduced rates, particularly if the period is midweek or off-season.

Low Barns

Thornborough, nr Corbridge NE45 5LX
HEXHAM (0434) 632408

Low Barns is a beautiful barn conversion which was completed in 1984. It is situated in open countryside, just off the B6530, east of Corbridge. The rooms are beamed, with exposed stone walls, and exquisitely decorated with matching prints and fabrics. All rooms have armchairs, hair-dryers, radio, TV and electric blankets. There is one ground-floor room, with bathroom, that has private access from the outside. Tom and Sue Jones are superb hosts and have retained an olde worlde atmosphere in their charming home. Evening meals are available at 7pm, using home-grown vegetables and local farmhouse butter and eggs. There is no alcohol licence, but guests may bring their own wine to dinner. Low Barns is an excellent base from which to walk Hadrian's Wall and for exploring the many places of interest in Corbridge. Children welcome. No smoking in the dining-room. Car park.

OWNERS Tom and Sue Jones OPEN All year ROOMS 1 double/ family, 2 twin; all rooms with bath/shower TERMS B&B £19, (single occupancy of twin/double) £30, (family room) £48 for 2 adults and 1 child; dinner £12.50; Access, Visa

COXWOLD North Yorkshire map 7

School House

Coxwold YO6 4AD
COXWOLD (034 76) 356

This seventeenth-century cottage of considerable charm is situated in the picturesque village of Coxwold. There are tubs full of flowers and roses around the door. The bedrooms are well appointed with period-style furnishings, two have bathrooms, one with a most attractive coronet. All have TV. Imaginative home-cooked evening meals are served at 7pm and vegetarians can be catered for. There is no licence, but guests may bring their own wine to dinner. Laurence Sterne's house, Shandy Hall, is in the village and open to visitors in the summer. Children welcome. Pets by arrangement. No smoking in the dining-room. Car park.

OWNERS J. and J. Richardson OPEN All year, exc Christmas and New Year ROOMS 1 family, 1 double, 1 twin; all rooms with wash-basin TERMS B&B £14–£16 (children under 10 half-price sharing); dinner £8; deposit

CROOKHAM Northumberland map 10

The Coach House

Crookham, Cornhill on Tweed TD12 4TD
CROOKHAM (089 082) 293

The original forge has been retained, the beams left and, inside, the house has been simply whitewashed and decorated with china, pottery and pictures. What used to be the smithy is now the dining-room. The unusually large lounge, with a big open fireplace at one end, was formerly the coach-house; the original openings are now filled with windows, and the pointed, barn-style roof with its rafters has been left open, giving the room a feeling of light and space. The bedrooms, also large and light, were converted from stables and outbuildings. Some of the bedrooms have windows overlooking the terrace where barbeques take place weekly in summer. Four-course dinners (served at 7.30pm) are a major feature of a stay at the Coach House and there is a wide choice at breakfast, too. There is an alcohol licence. Vegetarian dishes can be provided and afternoon teas are also served. There is a TV lounge, a snooker room and a table tennis room. There are five ground-floor rooms suitable for the disabled. The bathrooms have been adapted for the wheelchair-bound traveller and one has a roll-in shower with plastic wheelchair. Children welcome. Pets by arrangement. No smoking in the dining-room. Car park.

OWNERS Lynne and Jamie Anderson OPEN Mar–Nov, Christmas and New Year ROOMS 2 double (1 with bath/shower), 5 twin (4 with bath/shower, 1 with wash-basin), 2 single (with bath/shower) TERMS B&B £19–£30 (children under 2 free, 2–10 reductions); £2 supplement for single night; dinner £12.50; minimum £5 deposit; Access, Visa

DARLINGTON Co Durham map 10

Woodland Guest House

63 Woodland Road, Darlington DL3 7BQ
DARLINGTON (0325) 461908

This pleasant, family-run Victorian house is near the centre of the historic market town of Darlington. There are many original features remaining – stained-glass windows, marble fireplaces and entrance tiles. There is a lovely oak staircase with an attractive plate display. Guests may use the kitchen to prepare light snacks and tea and coffee. Mrs Hawke has built up a reputation for good-value accommodation. Breakfast only is served. Children welcome. Pets by arrangement.

OWNERS P. R. and M. Hawke OPEN All year ROOMS 2 family (with wash-basin), 1 double (with wash-basin), 2 twin (1 with bath/shower, 1 with wash-basin), 3 single (with wash-basin) TERMS B&B £14–£17, (single occupancy of twin/double) £16–£26 (children half-price if sharing family room)

DENT Cumbria map 10

Stone Close

Main Street, Dent LA10 5QL
DENT (058 75) 231

Situated in the picturesque village of Dent, Stone Close is a seventeenth-century house with exposed beams, flagged floors and open fires in two original cast-iron ranges. There are three comfortable, pleasantly furnished bedrooms. The tea-shop on the ground floor is open throughout the day for home-baked cakes and tasty snacks. In the evening the licensed restaurant (7.30pm) offers a selection of freshly prepared meals using local produce. Lunches and packed lunches are provided and vegetarians are catered for. Children welcome; reductions for small evening meals. Pets by arrangement. No smoking in bedrooms and during meals.

OWNERS Graham Hudson and Patricia Barber OPEN All year, exc Jan–mid-Feb ROOMS 1 family, 1 double, 1 single; all rooms with wash-basin TERMS B&B £13.50, (single) £15.50, (single occupancy of double) £15.50, (family room) £32; dinner £10.50; deposit £10

DONCASTER South Yorkshire map 7

Earlesmere Guest House

84 Thorne Road, Doncaster DN2 5BL
DONCASTER (0302) 368532

Earlesmere House, built in 1900, is a spotless family-run guesthouse, one mile from the town centre. The top floor is an ideal family room, with an adjoining bedroom and its own bathroom. The dining-room is spacious and bright with an organ which accomplished guests are welcome to play. There is no guest lounge, but all the bedrooms have TV and there is a small reading area in the foyer. Breakfast only is served and packed lunches can be provided. Children welcome. Pets by arrangement. Car park.

OWNERS Mr and Mrs P. Barnes OPEN All year, exc Christmas ROOMS 2 family, 1 double (with bath/shower), 2 twin; all rooms with wash-basin TERMS B&B £12–£15, (singe occupancy of twin/double) £15–£20 (children under 2 free, over 2 half-price)

DURHAM Co Durham map 10

Colebrick

21 Crossgate, Durham DH1 4PS
DURHAM 091-384 9585

Colebrick is a lovely Georgian house in the centre of Durham. The bedrooms, both on the ground floor, are beautifully appointed and furnished with antiques, and have TV and radio. The comfortable guest lounge, which is on the first floor, has magnificent views of the cathedral and the castle. There is a small balcony off the lounge where guests may sit and enjoy the view. Breakfast is a feast and the presentation is superb. Dinner is not available, but there are several excellent places for meals within walking distance. No children under four. No pets. No smoking. Car park.

OWNERS Mr and Mrs J. R. Mellanby OPEN All year ROOMS 2 double (with wash-basin) TERMS B&B £19, (single occupancy of double) £25 (reductions for children sharing parents' room); deposit

The Georgian Town House

10 Crossgate, Durham DH1 4DS
DURHAM 091-386 8070

Views of the castle and cathedral can be enjoyed from this listed, eighteenth-century terraced house in the centre of the city. The rooms, all with TV, are extremely attractive, and furnished in traditional style. There is also a guest lounge with TV. No fried breakfasts are served here; instead, food is grilled and there are low-sugar preserves for the health-conscious. Children welcome. No pets. Smoking in the guest lounge only.

OWNER Mrs J. A. Weil OPEN All year, exc Christmas–end Jan ROOMS 1 family, 2 double, 3 twin; all rooms with bath/shower TERMS B&B £20–£22.50, (single occupancy of twin/double) £35–£40, (family room) £50 (children under 6 half-price); deposit £10 per night

EASINGWOLD North Yorkshire map 7

The Old Vicarage

Market Place, Easingwold YO6 3AL
EASINGWOLD (0347) 21015

This eighteenth-century listed Georgian country house has extensive lawned gardens, with a croquet lawn and walled rose garden. The house was used as a vicarage until the beginning of this century. The bedrooms are comfortable and there is a spacious TV lounge, as well as a quiet room for guests wishing to read or relax. There are french doors leading from the lounge into the lovely gardens. A three-course evening meal is served at 6.30pm with a selection of wines. Packed lunches can be provided and vegetarians are catered for on request. Children welcome. Car park.

OWNERS Joan and Geoffrey Broad OPEN Apr–Oct
ROOMS 1 family, 2 double, 2 twin, 2 single; all rooms with bath/shower TERMS B&B £17.50, (single) £19; dinner £6.50; deposit £10

EAST WITTON North Yorkshire map 10

The Holly Tree

East Witton, nr Leyburn DL8 4LS
WENSLEYDALE (0969) 22383

This whitewashed, wistaria-covered, listed sixteenth-century house is reputedly one of the oldest houses in the Dales. It has been tastefully restored, combining modern amenities with olde worlde charm. The beamed bedrooms are prettily decorated, some with Laura Ashley wallpaper. There are additional bedrooms in the converted barn, ideal for guests looking for privacy. Dinners are served at 7.30pm (pre-dinner sherry at 7.15pm), using only the finest of ingredients prepared by Andrea Robson. A typical menu might include broccoli and almond soup, followed by local pheasant and venison pie with red wine and juniper sauce, with a choice of sweets, cheeseboard and coffee. Vegetarian choices can be provided with prior notice. There is a wine list. Early reservations are recommended. No children under 10. No pets. No smoking. Car park.

OWNERS Keith and Andrea Robson OPEN Easter–end Oct (throughout winter for groups of 6–8) ROOMS 2 double, 2 twin; all rooms with bath/shower TERMS B&B £18–£20; dinner £10; deposit £10

EDENHALL Cumbria map 10

The Old Vicarage

Edenhall, nr Penrith CA11 8SX
PENRITH (0768) 881329

Edenhall is situated in the unspoilt Eden Valley. The Old Vicarage is a charming Georgian house, with Victorian additions, set in a three-quarter-acre garden. Breakfast is served in the dining-room/lounge, overlooking the garden, which has an antique chaise-longue and a stone fireplace. Breakfast only is served, but there is an inn and restaurant one and a half miles away. Children welcome. Pets by arrangement. No smoking in bedrooms. Car park.

OWNER Mrs Grace McDonnell OPEN All year, exc Christmas
ROOMS 1 double/family, 1 twin; both rooms with bath/shower
TERMS B&B £15, (single occupancy of twin/double) £17 (children under 3 free, under 11 half-price)

EGLINGHAM Northumberland map 10

Ogle Guest House

Eglingham, nr Alnwick NE66 2TZ
POWBURN (066 578) 264

Once a coaching-inn, this listed eighteenth-century house built of slate and stone was totally derelict when purchased by the present owners, but has since been tastefully modernised. The pretty bedrooms are all on the first floor. The floors slope and creak and the house has a warm and friendly atmosphere. There is a cosy guest lounge with an open fire, and a conservatory where morning coffee or afternoon teas may be taken. Mrs McRoberts is noted for her cuisine. Dinner is served (7–9pm) and vegetarians are catered for. There is a licence and guests may enjoy a drink with dinner. There are several golf courses close by, and this is an ideal spot for ornithologists and walkers. Children welcome. Pets by arrangement. Car park.

OWNER Carol Ann McRoberts OPEN 1 Feb–20 Dec
ROOMS 1 family, 1 double, 1 twin; all rooms with bath/shower
TERMS B&B £17.50, (single occupancy of twin/double) £21.50, (children under 5 free, 6–10 half-price, 11–14 two-thirds-price); deposit

If we know a B&Bs has an alcohol licence, we say so.

FORD Northumberland map 10

The Estate House

Ford, nr Berwick-upon-Tweed TD15 2QE
CROOKHAM (089 082) 297

This spacious Victorian country house in the tranquil village of Ford has a large, pretty garden. Guests have private access to the castle, which is situated just beyond the garden. The large rooms are comfortable and the house has a peaceful atmosphere. There is a guest lounge with TV and a games-room. Mr Bradley is the manager of the Heatherslow Corn Mill, where guests may watch flour being milled. Mrs Bradley prepares superb home-cooked meals; typical dishes might include Eyemouth sole with loganberries or Cheviot lamb. There is no alcohol licence, but guests may bring their own wine to dinner. Home-made preserves, bread and muesli using local wheat are available at breakfast. Vegetarians can be catered for with prior notice. Open fires are lit on chilly evenings. Mrs Bradley also runs an interesting craft shop on the premises. Unsuitable for children under five. No pets. No smoking. Car park.

OWNERS Judith and John Bradley OPEN Apr–Oct ROOMS 2 twin (with wash-basin) TERMS B&B £14 (children under 12 £7.50); dinner £7; deposit £5 per person; £2 per person supplement for 1 night stay July/Aug

FYLINGTHORPE North Yorkshire map 10

Croft Farm

Fylingthorpe, nr Whitby YO22 4PW
WHITBY (0947) 880231

On the edge of the village of Fylingthorpe, the attractive farmhouse stands in a lawned garden with wonderful views over the old smuggling village of Robin Hood's Bay, the sea and moors. The eighteenth-century building was modernised a few years ago, but most of the old features remain, such as the Adam-style fireplace in the lounge and the open brick fireplace in the dining-room. Tea and coffee are available on request. The house has a cosy atmosphere. Good home-cooked breakfasts with fresh farm eggs and milk are served, and there is a wide choice of places for evening meals in the village. There is a guest lounge with TV.

No children under five. No pets. No smoking in bedrooms. Part central heating. A self-contained cottage is available. Car park.

OWNER Mrs P. M. Featherstone OPEN Easter–mid-Oct ROOMS 1 family, 1 double, 1 single TERMS B&B £14–£16, (single occupancy of twin/double) £15–£17, (family room) £40–£46 (£2 reduction for children sharing with parents); deposit; £1 supplement for 1 night stay

GARSTANG Lancashire map 7

Greenhalgh Castle Farm

Castle Lane, Garstang PR3 1RB
GARSTANG (0995) 602140

The house is overlooked by the ruins of Greenhalgh Castle, built in 1490 and a stronghold in the Civil War. It was partly dismantled in 1645, and the stones and timbers used to build the farmhouse. The 150-acre farm is mostly dairy, with a small flock of sheep (some fleeces are kept for hand spinning), plus horses, hens and ducks. The house has a lovely old staircase, many original doors and beams, exposed stone walls and mullioned windows. The downstairs shower-room was originally an old pantry used to salt pigs. The rooms are individually heated; one of the bedrooms has a Queen Anne bed. Garstang, only a few minutes' drive away, has a market every Thursday. Breakfast only is served. Children welcome. No pets. No smoking preferred. Car park.

OWNERS Jean and Bill Fowler OPEN Easter–Oct ROOMS 2 double, 1 twin; all rooms with wash-basin TERMS B&B £14–£15, (single occupancy of twin/double) £18–£28 (reductions for children under 12); deposit

GOATHLAND North Yorkshire map 10

Heatherdene Hotel

Goathland, nr Whitby YO22 5AN
WHITBY (0947) 86334

Built in 1899, this ivy-covered stone building was a vicarage until carefully converted to a family-run hotel. It stands in its own grounds surrounded by an expanse of open moorland. The furniture is in traditional style, maintaining the atmosphere of the house. The bedrooms are large, immaculate and comfortable.

There is a licensed bar as well as a lounge, which has a fire on chilly days. There is also a sauna for guests' use. Evening meals are served at 7pm, and offer traditional, home-style cooking. Vegetarians can be catered for. This is a good base for exploring the North Yorkshire Moors and coast. Children welcome. No pets. No smoking in the dining-room. Car park.

OWNER Mr J. Pearson-Smith OPEN Easter–end Oct
ROOMS 3 family (with bath/shower), 1 double (with wash-basin), 2 twin (1 with bath/shower, 1 with wash-basin), 1 single (with wash-basin)
TERMS B&B £15.50–£19.50, (single occupancy of twin/double) £21–£25.50

GRANGE-OVER-SANDS Cumbria map 7

Somerset House

Kents Bank Road, Grange-over-Sands LA11 7EY
GRANGE-OVER-SANDS (053 95) 32631

Somerset House offers spacious accommodation and good food. The 100-year-old property is within three minutes' walk of the promenade and shops, with views over the Kent estuary. Four of the comfortable bedrooms have shower cubicles and all have TV. There are two lounges for guests, one with a TV and a small bar/lounge. Dinner is served at 6.30pm and vegetarian choices can be provided. The house has an alcohol licence. Packed lunches can be provided. There is partial central heating and all the beds have electric blankets. Children welcome. Pets by arrangement. Smoking in the lounge/bar only. Parking permits are available for the nearby car park.

OWNERS Miss Elizabeth O'Neill and Mrs Rose Marie Wilkinson
OPEN All year ROOMS 4 family (with bath/shower), 2 double (with wash-basin), 1 twin (with wash-basin), 1 single (with wash-basin)
TERMS B&B £16, (single) £18, (single occupancy of twin/double) £22 (children half-price under 12 sharing with parents); dinner £7; deposit

Thornfield House

Kents Bank Road, Grange-over-Sands LA11 7DT
GRANGE-OVER-SANDS (053 95) 32512

Thornfield House is a pleasant Victorian property in an excellent location close to the promenade and town centre. The immaculate bedrooms are individually decorated in soft, restful colours and have comfortable beds; all rooms have TV. Breakfast is served in the bright dining-room overlooking Morecambe Bay. There is a quiet lounge where guests can relax, read or chat. Mr Irving is an avid golfer and would be happy to arrange golf for visitors. Evening meals are served at 7pm and vegetarian dishes can be provided. Guests may bring their own wine to dinner. Packed lunches can be arranged. No children under five. No pets. Car park.

OWNERS Moray and Margaret Irving OPEN All year, exc Christmas
ROOMS 1 family, 2 double, 2 twin, 1 single; all rooms with wash-basin
TERMS B&B £13–£14.50 (children under 10 half-price sharing parents' room); dinner £6; deposit £5 per person

GRASMERE Cumbria map 9

Rothay Lodge Guest House

Grasmere LA22 9RH
GRASMERE (053 94) 35341

Rothay Lodge is a traditional nineteenth-century Lakeland house, situated in spacious gardens which bridge the gurgling Greenhead Ghyll. The house has magnificent views of the river and surrounding fells, including the Fairfield Ridge, Butharlip How and Helm Crag. The attractive bedrooms are all individually decorated and have TV. Breakfast only is served, but there is a portfolio of local restaurants for guests. Smoking is allowed in the guest lounge only. No children under eight. No pets. No smoking. Car park.

OWNERS Mr and Mrs W. Allan OPEN mid-Feb–end Oct
ROOMS 1 family, 3 double, 2 twin; all rooms with bath/shower, exc 1 double and 1 twin TERMS B&B £16.50–£20.50 (children under 10 half-price sharing); deposit £20 per person

Titteringdales Guest House

Pye Lane, Grasmere LA22 9RQ
GRASMERE (053 94) 35439

Titteringdales is situated in a quiet position, close to the centre of Grasmere, in two acres of lawned garden. The small, cosy lounge with red velvet furnishings has an open fire, which is lit on chilly days. All the bedrooms and public rooms have views of the beautiful surrounding fells, including Silver Howe and Helm Crag. All bedrooms have TV and easy chairs. Dinner is served at

6.30pm; there is an alcohol licence. No children under 10. No pets. Car park.

OWNERS Colin and Deborah Scott OPEN All year, exc Dec and Jan ROOMS 5 double (4 with bath/shower, 1 with wash-basin), 1 twin (with bath/shower) TERMS B&B £15–£20, (single occupancy of twin/double) £20–£27.50; D, B&B £23–£29; deposit £30; Visa

HALTWHISTLE Northumberland map 10

White Craig Farm

Shield Hill, Haltwhistle NE49 9NW
HALTWHISTLE (0434) 320565

Mrs Laidlow has been welcoming guests to her interesting seventeenth-century croft-style property for almost 30 years. It is perched high on the hillside above Haltwhistle, overlooking the South Tyne Valley and the fells beyond. Hadrian's Wall is close by. The farmhouse, with its beamed lounge, has a welcoming atmosphere. There are prizewinning Blue Faced Leicester sheep and rare English Longhorn cattle, along with working sheep-dogs, cats and poultry. The bedrooms, all on the ground floor, are small and comfortable, with electric blankets and TV. Guests are welcome to attend free weekly demonstrations of various crafts, such as spinning and mat-making. Breakfast only is served. Self-catering cottages are available. Children welcome. No pets. No smoking allowed.

OWNER Mrs G. B. B. Laidlow OPEN Mar–Oct ROOMS 2 double, 1 twin; all rooms with bath/shower TERMS B&B £18.50, (single occupancy of twin/double) £24; deposit £10

HARROGATE North Yorkshire map 7

Lynton House

42 Studley Road, Harrogate HG1 5JU
HARROGATE (0423) 504715

This friendly, immaculate guesthouse is on a quiet, tree-lined avenue, within minutes of the exhibition and conference centre and gardens. The well-appointed bedrooms have a supply of toiletries such as shampoo and tissues and all have remote-control TV. There are lovely pictures throughout the house and a very large fish-tank in the dining-room/lounge. Mrs McLoughlin is a friendly lady who keeps a lovely house. Good value in a central location. No children under nine. No smoking.

OWNERS John and Jean McLoughlin OPEN All year, exc Dec–Feb
ROOMS 1 family, 1 double, 1 twin, 2 single; all rooms with wash-basin
TERMS B&B £15–£17, (single occupancy of twin/double) £25 (children £5 deduction sharing parents' room); deposit

HARTBURN Northumberland map 10

The Baker's Chest

Hartburn, Morpeth NE61 4JB
HARTBURN (067 072) 214

This attractive, sandstone cottage has been newly converted, and is situated in the charming village of Hartburn. Guests may enjoy lovely walks through the nearby woods and along the banks of the burn, watch birds and perhaps see deer and red squirrels. This interesting house is furnished with antiques and features a display of miniature cottages, plates and spoons – items collected from various parts of the world by the well-travelled owners. Apart from the rooms in the main house, with a bathroom close by, guests have the option of staying in one of the self-catering cottages. Breakfast only is available. As well as a guest lounge with TV, there is a large lawned garden with croquet, bowls and clock golf. Children welcome. German and French spoken. Pets by arrangement. Car park.

OWNERS Sue and Richard Cansdale OPEN Apr–Oct
ROOMS 1 double, 1 twin TERMS B&B £15, (single occupancy of twin/double) £27; deposit £10

HAVERIGG Cumbria map 7

Dunelm Cottage

Main Street, Haverigg LA18 4EX
ULVERSTON (0229) 770097

Dunelm Cottage started life as two old village properties, which were later joined together as a shop. In January 1990 it was skilfully converted to a cosy whitewashed cottage. The guesthouse is within walking distance of the harbour and the Hodbarrow Nature Reserve. The immaculate bedrooms are small and tastefully furnished, with pretty décor. There are two bathrooms for the three bedrooms. The comfortable guest lounge has TV, and there is a walled garden and small conservatory. Dinners are a feature of the house, imaginatively prepared and presented (6.30pm); vegetarians can be catered for. There is no alcohol licence, but guests may bring their own wine to dinner. No children under 10. Pets by arrangement. No smoking in bedrooms. Private parking in the car park immediately opposite the cottage.

OWNER Julie Fairless OPEN All year, exc Jan ROOMS 1 double, 2 twin; all rooms with wash-basin TERMS B&B £16–£17.50 (children 10% reduction); D, B&B £23.75; dinner £8; deposit £10

HAWES North Yorkshire map 10

Brandymires Guest House

Muker Road, Hawes, Wensleydale DL8 3PR
WENSLEYDALE (0969) 667482

Brandymires is a comfortable three-storey house built in 1850 of local stone, just outside the market town of Hawes. Two of the elegant bedrooms have four-poster beds, and all four have views of Wensleydale. Each room has its own sitting area. It would be a shame to stay here without enjoying the good, imaginative, three-course evening meals cooked by Ann Mcdonald (7pm by prior arrangement; not on Thursdays). A menu might include pheasant casserole or perhaps boiled ham with Cumberland sauce and spiced peaches. Vegetarian dishes can be arranged, with prior notice. There is a licence, and drinks may be enjoyed in the comfortable lounge, which has a grandfather clock and many interesting books. No children under eight. Pets by arrangement. No smoking. Car park.

OWNERS Gail Ainley and Ann Macdonald OPEN Easter–Oct
ROOMS 2 four-poster, 1 double, 1 twin; all rooms with wash-basin
TERMS B&B £15.50, (single occupancy of twin/double) £23.50; dinner £9.50; deposit £15

HAWKSHEAD Cumbria map 9

Greenbank Country House Hotel

Main Street, Hawkshead, nr Ambleside LA22 ONS
HAWKSHEAD (053 94) 36497

Although extensively modernised, this seventeenth-century white-washed house retains its beams and open fireplaces. One of the twin bedrooms is on the ground floor. There are additional rooms available in an adjacent annexe. The guest lounge is large and there is a TV as well as a quiet area. A good choice of dishes is available at breakfast and dinner (6.30pm); fresh produce is used, and the wine list has something to suit most tastes. Vegetarians can be catered for by arrangement. Evening tea with home-made cakes is served at 9.45pm. Guests who enjoy an informal, homely atmosphere are well catered for here. Children welcome. Pets by arrangement. No smoking in the dining-room. Car park.

OWNERS Gordon and Valerie Walsh OPEN All year
ROOMS 1 family (with wash-basin), 5 double (3 with bath/shower, 2 with wash-basin), 3 twin (2 with bath/shower, 1 with wash-basin), 3 single (with wash-basin) TERMS B&B £17.50–£20 (children half-price sharing with adults); dinner £8–£10; deposit

HAWKSHEAD HILL Cumbria map 9

Summer Hill Country House

Hawkshead Hill, nr Hawkshead LA22 0PP
HAWKSHEAD (053 94) 36311

Hawkshead Hill is a hamlet one mile north-west of Hawkshead. Summer Hill Country House was built as a gentleman's country residence in the seventeenth century. It stands in an elevated position overlooking fields and fells. There is a beautiful landscaped front garden, with a Victorian summer-house, where morning coffee and afternoon teas are served. The luxurious bedrooms are decorated in soft pinks and greens; all have TV, hair-dryer and trouser press. The elegant lounge has an open log fire. Breakfast only is served but there are several eating establishments in the area. Packed lunches can be provided. No children under 10. Pets by arrangement. No smoking.

OWNERS Henry and Carol Rogers OPEN All year, exc Christmas
ROOMS 4 double, 1 twin; all rooms with bath/shower TERMS B&B £19–£24 (children 25% reduction); deposit

HAWORTH West Yorkshire map 7

Moorfield Guest House

80 West Lane, Haworth BD22 8EN
HAWORTH (0535) 643689

The footpath across Parson's Fields, used by the Brontës on their way to the waterfall and Top Withens, runs a few yards from this detached Victorian house. All the bedrooms have an electric blanket, TV and hair-dryer. The dining-room opens out on to the terrace, overlooking the garden and the village cricket field. There is a guest lounge, which has a small bar. Evening meals are available, served at 7.15pm (except Tuesdays). Vegetarians are catered for. Children welcome (reductions according to age). No pets. No smoking in bedrooms and the dining-room. Car park.

OWNERS Mr and Mrs B. Hargreaves OPEN All year, exc Christmas ROOMS 1 family, 2 double, 2 twin, 1 single; all rooms with bath/shower, exc 1 double (wash-basin only) TERMS B&B £15–£16, (single occupancy of twin/double) £20, (family room) £40–£50; dinner £8.50; deposit; Access, Visa

HAYDON BRIDGE Northumberland map 10

Geeswood House

Whittis Road, Haydon Bridge NE47 6AQ
HEXHAM (0434) 684220

This immaculate stone-built house is about 150 years old and is set on top of a hill, with glorious views over the gardens and the Tynedale countryside. The house has beautiful landscaped gardens that slope down to Langley Burn, which has a waterfall. Evening meals (served at 7pm) are a speciality of the house and include fresh vegetables, local meat and home-made bread, soups and desserts. There is no alcohol licence, but guests may bring their own wine to dinner. Packed lunches are available and vegetarians can be catered for. The house is comfortably furnished; there is an unusual fireplace in the spacious lounge, and an attractive galleried staircase. No children under 10. Pets by arrangement. No smoking.

OWNERS John and Doreen Easton OPEN All year, exc Christmas ROOMS 1 double, 2 twin; all rooms with wash-basin TERMS B&B £14, (single occupancy of twin/double) £20; dinner £8.50; deposit

HEXHAM Northumberland map 10

Middlemarch

Hencotes, Hexham NE46 2EB
HEXHAM (0434) 605003

This is a spacious, listed Georgian house in the centre of town overlooking the abbey. The house has an interesting history. It started life as a thatched, stone farmhouse and was used as a chapel until the church was built. It was rebuilt about the time of Queen Anne and the back of the house is a Georgian addition. Original features include the flagstone entry and window shutters. The bedrooms are spacious, and all have TV and radio. The quiet lounge is large and there is an abundance of information available on things to do in the area. There are some very interesting antique furnishings throughout the house. Breakfast only is provided but there are several good eating establishments within walking distance. No children under 10. Pets by arrangement. Smoking in the lounge only. Car park.

OWNER Mrs Eileen Elliott OPEN All year ROOMS 1 family (with wash-basin), 1 four-poster (with bath/shower), 1 twin (with wash-basin) TERMS B&B £19, (four-poster) £24, (single occupancy of twin/double) £23 (children 10–12 £15); deposit

West Close House

Hextol Terrace, Hexham NE46 2AD
HEXHAM (0434) 603307

West Close House is a charming detached guesthouse built in 1920, situated in a quiet cul-de-sac. The spacious bedrooms are tastefully furnished with comfortable beds. There is a cosy lounge with TV and an attractive window seat overlooking the garden. There is also a drawing-room where guests may relax and read. Breakfast and dinner (7pm) are available, with the emphasis on wholefoods, imaginatively presented and prepared. Vegetarians are well catered for. There is no alcohol licence, but guests may bring their own wine to dinner. Light suppers are available including Welsh rarebit, sandwiches, home-made scones and cakes. Packed lunches can also be provided. French and Spanish are spoken. No children under two. No smoking in bedrooms. Car park.

OWNER Patricia Graham-Tomlinson OPEN All year
ROOMS 1 family (with wash-basin), 1 double (with bath/shower), 2 single (with wash-basin) TERMS B&B £17–£20.50, (single occupancy of double) £5 supplement (reductions for children under 14); dinner from £3.50 (light snacks), £9 (meal); deposit

Where a single-occupancy rate is not specified in the details, the cost will be the same as that per person in a twin or double room, or will be included in the range of prices given.

Use the maps and indexes at the back of the Guide *to plan your trip.*

HIGH BENTHAM North Yorkshire map 7

New Butts Farm

New Butts Farm, High Bentham, Lancaster LA27 AN
INGLETON (052 42) 41238

Built in 1886, New Butts Farm is a small mixed farm of cattle, sheep and goats. It is a base from which to walk Ingleborough (2,373 feet). The spacious rooms are clean and modestly furnished. The beamed lounge has an open fire; there is also a sitting area in the dining-room. Breakfasts and dinners (7pm, by prior arrangement) are served. Fresh local trout and home-grown produce are offered, when available. Vegetarian choices can be provided and guests may bring their own wine to dinner. There are tea and coffee facilities in the hallway which guests may help themselves to, at no extra charge. This is a cosy and comfortable farmhouse and guests are also welcome to explore the farm. Children welcome. Pets by arrangement. No smoking in the dining-room and small lounge. Car park.

OWNERS Jean and Terry Newhouse OPEN All year ROOMS 2 family (with wash-basin), 2 double (1 with bath/shower, 1 with wash-basin), 1 twin (with wash-basin), 1 single TERMS B&B £11.50, (family room) £30 (children £8.50); dinner £6.50; deposit £10

HOLDEN Lancashire map 7

Bay Gate Farm

Holden, Bolton by Bowland, nr Clitheroe BB7 4PQ
BOLTON BY BOWLAND (020 07) 643

This 130-acre beef and sheep farm is set in glorious countryside. Guests are welcome to look round the farm and if you arrive at lambing time you might have an opportunity to feed one of the baby lambs. This informal farmhouse has three colour-co-ordinated bedrooms: green, pink and blue. Breakfast only is served. A log fire blazes on chilly evenings. There is a lovely rose garden, pretty flower-pots and hanging baskets. The farm is a little tricky to find: telephone for directions. Children welcome. Pets by arrangement.

OWNER Mrs Ethel Townson OPEN All year ROOMS 3 twin
TERMS B&B £11 (children under 12 half-price); deposit

Use the maps and indexes at the back of the Guide *to plan your trip.*

HOLY ISLAND Northumberland map 10

Britannia House

Holy Island, Berwick-upon-Tweed TD15 2RX
BERWICK-UPON-TWEED (0289) 89218

This pretty, 150-year-old cottage is right on the village green next to the evocative ruins of the eleventh-century Benedictine church and monastery. The accommodation is in a separate part of the house, which has its own entrance. There is a guest lounge and a pleasant breakfast-room. During the season, Mrs Patterson runs a tea-room, serving home-made scones. Mr Patterson is a keen golfer and can arrange golfing holidays for small groups. This is a peaceful spot and fires burn brightly in the lounge on most evenings. Packed lunches are available and there are some excellent pubs and eating establishments close by. No pets. No smoking in the dining-room.

OWNERS Mr R. and Mrs P. A. Patterson OPEN Mar–Oct
ROOMS 1 family, 1 double, 1 twin; all rooms with wash-basin
TERMS B&B £12, (single occupancy of twin/double) £15 (children half-price sharing with adults)

HORSLEY Northumberland map 10

Northumbria House

Croft Lane, Horsley, Newcastle-upon-Tyne NE15 0NH
WYLAM (0661) 853172

This attractive house is set at the end of a quiet lane with beautiful views over the surrounding countryside. The rooms are of an average size and are modestly furnished. The cosy guest lounge has TV. There are three acres of grounds. Breakfast and packed lunches are available. There is a pub nearby, which is within easy walking distance and serves food. Just 10 miles from Newcastle, Northumbria House is easily found off the A69. Children welcome. No pets in bedrooms. No smoking in bedrooms. Car park

OWNER Mrs Maureen Edgar OPEN All year, exc Christmas
ROOMS 1 family, 1 twin TERMS B&B from £15 (reductions for children); deposit

When the family-room rate is given in the details it applies to the cost of the whole room, unless a rate per person is specified.

HUDDERSFIELD West Yorkshire map 7

The Mallows

55 Spring Street, Springwood, Huddersfield HD1 4AZ
HUDDERSFIELD (0484) 544684

This elegant, listed Georgian building is on a quiet street within each reach of the town centre. Virtually derelict when purchased two years ago by the present owner, it has been beautifully restored. The exquisite dining-room has an original ceiling rose and cornices; superb breakfasts are served. The two attic rooms, with sloping ceilings, have skylight windows. Children welcome. No dogs. Car park.

OWNER Margaret Chantry OPEN All year, exc Christmas and New Year ROOMS 1 family (with bath/shower), 4 twin (2 with bath/shower, 2 with wash-basin), 1 single (with wash-basin) TERMS B&B £12.50–£17.50, (single) £15, (single occupancy of twin) £19.50–£29.50, (family room) £35 plus £5 for each child under 10

HUTTON-LE-HOLE North Yorkshire map 10

Hammer and Hand Country Guest House

Hutton-le-Hole, nr York YO6 6UA
LASTINGHAM (075 15) 300

Hammer and Hand House stands in a sheltered spot facing the village green and beck. It is a listed Georgian property, built in 1784 as the village beer house in mellow York stone. The house provides accommodation of great character and has many original features such as old stone fireplaces, cruck beams and panelled doors. The three double bedrooms (Hutton Room, Fitzherbert Room and The Snug) are exquisitely furnished – even the showers are beamed. Candle-lit dinners are served at 6.30pm; vegetarians can be catered for with prior notice. There is a wine list. The dining-room overlooks pretty gardens, where local sheep keep the grass trimmed. The lounge has an inglenook fireplace. No children under five. Pets by arrangement. No smoking in bedrooms and the dining-room. Car park.

OWNERS John and Alison Wilkins OPEN All year, exc Christmas ROOMS 2 double, 1 twin; all rooms with bath/shower TERMS B&B £18–£22, (single occupancy of twin/double) £30 (reductions for children); dinner £10; deposit 1 night charge

ILKLEY West Yorkshire map 7

Poplar View Guest House

8 Bolton Bridge Road, Ilkley LS29 9AA
ILKLEY (0943) 608436

This Victorian house, five minutes from the centre, is an immaculate property. The bedrooms are tastefully decorated with matching wallpaper and curtains. During the summer the 40 or so hanging baskets are full of flowers. The house is half a mile from Ilkley Moor and a quarter of a mile from the 73-mile 'Dales to Windermere' walk. Children welcome. Pets by arrangement. No smoking in the dining-room preferred.

OWNER Mrs Y. O'Neill OPEN All year ROOMS 1 family, 1 double, 1 twin; all rooms with wash-basin TERMS B&B £14, (single occupancy of twin/double) £18 (half-price for children sharing with adults)

Summerhill Guest House

24 Crossbeck Road, Ilkley LS29 9JN
ILKLEY (0943) 607067

A Victorian house dating from 1865, set back from the road in a quiet location on the edge of Ilkley Moor. There are many original features in the house, including the beautiful ceiling rose in the lounge and the marble fireplace. There is a piano in the dining-room, which guests are welcome to play, and a lovely grandfather clock. Guests may also help themselves to tea and coffee from a trolley in the dining-room. Traditional dinners are served at 6.30pm; vegetarians can be catered for and packed lunches are available. There is no alcohol licence, but guests may bring their own wine to dinner. Mr and Mrs Voss are happy to assist guests with information on sightseeing. Children welcome. Pets by arrangement. No smoking in the dining-room. Car park.

OWNERS Mr and Mrs R. A. Voss OPEN All year, exc Christmas ROOMS 1 double, 5 twin (2 with bath/shower), 1 single; all rooms with wash-basin TERMS B&B £12–£14 (children under 12 half-price); dinner £6; deposit

Breakfast at B&Bs tends to mean a cooked breakfast of bacon, eggs and so on. If you prefer a different style of breakfast, discuss this when you make the booking.

Most B&Bs offer tea/coffee-making facilities in the bedrooms.

KENDAL Cumbria map 9

Brantholme

7 Sedbergh Road, Kendal LA9 6AD
KENDAL (0539) 722340

This lovely Victorian house is set in three-quarters of an acre of secluded wooded gardens. The entrance to the house is through an arched doorway, which leads to the conservatory and into the octagonal hall with its beautiful pine staircase. The spacious bedrooms all have private bathroom and are traditionally furnished. There is a large and comfortable guest lounge with TV. Evening meals are served (6.30pm), featuring fresh local produce. There is no alcohol licence, but guests may bring their own wine to dinner. Vegetarian choices can be provided. Breakfast includes home-made preserves. Packed lunches are available. Children welcome. No pets. No smoking in the dining-room. Car park.

OWNER Cathryn Bigland OPEN Mar–Oct; Nov and Feb by prior arrangement ROOMS 3 twin (with bath/shower) TERMS B&B £15–£17, (single occupancy of twin) £21–£23, (reductions for children); dinner £5.50; deposit £20 per person

Hillside Guest House

4 Beast Banks, Kendal LA9 4JW
KENDAL (0539) 722836

Close to the town centre, this Victorian terraced home has been converted into a comfortable guesthouse. The bedrooms all have TV. Excellent breakfasts are served in the dining-room. There is also a guest lounge with TV. No pets. No smoking in the dining-room.

OWNERS Mr and Mrs Denison OPEN All year, exc 2 months in winter ROOMS 3 double (2 with bath/shower), 1 twin (with bath/shower), 2 single (1 with bath/shower) TERMS B&B £14–£17, (single occupancy of twin/double) £20–£23; deposit

Holmfield

41 Kendal Green, Kendal LA9 5PP
KENDAL (0539) 720790

Hospitable hosts, a superb location and a welcoming atmosphere make this bed and breakfast establishment special. Holmfield is an elegant Edwardian house set in an acre of grounds, with a swimming-pool and croquet lawn for guests' use. The spacious bedrooms are individually decorated in soft, restful colours, and are all named: the Meadow, the Pavilion and the Orchard. There are no *en suite* rooms, but there are enough bathrooms to go round. Breakfast only is served in the elegant dining-room, which has an open fire, as does the comfortable lounge. Vegetarian choices and special diets can be catered for at breakfast. Packed lunches can be provided. Brian Kettle is a keen walker and can provide guests with maps and information on the best walks in the area. No children under 12. No pets. No smoking. Car park.

OWNERS Eileen and Brian Kettle OPEN All year ROOMS 2 double, 1 twin TERMS B&B £14–£16; deposit

Natland Mill Beck Farm

Kendal LA9 7LH
KENDAL (0539) 721122

The seventeenth-century house, its date carved on the old oak doors built into the walls, stands in three-quarters of an acre of pretty gardens on a 100-acre dairy farm. Children are welcome and are gladly shown around the farm. Flowers are everywhere and the bedrooms are all spacious and comfortable. The guest lounge has an original stone fireplace, and there are lots of antique furnishings. Breakfast only is served and home-made biscuits and pots of tea are available on guests' arrival. The property is one mile south of Kendal. No pets. Car park.

OWNERS J. and E. Gardner OPEN Mar–Oct ROOMS 1 family, 1 twin, 1 single; 2 rooms with wash-basin TERMS B&B £12.50–£13 (children under 2 free, 2–10 half-price); deposit £5

KESWICK Cumbria map 9

Berkeley Guest House

The Heads, Keswick CA12 5ER
KESWICK (076 87) 74222

Barbara and Dennis Crompton are a friendly couple who took over the Berkeley Guest House in April 1990. Built of local slate, in an idyllic position overlooking Borrowdale and a nine-hole golf course, the house is just two minutes from the town centre and five minutes from Derwent Water. The bedrooms are of a good size, with pine and traditional furnishings. The attic room is very bright and has superb views. Two of the double rooms now have private bathrooms, new carpets have been fitted and all rooms have TV. There is also a sunny terrace for guests' use. Evening meals, including vegetarian choices, are available at 6.30pm if pre-arranged (minimum of four people). There is an alcohol licence. Packed lunches can be provided. Mountain bike hire (£6) and rock-climbing instruction (£14 per session) are available. Children welcome. No pets. No smoking in public rooms.

OWNERS Barbara and Dennis Crompton OPEN All year, exc Christmas and New Year ROOMS 1 family (with bath/shower), 3 double (1 with bath/shower, 2 with wash-basin), 1 twin (with wash-basin) TERMS B&B £13.50–£17.50, (single occupancy of twin/double) £19, (family room) £31–£46; dinner £7.50; deposit £10 per person

Claremont House

Chestnut Hill, Keswick CA12 4LT
KESWICK (076 87) 72089

Situated on the A591, on the edge of town, Claremont House is in an elevated, peaceful setting. It was originally the lodge to Fillside Manor. Some of the spotless bedrooms have views, and there are some nice touches such as the lace coronets and colourful duvets. All of the bedrooms now have private bathroom and radio; one has a brass bed. Breakfast consists of home-made bread, preserves, croissants, brioches and cereals, followed by a cooked breakfast. Morning tea and packed lunches are available, and vegetarians are catered for. A five-course evening meal is served at 7pm in the licensed dining-room. There is a guest lounge with a pretty window seat, TV and a selection of books on the area for guests to browse through. The bus to Keswick stops outside the door should guests want a break from driving. No children under 10. Pets by arrangement. No smoking in the dining-room. Car park.

OWNERS Mr G. W. and Mrs H. Mackerness OPEN All year, exc Christmas Day ROOMS 3 double, 1 twin, 1 single; all rooms with bath/shower TERMS B&B £24–£26, (single occupancy of twin/double) £36 (children under 12 half-price); dinner £14.50; deposit £10 per person

Reduced rates for children are normally given when they share their parents' bedroom. If no reductions are specified in the details or text, assume you'll have to pay full rates.

If any bedrooms are suitable for the disabled we mention this in the entry.

KIRKBY STEPHEN Cumbria map 10

Fletcher House

Fletcher Hill, Kirkby Stephen CA17 4QQ
KIRKBY STEPHEN (076 83) 71013

Fletcher House is an attractive, listed Georgian house, built in 1830, situated in the centre of town. It has been carefully modernised, retaining many original features, such as fireplaces and the entrance hall archway, which has been restored to its original splendour. The rooms are tastefully decorated; one bedroom has a half-tester bed, another a delicate lace backdrop. The dining-room has a beautiful crystal chandelier. There is a comfortable guest lounge with TV for guests' use. Breakfast only is served, but there are several eating establishments close by. Children welcome. No pets. No smoking. Car park.

OWNERS Mr and Mrs Bradwell OPEN Easter–Oct ROOMS 2 double (1 with bath/shower, 1 with wash-basin), 2 twin (1 with bath/shower, 1 with wash-basin), 1 single TERMS B&B £15–£22 (children under 11 half-price); deposit £5

LANCASTER Lancashire map 7

Edenbreck House

Sunnyside Lane, Lancaster LA1 5ED
LANCASTER (0524) 32464

Built in Victorian style, this large, detached modern house is set in landscaped gardens. It is a comfortable, luxurious house. There is a galleried lounge and an elegant dining-room. The bedrooms are spacious; one has a four-poster bed and patchwork quilt, another has a Jacuzzi. There is also a small conservatory for guests' use. Edenbreck House is in a peaceful location, 10 minutes' walk from the town centre. Children welcome. Pets by arrangement. No smoking in the dining-room. Car park.

OWNERS Mr and Mrs B. Houghton OPEN All year, exc Christmas ROOMS 2 double, 1 four-poster, 2 twin; all rooms with bath/shower TERMS B&B £17.50, (four-poster) £20 (children under 5 free, 5–12 £8, 12–16 £13, over 16 £15); deposit £10; Access, Visa

Reduced rates for children are normally given when they share their parents' bedroom. If no reductions are specified in the details or text, assume you'll have to pay full rates.

Elsinore House

76 Scotforth Road, Lancaster LA1 4SF
LANCASTER (0524) 65088

Located on the A6 Preston Road out of Lancaster, off the M6 at junction 33, this is an immaculate family-run guesthouse, one mile from the city centre. The house has recently been totally redecorated; both of the bedrooms have *en suite* bathrooms and are named after local beauty spots. The guest lounge has leaded, stained-glass windows, and also plenty of books to browse through. Breakfast only is available and is served in the bright, attractive dining-room. No children under 12. No pets. Smoking in the lounge only. Car park.

OWNER Mrs Linda Moorhouse OPEN All year, exc Christmas
ROOMS 1 double (with bath/shower), 1 twin (with bath/shower)
TERMS B&B £15, (single occupancy of twin/double) £30; deposit

LECK Lancashire map 7

Cobwebs Country House and Restaurant

Leck, Cowan Bridge LA6 2HZ
KIRKBY LONSDALE (052 42) 72141

This beautiful country house is fronted by a cobbled forecourt and set in four acres of peaceful grounds. The décor is Victorian, and the elegantly appointed bedrooms are individually decorated in soft, pastel colours, with matching coronets. All have TV, telephone and private bathroom. The intimate dining-room seats 16. Yvonne Thomson firmly believes in using the best of fresh ingredients in her meals. A typical menu might include dishes such as warm salmon and almond profiteroles with minted yoghurt sauce, followed by chicken, duck, turkey and spinach rolled together, sliced and served with shellfish and leek sauces. There is a small conservatory with wicker furniture for guests' use. Paul has a well-stocked wine cellar. Extremely high standards are maintained, combined with old-fashioned courtesy. Children over 12 are welcome. No pets. No smoking in the dining-room. Car park.

OWNERS Paul Kelly and Yvonne Thomson OPEN mid-Mar–end Dec
ROOMS 3 double, 2 twin; all rooms with bath/shower TERMS B&B £30, (single occupancy of twin/double) £40; dinner £25; deposit; Access, Visa

LEEDS West Yorkshire map 7

118 Grovehall Drive

118 Grovehall Drive, Leeds LS11 7ET
LEEDS (0532) 704445

Guests in this family home, about a mile from the city centre, are offered a chance to enjoy the beautiful Yorkshire countryside and historic towns: Rod Sabine is happy to prepare sightseeing itineraries, and, at weekends, to drive guests around, for a modest charge, in their own car. Friends of the Sabines who have a sheep farm on the moors offer a warm welcome, with simple home cooking, and an opportunity to explore the farm. The spotless bedrooms are on the top floor and are ideal for a family, or friends travelling together, as the two bedrooms lead directly from one to another. Substantial breakfasts are served. Children welcome. No pets. No smoking.

OWNERS Ann and Rod Sabine OPEN All year ROOMS 1 family, 1 double, 1 single TERMS B&B £12, (single) £13.50, (single occupancy of double) £13.50 (children in cot free, under 12 £7); deposit

LEVISHAM North Yorkshire map 10

Grove House

Levisham Station, Pickering YO18 7NN
PICKERING (0751) 72351

Grove House is a beautiful old manor house in an acre of gardens, bounded by woodland, pine forest and moorland; the house is adjacent to Levisham Station, which is on the North York Moors Steam Railway, featured in many films. Levisham village is one and a half miles away. The lounge has been extended and is a very comfortable room in which to relax. Furnishings are Victorian-style. Many people come here for the superb meals, all prepared fresh daily, and served at 7pm. There is an alcohol licence. Guests can enjoy a drink in the lounge or, on warm evenings, on the patio. No children or pets. No smoking. Car park

OWNERS June and Neville Carter OPEN Easter–Oct
ROOMS 3 double (1 with bath/shower, 2 with wash-basin), 1 twin
TERMS B&B £16–£18, (single occupancy of twin/double) £30; dinner £10; deposit £10 per person

LOWER DOLPHINHOLME Lancashire map 7

The Old Mill House

Lower Dolphinholme, nr Lancaster LA2 9AX
LANCASTER (0524) 791855

The Old Mill dates from the seventeenth-century and was originally a cornmill on the estates of the Lord of Wyreside. The house stands in three acres of beautiful gardens on the River Wyre. The beautifully decorated bedrooms are colour-co-ordinated, and there is a de luxe four-poster room with its own bathroom. The owners are keen bird-watchers and have recorded over 55 species in the gardens. There is a varied menu and wine list for evening meals (7.30–9.30pm by arrangement); vegetarians can be catered for with prior notice. Packed lunches can be provided. No smoking in public rooms. Car park.

OWNERS A. B. and B. C. Williamson OPEN All year ROOMS 1 four-poster (with bath/shower), 1 double (with wash-basin), 1 twin (with wash-basin) TERMS B&B £15–£17.50, (single occupancy of twin/double) £20–£22 (children under 2 free); dinner £9.50–£12.50; deposit £10 per night per room

LOWICK Northumberland map 10

The Old Manse

5 Cheviot View, Lowick, Berwick-upon-Tweed TD15 2TY
BERWICK-UPON-TWEED (0289) 88264

This late-Georgian manse is attached to what is believed to be the first Presbyterian church built in England. The spacious bedrooms are comfortably furnished. Both owners are interested in country pursuits and local history, and are willing to take guests on half-day tours of the area in a mini-bus. There is a homely guest lounge with TV. Substantial breakfasts are served; dinners are available (6.30pm), and dishes are traditional or Continental. Vegetarian meals are also served. The premises are not licensed, but guests may bring their own wine. No children. No pets. No smoking in bedrooms.

OWNERS John and Janet Dunn OPEN Easter–end Oct
ROOMS 2 double (1 with bath/shower), 1 twin (with bath/shower)
TERMS B&B £13–£15, (single occupancy of twin/double) £26–£30; D, B&B £33.50–£35.50; deposit 1 night charge

LUPTON Cumbria map 10

Lupton Tower Vegetarian Country House

Lupton, nr Kirkby Lonsdale LA6 2PR
CROOKLANDS (044 87) 400

This unusual house is set in open countryside and is approached from a private driveway lined with lovely trees. The comfortable lounge with tasteful floral curtains has an open fire and a beautiful antique carved dresser. The top tower bedroom has panoramic views and an original Victorian fireplace. Vegetarian meals only are served in the dining-room (8pm) and roaring log fires are lit here in winter. There is a full alcohol licence. Packed lunches can be provided. Guests are made to feel most welcome and there is a relaxed, informal atmosphere. Non-vegetarians should not be deterred from visiting – the food is excellent and might even convert some meat-eaters. Children welcome. Pets by arrangement. No smoking. Car park.

OWNERS Mr and Mrs G. Smith OPEN All year, exc Christmas
ROOMS 1 family (with bath/shower), 4 double (3 with bath/shower, 1 with wash-basin), 2 twin (1 with bath/shower, 1 with wash-basin)
TERMS B&B £14.50–£18.50, (family room) from £55 (children under 2 free, under 12 half-price); dinner £17.50; deposit £10 per room

MIDDLEHAM North Yorkshire map 10

Waterford House

19 Kirkgate, Middleham DL8 4PG
WENSLEYDALE (0969) 22090 Fax (0969) 24020

A beautiful, traditional, stone-built residence, Waterford House is situated on the edge of the Yorkshire Dales National Park in an elevated position overlooking the market square. The spacious, beamed bedrooms are exquisitely decorated with soft, pastel, floral patterns. Each bedroom is supplied with fresh fruit, sherry, filter coffee, a wide selection of teas and fresh milk. All have TV. The Georgian-style drawing-room has a grand piano which guests may play. Candle-lit dinners are served (7.30–10.30pm) in the Regency-style dining-room or the seventeenth-century Oak Room. There is an extensive menu and wine list (comprising over 400 wines) and everything is prepared to order. Choices might include crab with ginger, pink grapefruit and avocado, followed by fillets of Aberdeen Angus, venison and free-range chicken with wild mushrooms and red wine. Vegetarian dishes can be provided. There is a quiet lounge. Children welcome. Pets welcome. Smoking discouraged in the dining-rooms. Car park.

OWNERS Everyl and Brian Madell OPEN All year ROOMS 1 four-poster, 1 family, 2 double, 1 twin; all rooms with bath/shower
TERMS B&B £22.50–£25, (single occupancy of twin/double) £32.50, (family room) £16.50 per person (reductions for children); dinner from £13.50, à la carte from £17.50; Visa

MIDDLETON-IN-TEESDALE Co Durham map 10

Brunswick House

55 Market Place, Middleton-in-Teesdale DL12 0QH
TEESDALE (0833) 40393

Built in 1760, Brunswick House overlooks the market-place and St Mary's Church with its unique detached bell-tower. Andrew and Sheila Milnes are a friendly couple who have been busy refurbishing the house, which has a beamed, whitewashed interior. Bedrooms have pine furnishings; all have TV. There is a cosy guest lounge with TV and an open log fire. Breakfast and evening meals (7.30pm) are served in the licensed dining-room, using fresh local produce and meat whenever possible. Vegetarian choices can be provided. Lunch and packed lunches are available.

There is a tea-shop adjacent to the house, where sandwiches and home-baked cakes are available. Children welcome. No pets. Car park.

OWNERS Andrew and Sheila Milnes OPEN All year ROOMS 1 family (with wash-basin), 2 double (with bath/shower), 1 twin (with bath/shower) TERMS B&B £18, (single occupancy of twin/double) £25 (reductions for children sharing parents' room); dinner £10; deposit £5 per person per night (up to £50)

MIDDLETON-ON-THE-WOLDS Humberside map 8

Middleton Wold Cottages

Middleton-on-the-Wolds, nr Driffield YO25 9DD
MIDDLETON-ON-THE-WOLDS (037 781) 635

The original four cottages have been skilfully converted into a most comfortable and pleasant B&B in a peaceful location with over an acre of garden and paddocks. The bedrooms have pretty wallpaper, quilts and pine furnishings. All bedrooms have a radio-alarm. A building which was formerly the chapel has been converted into an elegant guest lounge with TV. There is an interesting old glass bottle collection in the breakfast room. No children under 12. No pets. No smoking. Car park.

OWNER Tony King OPEN All year ROOMS 2 double, 1 single TERMS B&B £14

MILLOM Cumbria map 7

Buckman Brow House

Thwaites, Millom LA18 5HX
BROUGHTON-IN-FURNESS (0229) 716541

The house was built in 1845 as a schoolhouse, and converted to a family home in 1927. It has spectacular views of the Duddon valley and estuary. Gwen Dunn retired from a restaurant business and began her new venture by offering cream teas (which are still available) in her delightful garden. Breakfast is served in the huge dining-room/lounge; lunch and dinner (6.30pm or 8pm) are available. There is no alcohol licence, but guests may bring their own wine. There is also a conservatory for guests' use. The large bedrooms are exquisitely decorated and two have TV. Children welcome. Pets by arrangement. Smoking restrictions. Car park. Situated two miles north-west of Broughton-in-Furness, off the A595.

OWNER Mrs Gwen Dunn OPEN All year ROOMS 1 family (with bath/shower), 2 double (1 with bath/shower) TERMS B&B from £17.50, (single occupancy of double) £22.50 (children under 3 free, under 12 half-price); D, B&B from £25 per night for 3 nights or more; dinner £10.50/£15; deposit 10%

NEWCASTLE-UPON-TYNE Tyne & Wear map 10

Bywell

54 Holly Avenue, Jesmond, Newcastle-upon-Tyne NE2 2QA
091-281 7615

Bywell is a pleasant Victorian house in a quiet residential cul-de-sac just five miles from the Metro Centre shopping complex. The bus to town passes the top of the road and an underground station is close by. A varied substantial breakfast is served. No evening meals are available, but there are plenty of pubs and restaurants in the area. Both bedrooms (one is on the ground floor) have TV. There is also a comfortable guest lounge with TV. Children welcome. No pets. No smoking.

OWNER Mrs M. Cook OPEN All year, exc Christmas ROOMS 1 double, 1 twin; both rooms with wash-basin TERMS B&B £14–£16.50 (children £7 sharing with two adults); deposit 10%

NORTHALLERTON North Yorkshire map 10

Windsor Guest House

56 South Parade, Northallerton DL7 8SL
NORTHALLERTON (0609) 774100

This well-maintained Victorian guesthouse is half a mile from the town centre on the Bedale road. The guest lounge and dining-room have the original cornices and ceiling roses. The bedrooms are all large, and have TV. The top room is particularly attractive and spacious, and a twin room overlooks the pretty rear garden. There is also a comfortable TV lounge. Mrs Peacock is a jolly lady who has created a very homely and relaxing atmosphere. Dinner is served 6.30–7pm. There is no licence, but guests may bring their own wine. Vegetarian dishes can be arranged. Packed

If there are any bedrooms with TV and/or telephone we mention this in the entry.

lunches can be provided. Children welcome. Pets by arrangement. No smoking in the dining-room.

OWNER Mrs C. Peacock OPEN All year, exc Christmas ROOMS 1 family (with wash-basin), 2 double (with bath/shower), 3 twin (1 with bath/shower, 2 with wash-basin) TERMS B&B £14.50, (single occupancy of twin/double) £19, (family room) £14 (children under 3 free, under 14 half-price); dinner £8.50; deposit £5 per room; Access, Visa

OGLE Northumberland map 10

The Gables

Ogle, Ponteland, nr Newcastle-upon-Tyne NE20 OAU
WHALTON (067 075) 392

The Gables is a modern ranch-type bungalow in the picturesque hamlet of Ogle, with views over the surrounding farmland. It is a friendly, spacious home in a country garden of lawns, shrubs and fruit orchard. The bedrooms have matching fabrics, easy chairs and TV. Breakfast is cooked to order and guests can have just about anything they wish. Special diets are catered for. Guests may enjoy watching a video on Northumbria in their room. Conveniently located for the airport and Newcastle. Children welcome. Pets by arrangement. No smoking. Car park.

OWNER Mrs L. S. P. Bewick OPEN All year ROOMS 1 double (with bath/shower), 1 twin (with bath/shower), 2 single (with wash-basin) TERMS B&B £17.50–£20, (single occupancy of twin/double) £22–£30 (children under 5 £5); deposit on very advanced bookings

OVER KELLET Lancashire map 7

Thie-ne-Shee

Moor Close Lane, Over Kellet, nr Carnforth LA6 1DF
CARNFORTH (0524) 735882

Thie-ne-Shee is Manx for haven of peace and this house is aptly named. It sits in an elevated position overlooking Morecambe Bay and the southern Lakeland hills. Both bedrooms are on the ground floor; the family room is exceptionally large and has lovely views. Dr Cobb is a keen gardener and there is a beautiful garden. The dining-room-cum-lounge has TV. Dr and Mrs Cobb also welcome guests into their lounge, where they are happy to assist with the planning of daily activities. Breakfast comprises an excellent Continental choice as well as traditional English fare. Tea or coffee is available upon request at no extra charge. The house is a quarter of a mile from the village and close to Capernwray Hall. Children welcome. No pets. No smoking. Car park.

OWNERS Dr and Mrs M. C. Cobb OPEN All year, exc Christmas and New Year ROOMS 1 family, 1 twin TERMS B&B £10–£12, (single occupancy of twin) £13–£15, (family room) £12–£14 adults (children 3–12 £8, 12–16 £10)

PATELEY BRIDGE North Yorkshire map 7

Dale View

Old Church Lane, Pateley Bridge HG3 5LY
HARROGATE (0423) 711506

Spectacular views can be enjoyed from this former farmhouse, especially from the front rooms. The spotless bedrooms are basic and functional. The beamed, comfortable lounge, where hot drinks and biscuits are served, has glowing fires on chilly evenings. Of particular interest is a pump organ from a local chapel. Leading off the lounge is a conservatory which has a pool-table and dartboard. Breakfast only is served. Children welcome. Pets not allowed in the dining-room or lounge. Car park.

OWNERS John and Evelyn Simpson OPEN Apr–Oct ROOMS 1 family, 3 double (1 with bath/shower), 1 twin (with bath/shower) TERMS B&B £12.50–£14 (children under 3 free, under 11 £6.50)

PENRITH Cumbria map 10

Brandelhow Guest House

1 Portland Place, Penrith CA11 7QN
PENRITH (0768) 64470

The large bedrooms at this friendly, comfortable guesthouse are prettily decorated with matching wallpaper and fabric; all have TV. The lounge has been decorated in a Victorian print, and is a very comfortable spot in which to relax. Breakfast only is served. Packed lunches can be provided. Children welcome. Pets by arrangement. Two bedrooms are non-smoking.

OWNER Mrs Carole Tully OPEN All year, exc Christmas ROOMS 1 family, 4 double; all rooms with wash-basin TERMS B&B £13–£14, (single occupancy of double) £20 (children under 14 £8); deposit £10

PENTON Cumbria map 10

Bessiestown Farm

Catlowdy, Penton, Carlisle CA6 5QP
NICHOLFOREST (0228) 577219

Only three miles from the border with Scotland, Bessietown Farm is best reached by taking the A7 from Carlisle to Longtown and then following the signs for Penton. There are now just five quite spacious bedrooms, which have been completely refurbished. Dinner is a four-course meal (7pm); the sweet trolley has an amazing array of creamy home-made puddings, and the cheeseboard that follows provides almost as wide a choice. Vegetarians can be catered for with prior notice. There is a bar as well as a TV lounge. The large indoor swimming-pool is open from mid-May to mid-September. One of the farm buildings has been converted into a games-room, and has table tennis, pool and darts. Riding can be arranged on one of the ponies. Children welcome. Smoking in the bar lounge only. No pets. Self-catering is available. Car park.

OWNERS Jack and Margaret Sisson OPEN All year ROOMS 1 family, 2 double, 2 twin; all rooms with bath/shower TERMS B&B £21, (single occupancy of twin/double) £26, (family room) £21 (children under 12 reduced rate sharing with parents); dinner £12; deposit

RICHMOND North Yorkshire map 10

Ridgeway Guest House

47 Darlington Road, Richmond DL10 7BG
RICHMOND (0748) 823801

A 10-minute walk from the town centre, this detached house was built from Yorkshire stone in 1928 and has an acre of lawn and garden. The house is full of interesting items, including antiques such as the chaise-longue in the hallway and the clock on the landing. The sitting-room is very comfortable and there is a TV and piano. Good food is served here; dinner is at 6pm and vegetarians can be catered for. There is no alcohol licence, but guests may bring their own wine to dinner. Pets by arrangement. No smoking. Car park

OWNERS Janet and Michael Warrior OPEN Feb–Nov
ROOMS 1 four-poster, 2 double, 2 twin; all rooms with bath/shower
TERMS B&B £17, (single occupancy of twin/double) £25; dinner £9.50; deposit £10 per room

West End Guest House

45 Reeth Road, Richmond DL10 4EX
RICHMOND (0748) 824783

There is a pretty front garden with a monkey-puzzle tree at this family-run guesthouse on the outskirts of Richmond. The house was built in the mid-nineteenth century and retains much of its charm and character. Everything is colour-co-ordinated and the bedrooms are furnished to a high standard. Some of the rooms have the original fireplaces. There is one ground-floor room. Evening meals are served at 7pm, and vegetarians can be catered for by prior arrangement. There is an alcohol licence. Smoking in the lounge only. Pets by arrangement. Car park.

OWNERS Trevor and Kath Teeley OPEN All year, exc Christmas and New Year ROOMS 1 family (with bath/shower), 1 twin (with bath/shower), 2 double (with bath/shower), 1 single (with wash-basin) TERMS B&B £17.50, (single) from £15, (single occupancy of twin/double) £25–£34, (family room) £45; dinner £9.50; deposit

RIPON North Yorkshire map 7

Crescent Lodge

42 North Street, Ripon HG4 1EN
RIPON (0765) 602331

This Georgian lodge, dating back to 1725, has the distinction of having been the residence of the Archbishop of York. It still bears a plaque in the form of a bishop's mitre on the side of the house. Christine Bunce, originally from London, is very pleasant, and the atmosphere in this immaculate guesthouse is one of quiet and comfort. The building is just five minutes from the market square, where, at 9pm, you can hear the hornblower setting the watch, a custom unbroken for over a thousand years. The road can be busy. Complimentary tea and coffee are available. Breakfast only is served. All bedrooms have TV. Children welcome. No pets. No smoking in the dining-room. On-street parking.

OWNER Christine Bunce OPEN All year, exc Christmas and New Year ROOMS 4 family (2 with bath/shower, 2 with wash-basin), 4 double (1 with bath/shower, 3 with wash-basin), 1 twin (with wash-basin), 1 single (with wash-basin) TERMS B&B £12–£18 (children sharing £7); deposit

Most B&Bs offer tea/coffee-making facilities in the bedrooms.

ROBIN HOOD'S BAY North Yorkshire map 10

Plantation House

Thorpe Lane, Robin Hood's Bay, nr Whitby YO22 4RN
WHITBY (0947) 880036

Built by a plantation owner in 1780, this Georgian house was formerly a vicarage. The bay is a five-minute walk away. The bedrooms range in size from average to spacious; one is on the ground floor, and all have TV. There is a beautiful Venetian-style arched window on the landing, and an antique grandfather clock stands in the hallway. The hosts are very hospitable and families are made welcome. A free baby-listening service can be provided, as well as cots and high chairs. Breakfast only is available, but there are plenty of places in the area for dinners. Packed lunches can be provided. Well-behaved pets only. Car park.

OWNERS David and Wendy Scrivener OPEN Feb–Nov
ROOMS 1 family, 2 double; all rooms with bath/shower TERMS B&B £15, (single occupancy of double) £20 (children half-price sharing with parents); deposit £10

ROTHBURY Northumberland map 10

Silverton Lodge

Silverton Lane, Rothbury NE65 7RJ
ROTHBURY (0669) 20144

Formerly a school, this property has been lovingly restored and is furnished to a high standard with Laura Ashley wallpapers. An unusual Victorian fireplace has been installed in the lounge. The bedrooms are well appointed and have sloping ceilings. High teas are served and there are several eating establishments close by. Children welcome. Pets by arrangement. No smoking. Car park.

OWNER Mrs J. Hewison OPEN All year ROOMS 1 double, 1 twin; both rooms wth bath/shower TERMS B&B £13–£17, (single occupancy of twin/double) £19.50–£25.50 (babies free, children £5–£10); deposit 1 night charge

Where we know of any particular payment stipulations we mention them in the details. It is always best to check when booking, however.

Where we know an establishment accepts credit cards, we list them. There may be a surcharge if you pay by credit card. It is always best to check whether the card you want to use is acceptable when booking.

ST BEES Cumbria map 9

Kinder How

Egremont Road, St Bees CA27 0AS
EGREMONT (0946) 822376

This is a warm and friendly modern house, very much a family home, with sweeping views of St Bees Head and the golf course. The bedrooms are immaculate and all on the ground floor. The well-furnished, comfortable guest lounge is on the second floor, designed to take full advantage of the breathtaking views from the picture window. Excellent evening meals (6–7.30pm) are available with advance notice at very reasonable prices. There is no licence, but guests may bring their own wine. Vegetarians can be catered for and packed lunches are available. St Bees is the start of the coast-to-coast walk. Children welcome. Pets by arrangement. No smoking in bedrooms or the dining-room. Car park.

OWNERS Denise and Roy Pearson OPEN All year, exc Christmas
ROOMS 3 double (1 with wash-basin), 1 twin (with wash-basin)
TERMS B&B £14–£18; dinner £6.50; deposit £5 per person

ST JOHN'S CHAPEL Co Durham map 10

Pennine Lodge

St John's Chapel, Weardale, Bishop Auckland DL13 1QX
WEARDALE (0388) 537247

Pennine Lodge is a sixteenth-century stone house, covered with Virginia creeper. The River Wear is close by and there is a small waterfall and a footbridge behind the house; the village is a five-minute walk. The rooms are well maintained and comfortable, some with flagstone floors, and are furnished with antiques. One bedroom is on the ground floor. Traditional breakfasts and dinners (7pm) are served in the licensed dining-room, which has beams and an open fire. Vegetarians can be catered for by arrangement. Packed lunches are available. The attached tea-room offers afternoon teas. This is an area of outstanding beauty and is good walking country. No children. Pets by arrangement. No smoking in the dining-room and bedrooms. Car park.

OWNER Mrs Y. Raine OPEN Apr–Sept ROOMS 1 four-poster, 2 double, 2 twin; all rooms with bath/shower TERMS B&B £17.50–£23; dinner £8.50; deposit

SALE Greater Manchester map 7

Brooklands Lodge

208 Marsland Road, Sale M33 3NE
MANCHESTER 061-973 3283

Built in 1851, Brooklands Lodge is an attractive residence standing in its own grounds with ample parking. The well-maintained property has large bedrooms (four on the ground floor), all with TV, easy chairs and a breakfast bar. Guests help themselves to a Continental breakfast which is taken in their own room and served until 10am. A cooked breakfast is available at an extra charge. Dinner is available between 5.30pm and 6.30pm, and, again, served in the bedroom. Guests have use of a sunbed and whirlpool bath. There is also a laundry facility. No pets.

OWNERS Les and Ann Bowker OPEN mid-Nov–early Dec
ROOMS 1 family (with bath/shower), 1 double (with wash-basin), 2 twin (1 with bath/shower, 1 with wash-basin), 5 single (with wash-basin)
TERMS B&B £16–£18, (single) £20–£26, (family room) £45 (babies free); deposit £10; dinner £8

SAWREY Cumbria map 9

Buckle Yeat

Near Sawrey, Ambleside LA22 0NS
HAWKSHEAD (053 94) 36446/36538

Buckle Yeat is a beautifully restored cottage, within walking distance of Beatrix Potter's cottage. There is an adjacent farm and a sawmill to the rear of the property. Many original features, such as oak beams and the flagstone floor in the spacious lounge, have been retained. There is a log fireplace, lit on chilly days. The bedrooms are of a good size and are tastefully decorated and furnished. There is one ground-floor room with a king-size bed and *en suite* bathroom. Excellent breakfasts are served in the dining-room, which has an old cast-iron range. Morning coffee, light lunches and teas are served during the day. Children welcome. Pets by arrangement. No smoking in the dining-room. Car park. Near Sawrey is one kilometre west of Far Sawrey village.

OWNERS W. D. and M. S. Lambert OPEN All year ROOMS 1 family, 4 double, 2 twin, 1 single; all rooms with bath/shower TERMS B&B £16–£18, (single occupancy of twin/double) £30 (reductions for children); deposit £30 per room

High Green Gate Guest House

Near Sawrey, Ambleside LA22 0LF
HAWKSHEAD (053 94) 36296

This eighteenth-century converted farmhouse is situated in the hamlet of Near Sawrey, which is famous as the home of Beatrix Potter. There is a pretty front garden with a fish pond. The bedrooms are of a good size and are bright and comfortable. One room is on the ground floor. Four-course evening meals (7pm), with lots of fresh local vegetables and tasty home-made desserts, are served. Vegetarians can be catered for by prior arrangement. There is no licence, but guests may bring their own wine. Packed lunches can be provided. There is a beamed TV lounge and a quiet sitting-room. Children welcome. Pets by arrangement. Car park.

OWNER Miss Gillian Fletcher OPEN Apr–Oct ROOMS 4 family (3 with bath/shower), 1 double (with bath/shower) TERMS B&B £15–£18 (reductions for children under 10 sharing); dinner £10; deposit £5 per person

SCARBOROUGH North Yorkshire map 10

Dolphin Hotel

151 Columbus Ravine, Scarborough YO12 7PZ
SCARBOROUGH (0723) 374217

The town centre is approximately a 15-minute walk from the Dolphin Hotel. The cricket ground and Peasholm Park are nearby. The rooms are well decorated and colour-co-ordinated, with pretty wallpaper and matching bedspreads. All have TV, telephone, trouser-press, iron and board, and hair-dryer. The Dolphin has many connections with the Royal Air Force – photographs and memorabilia are in the dining-room. Lunch and packed lunches are available, and dinner (from 7pm) is served in the licensed dining-room. Special diets are catered for – there is an extensive vegetarian menu. Reductions for children, but no children under five. No pets. No smoking in the dining-room.

OWNER Mrs Beryl Willis OPEN All year, exc Christmas and New Year ROOMS 4 double, 2 twin; all rooms with bath/shower TERMS B&B £18.50, (single occupancy of twin/double) £32; dinner £3.50–£20; deposit £20 for 2 people

If there are any bedrooms with TV and/or telephone we mention this in the entry.

St Margarets Guest House

8 Trafalgar Square, Scarborough YO17 7PY
SCARBOROUGH (0723) 379983

This is an immaculate property, with pretty flower boxes, on a quiet side-street, just 10 minutes from the beach and town centre. There is a comfortable TV lounge. A bathroom has been added, so there is now a bathroom on each floor. Evening meals are available (5.30pm) and are served in the spacious, bright dining-room. There is a table licence, so guests may enjoy a glass of wine with their meal. Packed lunches are available and vegetarians can be catered for with prior notice. No children under two. No pets. No smoking in bedrooms.

OWNERS Ron and Nancy Pearson OPEN All year, exc Christmas
ROOMS 2 family, 1 double, 2 twin, 2 single; all rooms with wash-basin
TERMS B&B £11–£12, (single occupancy of twin/double) £22–£24, (family room) £33–£36 (children half-price sharing with 2 adults); D, B&B £14–£15; deposit 10%

SEDBERGH Cumbria map 10

Marshall House

Main Street, Sedbergh LA10 5BL
SEDBERGH (053 96) 21053

Marshall House is a listed eighteenth-century house in the town centre, named after a former master of Sedbergh School. Original features, such as a grand staircase, oak panelling, ceilings and several old fireplaces, remain. Special features are the eighteenth-century plumbing, which is still intact, and a curved corner in one of the bedrooms where the old copper once stood. The charming bedrooms are well appointed, and all have pine furnishings and TV. Breakfast and dinner (by special arrangement only) are served in the panelled dining-room. There is no alcohol licence, but guests may bring their own wine to dinner. Vegetarian dishes and packed lunches can be provided. No children under 12. No pets. There is one no-smoking bedroom. Car park.

OWNERS Mr and Mrs David Kerry OPEN All year, exc Christmas
ROOMS 1 double, 2 twin; all rooms with bath/shower TERMS B&B £17.50–£19.50, (single occupancy of twin/double) £25; dinner from £15; deposit £5 per person per night

Use the maps and indexes at the back of the Guide *to plan your trip.*

Randall Hill

Sedbergh LA10 5HJ
SEDBERGH (053 96) 20633

Located within the Yorkshire Dales National Park and only 10 miles from Kendal, Randall Hill is a turn-of-the-century house set in three acres of grounds, amid the beautiful scenery of the Vale of Sedbergh. The rooms, all on the ground floor, are spacious and comfortable, with white cotton sheets. Breakfast includes free-range eggs, and home-made bread and marmalades. Packed lunches are available. Randall Hill is four and a half miles from the M6, junction 37 and half a mile from Sedbergh. No smoking in bedrooms. Car park.

OWNERS Peter and Joan Snow OPEN All year, exc Christmas ROOMS 2 double, 2 twin; 3 rooms with wash-basin TERMS B&B £14–£15 (children £10 on z-bed); deposit £10

SETTLE North Yorkshire map 7

The Yorkshire Rose Guest House

Duke Street, Settle BD24 9AJ
SETTLE (0729) 822032

Once the local doctor's house, this lovely Georgian building is only two minutes' walk from the Dales town of Settle. The bedrooms, all with TV, are well appointed and have been freshly decorated; one has an original fireplace. Mrs Palmer makes dolls, which are available for sale, and Mr Palmer is an artist. The comfortable lounge with TV leads in to the licensed dining-room through Georgian-style doors. Evening meals are available (6.30–7pm) if pre-arranged; vegetarian choices can be provided. Packed lunches can be arranged. Children welcome. No pets. No smoking in the dining-room and bedrooms. Car park.

OWNERS Ann and Robin Palmer OPEN Feb–Dec ROOMS 1 family (with wash-basin), 2 double (1 with bath/shower, 1 with wash-basin), 1 single (with wash-basin) TERMS B&B £15–£19.50 (children under 3 free, 3–12 half-price, 12–15 £12); dinner £9; deposit

Those B&Bs that we know can offer some kind of off-street car parking, have 'car park' at the end of the entry. If we are aware of particular car parking difficulties, we mention them.

Most establishments have central heating. We say when this is not the case.

SHEFFIELD South Yorkshire map 7

Lindum Hotel

91 Montgomery Road, Nether Edge, Sheffield S7 1LP
SHEFFIELD (0742) 552356

This immaculate Victorian hotel is on a quiet, tree-lined street close to the city centre. The bedrooms are individually decorated; all have TV and radio-alarm. There is a very comfortable TV lounge. Breakfast only is served in the attractive pink and blue dining-room. The premises are licensed. Children welcome. Pets by arrangement. Some of the bedrooms are non-smoking. Car park.

OWNERS Moira and Peter Jones OPEN All year, exc Christmas ROOMS 1 family, 3 double, 3 twin (1 with bath/shower), 5 single; all rooms with wash-basin TERMS B&B £18, (single) £16–£22.50, (family room) £42; payment on arrival

The Sharrow View Hotel

Sharrow View, Nether Edge, Sheffield S7 1ND
SHEFFIELD (0742) 551542

This is a pleasant, privately owned hotel in a quiet suburb, close to the city centre. The bedrooms are comfortable and TVs are available for a modest charge. Guests departing early may take Continental breakfast in the lounge. Dinners are available Monday to Thursday (except bank holidays) and vegetarian choices can be provided. Snacks are available during the day on request. There is a spacious TV lounge and a small licensed bar. Children welcome. Pets welcome. No smoking. Car park.

OWNER Mrs Judith E. Hodgson OPEN All year, exc Christmas and New Year ROOMS 2 family, 4 double, 1 twin, 14 single; all single rooms and 7 other rooms with wash-basin TERMS B&B £19.50, (single) £24.75, (family room) £52; dinner £10.95; deposit

Many B&Bs will cater for vegetarians. It is always best, however, to check when booking and make it clear what your requirements are, especially if you need a special diet.

Bath/shower information in the details refers only to a private bathroom or shower; other bathroom facilities at the establishments will be shared. We say if rooms have wash-basins.

SILVERDALE Lancashire map 7

Lindeth House

Lindeth Road, Silverdale, Carnforth LA5 0TX
SILVERDALE (0524) 701238

This charming turn-of-the-century house is set in three-quarters of an acre of lovely gardens. The spacious bedrooms are all individually decorated and furnished, one with antique pine and pretty blue curtains. Exceptionally high standards prevail at this lovely open-plan home and there is an informal, welcoming atmosphere. Two elegant lounges are for the use of guests. The licensed restaurant within the guesthouse is very popular and offers excellent cuisine, Wednesday to Saturday 7–8.30pm, although meals can be provided on additional nights with notice. Packed lunches are available and vegetarians can be catered for. Within easy walking distance of the Wolf House Gallery. Children welcome. No pets. No smoking in bedrooms and the dining-room. Car park.

OWNERS Pat and Mark Edwards OPEN All year, exc Jan
ROOMS 1 double, 2 twin; all rooms with bath/shower TERMS B&B £18–£20, (single occupancy of twin/double) £25; dinner £15.50; deposit

SKIPTON North Yorkshire map 7

Low Skibeden Farm House

Skibeden Road, Skipton BD23 6AB
SKIPTON (0756) 793849

This sixteenth-century stone-built farmhouse is three-quarters of a mile from the town centre. The large, lawned garden is bordered with shrubs. On the landing is an original Georgian window. The rooms are spacious, with a mixture of modern and traditional furniture. A real Yorkshire welcome is extended here, with tea or coffee and home-made cakes offered when guests arrive. Supper-time drinks with biscuits are offered too. Laundry facilities are available at a modest cost. Children welcome. No pets. No smoking.

OWNERS Mr W. and Mrs H. M. Simpson OPEN All year
ROOMS 1 family (with bath/shower), 1 double, 1 twin; all rooms with wash-basin TERMS B&B £12.50–£15, (single occupancy of twin/double) £15–£20; deposit £20–£25

Westfield House

50 Keighley Road, Skipton BD23 3NB
SKIPTON (0756) 790849

This characterful Victorian residence is two minutes from the town centre. The bedrooms have all been redecorated with matching fabrics in soft colours; all rooms have TV. Breakfast only is served in the dining-room/lounge, which has an open fire. Children welcome. No smoking. No pets.

OWNERS J. D. and K. Hardaker OPEN All year, exc Christmas
ROOMS 3 double, 1 twin, 1 single TERMS B&B £13.50–£14, (single occupancy of twin/double) £20 (children under 5 £3, under 15 £7); deposit

SLAIDBURN Lancashire map 7

Pages Farm

Woodhouse Lane, Slaidburn, Clitheroe BB7 3AH
SLAIDBURN (020 06) 205

This seventeenth-century farmhouse on a 65-acre farm is in beautiful countryside near the Forest of Bowland, not far from Slaidburn. The owners took over the house in September 1990 and offer guests a warm welcome. The farmhouse has oak beams, and the comfortable lounge has open fires on chilly evenings. Mrs Cowking is willing to baby-sit if pre-arranged. Breakfasts are excellent. Traditional cooked dinners are served from 6.30pm, by arrangement. Guests may bring their own wine to dinner. Children welcome. Pets by arrangement. Smoking in lounge only. Car park.

OWNERS Mary and Peter Cowking OPEN All year, exc Christmas
ROOMS 1 family, 1 double, 1 twin; all rooms with bath/shower
TERMS B&B £16, (single occupancy of twin/double) £19 (children up to 3 free, 3–12 half-price); deposit

SLINGSBY North Yorkshire map 7

Beech Tree House Farm

South Holme, Slingsby, York YO6 7BA
HOVINGHAM (0653) 628257

A long private driveway leads to Beech Tree House Farm. This nineteenth-century farmhouse is situated on a 270-acre mixed farm. Simple, clean accommodation and traditional home-cooked food, with vegetables from the garden and home-made bread and desserts, are on offer. There is a large play area for the children. Guests may wander or cycle around the farm on bicycles borrowed from Mr and Mrs Farnell. Croquet and pool are also available. Mr Farnell often takes guests who are interested on a tour of the farm. Dinner is available (6.30–7pm) and vegetarians can be catered for. Guests may bring their own wine to dinner. The farm is five miles from Castle Howard and 15 miles from York. Children welcome. No pets.

OWNERS Mr and Mrs R. W. Farnell OPEN All year, exc Christmas ROOMS 1 family, 1 double, 1 twin, 2 single TERMS B&B £12 (reductions for children); dinner £6; deposit

SOUTH CAVE Humberside map 8

Rudstone Walk Farmhouse

South Cave, nr Beverley HU15 2AH
HOWDEN (0430) 422230

Set in a quiet location at the foot of the Yorkshire Wolds, 400-year-old Rudstone Walk Farmhouse is a good base for East Yorkshire, and is only 20 minutes from Hull. The bedrooms, all furnished with antiques, are individually decorated. Six rooms have TV, eight are on the ground floor and one is suitable for the disabled. The spacious and elegantly furnished lounge has an inglenook fireplace. The licensed dining-room, where candle-lit dinners are served (weekdays only, 7pm), has an interesting collection of corn dollies. Vegetarians can be catered for on request and packed lunches can be provided. There are several self-catering cottages converted from farm buildings, which can be booked on a B&B basis. Children welcome. No pets. Car park. Tennis court. Very popular with business people and tourists; advance reservations are recommended.

OWNER Mrs Pauline Greenwood OPEN All year, exc Christmas ROOMS 1 family, 7 double, 7 twin, 3 single; 15 rooms with bath/shower TERMS B&B from £18, (single) from £21, (single occupancy of twin/double) £25, (family room) from £50; dinner £12.50; deposit ⅓ of total price; Amex

B&B rates specified in the details for each entry are per person per night; unless the details state otherwise, they are based on two people sharing a double or twin-bedded room.

SOUTHPORT Merseyside map 7

Ambassador Private Hotel

Bath Street, Southport PR9 ODP
SOUTHPORT (0704) 43998/30459

Built by a wealthy cotton-mill owner in 1845, this friendly, comfortable house has a small walled garden with pretty climbing plants and shrubs. It is very much a family-run hotel, and has been owned and operated by Margaret and Harry Bennett for close on 30 years. Margaret is in charge of preparing good home-cooked breakfasts, lunches, dinners (6–7pm) and bar snacks. Vegetarian meals are available. Later in the evening Harry plays the organ in the bar. There is one ground-floor room. No children under five. Pets by arrangement. No smoking in the dining-room. Car park.

OWNERS Margaret and Harry Bennett OPEN All year, exc New Year ROOMS 2 family, 2 double, 3 twin, 1 single; all rooms with bath/ shower TERMS B&B £25–£33, (family room) £75 (children under 12 half-price); dinner £9; deposit; Access, Visa

SOWERBY BRIDGE West Yorkshire map 7

Park Villa Guest House

141 Bolton Brow, Sowerby Bridge, Halifax HX6 2BE
HALIFAX (0422) 832179

Most of the Victorian features have been retained at this house – an original frieze, ceiling rose and stained-glass windows. The spacious rooms are colour-co-ordinated in soft pastel colours and all have radio-alarm and hair-dryer. The two single rooms have TV. There is a comfortable TV lounge with an antique Welsh dresser. Substantial breakfasts are served, and there are a number of eating establishments close by. Packed lunches can be provided. Situated on the A58 Halifax road, a five-minute drive to town. Children welcome. Pets by arrangement. Smoking in guest lounge only. Car park.

OWNERS Mr P. E. and Mrs C. E. Lane OPEN All year ROOMS 4 twin (3 with wash/basin), 2 single TERMS B&B £14–£17 (reductions for children); deposit

Where a single-occupancy rate is not specified in the details, the cost will be the same as that per person in a twin or double room, or will be included in the range of prices given.

STARBOTTON North Yorkshire map 7

Hilltop Country Guest House

Starbotton, nr Skipton BD23 5HY
KETTLEWELL (0756) 760321

Beautifully situated with fine views of Upper Wharfedale, the house overlooks the unspoilt village of Starbotton. Built for the Rathwell family in the seventeenth century, Hilltop, a listed property, and its adjacent barn have been converted into a comfortable guesthouse, with spacious bedrooms, all with TV. In the summer, guests can relax by the stream, the Cam Gill Beck, which runs through the property. Excellent dinners are served in the beamed dining-room (7pm) using local produce, after which you can enjoy a drink by the inglenook fireplace. Vegetarian meals are also available. Packed lunches can be made up on request. This is a popular haven for walkers, being close to the Three Peaks. Children welcome (reductions available). No smoking in bedrooms. No pets. Car park.

OWNERS Marie Louise and Tim Rathmell OPEN Mar–Nov
ROOMS 1 family, 2 double, 2 twin; all rooms with bath/shower
TERMS B&B £27; D, B&B £39; deposit £20 per room

STOCKSFIELD Northumberland map 10

The Dene

11 Cade Hill Road, Stocksfield NE43 7PB
STOCKSFIELD (0661) 842025

The Dene is an Edwardian house in a quiet position, surrounded by a beautiful garden and woodlands. The spacious rooms are comfortably furnished and decorated to a high standard. All bedrooms have easy chairs, radio-alarm and TV. The house is furnished with antiques, together with pictures and artefacts collected over many years from around the world. There are several lounges. Children welcome. No pets in bedrooms. Car park.

OWNERS P. A. and A. G. Mitchell OPEN All year, exc Christmas
ROOMS 3 twin (with bath/shower) TERMS B&B £14–£17.50 (children under 5 ⅓ reduction, under 12 ⅔); deposit £10 per person

Any smoking restrictions that we know of are given in each entry.

SUNDERLAND Tyne & Wear map 10

Mayfield Hotel

Sea Lane, Seaburn, Sunderland SR6 8EE
SUNDERLAND 091-529 3345

This is a pleasant turn-of-the-century house, approximately one mile from Sunderland and close to the sea. The immaculate bedrooms are well furnished and comfortable, all with TV. A large, freshly cooked breakfast is served and dinner is available by prior arrangement (6pm). Guests may bring their own wine to dinner. Plenty of parking. Children welcome.

OWNERS Margaret and John Close OPEN All year ROOMS 1 family (with bath/shower), 5 double (with bath/shower), 4 twin (3 with bath/shower, 1 with wash-basin), 1 single (with wash-basin) TERMS B&B £20, (single) £17, (single occupancy of twin/double) £30, (family room) 2 adults and 2 children £40; D, B&B £25; deposit

THIRLMERE Cumbria map 9

Brackenrigg

Thirlmere, Keswick CA12 4TF
KESWICK (076 87) 72258

This beautiful Victorian house is set in two acres of landscaped gardens and paddocks. It is in an elevated position and has magnificent views. The spacious bedrooms, four of which have *en suite* facilities, are well appointed. Breakfast and imaginative four-course dinners are served in the beamed, elegant dining-room (7.30pm). There is no alcohol licence, but guests may bring their own wine to dinner. The comfortable drawing-room has TV and a log fire. Brackenrigg is a splendid base from which to explore the Lake District. There are also three self-catering cottages. No children under five. No pets in the house. No smoking in the dining-room. Car park.

OWNERS Anne and Roy Wilson OPEN 1 Apr–end Oct
ROOMS 1 family, 3 double (with bath/shower), 1 twin (with bath/shower), 1 single (with wash-basin) TERMS B&B £16.50–£22, (children under 12 half-price if sharing with parents); dinner £12.50; deposit £20 per person

Many B&Bs are in remote places; always ask for clear directions when booking.

THIRSK North Yorkshire map 10

St James House

36 The Green, Thirsk YO7 1AQ
THIRSK (0845) 524120

This listed eighteenth-century Georgian house fronts The Green (a conservation area) and is two minutes' walk from the market-place. The house is tastefully decorated and furnished with antiques. The rooms are colour-co-ordinated, each bedroom named after its décor – green, blue and pink. There is TV in each of the bedrooms. A twin-bedded ground-floor room is available. Pony-trekking, golf and tennis can be arranged. Breakfast only is served, but there are some pubs and restaurants close by. No children under eight. No pets. No smoking.

OWNER Mrs Elizabeth Ogleby OPEN Mar–Oct ROOMS 2 family, 1 four-poster, 1 double; 2 rooms with bath/shower, 2 with wash-basin TERMS B&B £16, (single occupancy of double) £25, (family room) £44; deposit

THRESHFIELD North Yorkshire map 7

Bridge End Farm

Threshfield, nr Grassington BD23 5NH
GRASSINGTON (0756) 752463

This country cottage of great character has been restored to its original style. It has exposed beams, oak doors and window seats, and an attractive stone fireplace. Most of the furniture in the house is made by the owner, a master cabinet-maker with a workshop in the village. Breakfast and dinner (6.30–7pm) are served in the original flagstone-floor dining-room. Menus include roast duck, goose, venison and pheasant. There is no alcohol licence, but guests may bring their own wine to dinner. Vegetarian dishes can be provided. Packed lunches are also available. Stone steps lead up to the bedrooms and lounge. One room is on the ground floor. There is a music room downstairs which guests are welcome to enjoy. A large garden runs down to the River Wharfe,

Reduced rates for children are normally given when they share their parents' bedroom. If no reductions are specified in the details or text, assume you'll have to pay full rates.

If any bedrooms are suitable for the disabled we mention this in the entry.

just below Grassington Bridge, where guests may enjoy fishing. Children welcome. No pets. No smoking. Car park.

OWNERS A. L. and E. Thompson OPEN All year ROOMS 1 family, 2 double, 1 twin; all rooms with wash-basin TERMS B&B from £18 (babies free, toddlers 25%, 5–10 50%, 10–16 75%); dinner £11; deposit £15 per person

THROPTON Northumberland map 10

Bickerton Cottage Farm

Thropton, Morpeth NE65 7LW
ROTHBURY (0669) 40264

This 200-year-old stone cottage is in a most beautiful position, with panoramic views of countryside. The spacious, beamed sitting-room has the original stone fireplace. Guests have their own private entrance and staircase. Breakfast only is served and packed lunches can be provided. Bickerton Cottage is one mile from the B6344 and 12 miles from Otterburn. Children welcome. No dogs. No smoking. Car park.

OWNER Mrs Amanda France OPEN Mar–Nov ROOMS 1 double, 1 twin TERMS B&B £12.50–£15, (single occupancy of twin/double) £18–£22.50 (children under 5 £5); deposit

THURSBY Cumbria map 10

How End Farm

Thursby, Carlisle CA5 6PX
WIGTON (069 73) 42487

How End is a listed eighteenth-century farmhouse and a comfortable, simply furnished home, with original oak beams and a lovely wooden staircase. All rooms have hair-dryer. Margaret Swainson is a busy farmer's wife who enjoys making her guests feel at home. Coarse fishing is available nearby. Children welcome. No smoking in bedrooms.

OWNER Mrs Margaret Swainson OPEN All year ROOMS 1 family, 1 double, 1 twin TERMS B&B £12.50 (babies free, children under 2 £6, under 12 £8); deposit £5

TROUTBECK Cumbria map 10

Yew Grove

Troutbeck, nr Windermere LA23 1PG
AMBLESIDE (053 94) 33304

Yew Grove dates from the seventeenth century and is a whitewashed house built from local stone, situated in the unspoilt village of Troutbeck. The house was formerly the village post office and an office for Martin's Bank, until earlier this century when it offered 'apartments and refreshments'. Angela and Derek Pratt have established a comfortable and restful house in a peaceful location. Breakfast only is served. Packed lunches can be provided. There is a pub that serves evening meals half a mile away. The guest lounge is small and cosy and has TV. No pets. No smoking in the public rooms. Car park.

OWNERS Derek and Angela Pratt OPEN All year, exc Christmas ROOMS 3 double/1 family (2 with wash-basin), 1 twin (with wash-basin) TERMS B&B £14–£17.50 (30% reduction for children under 12 sharing with parents); deposit £10

ULVERSTON Cumbria map 9

Trinity House Hotel

Prince's Street, Ulverston LA12 7NB
ULVERSTON (0229) 57639

Built as a gentleman's residence in 1812, Trinity House is a Grade II listed building. Later it became the rectory to Holy Trinity Church. Today, the church building, with its beautiful William Morris stained-glass and its mature evergreens, provides a splendid backcloth to the small, informal hotel that the rectory has become. It has been sympathetically modernised to retain its original elegance. The sash windows in the front bedroom have been carefully double glazed, with french windows opening into individually decorated, spacious rooms; marble and slate fireplaces have been re-opened for those who want a cosy fire. All rooms have TV and five have telephone. There is one ground-floor room for the disabled, with easy access by a ramp from the car park. Evening meals (7.30–9pm) include local roast duck and poached salmon. A small bar area has been added. Packed lunches can be provided. Children welcome. Pets by arrangement. Car park.

OWNERS Stephanie Thompson and Keith Sutton OPEN All year, exc Jan ROOMS 1 family, 4 double, 2 twin, 1 single; all rooms with bath/shower TERMS B&B £22.50–£28, (single) £32.50–£35, (single occupancy of twin/double) £35–£40, (family room) £50–£60 (children under 5 free, £5 sharing with parents); dinner £12; deposit; Access, Visa

WALDRIDGE Co Durham map 10

Waldridge Hall Farm

Waldridge, Chester-le-Street DH2 3SL
DURHAM 091-388 4210

The seventeenth-century farmhouse is on a 200-acre working arable farm in pretty countryside, within walking distance of Waldridge Fell, the county's last remaining area of lowland heath. The large, lofty bedrooms are furnished with antiques; one room has a half-tester bed. All rooms have TV. Breakfast is served in a homely dining-room, which has an open fire and the original window shutters. There is a pleasant, informal atmosphere in this

If you are forced to turn up late into the evening, please telephone to warn the proprietor.

family-run farmhouse. Children welcome; a cot and high chair can be provided. No pets. No smoking.

OWNERS Arthur and Joan Smith OPEN All year ROOMS 1 family, 1 double, 1 twin TERMS B&B £16, (single occupancy of twin/double) £22 (children under 12 £7.50); deposit £10 per room

WALLINGTON Northumberland map 10

Shield Hall

Wallington, Morpeth NE61 4AQ
OTTERBURN (0830) 40387

Built in 1695, Shield Hall is set in the heart of the Northumberland border country, overlooking Wallington Hall, a National Trust property noted for its fine parks and gardens. A charming and elegant house has been created from the original eighteenth-century farm buildings, which form three sides of a courtyard. The guest rooms, although a little small, are completely self-contained. The long side of the courtyard contains the main house, including the sunny dining-room with its beamed ceiling, Delft rack and inglenook fireplace. Dinners are served at 6.30pm and there is an alcohol licence. Vegetarian choices and packed lunches can be provided. There are lovely views all round and the front garden is inhabited by doves. Shield Hall is a little tricky to find; it is two miles from Wallington and four miles south-west of Cambo. Children welcome. No pets. No smoking in public areas.

OWNERS Stephen and Celia Gay OPEN All year, exc Christmas ROOMS 1 family, 1 four-poster, 1 double, 2 twin, 1 single; all rooms with bath/shower, exc 1 twin TERMS B&B £17.50–£19.50, (single occupancy of twin/double) £30–£32, (family room) £14.50–£17.50 per person; dinner £9.50

WENTBRIDGE West Yorkshire map 7

The Corner Cafe

Wentbridge, Pontefract WF8 3JJ
PONTEFRACT (0977) 620316

Oak beams and stone walls are a feature of this guesthouse, which dates from the sixteenth century. It is located in a small village, yet is within easy access of the main roads and one mile from the A1. Breakfast only is served and there are some pubs nearby serving evening meals. The bedrooms are small, but spotlessly clean and decorated to a high standard; all have TV. A family *en suite* room has been added to the annexe adjacent to the main house. Two additional bedrooms in the annexe use the bathroom in the main house close by. Children welcome. Car park.

OWNER Mrs I. Goodworth OPEN All year, exc Christmas
ROOMS 1 family (with bath/shower), 1 double (with bath/shower), 1 twin (with bath/shower), 4 single TERMS B&B from £15, (single) £14–£16, (single occupancy of twin/double) £16; deposit £5 per person per night

WEST WITTON North Yorkshire map 10

Ivy Dene

West Witton, nr Leybyurn DL8 4LP
WENSLEYDALE (0969) 22785

Ivy Dene is a listed 300-year-old farmhouse in the Dales National Park. Tastefully decorated, the house still retains the country-cottage atmosphere. All of the bedrooms overlook glorious countryside and three have TV. There is an oak-beamed lounge with an open log fire and TV. A small, well-stocked bar enables guests to enjoy a drink. The bedrooms are prettily decorated with flowered fabrics and the top-floor beamed bedroom is very spacious and has sloping ceilings. No children under five. No pets. Smoking in the lounge only. Private parking. Advance bookings require a two-night minimum stay.

OWNERS Bob and June Dickinson OPEN All year, exc Christmas
ROOMS 1 family (with bath/shower), 1 four-poster (with bath/shower), 1 double (with wash-basin), 2 twin (1 with bath/shower, 1 with wash-basin), 1 single (with wash-basin) TERMS B&B £16–£20, (single occupancy of twin/double) £28–£36 (children 5–10 half price if sharing with adults); dinner £10; deposit £20 per room

WHITBECK Cumbria map 9

Hillcrest Country House

Whitbeck, nr Millom LA19 5UP
MILLOM (065 78) 288

This beautifully restored 300-year-old house was formerly the vicarage. The bedrooms have Victorian-style décor, and two have four-poster beds. A gracious, olde worlde atmosphere prevails, and there are oak beams, stone flags and numerous antiques.

Breakfast and dinner are served in the dining-room, which has an original open fireplace and a lovely grandfather clock. There is a cosy lounge, 'The snug', with TV and video. This is a good base from which to explore the western Lake District. No children under 10. Car park.

OWNER Mrs Hilary Roach OPEN All year, exc Christmas ROOMS 2 four-poster, 1 twin; all rooms with wash-basin TERMS B&B £20–£25; D, B&B £25–£30; dinner £10.50–£12.50

WHITBY North Yorkshire map 10

Elford

10 Prospect Hill, Whitby YO21 1QE
WHITBY (0947) 602135

Elford is a charming Victorian property. Its original occupants were associated with the whaling industry, for which Whitby was once famous. There is a beautiful pine stairway, a ceiling rose and an exceptionally attractive frieze in the dining-room. The hallway features antique furnishings. The rooms range in size from average to spacious, some with sloping ceilings. The house is immaculate throughout and well maintained. The guest lounge is very spacious, with an original tiled fireplace. Breakfast only is served, but there are some excellent places for dinner nearby. No children under three. No pets. Car park.

OWNER Mrs M. D. Dixon OPEN Mar–Oct ROOMS 1 family, 3 double, 3 twin, 1 single TERMS B&B £12.50–£14

WINDERMERE Cumbria map 9

The Archway

13 College Road, Windermere LA23 1BY
WINDERMERE (053 94) 45613

This small Victorian house is on a quiet street, a two-minute walk from the lake and the train station. The house is furnished in Victorian style, with patchwork quilts and hand-made bedcovers. There are antiques throughout the house, including a Welsh pine dresser and a high bed which belonged to the grandmother of owner Aurea Greenhalgh. The beautifully appointed bedrooms all have TV, telephone and radio-alarm. The emphasis is on wholefoods; candle-lit dinners are served (6.45pm) and everything is home-made and prepared with flair and imagination.

Vegetarian choices are available. There is a table licence, so guests may enjoy a drink with their dinner. Packed lunches can be arranged. Fires are lit in the comfortable sitting-room on chilly days. No children under 12. No pets. No smoking. Car park.

OWNERS Anthony and Aurea Greenhalgh OPEN All year
ROOMS 2 double, 2 twin, 1 single; all rooms with bath/shower
TERMS B&B £23–£25, (single occupancy of twin/double) £34; dinner £10.50; deposit £20

Birch House

11 Birch Street, Windermere LA23 1EG
WINDERMERE (053 94) 45070

Ideal for train travellers, Birch House is located on a quiet street just a three-minute walk from the station. The rooms are small and clean, and all have new beds, *en suite* facilities and TV. Breakfast only is served; packed lunches are also available. No children under 10. No pets. No off-street parking is allowed, but James Himlin has arranged for car parking at a nearby hotel.

OWNERS James and Deborah Himlin OPEN All year
ROOMS 3 double, 1 single; all rooms with bath/shower TERMS B&B £12–£15 (children under 10 £10); deposit; Access, Visa

Glenville

Lake Road, Windermere LA23 2EQ
WINDERMERE (053 94) 43371

This small, friendly, family-run hotel is located halfway between Windermere and Bowness. The bedrooms have all been freshly decorated with bright pastel wallpapers; all have TV. The top-floor rooms are very bright and airy with sloping sun-roofs. There is a well-furnished, comfortable TV lounge. The dining-room overlooks a pretty garden. Breakfast only is served and packed lunches are available. There is a small bar/lounge. Children welcome. No pets. No smoking in the dining-room. Car park.

OWNERS Joseph and Vera Crawford OPEN Feb–Nov
ROOMS 1 family, 5 double (2 with bath/shower), 2 twin (with bath/shower), 1 single (with bath/shower) TERMS B&B £17.50–£22, (single occupancy of twin/double) £20–£25 (babies free, children under 5 half-price); deposit £15 per person

Any smoking restrictions that we know of are given in each entry.

Kirkwood Guest House

Prince's Road, Windermere LA23 2DD
WINDERMERE (053 94) 43907

This attractive house is on a quiet side-street. Most of the bedrooms are large and have matching fabrics; all have TV. Evening meals are no longer available, but there are several eating establishments in the area. Children welcome. Pets by arrangement. No smoking in the dining-room. Transport to and from the rail station can be provided with advance notice.

OWNERS Mr and Mrs N. Cox OPEN All year ROOMS 2 family, 7 double/twin/family (2 with bath/shower) TERMS B&B £14–£18 (children up to 5 £5, 5–12 £9); deposit £15 per person; Access, Visa

WOLSINGHAM Co Durham map 10

Friarside Farm

Wolsingham, Weardale DL13 3BH
WEARDALE (0388) 527361

Friarside Farm is a mixed dairy and sheep farm. The sixteenth-century farmhouse is set amid spectacular scenery over the Wear Valley. An atmosphere of peace and tranquility pervades, and guests experience superb hospitality and excellent home cooking. The cosy guest lounge has TV. Delicious farmhouse breakfasts are served in the conservatory, with panoramic views. Packed lunches are also available by arrangement and dinner is served at 6.30pm. Vegetarians can be catered for by arrangement. Guests may bring their own wine to dinner. Children welcome. There is a small charge for small dogs. No smoking. Car park.

OWNERS Mr and Mrs J. J. Anderson OPEN All year ROOMS 2 double (with wash-basin) TERMS B&B £13–£14 (children under 12 £2 reduction); dinner £7–£8; deposit

WOOLER Northumberland map 10

Dene House

20 Church Street, Wooler NE71 6DA
WOOLER (0668) 81572

This detached Georgian-style house is on the edge of town, close to the twelfth-century church of St Mary's. The rooms are of a good size and are comfortable and clean. There is a guest lounge with TV. There is also a game-room with a snooker table and dartboard. Breakfast only is served, but there are lots of places for evening meals close by. Children welcome. No pets.

OWNER Mrs E. Weatherson OPEN Easter–Oct ROOMS 1 double, 1 twin, 1 single TERMS B&B £12

YORK North Yorkshire map 7

Curzon Lodge and Stable Cottages

23 Tadcaster Road, Dringhouses, York YO2 2QG
YORK (0904) 703157

This listed early seventeenth-century house is in a quiet location overlooking the Knavesmire Racecourse and is set in beautiful landscaped gardens. The house was formerly owned by the Terrys, one of the famous York 'chocolate families'. The bedrooms, four of which are on the ground floor, are tastefully decorated. There are two beautiful four-poster rooms and two rooms with Victorian brass beds; all have TV, radio, hair-dryer and easy chairs. Breakfast is served in the dining-room with its exposed beams and original quarry-tile floors. Wendy and Richard Wood welcome guests with a glass of sherry. There is a very comfortable drawing-room furnished with antiques. The stable cottage adjacent to the house has two bedrooms and a bathroom, also on the ground floor. No children under seven. No pets. No smoking in the dining-room. Car park.

OWNERS Wendy and Richard Wood OPEN All year, exc Christmas and New Year ROOMS 1 family, 5 double, 3 twin, 1 single; all rooms with bath/shower TERMS B&B £22–£26, (single) £30–£36, (family room) 4 persons sharing £19.50 per person (children sharing with 2 adults, 50–66% off adult price depending on age); deposit £20 per room

Farthings Hotel

5 Nunthorpe Avenue, York YO2 1PF
YORK (0904) 653545

Built in 1895, this spotless house is close to the centre of town and only a short walk from Micklegate Bar, the nearest gateway in the city walls. There are two ground-floor bedrooms with a bathroom on the same floor. There is a cosy guest lounge with a small bar where guests are often joined by the owners, Bob and Audrey Reid. Excellent breakfasts are served in the bright dining-room;

there is unlimited 'help-yourself' fresh coffee. Children welcome. No smoking in the dining-room.

OWNERS Bob and Audrey Reid OPEN All year, exc Christmas ROOMS 2 family (1 with bath/shower), 6 double (2 with bath/shower), 1 twin TERMS B&B from £15, (single occupancy of twin/double) from £26 (children under 12 £8 sharing family room); deposit

St Raphael Guest House

44 Queen Anne's Road, Bootham, York YO3 7AF
YORK (0904) 645028

This attractive mock-Tudor hotel is on a quiet street, a 10-minute walk from the Minster and city centre. The immaculate bedrooms are prettily decorated with matching fabrics. All have TV; sweets are also provided. The three bedrooms that are not *en suite* are on the top floor. The bright dining-room has an original stripped-pine fireplace. Evening meals are served (6–7pm); there is no alcohol licence, but guests may bring their own wines to dinner. Vegetarian choices can be provided. Packed lunches can be arranged. Children welcome. Parking space for one car.

OWNERS Raymond and Janet Farrell OPEN All year ROOMS 2 family (1 with bath/shower, 1 with wash-basin), 3 double (2 with bath/shower, 1 with wash-basin), 1 twin (with wash-basin), 1 single (with wash-basin) TERMS B&B £14–£17, (single) £11–£13, (single occupancy of twin/double) £20–£34; dinner £6.50; deposit 1 night charge; Access, Visa

Greater London

Alison House Hotel

82 Ebury Street SW1W 9QD
071-730 9529

The Alison House Hotel is part of a terrace dating from about 1880 and is in an excellent location, within walking distance of Buckingham Palace, Hyde Park and Victoria Station. It has been under new ownership since 1990 and offers fairly basic accommodation. Breakfast only is served in the small breakfast room. All bedrooms have TV. Children welcome. No pets. No smoking in the breakfast room or corridors.

OWNER Mr Gareth Owen OPEN All year ROOMS 3 double, 6 twin, 2 single; all rooms with wash-basin) TERMS B&B £23, (single) £28, (single occupancy of twin/double) £35; deposit; Visa

Avonmore Hotel

66 Avonmore Road W14 8RS
071-603 4296/3121 Fax 071-603 4035

This is a small hotel in a quiet residential street conveniently placed for both Olympia and Earls Court, with West Kensington underground station a few minutes' walk away. The owners have been gradually refurbishing the whole hotel and the bedrooms have either an *en suite* bath/shower-room or a separate, private bathroom. All have TV, telephone and a fridge stocked with soft drinks. Breakfast is served in the basement where there is also a bar. Children welcome. No pets.

OWNER Mrs Margaret McKenzie OPEN All year ROOMS 3 family (2 with bath/shower, 1 with wash-basin), 2 double (with bath/shower), 3 twin (with bath/shower), 1 single (with wash-basin) TERMS B&B £29, (single occupancy of twin/double) £47, (single) £37–£38, (family room) £59–£67 (children under 10 10% reduction); deposit 1 night charge

Bickenhall Hotel

119 Gloucester Place W1H 3PJ
071-935 3401

Bickenhall Hotel is an elegant Georgian building in a very central position, within two minutes' walk of Baker Street underground station. The hotel has been totally refurbished to a high standard, the large *en suite* bedrooms have rich wood furnishings and all are colour-co-ordinated. All bedrooms have telephone, trouser press and colour TV with satellite and radio channels. There is a comfortable guest lounge with an original fireplace. Breakfast and dinner (6–9pm) are served in the dining-room located on the ground floor, which leads out on to a pretty furnished patio. This is a family-run hotel which combines all the comforts of a hotel with a friendly atmosphere. Only small, trained dogs allowed. Children welcome. Reductions for children depending on time of the year. There is no car park but parking can be arranged.

OWNER Mrs Irene Aghabegian OPEN All year ROOMS 9 family (with bath/shower), 4 double (with bath/shower), 3 twin (1 with bath/shower, 2 with wash-basin), 7 single (4 with bath/shower, 3 with wash-basin) TERMS B&B £35, (single) £35–£50, (single occupancy of twin/double) £40–£55, (family room) £75–£90; deposit 1 night charge; Access, Amex, Diners, Visa

Chesham House Hotel

64–66 Ebury Street SW1W 9QD
071-730 8513

The building, dating from 1825, is part of a classic Georgian terrace with mews coach-houses at the back. Mozart lived at number 180, where he is alleged to have composed his first symphony, and Noel Coward used to live opposite. Chesham House Hotel offers basic accommodation, with approximately three bedrooms to each bathroom. All have TV. Breakfast only is served in the basement breakfast room. Children welcome. No pets.

OWNER Mr E. J. Fletcher OPEN All year, exc Christmas
ROOMS 3 family, 7 double, 8 twin, 5 single; all rooms with wash-basin
TERMS B&B £22–£24, (single) £28–£30, (single occupancy of twin/double) £33–£35, (family room) £54–£60; deposit 1 night charge; Access, Amex, Diners, Visa

Collin House

104 Ebury Street SW1W 9QD
071-730 8031

A mid-Victorian house in the convenient location of Ebury Street, Collin House is owned by a very helpful couple who go out of their way to be of assistance to their guests. The bedrooms vary in size, are well decorated and nearly all have *en suite* bathrooms.

This is a fairly basic little guesthouse. Breakfast only is served. Children welcome. No smoking in the breakfast room. No pets.

OWNERS Dafydd and Beryl Thomas OPEN All year, exc Christmas ROOMS 1 family (with wash-basin), 5 double (4 with bath/shower, 1 with wash-basin), 4 twin (2 with bath/shower, 2 with wash-basin), 3 single (with bath/shower) TERMS B&B £23–£27, (single) £32–£34, (family room) £64; deposit 1 night charge

Colonnade Hotel

2 Warrington Crescent W9 1ER
071-286 1052 Fax 071-286 1057

The Colonnade was built in 1853 as two private houses and since then it has been a girls' boarding school, a nursing home and – as the blue plaque outside attests – where Sigmund Freud lived. This family-run hotel offers an extremely high standard of accommodation. Bedrooms vary in size, but the suites and four-poster rooms are very large and plush, with Jacuzzi-style baths. All have TV, radio, telephone, hair-dryer and trouser press. An excellent breakfast is served in the dining-room, and both à la carte and set dinners are available. Packed lunches are also available on request. The bar leads off the dining-room, and beyond is a most attractive patio, which is a delightful place to sit and enjoy a drink on a warm day. There is a comfortable lounge off the reception area. The Colonnade is within a one-minute walk of both the underground and buses and is close to the canal basin of Little Venice (where a traditional narrow boat carries passengers along the Regent's Canal to Regent's Park and the Zoo). The Colonnade continues to provide excellent value for money. Smoking restrictions. Children welcome. No pets. Car park.

OWNER J. H. Richards OPEN All year ROOMS 10 family, 9 four-poster, 20 twin, 10 single; all rooms with bath/shower TERMS B&B £30–£45, (single occupancy of twin/double) £55 (reductions for children under 10 £3, 10–16 £6); Access, Amex, Diners, Visa

Demetriou Guest House

9 Strathmore Gardens W8 4RZ
071-229 6709

Tucked away on a quiet cul-de-sac in a residential area, the Demetriou Guest House is in an excellent location, being within a few minutes' walk of Kensington Gardens and Hyde Park, and both Notting Hill Gate and Queensway underground stations. The house is in good decorative order, the rooms are simply furnished and all have TV. Tea- and coffee-makers are available on request. Breakfast only is served in the dining-room, where smoking is not allowed. Children welcome. No pets.

OWNERS A. and I. Demetriou OPEN All year, exc Christmas
ROOMS 2 family, 3 double, 3 twin, 1 single; all rooms with wash-basin
TERMS B&B £20, (single) £27, (family room) £19 per person (50% reduction for children under 10); deposit 1 night charge

Ebury House Hotel

102 Ebury Street SW1W 9QD
071-730 1350

A listed building dating from around 1800, Ebury House Hotel has been run by David and Marilyn Davies for the past 12 years and they manage to have time to talk to their guests and to help with sightseeing. The bedrooms are on the small side but have been freshly decorated, and are bright and clean. All have wash-basin, colour TV and hair-dryer. The small breakfast room, where breakfast only is served, is panelled in pine and decorated with pieces of china. Children welcome. No pets.

OWNERS David and Marilyn Davies OPEN All year, exc Christmas
ROOMS 1 family, 4 double, 4 twin, 3 single; all rooms with wash-basin
TERMS B&B £23–£25, (single occupancy of twin/double) £33–£38, (family room) £60–£70

Enrico Hotel

77–79 Warwick Way SW1V 1QP
071-834 9538

Enrico Hotel has to be one of the most immaculately kept bed and breakfast establishments in London – everything about it seems to sparkle and shine. The bedrooms are simply furnished and modest in size. None have *en suite* bathroom or toilet but some rooms do have shower cubicles, and there are bathrooms on each floor. Breakfast only is served in the cheerful, bright basement dining-room and guests may sit in the lounge, where there is a TV. This hotel is ideally located for sightseeing and for day-trips from Victoria Station, which is a seven-minute walk away. Good-value

When the family-room rate is given in the details it applies to the cost of the whole room, unless a rate per person is specified.

accommodation. No smoking in the breakfast room. Car park nearby.

OWNERS Mr and Mrs Desira OPEN All year ROOMS 13 double (5 with shower, 8 with wash-basin), 9 twin (5 with shower, 4 with wash-basin), 4 single (with wash-basin) TERMS B&B £15–£20, (single) £24–£26; full payment on day of arrival; Access, Visa

Harcourt House Hotel

50 Ebury Street SW1W 0LU
071-730 2722

This five-storey Victorian guesthouse, dating from about 1830, is in a main thoroughfare in an area of interesting small shops, wine bars and restaurants. The house has been a hotel since 1896 and was allegedly the refuge of a spy during the First World War. Ebury Street is within walking distance of Buckingham Palace, St James's Park and Victoria Station. The guesthouse offers fairly basic accommodation, with small bedrooms, all of which have their own TV. Breakfast only is served in the attractive basement breakfast room. No smoking in the breakfast room. No children under six. No pets.

OWNERS David and Glesni Wood OPEN All year, exc Christmas ROOMS 1 family (with bath/shower), 4 double (3 with bath/shower), 3 twin (2 with bath/shower), 1 single (with bath/shower) TERMS B&B £23–£28, (single) £44, (family room) £76; deposit 1 night charge; Amex

Harlingford Hotel

61–63 Cartwright Gardens WC1H 9EL
071-387 4616

A medium-sized hotel consisting of three converted Georgian houses in a most attractive crescent, offering a peaceful oasis close to the busy streets of Bloomsbury. It is in an excellent location for public transport and getting around London, and guests have access to the tennis courts in the crescent gardens. In the past couple of years bathrooms have been added to nearly all the bedrooms and the whole place has been redecorated and refurnished. All bedrooms have TV and telephone. There is a lounge with TV and a spacious dining-room, where breakfast

Where a single-occupancy rate is not specified in the details, the cost will be the same as that per person in a twin or double room, or will be included in the range of prices given.

where breakfast only is served. No smoking in the dining-room. Children welcome. No pets.

OWNERS Paul and Tina Gabriele OPEN All year ROOMS 2 family (with bath/shower), 7 double (with bath/shower), 5 twin (1 with bath/shower, 4 with wash-basin), 3 single (with bath/shower) TERMS B&B £17–£23, (single) £24–£30, (family room) £42–£48 (children under 12 half-price); deposit 1 night charge

Merryfield House Hotel

42 York Street W1H 1FN
071-935 8326

A listed building dating from around 1899, this hotel was originally a pub called The Lord Keith. Located in a reasonably quiet street, it is very close to Baker Street, Oxford Street and Madame Tussaud's. The bedrooms have recently been equipped with folding beds, which creates more space for the table and chairs at breakfast, which is served in the rooms. All rooms have their own TV. Children welcome. No dogs.

OWNER G. K. Tyler-Smith OPEN All year ROOMS 1 family, 7 double; all rooms with bath/shower TERMS B&B £21.50–£22.50, (single occupancy of double) £33–£35, (family room) £62–£66

Oxford House Hotel

92–94 Cambridge Street SW1V 4QG
071-834 6467/9681

This is a family-run hotel with a warm, friendly atmosphere. When Mr Kader came to England from India he helped out at the Oxford House Hotel, and he enjoyed it so much he eventually bought it. That was over 20 years ago and he now runs the hotel with his wife. A 150-year-old terraced house, Oxford House Hotel is a comfortable place in a quiet residential street, 10 minutes' walk from Victoria Station. The bedrooms are basic, good-sized and decorated with matching wallpaper and curtains. There is a pleasant basement breakfast room, where breakfast only is served, and a TV lounge on the ground floor. Children welcome. Pets by arrangement.

OWNER Mr Yunus Kader OPEN All year ROOMS 6 family, 5 double, 4 twin, 2 single; all rooms with wash-basin TERMS B&B £19, (single) £28, (family room) £16 per person; deposit 1 night charge; payment in full on arrival; Access, Visa

Parkwood Hotel

4 Stanhope Place W2 2HB
071-402 2241

In a quiet street just off Marble Arch, the Parkwood Hotel is in a superb location – five minutes to Marble Arch and Oxford Street. The hotel has been upgraded and is bright and freshly decorated. The rooms are of quite a reasonable size, all with TV and telephone. There is a small, sunny terrace at the back with a picnic table which guests are welcome to use, and a small basement breakfast room, hung with old posters, where breakfast only is served. There are a lot of stairs to climb and no lift. No smoking in the dining-room. Children welcome.

OWNER Peter Evans OPEN All year ROOMS 4 family (3 with bath/shower, 1 with wash-basin), 3 double (with bath/shower), 7 twin (6 with bath/shower, 1 with wash-basin), 4 single (1 with bath/shower, 3 with wash-basin) TERMS B&B £27–£32, (single) £40–£55, (family room) £64–£74; deposit 1 night charge; Access, Visa

Romany House Hotel

35 Longmoore Street SW1V 1JQ
071-834 5553

Romany House Hotel is said to be 500 years old and at one time the haunt of highwaymen. With its steep, narrow staircases and latticed windows, the house and cottage together form a building of character. The two basement rooms form the pretty dining-room and are the focal point. The two rooms above, reached by a narrow staircase, provide two of the 10 bedrooms. There are three bedrooms on the ground floor and the one cottage room has an outside entrance and is not too convenient for the bathroom, but it is adequate and comfortable. The hotel is simply furnished and kept spotlessly clean by the owners. Reductions for children up to six months old. No pets. No smoking in the breakfast room. On-street parking only at weekends.

OWNERS Peter and Mary Gulbitis OPEN All year, exc Christmas
ROOMS 6 double, 2 twin, 2 single; all rooms with wash-basin
TERMS B&B £16, (single) £21, (single occupancy of twin/double) £25; deposit £5; 1 night's full payment in advance in peak period

Reduced rates for children are normally given when they share their parents' bedroom. If no reductions are specified in the details or text, assume you'll have to pay full rates.

17 Ovington Street

17 Ovington Street SW3 2JA
071-584 2722

This is a small and narrow terraced house in a quiet residential street in the heart of fashionable Knightsbridge – a stone's throw from Harrods and Beauchamp Place. There is a good-sized basement bedroom, with sofabed, wash-basin, toilet and TV. There is a second single room on the first floor, also with TV. Both can be made twin-bedded if requested. The shared bathroom is between the ground and first floors. On the ground floor there is a long, beautifully furnished sitting-room, and breakfast only is served in the kitchen, which leads out on to a small garden patio with tables and chairs. There are some small reductions for children. No smoking. No pets.

OWNER Margaret Parsons OPEN All year, exc Christmas ROOMS 2 single (with wash-basin and toilet) TERMS B&B £20–£25; deposit; full payment on arrival preferred

Swiss House Hotel

171 Old Brompton Road SW5 0AN
071-373 9383/2769

In the heart of South Kensington, this hotel is on a main road, a bus route and close to South Kensington and Gloucester Road underground stations. It has been attractively decorated and there are dried-flower displays throughout the hotel. The rooms are comfortable, some with *en suite* bathrooms, and all have TV and telephone. It has an unusual basement dining-room where a substantial Continental breakfast is laid out on a Welsh dresser, which includes croissant, cheese and cereal. Cooked breakfast is extra, and room service is available throughout the day. Packed lunches can also be provided. Credit card payments are subject to a five per cent surcharge. Children under two stay free and cots are available free of charge. No smoking in the dining-room. Children welcome. Only well-trained dogs and guide dogs accepted.

OWNER Peter Vincenti OPEN All year ROOMS 4 family (with bath/shower), 4 double (2 with bath/shower, 2 with wash-basin), 4 twin (2 with bath/shower, 2 with wash-basin), 4 single (2 with bath/shower, 2 with wash-basin) TERMS B&B £23–£27, (single) £30–£43.50, (family room) £18–£21 per person (children under 2 free); deposit 1 night charge; Access, Visa

Terstan Hotel

29–31 Nevern Square SW5 9PE
081-835 1900

This is a family-run hotel in an attractive square with access to gardens. It continues to provide good value for money and has friendly, helpful staff. The bedrooms are quite pleasantly decorated and all have TV and telephone. The majority have private bathrooms and tea/coffee-making facilities. There is a bar open to residents until 1am, a pool-room, small lounge and breakfast room (where a full English breakfast is served), and lift access to all floors. This hotel is very conveniently placed for both the Earls Court and Olympia exhibition halls. Children welcome. No smoking in the dining-room. No dogs.

OWNER Mr S. Tabaka OPEN All year, exc Christmas
ROOMS 6 family, 6 double, 12 twin, 26 single; 34 rooms with bath/shower, 16 rooms with wash-basin TERMS B&B £26–£28, (single) £28–£42, (family room) £60–£70 (children under 2 free in parents' room; £3 charge for a cot); deposit; Access, Visa

Vicarage Private Hotel

10 Vicarage Gate W8 4AG
071-229 4030

This Victorian house with an impressive façade and entrance hall is located in a quiet square, in the heart of Kensington and just a few minutes' walk from Kensington High Street. Most bedrooms are of a good size. None have private bathroom but there is a shower-room with toilets on every floor. The hotel also provides hair-dryer and iron on request. There is a small sitting-room with TV on the ground floor and a large dining-room in the basement where a full English breakfast is served. Children welcome. No pets.

OWNERS Martin and Eileen Diviney OPEN All year
ROOMS 3 family, 3 double, 4 twin, 9 single; all rooms with wash-basin
TERMS B&B £25, (single) £28, (family room) £60–£65; deposit 1 night charge

Bath/shower information in the details refers only to a private bathroom or shower; other bathroom facilities at the establishments will be shared. We say if rooms have wash-basins.

Windermere Hotel

142–144 Warwick Way SW1V 4JE
071-834 5163 Fax 071-630 8831

Windermere Hotel is within a few minutes' walk of Victoria railway station, bus terminal and underground and is full of charm and character. The two houses are good examples of early Victorian architecture, and in 1990 they were completely refurbished and joined to form one hotel. The bedrooms are attractively furnished and decorated and all have TV and telephone. Some bedrooms also have a mini-fridge and trouser press. The basement coffee-shop has recently been created, a most attractive, spacious room where breakfast and simple evening meals are served. Snacks and drinks are available at any time of the day from the coffee-shop or from room service. A Continental-style breakfast is also available for guests with an early-morning departure. Children welcome; cots are provided free of charge. Guide dogs only. No smoking in the dining-room.

OWNERS Nick and Sylvia Hambi OPEN All year ROOMS 4 family (with bath/shower), 11 double (9 with bath/shower, 2 with wash-basin), 5 twin (4 with bath/shower, 1 with wash-basin), 3 single (2 with bath/shower, 1 with wash-basin) TERMS B&B £24.50–£39, (single occupancy of twin/double) £44–£59, (single) £38–£49, (family room) £79–£86; deposit 1 night charge; Access, Amex, Carte Blanche, Visa

Woodville House

107 Ebury Street SW1W 9QU
071-730 1048 Fax 071-730 2574

Woodville House is a Georgian building in Belgravia and ideally situated for Victoria railway station, the underground and buses. The guesthouse has a warm and friendly atmosphere, and Ian Berry and Rachel Joplin go out of their way to make sure their guests have a comfortable and enjoyable stay. The breakfast room is on the ground floor, as is a kitchenette where guests may prepare tea/coffee or light snacks, and use the ironing facilities. A pretty furnished patio garden is open to guests, where they may sit out on fine days. All bedrooms have TV, and some have air-conditioning. No smoking in the breakfast room. Children welcome. No pets.

OWNERS Ian Berry and Rachel Joplin OPEN All year
ROOMS 2 family, 3 double, 3 twin, 4 single; all rooms with wash-basin
TERMS B&B £25, (single), £34, (family room) £66–£80 (children under 2 free); deposit

Scotland

ABERDEEN Grampian map 11

Bracklinn Guest House

348 Great Western Road, Aberdeen AB1 6LX
ABERDEEN (0224) 317060

This Victorian end-of-terrace town house in a conservation area is on a main road, with easy access to the town centre, and well placed for visiting the castles of Royal Deeside and the seaside. The lounge (with TV) and the large bedroom above it have exceptionally fine ceilings. The bedrooms are spacious and comfortable. All have TV. The whole house is immaculately kept and has been attractively decorated. Breakfast only is served. Children welcome and reductions available by arrangement. Small dogs only. Car park.

OWNERS Gordon and Pel-Ling Petrie OPEN All year, exc Easter ROOMS 2 family (1 with bath/shower, 1 with wash-basin), 1 double (with bath/shower), 3 single (with wash-basin) TERMS B&B £14–£16, (single) £18, (single occupancy of double) £22–£32, (family room) £36–£40; deposit

ABERDOUR Fife map 11

Hawkcraig House

Hawkcraig Point, Aberdour KY3 0TZ
ABERDOUR (0383) 860335

Hawkcraig House is at the end of a narrow road, reached through an immense car park and down a short, extremely steep and rough track. The house stands at the foot of the cliffs, with spectacular views across the River Forth to Edinburgh and round the bay to Aberdour. A 15-minute walk along a shoreline footpath brings you to Aberdour station, from where Edinburgh is a 30-minute train ride. There are two very comfortable ground-floor bedrooms with a view, both *en suite* and with TV. There is also a sitting-room/breakfast room. Pre-dinner drinks are served in the sitting-room upstairs overlooking the sea and excellent, freshly-prepared Scottish food is served in the elegant, small dining-room. Evening meals (7–8.30pm) must be booked 24 hours ahead. Vegetarians can be catered for and packed lunches

When the family-room rate is given in the details it applies to the cost of the whole room, unless a rate per person is specified.

provided on request. There is no alcohol licence, but guests may bring their own wine. No children under eight. No pets. No smoking. Car park.

OWNER Mrs Elma Barrie OPEN Feb–Nov ROOMS 1 double, 1 twin; both rooms with bath/shower TERMS B&B £16–£18, (single occupancy of twin/double) £20–£22 (25% reduction for children sharing with parents); dinner £15.50

ABERLEMNO Tayside map 11

Wood of Auldbar Farmhouse

Aberlemno, by Brechin DD9 6SZ
ABERLEMNO (030 783) 218

This turn-of-the-century stone building is a working mixed farm set in a small front garden and orchard, surrounded by open countryside. Home-cooked dinner (from 6pm) and breakfast are served in the conservatory, which has been built on to the front of the house and has a lovely view. Packed lunches and vegetarian choices at dinner are available. Guests may bring their own wine. The accommodation is simple but clean. There is also a TV lounge. The Angus Glens, Royal Deeside, Balmoral and Glamis Castle are within easy reach. No pets in the house. No smoking in bedrooms. Car park.

OWNER Jean Stewart OPEN All year, exc Christmas and New Year ROOMS 1 family, 1 twin, 1 single TERMS B&B £12–£15, (family room) from £36 (babies free, reductions for children under 10); dinner from £7; deposit

ABINGTON Strathclyde map 9

Craighead Farm

Crawfordjohn Road, Abington ML12 6SQ
CRAWFORD (086 42) 356

This stone-built, whitewashed farmhouse with red and black trim dates from the fourteenth century and is on a 600-acre mixed farm, set in peaceful, rolling countryside. Although in quite a remote spot, it is well placed for the main Glasgow–Carlisle road. There are two comfortable bedrooms upstairs, a toilet halfway down and a large bathroom on the ground floor. Evening meals are served in the dining-room from 6.30pm, and menus are flexible. Packed lunches can be provided on request and vegetarian choices are available. Guests may bring their own wine to dinner. Fishing can be arranged. Children are welcome and baby-sitting is provided. No pets in bedrooms. No smoking in the dining-room. Car park.

OWNERS Mr and Mrs George Hodge OPEN May–Nov
ROOMS 1 double (with wash-basin), 1 twin (with wash-basin), 1 single
TERMS B&B £12.50–£13 (children under 5 free, over 5 one-third reduction); dinner £7–£8; deposit

ABOYNE Grampian map 11

Hazlehurst Lodge

Ballater Road, Aboyne AB34 5HY
ABOYNE (033 98) 86921

Hazelhurst Lodge stands in an attractive, wooded garden just off the A93 on the edge of town and was built in 1880 as the coachman's lodge to Aboyne Castle. The owners have kept its Victorian character, with Victorian cut glass and old linen table-cloths, as well as introducing some contemporary works of art and French porcelain tableware. The bedrooms are attractively furnished; two have shower units. A breakfast room at the back of the house serves breakfast and dinner, and lunch by arrangement. Packed lunches are also available and vegetarians can be catered for. The hotel is licensed. The immaculate, small dining-room at the front of the house is used mostly by non-residents. There are two comfortable sitting-rooms for guests' use. There is a four per cent surcharge on payments made by credit card. Children welcome. No pets in bedrooms. Priority given to non-smokers. Car park.

OWNERS Anne and Eddie Strachan OPEN Feb–Dec
ROOMS 3 double (2 with bath/shower, 1 with wash-basin), 2 twin
TERMS B&B £20, (single occupancy of twin/double) £27; dinner from £14; deposit; Access, Amex, Visa

ALLIGIN Highland map 11

Grianan

Alligin, Torridon IV22 2HB
TORRIDON (044 587) 264

This small, neat modern bungalow is in a spectacular position on the north shore of Upper Loch Torridon, with wonderful views over the loch to the mountains on the other side. It is in a very remote spot and reached by a beautifully scenic, narrow road from Torridon. One bedroom has a front view, the other is at the back of the house. The lounge, with dining table, serves breakfast and evening meals (by arrangement at 7pm). Vegetarian options are available and guests may bring their own wine. A small patio and front garden offer space for sitting out. Children welcome. No pets. No smoking in bedrooms. Car park.

OWNER Mrs M. A. MacDonald OPEN Apr–Sept ROOMS 1 double, 1 twin TERMS B&B from £12; dinner from £7.50; deposit

ANCRUM Borders map 10

Ancrum Craig

Ancrum, Jedburgh TD8 6UN
ANCRUM (083 53) 280

Approached up a narrow lane and along a rough track, Ancrum Craig is a substantial early Victorian country house with wonderful views. It has many of its original features, and both the dining-room and the drawing-room are elegant. The three bedrooms are spacious, one with an exceptionally large double bed, and all have private or *en suite* bathroom, one with an old-fashioned bath. Breakfast only is available. Guests have use of the games-room, with table tennis and darts, and the garden with its lovely views. Children welcome. Car park.

OWNER Mrs Jill Hensens OPEN Apr–Oct ROOMS 2 double, 1 twin; all rooms with bath/shower TERMS B&B £13–£15, (single occupancy of twin/double) £18–£24 (cot in double £5)

ANNAN Dumfries & Galloway map 9

Northfield House

Annan DG12 5LL
ANNAN (0461) 202851

Set in lovely grounds with the River Annan at the bottom, this is an attractive country house thought to be partly Georgian and partly Victorian. All the rooms are large and have a spacious feel. As they are all on one level they are suitable for disabled guests. The three bedrooms are comfortably furnished, all with their own bathroom and TV. The beds all have crowns and drapes. The dining-room has separate tables for breakfast and dinner, which is served at 7.30pm. The menu changes from day to day and can include dishes such as caviare pie with smoked salmon, poached Annan sea trout with hollandaise sauce and Glenfiddich chocolate mousse. Vegetarians can be catered for by arrangement. Packed lunches are also available. There is no alcohol licence, but guests may bring their own wine to dinner. The large sitting-room has views down to the river and a stretch of the river is available for guests for salmon and trout fishing. There is also a large garden and croquet lawn. No children under 13. No pets. No smoking in the dining-room and bedrooms. Car park.

OWNERS James and Mary Airey OPEN All year, exc Christmas and Jan ROOMS 2 double, 1 twin; all rooms with bath/shower TERMS B&B £26–£30, (single occupancy of twin/double) £36–£41; dinner £18; deposit

ARDNADAM Strathclyde map 11

Firpark Hotel

Shore Road, Ardnadam, Dunoon PA23 8QG
DUNOON (0369) 6506/2214

This solidly built house dates from 1850 and was originally the summer residence of a ship owner. It has a most unusual lounge, a half-panelled room with a carved wooden fireplace and ministrels' gallery with piano. Some of the bedrooms are large and some have wonderful views. All have TV. The bar has recently been brightly redecorated and sailing photographs adorn the walls. Dinner is served from 6pm and vegetarians can be catered for. Packed lunches and cheap bar meals are also available. This hotel stands on a corner site at Lazaretto Point and has sea views on two sides. There is a pleasant garden with tables and chairs for sitting out. Children welcome. No pets in public rooms. Car park.

OWNER Mrs Pat Lamont OPEN All year, exc Christmas Day and New Year's Day ROOMS 3 double (1 with bath/shower, 2 with wash-basin), 2 twin (1 with bath/shower, 1 with wash-basin), 2 single (with wash-basin) TERMS B&B £18–£20, (single occupancy of twin/double) £19.75–£21 (children half-price); dinner £10.50–£15; Access, Visa

Most B&Bs don't accept credit cards, but when they do we list the cards taken.

If you intend to spend several days at a B&B, it is worth asking whether there are reduced rates, particularly if the period is midweek or off-season.

ARINAGOUR Strathclyde (Coll) map 11

Tigh-na-Mara Guest House

Arinagour, Isle of Coll PA78 6SY
COLL (087 93) 354

Built in the early 1980s by the owners themselves on the site of Robert Sturgeon's old childhood home, the house offers stunning views out to sea, and on clear days to the Treshnish Isles, Mull and Staffa. The house is the first you come to after leaving the ferry and stands a little outside the main settlement of Arinagour. Robert Sturgeon is responsible for maintaining the large and colourful garden with croquet lawn, and he is happy to take guests out trout fishing and lobstering and organise boat trips to see the seals. Bicycles and mopeds can be hired, and golf clubs are available. Evening meals are served on Sundays only at 6.30pm and offer a mainly seafood menu. Vegetarians can be catered for and packed lunches are available. There is an alcohol licence and all bedrooms have their own mini-bar. Children welcome. No dogs in the dining-room and only by prior arrangement. No smoking in the dining-room and one twin room. Car park.

OWNERS Robert and Ruth Sturgeon OPEN All year, exc Christmas and New Year ROOMS 2 family (1 with bath/shower, 1 with wash-basin), 3 double (1 with bath/shower, 2 with wash-basin), 2 twin (with wash-basin), 1 single (with wash-basin) TERMS B&B £15.30, (single occupancy of twin/double) £21.80 (children half-price sharing with adults); dinner £12–£15; deposit

ARISAIG Highland map 11

The Old Library Lodge and Restaurant

Arisaig PH39 4NH
ARISAIG (068 75) 651

This stone-built converted barn is in the middle of the small village of Arisaig, overlooking the sea towards the islands of the Inner Hebrides. It is primarily a restaurant, serving simple, good home-cooked food at both lunch and dinner (6.30–9.30pm). Vegetarian choices are available and packed lunches can be provided on request. The premises are also licensed. The interior of the restaurant is partly whitewashed, with some natural stone walls, and there is some space for sitting outside. There are now three prettily decorated bedrooms on the first floor and a further four in an extension to the back of the house. Some of the bedrooms have TV. There are ferry links with the islands of Skye, Rhum, Eigg and Muck. Children welcome. Car park.

OWNERS Angela and Alan Broadhurst OPEN Easter–end Oct
ROOMS 4 double, 2 twin, 1 single; all rooms with bath/shower
TERMS B&B £28, (single) £22, (single occupancy of twin/double) £38; dinner £18.50; deposit £20; Access, Visa

ARROCHAR Strathclyde map 11

Succoth Farm House

Arrochar G83 7AL
ARROCHAR (030 12) 591

This whitewashed building is in a quiet spot on the edge of the village of Arrochar. The house overlooks Loch Long and there are views of the surrounding hills. The house was taken over by the Armstrongs in 1990 and they have completely redecorated. The bedrooms are comfortable and spacious, and they have been charmingly furnished. Breakfast only is served and packed lunches can be provided. There are facilities close by for canoe-hire, riding, cycling, fishing and water-skiing. No children under 10. No pets inside the house. No smoking. Car park.

OWNERS Hammy and Adrienne Armstrong OPEN All year
ROOMS 2 double (with wash-basin), 1 twin (with bath/shower)
TERMS B&B from £13, (single occupancy of twin/double) from £15

Tarbet House

Loch Lomond, Tarbet, by Arrochar G83 7DE
ARROCHAR (030 12) 349

This is a large house built in the 1960s and in a wonderful position overlooking mature gardens of trees and shrubs down to Loch Lomond. The bedrooms are spacious and all have loch views (one room has a balcony). The large sitting-room/dining-room enjoys the splendid views, as does the outside sun terrace. Dinner is available by prior arrangement up to four evenings per week. The menu is simple, usually with three choices per course. Packed lunches are available and vegetarians can be catered for. There is no licence, but guests may bring their own wine. John and Christine Harvey are both experienced mountaineers and sailors, and the focus here is on activity holidays for adults, including mountain walking, scrambling, sailing and orienteering. Guests choosing their own activities are also welcome. The grounds include a tennis court and launching facilities for boats. Pets by arrangement. No smoking inside the house. Car park.

OWNERS Christine and John Harvey OPEN Jan–Oct
ROOMS 2 double (1 with bath/shower, 1 with wash-basin), 1 twin (with bath/shower), 1 single (with wash-basin) TERMS B&B £15–£22.50, (single occupancy of twin/double) £18–£25, (single) £18–£21; dinner £10; deposit £5

AUCHENCAIRN Dumfries & Galloway map 9

Bluehill Farm

Auchencairn, Castle Douglas DG7 1QW
AUCHENCAIRN (055 664) 228

Bluehill Farm is a whitewashed building standing a quarter of a mile along a narrow road above the village, with rural views down to the sea. This is a working dairy farm and looks like two houses set at right angles to each other (the smaller of the two probably being the oldest part with a later, larger addition). The house is sparkling and immaculately clean, and there are plants throughout. The bedrooms are comfortable, spacious, attractively decorated and have TV. There is also a lounge for guests' use. Breakfast only is available, and is elegantly served in the conservatory sitting area, which has views to the sea. No pets or smoking in bedrooms. Car park.

OWNER D. Cannon OPEN Easter–Sept ROOMS 2 double, 1 twin; all rooms with bath/shower TERMS B&B £18–£20, (single occupancy of twin/double) £25; deposit

AVIEMORE Highland map 11

Kinapol Guest House

Dalfaber Road, Aviemore PH22 1PY
AVIEMORE (0479) 810513

This is a modern, chalet-type house, built by the owners in 1973. The back of the house has lovely views over the garden to the River Spey and the Cairngorm Mountains. Although Kinapol Guest House is close to the railway line (immediately behind the station), it is in a quiet spot and only a two-minute walk from the village. Mrs Hall will often leave a home-baked treat with the tea and coffee, available on a hot trolley all day in the large lounge/ breakfast room with TV. Breakfast only is served and packed lunches can be provided. The bedrooms are small and functional, and a bathroom is on each floor. Some rooms have mountain views. Children welcome, but there are no facilities for babies. No dogs. No smoking at breakfast. Car park.

OWNERS Mr and Mrs D. G. Hall OPEN All year ROOMS 2 family, 3 double; all rooms with wash-basin TERMS B&B £12.50–£13, (single occupancy of double) £16–£20 but not at peak period, (family room) £31–£33 (children half-price sharing with parents, free under 5); deposit 1 night charge

AYR Strathclyde map 9

Windsor Hotel

6 Alloway Place, Ayr KA7 2AA
AYR (0292) 264689

Windsor Hotel is an end-of-terrace Victorian building with a small, colourful front garden. It is centrally located for the town and the sea, and from the upstairs lounge there are sea views. The dining-room has an old ceiling and marble fireplace, and the big, solid chairs come from an old passenger liner. Most bedrooms have private bathroom and all have TV. Dinner is served from 6pm and vegetarian choices can be arranged. Packed lunches are also available and guests may bring their own wine to dinner (there is no alcohol licence). Children welcome. Pets by arrangement and not in the dining-room. No smoking in the dining-room.

OWNERS George and Maggie Davie OPEN All year, exc Christmas and New Year ROOMS 4 family (with bath/shower), 3 double (2 with bath/shower, 1 with wash-basin), 1 twin (with bath/shower), 2 single (with wash-basin) TERMS B&B £20 approx, (single occupancy of twin/double) £26 approx (children half-price sharing with adults); dinner £9.50; deposit; Access, Visa

BADACHRO Highland map 11

Harbour View

Badachro, Gairloch IV21 2AA
BADACHRO (0445 83) 316

Harbour View is a small, whitewashed house and was originally a fisherman's cottage. It stands above the narrow road, in a lovely position looking over a small bay, the islands and beyond to Gairloch. It is a charming, cosy little house, full of knick-knacks.

There is a small sitting-room and a dining-room, where evening meals are available from 7pm, and all the bedrooms, though small, have *en suite* facilities and TV. Ironing, shoe cleaning and hair-dryer are available on request. One of the bedrooms is in a chalet annexe. Vegetarians can be catered for and packed lunches provided. Harbour View is unlicensed, but guests may bring their own wine. This is a great place for walking and fishing, and all kinds of boats are available for hire. Children welcome. Dogs only, but not allowed in public rooms. No smoking in bedrooms. Car park.

OWNERS Eliza and Graham Willey OPEN All year, exc Christmas and New Year ROOMS 1 family, 2 double, 2 twin (1 in chalet annexe); all rooms with bath/shower TERMS B&B £16 Apr–Oct, £14.50 low season (children under 4 free, 4–11 half-price); dinner £8; deposit 15%

BALESHARE Western Isles (North Uist) map 11

Clachan Uaine

Baleshare, North Uist PA82 5HG
LOCHEPORT (087 64) 688

Situated on the west coast of North Uist, Clachan Uaine is close to the shore and white, sandy beaches, and overlooks a small loch where otters can be seen. Originally built in 1907 as a village church, it was converted in 1980 and now provides small but comfortable bedrooms, a compact TV lounge and a small dining-room, with an eating area in the sun porch (which is particularly popular with bird-watchers). Katie Rankin provides good, home-cooked evening meals (from 6.30pm or later by arrangement) and vegetarian choices are available. There is no licence, but guests may bring their own wine. Children welcome but must be accompanied by adults at all times. No pets in bedrooms. Smoking only in the sitting-room. Car park.

OWNERS Katie and Bill Rankin OPEN All year, exc Christmas and New Year ROOMS 2 double, 1 twin TERMS B&B £11.50; dinner £7.50; deposit

The description for each entry states when pets are not allowed. Where no details are given, you can assume that pets are allowed. It's always best to check first in any case.

B&B rates specified in the details for each entry are per person per night; unless the details state otherwise, they are based on two people sharing a double or twin-bedded room.

offers traditional home-cooked Highland food. Packed lunches can be provided by arrangement. Vegetarian choices are available. Children welcome. No smoking in the dining-room. Car park.

OWNERS Ron and Elizabeth Gould OPEN All year ROOMS 1 family, 1 double, 2 twin; all rooms with bath/shower TERMS B&B £16, (single occupancy of twin/double) £19, (family room) £40 (children 25% reduction); dinner £8; deposit

BRAE Shetland (Mainland) map 11

Vaddel

Busta Road, Brae ZE2 9QN
BRAE (080 622) 407

Vaddel is a modern bungalow set in a large garden with wonderful views over Busta Voe and offering basic accommodation. It is owned by Mrs Brown, who is delighted to help with information on what to see and do. Breakfast and evening meals are home cooked and there is a wide choice of dishes on offer. Lunch is also available, as is a packed lunch if preferred. Guests may bring their own wine to dinner (no licence). A comfortable place to stay at, with very much a home-from-home atmosphere. No pets. No smoking in the dining-room.

OWNER Mrs H. E. Brown OPEN All year, exc Christmas
ROOMS 1 double, 1 twin TERMS B&B £11–£13.50; dinner £6

BRAEMAR Grampian map 11

Clunie Lodge Guest House

Clunie Bank Road, Braemar AB3 5YP
BRAEMAR (033 97) 41330

Standing in its own gardens, this stone-built house was formerly the manse. It lies on the edge of Braemar and has wonderful views up Clunie Glen and is just a short distance from the Clunie river. It is a friendly, relaxed house, with a comfortable lounge and dining-room panelled in pine. The bedrooms are spacious but simply furnished and most of them have lovely views. One bedroom has a private bathroom, and some rooms have *en suite* facilities. Dinner is served 6.30–7.30pm and vegetarians can be catered for. Packed lunches are available and guests may bring their own wine (no licence). The house is very close to the riverside and golf course. Children welcome. No smoking in bedrooms and the dining-room. Car park.

OWNERS Roma and Jack Brown OPEN All year, exc Nov–Jan and late Apr ROOMS 2 family (1 with bath/shower, 1 with wash-basin), 2 double (with bath/shower), 2 twin (with bath/shower), 1 single (with wash-basin) TERMS B&B £15, (single) £12, (family room) £30–£40; dinner £9; deposit £5 per person

BRECHIN Tayside map 11

Blibberhill

Brechin DD9 6TH
ABERLEMNO (030 783) 225

This eighteenth-century farmhouse is set in lovely, peaceful countryside and is a working 300-acre arable and stock-rearing farm. It is five miles south of Brechin and has a pretty garden with roses, shrubs and lawns. One of the bedrooms is large and two have *en suite* facilities. There is a conservatory and sitting-room, and Mrs Stewart will prepare home-cooked evening meals by arrangement, at 6.30pm, served at one large table in the dining-room. Vegetarian choices are available and guests may bring their own wine (no licence). No pets. No smoking in bedrooms. Car park.

OWNER Mrs M. Stewart OPEN All year ROOMS 2 twin (with bath/shower), 1 double (with wash-basin) TERMS B&B from £12, (single occupancy of twin/double) £15; dinner £7; deposit

BRIDGE OF ORCHY Strathclyde map 11

Inveroran Hotel

Bridge of Orchy PA36 4AQ
TYNDRUM (083 84) 220

The hotel is approached down a three-mile narrow road off the main Glasgow to Fort William road at Bridge of Orchy, and is situated in an isolated position at the head of Loch Tulla. The West Highland Way and General Wade's Road pass the door of the hotel. There is salmon fishing on the hotel's two-mile beat of the River Orchy and trout fishing from its boat on Loch Tulla. Packages are available for groups and clubs interested in skiing at Glencoe. The hotel is popular with walkers, climbers, fishermen and skiers, and they often frequent the walkers' bar. There is also

a games-room, lounge bar and a small lounge. Set evening meals are served 6.30–8.15pm (vegetarians can be catered for by arrangement) in the dining-room, but most choose to eat at the bar, where meals are also available from 6.30pm. Packed lunches are provided on request. Children welcome. No pets in the dining-room. No smoking in the dining-room and the lounge bar (meal-times). Car park.

OWNER Mrs Janet Blackie OPEN All year, exc Christmas
ROOMS 2 family (1 with bath/shower, 1 with wash-basin), 3 double (2 with bath/shower, 1 with wash-basin), 2 twin (1 with bath/shower, 1 with wash-basin), 2 single (with wash-basin) TERMS B&B £19, (single occupancy of twin/double) £19.50; dinner £2–£7.95 for main course; deposit

BROADFORD Highland (Skye) map 11

Liveras House

Broadford, Isle of Skye IV49 9AA
BROADFORD (0471) 822 219

This is a substantial stone-built whitewashed house standing in an attractive garden, with lovely views. The TV lounge is shared by family and guests alike and breakfast is served in the large, homely kitchen. Evening meals (with vegetarian choices) can also be served on request. Packed lunches can be provided. Ian Chard also runs a bookbinding and arts supply shop at the end of the road. No central heating. Children welcome. No pets. No smoking in the house. Car park.

OWNERS Ian and Rosemary Chard OPEN Easter–Oct
ROOMS 2 double (1 with bath/shower), 1 single TERMS B&B £15–£22 (reductions for children sharing with parents); dinner £10–£12, deposit 1 night charge

BRODICK Strathclyde (Arran) map 9

Glencloy Farmhouse

Brodick, Isle of Arran KA27 8DA
BRODICK (0770) 2351

An old stone-built farmhouse, Glencloy is set in a pretty, peaceful glen about half a mile down a narrow road and track from Brodick. Vegetables are home grown, and geese and hens roam the garden. The house is comfortable, with spacious bedrooms which have been attractively decorated with stencilling in simple country-house style. Two of the rooms have TV. The large sitting-room has a good selection of local guides and an open log fire. Home-cooked dinners are elegantly served in the dining-room from 7pm and guests may bring their own wine (no licence). Vegetarians can be catered for and packed lunches provided. Guests have use of the garden, which has croquet and badminton. No children under four. No smoking in the dining-room. Car park.

OWNERS Mr and Mrs Padfield OPEN Mar–early Nov
ROOMS 2 double (1 with bath/shower, 1 with wash-basin), 2 twin (1 with bath/shower, 1 with wash-basin), 1 single (with wash-basin)
TERMS B&B £17, (single occupancy of twin/double) £20 (children under 8 half-price, 8–11 25% reduction); dinner £10; deposit £10 per person

Kilmichael House Hotel

Glen Cloy, by Brodick, Isle of Arran KA27 8BY
BRODICK (0770) 2219

This 200-year-old mansion is set in its own grounds down a long driveway, about a mile from Brodick, in a peaceful, beautiful spot at the foot of the hills. Interior features include decorative arches and part of the upstairs sitting-room is thought to have been an old chapel. Nearly all the bedrooms are on the ground floor and are either *en suite* or have use of a private bathroom. Two of the bedrooms have a four-poster bed. The grounds are bordered on two sides by streams and the garden includes a croquet lawn. The dining-room, where dinner is served at 7.30pm, is on the first floor; vegetarian choices are always available. The premises are licensed, and packed lunches can be provided. 'Murder' dinners are sometimes organised. No children under five. Pets by arrangement. No smoking in the dining-room and bedrooms. Car park.

OWNERS Geoffrey Botterill and Antony Butterworth OPEN All year ROOMS 7 double (5 with bath/shower, 2 with wash-basin), 2 twin (with bath/shower) TERMS B&B £21–£25 (children under 10 half-price); dinner £10; deposit £10 per person

BRORA Highland map 11

Tigh Fada

Golf Road, Brora KW9 6QS
BRORA (0408) 621332

Tigh Fada is in a peaceful situation enjoying fine, uninterrupted views of the sea and hills. The house is on the edge of a golf course, with tennis courts, bowling-green and curling rink all within a five-minute walk. The garden leads down to the sandy beach, and there are delightful beach walks. The lounge is spacious and comfortable, with a large bay window and a peat fire in cool weather. Two of the bedrooms have lovely views, and breakfast only is served in the dining-room. Complimentary tea and home-baked food are offered each night. Preferably no toddlers. No dogs in the house. No smoking. Car park.

OWNERS John and Ishbel Clarkson OPEN All year, exc Christmas and New Year, Nov–Mar by arrangement ROOMS 1 double, 2 twin; all rooms with wash-basin TERMS B&B £12.50–£14.50 Jan–Apr, up to £15.50 from May; deposit £5 per person

CALLANDER Central map 11

Leny House

Leny Estate, Callander FK17 8HA
CALLANDER (0877) 31078

Leny Estate, the ancestral home of the Buchanan family for 1,000 years, is set in 20 acres of parkland with lovely views to the

Trossachs, and is only one mile from Callander. The Leny Falls and river are close by, as is the wild Leny Glen – good for walking. The house, which in 1513 was a small fortress, was enlarged in 1691 and again in 1845 to its present manor-house form. The Gallows Hill, used for executions in the fifteenth century and known as the Knoll of Justice, is visible in the grounds. Leny House has spacious rooms, fairly simply furnished and decorated, but comfortable. Breakfast only is served. There is partial central heating. Children welcome. Car park.

OWNERS Alan and Frances Roebuck OPEN Easter–Oct
ROOMS 2 double/family (1 with bath/shower, 1 with wash-basin), 2 twin (1 with bath/shower, 1 with wash-basin) TERMS B&B £17–£19 (reductions for children under 12)

CAMPBELTOWN Strathclyde map 9

Ballegreggan House

Campbeltown PA28 6NN
CAMPBELTOWN (0586) 52062

Ballegreggan House stands in a superb position with views of hills and sea, up a half-mile potholed track on the outskirts of Campbeltown. It was built in 1861 as the home of the owner of the estate. The rooms are well proportioned, the dining-room and lounge having the best views, and there is an abundance of plants everywhere. The bedrooms are spacious, clean and comfortable, and some are now *en suite*. There is a guests' lounge with TV. Evening meals are available 6–7pm and guests may bring their own wine (no licence). Vegetarian choices and packed lunches can be provided. Children welcome. No smoking. Car park.

OWNERS Moray and Bruce Urquhart OPEN All year
ROOMS 1 family (with wash-basin), 2 double (with bath/shower), 4 twin (3 with bath/shower), 1 single (with wash-basin) TERMS B&B £16–£20 (children half-price sharing with parents); dinner £10; deposit

Sandiway

Fort Argyll Road, Low Askomil, Campbeltown PA28 6SN
CAMPBELTOWN (0586) 52280

Sandiway is a modern bungalow in a quiet, residential area on the edge of town and close to Campbeltown Loch. It is surrounded by a pretty garden with lovely roses and there is a patio at the back for sitting out. The house has a friendly atmosphere, and there is a lounge and a dining-room where home-cooked evening meals using fresh local produce can be served 6–7pm. Vegetarians can be catered for by arrangement and guests may bring their own wine (no licence). No children, pets or smoking. Car park.

OWNERS Mr and Mrs Bell OPEN All year, exc Christmas and New Year ROOMS 1 twin (with bath/shower) TERMS B&B £13–£17; dinner £7–£9; deposit

CARDROSS Strathclyde map 11

Kirkton House

Cardross G82 5EZ
CARDROSS (0389) 841951 Fax (0389) 841868

Built around a pretty courtyard decorated with flowers and furnished with tables and chairs, this 100-year-old house stands in a lovely position just above Cardross overlooking the Clyde, and is convenient for Glasgow (18 miles away), Loch Lomond and the Argyll Hills. Originally a farmhouse, it has been considerably altered, giving the appearance of a rather modern building both inside and out. There is a large garden and paddock, with pony rides for children. One very large room has the lounge at one end and the licensed dining-room at the other where home-cooked evening meals are served at 7.30pm. Vegetarians can be catered for and packed lunches can be provided. Laundry, ironing and baby-sitting can be arranged. Children welcome. Car park.

OWNERS S. H. and G. MacDonald OPEN All year, exc Christmas ROOMS 4 family/double/twin (with bath/shower), 2 twin (with wash-basin) TERMS B&B £18.50–£24.50, (single occupancy of twin/double) £21–£32.50 (babies in cot free, 1 child sharing £7.50, 2 children sharing £12.50); dinner £13.50; deposit £20 per room; Access, Visa

CARRBRIDGE Highland map 11

Féith Mho'r Country House

Station Road, Carrbridge PH23 3AP
CARRBRIDGE (047 984) 621

In a quiet peaceful setting, surrounded by well-maintained gardens and views of mountains and hills in every direction, Féith Mho'r is a small nineteenth-century country house, approached down a quiet road about one and a quarter miles from Carrbridge. The Rawsons moved here from Keeper's House Hotel at the end of 1990. The house is comfortable and spacious; all bedrooms are *en suite* and have TV. There is a large dining-room and a pleasant lounge, and although there is no bar the establishment does have a table licence. Set dinners are served at 7pm and vegetarians can be catered for by arrangement. Packed lunches can also be provided. No children under 12. No pets in public rooms. No smoking in the lounge and the dining-room. Car park.

OWNERS Peter and Penny Rawson OPEN 20 Dec–10 Nov
ROOMS 3 double, 3 twin; all rooms with bath/shower
TERMS B&B £18; dinner £10; deposit £20

CHAPELTON Strathclyde map 9

Millwell Farm

Chapelton, nr Strathaven ML10 6SJ
EAST KILBRIDE (035 52) 43248

This old stone-built farmhouse is on a 96-acre working dairy farm only 12 miles from Glasgow, between East Kilbride and Chapelton, off the A726. The accommodation is simple and includes a large beamed sitting-room/dining-room where evening meals can be served at 6pm. The three bedrooms are on the ground floor, simply furnished and suitable for the disabled. Children welcome. No smoking at the table. Car park.

OWNER Fred Taylor OPEN All year, exc Christmas
ROOMS 1 double, 2 twin TERMS B&B £10; D, B&B £14

CLACHAN Western Isles (North Uist) map 11

Sealladh Traigh

Claddach Kirkibost, nr Clachan, North Uist PA82 5EP
LOCHEPORT (087 64) 248

This is a modern, compact house, with lovely views to Kirkibost Island and close to the wonderful sandy beaches of North Uist. It is two miles north of Clachan, 200 yards west of the Clachan to Baymead Road. The bedrooms, all with TV, are small and bright and there is a pleasant lounge with dining table, where good home-cooked dinners are served at about 7pm. There is no alcohol licence, but guests may bring their own wine. Lunches and vegetarian choices can be provided. Mrs Quarm is full of advice and helpful tips, having lived all her life on North Uist. The

Quarms used to own the next-door stone-built pub, which is a lively place on Saturday nights. Children welcome. Car park.

OWNERS W. J. and A. Quarm OPEN All year ROOMS 3 double, 1 twin, 1 single; all rooms with wash-basin TERMS B&B £14 (children under 3 free, 3–14 £9); dinner £9.50

CLACHAN-SEIL Strathclyde map 11

Old Clachan Farmhouse

Clachan-Seil, by Oban PA34 4RH
BALVICAR (085 23) 493

This early eighteenth-century, whitewashed farmhouse was originally a drovers' inn and is situated about four miles down a narrow road right on the edge of the water and has a dinghy-launching slip to Seil Sound. Boat fishing can be arranged and walking gear lent out. It is a very comfortable, relaxed house, with flexible hours for breakfast and dinner (7.30–10pm) to suit guests. Good local produce is always used in the cooking, and specialities such as oysters, lobster and salmon are usually on the menu, including vegetarian choices. Guests may bring their own wine (no licence). The bedrooms are comfortable (one has TV) and the lounge has an open log fire. Children welcome. Only well-trained dogs, but not allowed in public rooms. No smoking in the dining-room. Car park.

OWNERS Stan and Stella Malcolm OPEN All year, exc Christmas and New Year ROOMS 2 double (1 with bath/shower, 1 with wash-basin), 1 twin (with wash-basin) TERMS B&B £16–£22.50 (children 3–14 £10 sharing with parents); deposit 50% of first night charge; Access, Visa

COLDINGHAM Borders map 11

St Andrew's Wells

School Road, Coldingham TD14 5NS
COLDINGHAM (089 07) 71244

Although parts of it date back to 1611, the present house is essentially Victorian and stands right on the A1107. It once had four wells in the grounds, where the village people used to collect their water, and more recently it was a manse. The bedrooms are spacious, and one, which faces the road, is ideal for families. The other two rooms are at the back of the house, overlooking the large garden. There is a comfortable sitting-room, and evening meals can be served at 7pm by arrangement in the dining-room at two separate tables. St Andrew's Wells is unlicensed, but guests may bring their own wine. Lunches and vegetarian choices can be provided. Coldingham Bay has a good beach and the picturesque small harbour of St Abbs is only one and a half miles away. Children welcome. Small dogs only. No smoking. Car park.

OWNERS Mr Herman and Mrs Glynis Duff OPEN All year, exc Christmas ROOMS 1 family, 2 double; all rooms with wash-basin TERMS B&B £13 (children up to 5 £5, 6–12 £7); dinner £7

COLMONELL Strathclyde map 9

Burnfoot Farm

Colmonell, Girvan KA26 0SQ
COLMONELL (046 588) 220/265

One mile from the village of Colmonell is this traditional Scottish farmhouse on a 157-acre family-run dairy and beef farm in the Stinchar Valley, which is famous for its salmon fishing. The house is very clean, with a pleasant, warm atmosphere, and offers simple accommodation. The family suite comprises two interconnecting bedrooms; this and the double room have TV. Home cooking and baking are a speciality, and fresh fruit and vegetables come from the garden. Evening meals are served at 6.30pm in the dining-room at one table. There is no alcohol licence, but guests may bring their own wine. Vegetarian choices and packed lunches can be provided. Children welcome. No smoking in bedrooms and the dining-room. Car park.

OWNER Mrs Grace B. Shankland OPEN Easter–Oct
ROOMS 1 family suite, 1 double; both with wash-basin TERMS B&B £13, (single occupancy of double) £16 (babies under 1 free, children under 6 £5.50, 6–12 £8.50); dinner £6; deposit

CORRIE Strathclyde (Arran) map 9

Blackrock House

Corrie, Isle of Arran KA27 8JB
CORRIE (077 081) 282

Blackrock House is a small, neat, whitewashed guesthouse on the sea-front with wonderful sea views. It was originally built as a tea-room in 1925. The bedrooms, two of which are on the ground floor, are all at the back of the house. There are lovely views from the upstairs lounge and downstairs dining-room, where dinner can be served at 6.30pm. There is no alcohol licence, but guests may bring their own wine. Packed lunches can be provided. Hot drinks with scones or cakes are also available in the evening. Children welcome. Pets in bedrooms only and must be accompanied. No smoking in public rooms. Car park.

OWNERS Mary and David Wilkinson OPEN Mar–Oct
ROOMS 4 family, 1 double, 1 twin, 2 single; all rooms with wash-basin
TERMS B&B from £14.25 (children under 10 half-price); dinner £9.50; deposit £20 per person per week

CRAIL Fife map 11

Selcraig House

47 Nethergate, Crail KY10 3TX
CRAIL (0333) 50697

Right in the middle of the charming little town of Crail, with its picturesque harbour and beaches, Selcraig House is a solid 200-year-old stone building with a relaxed and warm atmosphere. Margaret Carstairs has given it an Edwardian feel, particularly in the two bathrooms and the pretty dining-room, where home-cooked evening meals are available, if booked in advance, at 6.30pm. Vegetarians can be catered for and guests may bring their own wine (no licence). Packed lunches can be provided. The three second-floor bedrooms are very small and have low ceilings, but two have splendid sea views. There is no central heating on the second floor and the lounge is on the first floor. Children welcome. No pets or smoking in the dining-room. Car park in the square at the front of the house.

OWNER Margaret Carstairs OPEN All year, exc Christmas Day
ROOMS 2 family, 1 double, 1 twin, 1 single; all rooms with wash-basin
TERMS B&B £13–£19 (children under 2 free, 3–10 half-price sharing); dinner £10; deposit

CROSSHILL Strathclyde map 9

Ashlea

18 Kirkmichael Road, Crosshill, Maybole KA19 7RJ
CROSSHILL (065 54) 251

Crosshill is a small village 11 miles south of Ayr, its streets lined with rows of compact stone cottages and houses. The two bedrooms at Ashlea are spotlessly clean and comfortable. The bathroom is downstairs, as are the small sitting-room and the dining-room. Mrs Morton will provide evening meals on request, and shortbread is always in the bedrooms with the tea- and coffee-making facilities. There are no fixed times for breakfast and evening meals. Vegetarians can be catered for and guests may bring their own wine (no licence). Packed lunches can be provided. Children welcome. No pets. No smoking in the dining-room.

OWNERS Mr and Mrs John Morton OPEN Feb–Nov ROOMS 1 family, 1 double; both rooms with wash-basin TERMS B&B £11–£12 (reductions for children according to age); dinner £8.50–£10

CULLEN Grampian map 11

Bayview Hotel

57 Seafield Street, Cullen AB56 2SU
CULLEN (0542) 41031

The modest exterior of this simple house above the harbour belies the spacious and cleverly designed interior. The attractive bar is furnished in pine and the pretty licensed dining-room, where evening meals are available 6.30–9pm, has recently been revamped. There are also bar lunch and supper menus, and packed lunches can be provided. Vegetarian choices are available. The top floor is taken up by an enormous and very comfortable lounge – a light room with marvellous views. The simply furnished bedrooms, all with TV and telephone, are of a good size, and some have lovely views over the harbour and bay. Children welcome. Only residents' children in bar. No pets.

OWNERS David and Frances Evans OPEN All year, exc Nov and Christmas ROOMS 1 four-poster, 2 double, 2 twin, 1 single; all rooms, exc 1 twin (wash-basin only), with bath/shower TERMS B&B £27.50, (single) £33 (children half-price in extra bed in double); dinner £10–£20 approx; Access, Visa

CULNAKNOCK Highland (Skye) map 11

Glenview Inn

Culnaknock, by Portree, Isle of Skye IV51 9JH
STAFFIN (047 062) 248

Formerly the village store, Glenview was acquired as a tea-shop and later expanded to become a restaurant. It is situated just off the road between Portree and Staffin, and although very close to the coast it is out of sight of the sea. However, it has lovely mountain views. It has been brightly decorated and the bedrooms are furnished in pine. All have TV. Excellent Scottish lunches and evening meals (from 7.30pm) are available in the restaurant and all the food is freshly prepared. Vegetarian choices are also available. There are tables and chairs for sitting outside, a pleasant lounge and a sitting-room with sun porch. Children welcome. 'Well-behaved' pets only, but not in the bar or restaurant. Car park.

OWNER Linda Thompson OPEN All year ROOMS 2 double, 2 twin, 2 single; all rooms, exc singles (wash-basin only), with bath/shower TERMS B&B £30, (single) £28, (single occupancy of twin/double) £40 (children under 1 free); deposit £10; Access, Visa

DALMALLY Strathclyde map 11

Orchy Bank Guest House

Orchy Bank, Stronmilchan, Dalmally PA33 1AS
DALMALLY (083 82) 370

This guesthouse sits on the very quiet B8077 Stronmilchan road, beside an eighteenth-century stone bridge on the banks of the River Orchy. Its garden stretches down to the river and there are pretty views of the old bridge. Orchy Bank is a simple, comfortable house, with a very pleasant, informal atmosphere. There is partial central heating. Evening meals, including vegetarian choices, are available in the licensed dining-room at 7pm and the very large, warm lounge has an open fire. Packed lunches can be provided. This is a good base for bird-watching, hill walking and fishing. Children welcome. No smoking in the dining-room. Car park.

OWNERS John and Jinty Burke OPEN All year, exc Christmas ROOMS 1 family, 3 double, 2 twin, 2 single; all rooms with wash-basin TERMS B&B £15–£16, (single occupancy of twin/double) £22.50–£24 (children under 3 free, under 11 half-price); D, B&B from £24.50; deposit £12

Where a single-occupancy rate is not specified in the details, the cost will be the same as that per person in a twin or double room, or will be included in the range of prices given.

It is always best to book a room in advance, especially in winter. B&Bs with few rooms may close at short notice for periods not specified in the details.

DERVAIG Strathclyde (Mull) map 11

Ardrioch Farm Guest House

Ardrioch, Dervaig, Isle of Mull PA75 6QR
DERVAIG (068 84) 264

From the outside, this is a very unprepossessing-looking cedar bungalow, a mile from Dervaig; inside, however, it is quite charming, full of the owners' bits and pieces and antique furniture. The farm extends to 70 acres and supports a herd of cows, rearing beef calves, a flock of cheviot sheep, a pony, collies and cats. Apart from running the farm and guesthouse, the owners offer guests activity holidays, including sailing on their Shetland skiff and Orkney ketch, which are kept two miles down the road at the natural harbour of Croig. Jeremy Matthew is also a folk musician, and plays banjo and mandolin in a local band, while Jenny Matthew is an imaginative cook who prepares excellent home-cooked food. Evening meals are served at 7pm and may include crab (locally caught) pâté, local venison and hot chocolate fudge cake. Guests may bring their own wine as there is no alcohol licence. Vegetarian choices and packed lunches can be provided. The comfortable, wood-panelled sitting-room is well supplied with books, maps and games. The small bedrooms are furnished in pine. No children under five. No pets. No smoking. Car park.

OWNERS Jenny and Jeremy Matthew OPEN Easter–Oct
ROOMS 2 double (1 with bath/shower, 1 with wash-basin), 1 twin (with wash-basin) TERMS B&B £16–£21 (children £4 reduction); dinner £8; deposit £10–£25 per person

Bellachroy Hotel

Dervaig, Isle of Mull PA75 6QW
DERVAIG (068 84) 225/314

This sixteenth-century former drovers' inn is the oldest continuously inhabited house on the Isle of Mull. It is a pleasant, whitewashed building at the end of one of the most picturesque villages in Mull on the road to Tobermory. It is a very friendly, small hotel, with a relaxed, informal atmosphere. All the guests' accommodation is on the first and second floors. The bedrooms are fairly small and simply furnished, and there is one very large, comfortable and light lounge, a smaller lounge and a pleasant dining-room where good home-cooked food is served. Evening meals are served at 7pm and can include vegetarian choices. Packed lunches can be provided. Meals at both lunch and dinner (7.45–9pm) are also available in the bar, which has a separate entrance from the hotel. Children welcome. No pets in public rooms. Smoking discouraged in bedrooms. Car park.

OWNERS Anne and Andrew Arnold OPEN All year, exc Christmas
ROOMS 2 family, 3 double, 3 twin; all rooms with wash-basin
TERMS B&B £19, (single occupancy of twin/double) £21.50 (children under 3 free, 3–10 half-price, 11–14 25% discount); deposit £10–£30

DORNOCH Highland map 11

Trevose Guest House

Cathedral Square, Dornoch IV25 3SD
DORNOCH (0862) 810269

In the centre of Dornoch overlooking the tree-lined village green is this attractive, sandstone house dating from 1830 and set in a very pretty, colourful front garden. The Mackenzies offer good value with comfort in a warm, friendly atmosphere. Jean Mackenzie, who comes from the Western Isles and is a Gaelic speaker, can prepare home-cooked evening meals at 7pm. The house is licensed and there is a TV lounge. Children welcome. Car park.

OWNERS Donald and Jean A. Mackenzie OPEN Mar–Oct
ROOMS 2 family, 1 double, 1 twin, 1 single; all rooms, exc double and single (wash-basin only), with bath/shower TERMS B&B £12.50–£15.50 (children half-price sharing a room); dinner £8; deposit

DRUMNADROCHIT Highland map 11

Glenkirk

Drumnadrochit IV3 6TZ
DRUMNADROCHIT (045 62) 802

Glenkirk is an old chapel, cleverly designed and simply furnished, mostly in pine. The family have rooms on the ground floor, which is also where the breakfast room is located. The guests' lounge is halfway up the stairs, and is a light, bright room with the original large back window of the church. On the first floor are the three small, light bedrooms, all with skylights and sharing a bathroom and shower-room. Leaflets are laid out on an old pew in the hall for guests to browse through. Breakfast only is available. Children welcome. No pets in the house. Smoking in the lounge only. Car park.

OWNERS Mr and Mrs R. Urquhart OPEN All year, exc 24–27 Dec ROOMS 1 family, 1 double, 1 twin; all rooms with wash-basin TERMS B&B £11–£12, (single occupancy of twin/double) £15 Apr–Oct (babies up to 1 free, children under 5 £6, 5–14 £9 sharing with parents)

DRYMEN Strathclyde map 11

Dunleen

Milton of Buchanan, Drymen, nr Glasgow G63 0JE
BALMAHA (036 087) 274

This long, low bungalow is in a very attractive setting with garden to the front and back, beside a pretty stream about a mile from Loch Lomond. There is a very large lounge and a breakfast room with lots of windows overlooking the stream. The bedrooms are comfortably furnished. Breakfast only is available, although packed lunches can be provided by arrangement. No children or pets. No smoking in bedrooms. Car park.

OWNER Mrs K. MacFadyen OPEN May–Oct ROOMS 1 double, 1 twin; both rooms with wash-basin TERMS B&B £14–£15, (single occupancy of twin/double) £17–£18 (babies free, children half-price sharing with adults); deposit

DUMFRIES Dumfries & Galloway map 9

St Margaret's

67 Rotchell Road, Dumfries DG2 7SA
DUMFRIES (0387) 53932

This small and cosy private guesthouse is in a quiet residential area convenient for touring, and within walking distance of the town centre. This is a spotlessly clean establishment, offering home comforts, with old-fashioned furnishings. All the rooms are small, including the TV lounge and breakfast room, but the welcome is friendly. One bedroom has TV. Breakfast only is available. Children welcome. No pets in bedrooms. Smoking only in the TV lounge. Car park.

OWNER Gladys M. Henderson OPEN All year, exc Christmas and New Year ROOMS 1 double, 1 twin, 1 single; all rooms with wash-basin TERMS B&B £13–£13.50 (infants free); deposit £10

DUNBAR Lothian map 11

Marine Guest House

7 Marine Road, Dunbar EH42 1AR
DUNBAR (0368) 63315

This is a small guesthouse situated in a quiet street at one end of the town and close to the centre and harbour. There are sea views, and the back of the house overlooks the golf course. It is a comfortable place with a pleasant atmosphere and bright, smallish bedrooms. Evening meals can be served at 6pm in the ground-floor dining-room and guests may bring their own wine (no licence). Vegetarians can be catered for. Children welcome. Pets in bedrooms only. No smoking in the dining-room.

OWNERS Jim and Alison Pilley OPEN All year, exc Christmas and New Year ROOMS 3 family, 1 double, 4 twin, 2 single; all rooms with wash-basin TERMS B&B £13–£14 (children under 2 free, 2–15 half-price); dinner £5

DUNDEE Tayside map 11

Invermark Hotel

23 Monifieth Road, Broughty Ferry, Dundee DD5 2RN
DUNDEE (0382) 739430

The Invermark is a large house in its own grounds on the main road between Dundee and Carnoustie, and only five minutes from the shops and beach. There is a large, comfortable lounge with books and games and the bedrooms are all freshly decorated and clean, some with *en suite* bathrooms. Evening meals are served by arrangement and can include vegetarian choices. Packed lunches can also be provided. There is a large garden to the rear of the house. Children welcome. No pets. Smoking in the lounge only. Car park.

OWNERS Muriel and David Metcalf OPEN All year ROOMS 1 family (with bath/shower), 3 twin (1 with bath/shower, 2 with wash-basin) TERMS B&B £15–£17.50, (single occupancy of twin) £25–£30, (family room) £45–£50 (children under 2 free, under 12 half-price); dinner £10; deposit £10

Where we know an establishment accepts credit cards, we list them. There may be a surcharge if you pay by credit card. It is always best to check whether the card you want to use is acceptable when booking.

DUNROSSNESS Shetland (Mainland) map 11

Columbine

Dunrossness ZE2 9JG
SUMBURGH (0950) 60582

Columbine is a small, neat, whitewashed bungalow in a rural setting and close to the sea. It is only a five-minute walk from the shop, post office and bus route, and Sumburgh Airport is four miles away. With only one comfortable *en suite* room, Mrs Reeve can give much attention to her guests' needs. Evening meals (6.30pm) and laundry facilities are available. Columbine has no alcohol licence, but guests may bring their own wine. Vegetarians can be catered for. Sea angling, loch fishing and boat trips to see seals, birds and cliff scenery can be arranged, and there is pony-trekking nearby. Small children welcome. Car park.

OWNER Mrs V. E. Reeve OPEN All year, exc Christmas
ROOMS 1 twin (with bath/shower) TERMS B&B £11.50–£12.50 (children ⅓–⅔ reduction); dinner £5–£6.50

DUNSYRE Strathclyde map 11

Dunsyre Mains

Dunsyre, Carnwath ML11 8NQ
DUNSYRE (089 981) 251

This attractive stone building dates from the early eighteenth century and stands just above the tiny village of Dunsyre. It is a very friendly, homely, comfortable and simple farmhouse set in beautiful, unspoilt, peaceful countryside of rolling hills, yet within easy reach of Edinburgh and the Borders. Part of a 400-acre beef and sheep farm, Dunsyre Mains has a pretty farmyard lying to the rear and side of the house with lots of colourful flowers and plants. There are three large bedrooms, a lounge and a dining-room where evening meals are available by arrangement at 7pm. Vegetarian choices and packed lunches can be provided. There is no alcohol licence, but guests may bring their own wine. Children welcome. Pets by arrangement. No smoking in the dining-room and bedrooms. Parking in farmyard.

OWNER Mrs Armstrong OPEN All year, exc Christmas
ROOMS 1 family, 1 double, 1 twin; all rooms with wash-basin
TERMS B&B £12–£14 (children 6 and under half-price, 7–11 three-quarters-price); dinner £8; deposit

DUNVEGAN Highland (Skye) map 11

Tables Hotel and Restaurant

Dunvegan, Isle of Skye IV55 8WA
DUNVEGAN (047 022) 404

Tables stands at the junction of the A850 and A863 in the small village of Dunvegan. It has a pleasant, relaxed, informal atmosphere. From the small front garden, a popular place for indulging in imaginative lunchtime snacks, there is a lovely view of Loch Dunvegan and the MacLeod's Tables. The bedrooms are small and all have sea views. Excellent food is served in the small licensed dining-room, with Austrian-inspired décor, and the comfortable lounge has TV. Evening meals, including vegetarian choices, are served 7–9pm (later in summer) and packed lunches can be provided. Children welcome. No pets. No smoking in the dining-room. Car park.

OWNERS Brenda and Dennis Hickman OPEN All year
ROOMS 2 family (1 with bath/shower, 1 with wash-basin), 1 double (with wash-basin), 1 single (with wash-basin) TERMS B&B £18–£25 (children up to 3 25% of adult rate, up to 9 60%, up to 14 80%); D, B&B from £31; deposit 20%; Access, Visa

EDINBURGH Lothian map 11

Balmoral Guest House

32 Pilrig Street EH6 5AL
031-554 1857

The Balmoral is only half a mile from the sea and less still from the city centre, with several bus stops nearby. It is a small terraced guesthouse, with a friendly, pleasant atmosphere. The amenities are fairly basic, although the simply furnished rooms are immaculately clean. The Mackenzies are experts on what to see and do in Edinburgh, and are only too happy to make recommendations. Breakfast only is available. Children welcome. No smoking in the dining-room. Car parking is available.

OWNERS Alex and Margaret Mackenzie OPEN All year
ROOMS 2 family, 3 double, 2 twin; all rooms with wash-basin
TERMS B&B £13.50–£15, (single occupancy of twin/double) £20, (family room) 3 adults £13 each, 2 adults and 1 child £33 (children under 4 free, 5–14 £7)

The Buchan

3 Coates Gardens EH12 5LG
031-337 1045/8047

The Logans took over the hotel in the summer of 1991 and aim to maintain the same high standards as their predecessors. The Buchan is a spacious Victorian terraced house built in 1870 for a merchant. It is in an excellent location, with easy access to the centre and places of interest. The bedrooms, all with TV, are of a good size and freshly decorated and bright. There is one delightful room downstairs, with a large bathroom and small patio with banked flower-bed. Breakfast only is served in the large dining-room, although packed lunches can be provided. Central heating in public areas only. Children welcome. Pets by arrangement. No smoking in the dining-room and some bedrooms. Parking is available close by.

OWNERS Ritchie and Linda Logan OPEN All year ROOMS 5 family, 2 double (1 with bath/shower), 2 twin (1 with bath/shower), 2 single; 9 rooms with wash-basin TERMS B&B £18–£20, (single) £22–£24 (children under 4 free, over 4 half-price); deposit; Access, Amex, Visa

Craigelachie Private Hotel

21 Murrayfield Avenue EH12 6AU
031-337 4076

This spacious terraced Victorian house is in a quiet residential street close to a bus route and not far from the centre. There are gardens to the front and rear. Max and Jean Cruickshank are friendly, welcoming people and keep an immaculate house. It is simply furnished, with some large and some smaller bedrooms (all with TV), a pleasant dining-room where breakfast only is served and an upstairs lounge. No children under five. Pets by arrangement. No smoking in the dining-room.

OWNERS Max and Jean Cruickshank OPEN All year, exc Christmas ROOMS 3 family, 1 double, 2 twin, 1 single; all rooms with wash-basin TERMS B&B £16–£21, (single occupancy of twin/double) £24.50 (children 5–9 £8, 10–13 £10.50); deposit; surcharge for rugby fixtures and other events

We asked the proprietors to estimate their 1992 prices in the autumn of 1991, so the rates may have changed since publication.

Bath/shower in the details under each entry means that the rooms have private facilities.

The Meadows Guest House

17 Glengyle Terrace EH3 9LN
031-229 9559 Fax 031-557 0563

The Meadows Guest House forms part of an attractive terrace facing an expanse of open park in a quiet street, yet close to the centre. It has a friendly atmosphere and is a comfortable house. The entrance is through the basement, where two large rooms with bathrooms are located. The remaining five bedrooms are upstairs; all bedrooms have TV. There is also a small sitting-room and breakfast room. Breakfast only is available. Smoking discouraged.

OWNERS Gloria and Jon Stuart OPEN All year, exc Christmas ROOMS 3 family (with bath/shower), 1 double (with bath/shower), 2 twin (1 with bath/shower, 1 with wash-basin), 1 single (with wash-basin) TERMS B&B £18–£22.50, (single occupancy of twin/double) £30–£35, (family room) £51–£60; deposit 1 night charge; Access, Visa

Sibbet House

26 Northumberland Street EH3 6LS
031-556 1078

The standard at Sibbet House continues to be very high. This is an elegant Georgian house built in 1809, in the heart of Edinburgh's New Town and only a five-minute walk from Princes Street. The owner has experience in antiques and interior decoration, reflected throughout the house, which is beautifully furnished and decorated. The bedrooms, reached by a unique hanging staircase crowned by a cupola, are large and provided with every comfort and all have their own bathroom, TV and telephone. There is a French-style, rather formal drawing-room and breakfast is taken in a large dining-room. There is also a spacious flat a few streets away which is excellent value and ideal for four or six people travelling together. Children welcome. No pets. Smoking in bedrooms only. Garage available.

OWNER Aurora Sibbet OPEN All year ROOMS 2 family, 1 double; all rooms with bath/shower TERMS B&B £20–£25, (single occupancy of double) £39 (children under 2 free, under 12 half-price sharing with 2 adults); deposit; payment in advance for 1 night; Access, Visa

Those B&Bs that we know can offer some kind of off-street car parking, have 'car park' at the end of the entry. If we are aware of particular car parking difficulties, we mention them.

Sonas Guest House

3 East Mayfield EH9 1SD
031-667 2781

A terraced house that was built in 1876 for a railway director and located about a mile south of the city centre. Although in a quiet road, it is very accessible to public transport – there is a car park where guests can leave their cars and then take the bus into town. The owners have recently done up the whole house, giving all bedrooms a bathroom and TV. They are small, pretty, bright and fresh rooms and there is also a breakfast/sitting-room with TV. Breakfast only is available. Children welcome. Pets by arrangement. No smoking during breakfast.

OWNERS Mr and Mrs Robins OPEN All year, exc Christmas
ROOMS 1 family, 3 double, 3 twin; all rooms with bath/shower
TERMS B&B £18–£27, (single occupancy of twin/double) £25–£35 (children up to 11 half-price sharing with 2 adults); deposit 1 night charge

Stuart House Hotel

12 East Claremont Street EH7 4JP
031-557 9030

This 150-year-old terraced house is in an excellent location in Edinburgh's New Town, only a 10-minute walk from Princes Street. It has been run since 1990 by Gloria Stuart, a most helpful, friendly lady, who also owns the Meadows Guest House, run by her husband Jon. Stuart House has nicely proportioned rooms with high ceilings, and the bedrooms, all with TV and telephone, are most comfortable. There is a small, bright sitting-room and a dining-room where home-cooked food is available in the evenings at a time (up to 9.30pm) to suit guests. Vegetarians can be catered for. Stuart House is unlicensed, but guests may bring their own wine. Children welcome (no cots or high chairs available). No pets. No smoking.

OWNER Mrs Gloria Stuart OPEN All year, exc Christmas
ROOMS 1 family, 3 double, 2 twin, 1 single; all rooms with bath/shower TERMS B&B £24–£26, (single occupancy of twin/double) £40–£45, (family room) £66–£72; dinner £5.75–£8.25 approx; deposit 1 night charge; Access, Visa

Many B&Bs will cater for vegetarians. It is always best, however, to check when booking and make it clear what your requirements are, especially if you need a special diet.

Turret Guest House

8 Kilmaurs Terrace EH16 5DR
031-667 6704

The Turret is a mid-terrace villa over 100 years old within easy access of the centre, in a quiet road near a bus stop. The house has a wide staircase and the original cornices. The bedrooms, all with TV, are of a good size and are prettily decorated; one room is now *en suite*. There is a pleasant lounge/dining-room where superb breakfasts are served, including waffles and a wide choice of teas. Children over two preferred. No pets. No smoking in the lounge/dining-room.

OWNERS Jackie and Ian Cameron OPEN All year, exc Christmas ROOMS 1 family, 2 double, 2 twin, 1 single; all rooms, exc family (with bath/shower), with wash-basin TERMS B&B £13–£21 (children half-price)

Woodlands

55 Barnton Avenue, Davidsons Mains EH4 6JJ
031-336 1685

Woodlands is a substantial house three miles from the city centre and is set in a large garden, with marvellous views over the Firth of Forth. The three bedrooms, all with TV, are clean and comfortably furnished and all overlook the two acres of gardens. The larger room has an *en suite* bathroom and the two smaller rooms share a bathroom. There is a small breakfast room with TV, a patio for sitting outside and plenty of parking space. Breakfast only is available. No smoking in bedrooms.

OWNER Mrs Helen Hall OPEN All year, exc Christmas and New Year ROOMS 1 double (with wash-basin), 2 twin (1 with bath/shower, 1 with wash-basin) TERMS B&B £16–£18, (single occupancy of twin/double) £20–£25; deposit

ELGIN Grampian map 11

Carronvale

18 South Guildry Street, Elgin IV30 1QN
ELGIN (0343) 546864

In a quiet residential street, this pleasant stone-built Victorian house is a five-minute walk from the town centre, railway and bus stations. The three bedrooms are simply but comfortably furnished and breakfast and evening meals (6–7pm) are served in the small, narrow dining-room at one long table. Vegetarian choices and packed lunches can be provided with notice. Carronvale is unlicensed, but guests may bring their own wine to dinner. A TV lounge is available for guests, and pictures by the owner and local artists decorate the house. Children welcome. No pets. No smoking. Car park.

OWNERS Anne and Roy Munn OPEN All year ROOMS 1 double, 2 twin; all rooms with wash-basin TERMS B&B £12, (single occupancy of twin/double) £16 (reductions for children sharing parents' room); dinner £8.50; deposit £10

EYEMOUTH Borders map 11

The Hermitage

Paxton Terrace, Eyemouth TD14 5EL
EYEMOUTH (089 07) 50324

This square, solid, stone-built house is in a commanding position above the attractive little port of Eyemouth. Formerly the manse, it has wonderful views over the bay, rocks and cliffs to the golf course on the other side of town. It offers simple accommodation, with clean and comfortable bedrooms. The large upstairs TV lounge/breakfast room has lovely views and guests may help themselves to tea, coffee and biscuits all day. Breakfast only is available. Cliff walks and St Abbs Nature Reserve are all close by. Children welcome. No smoking in the lounge. Parking is available.

OWNERS Nan and Phil Lowther OPEN Apr–Sept ROOMS 2 double, 1 twin, 1 single; all rooms with wash-basin TERMS B&B £13–£15 (children under 2 free, 2–12 £8)

FALA Lothian map 11

Fala Hall Farmhouse

Fala, Pathhead EH37 5SZ
HUMBIE (087 533) 249

This seventeenth-century stone-built farmhouse is approached down a half-mile pot-holed track from the tiny hamlet of Fala, which lies just off the A68. It is part of a 285-acre farm, situated in pretty, peaceful countryside. An attractive garden lies to the front of the house. The two bedrooms are large, as are the bathroom with bath, shower and bidet, and the TV lounge/dining-room, where breakfast only is served. Children welcome. Car park.

OWNER Helen Lothian OPEN All year ROOMS 1 family/twin, 1 double TERMS B&B £12, (single occupancy of twin/double) £18 (children under 12 £6 sharing)

FIONNPHORT Strathclyde (Mull) map 11

Achaban House

Fionnphort, Isle of Mull PA66 6BL
FIONNPHORT (068 17) 205

This old manse, built around 1840, stands in its own grounds on the edge of the village, and only a mile from the ferry to Iona overlooking Loch Poit na h-I, locally known as Loch Pottie. A spacious house, it has good-sized, simply decorated bedrooms with pine furniture. The former dining-room has been turned into a smoking lounge and children's play-room; the present licensed dining-room, where evening meals are served at 7.30pm and guests sit at large wooden tables, was once a kitchen, and still has its old-fashioned range. Vegetarian choices and packed lunches can be provided. Fishing can be arranged. Children welcome. Dogs only. Smoking only in guests' smoking room. Car park.

OWNERS C. and C. Baigent OPEN All year, exc Christmas ROOMS 1 family, 3 double, 2 twin, 1 single; all rooms, exc family (with bath/shower), with wash-basin TERMS B&B £16.50, (family room) from £50 (children half-price sharing with parents); dinner £12.50

FLODABAY Western Isles (Harris) map 11

Fernhaven

1 Flodabay, Isle of Harris PA85 3HA
MANISH (085 983) 340

A small, partly stone-built bungalow/cottage that stands on the edge of the little hamlet of Flodabay with its small harbour and views of hills and lochs. To find Flodabay, you leave the A859 south of Tarbert to take the C79 east coast road and continue for six miles. The accommodation is quite simple, with a couple of small bedrooms and a small sitting-room/dining-room where evening meals are available at 7pm. Vegetarians can be catered for and packed lunches are provided by arrangement. There is no alcohol licence, but guests may bring their own wine to dinner. Freshwater and sea angling can be arranged. No children under 12 in peak season. No dogs in the dining-room. No smoking in the dining-room and bedrooms. Car park.

OWNER Mrs Catherine Macaulay OPEN Apr–Oct ROOMS 1 double, 1 twin; both rooms with wash-basin TERMS B&B £15–£16; D, B&B £25; dinner £12.50; deposit

FORFAR Tayside map 11

Abbotsford

39 Westfield Crescent, Forfar DD8 1EG
FORFAR (0307) 62830

This modern bungalow stands just off a main road on the edge of a housing development, with parking to the rear. The beautifully kept garden now has a patio for sitting out, all bedrooms have a wash-basin, and one has an *en suite* shower-room. There is a small breakfast/TV room off the kitchen. Breakfast only is available. Glamis Castle is only six miles away. Abbotsford offers modest accommodation in a pleasant atmosphere. Children welcome. Smoking only in the lounge. Car park.

OWNER Mrs B. R. Tyrie OPEN All year, exc Christmas and New Year ROOMS 1 double (with wash-basin), 2 twin (1 with bath/shower, 1 with wash-basin) TERMS B&B £12, (single occupancy of twin/double) £16 (children under 5 free, 5–10 £7.50); deposit

FORT AUGUSTUS Highland map 11

Pier House

Fort Augustus PH32 4BX
FORT AUGUSTUS (0320) 6418

This unusual and interesting property extends to 50 acres and occupies an entire peninsula on the shores of Loch Ness, on the edge of Fort Augustus. The house, which was built about a hundred years ago, is a beautifully maintained, low, whitewashed building with a large patio overlooking the loch; the entrance is through a little circular tower. Inside, it is very simple and the floors and furniture are predominantly pine. There is an enormous sitting-room and an open-plan dining-room with kitchen. The simple bedrooms are all *en suite* or with private bathroom. Simple and substantial home-cooked evening meals are available by arrangement. Vegetarians can be catered for. Mrs MacKenzie teaches the harp and speaks French, German, Italian and Gaelic. There are highland cattle, and boats, canoes and riding are available. No children under five. No pets or smoking in the house. Car park.

OWNER Mrs Jenny MacKenzie OPEN Apr–Oct ROOMS 1 family, 1 double, 1 twin; all rooms with bath/shower TERMS B&B £15, (single occupancy of twin/double) £25, (family room) £50; dinner £7.50; deposit 1 night charge

FORT WILLIAM Highland map 11

Glenlochy Guest House

Nevis Bridge, Fort William PH33 6PF
FORT WILLIAM (0397) 702909

Glenlochy was built as a whisky distillery manager's residence in 1930 and is in a convenient position, on the edge of town and opposite the old distillery itself. Mr MacBeth is a keen fisherman and was a gamekeeper. The bedrooms are on the small side and functional, and there is a comfortable lounge and a dining-room for breakfast only. There are also two self-catering units in a side wing of the house which are ideal for families. Children welcome. Guide dogs only. Car park.

OWNERS Mr and Mrs D. MacBeth OPEN All year, exc Christmas ROOMS 2 family (with bath/shower), 5 double (4 with bath/shower, 1 with wash-basin), 4 twin (with bath/shower), 1 single (with wash-basin) TERMS B&B £13.50–£20, (single) £16.50–£24, (family room) £38.25–£60 (children under 12 half-price sharing with 2 adults); deposit £10

Guisachan House

Alma Road, Fort William PH33 6HA
FORT WILLIAM (0397) 703797

Guisachan House overlooks Loch Linnhe and the Ardgour Hills, and is within a five-minute walk of the town centre and bus and train stations. It has views from its lounge and licensed dining-room, and there is a pleasant patio in front of the house. Evening meals, including vegetarian choices, are served at 6.30pm. Packed lunches can be provided. The bedrooms, all with TV, have been made *en suite*. Children welcome. No pets. No smoking in the dining-room. Car park.

OWNERS J. and E. Rosie OPEN All year, exc Christmas
ROOMS 3 family, 5 double, 3 twin, 2 single; all rooms with bath/shower TERMS B&B £16–£22, (single occupancy of twin/double) £26–£28 (children half-price sharing); D, B&B £24–£28; deposit

GAIRLOCH Highland map 11

Birchwood Guest House

Gairloch IV21 2AH
GAIRLOCH (0445) 2011

Birchwood is in a lovely position, a little way outside the harbour part of Gairloch and above the main road with lovely views over Old Gairloch harbour to Skye and the outer isles. An old house, it looks modern inside with small, bright, plainly furnished bedrooms, all *en suite*. There is a small TV lounge and a terrace for sitting out, overlooking the well-kept small garden. Breakfast only is served, although packed lunches can be provided. Children welcome. No pets in bedrooms. Smoking only in downstairs lounge and conservatory. Car park.

OWNER Mrs Elsie Margaret Ramsay OPEN Apr–Oct
ROOMS 1 family, 3 double, 2 twin; all rooms with shower
TERMS B&B £22–£24, (single occupancy of twin/double) £10 surcharge Apr/May/Sept/Oct or full room price June/July/Aug (children under 5 free, 5–10 half-price sharing with parents); deposit

GELSTON Dumfries & Galloway map 11

Rose Cottage Guest House

Gelston, Castle Douglas DG7 1SH
CASTLE DOUGLAS (0556) 2513

This small, whitewashed one-storey cottage, with beds of roses in front of the house, stands on the B727, on the edge of the village, two miles south of Castle Douglas. It is situated in pretty, quiet countryside, with a small stream bordering one side of the property. The owners are helpful and friendly and the accommodation is simple. The bedrooms, one of which is *en suite*, are small, with three in the main building and two further rooms sharing a bathroom in an outside annexe. There is a pleasant lounge leading into the conservatory, where breakfast and evening meals (6.30pm) are served, and from here doors lead outside to an area where there are tables and chairs for sitting out. Vegetarian choices are available at dinner and packed lunches can be provided. Rose Cottage is unlicensed, but guests may bring their own wine. Children welcome. No pets in the dining-room. Car park.

OWNERS Kerr and Sheila Steele OPEN Feb–Nov (occasional booking Dec and Jan) ROOMS 2 double (1 with bath/shower, 1 with wash-basin), 3 twin (with wash-basin) TERMS B&B £13.50–£16, (single occupancy of twin/double) £5 surcharge (children up to 3 free, 3–11 half-price); dinner £7.50; deposit £10

GLASGOW Strathclyde map 11

Albion House

405/407 North Woodside Road G20 6NN
041-339 8620

In a quiet road facing a wooded area, the Albion is a small hotel geared primarily to the business visitor. It is a terraced Victorian building, with many of the original ceilings. It has recently been renovated, providing comfortable bedrooms with TV, telephone and trouser press, among other facilities. Breakfast is served in the bar lounge, where bar snacks are available in the evening 6.30–9pm. Vegetarians can be catered for with prior warning. The hotel is convenient for the city centre, museums, art galleries and restaurants. Children welcome. No pets.

OWNERS Mr Alan McGregor and Mr Robert McQuade OPEN All year, exc Christmas ROOMS 5 family, 4 double, 1 twin, 6 single; all rooms with bath/shower TERMS B&B £20–£25, (single) £35 (children under 5 free, 5–10 breakfast charge only, 10–14 half-price); deposit; Access, Visa

Kirklee Hotel

11 Kensington Gate G12 9LG
041-334 5555

Kirklee Hotel is located in an attractive curved terrace overlooking private gardens within one of the city's most outstanding conservation areas. Built of red sandstone in 1904, and originally the home of a shipping magnate, the hotel is convenient for art galleries and the Botanic Gardens and is only minutes from the centre. During the summer there is a beautiful display of flowers in the window boxes and garden. It still retains the wood-panelled hall and stairway and the original drawing-room. There is no dining-room, and full breakfast is served in guests' bedrooms, which all have tables and chairs. The hotel has an alcohol licence, and drinks are served either in the bedrooms or in the drawing-room. Children welcome. No pets. Plenty of on-street parking.

OWNERS Mr and Mrs Peter Steven OPEN All year ROOMS 3 family, 4 double, 2 twin, 1 single; all rooms with bath/shower TERMS B&B £27, (single) £42, (single occupancy of twin/double) £50, (family room) £64–£72 (children £9–£10 sharing with 2 adults); deposit £20–£25

The Town House

4 Hughenden Terrace G12 9XR
041-357 0862

Built in 1882, the Town House is a fine example of Glasgow's Victorian architecture, with spacious, well-proportioned rooms and lovely ceiling cornices. There are 10 very large and well-appointed bedrooms, all with TV and telephone, simply furnished and decorated in soft colours. There is a comfortable lounge with lots of reading material, and good Scottish breakfasts, including porridge and kippers, are served in the original dining-room. The Throws will also provide a simple evening meal (6.30–9pm) if required, and they have acquired an alcohol licence, although there is no bar. Vegetarians can be catered for. The house is located in a wonderful position, in a quiet terrace with a park in front and tennis courts behind, yet is close to the main road with buses into town. It is a 15-minute walk from bustling Byres Road with its many restaurants and shops, and is convenient for art galleries and museums. Children welcome. No smoking in the dining-room.

OWNERS Bill and Charlotte Throw OPEN All year ROOMS 2 family, 4 double, 4 twin; all rooms with bath/shower TERMS B&B £27, (family room) £56–£72 (reductions for children sharing with parents); dinner £15–£20; deposit; Access, Visa

We state at the end of an entry when children are welcome. If we know of any restrictions, we give them.

The description for each entry states when pets are not allowed or restricted in any way.

If a deposit is required for an advance booking this is stated at the end of an entry.

GOLSPIE Highland map 11

Deo Greine Farm

5 Backies, Golspie KW10 6SE
GOLSPIE (040 83) 633106

This modest little farmhouse is approached up a narrow lane off the A9 just outside Golspie and very close to Dunrobin Castle. The size of the interior is quite surprising. There are two ground-floor *en suite* bedrooms, and two rooms upstairs sharing a bathroom. The lounge has comfortable chairs and sofas and a piano. Excellent home-cooked meals, displaying a mixture of French, English and Scottish cooking, are served 7–9pm in the dining-room. Vegetarian choices and packed lunches can be provided. There is no alcohol licence, but guests may bring their own wine. Mrs Grant, originally from Belgium, is a great character. This is a simple, comfortable place to stay and great value. Children welcome. No smoking in bedrooms. Car park.

OWNER Nelly Grant OPEN Apr–Oct ROOMS 1 family, 3 twin; 2 rooms with bath/shower TERMS B&B about £12.50 (children under 4 free sharing with parents, 4–14 half-price); dinner £8.50–£11.50; deposit

GRANTOWN-ON-SPEY Highland map 11

Kinross House

Woodside Avenue, Grantown-on-Spey PH26 3JR
GRANTOWN-ON-SPEY (0479) 2042

This pleasant, detached stone-built house with small front garden is on a quiet residential road. The bedrooms, all with TV, are restful, spacious, light and four are *en suite*. There is a pleasant lounge with a piano, and David Elder serves evening meals (7pm) dressed in his MacIntosh kilt. A typical menu may consist of Stilton and leek soup, baked trout, and oranges in Cointreau with orange sorbet. Vegetarian choices and packed lunches can be provided by arrangement. Kinross House is licensed. No children under seven. No pets. No smoking. Car park.

OWNERS David and Katherine Elder OPEN All year, exc Dec and Jan ROOMS 2 family (1 with bath/shower, 1 with wash-basin), 2 double (1 with bath/shower, 1 with wash-basin), 2 twin (with bath-shower), 1 single (with wash-basin) TERMS B&B £16–£21 (children 7–14 half-price sharing with 2 adults); dinner £10; deposit

GROGPORT Strathclyde map 9

Kilbrannan View Guest House

Grogport, Carradale, by Campbeltown PA28 6QL
CARRADALE (058 33) 289

This very pretty, small stone-built house is in the tiny hamlet of Grogport, and has colourful flowers in front and a car park to the rear that stretches to the sea-shore. The licensed restaurant, where home-cooked food, including vegetarian choices, is available for breakfast, lunch, tea and dinner (from 7pm), is an extension to the back of the house with panoramic views over Kilbrannan Sound to Arran and beyond. Two large bedrooms have good views; one is on the ground floor and suitable for the disabled, the other is a family room upstairs. There are also two singles with a toilet upstairs and bathroom downstairs, and a comfortable sitting-room. Children must be kept under control in the dining-room. No pets in the house. No smoking in bedrooms. Car park.

OWNERS A. and D. Strang OPEN All year ROOMS 1 family (with bath/shower), 1 twin (with bath/shower), 2 single (with wash-basin) TERMS B&B £13–£15, (family room) £30 (children under 3 free); dinner from £10.50; deposit

HADDINGTON Lothian map 11

Barney Mains Farmhouse

Haddington EH41 3SA
ATHELSTANEFORD (062 088) 310 Fax (062 088) 639

The house, parts of which date back to the early eighteenth century, stands on a rise, with wonderful views in every direction to the Lammermuir Hills, the Bass Rock and Traprain Law. It is a working farm with a herd of cross Hereford-Friesian cattle, and there are also self-catering cottages available. The rooms are spacious and comfortable, sharing an old-fashioned bathroom and separate shower-room. Breakfast only is available, although packed lunches can be provided. Children welcome. No pets. No smoking in bedrooms. Car park.

OWNER Katie Kerr OPEN Apr–end Oct ROOMS 1 double, 2 twin TERMS B&B £12–£15 (children up to 2 free, 3–11 £6–£7)

If there are any bedrooms with TV and/or telephone we mention this in the entry.

HUNTLY Grampian map 11

Faich-Hill Farmhouse

Gartly, Huntly AB54 4RR
GARTLY (046 688) 240

This traditional, granite farmhouse, with views of the rolling hills and farmland, is about four miles south of Huntly. The long driveway to the farm is right beside the church, and the house forms one side of the farmyard. The entrance to the house is through the conservatory, which has lots of literature and brochures, and there are just two ground-floor bedrooms, one *en suite*. There is a TV lounge and a traditional dining-room where evening meals are served at 6.30pm. Vegetarian choices and packed lunches can be provided on request. There is no alcohol licence, but guests may bring their own wine to dinner. No pets. Smoking in the sun lounge only. Car park.

OWNERS Theo and Margaret Grant OPEN All year, exc Christmas
ROOMS 1 double (with wash-basin), 1 twin (with bath/shower)
TERMS B&B £13–£15; dinner £7; deposit

INNERLEITHEN Borders map 10

Caddon View Guest House

14 Pirn Road, Innerleithen EH44 6HH
INNERLEITHEN (0896) 830208

Caddon View was once a doctor's surgery; the waiting room is now the lounge, and the surgery itself a bedroom. It is a large, stone-built Victorian house, set back a little from the main road on the edge of town with views of the hills of the Tweed Valley. The house is surrounded by a beautifully kept garden, including an extensive vegetable garden with herbs and fruit. The Wrights are extremely friendly, welcoming people and offer comfortable, good-sized rooms, tastefully decorated. All bedrooms have TV; three bedrooms have gas fires. Breakfast choices include different kinds of porridge and smoked haddock. Dinner is also available 6.30–7pm in the small, neat and fresh dining-room. Vegetarian choices and packed lunches can be provided. There is no alcohol

B&B rates specified in the details for each entry are per person per night; unless the details state otherwise, they are based on two people sharing a double or twin-bedded room.

licence, but guests may bring their own wine. Children welcome. Pets by arrangement. Car park.

OWNERS Will and Audrey Wright OPEN All year, exc mid-Jan–mid-Feb ROOMS 1 family (with wash-basin), 1 double (with bath/shower), 2 twin (1 with bath/shower, 1 with wash-basin), 1 single (with wash-basin) TERMS B&B £13–£16 (children under 3 free, 3–11 half-price sharing with parents); dinner £8; deposit £5 per person

INVERASDALE Highland map 11

Knotts Landing

12 Coast, Inverasdale IV22 2LP
POOLEWE (044 586) 331

For an away-from-it-all holiday, this location would be hard to beat. Knotts Landing is about five miles down a narrow and remote road from Poolewe with wonderful views of sea and mountains, and a great place for walking and access to beaches. It is a small house with a well-maintained front garden. There are three basic ground-floor bedrooms, only one of which has a view. There is a TV lounge and a dining-room, where evening meals (by arrangement at 6.30pm) are served; vegetarians can be catered for. Guests may bring their own wine (no licence) and a packed lunch can be provided. Children welcome. No dogs. No smoking in bedrooms. Car park.

OWNER Mrs S. Maclean OPEN Feb–Oct ROOMS 2 twin (1 with wash-basin), 1 single (with wash-basin) TERMS B&B from £11 (children under 4 free, 4–12 half-price); dinner from £7; deposit

INVERNESS Highland map 11

Abb Cottage

11 Douglas Row, Inverness IV1 1RE
INVERNESS (0463) 233486

This charming little listed terraced cottage covered with creepers and roses is in a superb position, facing the river in a quiet street right in the centre of Inverness. The two downstairs bedrooms and bathrooms are suitable for the infirm, and the upstairs bedroom has lovely views over the river. The rooms are very simply furnished and decorated, and there is a small lounge/breakfast room with books and games. Evenings meals are available by arrangement 6–6.30pm and can cater for vegetarian and special diets. Abb Cottage is unlicensed, but guests may bring their own wine. No children under eight. No pets. No smoking.

OWNER Kate Storrar OPEN Mar–Dec ROOMS 3 twin (with wash-basin) TERMS B&B from £12, (single occupancy of twin) £18; dinner from £7; deposit

Craigside Lodge

4 Gordon Terrace, Inverness IV2 3HD
INVERNESS (0463) 231576

A detached Victorian house, Craigside Lodge has lovely views over the castle and river and is only a few minutes' walk from town. It is a pleasant guesthouse, with friendly owners, comfortable bedrooms, all with TV, and an excellent breakfast. Packed lunches can also be provided. The lounge is an attractive room on the ground-floor with good views, and the breakfast room on the lower-ground floor also has impressive views. Children welcome. Car park.

OWNERS Janette and Wilf Skinner OPEN All year ROOMS 3 double (2 with bath/shower, 1 with wash-basin), 3 twin (2 with bath/shower, 1 with wash-basin) TERMS B&B £13–£16 (children under 11 half-price)

Culduthel Lodge

14 Culduthel Road, Inverness IV2 4AG
INVERNESS (0463) 240089

This Georgian house, within easy access of the city centre, stands in its own grounds with splendid views of the River Ness. It has a spacious country-house feel with a comfortable lounge, where drinks are served before dinner (available 6.30–7.30pm), and an elegant dining-room. Vegetarians can be catered for with prior notice and packed lunches can be provided. Drinks are also taken on the terrace in fine weather. The bedrooms all have private bathroom, TV, hair-dryer, fresh fruit and flowers, and a newspaper is supplied daily. No children under eight. No pets. No smoking in the dining-room and some bedrooms. Car park.

OWNERS David and Marion Bonsor OPEN All year, exc Christmas and New Year ROOMS 3 family, 7 double, 1 twin, 1 single; all rooms with bath/shower TERMS B&B £25–£28, (single) £30–£35, (single occupancy of twin/double) £50 (reductions for children); dinner £12; deposit; Access, Visa

The Old Rectory

9 Southside Road, Inverness IV2 3BG
INVERNESS (0463) 220969

The Old Rectory is an attractive, small, stone-built detached house with a pretty front garden and a well-maintained rear garden, quite close to the centre of town. The bedrooms are pleasantly decorated and there is a comfortable lounge and a dining-room with Victorian fireplace, where breakfast only is served. Packed lunches can be provided. No children under three. No pets. No smoking. Car park.

OWNERS Mr and Mrs John Lister OPEN All year ROOMS 1 family, 2 double, 1 twin; all rooms with bath/shower TERMS B&B £14–£17, (single occupancy of twin/double) £16–£26, (family room) £50 (children ¾ adult rate); deposit

INVERSHIN Highland map 11

Gneiss House

Invershin, by Lairg IV27 4ET
INVERSHIN (054 982) 282

A purpose-built bungalow on the edge of Invershin, Gneiss House has pretty views across the Kyle of Sutherland to Carbisdale Castle. The Brinklows moved here from the Croit Mairi Guest House in Ardgay and built Gneiss House in 1989. The house, which stands just off the A836, has a large lounge with small outside terrace and pleasant views. Breakfast only is served in the small dining-room, and there are three small *en suite* bedrooms. 'Not ideal for children'. Pets by arrangement. No smoking. Ample parking.

OWNERS Ian and Win Brinklow OPEN All year, exc Christmas, New Year and 2 weeks Oct ROOMS 1 double, 1 double/twin, 1 twin; all rooms with bath/shower TERMS B&B £13–£18 (reductions for children by arrangement, but not July/Aug); deposit; all major credit cards

Most establishments have central heating. We say when this is not the case.

The description for each entry states when pets are not allowed. Where no details are given, you can assume that pets are allowed. It's always best to check first.

IONA Strathclyde map 11

Argyll Hotel

Isle of Iona PA76 6SJ
IONA (068 17) 334

The hotel, which is built of the local pink stone, sits right on the sea-front in the centre of the village looking towards Mull, and is only a few minutes' walk from the abbey. The original part was built in 1860 as an inn, and Robert Louis Stevenson recorded his visit here in a letter to his mother. The building is deceptively large, with various extensions added over the years. The bedrooms are fairly small and simply furnished; 10 of them, mostly singles, are located in the cedar extension in the garden. There is a most attractive dining-room, decorated in restful colours with old furniture and individual tables, leading out to the long, narrow sun lounge, which overlooks the Sound of Iona. Home-cooked food, using local produce and the hotel's own organically grown vegetables, is served both at lunch and dinner (7pm). Vegetarians can be catered for and the hotel is licensed. There are two small lounges, one for smokers and one for non-smokers. This is a friendly, relaxed place with a pleasant atmosphere, helpful staff and a delightful owner. Children welcome. No dogs in the dining-room. No smoking in the dining-room and one of the lounges. No central heating. No visitors' cars are allowed on the island, but there is free car parking near the ferry on Mull.

OWNER Mrs Fiona Menzies OPEN 10 Apr–10 Oct ROOMS 2 family (with bath/shower), 3 double (2 with bath/shower, 1 with wash-basin), 4 twin (3 with bath/shower, 1 with wash-basin), 10 single (3 with bath/shower, 7 with wash-basin) TERMS B&B £22–£31, (single occupancy of twin/double) £44–£58 (children sharing family room half-price, under 2 free, 2–6 40% reduction, 7–13 25% reduction – exc July/Aug); dinner £14; deposit £25 per person; Access, Visa

JEDBURGH Borders map 10

Hundalee House

Jedburgh TD8 6PA
JEDBURGH (0835) 63011

This handsome stone-built house, one mile south of Jedburgh off the A68, dates from the 1700s and stands in 10 acres of mature woodland and garden enjoying wonderful views towards Carter

Bar. Both house and grounds are well maintained. The bedrooms, all with TV, are spacious, extremely comfortably furnished and attractively decorated. There is a small *en suite* room on the ground floor through the kitchen, and a four-poster room with its own shower-room is upstairs. The remaining rooms in the main part of the house share a large bathroom and separate toilet. There is a large, comfortable lounge and breakfast only is served at one big table in the dining-room. Children welcome. No dogs. No smoking. Car park.

OWNERS Mr and Mrs A. P. Whittaker OPEN All year, exc Christmas and New Year ROOMS 1 family (with wash-basin), 1 four-poster (with bath/shower), 1 double (with bath/shower), 1 twin (with wash-basin) TERMS B&B £14–£18, (single occupancy of twin/double) £20–£25 (children £8 in family room); deposit

KEITH Grampian map 11

The Haughs Farm Guest House

Keith AB55 3QN
KEITH (054 22) 2238

The whitewashed farmhouse dates from 1614 and is part of a mixed 165-acre farm. James Scott Skinner, the famous fiddler and composer, was a regular guest at The Haughs, settling his B&B account with the composition of a hornpipe. Although all the bedrooms are on the ground floor, there are stairs up to this level and one bathroom is down another set of stairs. The rooms are large and three have *en suite* facilities. The dining-room, where evening meals (6.30pm) are served, is in the conservatory, which has particularly fine views, marred a little by the expanses of the distillery warehouses which lie below the house. Vegetarian choices can be provided. There is no alcohol licence, but guests may bring their own wine to dinner. No children under two. No pets. Smoking in the lounge only. Car park.

OWNERS Jean and Peter Jackson OPEN Apr–Oct ROOMS 2 family (with bath/shower), 2 double (1 with wash-basin), 1 twin (with bath/shower) TERMS B&B from £12.50–£14.50, (single occupancy of twin/double) £20; dinner £8; deposit

Bath/shower information in the details refers only to a private bathroom or shower; other bathroom facilities at the establishments will be shared. We say if rooms have wash-basins.

KELSO Borders map 10

Bellevue House Hotel

Bowmount Street, Kelso TD5 7DZ
KELSO (0573) 24588

This comfortable, homely hotel is five minutes' walk from the town centre and the gates of Floors Castle. The accommodation is simple but clean, and the rooms are of a good size. Five rooms have TV. One twin room with bathroom is on the ground floor and is suitable for the disabled. There is a lounge and bar for guests' use. Evening meals are available (6.30–8.30pm); vegetarian choices can be provided at dinner. Lunch and packed lunches are also available. Children welcome. Pets by arrangement. Car park.

OWNERS Mr and Mrs J. R. Dodds OPEN All year ROOMS 1 family, 3 double, 1 twin, 4 single (with wash-basin); all rooms, exc singles, with bath/shower TERMS B&B £23.50, (single occupancy of twin/double) £29 (children half-price); D, B&B £34; dinner £12; deposit £20 per room; Access, Visa

KEOSE Western Isles (Lewis) map 11

Handa

18 Keose Glebe, Lochs, Isle of Lewis PA86 9JX
STORNOWAY (0851) 83334

At the very end of a narrow side-road, Handa was built by its friendly young owners in 1983. Turn off the main Stornoway to Tarbert road (A859) at the sign 'Ceos' and drive one and a half miles through the village to the last house. It is a charming little place with honeysuckle growing around the front door. There is a loch at the front, and to the rear the garden goes down to another loch, where there are boats for hire. The furniture and fittings are mostly in pine and the two pretty, attic-type first-floor bedrooms have large skylights. There is also a downstairs *en suite* bedroom and a comfortable lounge/dining-room, where excellent home-cooked Scottish food is served at 7.30pm. Vegetarian choices can be provided. There is no alcohol licence, but guests may bring their own wine to dinner. Packed lunches can be arranged

Many B&Bs will cater for vegetarians. It is always best, however, to check when booking and make it clear what your requirements are, especially if you need a special diet.

(Sundays only). Children welcome. No pets. No smoking in bedrooms and the dining-room. Car park.

OWNERS Murdo and Christine Morrison OPEN Mar–Oct
ROOMS 2 double (1 with bath/shower, 1 with wash-basin), 1 twin (1 with wash-basin) TERMS B&B £15–£20 (child in cot free, children under 12 2/3 adult price); dinner £10

KILLIN Central map 11

Fairview Guest House

Main Street, Killin FK21 8UT
KILLIN (056 72) 667

This solid, stone-built guesthouse is in the middle of the village, with views of the Breadalbane Hills to the rear and Loch Tay and Ben Lawers to the front. The bedrooms are on the small side and simply furnished, but they are comfortable. There is a first-floor lounge and evening meals are available in the pine-furnished dining-room at 7.30pm. Vegetarian choices can be provided. There is no alcohol licence, but guests may bring their own wine to dinner. Packed lunches can be provided. Car park.

OWNERS Roger and Muriel Bedwell OPEN All year, exc Christmas
ROOMS 4 double (2 with bath/shower), 2 twin (1 with bath/shower, 1 with wash-basin), 1 single (with wash-basin) TERMS B&B £13–£15; dinner £7; deposit

KINGUSSIE Highland map 11

Homewood Lodge

Kingussie PH21 1HD
KINGUSSIE (0540) 661507

Homewood Lodge is a granite house standing well above the main road on the outskirts of Kingussie with wonderful mountain views. The Howarths, a young, enthusiastic couple with young children, took over in 1990. The bedrooms are spacious, all *en suite*, with simple, mostly pine furniture. There is a guests' lounge with an open fire, and imaginative evening meals (7–8.30pm) are available both to guests and non-residents. Vegetarian dishes can be provided. There is an alcohol licence. Packed lunches can be

Where a single-occupancy rate is not specified in the details, the cost will be the same as that per person in a twin or double room, or will be included in the range of prices given.

arranged. Children welcome. Pets by arrangement. No smoking. Car park.

OWNERS David and Gillian Howarth OPEN All year, exc Christmas ROOMS 2 family, 1 double, 1 twin; all rooms with bath/shower TERMS B&B from £19.75, (single occupancy of twin/double) £22.50, (children under 10 reductions sharing with parents); dinner £12.50–£13.50; deposit

KINLOCHBERVIE Highland map 11

Old School Restaurant and Guest House

Inshegra, Kinlochbervie IV27 4RH
KINLOCHBERVIE (0971) 521383

This stone-built former schoolhouse dates from 1879 and is midway between Rhiconich and Kinlochbervie, with lovely views over Loch Inchard. The licensed restaurant has an excellent reputation and serves local seafood. Evening meals are served 6–9pm; vegetarian dishes can be provided and packed lunches can be arranged. The accommodation, which is very well maintained, is in a new annexe and comprises six very comfortable, modern, ground-floor bedrooms. Four rooms have TV, and all have telephone. Children welcome. Dogs by arrangement. Car park.

OWNERS Tom and Margaret Burt OPEN All year, exc Christmas and New Year ROOMS 1 family (with bath/shower), 1 double (with bath/shower), 4 twin (2 with bath/shower, 2 with wash-basin) TERMS B&B £17–£23.50, (family room) £23.50 per adult and £8 per child; dinner £4.95–£8.75; Access, Visa

KINLOCH RANNOCH Tayside map 11

Cuilmore Cottage

Kinloch Rannoch PH16 5QB
KINLOCH RANNOCH (088 22) 218/(0882) 632218

This idyllic whitewashed croft is set in a colourful garden, with vines covering the front porch. It stands on the edge of the village, just above the loch. The house has been restored over the last 10 years by the owners and is simply decorated. Two of the bedrooms are surprisingly large and there is a small single, with the shared bathroom on the ground floor. There is a cosy sitting-room with an open fire. Dinners are served (7pm) in the small dining-room, with its old range. Up to eight non-residents can be catered for and the cuisine is mostly Scottish, with vegetables from the garden and home-made bread. Vegetarian dishes can be provided. Packed lunches can be arranged. Guests may bring their own wine to dinner. There are mountain bikes, a canoe and sailing dinghy for guests' use. No children under 10. No smoking in bedrooms. Car park.

OWNERS Jens and Anita Steffen OPEN All year, exc Christmas and New Year ROOMS 1 double, 1 twin, 1 single; all rooms with wash-basin TERMS B&B £17.50; D, B&B £30

KIRKWALL Orkney map 11

Brekk-ness Guest House

Muddisdale Road, Kirkwall KW15 1RS
KIRKWALL (0856) 4317

This modern, purpose-built guesthouse is in a quiet location, a 10-minute walk from the town centre. All the bedrooms have TV, hair-dryer and private bathroom with shower. Five bedrooms are on the ground floor. Evening meals are available 6–7pm and vegetarian dishes can be arranged. There is no alcohol licence, but guests may bring their own wine to dinner. Packed lunches can be provided. Children welcome. Pets by arrangement. No smoking in the dining-room and the lounge. Car park.

OWNERS J. S. and A. E. Bews OPEN All year ROOMS 2 family, 2 double, 7 twin; all rooms with bath/shower TERMS B&B £19, (single occupancy of twin/double) £22 (children under 3 free, 3–14 half-price); dinner £8

Briar Lea

10 Dundas Crescent, Kirkwall KW15 1JQ
KIRKWALL (0856) 2747

This stone-built townhouse in a large walled garden dates from the nineteenth century. It has an excellent central location and a friendly atmosphere. Original features of the house include the interior doors and there is a bell collection in the kitchen. The house is comfortably furnished and breakfast only is served. Packed lunches can be provided. There is much of architectural interest in the town; bird-watching and loch fishing can be

Where we know of any particular payment stipulations we mention them in the details. It is always best to check when booking, however.

enjoyed locally. Children welcome. No pets. No smoking in bedrooms. Car park.

OWNERS Mr and Mrs Arthur Flett OPEN All year ROOMS 2 twin, 2 single; twin rooms can take extra beds TERMS B&B £11–£12; deposit £10 for long stay, or £1 per person per night

LARGS Strathclyde map 11

South Whittlieburn Farm

Brisbane Glen, Largs KA30 8SN
LARGS (0475) 675881

This old farmhouse with lovely views of hills is about two miles inland from Largs. Sheep farming and stabling for horses are the main activities. The bedrooms are clean, fresh and comfortable, and one is now *en suite*. Dinner is served occasionally on request (at around 6pm) and vegetarian choices can be provided. There is no alcohol licence, but guests may bring their own wine. Packed lunches can be provided. There is also a TV lounge with a small organ. Guests can look round the farm and help with activities. Children welcome. Pets by arrangement. Car park.

OWNER Mrs M. Watson OPEN All year, exc Christmas ROOMS 1 family (with wash-basin), 1 double (with bath/shower), 1 twin (with wash-basin) TERMS B&B £13.50–£17.50 (children under 11 reductions); dinner from £9.50; deposit

LERWICK Shetland (Mainland) map 11

Whinrig

12 Burgh Road, Lerwick ZE1 0LB
LERWICK (0595) 3554

Breakfast only is served at this small, neat house in a quiet cul-de-sac. It is off the main road in a residential area, a few minutes' walk from the shops, museum and swimming-pool. The accommodation is comfortable, all rooms have TV and are on the ground floor. There are many places nearby for meals or snacks. Packed lunches can be provided. The owners can provide a taxi service to and from the bus or boat if required. Children welcome. No pets. No smoking. Car park.

OWNER W. B. Gifford OPEN All year, exc Christmas and New Year ROOMS 1 double (with wash-basin), 2 twin (1 with bath/shower) TERMS B&B £10–£14; deposit

LEVERBURGH Western Isles (Harris) map 11

Ben View

Leverburgh, Isle of Harris PA83 3TL
LEVERBURGH (085 982) 300

Ben View is in the village of Leverburgh, which overlooks the Sound of Harris. The harbour is the terminal for the passenger ferry for the isles of Berneray and North Uist. Mrs Green keeps a neat, immaculate guesthouse. The sitting-room is very pleasant and the two comfortable bedrooms are of a good size. Evening meals are served in the dining-room at 7pm. There is no alcohol licence, but guests may bring their own wine. Packed lunches can be provided. Sea angling can be arranged. Children welcome. Dogs by arrangement. Car park.

OWNER Mrs Norma Green OPEN May–Sept ROOMS 2 twin (with wash-basin) TERMS B&B from £17; dinner from £12; deposit

LOCHBOISDALE Western Isles (South Uist) map 11

Innis-Ghorm

Lochboisdale, South Uist PA81 5TH
LOCHBOISDALE (087 84) 232

Lochboisdale is about half a mile from this small, friendly working croft beside the sea loch. It is the main port for South Uist, and services run to Oban and Barra. The accommodation is simple and includes two bedrooms; one room is suitable for families. There are pleasant views south to lochs and mountains from the lounge/dining-room. Evening meals (served at 6pm) are provided by arrangement. There is no alcohol licence, but guests may bring their own wine. No children under 10. No pets. No smoking in bedrooms. Car park.

OWNER Mrs Catherine MacLeod OPEN All year, exc Christmas ROOMS 2 double (with wash-basin) TERMS B&B £11 (children under 10 half-price); dinner £6

It is always best to book a room in advance, especially in winter. B&Bs with few rooms may close at short notice for periods not specified in the details.

Breakfast at B&Bs tends to mean a cooked breakfast of bacon, eggs and so on. If you prefer a different style of breakfast, discuss this when you make the booking.

LOCHCARRON Highland map 11

A'Chomraich

Lochcarron IV54 8YD
LOCHCARRON (052 02) 225

On the edge of the pretty village of Lochcarron, this attractive stone-built and partly whitewashed 100-year-old house is in a charming garden. The front faces the sea. The house is comfortably furnished and there is a cosy lounge; the two very simple, pretty, attic-type bedrooms have a bathroom between them. Breakfast only is served. Packed lunches can be provided. Children welcome. No pets in bedrooms. No smoking in bedrooms. Car park.

OWNERS Mr and Mrs Rore OPEN Mar–Oct ROOMS 1 double, 1 twin; both rooms with wash-basin TERMS B&B £11–£13 (children under 5 free, 6–12 half-price); deposit

LOCH ERIBOLL Highland map 11

Port-na-Con House

Loch Eriboll, by Altnaharra, Lairg IV27 4UN
DURNESS (097 181) 367

Originally a customs house and harbour store, Port-na-Con is in a beautiful position on the west side of Loch Eriboll, approximately seven miles east of Durness on the A838. It is now a small, modernised, whitewashed guesthouse with a little beach. The accommodation is clean and comfortable and the bedrooms, as well as the first-floor lounge, have views over the loch. Evening meals consisting of local produce, including prawns from Loch Eriboll, are served at 7pm. Vegetarian choices can be provided. There is an alcohol licence. Packed lunches can be arranged. Children welcome, but there are no special facilities. Dogs by arrangement. No smoking. Car park.

OWNERS Kenneth and Lesley Black OPEN Apr–Oct
ROOMS 2 family, 1 twin, 2 double; all rooms with wash-basin
TERMS B&B £16, (single occupancy of twin/double) £22 (children 2–5 one-third-price, 6–8 half-price, 9–13 two-thirds-price); dinner £10; deposit £10; Access, Visa

Many B&Bs are in remote places; always ask for clear directions when booking.

LOCHGILPHEAD Strathclyde map 11

Buidhe Lodge

Craobh Haven, nr Lochgilphead PA31 8UA
BARBRECK (085 25) 291

This modern wooden building is on the edge of the yacht haven and old hamlet of Craobh Haven, on a tiny island linked by a causeway, which it shares with the adjoining watersports centre, to the mainland. The property has its own slipway and mooring, which guests can use, and is situated right on the shore. Simone Twinn prepares good home-cooked food using local produce, including seafood. There is a pleasant open-plan dining-room; the bedrooms are small and simply furnished in pine. All have TV and are on the ground floor. Mountain bike hire is available from the watersports lodge. Children welcome. Pets must have their own bed. Car park.

OWNERS Nick and Simone Twinn OPEN All year, exc Jan–Feb
ROOMS 6 twin (with bath/shower) TERMS B&B £23; D, B&B £33 (children under 12 half-price); deposit; Access, Visa

LOCHINVER Highland map 11

Ardglas

Lochinver IV27 4LI
LOCHINVER (057 14) 257

Ardglas is high up overlooking the picturesque fishing village of Lochinver, with fine views towards the famous Sugar Loaf Mountain. The McBains offer simple, very clean accommodation. The rooms are small, modern and comfortably furnished. Two rooms have TV and three are on the ground floor. There is a TV lounge, and breakfast only is served in the dining-room. The harbour and village can be seen from the house and terrace. Children welcome. Small pets only. No smoking in bedrooms and the dining area. Car park.

OWNERS Mr and Mrs D. McBain OPEN Mar–Nov
ROOMS 2 family, 3 double, 2 twin, 1 single; all rooms with wash-basin
TERMS B&B £13–£14 (children under 12 half-price sharing with adult); deposit

If you are forced to turn up late into the evening, please telephone to warn the proprietor.

LOCHRANZA Strathclyde (Arran) map 9

Butt Lodge Hotel

Lochranza, Isle of Arran KA27 8JF
LOCHRANZA (077 083) 240

Nestling under the hills, in a very quiet, rural spot on the edge of Lochranza, Butt Lodge, built about 100 years ago as a shooting lodge, is a pleasant whitewashed building standing in attractive grounds. There is a small pretty dining-room, where evening meals are served at 7pm and a large, comfortable sitting-room with an open fire. There is an alcohol licence. Packed lunches can be provided. No children under five. No pets. No smoking in bedrooms and the dining-room. Car park.

OWNERS Mr and Mrs P. Price OPEN Easter–Oct ROOMS 1 family, 3 double, 1 twin; all rooms with bath/shower TERMS B&B £22–£28, (family room) £33–£42 (children 5–14 half-price); dinner £11; deposit £15 per person; Visa

LUMSDEN Grampian map 11

Chapelton Farm

Lumsden, Huntly AB5 4JL
RHYNIE (046 46) 749

This small agricultural croft on 31 acres of land is close to Lumsden village. It is a warm, homely house where everyone is made very welcome. Edith Petrie, who has lived and worked in the area all her life, indulges her guests with cheese, biscuits, home-made scones and tea and coffee in the evenings. There are two attractive, simply furnished bedrooms. Breakfast and home-cooked dinners (6–8pm) are served with plenty of fruit and vegetables from the garden. Vegetarian dishes can be provided. There is no alcohol licence, but guests may bring their own wine to dinner. Packed lunches can be arranged. Children welcome. No pets. No smoking. Car park.

OWNER Edith Petrie OPEN All year ROOMS 1 family, 1 twin; both rooms with wash-basin TERMS B&B £10–£12 (£4 for children under 4, £8 under 12; D, B&B £6 under 4, £12 under 12); dinner £6; deposit £10

When the family-room rate is given in the details it applies to the cost of the whole room, unless a rate per person is specified.

LUSS Strathclyde map 11

Ardallie House

Luss G83 8NU
LUSS (043 686) 272

This attractive, small country house is approached up a drive from the A82 Luss bypass. Ardallie House is above Loch Lomond, with wonderful views over trees to the loch. It is a comfortable family home with a long, large sitting-room, with a dining area at one end. Evening meals are served at 7.30pm, by prior arrangement; vegetarian dishes can be provided. There is no alcohol licence, but guests may bring their own wine to dinner. Children occupying a bed are charged in full. Pets by arrangement. No smoking upstairs. Car park.

OWNER Mrs Short OPEN Mar–end Oct ROOMS 1 double, 2 twin; all rooms with wash-basin TERMS B&B £12–£18 (children under 4 free); dinner £8–£10; deposit £15 per person

LYNESS Orkney (Hoy) map 11

Stoneyquoy

Lyness, Hoy KW16 3NY
HOY (085 679) 234

Stoneyquoy is a traditional farmhouse with low stone buildings and slate roofs, a sheltered garden and views over Longhope Bay. The house is comfortable and cosy. Arthur Budge is pleased to give guests a tour of the 200-acre farm. Plenty of advice is available on good walks in the area. Guests share the sitting-room with the family, enjoying the open peat fire on cooler evenings. Louise Budge produces good home-cooked dinners (6pm), and supper is also served later in the evening. Vegetarian choices can be provided, if pre-arranged. There is no alcohol licence, but guests may bring their own wine. Packed lunches can also be arranged. Children welcome, but there are no facilities for very small children. No pets. Non-smokers preferred. Car park.

OWNERS Arthur and Louise Budge OPEN All year ROOMS 1 double, 1 twin; both rooms with wash-basin TERMS B&B £10–£12; dinner £6; deposit £2 per person per day

It is always best to check prices, especially for single occupancy, when booking.

MELROSE Borders map 9

Dunfermline House

Buccleuch Street, Melrose TD6 9LB
MELROSE (089 682) 2148

Dunfermline House is in the centre of Melrose, about 50 yards from Melrose Abbey, and offers comfortable accommodation. The Grahams have extended the house, adding on two spacious bedrooms at the back. All the bedrooms are *en suite* and have TV. The house has been prettily decorated throughout. Evening meals are available in the dining-room at 7pm and packed lunches can be provided. Guests may bring their own wine to dinner (no licence). Children welcome. No pets. No smoking.

OWNERS Susan and Ian Graham OPEN All year, exc Christmas
ROOMS 2 double, 2 twin, 1 single; all rooms with bath/shower
TERMS B&B £19, (single occupancy of twin/double) £24; dinner £10

MINNIGAFF Dumfries & Galloway map 9

Auchenleck Farm

Minnigaff, Newton Stewart DG8 7AA
NEWTON STEWART (0671) 2035

Built in 1863 by the Earl of Galloway as a shooting lodge, this is an imposing stone-built turreted house with a circular staircase enclosed in a round tower. The house is a working farm five miles from Newton Stewart and nestles in peaceful countryside in an isolated position. There is a TV lounge and a dining-room, where breakfast only is served; a packed lunch can be provided if requested. The bedrooms are comfortable, one with private bathroom, the other rooms sharing a large bathroom. Children welcome. No pets. No smoking in the dining-room and bedrooms. Car park.

OWNER Mrs Margaret Hewitson OPEN Easter–Nov
ROOMS 2 double, 1 twin; all rooms with wash-basin TERMS B&B £13–£15, (single occupancy of twin/double) £5 supplement (children under 5 half-price, 5–11 5% reduction); deposit

If you intend to spend several days at a B&B, it is worth asking whether there are reduced rates, particularly if the period is midweek or off-season.

Use the maps and indexes at the back of the Guide *to plan your trip.*

Auchenleck Farm, Minnigaff

MOFFAT Dumfries & Galloway map 9

Belmont

Sidmount Avenue, Moffat DG10 9BS
MOFFAT (0683) 20057

This substantial and very well-maintained late-nineteenth-century Georgian-style house stands in beautifully kept gardens at the end of a cul-de-sac, a few minutes' walk from the centre of Moffat. It has spacious rooms, with original cornices and huge wooden doors. All the bedrooms are large and comfortably furnished, with private bathroom. There is a comfortable upstairs sitting-room with TV and a traditional family dining-room with one big table where breakfast only is served. No pets. No smoking. Car park.

OWNERS Mr and Mrs Fell OPEN All year, exc Christmas and New Year ROOMS 2 double, 1 twin; all rooms with bath/shower TERMS B&B £14 (reductions for children under 12); deposit

It is always best to check prices, especially for single occupancy, when booking.

Fernhill

Grange Road, Moffat DG10 9HT
MOFFAT (0683) 20077

Fernhill is a detached sandstone house standing at the end of a residential street, in an elevated position close to the centre of town, yet with views of countryside and hills. The house is a pristine, comfortable family home full of ornaments and trinkets. The large sitting-room has a TV and the two spacious bedrooms have *en suite* facilities and TV. Breakfast only is served, but tea with home baking is served around 9.30pm in the lounge. Guests have use of the immaculately kept, colourful garden. No small children. No pets. No smoking in bedrooms. Car park.

OWNERS Mr and Mrs A. N. Gourlay OPEN June–Aug
ROOMS 1 double, 1 twin; both rooms with bath/shower
TERMS B&B £11.50–£12

Hartfell House

Hartfell Crescent, Moffat DG10 9AL
MOFFAT (0683) 20153

This substantial country house built in 1860 is at the end of a cul-de-sac in two acres of landscaped gardens. It is in a peaceful setting and only a few minutes' walk from the town centre. The house is immaculately kept and is known locally for its fine interior woodwork. The bedrooms are very large, with five now *en suite*, and there are lovely views from the spacious, first-floor lounge. The downstairs bedrooms and the dining-room have beautiful ceilings. Dinner is served from 6pm and vegetarian choices are available. The premises are licensed. Children welcome. No smoking in the dining-room. Car park.

OWNERS Andrea and Alan Daniel OPEN Mar–Nov
ROOMS 2 family (with wash-basin), 3 double (with bath/shower), 2 twin (1 with bath/shower, 1 with wash-basin), 2 single (1 with bath/shower, 1 with wash-basin) TERMS B&B £16.50–£21.50 (children under 12 half-price); dinner £10–£12.50

Those B&Bs that we know can offer some kind of off-street car parking, have 'car park' at the end of the entry. If we are aware of particular car parking difficulties, we mention them.

Many B&Bs will cater for vegetarians. It is always best, however, to check when booking and make it clear what your requirements are, especially if you need a special diet.

MONTROSE Tayside map 11

Oaklands

10 Rossie Island Road, Montrose DD10 9NN
MONTROSE (0674) 72018

This neat, stone-built detached house, with a small front garden, is on the A92 at the south end of Montrose. An extension has been added at the back of the house. Four of the bedrooms now have *en suite* facilities and seven have TV. Breakfast only is served, but packed lunches can be provided on request. There is a play area for children. No pets in the public rooms. No smoking in the dining-room. Car park.

OWNERS Mr and Mrs A. A. Crowe OPEN All year, exc Christmas ROOMS 1 family (with bath/shower), 2 double (with bath/shower), 3 twin (1 with bath/shower, 2 with wash-basin), 1 single (with wash-basin) TERMS B&B £12.50, (single occupancy of twin/double) £19.50; deposit for larger bookings

NAIRN Highland map 11

Greenlawns

13 Seafield Street, Nairn IV12 4HG
NAIRN (0667) 52738

This small family-run hotel is only a few minutes from the sea-front and golf course. The Caldwells are antique collectors and some of their purchases are on display in the house. The large dining-room (where breakfast only is served) leads into a sizeable lounge which houses an art gallery and from here there are doors out to the garden, with chairs for sitting out. Four of the bedrooms are on the ground floor and all have TV. Car park.

OWNERS William and Isabel Caldwell OPEN All year, exc Christmas ROOMS 4 double (1 with bath/shower, 3 with wash-basin), 3 twin (1 with bath/shower, 2 with wash-basin) TERMS B&B £20–£25 (babies free, reductions for children); deposit 10%; Access, Visa

Where we know an establishment accepts credit cards, we list them. There may be a surcharge if you pay by credit card. It is always best to check whether the card you want to use is acceptable when booking.

Where a single-occupancy rate is not specified in the details, the cost will be the same as that per person in a twin or double room, or will be included in the range of prices given.

NENTHORN Borders map 10

Whitehill Farm

Nenthorn, Kelso TD5 7RZ
STICHILL (057 37) 203

Whitehill is an early Victorian farmhouse on a working farm in a wonderful position with views of the Cheviots. This is an area full of Border history and has an abundance of castles and old houses. Three of the bedrooms have a view and the two singles are very spacious. The lounge is large and comfortable, and evening meals are served in the front-facing dining-room at 7.15pm. Guests may bring their own wine (no licence) and are welcome to walk round the farm, with access to tracks for walks. There are no cots for young children. No smoking in bedrooms. Car park.

OWNERS Mr and Mrs D. H. Smith OPEN All year, exc Christmas and New Year ROOMS 2 twin (1 with bath/shower, 1 with wash-basin), 2 single (with wash-basin) TERMS B&B £13.50–£14.50 (children under 10 75%); dinner £10; deposit

NEW GALLOWAY Dumfries & Galloway map 9

Cairn Edward

New Galloway, Castle Douglas DG7 3RZ
NEW GALLOWAY (064 42) 244

This attractive stone-built Victorian house is in eight acres of gardens and grounds, and on the edge of Galloway Forest Park with views of Loch Ken. The house has a welcoming atmosphere and is comfortably furnished. Two of the three bedrooms are *en suite* and the third has a shower unit with separate toilet. There is a large lounge and dining-room, where breakfast only is served; a packed lunch can be provided on request. Many outdoor activities are available in the area, including fishing, golf, sailing and windsurfing. No pets in bedrooms. No smoking in the dining-room and bedrooms. Car park.

OWNERS Penny and Donald Murray OPEN Easter–Oct ROOMS 2 double, 1 twin; all rooms with bath/shower TERMS B&B £14–£17, (single occupancy of twin/double) £25; deposit £10 per person

The description for each entry states when pets are not allowed. Where no details are given, you can assume that pets are allowed. It's always best to check first in any case.

NORTH BERWICK Lothian map 11

Cragside Guest House

16 Marine Parade, North Berwick EH39 4LD
NORTH BERWICK (0620) 2879

Built in 1880, this semi-detached, three-storey house on the sea-front overlooks East Bay, with glorious views of Fife, the Forth and Bass Rock. The harbour and high street are a five-minute stroll away. This guesthouse offers clean and simple accommodation. Breakfast only is served and vegetarians can be catered for. Car parking is available in a public car park opposite. No dogs. No smoking in the dining-room.

OWNERS Mr and Mrs M. T. Clelland OPEN All year, exc Christmas ROOMS 3 twin, 1 single; all rooms with wash-basin TERMS B&B £16.50–£17.50, (single occupancy of twin) £26 (children under 14 half-price); deposit

OBAN Strathclyde map 11

Don-Muir

Pulpit Hill, Oban PA34 4LX
OBAN (0631) 64536

This modern villa-style bungalow is on a hill above the town of Oban, with a pretty, well-kept front garden. The bedrooms are either *en suite* or have use of a private bathroom, and although they are on the small side, they are comfortable and have TV. There is a TV lounge and a small breakfast room where dinner is served at 6.30pm. Vegetarians can be catered for, and a packed lunch is available on request. Unlicensed, but guests may bring their own wine. There is space for some car parking. Children welcome. No dogs in the house. No smoking in the dining-room.

OWNER Mrs Peigi Robertson OPEN Feb–Nov ROOMS 3 double (2 with bath/shower, 1 with wash-basin), 1 twin (with wash-basin), 1 single (with wash-basin) TERMS B&B £15–£20, (single) £13; deposit £5 per person

It is always best to book a room in advance, especially in winter. Establishments with few rooms may close at short notice for periods not specified in the details.

We asked the proprietors to estimate their 1992 prices in the autumn of 1991, so the rates may have changed since publication.

Dungrianach

Pulpit Hill, Oban PA34 4LX
OBAN (0631) 62840

This 100-year-old house has spectacular views of the sea and islands and is located up the steep inclines of Pulpit Hill, in a large, mature and beautifully kept garden. The house is spacious, immaculate and attractively furnished and decorated. The bedrooms are comfortable and have TV. There is an airy TV lounge and a terrace with tables and chairs overlooking the bay and gardens. Breakfast only is served at one table in the dining-room. Dungrianach offers excellent value for money. Restrictions on children. Pets by arrangement. No smoking in the dining-room. Car park.

OWNER Mrs Elaine Robertson OPEN Apr–Sept ROOMS 1 double, 2 twin; all rooms with bath/shower TERMS B&B £14.50–£16.50; deposit

Lorne View

Ardconnel Road, Oban PA34 5DW
OBAN (0631) 65500

Lorne View is a small terraced house in a quiet street overlooking Oban bay, and only a few minutes' walk from the town centre. The three bedrooms are small and have been simply furnished and decorated. All have shower units and TV. There is a small lounge/dining-room, where evening meals are served at 6.15pm; vegetarians can be catered for. Guests may bring their own wine to dinner (no licence). No smoking in the lounge/dining-room.

OWNER Mrs E. M. Maclean OPEN All year, exc Christmas and New Year ROOMS 2 double, 1 twin; all rooms with shower TERMS B&B £13–£14, (single occupancy of twin/double) £25; dinner £8; deposit

OLD DAILLY Strathclyde map 9

Hawkhill Farm

Old Dailly, Girvan KA26 9RD
GIRVAN (0465) 87232

Lying a quarter of a mile off the B741 on the edge of the tiny village of Old Dailly, this working arable farm with views to

Killochan Castle was originally a coaching-inn and dates from the fifteenth century. It is a comfortable family home with spacious rooms, including two *en suite* bedrooms and an attractive first-floor sitting-room, with TV and piano. Breakfast and evening meals (by arrangement at 7pm) are served at one table in the owners' sitting-room. Guests may use the garden where there is croquet. A visit to nearby Bargany gardens is particularly recommended. Children welcome. No smoking in bedrooms. Car park.

OWNERS Morton and Isobel Kyle OPEN Mar–Oct
ROOMS 1 double, 1 twin; both rooms with bath/shower TERMS B&B £15–£16 (children under 12 half-price sharing); dinner £8; deposit

PEEBLES Borders map 10

Whitestone House

Innerleithen Road, Pebbles EH45 8BD
PEEBLES (0721) 20337

This large, stone house dating from 1892 was originally a manse and is set in a pretty garden with lovely views of the hills. The bedrooms, all with good views, are of a good size and have been comfortably furnished. The sitting-room/breakfast-room has its original black marble fireplace and overlooks the garden. Ironing facilities and hair-dryers are available. Breakfast only is served. Children welcome. No pets in the house. Car park.

OWNER Mrs Margaret Muir OPEN All year, exc owner's hol
ROOMS 1 family, 3 double, 1 twin; all rooms with wash-basin
TERMS B&B £12–£12.50, (single occupancy of twin/double) £12–£15 (children £7–£10)

PERTH Tayside map 11

Glunie Guest House

12 Pitcullen Crescent, Perth PH2 7HT
PERTH (0738) 23625

This is a small guesthouse on the busy A94, in a road of semi-detached stone houses – almost all of which are B&Bs – and conveniently placed for the centre of Perth and Scone Palace. The bedrooms have been prettily decorated and are well equipped with TV and hair-dryer. There is a varied breakfast menu and evening meals are served in the lounge/dining-room at 6pm.

Vegetarian choices are available and guests may bring their own wine (no licence). Car park.

OWNERS Joan and Scott Miller OPEN All year ROOMS 2 family, 2 double, 2 twin, 1 single; all rooms with bath/shower TERMS B&B £18, (single occupancy of twin/double) £25, (family room) £36 (children under 5 free, under 12 half-price); dinner £8; deposit 1 night

Pitcullen Guest House

17 Pitcullen Crescent, Perth PH2 7HT
PERTH (0738) 26506/38265

This family-run guesthouse has a well-kept, small front garden and pleasant views at the back. It is on the A94 and is convenient for the town centre. The small, airy lounge overlooks the back of the house, and breakfast and evening meals are served in the downstairs dining-room. The bedrooms are comfortable with basic facilities, and all have TV. No smoking in the dining-room. Car park.

OWNER Mrs Nancy Keddie OPEN All year ROOMS 2 family (1 with bath/shower, 1 with wash-basin), 2 double (1 with bath/shower, 1 with wash-basin), 2 twin (with wash-basin), 1 single (with wash-basin) TERMS B&B £16, (single occupancy of twin/double) £18 (children under 10 half-price); dinner £9; deposit

PITLOCHRY Tayside map 11

Arrandale House

Knockfarrie Road, Pitlochry PH16 5DN
PITLOCHRY (0796) 2987

Arrandale House is an 1860s stone-built building and used to be a minister's house. It is situated on the edge of town, surrounded by woodland in a peaceful spot, with wonderful views of the hills. Inside, it is spacious and some rooms have original ceilings. The bedrooms are mostly *en suite* and all have TV. Breakfast only is served. Children welcome. No smoking. Car park.

OWNERS Atholl and Pat Irvine OPEN Mar–Nov ROOMS 2 family (with bath/shower), 2 double (1 with bath/shower, 1 with wash-basin), 1 twin (with bath/shower), 1 single (with wash-basin) TERMS B&B £16–£18.50, (single) £14, (single occupancy of twin/double) £35, (family room) from £50 (children under 10 half-price); deposit £10

Balrobin Hotel

Higher Oakfield, Pitlochry PH16 5HT
PITLOCHRY (0796) 2901

This house was built in 1889 for a wealthy Edinburgh family and stands in its own grounds, commanding panoramic views of the Perthshire hills and Tummel Valley, yet only minutes away from the centre of town. All the bedrooms have views, *en suite* facilities and TV. The lounge and dining-room are spacious and a four-course evening meal is served from 6.30pm. Vegetarians can be catered for and packed lunches can be provided. The premises are licensed. No children under 10. Dogs by arrangement and in bedrooms only. No smoking in the dining-room. Car park.

OWNERS Mr and Mrs H. Hohman OPEN Apr–Oct
ROOMS 1 family, 10 double, 3 twin, 2 single; all rooms with bath/shower TERMS B&B £20.50–£27.50 (children 25%–50% reductions); dinner £10; deposit £25

Dundarave House

Strathview Terrace, Pitlochry PH16 5AT
PITLOCHRY (0796) 3109

This late-Victorian stone-built house stands just above the town and is set in a pretty garden, with roses climbing up the house. There are fresh flowers throughout and the house retains many of its original features, such as the attractive arched window above the fireplace in the lounge. The bedrooms are comfortable and well equipped with TV and hair-dryer. The house is maintained to a high standard. Both the lounge and dining-room, where breakfast only is served, have been elegantly furnished and have lovely views. A packed lunch can be provided on request. No children under seven. Car park.

OWNERS E. M. and M. Shuttleworth OPEN Mar–Oct
ROOMS 1 family, 2 double, 2 twin, 2 single; all rooms, exc singles (wash-basin only), with bath/shower TERMS B&B from £25 (children ⅓ price sharing); deposit

Reduced rates for children are normally given when they share their parents' bedroom. If no reductions are specified in the details or text, assume you'll have to pay full rates.

It is always best to book a room in advance, especially in winter. B&Bs with few rooms may close at short notice for periods not specified in the details.

PORT APPIN Strathclyde map 11

Linnhe House

Port Appin, Appin PA38 4DE
APPIN (0631) 73245

This substantial stone-built Victorian house has wonderful views overlooking the water and the island of Lismore. The four bedrooms are spacious and guests have the choice of bathroom or a view, as the two *en suite* rooms are at the rear of the house. The TV lounge is shared with the family, and evening meals (at 7pm) as well as a full English breakfast are served in the dining-room, which also has a view. Vegetarians can be catered for and packed lunches are available on request. The premises are licensed. Bicycle hire, pony-trekking and boating/fishing are some of the activities the hotel can arrange. Linnhe House is two miles down a single-track road off the A828. No children under five. No pets in the house. Car park.

OWNERS Doreen and Roger Evans OPEN All year ROOMS 4 twin (2 with shower, 2 with wash-basin) TERMS B&B £18 (reductions for children 5–12); D, B&B £25

PORTPATRICK Dumfries & Galloway map 9

Carlton House

21 South Crescent, Portpatrick DG9 8JR
PORTPATRICK (077 681) 253

Carlton House is a nineteenth-century terraced house right on the sea-front, in the centre of the little town of Portpatrick. The front bedrooms have wonderful sea views, looking across the bay and harbour to the hills of distant Ireland (21 miles away). All the rooms are spacious and have TV; five rooms are *en suite*. There is an attractive ground-floor dining-room where dinner is served 6–7pm. Vegetarian options are available and guests may bring their own wine (no licence). A packed lunch can also be provided. The first-floor lounge is sea facing and has a games-room. This is a well-kept, homely guesthouse. Children welcome.

OWNERS Mr and Mrs R. Thorburn OPEN All year ROOMS 2 family, 3 double, 2 twin; all rooms, exc twin (wash-basin only), with bath/shower TERMS B&B £15–£18, (single occupancy of twin/double) £20–£25, (family room) £37.50–£40 (children under 12 half-price); deposit £10

PORTREE Highland (Skye) map 11

Balloch

Viewfield Road, Portree, Isle of Skye IV51 9ES
PORTREE (0478) 2093

Balloch is a modern house 10 minutes from the town centre, close to the water and with good views from the garden, where there is furniture for sitting out. The small bedrooms are simply but comfortably furnished, and there is a lounge/dining-room, where breakfast only is served, though tea and biscuits are available in the evening. Ena MacPhie, a native of Skye, is a well-known singer in both Gaelic and English. Children welcome. Car parking for four cars.

OWNER Ena MacPhie OPEN Easter–Nov ROOMS 1 family, 1 double, 1 twin; all rooms with wash-basin TERMS B&B £13–£14 (children half-price); deposit

Craiglockhart Guest House

3 Beaumont Crescent, Portree, Isle of Skye IV51 9DF
PORTREE (0478) 2233

One of the best things about this simple guesthouse is its position, right on the harbour front, in a quiet cul-de-sac, facing the bay and a few minutes' walk from the town centre. It offers a friendly atmosphere and basic, clean accommodation. The bedrooms are small but all have TV. The front bedrooms have views. Breakfast only is served at the same time for everyone, with guests sharing tables, and there is a compact TV lounge. No children. No pets. No smoking in public rooms. Parking for four cars.

OWNERS Mr and Mrs D. D. Kemp OPEN All year ROOMS 3 double (2 with bath/shower, 1 with wash-basin), 4 twin (1 with bath/shower, 3 with wash-basin), 2 single (with wash-basin) TERMS B&B £15–£20; deposit

B&B rates specified in the details for each entry are per person per night; unless the details state otherwise, they are based on two people sharing a double or twin-bedded room.

Breakfast at B&Bs tends to mean a cooked breakfast of bacon, eggs and so on. If you prefer a different style of breakfast, discuss this when you make the booking.

RAASAY Highland map 11

Churchton House

Isle of Raasay, by Kyle of Lochalsh IV40 8NX
RAASAY (047 862) 260

Former home of Sorley Maclean, one of Scotland's leading contemporary poets, family-run Churchton House overlooks Churchton Bay with superb views to Skye, including the Cullin Mountains and Ben Tianavaig. It is located less than a mile from the ferry and is close to the shore. The accommodation is clean and comfortable and home-cooked evening meals, using local produce, are served at 6pm and 8pm. Vegetarians can be catered for and there is a reasonable wine list. There is no petrol on the island. This is a wonderful place for walking, bird-watching and fishing. Children welcome. No pets in the dining-room or left alone in bedrooms. No smoking in bedrooms. Car park.

OWNER Mrs Heather Harrison OPEN All year ROOMS 1 double (with bath/shower), 2 twin (1 with bath/shower, 1 with wash-basin) TERMS B&B £14 (children under 2 free, 2–12 half-price); dinner £9.50; deposit

ROSEMOUNT Tayside map 11

The Laurels

Golf Course Road, Rosemount, Blairgowrie PH10 6LH
BLAIRGOWRIE (0250) 4920

Built in 1873, this small, stone house is about a mile and a half from the centre of Blairgowrie and set back from the A93 Perth to Braemar road. The bedrooms are small and simply furnished, but are fresh and bright. The sitting-room is a very pleasant room with TV and large comfortable armchairs and sofas. Dinner is served at 6.30pm in the licensed dining-room. Vegetarians can be catered for. There are many famous golf courses nearby and the mountains of Glenshee provide skiing. Children welcome. No pets. Smoking only in bedrooms. Car park.

OWNERS Gordon and Sheila McPherson OPEN 10 Jan–30 Nov ROOMS 1 family (with wash-basin), 2 double (with bath/shower), 2 twin (with bath/shower), 1 single (with wash-basin) TERMS B&B £14–£16, (single occupancy of twin/double) £20, (family room) £36 (reductions for children under 10); dinner £7; deposit; Access, Amex, Visa

ROTHESAY Strathclyde (Bute) map 11

Alamein House

28 Battery Place, Promenade, Rothesay, Isle of Bute PA20 9DU
ROTHESAY (0700) 502395

On the sea-front, this whitewashed building with black trim is a small, simple guesthouse with clean, bright rooms and non-floral Laura Ashley décor. One bedroom is on the ground floor and suitable for the partially disabled, and all rooms have TV. The reading/dining-room is a non-smoking area, and there is a TV lounge at the back of the house for smokers. The windows are huge, and the front rooms offer wonderful views over the sea. Evening meals are available at 6pm (earlier or later, by arrangement) and may include home-made lentil and carrot soup, roast lamb and home-made apple pie. Vegetarians and diabetics can be catered for with notice, and packed lunches can be provided. There is no alcohol licence, but guests may bring their own wine. Children welcome. No pets in public rooms. Car parking for six or eight cars.

OWNER Hazel M. Davie OPEN All year, exc Christmas and 2 weeks hol ROOMS 1 family, 2 double (1 with bath/shower), 3 twin (1 with bath/shower), 3 single; 7 rooms with wash-basin TERMS B&B from £14.50, (single occupancy of twin/double) from £25.50 high season, (family room) £37 (children from half-price sharing with parents, three-quarters-price in single room); dinner from £6; deposit £20–£25 per person

ROY BRIDGE Highland map 11

Station House

Roy Bridge PH31 4AG
SPEAN BRIDGE (039 781) 285

This used to be the station master's house. Now trains run only about three times a day, so the disturbance is slight; in fact, this neat bungalow, with its colourful garden, is in a very quiet spot. There are two spotlessly clean, good-sized bedrooms and two bathrooms. Guests can use the lounge, which also doubles as the dining-room. Evening meals are served at 6.30pm and vegetarians can be catered for with notice. There is no alcohol licence, but guests may bring their own wine to dinner. Advance bookings are

Use the maps and indexes at the back of the Guide *to plan your trip.*

preferred. Partial central heating. Children welcome. No pets in the dining-room. Car park.

OWNER Mrs J. Grieve OPEN Apr–Oct ROOMS 1 double, 1 twin; both rooms with wash-basin TERMS B&B £12.50 (reductions for children under 12); dinner £6; deposit

ST ANDREWS Fife map 11

Cadzow Guest House

58 North Street, St Andrews KY16 9AH
ST ANDREWS (0334) 76933

Cadzow is just a 10-minute walk from the golf course, and two minutes from the town centre. It is a cosy, comfortable house with simple accommodation. All bedrooms, except two which are very small but bright and light, are now *en suite* and have TV. The basement sitting-room/breakfast room leads out to the back garden. Breakfast only is available. Children welcome. No smoking in the dining-room.

OWNERS Alexander and Elizabeth Small OPEN Feb–Nov
ROOMS 1 family, 4 double, 2 twin, 1 single; all rooms, exc 2 double (wash-basin only), with bath/shower TERMS B&B £13–£20, (single) £22–£27; deposit

West Park House

5 St Mary's Place, St Andrews KY16 9UY
ST ANDREWS (0334) 75933

This listed building dating from 1840 and in the heart of St Andrews has been tastefully restored. It was once owned by Sir David Brewster, inventor of the kaleidoscope. The bedrooms, all with TV, are spacious, comfortable and well decorated and there is a pretty, small sitting-room at the rear overlooking the garden. Breakfast only is available. Children welcome. No pets. No smoking in bedrooms.

OWNER Mrs R. E. MacLennan OPEN 1 Mar–30 Nov
ROOMS 1 family, 3 double, 1 twin; all rooms, exc 2 double, with bath/shower TERMS B&B £14.50–£19 (reductions for children)

Bath/shower information in the details refers only to a private bathroom or shower; other bathroom facilities at the establishments will be shared. We say if rooms have wash-basins.

ST CATHERINES Strathclyde map 11

Thistle House

St Catherines, by Cairndow PA25 8AZ
INVERARAY (0499) 2209

This spacious Victorian house has magnificent views across Loch Fyne to Inveraray and Inveraray Castle, and stands in two acres of garden. The lounge is a particularly pleasant, comfortable and spacious room with a small open fire and TV. The house is immaculately kept and very warm, and some bedrooms have lovely loch views. Children welcome. Pets by arrangement. No smoking in the dining-room. Parking for 12 cars.

OWNER Mrs Sandra Cameron OPEN Easter–31 Oct
ROOMS 1 family (with bath/shower), 2 double (1 with bath/shower, 1 with wash-basin), 2 twin (1 with bath/shower, 1 with wash-basin)
TERMS B&B £15–£17.50 (reductions for children in family room)

SALEN Strathclyde (Mull) map 11

Craig Hotel

Salen, Aros, Isle of Mull PA72 6JG
AROS (0680) 300347

This small, friendly, colour-washed, family-run hotel is on the main road in Salen, about halfway between Craignure and Tobermory. It overlooks the Sound of Mull and is conveniently placed for the ferries and for touring the island. The pretty garden has a sun-trap area to the side of the house and extends to the small stream which borders the property. The sitting-room has a piano, games, magazines and books, and home-cooked Scottish evening meals are served at 7.15pm in the pine-furnished licensed dining-room. Vegetarian choices and packed lunches can be provided. The bedrooms are small and simply furnished. Children welcome. No pets in public rooms. No smoking in the dining-room. Car park.

OWNERS James and Lorna McIntyre OPEN Easter–Oct
ROOMS 2 double, 4 twin; all rooms with wash-basin TERMS B&B £20–£23 (children under 5 20% reduction); D, B&B £30–£33; deposit £10 per person; Access, Visa

Any smoking restrictions that we know of are given in each entry.

SANDHEAD Dumfries & Galloway map 9

Cairnlea

Main Street, Sandhead DG9 9JB
SANDHEAD (077 683) 249

In the main road of the quiet village of Sandhead, Cairnlea is an attractive, whitewashed house with a pretty garden. The accommodation is simple, clean and bright, and downstairs there is a residents' lounge and a dining-room for breakfast only. Each room has its own heating. Children welcome. Pets are not encouraged. Parking for five cars.

OWNER Mrs Molly Willcox OPEN All year ROOMS 1 family, 1 double, 1 twin, 1 single TERMS B&B £12 (children under 13 half-price); deposit

SANQUHAR Dumfries & Galloway map 9

Drumbringan Guest House

53 Castle Street, Sanquhar DG4 6AB
SANQUHAR (0659) 50409

Drumbringan is a modest Georgian guesthouse on the edge of an ancient village in the lovely Nithsdale Valley, and was the home of the Lord Provost before being converted to its present use in 1920. It is on the main road into town, but double glazing keeps out the noise. Rosie Balfour, who comes from California, is also an aromatherapist and works on many of the walkers and cyclists who stay at the guesthouse. The accommodation is simple with three bedrooms and bathrooms on the first and second floors. There is a lounge/dining-room where evening meals, including vegetarian dishes, are available 6.30–8pm. There is no alcohol licence, but guests may bring their own wine. Packed lunches can be provided. Children welcome. Dogs must be kept on a lead. No smoking. Parking for six cars.

OWNER Mrs Rosie Balfour OPEN All year, exc Christmas and New Year ROOMS 2 family, 1 double, 1 twin, 2 single; all rooms with wash-basin TERMS B&B £12.50, (single occupancy of twin/double) £18 (children under 5 free, 5–12 £9); dinner £6; deposit £5

Most B&Bs offer tea/coffee-making facilities in the bedrooms.

Bath/shower in the details under each entry means that the rooms have private facilities.

SCOURIE Highland map 11

Minch View

Scouriemore, Scourie IV27 4TG
SCOURIE (0971) 2110

The main attraction of Minch View is its wonderful views over water and hills. It is a simple, whitewashed building on the outskirts of Scourie with small, plainly furnished bedrooms and a pleasant lounge/dining-room. Two bedrooms are on the ground floor. Evening meals are available if required at 7pm. Vegetarian choices and packed lunches can be provided with notice and guests may bring their own wine (there is no licence). Children welcome. No pets in the lounge. Car park.

OWNER Christine MacDonald OPEN Easter–Oct ROOMS 2 double (1 with wash-basin), 1 twin TERMS B&B £12 (children under 5 free); D, B&B £18; deposit

SELKIRK Borders map 10

Ivy Bank

Hillside Terrace, Selkirk TD7 2LT
SELKIRK (0750) 21270

Above the A7, this detached stone villa, originally a manse, has a small front garden and delightful views over the town to the Linglie Hills. The accommodation is spotlessly clean, and although the bedrooms are fairly small they are prettily decorated and comfortable. There is a TV lounge. Evening meals are available at 6.30pm and can include vegetarian choices on request. Packed lunches can be provided and guests may bring their own wine to dinner. Children welcome. No pets in public rooms. Parking for four cars.

OWNER Mrs Janet F. Mackenzie OPEN All year, exc Christmas, New Year and annual hols ROOMS 1 double, 1 twin; both rooms with wash-basin TERMS B&B £12.50 (children under 5 free, 5–12 two-thirds-price); dinner £7.50; deposit

We state at the end of an entry when children are welcome. If we know of any restrictions, we give them.

If you intend to spend several days at a B&B, it is worth asking whether there are reduced rates, particularly if the period is midweek or off-season.

SKEABOST BRIDGE Highland (Skye) map 11

The Old Manse

Skeabost Bridge, by Portree, Isle of Skye IV51 9XE
SKEABOST BRIDGE (047 032) 308

This pleasant, whitewashed house, a manse until about 10 years ago, stands above the main Uig to Dunvegan road and has lovely views over Loch Snizort. Steps lead up to the house from the road through a garden. The house is comfortable and the owners are friendly. There are two spacious front-facing *en suite* bedrooms, a lounge and a dining-room where breakfast only is served. Children welcome. No pets in public rooms. No smoking in the dining-room. Car park.

OWNERS Martin and Marilyn Chambers OPEN All year, exc Christmas ROOMS 1 family, 1 double; both rooms with bath/shower TERMS B&B £18 (children £9); deposit

SPEAN BRIDGE Highland map 11

Corriegour Lodge Hotel

Loch Lochy, by Spean Bridge PH34 4EB
SPEAN BRIDGE (039 781) 685

Originally a Victorian hunting lodge, this house, with black wood trunks supporting the porch, sits high above Loch Lochy on the east side just off the main road and enjoys wonderful loch and mountain views. It has recently been totally refurbished and a conservatory has been built on to house the restaurant and take advantage of the view. There is a cosy residents' lounge bar, and a bar for non-residents where snack meals are served. The bedrooms, all with TV, are comfortable and spacious, and some are enormous. Within the hotel's six acres of grounds is a small lochside beach with jetty, and a boat and fishing reels can be provided for those who want to fish. Mountain bikes can be hired locally. Evening meals, including vegetarian choices, are served 6–9pm in the bar, 7–8.30pm in the restaurant. Packed lunches can be provided. Not suitable for children under 10. No pets. No smoking in the dining-room. Car park.

OWNERS Rod and Lorna Bunney OPEN mid-Mar–New Year, exc Christmas ROOMS 4 double, 3 twin, 1 single; all rooms with bath/shower TERMS B&B £25–£35 (reductions for children over 10 sharing with parents); dinner from £16; deposit; Access, Visa

Old Pines

Gairlochy Road, Spean Bridge PH34 4EG
SPEAN BRIDGE (039 781) 324

A mile from Spean Bridge, this guesthouse is a long, pine-built, one-storey wood cabin. It is set in 30 acres, 300 yards from the Commando Memorial above Spean Bridge, and has wonderful views across the Great Glen to Aonach Mor and Ben Nevis. Its outward appearance belies the cosiness and warmth of the interior. The finish and furniture are almost entirely pine, and the bedrooms are small but comfortable and all have wonderful views. Four bedrooms are suitable for the disabled. There is a comfortable, large lounge and the restaurant has been added in a conservatory. Sukie Scott has already built up quite a reputation for her food, catering also for non-residents. Evening meals are available at 8pm and vegetarians can be catered for. A typical menu may include courgette and celery soup, baked Loch Lochy trout stuffed with leeks, orange and garlic, and rhubarb and banana brûlée. There is no alcohol licence, but guests may bring their own wine. Packed lunches can be provided. Children welcome. No smoking. Car park.

OWNERS Niall and Sukie Scott OPEN All year, exc 2 weeks Nov ROOMS 2 family (with bath/shower), 2 double (with bath/shower), 2 twin (1 with bath/shower, 1 with wash-basin), 2 single (1 with bath/shower, 1 with wash-basin) TERMS B&B £16–£22.50 (children under 10 free, 10–13 £10); dinner £10.50–£12.50; deposit; Access, Visa

Riverside

Invergloy, Spean Bridge PH34 4DY
SPEAN BRIDGE (039 781) 684

Riverside is just off the A82, five miles north of Spean Bridge on the east side of Loch Lochy. The house, which was built in the 1960s, stands close to the loch, has wonderful views and is approached down a long, winding drive through mature trees and shrubs. The Bennetts have recently added a new wing to the house, providing a large and comfortable guests' lounge with lovely views. One of the bedrooms has loch views and both rooms are on the ground floor. Breakfast only is available, although

If any bedrooms are suitable for the disabled we mention this in the entry.

Many B&Bs are in remote places; always ask for clear directions when booking.

packed lunches can be provided. Children welcome. No pets. No smoking in bedrooms. Car park.

OWNERS Joan and David Bennett OPEN All year, exc Christmas
ROOMS 1 family, 1 double; both rooms with bath/shower
TERMS B&B £16–£18, (single occupancy of double) £22; deposit £5

Tirindrish House

Spean Bridge PH34 4EU
SPEAN BRIDGE (039 781) 520

This is an interesting house set in 15 acres of grounds in an elevated position above the A86. The garden enjoys wonderful views over the Ben Nevis range of mountains and has been planted with many new trees and shrubs. A tennis court is available for guests' use. The back part of the house dates from the fifteenth or sixteenth century, and is where two bedrooms are located, each with its own staircase, large bathroom and TV. The rooms are very big and plainly decorated. Guests have use of a front-facing sitting-room, and breakfast and evening meals, by arrangement, are served in the dining-room. Vegetarian choices and packed lunches can be provided. Self-catering accommodation is also available. Children welcome. Car park.

OWNER Jean Wilson OPEN All year, exc Christmas and New Year
ROOMS 1 family, 1 double, 1 twin; all rooms with bath/shower
TERMS B&B £16.50 (reductions for children under 12); D, B&B £25; dinner £10; deposit £10 per person

STANLEY Tayside map 11

Newmill Farm

Stanley, by Perth PH1 4QD
STANLEY (0738) 828281

This old stone-built farmhouse, dating back four or five hundred years, is a handy stopping-off point, just off the A9 (take the Tullybelton turn). It is a comfortable, unfussy house with large rooms, fresh, simple bedrooms, one with TV, and plenty of bathrooms and toilets for those without *en suite* bathroom. Mrs Guthrie welcomes families and offers tea or coffee on arrival and in the evenings with home baking. There is a TV lounge and a dining-room where evening meals are served 6.30–7pm. Vegetarian choices and packed lunches can be provided. There is no alcohol licence, but guests may bring their own wine to dinner. Children welcome. Smoking only in the lounge. Car park.

OWNER Mrs A. Guthrie OPEN Feb–end Oct ROOMS 1 family, 1 double (with bath/shower), 1 twin (with bath/shower) TERMS B&B £15–£16, (family room) £24–£35 (children under 2 free, 2–6 £4, 6–12 £8); dinner £8

STIRLING Central map 11

Castlecroft

Ballengeich Road, Stirling FK8 1TN
STIRLING (0786) 74933

A modern house, standing just below the castle, Castlecroft has excellent views, best enjoyed from the enormous lounge, which has windows all the way round and a telescope. It stands on the opposite side of the castle to the town, which can be reached by a series of footpaths. There are four ground-floor bedrooms, two of which are particularly suited to the disabled; there is a special wheelchair lift to the main floor. All bedrooms have TV and bathroom, the accommodation is clean, comfortable and practical, and the house has a rather business-like atmosphere. Breakfast only is available. There is a large garden with seats and tables for sitting out. Children welcome. No pets in the breakfast room. Car park.

OWNER Bill Salmond OPEN All year, exc Christmas and New Year ROOMS 1 family, 3 double, 2 twin; all rooms with bath/shower TERMS B&B £17.50, (single occupancy of twin/double) £20–£30, (family room) £45–£50 (children half-price sharing with parents)

STONEHAVEN Grampian map 11

Arduthie House

Ann Street, Stonehaven AB3 2DA
STONEHAVEN (0569) 62381

Arduthie House is a solid Victorian building, standing above a quiet residential road (it's quite a climb up a flight of steps) with sea views from the upper floors, and is a couple of minutes from the shops. The décor is simple, the rooms are spacious and the two *en suite* bedrooms are on the second floor. The large lounge is on the first floor and the dining-room is on the ground floor. Evening meals are served at 6.30pm and can include vegetarian choices, by arrangement. There is no alcohol licence, but guests may bring their own wine. Packed lunches can be provided. Children welcome. No pets. No smoking in bedrooms.

OWNERS Brian and Mary Marr OPEN All year, exc Christmas and New Year ROOMS 2 family/twin/double (with bath/shower), 1 double (with wash-basin), 1 twin (with wash-basin) TERMS B&B £13–£17 (children half-price); dinner £6; deposit

STORNOWAY Western Isles (Lewis) map 11

Ardlonan

29 Francis Street, Stornoway, Isle of Lewis PA87 2NF
STORNOWAY (0851) 703482

A substantial, terraced Victorian town house, Ardlonan is in a quiet residential area, only a short walk from the centre of town and ferry dock. Mrs Skinner is a friendly lady who keeps an immaculately clean and neat house with lots of fresh flowers. There is a very pleasant lounge, a small breakfast room and a beautifully kept rear garden with tables and chairs for sitting out. The bedrooms, three with TV, are spacious, and the top-floor room, which has a very low ceiling, also has lovely views over houses to the port. Breakfast only is available; packed lunches can be provided. Children welcome. No pets. No smoking in the dining-room and bedrooms.

OWNER Mrs Jess Skinner OPEN All year, exc Christmas and New Year ROOMS 1 family, 2 double, 2 twin; all rooms with wash-basin TERMS B&B £15, (family room) from £14 per person (reductions for children under 11); deposit

STRANRAER Dumfries & Galloway map 9

Harbour Guest House

Market Street, Stranraer DG9 7RF
STRANRAER (0776) 4626

Only a short distance from the quayside, this late eighteenth-century sea-front property is ideally located for ferry passengers. It is a well-maintained and well-equipped house with a homely atmosphere. The interior is rather sombre, with much woodwork and dark wallpaper. Evening meals are available 5.30–6pm in the wood-panelled, small back dining-room and there is a comfortable TV lounge. Vegetarians can be catered for and packed lunches can be provided. Harbour Guest House is unlicensed, but guests may bring their own wine. Children welcome. No smoking in the dining-room.

OWNERS Mr and Mrs W. Alexander OPEN All year, exc Christmas and 1 Jan ROOMS 2 family, 1 double, 2 single; all rooms with wash-basin TERMS B&B £14–£15, (single occupancy of double) £20, (family room) £39 (reductions for children); dinner £5; deposit

STRATH Highland map 11

Strathgair House

Strath, by Gairloch IV21 2BT
GAIRLOCH (0445) 2118

This charming eighteenth-century house in a peaceful spot was once a manse. Miss Wylie offers old-fashioned comfort and good Scottish cooking. The rooms are large and comfortable with some interesting colour schemes and furniture, especially in the elegant dining-room, which has a large rectangular table. The house has lovely views over the loch. Evening meals are served at 6.30pm and guests may bring their own wine (no licence). No children under 14. Dogs in bedrooms only. Non-smokers preferred. Car park.

OWNER Miss I. M. Wylie OPEN Easter–end Aug ROOMS 1 double, 2 twin, 1 single; all rooms with wash-basin TERMS B&B £13–£15; dinner £9; deposit

STRATHPEFFER Highland map 11

Craigvar

The Square, Strathpeffer IV14 9DL
STRATHPEFFER (0997) 421622

Built in 1839, this small, stone, listed house has a well-kept front garden with lovely views of the hills and overlooking the square in the charming Victorian spa village of Strathpeffer. It is a most comfortable, attractively furnished and decorated house, with good-sized rooms and the original Victorian fireplaces. The downstairs double bedroom is the smallest room, one upstairs bedroom has a large bathroom with old-fashioned bath and separate shower, and the twin-bedded room has a dressing area. All bedrooms have TV and telephone. There is a lounge with an open fire and breakfast only is available. Children welcome. No pets. Car park.

OWNER Margaret S. L. Scott OPEN May–Oct ROOMS 1 four-poster, 1 double, 1 twin; all rooms with bath/shower TERMS B&B £14–£20, (single occupancy of twin/double) £25; deposit £15; Visa

STROMNESS Orkney map 11

Millburn

Sandwick, by Stromness KW16 3JB
SANDWICK (085 684) 656

This modern country house is set in 10 acres of private grounds with lovely views over Loch Harray. The atmosphere is warm and friendly and the house is immaculately clean. Excellent home-cooked food is available for breakfast and packed lunches can be provided. There are two bathrooms for the exclusive use of guests, who also have use of a lounge. Trout fishing and boat hire are available. Children welcome. Pets restricted. No smoking in the dining-room and bedrooms. Car park.

OWNER Mrs H. G. Kirkpatrick OPEN Apr–Oct ROOMS 1 double, 2 twin TERMS B&B £13–£16, (single occupancy of twin/double) £3 surcharge in high season (reductions for children sharing parents' room)

TARBERT Western Isles (Harris) map 11

Minchview House

Tarbert, Isle of Harris PA85 3DB
HARRIS (0859) 2140

Originally an old croft house, Minchview has been altered to become quite a substantial-looking house. It stands in a pretty garden on a hillside in the centre of, but above, Tarbert with spectacular views over the harbour to the open sea and to Skye in the distance. There are five bedrooms, with some lovely views, all sharing a bathroom; the comfortable lounge has a good supply of books. Evening meals are available at 6.30pm and all special diets can be catered for with notice. There is no alcohol licence, but guests may bring their own wine. Packed lunches can also be provided. One- and two-week walking holidays can be arranged for small parties of between six and eight people. There is no central heating, but electric fires are provided. No children under

12. Pets by arrangement. No smoking in the dining-room and bedrooms. Car park.

OWNERS Corinne and David Miller OPEN All year
ROOMS 2 double, 1 twin, 2 single TERMS B&B £12–£15; dinner £6–£8; deposit £10

TOBERMORY Strathclyde (Mull) map 11

Bad-Daraich House

Tobermory, Isle of Mull PA75 6PR
TOBERMORY (0688) 2352

Bad-Daraich, built around 1860, enjoys a spectacular position above and a little way beyond the town with views down the Sound of Mull. It belongs to a very enthusiastic young couple. Lynn is originally from Mull and is also a hairdresser with a small salon in the house, which she operates in winter when the B&B is closed. Calum is a local fisherman. Unfortunately, the bedrooms have no views, but the sitting-room and dining-room, where breakfast only is served, enjoy a good outlook. Children welcome. No smoking in bedrooms. Car park.

OWNERS Lynn and Calum MacLachlainn OPEN Mar–end Oct
ROOMS 2 family, 4 double; all rooms with bath/shower TERMS B&B £24, (single occupancy of double) £32 (children half-price); deposit £20

Staffa Cottages Guest House

Tobermory, Isle of Mull PA75 6PL
TOBERMORY (0688) 2464

This pretty row of small, stone-built terraced cottages lies above the harbour of Tobermory, with lovely views across the bay to the Sound of Mull and the Morvern Hills on the mainland. There is a small front garden and an area for sitting out to admire the view. The very small bedrooms, which are simply furnished in pine, now have *en suite* shower-rooms. The lounge is full of furniture and bits and pieces, and evening meals are served at 7pm in the dining-room if required. Vegetarian choices and packed lunches can be provided, and guests may bring their own wine. There is quite a steep walk to the house up a footpath from the car park,

If you intend to spend several days at a B&B, it is worth asking whether there are reduced rates, particularly if the period is midweek or off-season.

and there is no vehicle access to the front door. Children by arrangement. No smoking. Car park.

OWNERS Chad and Celia Chadwick OPEN All year, exc Christmas ROOMS 3 double, 2 twin; all rooms with bath/shower TERMS B&B £16–£20 approx; dinner £12; deposit

TROON Strathclyde map 9

Knockmarloch

57 St Meddans Street, Troon KA10 6NN
TROON (0292) 312840

Knockmarloch is a Victorian detached house near the town centre, built as the registrar's residence, and next to the former Presbyterian manse. It has an immaculately kept rear garden, is 400 yards from the beach and can boast nine golf courses within a mile of the house. The bedrooms, two with TV, are very bright and quite spacious; one is on the ground floor, and one now has an *en suite* bathroom. The TV lounge is also the breakfast room, and although no evening meals are available, there is a hotel almost next door which serves food. Children welcome. No pets in public rooms. Car park.

OWNERS Mr and Mrs R. A. Jamieson OPEN All year ROOMS 1 double (with wash-basin), 2 twin (1 with bath/shower, 1 with wash-basin) TERMS B&B £14–£18; deposit 1 night charge

UIG Highland (Skye) map 11

Woodbine Guest House

Uig, Isle of Skye IV51 9XP
UIG (047 042) 243

In Uig village, this small, newly whitewashed house stands above the main road and has a small front garden. Everything is fresh, bright and clean. The bedrooms, all *en suite* with tiny shower-rooms, are small and have TV. The front rooms have lovely views. There is a pleasant dining-room, where evening meals are served, if required, at 7pm, and a comfortable lounge. Vegetarians can be catered for and packed lunches can be provided. The Woodbine

Where a single-occupancy rate is not specified in the details, the cost will be the same as that per person in a twin or double room, or will be included in the range of prices given.

has no alcohol licence, but guests may bring their own wine. Children welcome. No smoking in the dining-room. Car park.

OWNERS Anne and Peter Caldwell OPEN All year ROOMS 1 family, 3 double, 1 twin; all rooms with bath/shower TERMS B&B £13.50, (single occupancy of twin/double) £18.50 (children under 3 free, 4–12 half-price); dinner £8.50

ULLAPOOL Highland map 11

The Sheiling Guest House

Garve Road, Ullapool IV26 2SX
ULLAPOOL (0854) 612947

The Mackenzies had this guesthouse purpose-built in 1988. It is an attractive house on the edge of town, below the main road, and enjoys panoramic views over Loch Broom. The bedrooms are small and bright, some have lovely views and three are on the ground floor; all are *en suite*. The pleasant lounge and breakfast room both have good views. Breakfast only is available; packed lunches can be provided. Trout fishing can be arranged for guests. 'Quiet' children welcome. No pets. No smoking. Car park.

OWNERS Duncan and Mhairi Mackenzie OPEN All year, exc Christmas and New Year ROOMS 4 double, 3 twin; all rooms with bath/shower TERMS B&B £16–£18, (single occupancy of twin/double) £22–£25 (reductions for children); deposit £20

Tigh-na-Mara

The Shore, Ardindrean, Loch Broom, nr Ullapool IV23 2SE
ULLAPOOL (0854) 85282

Reached down a narrow road, off the A835 south of Ullapool on the west side of Loch Broom, Tigh-na-Mara is a small, whitewashed house on the shingle beach, at one time the village store. In those days, there was no road and supplies would come by boat. Now, the more recently built houses lie off the road, above the loch, and the only approach to Tigh-na-Mara is down a steep hillside across a muddy field, a distance of some 200 yards. The house belongs to a young couple who have made a charming guest wing of a long, comfortable dining-room/sitting-room with wood-burning stove and, up a spiral staircase, two tiny bedrooms and bathroom with skylights and views over the loch. There is also a bedroom in the boat-shed, with *en suite* bathroom and picture window looking out on to the loch. The owners specialise

in vegetarian and vegan cooking, although local fish and seafood can be provided by arrangement. Evening meals are served around 8.30pm and guests are welcome to bring their own wine (there is no alcohol licence). Packed lunches can also be provided. Boats and bikes can be arranged for guests. This is a beautiful, peaceful spot, well away from the bustle of Ullapool. Children welcome. No pets. No smoking. Parking for four cars.

OWNERS Shân and Tony Weston OPEN Mar–Nov ROOMS 2 double (1 with bath/shower), 1 twin (with wash-basin) TERMS B&B £14.50–£20.50, (single occupancy of twin/double) £19.50–£25.50 (children under 5 free sharing room); dinner £8.50–£12; deposit 20%, min £25

WALSTON Strathclyde map 9

Walston Mansions Farmhouse

Walston, Carnwath ML11 8NF
DUNSYRE (089 981) 338

This attractive stone-built house stands beside a very minor, narrow road in the middle of peaceful, beautiful, unspoilt countryside with lovely views of hills. The house, which is no longer part of a farm, offers homely accommodation with good home cooking. Evening meals are served at 7pm and can include vegetarian choices by arrangement. Packed lunches can be provided and guests may bring their own wine. All bedrooms have TV. There is a comfortable TV lounge, shared with the family, and open fires burn in both dining-room and sitting-room. This is a good central spot for both Edinburgh and Glasgow. Children welcome (play area available). Car park.

OWNER Mrs Margaret Kirby OPEN All year ROOMS 1 family (with bath/shower), 1 double (with bath/shower), 1 twin (with wash-basin) TERMS B&B £10–£12 (reductions for children); dinner £6

WATERNISH Highland (Skye) map 11

Lismore

1 Camuslusta, Waternish, Isle of Skye IV55 8GE
WATERNISH (047 083) 318

Owned by a friendly couple from England, Lismore is an old croft on the Waternish peninsula. Follow the A850 to the B886 Waternish peninsula road – Lismore is the second house on the left below the Waternish sign. It is in an absolutely wonderful position, looking over high cliffs, sea and spectacular sunsets. The house has a small sun porch entrance with windows all round and a couple of easy chairs; this is where breakfast is served. The house is all on one level, and there are two simple bedrooms. Packed lunches can be provided. Self-catering accommodation is also available. Children welcome. No pets. Smoking in the lounge only. Car park.

OWNERS Bill and Janet Dame OPEN Easter–end Oct ROOMS 1 double, 1 twin; both rooms with wash-basin TERMS B&B £13, (single occupancy of twin/double) £2 surcharge July/Aug (children half-price sharing parents' room); deposit

WEST LINTON Borders map 11

Medwyn House

Medwyn Road, West Linton EH46 7HB
WEST LINTON (0968) 60542 Fax (0968) 60005

Adjoining West Linton Golf Course (half-price green fees for guests), this Victorian baronial-style country house was originally an old inn, close to the crossing of the River Lyne. In 1832, the inn was closed down and the property sold to Lord Medwyn who rebuilt the house as you see it today. It stands in 30 acres of immaculate gardens, lawns and woods on the edge of West Linton. Mike and Anne Waterston are a delightful couple. Mike does all the building work and repairs to the house and Anne does everything else, including cooking excellent evening meals (8pm), which are elegantly served at separate lace-cloth-covered tables in the large dining-room. Vegetarian choices and packed lunches can be provided by arrangement. Guests may bring their own wine to dinner. A glass of sherry is offered to guests before dinner in front of the roaring fire in the enormous high-ceilinged hall. There is also a large drawing-room, and a carved wooden staircase leads to three large and beautifully furnished bedrooms, each having a bathroom almost as large. There are also two rooms with bathrooms in an annexe. All bedrooms have TV and telephone, and one is suitable for the disabled. Children under 12 by arrangement. No dogs in public rooms or unattended in bedrooms. No smoking in the dining-room and bedrooms. Car park.

OWNERS Anne and Mike Waterston OPEN All year, exc mid-Jan–mid-Mar ROOMS 1 family, 2 double, 2 twin; all rooms with bath/shower TERMS B&B £28–£32, (single occupancy of twin/double) £42; dinner £17

WHALSAY Shetland — map 11

Lingaveg Guest House

Marrister, Symbister, Isle of Whalsay ZE2 9AE
SYMBISTER (080 66) 489

This substantial stone-built Edwardian house is on the tiny island of Whalsay. Lined in timber, it was originally a manse and has wonderful views. The Tathams offer a warm welcome and comfortable accommodation. Lunches and evenings meals (6pm) are available and can include vegetarian choices if requested. There is no alcohol licence, but guests may bring their own wine. Trout fishing can be arranged, and there is an 18-hole golf course nearby. Children welcome. No pets. No smoking in bedrooms. Car park.

OWNER Mrs P. A. Tatham OPEN All year, exc Christmas and New Year ROOMS 3 twin (with wash-basin) TERMS B&B £14 (children under 3 free, 3–12 half-price); dinner £7

Bath/shower in the details under each entry means that the rooms have private facilities.

WICK Highland map 11

Bilbster House

By Wick KW1 5TB
WATTEN (095 582) 212

This is a delightful find in the middle of the flat landscape of Caithness. Once a farmhouse, Bilbster House dates from the mid-eighteenth century. The owners have renovated and decorated the attractive, spacious and well-proportioned rooms in a rather old-fashioned and somewhat theatrical way, which is not surprising as they both worked in the theatre. The attractive dining-room has small tables covered with crisply laundered linen table-cloths. Breakfast is beautifully served with each table having its own china, and there are flowers, linen napkins and silver cutlery. The large, comfortable drawing-room has TV and there are lovely mature gardens. Excellent value for money. Children welcome. No pets and smoking in the dining-room. Car park.

OWNERS Jeanne and Archie Stewart OPEN May–end Sept
ROOMS 2 double, 1 twin; all rooms with wash-basin TERMS B&B £11 (children under 12 £6); deposit

Wales

ABERGAVENNY Gwent map 6

Halidon House

63 Monmouth Road, Abergavenny NP7 5HR
ABERGAVENNY (0873) 857855

This 100-year-old mansion on a main road was built for the family of Sir Henry Tate, of Tate and Lyle, and was designed to take advantage of the magnificent views of mountains and rivers. The bedrooms are spacious and comfortable. Breakfast is five-course, and a packed lunch can be made on request. There is a TV lounge overlooking the half-acre of formal gardens. Guests may use the heated outdoor swimming-pool, which is open from the end of May to September. The town centre is a five-minute walk away. No smoking in the dining-room. No pets. Car park.

OWNER Mrs I. Heritage OPEN Apr–Oct ROOMS 1 family, 2 double, 1 twin, 1 single; all rooms with wash-basin TERMS B&B £17.50, (single occupancy of twin/double) £20, (family room) £40; deposit £15 per room

ABERYSTWYTH Dyfed map 6

Bryn-y-Don

36 Bridge Street, Aberystwyth SY23 1QB
ABERYSTWYTH (0970) 612011

This small, well-established guesthouse is close to the shops and just a few minutes' walk from the sea-front. The bedrooms are of an average size, all with TV. Evening meals are available and vegetarians can be catered for. There is no alcohol licence, but guests may bring their own wine to dinner. Packed lunches can be made on request. There is a pleasant guest lounge. Children welcome. No pets in the dining area and lounge.

OWNERS D. and I. M. Daniel OPEN All year, exc Christmas
ROOMS 1 family, 2 double, 1 twin; all rooms with wash-basin
TERMS B&B from £12; dinner from £5; deposit

B&B rates specified in the details for each entry are per person per night; unless the details state otherwise, they are based on two people sharing a double or twin-bedded room.

Most B&Bs don't accept credit cards, but when they do we list the cards taken.

Glyn-Garth Guest House

South Road, Aberystwyth SY23 1JS
ABERYSTWYTH (0970) 615050

Glyn-Garth is a Victorian double-fronted terraced house and is within the walls of the old castle in a conservation area. The harbour and castle are just a one-minute walk away. The bedrooms have all been decorated with pastel wallpaper and colour-co-ordinated fabrics; all have TV. There is a well-furnished lounge and a cosy basement bar. Breakfast only is served and packed lunches are provided on request. No smoking in the lounge, dining-room and most bedrooms. No children under three. No pets.

OWNERS Mr and Mrs M. J. P. Evans OPEN All year, exc Christmas ROOMS 3 family (with bath/shower), 5 double (3 with bath/shower), 1 twin, 2 single TERMS B&B £15–£21, (single) £15–£16.50, (family room) £40–£60; deposit

Yr Hafod

1 South Marine Terrace, Aberystwyth SY23 1JX
ABERYSTWYTH (0970) 617579

Breakfast only is served at this modest guesthouse on the sea-front between the castle and the harbour. The bedrooms are small but immaculate and comfortable. Packed lunches can be provided on request. Children welcome. No dogs. No smoking in the dining-room and several bedrooms.

OWNER John Evans OPEN All year, exc Christmas ROOMS 3 family, 3 double (1 with bath/shower), 2 single; all rooms with wash-basin TERMS B&B from £14.50, (single occupancy of double) from £18.50 (children half-price sharing with adults); deposit

BALA Gwynedd map 6

Crud-yr-Awel

College Hill, Bala LL23 7RY
BALA (0678) 520027

Surrounded by glorious countryside, this comfortable house is on the outskirts of Bala, within walking distance of town. The family room is quite spacious, although the twin is small. The lounge, which leads to a conservatory, has TV and a piano, which guests are welcome to play. Breakfast only is served, but the owners are happy to recommend restaurants and pubs in the area. Children welcome. No pets. No smoking in the dining-room. Parking available.

OWNERS John and Ann Frost OPEN Mar–Nov ROOMS 1 family (with bath/shower), 1 twin TERMS B&B £10, (family room) £12.50 (children under 6 50% reduction, 6–12 25%)

BARMOUTH Gwynedd map 6

Bryn Melyn Hotel

Panorama Road, Barmouth LL42 1DQ
BARMOUTH (0341) 280556 Fax (0341) 280276

Bryn Melyn is a small, comfortable hotel, situated in its own grounds in an elevated position with superb views of the Mawddach estuary and Cader range of mountains. Barmouth has 10 miles of sandy beaches. The hotel is in a quiet part of town, but within a 15-minute walk of the beach and shops. A traditional breakfast is served and there is an interesting dinner menu available 7–8.30pm. The hotel has a guest lounge and a bar, and all rooms have TV and telephone. Children welcome. Pets by arrangement. Car park.

OWNERS David and Carol Clay OPEN Mar–Nov ROOMS 1 family (with bath/shower), 5 double (with bath/shower), 3 twin (2 with bath/ shower, 1 with wash-basin) TERMS B&B £23, (single) £17.50, (single occupancy of twin/double) £28 (children half-price); dinner £11.50; Access, Visa

The Sandpiper

7 Marine Parade, Barmouth LL42 1NA
BARMOUTH (0341) 280318

The Sandpiper is centrally situated on the sea-front. The accommodation consists of well-appointed rooms, with an extremely high standard of furnishing and décor. There is one ground-floor bedroom with its own bathroom. All bedrooms have TV and the front bedrooms have magnificent views. Breakfast only is served in the dining-room, which overlooks Cardigan Bay. The

The description for each entry states when pets are not allowed or restricted in any way.

Use the maps and indexes at the back of the Guide *to plan your trip.*

lounge is now situated on the top floor and is a quiet spot in which to relax and read. Children welcome. No pets.

OWNERS John and Susan Palmer OPEN Easter–Oct
ROOMS 3 family (2 with bath/shower, 1 with wash-basin), 5 double (3 with bath/shower, 2 with wash-basin), 1 twin (with bath/shower), 2 single (with wash-basin) TERMS B&B £13–£16.50 (children half-price sharing with adults); deposit

BENLLECH Gwynedd (Anglesey) map 6

Castaway Guest House

Beach Road, Benllech, Anglesey LL74 8SW
LLANERCHYMEDD (0248) 852628

The Castaway is a beautifully maintained modern house in a peaceful, elevated position just off the A5205. The beach and shops are just a two-minute walk away. The bedrooms are colour-co-ordinated with matching fabrics; all have TV, and two of the rooms are on the ground floor. There are no private bathrooms, but two bathrooms are available for guests' use. Substantial breakfasts are served in the conservatory and there is a guest lounge which overlooks the bay. There is also a self-catering unit that sleeps four. Packed lunches can be provided. Children welcome. Small dogs by arrangement. Smoking in the conservatory only. Car park.

OWNER Mrs Marjorie Woolfenden OPEN Mar–Nov
ROOMS 1 family, 3 double; all rooms with wash-basin
TERMS B&B £12.50–£15, (single occupancy of double) £20 (children under 4 free, over 4 half-price); deposit

BETWS-Y-COED Gwynedd map 6

Park Hill Hotel

Llanrwst Road, Betws-y-Coed LL24 0HD
BETWS-Y-COED (0690) 710540

This charming hotel, built of Welsh stone, is a few minutes' walk from the village and is situated in an acre of well-kept gardens overlooking the River Conwy and a nine-hole golf course. The rooms are furnished in rich mahogany and all have TV. There are two lounges, both elegantly furnished; one has TV. Dinner is served 7–8pm and there is a small bar/lounge. Lunch and packed lunches are available and vegetarian choices can be provided. The hotel has a heated indoor swimming-pool, with a Jacuzzi and sauna; the doors from the pool open on to the lovely gardens. There is a conservatory with attractive wicker furniture. No children under six. No pets. No smoking in the dining-room. Car park.

OWNERS James and Elizabeth Bovaird OPEN All year
ROOMS 1 four-poster (with bath/shower), 6 double (with bath/shower), 2 twin (with bath/shower), 2 single (with wash-basin)
TERMS B&B £25.50–£26.50, (four-poster) £30, (single) £18.50, (single occupancy of twin/double) £28.50 (children sharing with adults half-price); dinner £13.50; deposit; Access, Amex, Diners, Visa

Ty'n-y-Celyn House

Llanrwst Road, Betws-y-Coed LL24 0HD
BETWS-Y-COED (0690) 710202 Fax (0690) 710800

Ty'n-y-Celyn is a large Victorian house nestling in an elevated position overlooking Betws-y-Coed, Llugwy Valley and the surrounding mountains. Owners Maureen and Clive Muskus have created a charming and elegant house. The luxurious bedrooms are tastefully and individually decorated. All rooms have TV, hair-dryer, radio/cassette player and thoughtful extra touches such as fresh fruit. There is a very comfortable guest lounge. Breakfast only is served, but there are several pubs and restaurants serving good food nearby. For guests arriving by train, arrangements can be made to meet them at the station. Children welcome. 'Well-behaved' pets by arrangement. No smoking in the dining-room. Car park.

OWNERS Maureen and Clive Muskus OPEN 2 weeks before Easter–2 Jan ROOMS 2 family, 3 double, 3 twin; all rooms with bath/shower
TERMS B&B £17–£19, (single occupancy of twin/double) £17–£35 (children 2–12 half-price); deposit for first-time booking

BONTDDU Gwynedd map 6

Farchynys Cottage Garden

Farchynys Cottage, Bontddu, nr Barmouth LL42 1TN
BONTDDU (0341) 49245

Farchynys Cottage is a former estate gardener's dwelling in an elevated position, in four acres of beautiful gardens with views of the Mawddach estuary. The bedrooms are average in size and decorated in soft, restful colours. There is one enormous family room. All meals are taken in the cosy dining-room, which has an antique Welsh dresser and grandfather clock. Dinner is served at 6.30pm. There is no alcohol licence, but guests may bring their own wine to dinner. There is a comfortable lounge with TV. The terrace is a very pleasant spot to sit on fine days. The public footpath through the top gate leads to a forestry plantation with spectacular views along the magnificent Cader Idris range. Guests can enjoy tea with home-made scones, cakes or pastries on their return. Children welcome. No smoking in the dining-room. Car park.

OWNERS Mr and Mrs G. Townshend OPEN Mar–Nov
ROOMS 1 family, 1 double, 1 single; all rooms with wash-basin
TERMS B&B £12.50, (single occupancy of double) £20, (children under 5 one-third price, 5–12 half-price); dinner £7.50; deposit

BORTH Dyfed map 6

Hafan Wen

Borth SY24 5JA
BORTH (0970) 871739

Hafan Wen, which means 'white haven', is situated at the edge of town, on the sea-front. It is a Victorian house that has been tastefully modernised; the bedrooms are bright, airy and attractively decorated with matching fabrics and headboards. One double bedroom is on the ground floor adjacent to a bathroom. There are ample bathroom facilities. The well-furnished lounge is on the first floor and has sea views. Guests are greeted with a cup of tea or coffee on arrival. Breakfast only is served, but there are several pubs and restaurants within walking distance. No children under three. No smoking in bedrooms. Free parking available in front of the house.

OWNER Christine Cameron Cox OPEN All year, exc Christmas
ROOMS 1 family, 2 double TERMS B&B £12.50 (children £6); deposit £5 per adult

BUILTH WELLS Powys map 6

Querida

43 Garth Road, Builth Wells LD2 3AR
BUILTH WELLS (0982) 553642

If you are fortunate enough to arrive on the day Welsh teacakes are on the stove, you will receive a tray with tea or coffee and a plate of these delicious, freshly baked cakes. Breakfasts are large at this modest guesthouse close to the town centre. There is also a comfortable TV lounge. Children welcome. Pets by arrangement. Car park.

OWNER Mrs C. M. Hammond OPEN All year ROOMS 1 double, 1 twin; both rooms with wash-basin TERMS B&B £11–£12; deposit

CAERNARFON Gwynedd map 6

Isfryn Guesthouse

11 Church Street, Caernarfon LL55 1SW
CAERNARFON (0286) 5628

Isfryn, which means 'house under the hill', is an immaculate Victorian house within the old town walls and close to Caernarfon Castle. The bedrooms are tastefully decorated; all have TV. There is a family suite on the second floor, which comprises a double and single bedroom, and an additional single which has its own bathroom. Evening meals are served at 6pm, by arrangement, and vegetarian choices can be provided. There is no alcohol licence, but guests may bring their own wine to dinner. There is a comfortable and well-furnished lounge. Children welcome. Pets by arrangement. No smoking in the dining-room.

OWNERS Graham and Jennifer Bailey OPEN Mar–Oct
ROOMS 5 double/family (with bath/shower), 2 single (with wash-basin)
TERMS B&B £14–£17.50 (children £7.50); dinner £9–£10; deposit

CARDIFF South Glamorgan map 6

Ashley Court Hotel

138 Cathedral Road, Cardiff CF1 9JB
CARDIFF (0222) 233324

This is an excellent location from which to explore the National Museum, Folk Museum and the Maritime Museum. The Victorian hotel is situated in a conservation area and is within walking distance of the city centre. The bedrooms are tastefully furnished and have TV. Dinner is served 7–8pm by prior arrangement and vegetarian choices can be provided. Light refreshments are also available throughout the day and packed lunches can be arranged. There is a separate guest lounge and

When the family-room rate is given in the details it applies to the cost of the whole room, unless a rate per person is specified.

dining-room as well as a bar/lounge. Children welcome. No pets. No smoking in the dining-room. Car park.

OWNERS Mr and Mrs R. Skrines OPEN All year, exc Christmas and New Year ROOMS 2 family, 3 double, 2 twin, 2 single; all rooms with bath/shower TERMS B&B £18–£19, (single occupancy of twin/double) £26–£28, (family room) £42–£58 (children under 12 half-price); dinner £10; deposit £10 per person; Access, Visa

Preste Gaarden Hotel

181 Cathedral Road CF1 9PN
CARDIFF (0222) 228607

John and Sarah Nicholls took over the Preste Gaarden in May 1990 and are maintaining high standards. It is a comfortable guesthouse, a short distance from the castle, civic centre and shopping centre. Furnishings and décor are Victorian in style. Long, green curtains separate the lounge from the dining-room. The lounge is very attractive, decorated with tasteful wallpaper, and has an original marble fireplace. All bedrooms have TV. Evening meals are not available but there is a wide selection of nearby pubs and restaurants. The hotel has an alcohol licence. Children welcome. Pets by prior arrangement.

OWNERS John and Sarah Nicholls OPEN All year, exc Christmas ROOMS 2 family (1 with bath/shower), 2 double (with bath/shower), 3 twin (2 with bath/shower), 4 single (2 with bath/shower, 2 with wash-basin) TERMS B&B £15–£17 (children under 7 free, 7–14 half-price)

CARDIGAN Dyfed map 6

Maes-y-Dre Guest House

Aberystwyth Road, Cardigan SA43 1LU
CARDIGAN (0239) 612852

Guests are welcome to sit in the gardens of this attractive turn-of-the-century house on the outskirts of Cardigan. There are plenty of pretty plants about the house. The spacious bedrooms have modern furniture and all have TV. There are several pubs and restaurants nearby for evening meals. Children welcome. No pets. Car park.

OWNERS N. and M. Thomas OPEN All year ROOMS 1 family, 1 twin, 1 single TERMS B&B £14 (children under 4 free, under 10 half-price)

CEFN-DDWYSARN Gwynedd map 6

Cwm Hwylfod

Cefn-Ddwysarn, Bala LL23 7LN
LLANDDERFEL (067 83) 310

Children especially enjoy accompanying Mr Best on his tour of this sheep farm, and there are wellington boots available in all sizes. The 400-year-old farmhouse is in an elevated position, with fabulous views. Free-range eggs are served at breakfast. Dinner is also available by arrangement at 7pm (or to suit guests), with home-made pies and delicious puddings on the menu. Vegetarians can be catered for. There is no alcohol licence, but guests may bring their own wine. Packed lunches can be provided for walkers leaving from the house. The Bests may offer a set-down and pick-up service for walkers. There are washing and drying facilities at the farmhouse. Toys for young children and board games are available. Children welcome. Small pets by arrangement. No smoking in the bedrooms and at meal times. Car park.

OWNERS Mr and Mrs E. Best OPEN All year, exc Christmas
ROOMS 1 family, 2 twin; all rooms with wash-basin TERMS B&B £14 (babies under 2 £1.50, reductions for children under 10); dinner £7.50

CHEPSTOW Gwent map 6

Upper Sedbury House

Sedbury Lane, Sedbury, nr Chepstow NP6 7HN
CHEPSTOW (0291) 627173

This 200-year-old country house is set in an attractive garden of one and a half acres down a quiet country lane, one mile east of Chepstow. There are several outbuildings, and a swimming-pool is available for guests' use. In the garden are several sitting-areas. The house has creaky floors, uneven stone walls, a vaulted cellar and lots of olde worlde charm. The bedrooms are of a good size; one has its own bathroom and one has TV. There is a guest lounge and a pretty dining-room where breakfast and dinner (from 7pm) are served using home-grown produce and home-made preserves. Dinners must be pre-arranged. Vegetarians can be catered for and packed lunches can be provided. There is no alcohol licence, but guests may bring their own wine. A two-bedroom self-catering

Most B&Bs offer tea/coffee-making facilities in the bedrooms.

unit is also available. Children welcome. No smoking in the dining-room. Car park.

OWNERS Mr and Mrs M. A. Potts OPEN All year, exc Christmas ROOMS 2 double (1 with bath/shower), 1 twin TERMS B&B £14.50–£16.50 (children under 3 free, discretionary reductions up to 12); dinner £8.50; deposit

COLWYN BAY Clwyd map 6

West Point Hotel

102 Conway Road, Colwyn Bay LL29 7LE
COLWYN BAY (0492) 530331

West Point is an attractive, detached late-Victorian hotel in a central location. The immaculate bedrooms have solid, traditional furnishings and all have TV. There is a small lounge/bar. Dinner is served 6–7pm, and vegetarian choices can be provided. This is very much a family-run hotel and there is a welcoming atmosphere. Packed lunches are available and there is an alcohol licence. Children welcome. Pets in bedrooms only. No smoking in the dining-room. Car park.

OWNERS Mr and Mrs P. Chidlow and Mrs N. Carter OPEN Feb–Oct ROOMS 3 family (1 with bath/shower), 4 double (3 with bath/shower, 1 with wash-basin), 2 twin (1 with bath/shower, 1 with wash-basin), 1 single (with wash-basin) TERMS B&B £15.50–£18.50, (single occupancy of twin/double) £16.50–£19.50 (children 5–14 half-price); dinner £8.50–£12; deposit; Access, Visa

CORRIS Gwynedd map 6

Bronwydd

Bridge Street, Corris, Machynlleth SY20 9SS
CORRIS (0654) 761381

Bronwydd, which means ‘goose breast’, was formerly the local butcher’s, and was built of local slate over 200 years ago. The village of Corris nestles in the foothills of Cader Idris, and is an ideal centre for walking, climbing, fishing and bird-watching. The bedrooms are of an average size and are well appointed, all with easy chairs and TV. There is an attractive lounge, which is shared with the family. Breakfast and dinners, if pre-arranged, are served in the pleasant dining-room, which has a 150-year-old Grecian harp and a grandfather clock. Vegetarian choices can be provided. There is no alcohol licence, but guests may bring their own wine to dinner. Packed lunches can be arranged. On arrival guests are greeted with a cup of tea. Children welcome (there are reductions in the tariff). Pets by arrangement. No smoking. Car park.

OWNER Mrs S. A. Darbyshire-Robert OPEN All year, exc Christmas ROOMS 1 family, 1 double, 1 twin, 1 single; all rooms with wash-basin TERMS B&B £12–£15, (family room) £35; dinner from £5

CYNWYD Clwyd map 6

Fron Goch Farmhouse

Cynwyd, nr Corwen LL21 0NA
LLANDRILLO (049 084) 418

Owner Mrs Sarah Stille is a qualified walking guide and will arrange conducted walks. Fron Goch is a stone farmhouse in the lovely Vale of Edeyrnion, sheltered by the Berwyn Mountains. Three of the spacious, well-decorated bedrooms are named after local trees: 'The Birch', 'The Oak' and 'The Willow'. Dinners are served at 7.30pm every day except Tuesday and include plenty of fresh vegetables, local meat and home-made bread. Fron Goch is licensed and vegetarian meals are available on request. Lunch and packed lunches can be provided. Good drying facilities are available for walkers and cyclists, and the house and gardens are open to guests throughout the day. Children welcome. Pets by arrangement. No smoking in the dining-room. Car park.

OWNER Mrs Sarah Stille OPEN All year ROOMS 2 family (1 with bath/shower, 1 with wash-basin), 3 double (with bath/shower), 1 twin (with wash-basin) TERMS B&B £15–£18, (single occupancy of twin/double) £18.50–£21.50 (children under 3 charge for food only, 3–12 sharing with parents £6–£10); dinner £11; deposit £10 or 10%

DOLGELLAU Gwynedd map 6

Ivy House

Finsbury Square, Dolgellau LL40 1RF
DOLGELLAU (0341) 422535

Dolgellau is situated in the Snowdonia National Park at the foot of Cader Idris, and is an excellent base for walking and pony-trekking. Ivy House, built in 1829 of local granite, is an attractive residence close to the centre of this ancient small town. The bedrooms are well appointed and decorated to a high standard. All have TV. The owners have purchased the adjacent property to live in and the house is now exclusively for guests. Drinks are available from the cellar bar. Four-course dinners are served 5–9.30pm in the restaurant, which is open to non-residents. Vegetarian meals are available. Packed lunches can be made up on request. Children welcome. Pets by arrangement. No smoking in the dining-room.

OWNERS J. S. and M. Bamford OPEN All year ROOMS 1 family (with wash-basin), 3 double (2 with bath/shower, 1 with wash-basin), 2 twin (1 with bath/shower, 1 with wash-basin) TERMS B&B £16–£22, (single occupancy of twin/double) £18–£25 (reductions for children); deposit; Visa

Tyddyngarreg Farm

Tabor, Dolgellau LL40 2PU
DOLGELLAU (0341) 422366

Tyddyngarreg is a 750-acre farm, dating from the sixteenth century, halfway between Dinas Mawddwy and Dolgellau. The atmosphere here is that of a down-to-earth working farm, and guests are welcome to put on some wellies and take a tour. The house has thick stone walls, a large stone fireplace in the dining-room and lounge, beams galore and original doors and panelling. This is a fascinating old place furnished with antiques, including a chaise-longue and a collection of cheese dishes. The bedrooms are comfortable, with patchwork quilts on the beds. Evening meals, 6.30–8pm, include home-cured ham and lamb as well as home-made desserts. There is no alcohol licence, but guests may bring their own wine to dinner. Vegetarian choices can be provided and packed lunches can be arranged. Children welcome. No smoking in bedrooms. Car park.

OWNER Mrs Mary Price OPEN Mar–end Oct ROOMS 1 family (with wash-basin), 1 double (with bath/shower), 1 twin (with wash-basin) TERMS B&B £10, (family room) £32 (children 7–12 £7, 2–7 half-price, up to 2 free); dinner £5; deposit

DYFFRYN ARDUDWY Gwynedd map 6

Cors-y-Gedol Hall

Dyffryn Ardudwy LL44 2RJ
DYFFRYN (034 17) 230

A drive flanked by lime trees brings guests to this lovely listed Jacobean and Elizabethan building, approached through a stone arched gateway with a clock-tower believed to have been designed by Inigo Jones. Cors-y-Gedol is situated on a 3,000-acre sheep and cattle farm. This is a historic house; there is a beautiful Elizabethan hall with beams taken from the Spanish Armada, original panelling, a table dating from the sixteenth century and a huge stone fireplace. The bedrooms are spacious and well appointed, with comfortable beds. There is also an elegant lounge with an Adam-style ceiling. Breakfasts only are served, but there are plenty of places to eat within a few minutes' drive. Guests may use the garden, table tennis and an ornamental lake with a small boat. No pets. Car park.

OWNER Mrs J. F. Bailey OPEN All year, exc Christmas and New Year ROOMS 2 double, 1 twin/family; all rooms with bath/shower TERMS B&B £14–£15 (children under 10 half-price); deposit

ERWOOD Powys map 6

Orchard Cottage/The Barn

Erwood, Builth Wells LD2 3EZ
ERWOOD (0982) 560600

Orchard Cottage is situated on the A470 between Talgarth and Builth Wells. Two bedrooms have on the ground floor; one has attractive Laura Ashley décor and a private bathroom. There are also two beautifully appointed bedrooms with beams and sloping roofs and a bathroom in the middle, ideal for families or friends travelling together. All rooms have TV. The Barn is a converted outbuilding set on the banks of the River Wye. It is a self-catering unit, but is also used for B&B. There is a sitting-room with TV in both Orchard Cottage and the Barn. Breakfast only is served, but there are several eating establishments nearby and packed lunches can be provided. Trout and salmon fishing can be arranged, and guests may use the pretty garden. Children welcome. Pets in the Barn only by prior arrangement. Non-smokers preferred. Car park.

OWNERS Wendy and Reg Coe OPEN All year ROOMS 3 double (2 with bath/shower), 2 twin (1 with bath/shower) TERMS B&B £13.50, (single occupancy of twin/double) £18.50 (children half-price sharing with parents); dinner £6.50; deposit 20%

Please let us know if you need more report forms and we will send you a fresh supply.

If a deposit is required for an advance booking this is stated at the end of an entry.

GLASCOED Gwent map 6

Marnham House Farm

Glascoed, nr Pontypool NP4 0TY
LITTLE MILL (049 528) 230

This spacious Victorian country house is set in seven acres of paddock and woodland, with delightful views to the Skirrid and the Sugar Loaf mountain. Several original features remain, such as a stained-glass front door, cornices and a lovely ceiling rose. The house is furnished with interesting antiques. The bedrooms are of a good size, have fireplaces and one has an *en suite* bathroom. The house has a warm, comfortable atmosphere. The well-furnished lounge overlooks the large gardens. A substantial breakfast is served and there are several pubs and restaurants within a short drive. Glascoed is a small hamlet of farms and houses a short distance from the delightful town of Usk. Children welcome. No pets in the house; they must be left in stables. Smoking in the sitting-room only. Car park.

OWNERS Tim and Jenny Walton OPEN All year
ROOMS 3 twin/1 family (1 with bath/shower, 2 with wash-basin)
TERMS B&B £14–£16.50, (single occupancy of twin) £16–£19 (reductions for children); deposit

HARLECH Gwynedd map 6

Aris Guest House

Pen y Bryn, Harlech LL46 2SL
HARLECH (0766) 780409

The town of Harlech, the castle and the sea can be seen from this modern house. The rooms are average in size; all have TV and radio, and the family room has its own shower. There is a guest lounge, with TV and log fires, and a patio for enjoying the view on fine days. Evening meals are available (by arrangement) with salads served in the summer. Timing of meals can be arranged to suit guests, and vegetarian choices can be provided. There is no alcohol licence, but guests may bring their own wine to dinner.

Reduced rates for children are normally given when they share their parents' bedroom. If no reductions are specified in the details or text, assume you'll have to pay full rates.

If there are any bedrooms with TV and/or telephone we mention this in the entry.

Lunch and packed lunches can be arranged. Children welcome. No smoking in the public rooms. Car park.

OWNER Ruth Owen OPEN All year ROOMS 1 family (with bath/shower), 1 double, 1 twin, 1 single; all rooms with wash-basin
TERMS B&B £13, (single) £15, (single occupancy of twin/double) £15, (family room) £35 (children under 11 half-price, 12–16 three-quarters-price); dinner £7

Noddfa Hotel

Lower Road, Harlech LL46 2UB
HARLECH (0766) 780043

The hotel is set in three and a half acres of garden and woodland, in an elevated position overlooking the Royal St David's Golf Course in Snowdonia. It is an early Victorian stone building with a bell tower. Superb sea and mountain views can be enjoyed from the terrace. The high-ceilinged public rooms are decorated with a collection of bows and medieval weapons. The owners are enthusiastic archers and give traditional archery lessons; for the medieval displays held in Harlech Castle they practice sword fighting in the hotel grounds – much to the amazement of the guests! Noddfa, meaning 'place of safety', was the site of a shepherds' hut under the protection of Harlech Castle. Personal escorted tours of the castle can be arranged. Dinner is available (7–8.30pm) with local salmon and Welsh lamb on the menu, served in the licensed dining-room. Packed lunches can be provided. The hotel also has a guest lounge, a bar and a games-room. Children welcome, but there are no facilities for babies. No dogs. Car park.

OWNERS Eric and Gillian Newton Davies OPEN All year
ROOMS 4 double (2 with bath/shower, 2 with wash-basin)
TERMS B&B £15–£21, (single occupancy of double) £25–£37 (reductions for children out of season); D, B&B £27.50–£33.50; dinner £15; deposit; Access, Visa

HOLYHEAD Gwynedd (Anglesey) map 6

Roselea

26 Holborn Road, Holyhead, Anglesey LL65 2AT
HOLYHEAD (0407) 764391

Roselea is a cosy guesthouse, close to the ferry and town. Mrs Foxley will stay up for guests coming in on the late ferry, provided that advance notice is given. The bedrooms are well appointed and have orthopaedic beds. There is a guest lounge with TV. Dinners are available, if pre-arranged; home-cooked meals are served with lots of local fresh vegetables and meat. Vegetarian choices can be provided at dinner. There is no licence, but guests may bring their own wine. Children welcome. No pets. No smoking in bedrooms.

OWNER Mrs S. Foxley OPEN All year ROOMS 1 double/family, 2 twin; all rooms with wash-basin TERMS B&B from £10, (single occupancy of twin/double) £14 (reductions for children sharing with parents); dinner from £6; deposit

HOWEY Powys — map 6

Three Wells Farm

Chapel Road, Howey, Llandrindod Wells LD1 5PB
LLANDRINDOD WELLS (0597) 822484/824427

This working dairy farm has sheep, pedigree Welsh Black Cattle, ducks, hens and two ponies. The farmhouse overlooks a fishing lake, in peaceful, lovely countryside. The house is immaculately kept. All the bedrooms have radio, telephone and TV. There is a lounge bar, a TV room and a comfortable guest lounge with an adjoining sun lounge and a lift. Home-cooked food is offered from a varied menu in the attractive licensed dining-room; dinner is served at 7pm and vegetarians can be catered for. Packed lunches are also available. Riding and fishing can be arranged at the farm. No children under 10. No pets. No smoking in public areas. Car park.

OWNERS Ron, Margaret and Sarah Bufton OPEN Feb–Nov ROOMS 1 four-poster, 6 double, 6 twin, 1 single; all rooms with bath/shower TERMS B&B £15.50–£19 (reductions for children sharing with parents); dinner £8–£8.50; deposit £10 per person

KNELSTON West Glamorgan — map 6

Fairfield Cottage

Knelston, Gower SA3 1AR
GOWER (0792) 391013

This picturesque eighteenth-century cottage is in the heart of beautiful Gower, in the village of Knelston, close to bays with sandy beaches, dunes, cliffs and lovely country walks. The three bedrooms, although a little small, are comfortable and very prettily decorated. There is now a small family room with a king-size bed, attractive green chintz décor and a natural stone wall. There is a cosy guest lounge with an inglenook fireplace. Morning tea is served in guests' rooms and a pre-dinner aperitif and a bedtime drink are included at no extra charge. Breakfast, with home-made preserves and yoghurts, and home-cooked traditional dinners are served, using home-produced fruit and vegetables when in season. There is no licence, but guests may bring their own wine. Packed lunches are available on request. No children under two. No pets. No smoking preferred. Car park.

OWNER Mrs C. W. Ashton OPEN Mar–Oct ROOMS 1 family (with wash-basin), 1 double, 1 twin (with wash-basin) TERMS B&B £14–£15; dinner £7.50–£8.50; deposit

LAUGHARNE Dyfed map 6

Halldown

Laugharne SA33 4QS
LAUGHARNE (0994) 427452

There is a large garden surrounding this 200-year-old Welsh stone farmhouse; it is in a peaceful setting, with lovely views. The bedrooms are large, with modern furnishings, and one is on the ground floor. The lounge has a huge stone fireplace and an interesting collection of stones from all over the world. The Welsh corgis form a friendly welcoming committee. There is a barn conversion adjacent to the main house, ideal for those who value privacy; breakfast is taken in the main house. Children welcome. Car park.

OWNERS Mr and Mrs T. Best OPEN All year ROOMS 2 family (1 with bath/shower), 3 double (with wash-basin)
TERMS B&B £12–£13.50 (children half-price)

LLANDRINDOD WELLS Powys map 6

Brynllys Guest House

High Street, Llandrindod Wells LD1 6AG
LLANDRINDOD WELLS (0597) 823190

This is a family-run guesthouse in the centre of town with ample parking space opposite. The rooms are clean, with modern furnishings, comfortable beds and TV. Mrs Rogers prepares good home-cooked breakfasts and dinners (6.30pm) with local fresh produce used whenever possible. Vegetarians can be catered for. Brynllys is licensed. Packed lunches can be provided. Children welcome. Small or old dogs only. No smoking at breakfast in the dining-room.

OWNER Carol Rogers OPEN All year ROOMS 2 double/family, 2 twin, 2 single; all rooms with wash-basin TERMS B&B £13–£15, (single occupancy of twin/double) £20, (family room) £52–£60 (children under 15 half-price sharing with adults); dinner £7.50; deposit for bookings 2 weeks or more in advance

LLANDUDNO Gwynedd map 6

Beach Cove

8 Church Walks, Llandudno LL30 2HD
LLANDUDNO (0492) 879638

The beaches and other amenities are very close to this immaculate property. The rooms range from small to spacious and all have TV. The house has been completely redecorated and a solarium has been added. There is a comfortable, tastefully furnished guest lounge with TV and a grandfather clock. The proprietors have experience of elderly people's needs as they formerly ran a nursing home; the ground-floor bedroom is suitable for the disabled. Mrs Carroll is an excellent cook and tasty dinners, with lots of fresh vegetables and home-baked desserts, are served at 5.30pm. Special diets and vegetarians can be catered for. Guests may bring their own wine as there is no alcohol licence. Packed lunches can be provided. Children welcome. No pets. No smoking in the dining-room and one lounge.

OWNERS Mr and Mrs Carroll OPEN All year, exc Christmas ROOMS 5 double (4 with bath/shower, 1 with wash-basin), 1 twin (with bath/shower), 1 single (with wash-basin) TERMS B&B £15, (single) £12.50, (single occupancy of twin/double) £20 (children £8); dinner £6.50; deposit £10

Bryn-y-Mor Hotel

North Parade, Llandudno LL30 2LP
LLANDUDNO (0492) 876790 Fax (0492) 860825

A few minutes' walk from the beach, town centre and the Great Orme Tramway, this attractive Victorian residence in an elevated position has lovely views of the bay and mountains. The bedrooms, some with sea views, are individually decorated with pretty duvets, and all have TV. There is a guest lounge and a small bar lounge with views. Breakfast and dinner (6–7pm) are served in the pleasant licensed dining-room with its attractive curtains and green décor. Everything is prepared fresh daily, and vegetarians and special diets can be catered for. Packed lunches can be provided. Drying facilities and hair-dryers are available. Partial central heating. Children welcome. Pets by arrangement. No smoking areas in the restaurant and guests' lounge.

OWNERS Peter and Jacqueline Ratcliffe OPEN All year, exc Christmas ROOMS 4 family (1 with bath/shower, 3 with wash-basin), 7 double (4 with bath/shower, 3 with wash-basin), 4 twin (1 with bath/shower, 3 with wash-basin), 3 single (with wash-basin) TERMS B&B £17–£24, (single occupancy of twin/double) £29–£32 (children under 4 £3, 4–12 25% reduction); dinner from £8.50; deposit £20 per person high season and bank hols; all major credit cards

Carmel

Craig-y-Don Parade, Promenade, Llandudno LL30 1BG
LLANDUDNO (0492) 877643

This pleasant private hotel is situated on the sea-front and has a view of the whole bay. The rooms range from small, cosy singles to spacious family rooms, some with sea views. The owners have been busy upgrading and improving the accommodation, and there are now five bedrooms with *en suite* bathrooms. There is also a lounge with TV. Evening meals are served Monday to Saturday at 6.30pm. Sunday lunch is also available. Special diets can be catered for with advance notice. There is no alcohol licence, but guests may bring their own wine. No children under four. Pets by arrangement. Car park. No smoking in the dining-room.

OWNERS Laura and Phill Lesiter OPEN Apr–Oct ROOMS 3 family (2 with bath/shower, 1 with wash-basin), 5 double (2 with bath/shower, 3 with wash-basin), 1 twin (with bath/shower), 1 single (with wash-basin) TERMS B&B £12.50–£19 (children 4–14 40% reduction, 14 and over 25%); dinner £5; deposit £20–£30

Bath/shower information in the details refers only to a private bathroom or shower; other bathroom facilities at the establishments will be shared. We say if rooms have wash-basins.

Many B&Bs are in remote places; always ask for clear directions when booking.

LLANFAIR CAERINION Powys map 6

Cwmllwynog

Llanfair Caereinion SY21 0HF
LLANFAIR CAEREINION (0938) 810791

Cwmllwynog, situated three miles west of Llanfair Light Railway Station, is a seventeenth-century traditional Welsh farmhouse on a working dairy farm of 105 acres. It is surrounded by hanging baskets and tubs full of flowers, and there is a lovely flower garden leading down to a stream. The bedrooms are large, with solid, old-fashioned furnishings. The double bedroom has its own bathroom and attractive matching Sanderson fabrics and wallpaper. There are beams galore throughout this warm and welcoming house, and the lounge has a huge Welsh stone fireplace with a wood-burning stove. Home-cooked meals are served, using fresh produce from the garden, home-made bread, preserves and puddings. Dinner is available 6.30–7pm and can include vegetarian choices. There is no alcohol licence, but guests may bring their own wine. Lunches are also available. Children welcome. No pets. Smoking only on ground floor. Car park.

OWNER Joyce Cornes OPEN All year ROOMS 1 double (with bath/shower), 1 twin (with wash-basin) TERMS B&B £14 (children 10% reduction); dinner £6

LLANGEITHO Dyfed map 6

Glanrhyd Isaf

Llangeitho, nr Tregaron SY25 6QU
TREGARON (0974) 298762

Glanrhyd Isaf, meaning 'lower bank of the ford', is a charming bungalow in an elevated position with lovely views. It is very well maintained, and has two bedrooms decorated in pastel colours, with modern furnishings; the twin has a black and white TV, the double a colour TV. The lounge has french windows leading into the lovely garden. Breakfasts are large. Guests are greeted with a cup of tea or coffee on arrival. The elevated position and steps approaching the bungalow make Glanrhyd Isaf unsuitable for the disabled. It is 10 miles from the Cardigan Bay coast, in ideal bird-

Where we know of any particular payment stipulations we mention them in the details. It is always best to check when booking, however.

watching and walking country. Children welcome. No pets. Car park.

OWNER Mrs W. R. Owen OPEN All year ROOMS 1 double (with shower), 1 twin TERMS B&B £11–£15 (children up to 12 half-price); deposit 10%

LLANRHAEADR-YM-MOCHNANT Clwyd map 6

Bron Heulog

Waterfall Road, Llanrhaeadr-ym-Mochnant SY10 0JX
LLANRHAEADR (069 189) 521

This spacious Victorian house lies on the outskirts of the village in the beautiful Tanat and Rhaeadr valleys, 13 miles west of Oswestry. It is a comfortable, old-fashioned house, with a mixture of antique and traditional furnishings. The bedrooms, all with TV, are very spacious and one of the double rooms has a coronet bed. There are several items of interest within the house, including a French campaign chest in the dining-room. There is also a small snug library. Guests are welcome to visit the family rare-breeds farm nearby. Pony-trekking and fishing can be arranged. Pistyll Rhaeadr, a waterfall at the head of the Rhaeadr Valley, is four miles away. Delicious home-cooked dinners are available by arrangement, usually 6.30–8.30pm. Vegetarians can be catered for on request. Packed lunches can be provided and guests may bring their own wine to dinner (there is no alcohol licence). Children welcome. Car park.

OWNER Lorraine Pashen OPEN All year ROOMS 2 double, 1 twin/family; all rooms with wash-basin TERMS B&B £13–£18 (children £9–£10); dinner £7.50–£9 (children £5–£6); deposit £10–£15

Llys Morgan

Llanrhaeadr-ym-Mochnant SY10 0JZ
LLANRHAEADR (069 189) 345

A charming historic house dating from the sixteenth-century, Llys Morgan is 200 yards from the village, in grounds of one acre and set in lovely gardens with a fish pond. It was formerly the Old Vicarage, where the Bible was translated into Welsh in 1588; the dining-room has seven bibles inset in the fireplace. The bedrooms, all with TV, are very spacious and comfortable. There is also a guest lounge where a fire burns brightly on chilly evenings, while on pleasant days guests can wander out to the garden and walled patio – a perfect spot in which to unwind after a busy day. Modestly priced home-cooked dinners are available by prior arrangement, and special diets and vegetarians can be catered for. Packed lunches can be provided. There is no alcohol licence, but guests may bring their own wine. Children welcome. Pets by arrangement. Car park.

OWNER Mrs J. L. Morgan OPEN All year ROOMS 1 family (with bath/shower), 3 double (1 with bath/shower, 2 with wash-basin), 1 twin (with bath/shower) TERMS B&B £12.50–£15.50, (family room) £37.50–£45 (children under 11 half-price); dinner £5–£7

LLANRUG Gwynedd map 6

Lakeside

Llanrug, nr Caernarfon LL55 4ED
CAERNARFON (0286) 870065

This delightful stone house, dating from the seventeenth-century, stands in six acres of woodlands with a beautiful landscaped garden, inhabited by the three dogs, peacocks, geese, chickens and quail. There is a comfortable guest lounge with a log-burning fire. The well-appointed bedrooms, all with TV, are furnished mostly with antiques; one room has a particularly ornate wash-basin. This is a most warm and friendly house with virtually no area off-limits. There is a private lake on the property and a rowing-boat and a canoe are available for guests' use. Dinner, if pre-arranged, is available; unlicensed, but guests are welcome to bring their own wine. Lunches are available and advance notice is required to cater for vegetarians. Bryn-Bras Castle is nearby and worth a visit. Children welcome (no cots or high chairs provided). 'Well-trained' adult dogs only. Car park.

OWNER Lyn Kane OPEN All year ROOMS 1 family (with wash-basin), 2 double (1 with bath/shower, 1 with wash-basin), 1 twin (with wash-basin) TERMS B&B £16–£22 (children half-price sharing with 2 adults); dinner £12.

We asked the proprietors to estimate their 1992 prices in the autumn of 1991, so the rates may have changed since publication.

When the family-room rate is given in the details it applies to the cost of the whole room, unless a rate per person is specified.

Where we know an establishment accepts credit cards, we list them. There may be a surcharge if you pay by credit card. It is always best to check whether the card you want to use is acceptable when booking.

LLANSADWRN Dyfed map 6

Brynheulog

Llansadwrn, Llanwrda SA19 8LN
LLANGADOG (0550) 777216

Brynheulog is a beautiful house in a peaceful setting off the A40 halfway between Llandovery and Llandeilo. The house is close to a nature reserve and the nesting spot of the red kite. There is an interesting collection of RAF memorabilia in the hallway. The rooms are of a good size, well decorated and elegantly furnished. Afternoon cream teas are available, and dinner can be served at 7pm by prior arrangement; unlicensed, but guests may bring their own wine. Vegetarians can be catered for with notice. No facilities for children under five. No pets. Smoking in the guest lounge only. Car park.

OWNER Mrs M. Goodwin OPEN Mar–Nov ROOMS 2 double, 1 twin; all rooms with wash-basin TERMS B&B £13 (children under 12 £10); dinner £6.50–£8

LLANSILIN Clwyd map 6

Bwlch y Rhiw Farmhouse

Llansilin, nr Oswestry SY10 7PT
OSWESTRY (0691) 70261

Bwlch y Rhiw Farmhouse is a large early Victorian building perched high above the Cynllaith valley, in 120 acres of farmland. This is a comfortable, informal house that has been attractively modernised yet retains many original features, such as flagstone floors, inglenook fireplace and natural wood doors, and is furnished in keeping with the character of the house. Of special interest is a beautiful Victorian firescreen. There are three comfortable bedrooms, all with *en suite* facilities and TV. There is also a guest lounge with TV and a piano which guests are welcome to play. Hearty breakfasts are served in the delightful dining-room. Evening meals are not available, but soup and sandwiches can be arranged for an evening-in. Llansilin is an interesting village and the church of St Silins is well worth a visit. This house is situated four and a half miles west of Oswestry on the B4580.

Those B&Bs that we know can offer some kind of off-street car parking, have 'car park' at the end of the entry. If we are aware of particular car parking difficulties, we mention them.

No children under seven. No pets. Smoking preferred downstairs only. Car park.

OWNERS Mrs Brenda Jones and Mrs Alison Gallagher OPEN Apr–end Oct ROOMS 1 family, 1 double, 1 twin; all rooms with bath/shower TERMS B&B from £32, (single occupancy of twin/double) from £24, (family room) from £46 (children from £12); deposit £15–£60 depending on length of stay

LLANWRTYD WELLS Powys map 6

Maesygwaelod Farmhouse

Llanwrtyd Wells LD5 4SL
LLANWRTYD WELLS (059 13) 613

A 100-year-old stone house, with adjacent 300-year-old barns, set amid 10 acres inhabited by ducks and chickens, and peacefully situated at the foot of the Cambrian Mountains, half a mile from Llanwrtyd Wells. If you are looking for clean, comfortable, no-frills accommodation, then Maesygwaelod certainly fits the bill. Breakfast only is available and is served in the cosy dining-room/ lounge, with an open fire lit on cool days. Packed lunches can be provided. This is good walking country, with pony-trekking, angling and golf available nearby. Children welcome. 'Well-behaved' pets only. No smoking. Car park.

OWNERS Lyndon and Judy Gore OPEN All year ROOMS 1 double, 1 twin, 1 single TERMS B&B £12

MOYLEGROVE Dyfed map 6

The Old Vicarage Country Guest House

Moylegrove, nr Cardigan SA43 3BN
MOYLEGROVE (023 986) 231

The Old Vicarage is a beautiful, spacious, elegant Edwardian home set in an acre of paddocks and garden, in an elevated position with views over the village of Moylegrove and out to the sea. Moylegrove is situated in the centre of the Pembrokeshire Coast National Park and the 180-mile-long Pembrokeshire Coastal Path runs along the cliffs a mile from the house. The spacious bedrooms are elegantly furnished in traditional Edwardian style and individually decorated in soft restful colours; one is a patio suite suitable for the disabled. There is a separate dining-room and a sitting-room; both have open log fires. Four-course dinners, with an interesting and varied menu, are served, by arrangement, at 7.30pm. Vegetarians can be catered for and wine is available. Lunches can be provided. There is a utility room with washing, drying and ironing facilities for guests' use. Children welcome. No dogs. No smoking in bedrooms. Car park.

OWNERS Anthony and Peggy Govey OPEN All year, exc Christmas ROOMS 1 family (with wash-basin), 2 double (1 with bath/shower, 1 with wash-basin), 2 twin (with bath/shower), 1 single (with wash-basin) TERMS B&B £17.50–£22.50 (children up to 3 free, 3–12 £10); dinner £11.50; deposit £20 per person

NANTGAREDIG Dyfed map 6

Cwmtwrch Farm Hotel

Nantgaredig, nr Carmarthen SA32 7NY
NANTGAREDIG (0267) 290238

Cwmtwrch Farm is no longer a working farm, but a most interesting country-house hotel. There are six warm and pretty bedrooms, furnished in pine. Three of the bedrooms are in the main farmhouse; the other three, one of which is suitable for the disabled, are at ground level in converted outbuildings. Three rooms have TV. There are flagstone floors, and a collection of old farm implements hangs on the walls. Dinner is served from 7.30pm and vegetarians can be catered for. The licensed restaurant has an imaginative menu and includes dishes such as roast and boned duck stuffed with chicken and brandied fruits. Fresh produce, and home-made bread and preserves are used. Lunches can also be provided. Children welcome. Pets in three bedrooms only. No smoking in the restaurant. Car park.

OWNER Mrs Jenny Willmott OPEN All year ROOMS 1 family, 3 double, 2 twin; all rooms with bath/shower TERMS B&B £19–£21, (single occupancy of twin/double) £28–£30 (children free accommodation); dinner £13.50–£17.50; deposit 10%

NEWPORT Dyfed map 6

Llysmeddyg Guest House

East Street, Newport, nr Fishguard SA42 0SY
NEWPORT (0239) 820008

There are two Newports in Wales; this is the one on the west coast, in Dyfed. Llysmeddyg is a beautifully preserved Georgian house in the centre of the town. The immaculate bedrooms are tastefully decorated, each with armchairs and hair-dryer. The lounge windows have the original casement shutters, and there are log fires in both the dining-room and lounge. Three-course candle-lit dinners are served at 7.45pm and vegetarian meals are available on request. There is an extensive wine list. Packed lunches can also be provided. This is beautiful walking country, and the owners are very knowledgeable about the area and happy to assist guests with itineraries. A two-bedroom self-catering unit is available. No children under five. No pets. No smoking in bedrooms. Car park.

OWNERS Ian and Penny Ross OPEN All year, exc Christmas Day
ROOMS 2 double, 2 twin; all rooms with wash-basin
TERMS B&B £16; dinner £10.50; deposit 1 night charge

NEWPORT Gwent map 6

Kepe Lodge Guest House

46A Caerau Road, Newport NP9 4HH
NEWPORT (0633) 262351

This is the Newport close to Cardiff. Kepe Lodge is an immaculate house tucked away in a quiet position just off the main road, and is set in a lovely garden full of mature shrubs and flowers. The bedrooms are tasteful with modern furnishings; three have their own bathroom, and all have TV, radio-alarm, chairs and writing desks. Excellent breakfasts are served, including a buffet for cereals and juices, followed by a traditional cooked course. There is a separate lounge which leads out to the garden where there is a furnished patio for guests' use. Guide dogs only. No smoking in the dining-room, guest lounge and hallways. Car park.

OWNERS Ken and Peggy Long OPEN All year, exc Christmas
ROOMS 1 double (with bath/shower), 2 twin (with bath/shower), 5 single (with wash-basin) TERMS B&B £15–£20 approx; deposit

Many B&Bs will cater for vegetarians. It is always best, however, to check when booking and make it clear what your requirements are, especially if you need a special diet.

If you are forced to turn up late into the evening, please telephone to warn the proprietor.

It is always best to check prices, especially for single occupancy, when booking.

OXWICH West Glamorgan map 6

Surf Sound Guest House

Long Acre, Oxwich, Gower SA3 1LS
GOWER (0792) 390822

This 1960s house stands in its own grounds and the dining-room and lounge overlook the gardens. The bedrooms are of a good size and well appointed. Five are on the ground floor and suitable for the disabled. Mr Woodburn is a trained chef and takes great pride in preparing excellent dinners at 7pm. Vegetarians can be catered for, and packed lunches are available on request. There is an alcohol licence. Children welcome. No pets. No smoking in the dining-room. Car park.

OWNER Mr M. L. Woodburn OPEN All year ROOMS 3 family (2 with bath/shower, 1 with wash-basin), 1 double (with bath/shower), 1 twin (with wash-basin), 1 single (with wash-basin)
TERMS B&B £16–£20 (children under 14 half-price sharing parents' room); dinner £8; deposit

PENCELLI Powys map 6

Cambrian Cruisers Marina

Ty Newydd, Pencelli, Brecon LD3 7LJ
LLANFRYNACH (087 486) 315

Situated on a beautiful canal and nestling beneath Pen-y-Fan – the highest peak of the Brecon Beacons – Cambrian Cruisers offers narrow boat hire and bed and breakfast accommodation. The bedrooms, in a restored eighteenth-century farmhouse, are beautifully furnished with new and antique pine, and all have *en suite* facilities, chair or couches and TV. The top floor is particularly charming with its sloping beamed roofs. Guests have their own entrance to the accommodation. There are several buildings of interest around the courtyard which are gradually being restored. There is a small gift shop and tea-room serving freshly made sandwiches and home-baked cakes, which can be enjoyed overlooking the canal on fine days. Canoeing, pony-trekking, cycling and fishing can be arranged. Breakfast only is

B&B rates specified in the details for each entry are per person per night; unless the details state otherwise, they are based on two people sharing a double or twin-bedded room.

available, although packed lunches can be provided. Children welcome. No dogs. No smoking in bedrooms. Car park.

OWNERS Mr and Mrs P. Griffiths OPEN Mar–Dec, exc Christmas ROOMS 1 family, 2 double, 1 twin; all rooms with bath/shower TERMS B&B £16–£17.50, (family room) £32–£48 (children under 5 free, 5–14 half-price); deposit £15 per room

PENMACHNO Gwynedd map 6

Tyddyn Gethin Farm

Penmachno, Betws-y-Coed LL24 0PS
PENMACHNO (069 03) 392

This stone-built farmhouse is on a working sheep farm, and guests are welcome to put on some boots and explore it for themselves. The views from the farm are breathtaking, and this is the perfect place for people who enjoy walking. Dinner is available by arrangement and packed lunches can be provided. There is no alcohol licence, but guests may bring their own wine. The bedrooms are clean and comfortable, and the atmosphere is welcoming. A fire is lit on cooler evenings and guests are offered tea or coffee before they go to bed. If Megan Jones has made some of her delicious Welsh teacakes, try one – they are some of the best in Wales. There is a huge, old Welsh dresser in the lounge, and smoking is allowed in the small lounge only. Pets by arrangement. Car park.

OWNER Megan Jones OPEN All year ROOMS 2 double, 1 twin; all rooms with wash-basin TERMS B&B £11.50–£13 (reductions for children); dinner £6–£7; deposit

PENMON Gwynedd (Anglesey) map 6

Dinmor

Penmon, nr Beaumaris, Anglesey LL58 8SN
BEAUMARIS (0248) 490395

Dinmor is situated on a quiet country road just outside Penmon village. There are four acres of land with geese, ducks and guinea-fowl. It is a good place for walkers, riders or people who just want peace and tranquillity. Guests have a chance to work with the horses – groom, feed, muck out – and riding can be arranged. Sailing can also be arranged locally. There are many footpaths in the area and Mrs Korn has charted several circular routes from the house. Bicycles can also be provided. The large lounge has an open fire. Vegetarian meals only are served, and the Korns join guests for dinner (7.30–8pm). Vegans can be catered for. There is no alcohol licence, but guests may bring their own wine. Packed lunches can be provided. No children under eight at Christmas. No dogs on the furniture. No smoking in bedrooms. Car park.

OWNERS T. and M. Korn OPEN All year ROOMS 1 family (with bath/shower), 1 double (with bath/shower), 1 twin (with bath/shower), 2 single (1 with wash-basin) TERMS B&B £15, (single occupancy of twin/double) £25 (children under 12 half-price sharing with parents); dinner £7; deposit

PENTRE HALKYN Clwyd map 6

The Hall

Lygan-y-Wern, Pentre Halkyn CH8 8BD
HALKYN (0352) 780215

The Hall dates from the sixteenth-century and stands in its own grounds of 13 acres, which are inhabited by bantams, geese, ducks and hens, overlooking the estuary of the River Dee. It is just off the B5123 at the junction with the A55. The house combines modern comforts with many original features such as flagstone floors, a listed dovecote and seventeenth-century privies outside, which guests are welcome to see. The five bedrooms are enormous, all painted sparkling white with pine furnishings. There is a separate sitting-room/dining-room with TV. Guests are greeted with a cup of tea or coffee on arrival. Breakfast only is available, although packed lunches can be provided. Well-behaved children. No pets. No smoking in bedrooms. Car park.

OWNER Mrs James Vernon OPEN All year, exc Christmas
ROOMS 1 double, 3 twin, 1 single; all rooms with wash-basin
TERMS B&B £13–£16 (reductions for children); Access, Visa

PEN-Y-BONT-FAWR Powys map 6

Glyndwr

Pen-y-bont-fawr SY10 0NT
PENNANT (069 174) 430

Glyndwr is a whitewashed seventeenth-century stone cottage situated in the heart of the Tanat Valley. It is easily found in the main street next to the stone river bridge and there are hanging baskets full of flowers outside. The cottage is tastefully decorated throughout, and there are oak beams and open fires. There is a private sitting-room with TV, or you may enjoy a quiet hour in the secluded garden bordered by the Barrog river. A converted cottage is available adjacent to the house, which has its own entrance and is ideal for those who want privacy. The surrounding country is mountainous, with lakes, waterfalls and forests. Evening meals, using fresh, local meat and home-grown produce and fruit from the garden, are served at 7.30pm. Vegetarian choices and packed lunches can be provided by arrangement. There is no alcohol licence, but guests may bring their own wine. Glyndwr has storage and panel heaters, but no central heating. Children welcome. No pets. No smoking in bedrooms. Car park.

OWNER Mrs E. M. Henderson OPEN All year, exc Christmas and New Year ROOMS 2 double, 1 twin; all rooms with bath/shower TERMS B&B £14–£18, (single occupancy of twin/double) £20 (children under 12 half-price); dinner £8; deposit

PONTYPOOL Gwent map 6

Pentwyn Farm

Little Mill, Pontypool NP4 0HQ
LITTLE MILL (049 528) 249

This long, low, sixteenth-century whitewashed building looks out across fields and valleys to the lovely outline of the Gwent Hills. It is in the small village of Little Mill, three miles north-east of Pontypool. The kitchen is a typical farmhouse kitchen: an enormous room with a low, beamed ceiling. Imaginative dinners, including such things as soufflés, curried soup, chicken tarragon and pan-fried sewin (a local trout) are served at 7.30pm in a separate dining-room. Vegetarians can be catered for and the farmhouse is licensed. Next to the kitchen is the guests' part of the house, cleverly converted from a granary. Downstairs there is a large, beamed sitting-room and upstairs are four bedrooms, which are light, bright and decorated with pretty wallpapers. There is a swimming-pool in the garden and a table-tennis table in the barn. No children under four. No pets. No smoking in the dining-room. Car park.

OWNERS Stuart and Ann Bradley OPEN Mar–Nov ROOMS 2 double (1 with bath/shower, 1 with wash-basin), 2 twin (1 with bath/shower, 1 with wash-basin) TERMS B&B £12.50–£16, (single occupancy of twin/double) £17.50–£21 (children under 10 half-price sharing with adults); dinner £9

Pentwyn Farm, Pontypool

RHAYADER Powys map 6

Liverpool House

East Street, Rhayader LD6 5EA
RHAYADER (0597) 810706

Close to the centre of town is this pleasant, double-fronted, turn-of-the-century house with private parking. It is bright and airy and the rooms are all colour-co-ordinated in blue, pink and apricot. All bedrooms have TV. There is a very large sitting-room for guests to relax in. Lunch and dinner, including vegetarian choices, can be provided. Liverpool House is unlicensed, but guests may bring their own wine. Children welcome. No smoking in the dining-room.

OWNER Mrs Ann Griffiths OPEN All year, exc Christmas ROOMS 2 family, 2 double; all rooms, exc 1 double (wash-basin only), with bath/shower TERMS B&B £12–£17.50, (family room) from £32.50 (children half-price sharing with parents); dinner from £5; deposit

Bath/shower in the details under each entry means that the rooms have private facilities.

RHYL Clwyd map 6

Romsley Guest House

8 Butterton Road, Rhyl LL18 1RF
RHYL (0745) 330300

This attractive house, with some unusual Victorian windows, is close to the promenade and beach (it can be noisy). The rooms are colour-co-ordinated; one has an elegant four-poster bed with a lacy canopy, another a colonial bed, and all have TV. The lounge has TV and a marble chess set. The licensed dining-room, where delicious, freshly cooked breakfasts and simple home-style dinners (from 5pm) are served, has been extended. Lunches are also available and vegetarians can be catered for. Blue shark fishing can be arranged; guests who are interested must make a reservation and send a deposit. The house does not have central heating, but each room has individual heaters. Children welcome. No pets. No smoking in the dining-room. Arrangements can be made for guests arriving by train or bus to be met.

OWNERS Mr and Mrs C. E. L. Bill OPEN All year, exc Christmas ROOMS 1 four-poster, 5 double/family, 1 double/single; all rooms with wash-basin TERMS B&B £12–£14 (children 3–12 half-price); dinner £5; deposit £12 per person; balance to be paid on arrival

RUTHIN Clwyd map 6

Gorphwysfa

8A Castle Street, Ruthin LL15 LDP
RUTHIN (082 42) 2748 (from summer 1992: (0824) 702748)

Gorphwysfa, which means 'resting place', is a magnificent house dating from the fifteenth-century and situated 200 yards from Ruthin Castle entrance. This is a most interesting house with many original features, such as wattle and daub walls, carved wood in the hallway from old ship timbers, and an inglenook fireplace. The house is exquisitely furnished and the bedrooms are very spacious, with one enormous family room with *en suite* bathroom. There is an elegant TV lounge, which has window seats and casement shutters, and a reading room with plenty of interesting books to browse through. Breakfast only is served, but there are several places to eat within walking distance. There is limited street parking after 6pm and parking is also available at the town square a short distance away. Guests are given a front-door key so they can come and go as they please. Children welcome. Dogs only.

OWNERS Walter and Eleanor Jones OPEN All year ROOMS 1 family (with bath/shower), 1 double (with wash-basin), 1 twin (with wash-basin) TERMS B&B £13.50–£15 (small children in carry-cots free, children under 14 half-price)

ST DAVID'S Dyfed map 6

Y Glennydd

51 Nun Street, St David's SA62 6NU
ST DAVID'S (0437) 720576

This immaculate, cosy, family-run guesthouse is situated in the centre of St David's and close to the cathedral. The bedrooms, all with TV, are well appointed, and one has an original Victorian fireplace. There is one ground-floor bedroom and a guest lounge with TV. Guests have use of a small bar. Dinners are served 7–8.30pm, and a picnic basket can be made up on request. Vegetarians can be catered for. The house is exceptionally well maintained and Tim and Tracey Foster are a congenial and helpful couple. Children welcome. Guide dogs only.

OWNERS Tim and Tracey Foster OPEN Feb–Dec ROOMS 4 family (with bath/shower), 3 double (1 with bath/shower, 2 with wash-basin), 2 twin (with wash-basin) TERMS B&B £14.50–£17, (single occupancy of twin/double) £16–£30 (children half-price); dinner £10.50; Access, Diners, Visa

SAUNDERSFOOT Dyfed map 6

Primrose Cottage

Stammers Road, Saundersfoot SA69 9HH
SAUNDERSFOOT (0834) 811080

Situated in the centre of Saundersfoot, Primrose Cottage is a pretty Victorian cottage, tastefully modernised. The harbour and beaches are very close. The bedrooms are small, and one has its own bathroom. There is also a guest lounge with TV, lots of books and slides of the area. Itineraries can be worked out or, for people who would prefer a guided tour, Malcolm Quinn is willing to escort people in his car for a modest charge. Breakfast only is served, but there are several eating establishments within walking distance. Hair-dryer, trouser press and iron are available on request. 'Well-behaved' children and pets welcome. No smoking in bedrooms. Car park.

OWNERS Malcolm and Jennifer Quinn OPEN All year, exc Christmas ROOMS 1 double (with bath/shower), 1 twin, 1 single TERMS B&B £13.50–£14.50 (children under 2 free, 2–8 £7); deposit £5 per person

Sandyhill Guest House

Tenby Road, Saundersfoot SA69 9DR
SAUNDERSFOOT (0834) 813165

Sandyhill Guest House was a two-up two-down farmhouse in the seventeenth century and has had various additions over the years. The house is well maintained; the bedrooms are average in size and all have TV and wash-basin. There is a most friendly and welcoming atmosphere. Sandyhill is in a peaceful situation with a beautiful garden and swimming-pool for guests' use. There is a small bar lounge as well as a guest lounge. Evening meals, including vegetarian choices with notice, are served at 6pm. No children under three. Pets by arrangement and not in public rooms. Car park.

OWNERS David and Peggy Edwards OPEN 1 Mar–31 Oct ROOMS 2 family, 2 double, 1 twin; all rooms with wash-basin TERMS B&B £14–£15, (single occupancy of twin/double) £5 supplement (children half-price sharing with parents); D, B&B £18–£20; deposit

SWANSEA West Glamorgan map 6

Acorns Guest House

176 Gower Road, Sketty, Swansea SA2 9HS
SWANSEA (0792) 201345

Set back off the A4118, one and a quarter miles from the town centre, Acorns House is a family-run establishment with a pretty garden and a large oak tree in front of the house. It is in a good position for touring the Gower peninsula. The spacious bedrooms are well appointed and have TV; two now have *en suite* bathroom. The public rooms have solid, dark oak furnishings and include a licensed bar and a reading room with TV. Dinners and packed lunches are available, by prior arrangement only. Vegetarians can be catered for. The owners are local people who speak both Welsh and English. Children welcome. No pets. No smoking in the dining-room and some bedrooms. Car park.

OWNERS P. J. and B. J. Davies OPEN All year, exc Christmas ROOMS 1 family (with wash-basin), 2 double (1 with bath/shower), 1 with wash-basin), 2 twin (1 with bath/shower, 1 with wash-basin), 3 single (with wash-basin) TERMS B&B £16–£18, (single occupancy of twin/double) £22 (children half-price sharing); deposit; Access, Visa

The Bays Guest House

97 Mumbles Road, Norton SA3 5TW
SWANSEA (0792) 404755

This is most attractive turn-of-the-century house is situated in its own grounds in a quiet area of the seaside district of Mumbles and within walking distance of the beach, promenade and most amenities. The house is well appointed and in good decorative order. The bedrooms, two of which have sea views, are individually decorated and colour-co-ordinated. There is a comfortable lounge, overlooking the extensive garden, which has TV and tea- and coffee-making facilities. Breakfast only is available and is served in the conservatory-style garden room. Judy Burrell has created a warm and welcoming atmosphere. Not suitable for young children. No pets. No smoking. Car park.

OWNER Mrs Judy Burrell OPEN All year, exc 25 and 26 Dec ROOMS 2 double (with wash-basin), 1 twin (with bath/shower) TERMS B&B £16–£18, (single occupancy of twin/double) £20–£25; deposit; cheques over banker's limit to be cleared in advance

Tide's Reach Guest House

388 Mumbles Road, Mumbles SA3 5TN
SWANSEA (0792) 404877

Originally built as the Bath House Hotel in 1855, this house has had several owners and has been much altered. The present owners have created a cosy, olde worlde atmosphere. Tide's Reach is pleasantly situated on the sea-front and is a five-minute stroll from the centre of Mumbles. The house is beautifully appointed throughout, with Laura Ashley and Sanderson décor. All bedrooms have TV. There is an elegant lounge, exquisitely furnished with antiques and an original marble fireplace. Evening meals, available June to September, are served at 6.30pm in the attractive dining-room and can include vegetarian choices. Guests are welcome to bring their own wine, which the owners are happy to chill. Children welcome.

OWNERS Jan and William Maybery OPEN All year ROOMS 1 family (with bath/shower), 5 double, 1 twin (with bath/shower)
TERMS B&B £15–£16 (children half-price); dinner £8; deposit 1 night charge

Tredilion House Hotel

26 Uplands Crescent, Uplands, Swansea SA2 0PB
SWANSEA (0792) 470766

This attractive late-Victorian town house has been tastefully converted by the present owners into a comfortable hotel of extremely high standards. The guest lounge has the original moulded ceiling and is attractively decorated with Laura Ashley fabrics and beautiful soft furnishings. Games and books are provided. The well-appointed bedrooms, with traditional pine furnishings, are all *en suite* and have TV, hair-dryer, radio, telephone and pretty blue-pattern wallpapers. Dinner is served at 7pm (ordered by noon) in the pleasant licensed dining-room and features tasty home-style cooking. Vegetarian choices and packed lunches can be provided with notice. There is also a licensed bar with a selection of beers, wines and spirits. For those wishing to avoid the hassle of driving, there is a bus stop just in front of the hotel, with a frequent service to the town centre. Children welcome. No pets in the public rooms; small, well-behaved dogs allowed in bedrooms. Car park.

OWNERS Dorothy and Paul Mesner OPEN All year
ROOMS 1 family, 2 double, 1 twin, 3 single; all rooms with bath/shower TERMS B&B £24–£25, (single) £32.50–£39 (children under 3 free, over 3 £6 in family room); dinner £12.50; deposit 1 night charge; Access, Visa

Uplands Court Guest House

134 Eaton Crescent, Uplands, Swansea SA1 4QR
SWANSEA (0792) 473046

This attractive Edwardian property with stained-glass windows is on a quiet residential street. The bedrooms are basic, clean and functional, all with TV and radio-alarm. There is a licensed guest lounge and dinner is served Monday to Thursday throughout winter at 6pm. Vegetarians can be catered for by arrangement and packed lunches can be provided. Children welcome. No pets. No smoking in the dining-room.

OWNERS Allan and Susan Gray OPEN All year ROOMS 2 family (1 with shower), 2 double (1 with shower), 1 twin, 3 single (1 with shower); 5 rooms with wash-basin TERMS B&B £16, (single occupancy of twin/double) £20 (children under 3 free, 3–14 half-price); dinner £7; deposit £10 per person; Access, Visa

TALSARNAU Gwynedd map 6

Tegfan

Llandecwyn, Talsarnau, nr Harlech LL47 6YG
PENRHYNDEUDRAETH (0766) 771354

This attractive house is set in a peaceful location, on the A496, two miles from Porthmadog. The rooms are well appointed and furnished in pine. The top-floor loft room is exceptionally spacious, with sun-roof windows and armchairs in which to relax and enjoy the magnificent views. The separate double *en suite* room in the ground-floor annexe is ideal for anyone wanting a little extra privacy. There is a guest lounge with open log fires on chilly days. No children under 10. No pets. No smoking. Car park.

OWNERS Dawn and Roy King OPEN All year, exc Christmas ROOMS 1 family (with bath/shower), 3 double (with wash-basin) TERMS B&B £12–£14; deposit

TALYBONT Powys map 6

Brynhyfryd

Talybont LD3 7JA
TALYBONT-ON-USK (0874) 87230

Brynhyfryd, which means 'pretty house on the hill', is an elegant residence built in 1860, overlooking the beautiful Usk Valley. The house is surrounded by 14 acres and guests can walk down to the canal from the house. The bedrooms are attractively decorated with matching wallpaper and fabrics. Two of the bedrooms are *en suite* and there are plenty of facilities for the remaining two; all rooms have solid, old-fashioned furnishings. Excellent breakfasts are served on bone china with linen napkins. Packed lunches can be provided if required. This is an ideal base from which to explore the Black Mountains and the Brecon Beacons and is an excellent choice for walkers. Children welcome. Pets by arrangement. Car park.

OWNER Mrs E. M. Evans OPEN All year ROOMS 2 family (with bath/shower), 1 double (with wash-basin), 1 twin (with wash-basin) TERMS B&B £15–£16, (family room) £20, (children under 14 half-price); deposit 20%

TENBY Dyfed map 6

High Seas

8 The Norton, Tenby SA70 8AA
TENBY (0834) 3611

High Seas was built in 1850 and is on the North Beach, facing the sea. The house is comfortable, and the atmosphere is pleasant and informal. The rooms, most with sea views, have solid, old-fashioned furnishings. All have TV. There is an attractive, spacious lounge with original cornices, covings, an antique couch and a baby grand piano which guests with the expertise are welcome to play. Excellent, freshly prepared breakfasts are served, enough to set you up for the day. Children welcome. No pets.

OWNERS J. D. and M. MacDonald OPEN May–Sept
ROOMS 2 family (1 with bath/shower), 4 double (3 with bath/shower)
TERMS B&B £14–£16 (children under 5 free, 5–12 half-price)

Tall Ships Hotel

Victoria Street, Tenby SA70 7DY
TENBY (0834) 2055

This small, friendly hotel is 50 yards from the beach. The rooms are spacious, with pretty bedspreads; all have TV and armchairs in which to relax. The cellar has a large anchor for a support beam, and other beams are timbers from various boats. There is a pleasant lounge, with plenty of reading material. Excellent home-cooked dinners are served at 6.30pm and vegetarians can be catered for by prior arrangement. Children welcome. No pets. No smoking in the dining-room.

OWNERS Mr and Mrs Richards OPEN Mar–end Oct
ROOMS 6 family (5 with bath/shower, 1 with wash-basin), 2 double (1 with bath/shower, 1 with wash-basin), 1 single (with wash-basin)
TERMS B&B £13–£18.50 (children under 3 £20 per week, 3–13 half-price); dinner £6.50; deposit £20 per adult, £10 per child, per week; Visa

TINTERN Gwent map 6

The Old Rectory

Tintern, Chepstow NP6 6SG
TINTERN (0291) 689519

There are beautiful views of the River Wye and its valley from the Old Rectory. The house has five comfortable bedrooms with new furniture and a separate sitting-room for guests. Log fires are lit in winter, and the house has its own spring water. There is a free and easy atmosphere and children are welcome. Dinner is available at 6.30pm and vegetarian choices can be provided. There is no licence, but guests may bring their own wine to dinner. Packed lunches can be arranged. Pets by arrangement. Smoking in guests' sitting-room only. Car park.

OWNERS Tony and Maureen Newman OPEN All year, exc Christmas and New Year ROOMS 2 double (with wash-basin), 2 twin (1 with wash-basin), 1 single (with wash-basin) TERMS B&B £12.50, (single occupancy of twin/double) £19–£23 (children half-price sharing with adults); dinner £7.50; deposit £5 per person

TREARDDUR BAY Gwynedd (Anglesey) map 6

Moranedd Guest House

Trearddur Road, Trearddur Bay, Anglesey LL65 2UE
TREARDDUR BAY (0407) 860324

The beach, shops and golf course are a five-minute walk from this lovely house in a quiet cul-de-sac. The bedrooms are large and well furnished and there is a spacious lounge with TV. Breakfast only is served in the bright dining-room, but a portfolio in the lounge lists local restaurants. There is a terrace that overlooks the three-quarters of an acre of garden where guests are welcome to sit out and have a drink on fine days. Children welcome. Dogs only by arrangement. Car park.

OWNER Mrs Sheila Wathan OPEN All year ROOMS 2 double, 3 twin, 1 single; all rooms with wash-basin TERMS B&B £12–£14, (single occupancy of twin/double) £16–£20 (children half-price sharing with adults)

Where a single-occupancy rate is not specified in the details, the cost will be the same as that per person in a twin or double room, or will be included in the range of prices given.

TREMADOG Gwynedd map 6

Gwynys

Tremadog, Porthmadog LL49 9RN
PORTHMADOG (0766) 512594

This attractive turn-of-the-century house is in its own grounds, set back from the A487 half a mile from Porthmadog. There are two comfortable, tastefully decorated bedrooms, one of which is very large, and a lounge with TV. There is an interesting display of county arms and two antique bed-warmers in the hall. Breakfast only is served and packed lunches can be provided. Guests are greeted with a cup of tea or coffee on arrival. Children over three preferred. No pets. No smoking in bedrooms. Car park.

OWNER Mrs Nia Evans OPEN Easter–mid-Oct ROOMS 2 double, 1 twin; all rooms with wash-basin TERMS B&B £12.50 (children under 3 free, 4–10 half-price); deposit

WELSHPOOL Powys map 6

Gungrog House

Rhallt, Welshpool SY21 9HS
WELSHPOOL (0938) 553381

Gungrog House is a 300-year-old stone-built farmhouse in an elevated position, with magnificent views of the Severn Valley. It is only two miles from Welshpool and is part of a 21-acre farm. The house is comfortably and traditionally furnished and the rooms are spacious, with oak floors. Breakfast and evening meals, served at 6.30pm, are taken in the large beamed dining-room. All the dishes are home-made, and most vegetables come from the garden. There is no alcohol licence, but guests may bring their own wine to dinner. Vegetarian choices can be provided and packed lunches arranged. Guests may use the spacious, comfortable TV lounge. Children welcome. No pets. Restrictions on smoking. Car park.

OWNERS Stan and Eira Jones OPEN Mar–Oct ROOMS 1 family, 1 double; both rooms with bath/shower TERMS B&B £15–£17 (children 2–5 one-third-price, 5–12 half-price); dinner £9; deposit £10

It is always best to book a room in advance, especially in winter. Establishments with few rooms may close at short notice for periods not specified in the details.

Montgomery House

43 Salop Road, Welshpool SY21 7DX
WELSHPOOL (0938) 552693

Montgomery House is an immaculate hotel run by a mother-daughter team and is within easy walking distance of the town centre and railway station. The bedrooms, although rather small, are bright, colour-co-ordinated and decorated with Laura Ashley wallpapers. The back rooms have views of the surrounding countryside. Tasty breakfasts are served in the small, cosy dining-room. The hotel is well located for the narrow-gauge railway. Children welcome. No pets. Car park.

OWNERS M. G. and A. Kaye OPEN All year, exc Christmas
ROOMS 2 family, 1 double, 1 twin TERMS B&B £12.50, (single occupancy of twin/double) £13.50 (children £9); deposit £5 per room

Severn Farm

Welshpool SY21 7BB
WELSHPOOL (0938) 553098

This modernised farmhouse was originally a small cottage and has been extended over the years. It is on the outskirts of Welshpool and commands a superb view of the Long Mountains and Severn Valley. Guests have their own entrance to the house. The bedrooms are basic, but clean and functional. Substantial breakfasts are served at an elongated table in a cosy dining-room. Dinner is available and offers simple home-style cooking using fresh local produce and meat. Vegetarians can be catered for. There is no licence, but guests may bring their own wine to dinner. Packed lunches can be provided. Children welcome. Pets by arrangement. Car park.

OWNERS Joyce and Alun Jones OPEN All year, exc Christmas
ROOMS 1 family, 1 double, 1 twin; all rooms with wash-basin
TERMS B&B from £12.50, (single occupancy of twin/double) from £13 (reductions for children); dinner £7

Reduced rates for children are normally given when they share their parents' bedroom. If no reductions are specified in the details or text, assume you'll have to pay full rates.

Bath/shower information in the details refers only to a private bathroom or shower; other bathroom facilities at the establishments will be shared. We say if rooms have wash-basins.

Tynllwyn Farm

Welshpool SY21 9BW
WELSHPOOL (0938) 553175

The farm is about a mile from Welshpool and has an attractive garden, with a pond and fountain. It is mainly a dairy farm, but there are chickens, peacocks, pheasants, ducks, geese, calves and a goat. The farmhouse dates from 1861 and has beautiful views of the Severn Valley and Long Mountains. The spacious bedrooms are well furnished and decorated to a high standard. The comfortable guest lounge houses an interesting brass and plate collection. Large, farmhouse-style dinners (6.30pm) are served in the pleasant licensed dining-room and feature home-produced honey, eggs and fresh vegetables in season, as well as home-made puddings. Vegetarian choices can be provided. Packed lunches can be arranged. Children welcome. Pets by arrangement. Car park.

OWNER Mrs Freda Emberton OPEN All year, exc Christmas
ROOMS 2 family, 2 double, 2 twin; all rooms with wash-basin
TERMS B&B £12.50 (reductions for children under 10); dinner £7.50

The Channel Islands

ROZEL BAY Jersey map 1

La Petite Chaire

Rozel Bay
JERSEY (0534) 62682

La Petite Chaire is a converted coach-house, four and a half miles from St Helier and situated within 100 yards of the lovely unspoilt bay, which offers safe bathing, good rod fishing and is an ideal spot for sub-aqua sports. Some of the bedrooms have leaded windows and views of the bay. The lounge, bar and dining-room have been decorated in classic cottage style. There is a furnished sun terrace for guests' use. All bedrooms are *en suite* with six on the ground floor. Breakfast and set evening meals (from 6.30pm) offer home-style cooking using fresh produce. Packed lunches are available and vegetarians can be catered for. There are several buses a day to St Helier. Children welcome. Small dogs only. Car park.

OWNERS Mr and Mrs Michieli OPEN May–Oct ROOMS 1 family, 11 double, 2 twin; all rooms with bath/shower TERMS B&B £18–£23, (single occupancy of twin/double) £28–£31 (children under 3 half-price, under 10 one-third reduction); dinner £5; deposit

ST AUBIN Jersey map 1

Au Caprice

La Haule, St Aubin
JERSEY (0534) 20334/22083

This is a small, friendly hotel opposite a large, safe and sandy beach. St Helier is about a 15-minute drive away and there is a regular bus service. The bedrooms are bright and airy, most of them with sea views. There is a spacious dining-room facing the sea and drinks can be obtained from a bar lounge. Lunch and evening meals (6.30pm) are available and packed lunches can be provided. There is also a small, cosy sun lounge with wicker furnishings for guests' use. Afternoon tea and morning coffee are served. Children welcome. No pets. Car parking available across the road.

OWNER Mr Peter Deffains OPEN Feb–Nov ROOMS 8 double (6 with bath/shower, 2 with wash-basin), 5 twin (4 with bath/shower, 1 with wash-basin), 1 single (with wash-basin) TERMS B&B £15–£22 (children half-price sharing with parents); dinner £6; deposit

ST HELIER Jersey map 1

La Bonne Vie

Roseville Street, St Helier
JERSEY (0534) 35955

La Bonne Vie has been decorated to a very high standard; the décor and matching fabrics, all designed and made by Mrs Hetherington, are especially attractive. One of the bedrooms has an antique brass bed, another an elegant four-poster. All bedrooms have TV and there are extra touches, such as home-made fudge, for guests. Breakfast only is served. The elegant dining-room has linen table-cloths and napkins. The guest lounge has an Adam-style fireplace. No children under five. No pets. No smoking in the dining-room.

OWNERS Mr and Mrs Hetherington OPEN Mar–end Nov ROOMS 1 family, 2 four-poster, 6 double, 1 twin, 3 single; all rooms, exc 1 single (wash-basin only), with bath/shower TERMS B&B £15–£22.50 (children 6–12 25% reduction: deposit; Access, Visa

ST MARTIN Jersey map 1

Le Relais de St Martin

St Martin's House, St Martin
JERSEY (0534) 53271

Dating from 1490, this lovely granite house stands opposite the beautiful St Martin's church and is said to be one of the oldest dwellings on the island. Set in two and a half acres of lawns and gardens with swimming-pool and boules, the house is a mile from the fishing village of Rozel and the harbour of Gorey with its beautiful castle, Mont Orgueil. Gerald Durrell's world-famous zoo is only two miles away. The dining-room and bar (with billiard table) are beamed and have granite fireplaces. Packed lunches and good-value, home-style evening meals (from 6.30pm) are served, using home-grown produce. Vegetarians can be catered for by prior arrangement. There are also three self-catering flats available. Stays between April and October are on half-board basis only. Guide dogs only. Car park.

OWNERS Mr and Mrs J. Gicquel OPEN All year ROOMS 4 family, 4 double, 3 single; all rooms with bath/shower TERMS B&B £18.25–£24 (children under 3 £3, 3–7 half-price, 8–10 25% reduction); dinner £8.25; deposit; balance of payment due 21 days prior to arrival

ST MARTIN'S Guernsey map 1

Saints Farm

Icart Road, St Martinls
GUERNSEY (0481) 38472

This is a fifteenth-century farmhouse on a 50-acre dairy farm, set in the midst of farmland bordering cliffs with views of the sea. The farm itself has been in the family for around 90 years. The house is beamed and has modern furniture. Breakfast only is served in the dining-room overlooking the peaceful garden, and packed lunches can be provided on request. This is a lovely part of the island – the walk from the farm to Icart Bay with its lovely views is highly recommended. Book early as this is a very popular place to stay. No children under one. No pets. No smoking in the dining-room. Car park.

OWNERS Mr and Mrs G. J. Browning OPEN May–Oct
ROOMS 1 family, 2 double, 1 twin, 1 single; all rooms with wash-basin
TERMS B&B £15 (children half-price sharing parents' room)

Wellesley Hotel

Route de Sausmarez, St Martin's
GUERNSEY (0481) 38028 Fax (0481) 39501

This charming country house was built in 1887 and is set in attractive grounds. A pleasant stroll through the gardens leads to beautiful Fermain Bay, where you can take a boat or walk along the cliff path to St Peter Port. All the bedrooms are well appointed and have hair-dryer, TV and telephone. The elegant drawing-room has a cast-iron fireplace and a selection of oil paintings. There is a separate smoking lounge, with games and a billiard table. Breakfast only is available and is served in the oak-panelled dining-room. Children welcome. Guide dogs only. Car park.

OWNERS Mr and Mrs J. E. P. Chattell OPEN May–Oct
ROOMS 3 family, 1 double, 4 twin, 2 single; all rooms, exc family room, with bath/shower TERMS B&B £25.30–£28.05, (single) £27.50–£30.80 (children half-price); deposit

We asked the proprietors to estimate their 1992 prices in the autumn of 1991, so the rates may have changed since publication.

Bath/shower information in the details refers only to a private bathroom or shower; other bathroom facilities at the establishments will be shared.

ST OUEN Jersey map 1

Lecq Farm Guest House

Leoville, St Ouen
JERSEY (0534) 481745

This Jersey longhouse dates from the 1700s and is set in peaceful countryside, with a large landscaped garden full of mature shrubs, trees and flowers. Mrs Renouf has been running her bed and breakfast business for over 30 years and has established a steady clientele of satisfied customers, so early reservation is recommended. There is a Jersey granite fireplace in both the dining-room and lounge, used on cool days. The bedrooms are of a good size and are very comfortable. Breakfast only is served, but there are several pubs within a few minutes' drive. Greve de Lecq Bay, one of the most popular spots on the island, is a 10-minute walk away, and there is a frequent bus service from here to the town centre. Children welcome. Car park.

OWNERS Mr and Mrs D. C. Renouf OPEN Mar–Nov
ROOMS 1 family, 3 double, 1 twin, 3 single; all rooms with wash-basin
TERMS B&B £11.75–£13 (children under 6 half-price, 6–12 one-third reduction); deposit

ST PETER PORT Guernsey map 1

Kenwood House

Allez Street, St Peter Port
GUERNSEY (0481) 726146

This listed property, built in 1840, is in an excellent location, just five minutes from the beach and shops. The bedrooms are well appointed, have been individually decorated and are comfortably furnished. Bedrooms without private bathroom are on the top floor. The dining-room, where a substantial breakfast is served, overlooks the garden and the lounge for guests' use has an original fireplace and TV. Packed lunches can be provided by prior arrangement, and afternoon tea is served 3.30–5pm. The house is

Any smoking restrictions that we know of are given in each entry.

It is always best to book a room in advance, especially in winter. B&Bs with few rooms may close at short notice for periods not specified in the details.

well maintained and there is a public car park close by. No children under 10. No pets. No smoking in the dining-room.

OWNERS Mr A. J. and Mrs V. A. L. Rout OPEN All year, exc Christmas ROOMS 1 family (with wash-basin), 3 double (2 with bath/shower, 1 with wash-basin), 3 twin (2 with bath/shower, 1 with wash-basin) TERMS B&B £12–£20, (single occupancy of twin/double) £15–£26 (children half-price sharing with adults); deposit

Marine Hotel

Well Road, St Peter Port
GUERNSEY (0481) 724978

This is a family-run hotel situated 30 yards from the sea-front and new marina. A few minutes' walk away is St Peter Port's picturesque shopping centre, with a bus terminus for island tours. Most of the public rooms have sea views, as do the well-appointed, predominately pink bedrooms. TV in the beedroom is optional at a modest charge. There is also a furnished sun patio for guests' use. The TV lounge has a bookcase which runs the length of the room, with a good selection of books. The Marine Hotel also boasts the only red telephone box on the island. Excellent breakfasts include kippers, various cheeses and yoghurts as well as a full cooked breakfast. Packed lunches are also available. There is a car park nearby. Children welcome. No pets. No smoking in the dining-room.

OWNERS Margaret and Arthur Clegg OPEN All year
ROOMS 3 family, 4 double, 3 twin, 1 single; all rooms with bath/shower TERMS B&B £13.50–£21, (single occupancy of twin/double) £14.75–£26.50 (children under 5 half-price, 5–10 25% reduction sharing parents' room); deposit

Midhurst House

Candie Road, St Peter Port
GUERNSEY (0481) 724391

This listed hotel was originally a Regency town house and has been tastefully decorated and furnished in keeping with the period. The garden is secluded within its flower-clad granite walls, and flowers are always in abundance; the residents' lounge, which leads out to the garden, was designed to achieve an indoor-garden atmosphere. Midhurst House is in possibly the best residential area of St Peter Port, adjacent to Candie Gardens. Brian and Jan Goodenough have acquired a reputation for very high standards of comfort and, notably, for the quality of meals served in the licensed dining-room (and always with fresh flowers on the tables). Dinner is served at 7pm and the home-made soups, rolls, mousses, ice-creams and featherlight pastries are superb. Packed lunches are available, and vegetarians and special diets can be catered for on request. All the bedrooms have TV and telephone. Early reservation is essential as this is a very popular venue. No children under eight. No pets. No smoking in the dining-room. Garaging available for cars.

OWNERS Brian and Jan Goodenough OPEN Easter–end Oct
ROOMS 1 family, 3 double, 3 twin; all rooms with bath/shower
TERMS B&B £22–£28, (single occupancy of twin/double) £29–£35 (children 8–10 half-price sharing with adults); dinner £8; deposit

ST SAMPSON Guernsey map 1

Bordeaux Guest House

Bordeaux Bay, Vale, nr St Sampson
GUERNSEY (0481) 47461

Bordeaux Guest House is situated in the quiet and picturesque fishing harbour of Bordeaux and Roy and Helen Ackrill are a

couple from London who took over the hotel in April 1991 and have been gradually improving and upgrading the house. Three of the seven bedrooms have four-poster beds and one has an enormous brass bed; all have TV and private facilities. There is a guest lounge with a real fire and a small bar lounge. Home-cooked dinners are served by request 6–8.30pm in the dining-room, which still retains its Victorian marble fireplace. Packed lunches are available and vegetarians can be catered for. Arrangements can be made to meet guests at the airport or harbour. There is a bus service to St Peter Port outside the hotel. Children welcome. Pets by arrangement. Car park.

OWNERS Roy and Helen Ackrill OPEN All year ROOMS 2 family, 3 four-poster, 1 double, 1 twin; all rooms with bath/shower TERMS B&B £17.50 (children under 5 free, 5–15 half-price); dinner £6; deposit; Access, Amex, Visa

ST SAVIOUR Guernsey map 1

Les Piques Farm Guest House

Les Piques, St Saviour
GUERNSEY (0481) 64515

This fifteenth-century farmhouse and outbuildings have been sympathetically converted into an absolutely delightful guesthouse. There is an extensive, beautifully landscaped garden with several sitting areas and a croquet lawn. The dining area is spread over three rooms and includes a conservatory and a stone-walled dining-room with a huge stone fireplace. There are three beamed bedrooms in the oldest part of the house; all have *en suite* bathroom, trouser press, hair-dryer and TV. There are eight ground-floor bedrooms, all overlooking the rear garden. Guests can enjoy a drink in the friendly atmosphere of the beamed bar room. Dinner is served at 6.30pm and includes vegetarian options. A packed lunch can also be provided. No children under 10. No pets. Car park.

OWNER J. T. D. Trimbee OPEN Apr–end Oct ROOMS 13 double, 10 twin, 2 single; all rooms with bath/shower TERMS B&B £20–£30.50; dinner £9.50; deposit

B&B rates specified in the details for each entry are per person per night; unless the details state otherwise, they are based on two people sharing a double or twin-bedded room.

SARK map 1

Hivernage

Sark
SARK (0481) 832000

Hivernage, which means 'winter's rest', has been a guesthouse since 1914. It is situated on the west coast of the island and has splendid views of the adjacent island; there are some lovely secluded walks and beauty spots nearly. Visitors to Sark arrive by boat; there are no paved roads or motorised vehicles other than the tractors which pull you up from the dock or, if pre-arranged, the farm tractor to take you where you are staying. There are bicycles for hire and, as the island is quite small, it is very easy to walk everywhere. Boating trips around the island and horse and carriage trips can also be arranged. There are seven comfortable bedrooms (three are on the ground floor) and a conservatory/ lounge, as well as a bar. Dinner is served at 7pm, if pre-arranged, and vegetarians can be catered for. A packed lunch can also be provided. There are several restaurants on the island. Mr Carre is the local harbourmaster. Children welcome. No pets.

OWNER Mrs Marilyn Carre OPEN Easter–end Sept
ROOMS 1 family, 2 double, 2 twin, 2 single; all rooms with wash-basin
TERMS B&B £14 (children under 3 free); dinner £12; deposit

Indexes

Towns and villages

B&Bs

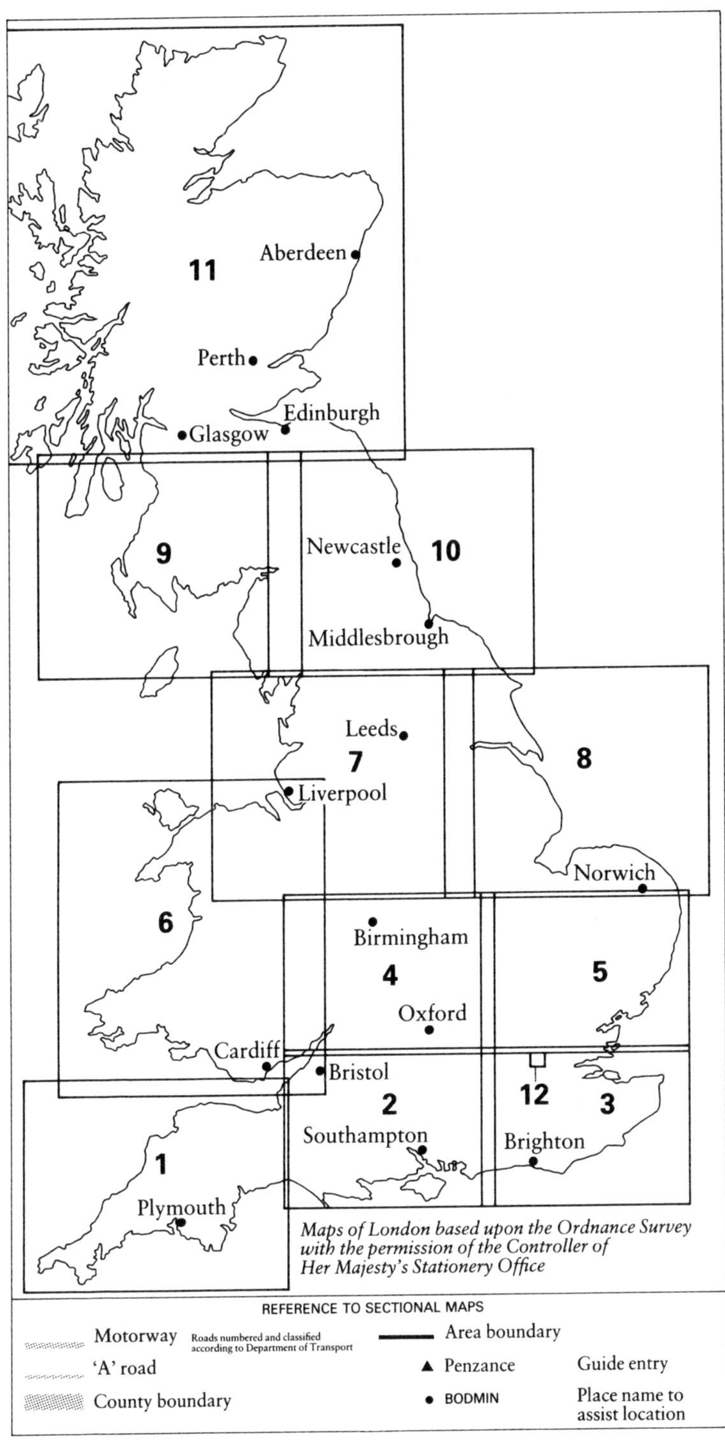
11
Aberdeen
Perth
Edinburgh
Glasgow
9
Newcastle
10
Middlesbrough
Leeds
7
8
Liverpool
6
Norwich
Birmingham
4
5
Oxford
Cardiff
Bristol
12
2
3
Southampton
Brighton
1
Plymouth
REFERENCE TO SECTIONAL MAPS
Motorway
Roads numbered and classified according to Department of Transport
'A' road
County boundary
Area boundary
Penzance
Guide entry
BODMIN
Place name to assist location

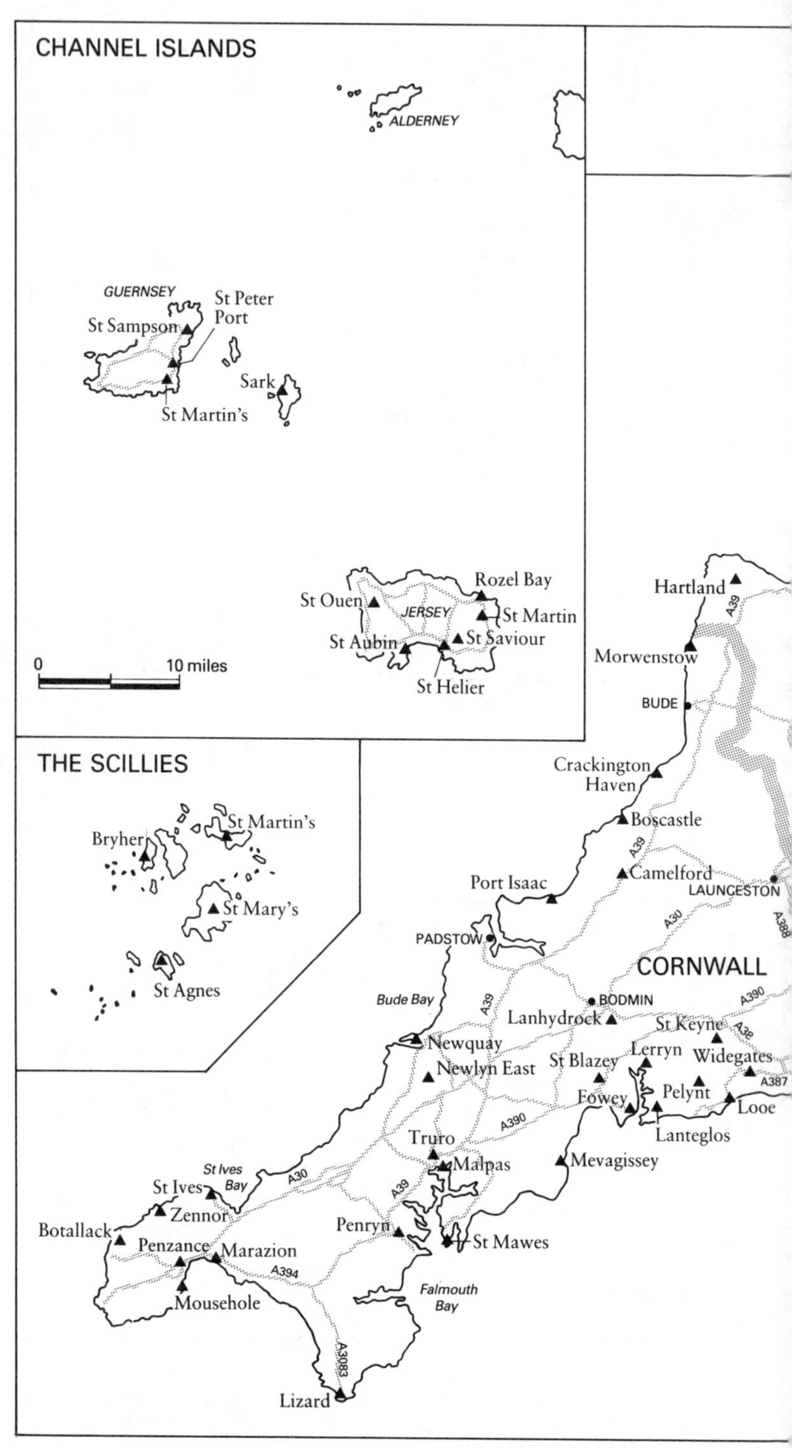
CHANNEL ISLANDS
ALDERNEY
GUERNSEY
St Sampson
St Peter Port
St Martin's
Sark
St Ouen
JERSEY
Rozel Bay
St Martin
St Aubin
St Saviour
St Helier
0
10 miles
THE SCILLIES
Bryher
St Martin's
St Mary's
St Agnes
Hartland
A39
Morwenstow
BUDE
Crackington Haven
Boscastle
A39
Camelford
LAUNCESTON
Port Isaac
A30
A388
PADSTOW
CORNWALL
Bude Bay
A39
BODMIN
A390
Lanhydrock
St Keyne
A38
Newquay
Lerryn
Widegates
St Blazey
Newlyn East
A387
Pelynt
Fowey
Looe
A390
Lanteglos
Truro
Malpas
Mevagissey
St Ives Bay
A30
St Ives
A39
Zennor
Penryn
Botallack
St Mawes
Penzance
Marazion
A394
Falmouth Bay
Mousehole
A3083
Lizard

MAP 1

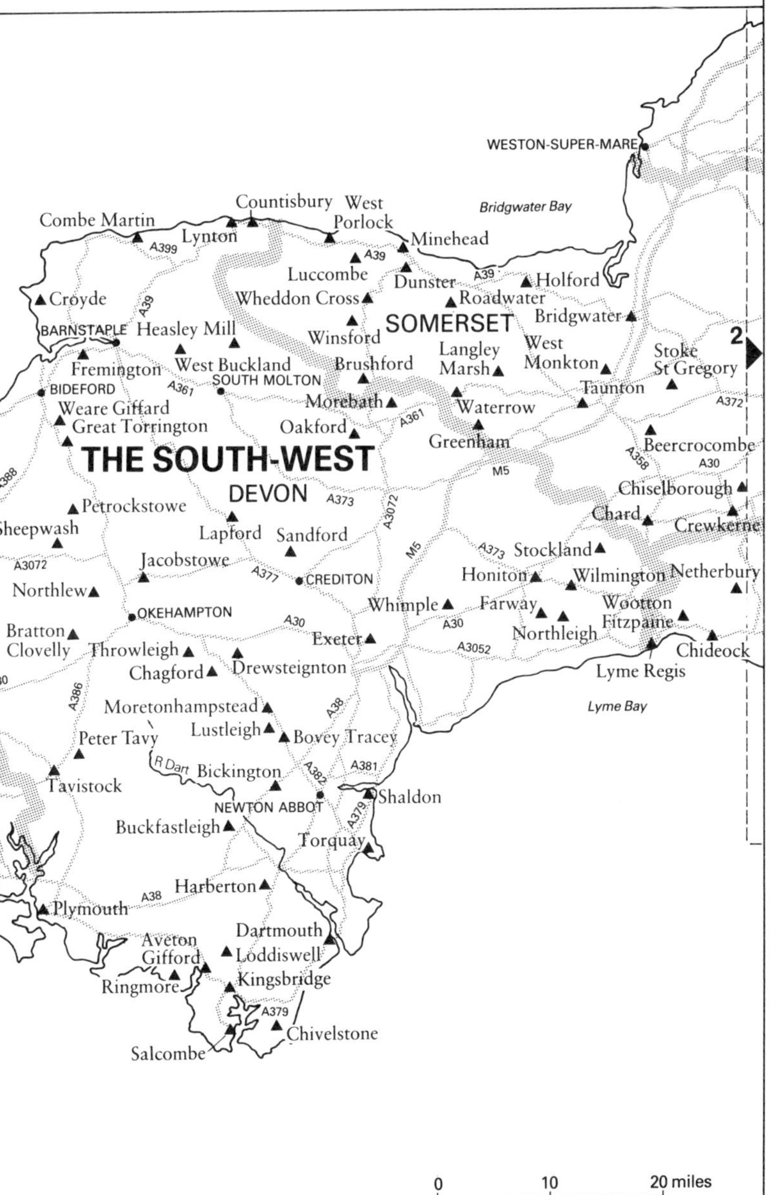

THE SOUTH-WEST
DEVON
SOMERSET
WESTON-SUPER-MARE
Bridgwater Bay
Lyme Bay
Combe Martin
Countisbury
West Porlock
Lynton
Minehead
Luccombe
Dunster
Holford
Croyde
Wheddon Cross
Roadwater
Bridgwater
BARNSTAPLE
Heasley Mill
Winsford
West Buckland
Fremington
Langley Marsh
West Monkton
Stoke St Gregory
Brushford
SOUTH MOLTON
BIDEFORD
Morebath
Taunton
Weare Giffard
Waterrow
Great Torrington
Oakford
Greenham
Beercrocombe
Chiselborough
Petrockstowe
Chard
Crewkerne
Sheepwash
Lapford
Sandford
Stockland
Jacobstowe
CREDITON
Honiton
Wilmington
Netherbury
Northlew
Whimple
Farway
Wootton Fitzpaine
OKEHAMPTON
Bratton Clovelly
Exeter
Northleigh
Chideock
Throwleigh
Drewsteignton
Lyme Regis
Chagford
Moretonhampstead
Lustleigh
Bovey Tracey
Peter Tavy
R Dart
Bickington
Tavistock
NEWTON ABBOT
Shaldon
Buckfastleigh
Torquay
Harberton
Plymouth
Dartmouth
Aveton Gifford
Loddiswell
Kingsbridge
Ringmore
Chivelstone
Salcombe
A399
A39
A361
A388
A373
A3072
M5
A377
A30
A3052
A38
A386
A382
A381
A379
A358
A372
2
0
10
20 miles

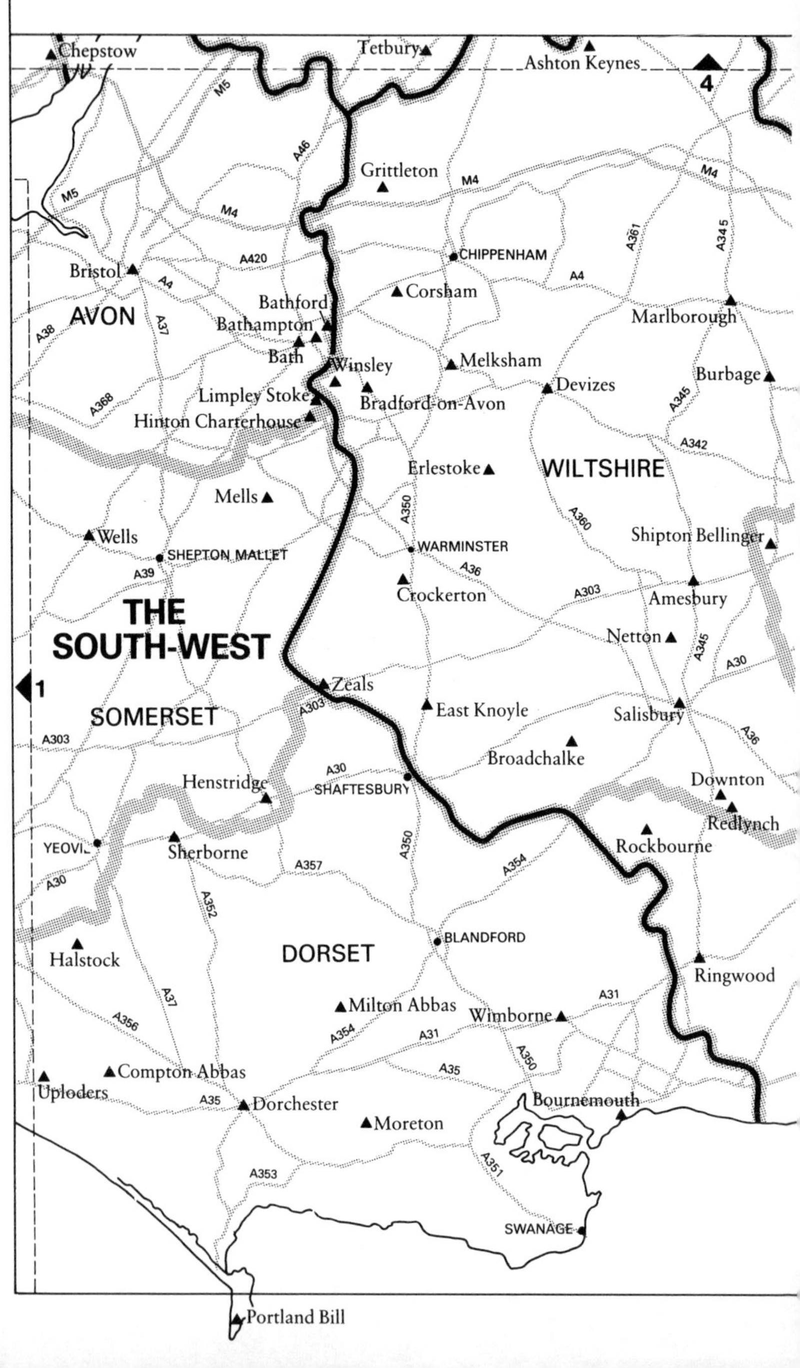
Chepstow
Tetbury
Ashton Keynes
4
M5
A46
Grittleton
M4
M4
M5
M4
CHIPPENHAM
A361
A345
A420
Bristol
A4
A4
Bathford
Corsham
Marlborough
AVON
A37
Bathampton
A38
Bath
Winsley
Melksham
Burbage
Devizes
A368
Limpley Stoke
Bradford-on-Avon
A345
Hinton Charterhouse
A342
Erlestoke
WILTSHIRE
Mells
A350
A360
Wells
WARMINSTER
Shipton Bellinger
SHEPTON MALLET
A39
A36
Crockerton
A303
Amesbury
THE
SOUTH-WEST
Netton
A345
A30
1
Zeals
A303
East Knoyle
Salisbury
SOMERSET
A303
A36
Broadchalke
A30
Henstridge
SHAFTESBURY
Downton
Redlynch
Rockbourne
YEOVIL
Sherborne
A350
A357
A354
A30
A352
BLANDFORD
Halstock
DORSET
Ringwood
A37
Milton Abbas
A31
Wimborne
A356
A354
A31
A350
A35
Compton Abbas
Uploders
A35
Dorchester
Bournemouth
Moreton
A351
A353
SWANAGE
Portland Bill

MAP 2

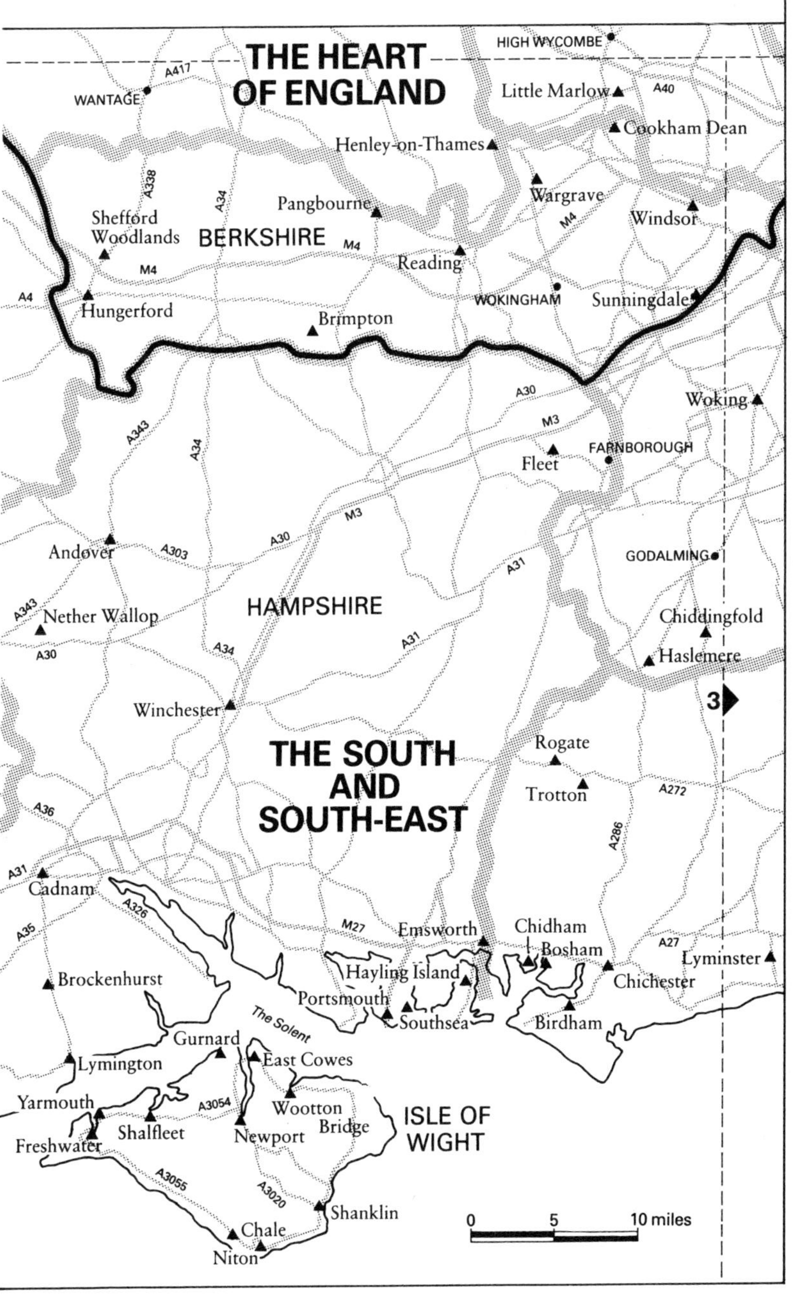

THE HEART OF ENGLAND
HIGH WYCOMBE
WANTAGE
A417
Little Marlow
A40
Cookham Dean
Henley-on-Thames
A338
A34
Pangbourne
Wargrave
Windsor
M4
Shefford Woodlands
BERKSHIRE
M4
Reading
M4
A4
Hungerford
Brimpton
WOKINGHAM
Sunningdale
A30
Woking
M3
A343
A34
FARNBOROUGH
Fleet
M3
A30
Andover
A303
A31
GODALMING
A343
Nether Wallop
HAMPSHIRE
Chiddingfold
A30
A34
A31
Haslemere
3
Winchester
THE SOUTH AND SOUTH-EAST
Rogate
Trotton
A272
A36
A286
A31
Cadnam
A326
A35
M27
Emsworth
Chidham
Bosham
A27
Lyminster
Brockenhurst
Hayling Island
Chichester
Portsmouth
Southsea
Birdham
The Solent
Gurnard
Lymington
East Cowes
Yarmouth
A3054
Wootton Bridge
ISLE OF WIGHT
Shalfleet
Newport
Freshwater
A3055
A3020
Shanklin
0
5
10 miles
Chale
Niton

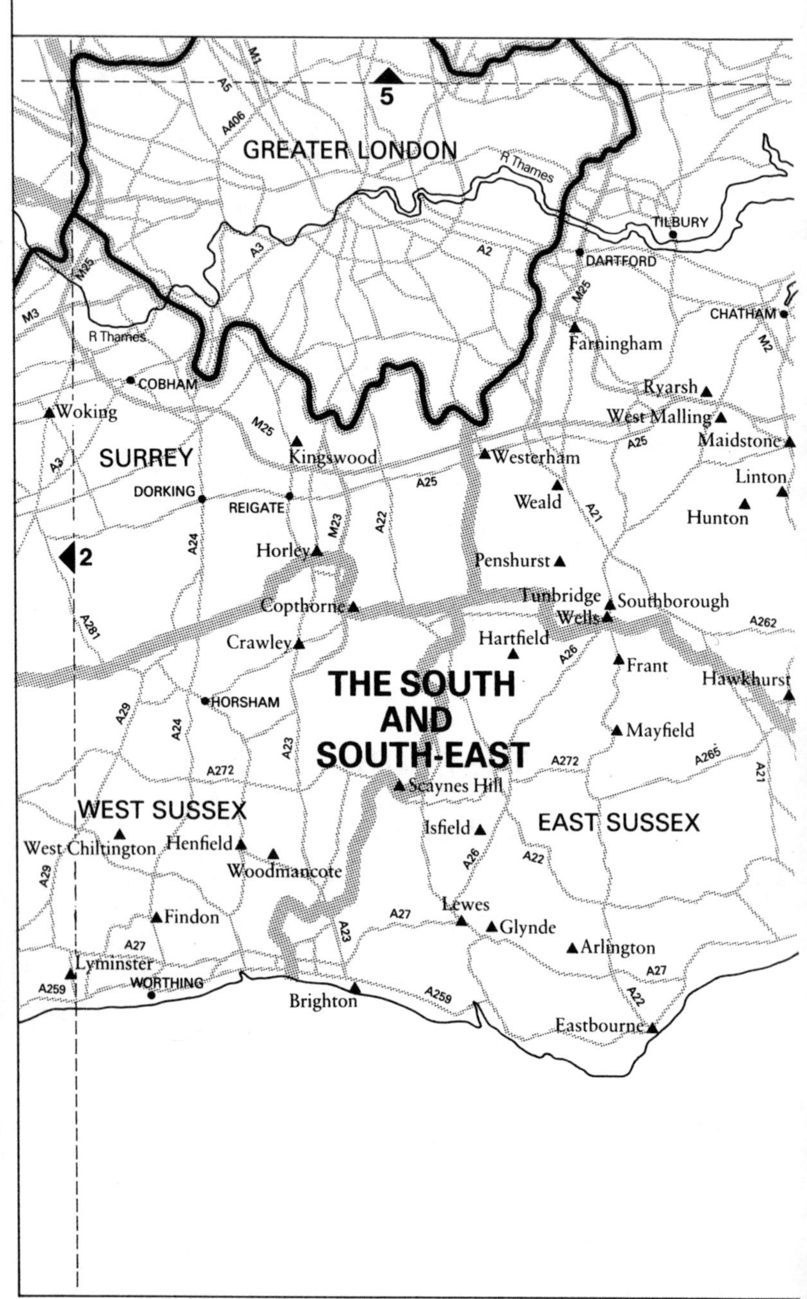
5
GREATER LONDON
R Thames
TILBURY
DARTFORD
CHATHAM
M1
A5
A406
A3
A2
M25
M3
R Thames
Farningham
M2
COBHAM
Ryarsh
Woking
West Malling
M25
Maidstone
A25
SURREY
Kingswood
Westerham
A3
Linton
A25
DORKING
REIGATE
Weald
Hunton
A21
M23
A22
A24
Horley
2
Penshurst
Tunbridge Wells
Southborough
Copthorne
A281
A262
Crawley
Hartfield
A26
Frant
Hawkhurst
THE SOUTH AND SOUTH-EAST
HORSHAM
A29
A24
Mayfield
A23
A272
A265
A272
A21
Scaynes Hill
WEST SUSSEX
Isfield
EAST SUSSEX
West Chiltington
Henfield
Woodmancote
A29
A26
A22
Lewes
A27
Findon
Glynde
A23
Arlington
A27
A27
Lyminster
WORTHING
A259
Brighton
A259
A22
Eastbourne

MAP 3

ESSEX
Southend-on-Sea
THAMES
Sheerness
MARGATE
HERNE BAY
Westgate-on-Sea
A2
M2
A2
Wormshill
Canterbury
Otterden
KENT
A28
A256
Deal
Petham
Charing
A247
A2
A258
Great Chart
ASHFORD
Smarden
Bethersden
A20
A20
Dover
Mersham
Biddenden
Cranbrook
A28
STRAIT OF DOVER
Stone-in-Oxney
Rye
A28
Icklesham
Winchelsea
A259
HASTINGS
0
5
10 miles

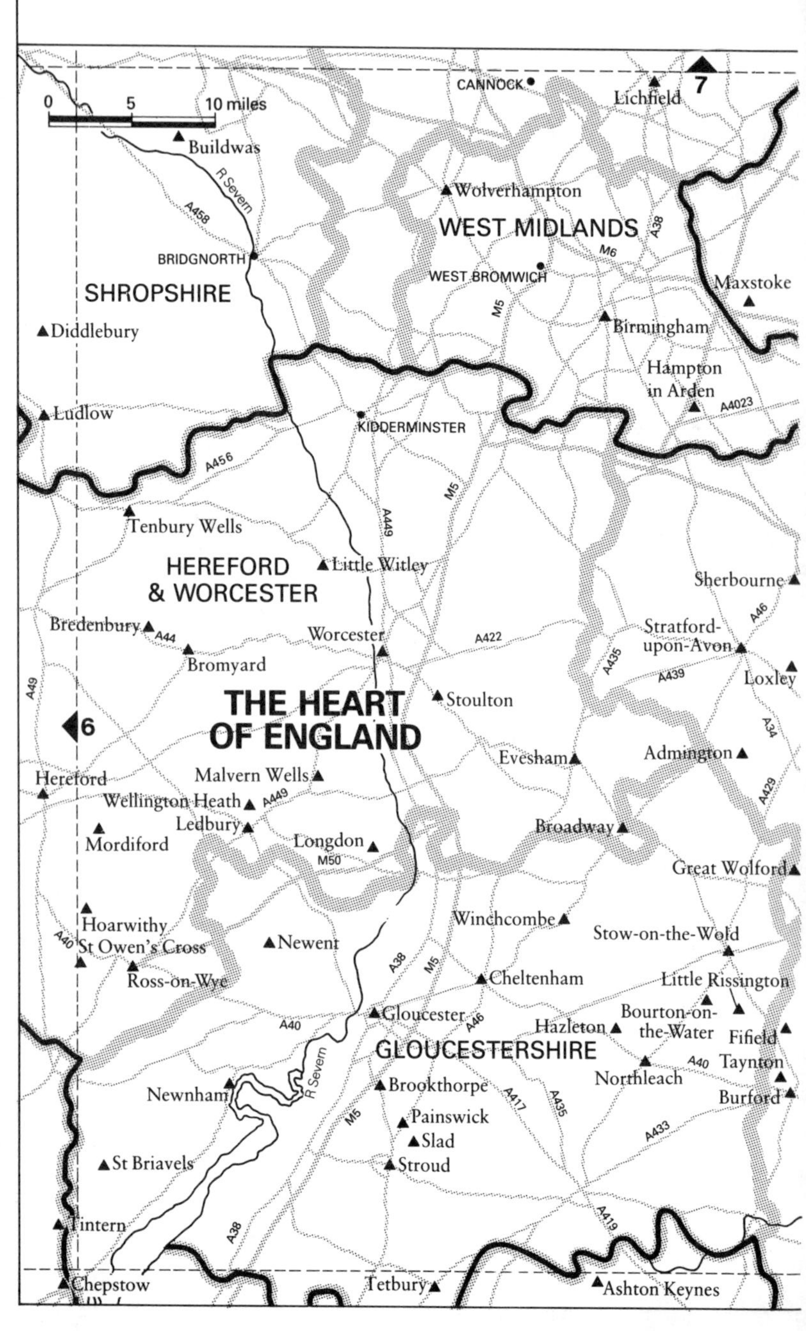

0
5
10 miles
CANNOCK
Lichfield
7
Buildwas
R Severn
A458
Wolverhampton
WEST MIDLANDS
A38
M6
BRIDGNORTH
WEST BROMWICH
SHROPSHIRE
Maxstoke
M5
Diddlebury
Birmingham
Hampton in Arden
A4023
Ludlow
KIDDERMINSTER
A456
M5
Tenbury Wells
A449
HEREFORD & WORCESTER
Little Witley
Sherbourne
A46
Bredenbury
A44
Bromyard
Worcester
A422
Stratford-upon-Avon
A435
A439
Loxley
A49
Stoulton
THE HEART OF ENGLAND
6
A34
Evesham
Admington
Hereford
Malvern Wells
Wellington Heath
A449
A429
Ledbury
Mordiford
Longdon
M50
Broadway
Great Wolford
Winchcombe
Stow-on-the-Wold
Hoarwithy
A40
St Owen's Cross
Newent
A38
M5
Ross-on-Wye
Cheltenham
Little Rissington
Gloucester
A46
Hazleton
Bourton-on-the-Water
A40
Fifield
GLOUCESTERSHIRE
Taynton
A40
Newnham
R Severn
Brookthorpe
Northleach
Burford
A417
A435
M5
Painswick
A433
Slad
St Briavels
Stroud
A419
Tintern
A38
Chepstow
Tetbury
Ashton Keynes

MAP 4

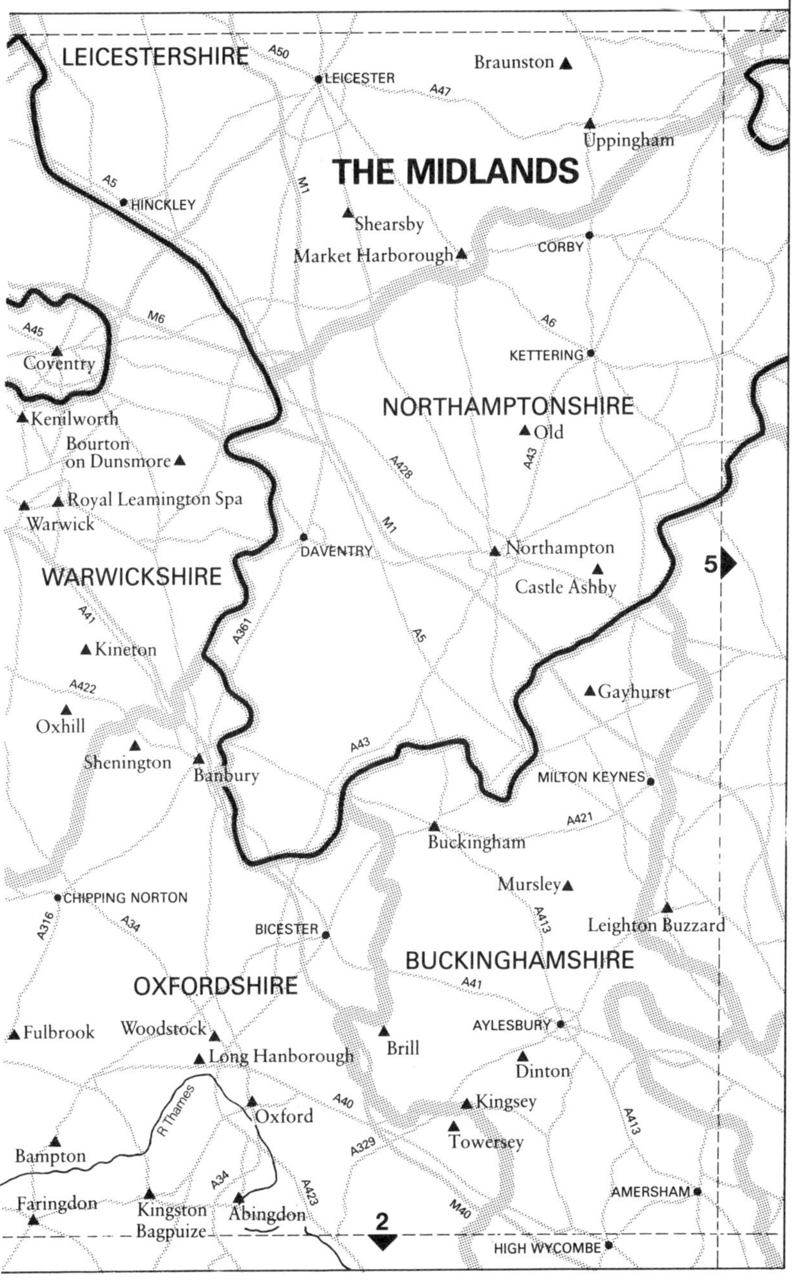
LEICESTERSHIRE
A50
LEICESTER
A47
Braunston
Uppingham
THE MIDLANDS
A5
HINCKLEY
M1
Shearsby
Market Harborough
CORBY
M6
A45
Coventry
A6
KETTERING
NORTHAMPTONSHIRE
Kenilworth
Old
Bourton on Dunsmore
A43
A428
Royal Leamington Spa
Warwick
M1
DAVENTRY
Northampton
5
Castle Ashby
WARWICKSHIRE
A41
A361
A5
Kineton
A422
Gayhurst
Oxhill
A43
Shenington
Banbury
MILTON KEYNES
A421
Buckingham
Mursley
CHIPPING NORTON
A316
A34
A413
Leighton Buzzard
BICESTER
BUCKINGHAMSHIRE
OXFORDSHIRE
A41
AYLESBURY
Fulbrook
Woodstock
Brill
Long Hanborough
Dinton
R Thames
A40
Kingsey
Oxford
A413
Towersey
A329
Bampton
A34
A423
AMERSHAM
Faringdon
Kingston Bagpuize
Abingdon
M40
2
HIGH WYCOMBE

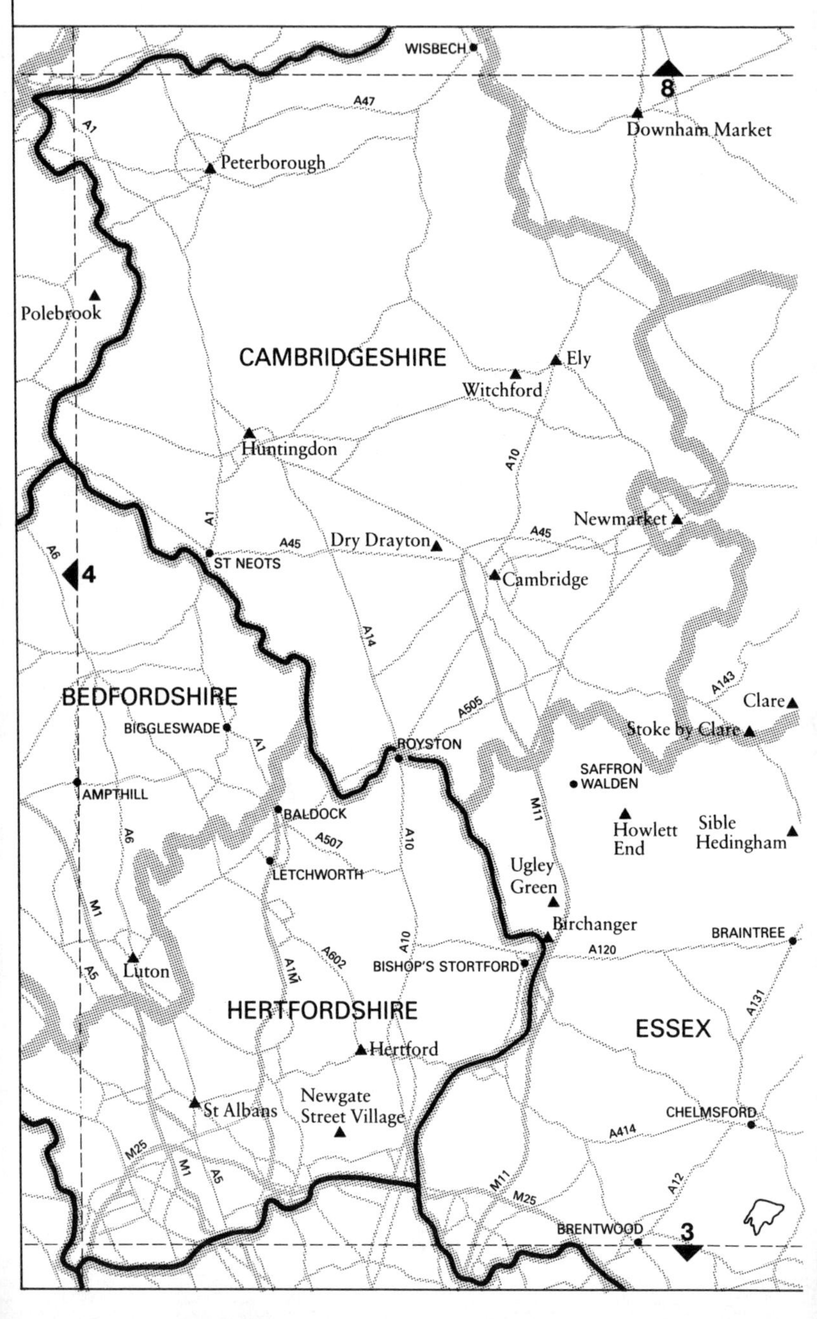
WISBECH
8
A47
Downham Market
A1
Peterborough
Polebrook
CAMBRIDGESHIRE
Ely
Witchford
Huntingdon
A10
Newmarket
A1
A45
Dry Drayton
A45
A6
ST NEOTS
4
Cambridge
A14
A143
BEDFORDSHIRE
A505
Clare
BIGGLESWADE
Stoke by Clare
A1
ROYSTON
SAFFRON WALDEN
AMPTHILL
M11
BALDOCK
A6
A507
A10
Howlett End
Sible Hedingham
LETCHWORTH
Ugley Green
M1
Birchanger
BRAINTREE
A10
A120
Luton
A602
BISHOP'S STORTFORD
A5
A1M
A131
HERTFORDSHIRE
ESSEX
Hertford
Newgate Street Village
St Albans
CHELMSFORD
A414
M25
M1
A5
M11
M25
A12
BRENTWOOD
3

MAP 5

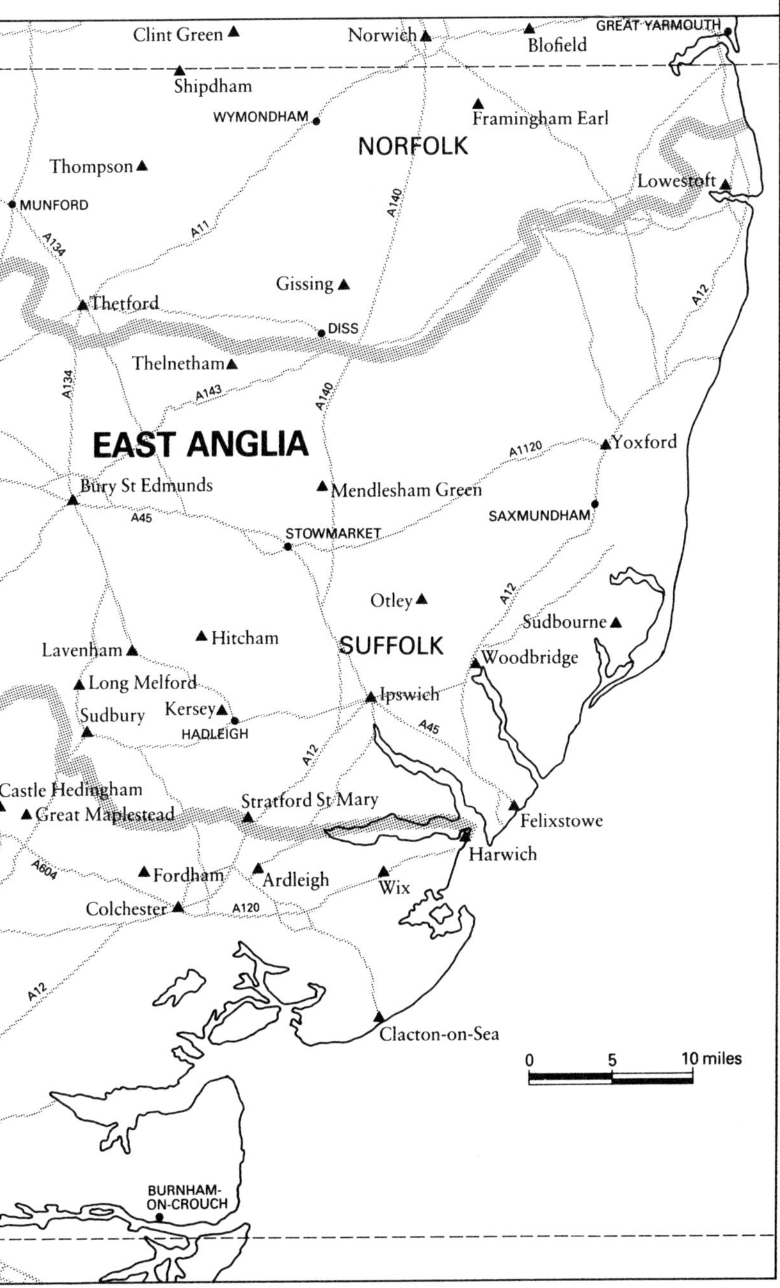
Clint Green
Norwich
Blofield
GREAT YARMOUTH
Shipdham
WYMONDHAM
Framingham Earl
NORFOLK
Thompson
Lowestoft
MUNFORD
A11
A140
A134
A12
Gissing
Thetford
DISS
Thelnetham
A134
A143
A140
EAST ANGLIA
A1120
Yoxford
Bury St Edmunds
Mendlesham Green
A45
SAXMUNDHAM
STOWMARKET
Otley
A12
Sudbourne
Hitcham
Lavenham
SUFFOLK
Woodbridge
Long Melford
Ipswich
Kersey
Sudbury
HADLEIGH
A45
A12
Castle Hedingham
Stratford St Mary
Great Maplestead
Felixstowe
Harwich
A604
Fordham
Ardleigh
Wix
Colchester
A120
A12
Clacton-on-Sea
0
5
10 miles
BURNHAM-
ON-CROUCH

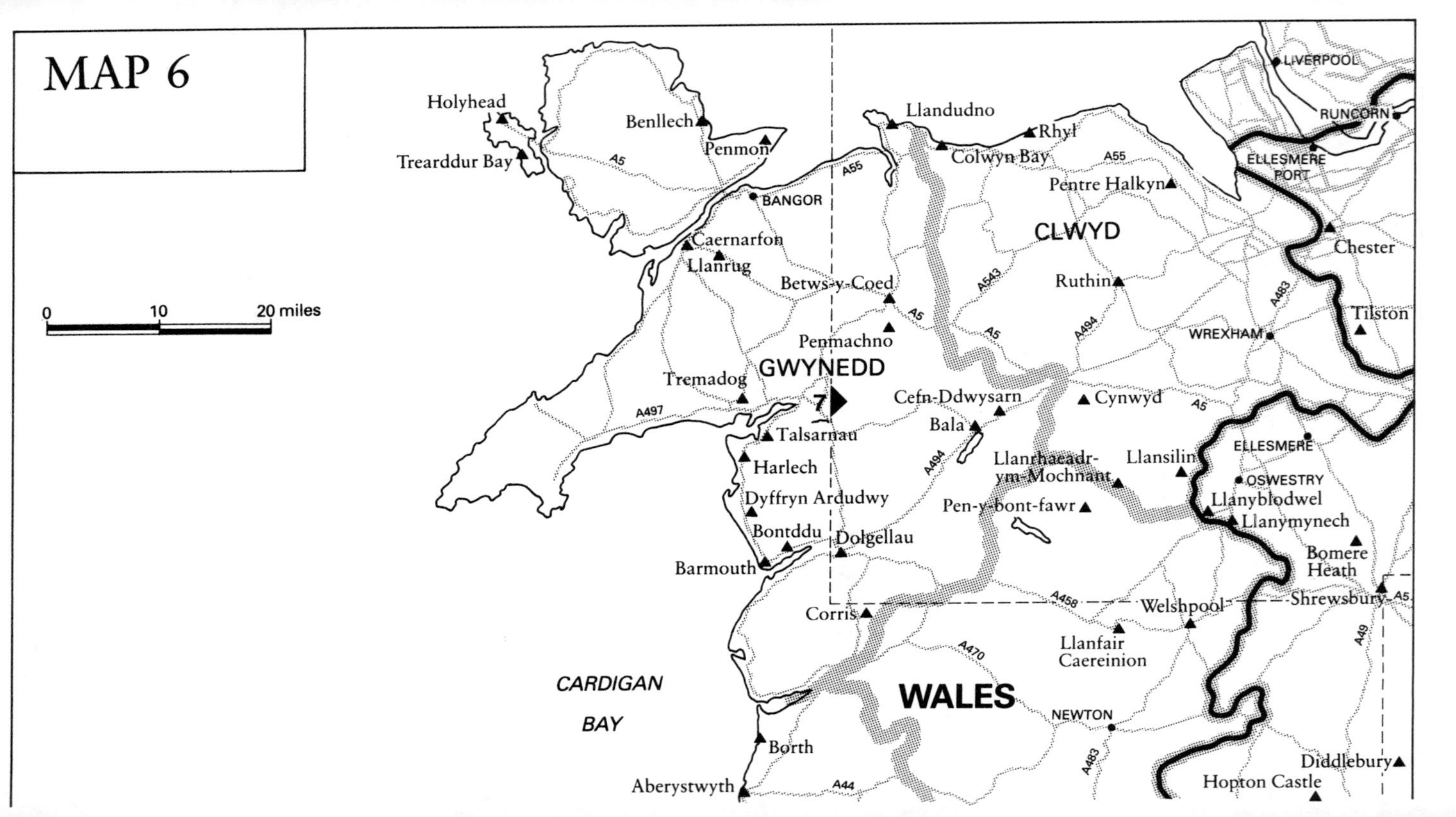
MAP 6
0
10
20 miles
Holyhead
Trearddur Bay
Benllech
Penmon
A5
BANGOR
A55
Caernarfon
Llanrug
Betws-y-Coed
Penmachno
GWYNEDD
Tremadog
A497
7
Talsarnau
Harlech
Dyffryn Ardudwy
Bontddu
Barmouth
Dolgellau
Corris
CARDIGAN
BAY
Borth
Aberystwyth
A44
Llandudno
Colwyn Bay
Rhyl
A55
Pentre Halkyn
CLWYD
Ruthin
A543
A5
A494
Cefn-Ddwysarn
Bala
Cynwyd
Llanrhaeadr-ym-Mochnant
Pen-y-bont-fawr
Llansilin
A458
Welshpool
Llanfair Caereinion
A470
WALES
NEWTON
A483
LIVERPOOL
RUNCORN
ELLESMERE PORT
Chester
Tilston
WREXHAM
ELLESMERE
OSWESTRY
Llanyblodwel
Llanymynech
Bomere Heath
Shrewsbury
A49
Diddlebury
Hopton Castle

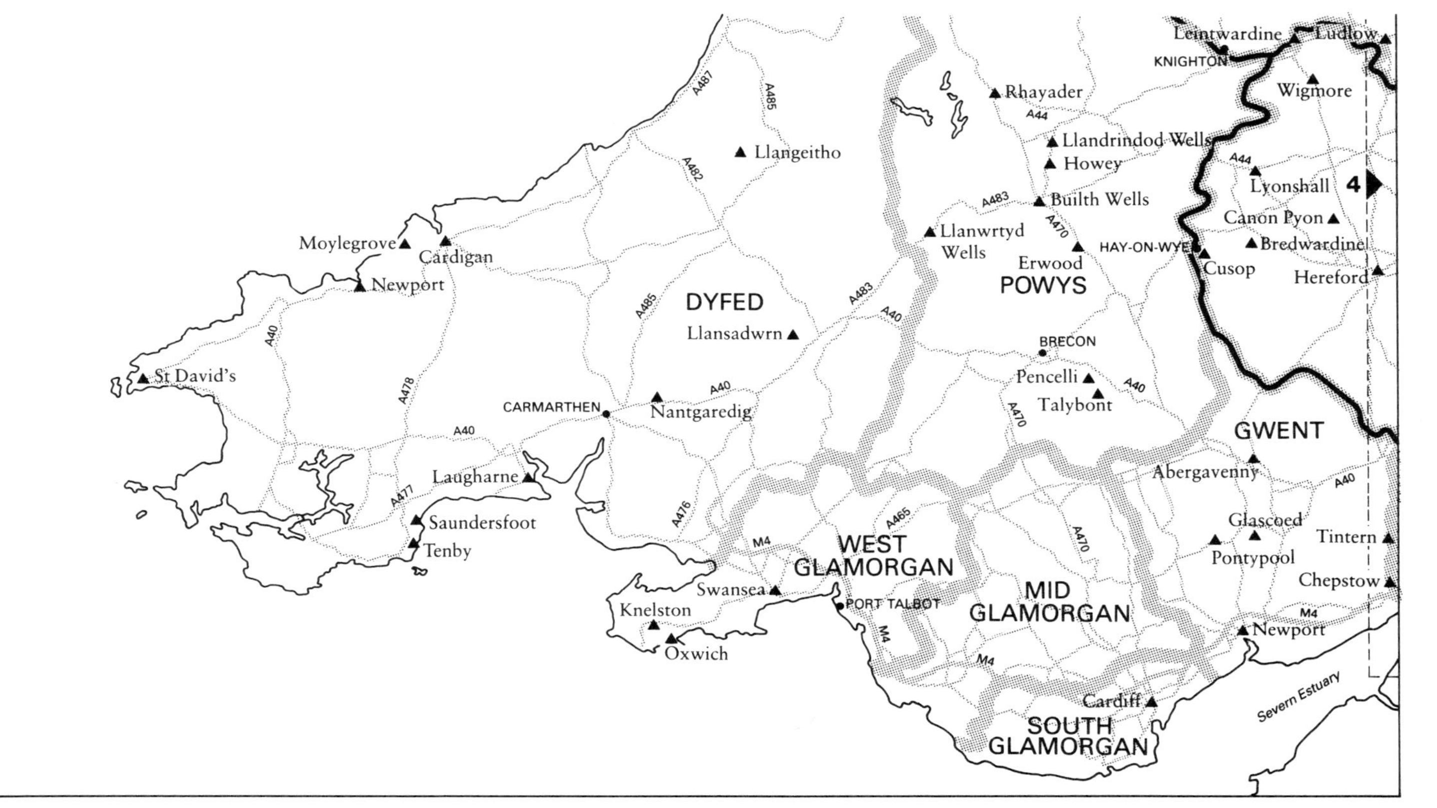

Leintwardine
Ludlow
KNIGHTON
Wigmore
Rhayader
A44
A487
A485
Llangeitho
A482
Llandrindod Wells
Howey
A44
Lyonshall
4
A483
Builth Wells
Canon Pyon
A470
Llanwrtyd
Wells
HAY-ON-WYE
Bredwardine
Erwood
Cusop
Hereford
POWYS
Moylegrove
Cardigan
Newport
DYFED
A485
A483
A40
Llansadwrn
BRECON
A40
St David's
Pencelli
A40
A478
A40
Talybont
CARMARTHEN
Nantgaredig
A470
GWENT
A40
Abergavenny
A40
Laugharne
A477
A476
A465
Saundersfoot
Glascoed
Tenby
A470
Tintern
M4
WEST
GLAMORGAN
Pontypool
Swansea
MID
GLAMORGAN
Chepstow
Knelston
PORT TALBOT
M4
Newport
M4
Oxwich
M4
Cardiff
Severn Estuary
SOUTH
GLAMORGAN

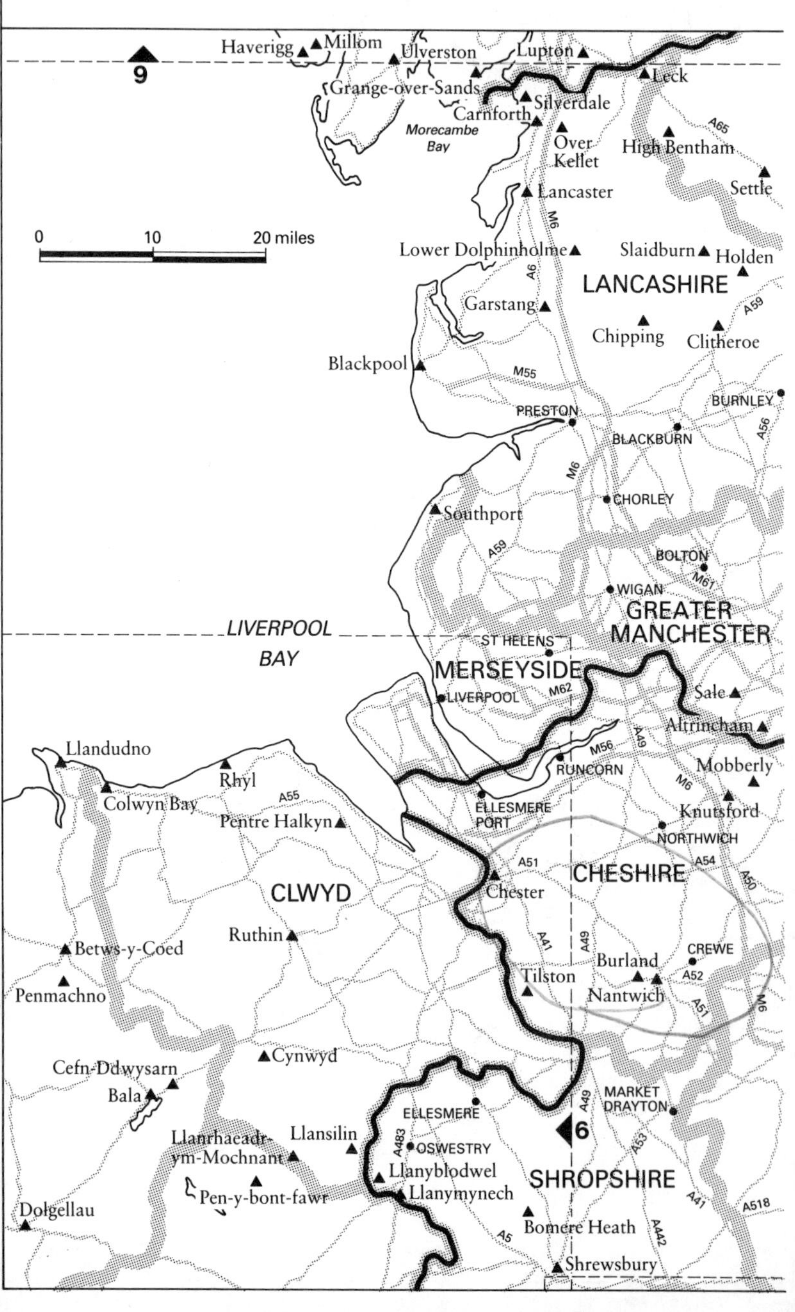

Haverigg
Millom
Ulverston
Lupton
9
Leck
Grange-over-Sands
Silverdale
Carnforth
Morecambe Bay
Over Kellet
High Bentham
A65
Settle
Lancaster
M6
0
10
20 miles
Lower Dolphinholme
Slaidburn
Holden
A6
LANCASHIRE
Garstang
A59
Chipping
Clitheroe
Blackpool
M55
BURNLEY
PRESTON
BLACKBURN
A56
M6
CHORLEY
Southport
A59
BOLTON
M61
WIGAN
GREATER MANCHESTER
LIVERPOOL BAY
ST HELENS
MERSEYSIDE
LIVERPOOL
M62
Sale
Altrincham
A49
Llandudno
M56
Mobberly
Rhyl
RUNCORN
M6
Colwyn Bay
A55
ELLESMERE PORT
Knutsford
Pentre Halkyn
NORTHWICH
A51
CHESHIRE
A54
A50
CLWYD
Chester
Ruthin
A41
A49
CREWE
Betws-y-Coed
Burland
Tilston
A52
Penmachno
Nantwich
A51
M6
Cynwyd
Cefn-Ddwysarn
Bala
MARKET DRAYTON
A49
ELLESMERE
6
Llansilin
A483
OSWESTRY
Llanrhaeadr-ym-Mochnant
A53
Llanyblodwel
SHROPSHIRE
Pen-y-bont-fawr
Llanymynech
A41
A518
Dolgellau
Bomere Heath
A5
A442
Shrewsbury

MAP 7

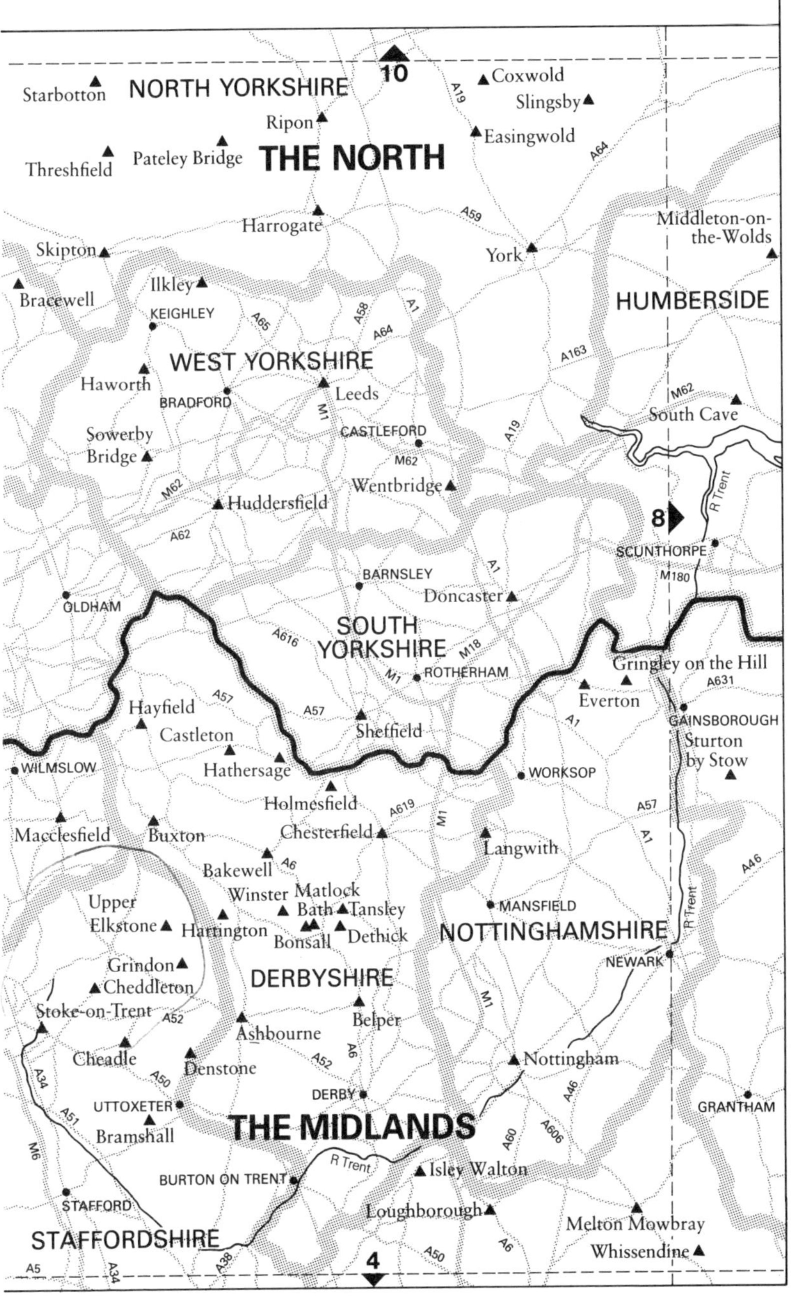

10
NORTH YORKSHIRE
THE NORTH
Starbotton
Threshfield
Pateley Bridge
Ripon
Coxwold
Slingsby
Easingwold
A19
A64
A59
Harrogate
Skipton
Bracewell
Ilkley
KEIGHLEY
York
Middleton-on-the-Wolds
HUMBERSIDE
A65
A58
A1
A64
A163
WEST YORKSHIRE
Haworth
BRADFORD
Leeds
M1
M62
South Cave
Sowerby Bridge
CASTLEFORD
A19
M62
Wentbridge
M62
Huddersfield
A62
8
R Trent
SCUNTHORPE
M180
A1
BARNSLEY
Doncaster
OLDHAM
SOUTH YORKSHIRE
A616
M18
M1
ROTHERHAM
Gringley on the Hill
A631
Everton
GAINSBOROUGH
Hayfield
A57
A57
Sheffield
Castleton
A1
Sturton by Stow
WILMSLOW
Hathersage
WORKSOP
Holmesfield
A619
M1
A57
Macclesfield
Buxton
Chesterfield
Langwith
A1
A46
Bakewell
A6
Winster
Matlock Bath
Tansley
Upper Elkstone
Hartington
Bonsall
Dethick
MANSFIELD
NOTTINGHAMSHIRE
R Trent
NEWARK
Grindon
Cheddleton
DERBYSHIRE
Stoke-on-Trent
A52
Ashbourne
Belper
M1
Cheadle
Denstone
A52
A6
Nottingham
A34
A50
DERBY
A46
GRANTHAM
UTTOXETER
A51
Bramshall
THE MIDLANDS
A60
A606
M6
R Trent
Isley Walton
BURTON ON TRENT
STAFFORD
Loughborough
Melton Mowbray
STAFFORDSHIRE
A6
Whissendine
A38
A50
A5
A34
4

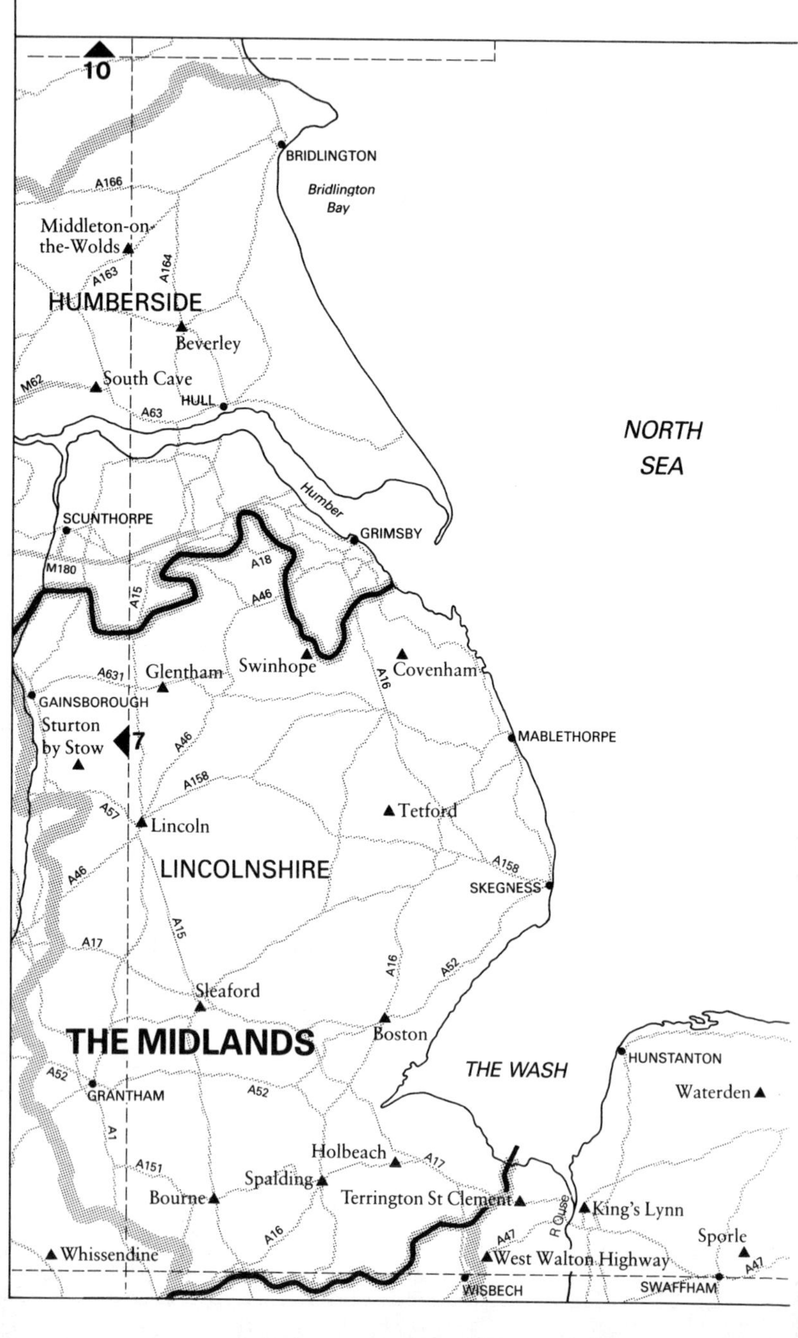
10
BRIDLINGTON
Bridlington Bay
A166
Middleton-on-the-Wolds
A163
A164
HUMBERSIDE
Beverley
M62
South Cave
HULL
A63
NORTH SEA
Humber
SCUNTHORPE
GRIMSBY
M180
A18
A15
A46
Swinhope
Covenham
A631
Glentham
A16
GAINSBOROUGH
Sturton by Stow
7
A46
MABLETHORPE
A158
Tetford
A57
Lincoln
LINCOLNSHIRE
A46
A158
SKEGNESS
A15
A17
A16
A52
Sleaford
Boston
THE MIDLANDS
THE WASH
HUNSTANTON
A52
GRANTHAM
A52
Waterden
A1
Holbeach
A17
A151
Spalding
Bourne
Terrington St Clement
R Ouse
King's Lynn
A16
A47
Sporle
Whissendine
West Walton Highway
A47
WISBECH
SWAFFHAM

MAP 8

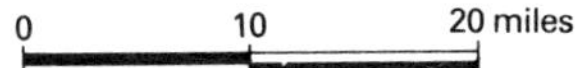
0
10
20 miles

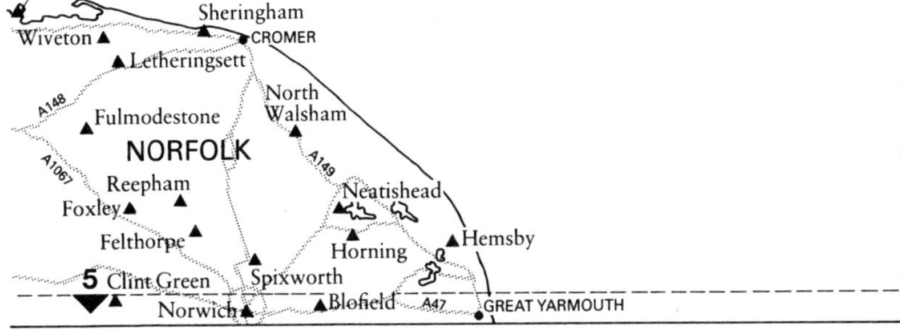
Wells-next-the-Sea
Sheringham
Wiveton
CROMER
Letheringsett
North Walsham
A148
Fulmodestone
NORFOLK
A1067
A149
Reepham
Neatishead
Foxley
Felthorpe
Hemsby
Horning
5
Clint Green
Spixworth
Norwich
Blofield
A47
GREAT YARMOUTH

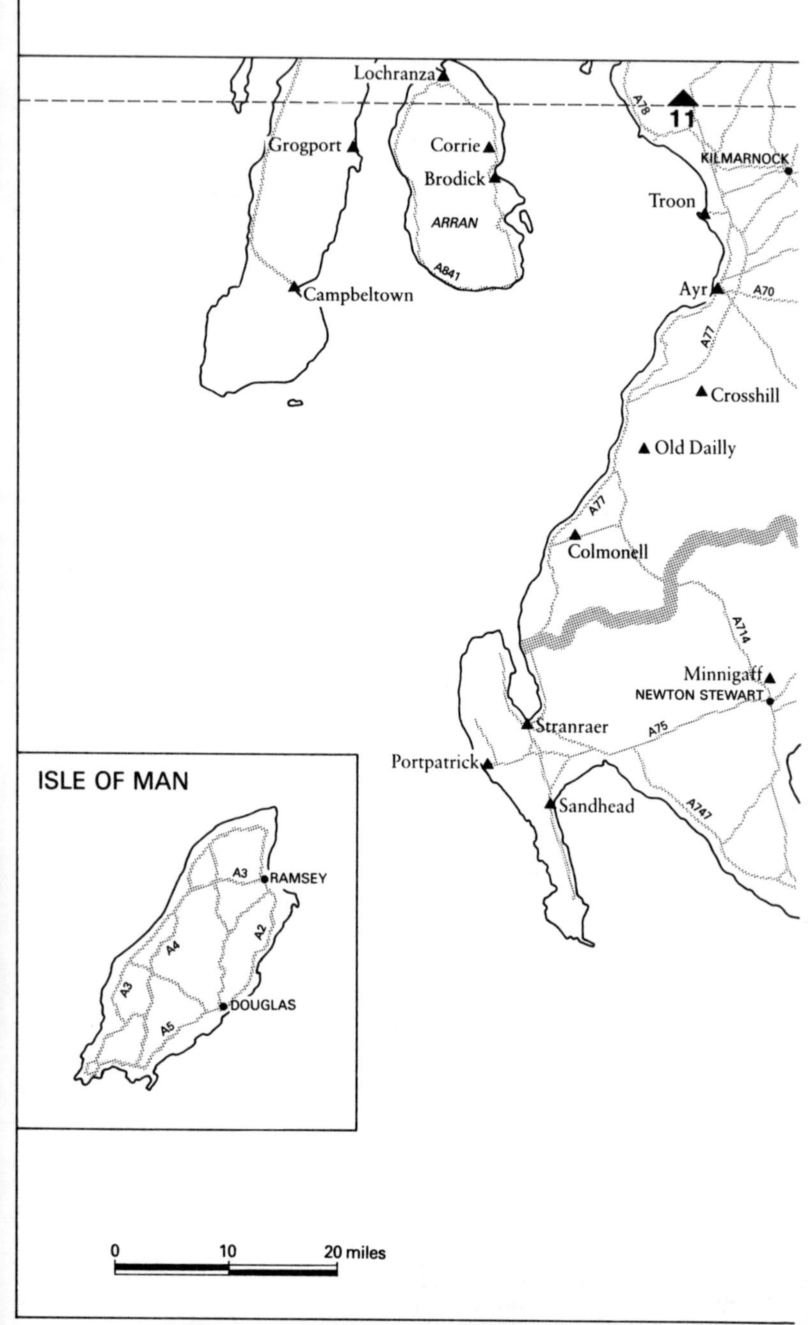

Lochranza
11
A78
Grogport
Corrie
Brodick
KILMARNOCK
Troon
ARRAN
A841
Campbeltown
Ayr
A70
A77
Crosshill
Old Dailly
A77
Colmonell
A714
Minnigaff
NEWTON STEWART
Stranraer
A75
Portpatrick
Sandhead
A747
ISLE OF MAN
A3
RAMSEY
A2
A4
A3
DOUGLAS
A5
0
10
20 miles

MAP 9

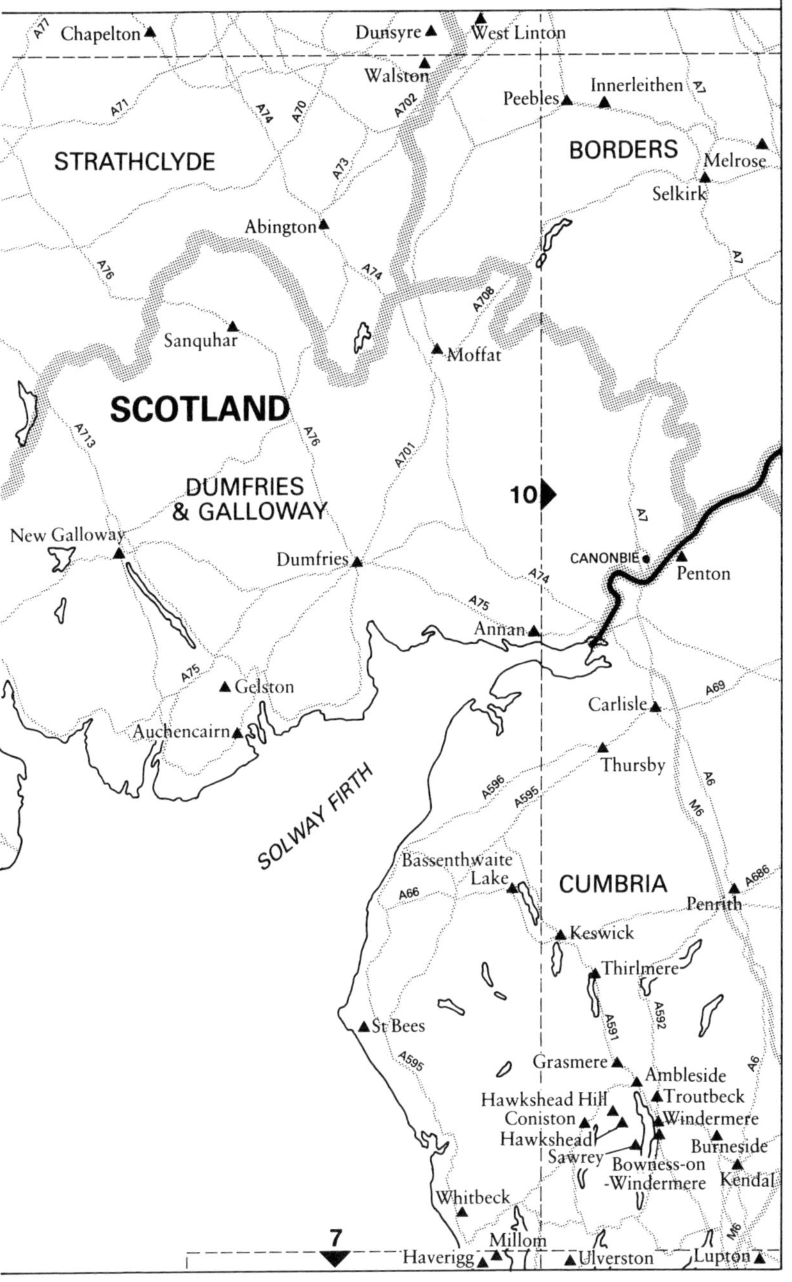

Chapelton
Dunsyre
West Linton
Walston
Peebles
Innerleithen
STRATHCLYDE
BORDERS
Melrose
Selkirk
Abington
Sanquhar
Moffat
SCOTLAND
DUMFRIES
& GALLOWAY
10
New Galloway
Dumfries
CANONBIE
Penton
Annan
Gelston
Auchencairn
Carlisle
Thursby
SOLWAY FIRTH
Bassenthwaite
Lake
CUMBRIA
Penrith
Keswick
Thirlmere
St Bees
Grasmere
Ambleside
Hawkshead Hill
Troutbeck
Coniston
Windermere
Hawkshead
Burneside
Sawrey
Bowness-on
-Windermere
Kendal
Whitbeck
7
Millom
Haverigg
Ulverston
Lupton
A77
A71
A74
A70
A702
A7
A73
A76
A74
A708
A713
A76
A701
A7
A74
A75
A75
A69
A6
M6
A596
A595
A66
A686
A591
A592
A595
A6
M6

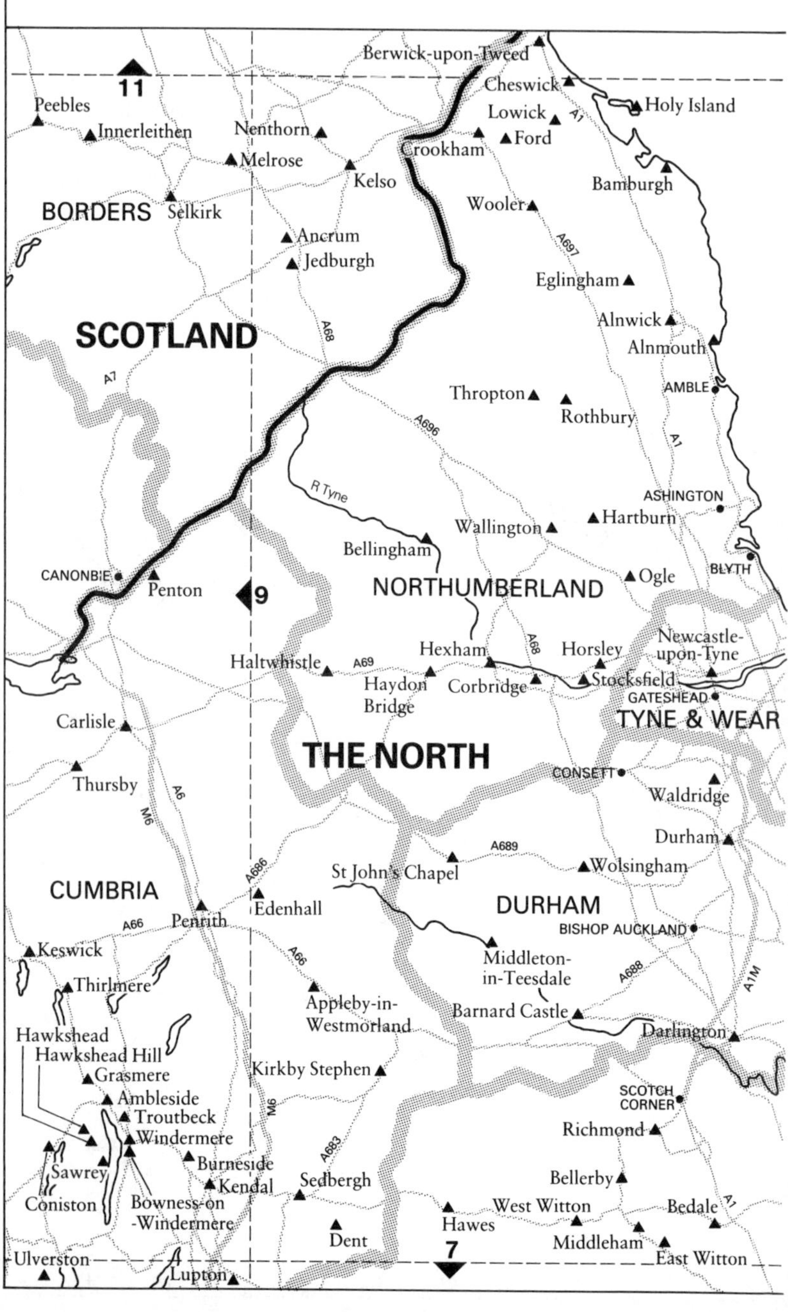

11
Berwick-upon-Tweed
Cheswick
Holy Island
Lowick
Ford
Peebles
Innerleithen
Nenthorn
Crookham
Melrose
Kelso
Bamburgh
BORDERS
Selkirk
Wooler
A1
A697
Ancrum
Jedburgh
Eglingham
Alnwick
SCOTLAND
A68
Alnmouth
A7
AMBLE
Thropton
Rothbury
A696
A1
R Tyne
ASHINGTON
Hartburn
Wallington
Bellingham
BLYTH
CANONBIE
Penton
9
NORTHUMBERLAND
Ogle
Newcastle-upon-Tyne
Hexham
A68
Horsley
Haltwhistle
A69
Haydon Bridge
Corbridge
Stocksfield
GATESHEAD
Carlisle
TYNE & WEAR
THE NORTH
Thursby
CONSETT
Waldridge
A6
M6
Durham
A689
A686
St John's Chapel
Wolsingham
CUMBRIA
Edenhall
DURHAM
A66
Penrith
BISHOP AUCKLAND
Keswick
A66
Middleton-in-Teesdale
A688
A1M
Thirlmere
Appleby-in-Westmorland
Barnard Castle
Hawkshead
Darlington
Hawkshead Hill
Grasmere
Kirkby Stephen
Ambleside
SCOTCH CORNER
Troutbeck
M6
Windermere
Richmond
A683
Burneside
Sawrey
Bellerby
Kendal
Sedbergh
Coniston
Bowness-on-Windermere
West Witton
Bedale
A1
Hawes
Dent
7
Middleham
Ulverston
East Witton
Lupton

MAP 10

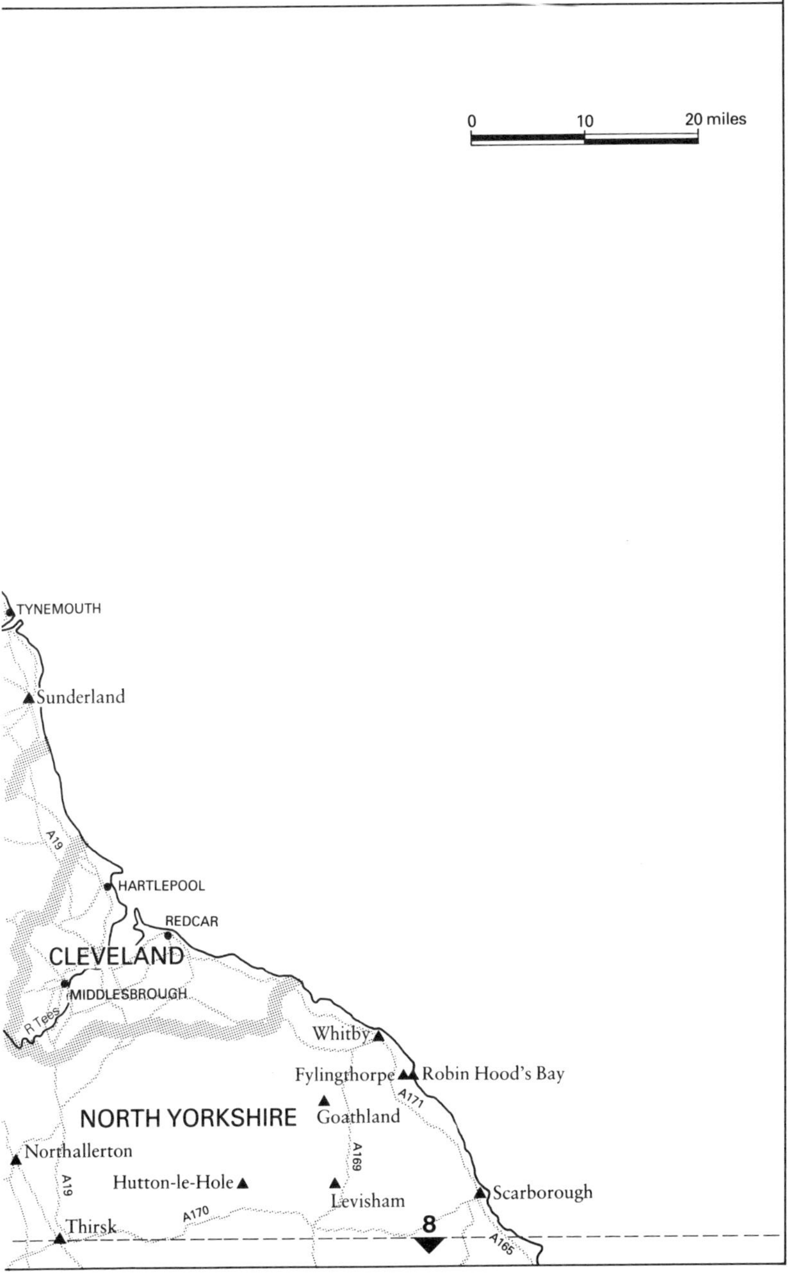

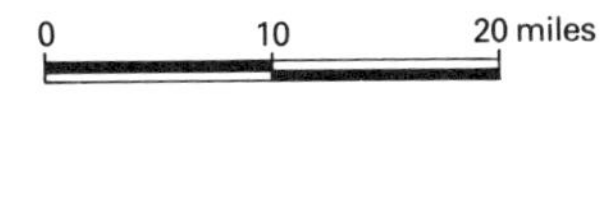

0
10
20 miles
TYNEMOUTH
Sunderland
A19
HARTLEPOOL
REDCAR
CLEVELAND
MIDDLESBROUGH
R Tees
Whitby
Fylingthorpe
Robin Hood's Bay
A171
NORTH YORKSHIRE
Goathland
A169
Northallerton
A19
Hutton-le-Hole
Levisham
Scarborough
A170
Thirsk
8
A165

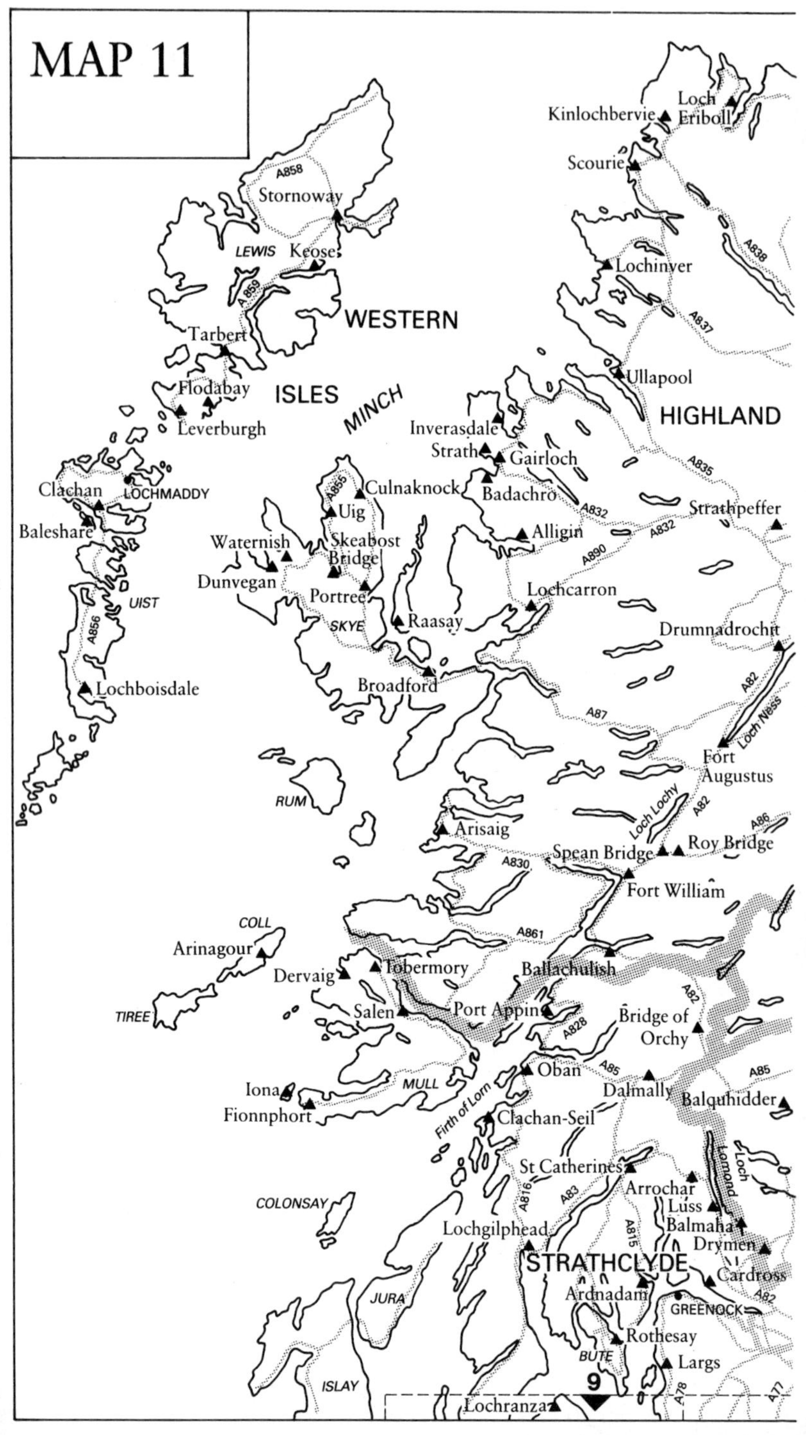

MAP 11
A858
Stornoway
LEWIS
Keose
A859
WESTERN
Tarbert
Flodabay
ISLES
MINCH
Leverburgh
Clachan
LOCHMADDY
Baleshare
UIST
A856
Lochboisdale
Kinlochbervie
Loch Eriboll
Scourie
A838
Lochinver
A837
Ullapool
HIGHLAND
Inverasdale
Strath
Gairloch
Badachro
A835
Culnaknock
A855
Uig
Waternish
Skeabost Bridge
Dunvegan
Portree
SKYE
Raasay
Alligin
A832
Strathpeffer
A890
Lochcarron
Drumnadrochit
Broadford
A82
A87
Loch Ness
Fort Augustus
RUM
Loch Lochy
Arisaig
A86
Spean Bridge
Roy Bridge
A830
Fort William
COLL
A861
Arinagour
Dervaig
Tobermory
Ballachulish
TIREE
Salen
Port Appin
A828
Bridge of Orchy
Oban
A85
Iona
MULL
Dalmally
Balquhidder
Fionnphort
Firth of Lorn
Clachan-Seil
St Catherines
Loch Lomond
Arrochar
COLONSAY
A816
A83
Luss
Balmaha
A815
Lochgilphead
Drymen
STRATHCLYDE
Cardross
Ardnadam
JURA
GREENOCK
Rothesay
BUTE
Largs
9
ISLAY
A78
A77
Lochranza

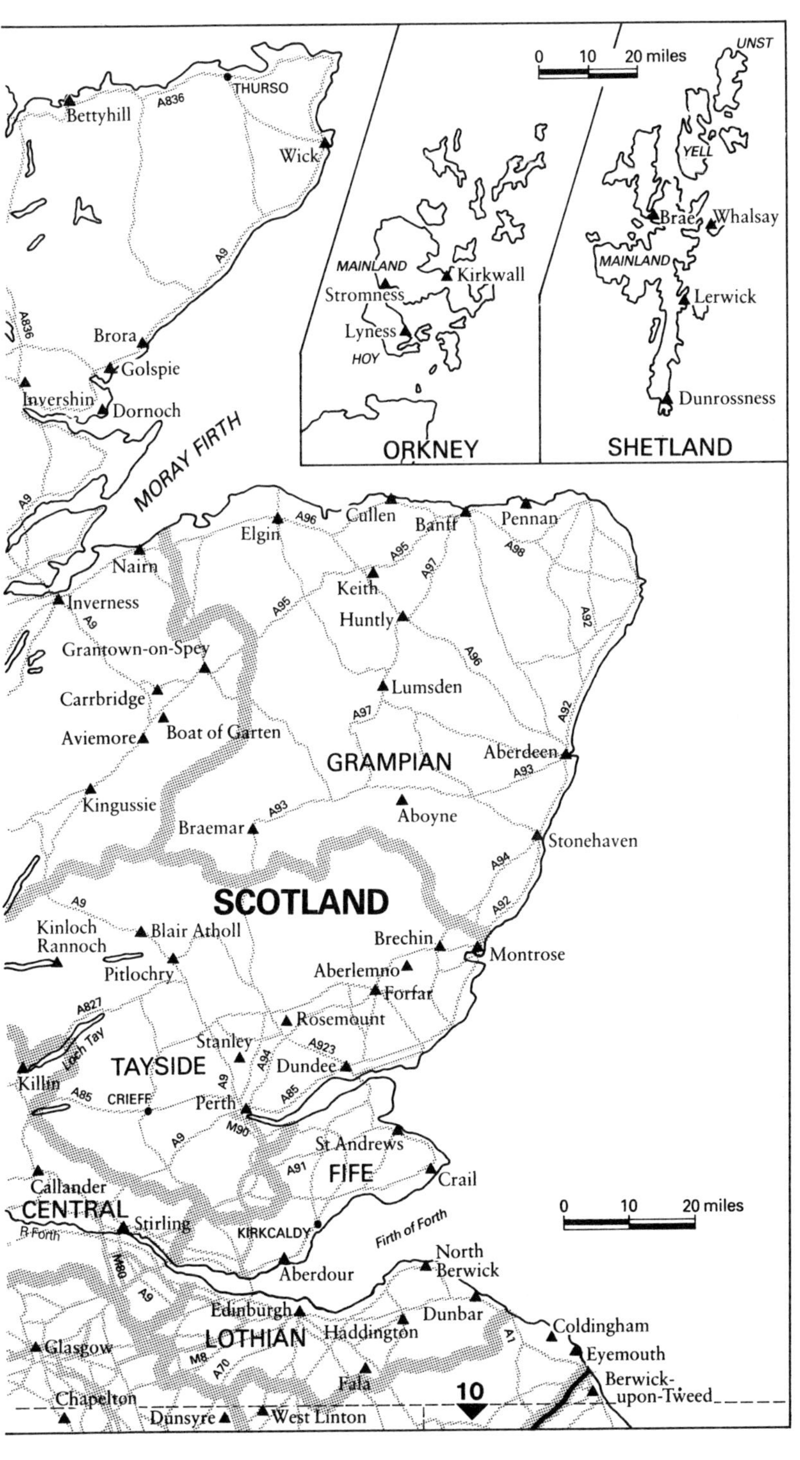

THURSO
A836
Bettyhill
Wick
A9
A836
Brora
Golspie
Invershin
Dornoch
MORAY FIRTH
UNST
0 10 20 miles
YELL
Brae
Whalsay
MAINLAND
Lerwick
Dunrossness
SHETLAND
MAINLAND
Kirkwall
Stromness
Lyness
HOY
ORKNEY
A9
Cullen
Banff
Pennan
A96
Elgin
A95
A97
A98
Nairn
Keith
Inverness
A95
A92
A9
Huntly
Grantown-on-Spey
A96
Lumsden
Carrbridge
A97
A92
Aviemore
Boat of Garten
GRAMPIAN
Aberdeen
A93
Kingussie
A93
Aboyne
Braemar
Stonehaven
A94
SCOTLAND
A9
A92
Kinloch
Rannoch
Blair Atholl
Brechin
Montrose
Pitlochry
Aberlemno
Forfar
A827
Rosemount
Stanley
A923
Loch Tay
TAYSIDE
A94
Dundee
A9
Killin
A85
CRIEFF
Perth
A85
M90
A9
St Andrews
A91
FIFE
Crail
Callander
CENTRAL
0 10 20 miles
Stirling
R Forth
KIRKCALDY
Firth of Forth
North
Berwick
M80
Aberdour
A9
Edinburgh
Dunbar
LOTHIAN
Haddington
A1
Coldingham
Glasgow
Eyemouth
M8
A70
Fala
Berwick-
upon-Tweed
10
Chapelton
Dunsyre
West Linton

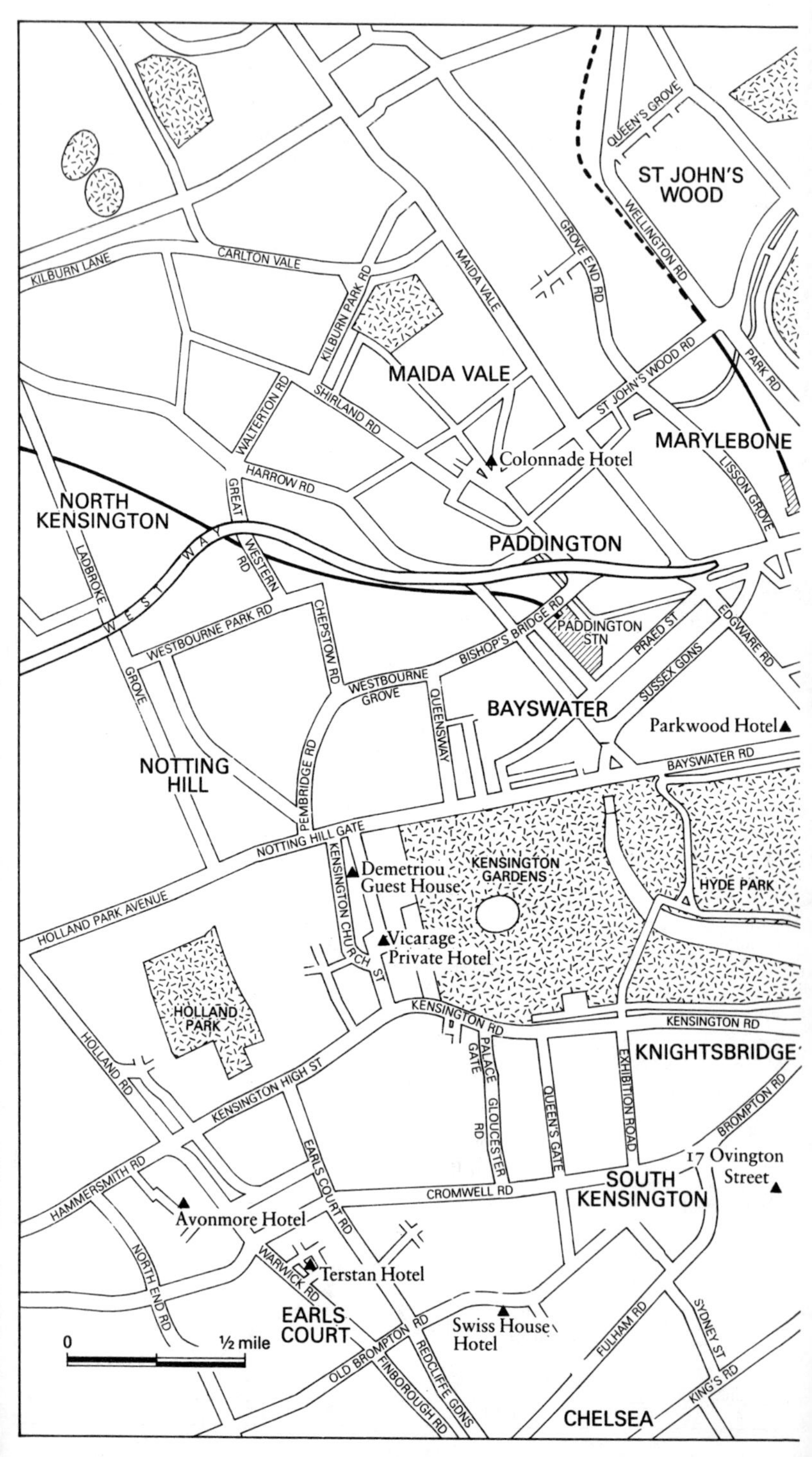

ST JOHN'S WOOD
MAIDA VALE
MARYLEBONE
NORTH KENSINGTON
PADDINGTON
BAYSWATER
NOTTING HILL
KENSINGTON GARDENS
HYDE PARK
HOLLAND PARK
KNIGHTSBRIDGE
SOUTH KENSINGTON
EARLS COURT
CHELSEA
Colonnade Hotel
Parkwood Hotel
Demetriou Guest House
Vicarage Private Hotel
17 Ovington Street
Avonmore Hotel
Terstan Hotel
Swiss House Hotel
PADDINGTON STN
QUEEN'S GROVE
WELLINGTON RD
GROVE END RD
PARK RD
ST JOHN'S WOOD RD
LISSON GROVE
MAIDA VALE
KILBURN PARK RD
CARLTON VALE
KILBURN LANE
SHIRLAND RD
WALTERTON RD
HARROW RD
GREAT WESTERN RD
WESTWAY
LADBROKE GROVE
WESTBOURNE PARK RD
CHEPSTOW RD
BISHOP'S BRIDGE RD
PRAED ST
EDGWARE RD
SUSSEX GDNS
WESTBOURNE GROVE
QUEENSWAY
BAYSWATER RD
PEMBRIDGE RD
NOTTING HILL GATE
KENSINGTON CHURCH ST
HOLLAND PARK AVENUE
KENSINGTON RD
HOLLAND RD
KENSINGTON HIGH ST
PALACE GATE
GLOUCESTER RD
QUEEN'S GATE
EXHIBITION ROAD
BROMPTON RD
HAMMERSMITH RD
EARLS COURT RD
CROMWELL RD
NORTH END RD
WARWICK RD
OLD BROMPTON RD
FINBOROUGH RD
REDCLIFFE GDNS
FULHAM RD
SYDNEY ST
KING'S RD
0
½ mile

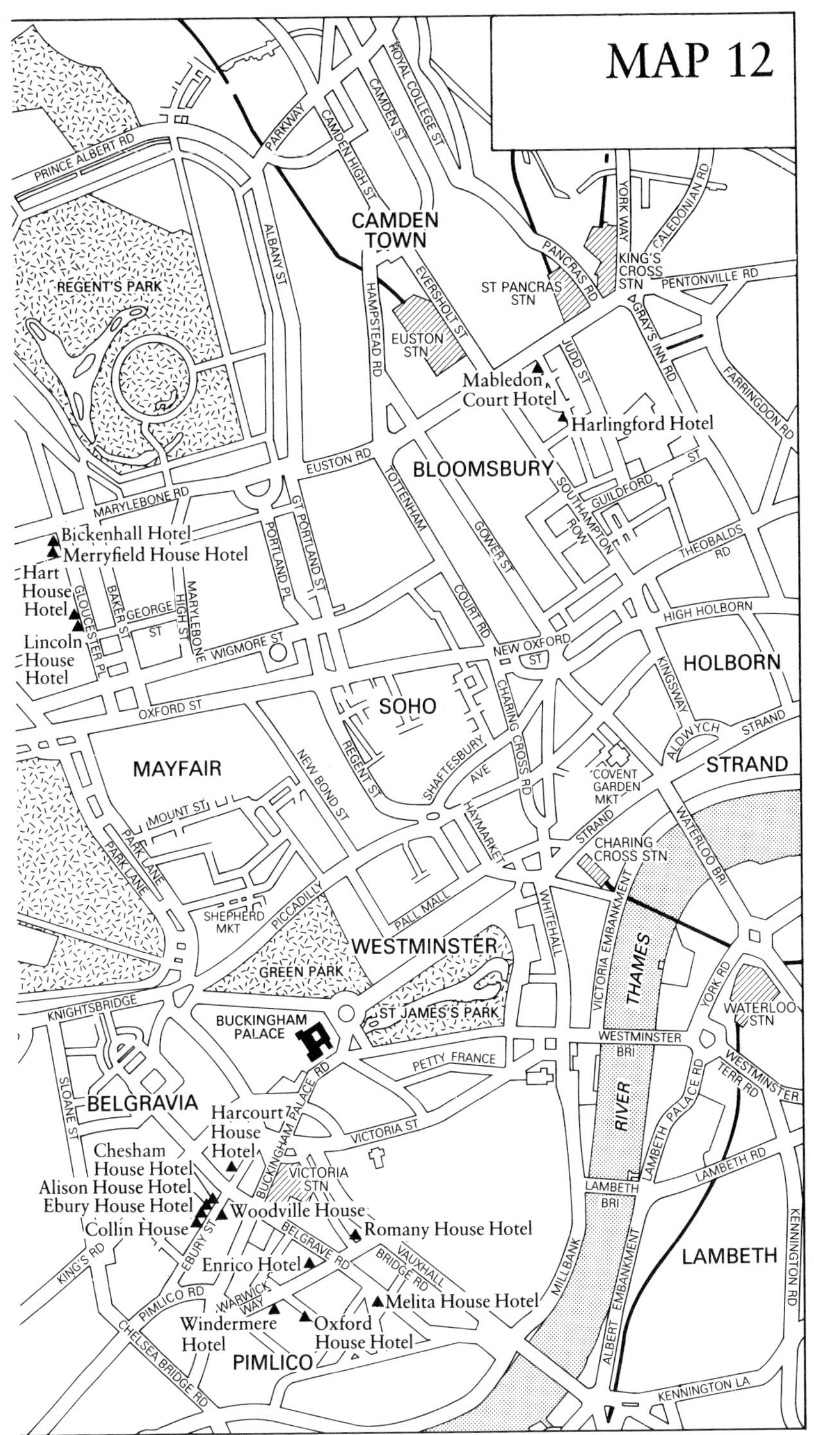
MAP 12
PRINCE ALBERT RD
PARKWAY
CAMDEN HIGH ST
CAMDEN ST
ROYAL COLLEGE ST
YORK WAY
CALEDONIAN RD
CAMDEN TOWN
ALBANY ST
REGENT'S PARK
HAMPSTEAD RD
EVERSHOLT ST
ST PANCRAS STN
PANCRAS RD
KING'S CROSS STN
PENTONVILLE RD
GRAY'S INN RD
EUSTON STN
JUDD ST
FARRINGDON RD
Mabledon Court Hotel
Harlingford Hotel
EUSTON RD
TOTTENHAM
BLOOMSBURY
SOUTHAMPTON ROW
GUILDFORD ST
MARYLEBONE RD
GT PORTLAND ST
PORTLAND PL
GOWER ST
THEOBALDS RD
Bickenhall Hotel
Merryfield House Hotel
Hart House Hotel
Lincoln House Hotel
GLOUCESTER PL
BAKER ST
GEORGE ST
MARYLEBONE HIGH ST
WIGMORE ST
COURT RD
HIGH HOLBORN
NEW OXFORD ST
HOLBORN
KINGSWAY
OXFORD ST
SOHO
CHARING CROSS RD
ALDWYCH
STRAND
MAYFAIR
NEW BOND ST
REGENT ST
SHAFTESBURY AVE
COVENT GARDEN MKT
MOUNT ST
PARK LANE
HAYMARKET
CHARING CROSS STN
WATERLOO BRI
SHEPHERD MKT
PICCADILLY
PALL MALL
WHITEHALL
VICTORIA EMBANKMENT
WESTMINSTER
THAMES
GREEN PARK
YORK RD
WATERLOO STN
KNIGHTSBRIDGE
BUCKINGHAM PALACE
ST JAMES'S PARK
WESTMINSTER BRI
PETTY FRANCE
WESTMINSTER TERR RD
SLOANE ST
BELGRAVIA
BUCKINGHAM PALACE RD
Harcourt House Hotel
RIVER
LAMBETH PALACE RD
VICTORIA ST
Chesham House Hotel
VICTORIA STN
LAMBETH RD
Alison House Hotel
Ebury House Hotel
Woodville House
LAMBETH BRI
Collin House
Romany House Hotel
KENNINGTON RD
BELGRAVE RD
KING'S RD
EBURY ST
Enrico Hotel
VAUXHALL BRIDGE RD
MILLBANK
ALBERT EMBANKMENT
LAMBETH
PIMLICO RD
WARWICK WAY
Melita House Hotel
Windermere Hotel
Oxford House Hotel
PIMLICO
CHELSEA BRIDGE RD
KENNINGTON LA